US PENSION REFORM

LESSONS FROM OTHER COUNTRIES

Martin Neil Baily

Jacob Funk Kirkegaard

PETERSON INSTITUTE FOR INTERNATIONAL ECONOMICS

Washington, DC

February 2009

Martin Neil Baily, former senior fellow (2001–07) at the Peterson Institute for International Economics, is a senior fellow at the Brookings Institution, where he held the same position from 1979 to 1989. He was chairman of the Council of Economic Advisers during the Clinton administration (1999–2001) and one of three members of the council from 1994 to 1996. He was a principal at McKinsey & Company's Global Institute (1996–99) and is now senior adviser to McKinsey. He joined the board of The Phoenix Companies, Inc. in 2005 and is an academic adviser to the Congressional Budget Office. He was a professor of economics at the University of Maryland (1989–96, vice chairman of a National Academy of Sciences/National Research Council panel investigating the effect of computers on productivity, and research associate at the National Bureau of Economic Research. He cofounded the microeconomics issues of the *Brookings Papers on Economic Activity*. He is coauthor of *Transforming the European Economy* (2004), which was named a Choice Outstanding Academic Title for 2005.

Jacob Funk Kirkegaard is a research fellow at the Peterson Institute for International Economics, where he had been a research associate since 2002. Before joining the Institute, he worked with the Danish Ministry of Defense, the United Nations in Iraq, and in the private financial sector. He is a graduate of the Danish Army's Special School of Intelligence and Linguistics with the rank of first lieutenant; the University of Aarhus in Aarhus, Denmark; and Columbia University in New York. He is the author of *The Accelerating Decline in America's High-Skilled Workforce: Implications for Immigration Policy* (2007) and coauthor of *Transforming the European Economy* (2004), which was named a Choice Outstanding Academic Title for 2005, and assisted with *Accelerating the Globalization of America: The Role for Information Technology* (2006).

PETER G. PETERSON INSTITUTE
FOR INTERNATIONAL ECONOMICS
1750 Massachusetts Avenue, NW
Washington, DC 20036-1903
(202) 328-9000   FAX: (202) 659-3225
www.petersoninstitute.org

C. Fred Bergsten, *Director*
Edward Tureen, *Director of Publications,*
Marketing, and Web Development
Typesetting by Xcel Graphic Services
Printing by United Book Press, Inc.
Cover by Peggy Archambault Design/pa2design
.com
Cover photo: © *Brian Hagiwara/Brand X/Corbis*

Printed in the United States of America
11   10   09   5   4   3   2   1

Library of Congress Cataloging-in-Publication Data

Baily, Martin Neil.
    US pension reform : lessons from other countries / Martin Neil Baily, Jacob Funk Kirkegaard.
      p. cm.
    1.   Social security—United States.
    2.   Social security. 3.   Pensions—United States. 4.   Pensions. I. Kirkegaard, Jacob F. II. Title. III. Title: U.S. pension reform.

HD7125.B275 2008
331.25'220973—dc22

                                2008050026

Contents

Figures

Boxes

Preface

Americans are living longer and baby-boomers are beginning to retire. These are positive developments but, unfortunately, they are also the cause of some of the most daunting public policy challenges facing America. As more baby-boomers retire and enter the Social Security system, the current pension surplus will turn to deficit over the next decade and, thanks to increased life expectancy, retiring baby-boomers will draw Social Security benefits for a longer period. Awareness of the long-term fiscal unsustainability of Social Security is widespread though the American public's grasp of the details is weak.

Focusing on the finances of Social Security by itself is, however, not enough. To fix the US pension system, other issues will also have to be addressed: adequacy of retirement income and old age poverty; labor market participation and economic incentives facing older workers; soundness of state and local government, as well as corporate, pension plans; the low US national saving rate; and redistribution between generations.

These challenges are not unique to America but shared throughout the industrialized world. Policymakers in all OECD countries have had to wrestle with the same set of pension policy–related issues and, in fact, face more rapidly aging populations and harsher economic circumstances than the United States. US policymakers contemplating how to implement required pension reforms ought to look to the reform processes and experiences of other countries for ideas on which policies work and which do not.

In this study, Martin Neil Baily and Jacob Funk Kirkegaard explore how other advanced countries such as the United Kingdom, France, Germany, and Japan, as well as a host of smaller countries have solved the same fundamental problems facing the US pension system. The authors present an extensive list of lessons learned and, based on these lessons, make the case for a package of policy reforms to secure the fiscal sustainability of Social Security, guard against old age poverty in the United States, provide the necessary economic incentives and opportunities for older workers, and raise the US national saving rate.

The study reveals that the design of US Social Security is fundamentally sound, and that the challenges it faces are smaller than those facing mandatory pension systems in most other OECD countries. Baily and Kirkegaard conclude that transforming the basic tenets of Social Security is neither warranted nor wise. They instead propose targeted changes to parts of the Social Security system, with the cost of reforms distributed across generations.

The authors find a large effect of the tax system on total public and private cost of pension provision across countries and propose integrating more closely the cost to the Treasury of tax breaks toward private pension savings and the long-term sustainability of the Social Security system. With most American retirees—as British, French, German, Japanese, and other OECD retirees—receiving the majority of their income in the form of Social Security benefits and other public payments, any reductions in overall retirement income should affect only the highest-income among them. In analyzing work incentives, labor market withdrawal ages, and intergenerationally fair periods of life spent in retirement, Baily and Kirkegaard uncover a powerful basis for further strengthening the direct link between life expectancy and retirement age in the United States.

The authors also argue for the introduction of *add-on* individual accounts. The idea of *replacing* the existing Social Security retirement program with individual accounts is dead because George W. Bush's proposal along those lines was not supported in Congress or by voters. Nevertheless, the concept of low- and middle-income workers having additional retirement savings, over and above their Social Security benefits, is a good one. Moreover, the government can play a legitimate role in making it easier and cheaper for lower-income families to save. Under the plan, workers would be automatically enrolled in a 401(k)-style individual account managed by the Social Security Administration but with the funds invested privately. Participants could opt out of the program without penalty. The plan would add not only to the retirement resources of future generations of elderly but also marginally to national saving.

The Peter G. Peterson Institute for International Economics is a private, nonprofit institution for the study and discussion of international economic policy. Its purpose is to analyze important issues in that area and to develop and communicate practical new approaches for dealing with them. The Institute is completely nonpartisan.

The Institute is funded by a highly diversified group of philanthropic foundations, private corporations, and interested individuals. About 22 percent of the Institute's resources in our latest fiscal year were provided by contributors outside the United States, including about 9 percent from Japan. The Institute carried out this comparative study at the request of the Ford Foundation, which also funded the project, as part of the Ford Foundation's broader initiative to provide better public education on the Social Security System, its financial status, and proposals for reform.

The Institute's Board of Directors bears overall responsibilities for the Institute and gives general guidance and approval to its research program, including the identification of topics that are likely to become important over the medium run (one to three years) and that should be addressed by the Institute. The director, working closely with the staff and outside Advisory Committee, is responsible for the development of particular projects and makes the final decision to publish an individual study.

The Institute hopes that its studies and other activities will contribute to building a stronger foundation for international economic policy around the world. We invite readers of these publications to let us know how they think we can best accomplish this objective.

C. FRED BERGSTEN
Director
December 2008

Acknowledgments

We thank the Ford Foundation for their economic support for this project and our colleagues at the Peterson Institute for International Economics and the Brookings Institution for many instructive comments, in particular C. Fred Bergsten and Adam S. Posen for their sustained support and guidance.

In writing this book, we have become deeply indebted to the numerous helpful comments and insightful manuscript reviews of Edward Whitehouse, Monika Queisser, and Mark Keese from the Organization for Economic Cooperation and Development (OECD); Robert Holzmann, Richard Hinz, Mark Dorfman, and David Robalino from the World Bank; Denise Lamaute from the Social Security Administration; Gary Burtless from the Brookings Institution; Peter A. Diamond from MIT; Jakob von Weizsäcker from Bruegel; Giuseppe Carone from the European Commission Directorate General Economic and Financial Affairs; Alicia H. Munnell from Boston College; and John A. Turner.

We would also like to thank the participants of the Peterson Institute study group in the spring of 2008, as well as Noel Richards of the UK Pension Protection Fund, Virginia P. Reno of the National Academy of Income Security, Herwig Immerwoll of the OECD, and Junichi Sakamoto of the Nomura Research Institute for their assistance during the project.

Special thanks go to Katharina Plueck, Tim Works, and Matthew Johnson for their outstanding research assistance, and to Madona Devasahayam, Cameron Fletcher, Ed Tureen, Susann Luetjen, and Natalie Fullenkamp for their invaluable and tireless assistance with editing the manuscript and preparing it for publication.

All opinions and any remaining factual mistakes and other errors are the authors' own, and the views expressed do not necessarily correspond with those of the Ford Foundation or of the staff and trustees of the Peterson Institute for International Economics.

1

Lessons from the World

We know exactly what to do, but we do not know how to win the next elections after we have done it.

——Jean-Claude Juncker, prime minister of Luxembourg[1]

When a new presidential administration takes office in January 2009, an important item on the policy agenda will be Social Security reform. The large cohort of Americans born after 1945 is starting to collect Social Security benefits, and over the next several years the surpluses of Social Security tax receipts over benefit payments will become deficits. Social Security is a pay-as-you-go (PAYGO) system, and the number of workers paying contributions into the system is declining relative to the number of those receiving benefits. Increases in life expectancy, although for the most part a positive development, also contribute to the financial concern.

In addition to the fiscal challenge, Social Security faces the challenge of adequacy. A large fraction of retirees relies on Social Security benefits for most of their income. For the average worker, the level of benefits is not very high—$990 for all beneficiaries in April 2008 ($1,083 for all workers and $533 for spouses).[2] Elderly poverty, particularly among widows, is a significant problem. Furthermore, even if retirement benefits were adequate today, they would not be in the future because of the rising costs of health care. Medicare covers retirees without alternative coverage,

---

1. BBC News, "Campaign To Cure EU Labour Woes," March 23, 2006.

2. Data are from the Social Security Administration, www.ssa.gov.

and its costs are rising enormously; most observers conclude that the cost of Medicare is unsustainable (see, for example, CBO 2008). Ideally, reforms will preserve effective care while reducing costs, but it is likely that retirees will nonetheless have to pay more for their health care. However, at the average level of pension benefits, it is hard to see how retirees dependent on Social Security income will be able to pay more for health care. Thus the dual challenge for the US Social Security system is to improve its solvency while maintaining an adequate standard of living for retirees who have come to depend on its benefits.

The United States is not alone in the fiscal challenges to its public retirement program; PAYGO plans are facing large deficits in many other countries, and these fiscal shortfalls share a common explanation. Most developed countries experienced strong economic growth in the 1950s and 1960s, which resulted in large inflows of revenues from the payroll taxes that funded the retirement programs. In addition, the cohort of retirees was small, and most workers continued to work into their mid-to-late 60s, so politicians could be generous to retirees without fear of program deficits in the short run. But economic growth has slowed since then, and populations are living longer. The number of retirees has increased rapidly as the retirement age has fallen in most countries, the baby boomer generation is moving into retirement years, and life expectancy is increasing. Furthermore, the number of active workers is actually starting to decline in some countries, so that the ratio of workers paying into the system has declined relative to the number of retirees receiving benefits. This trend is expected to continue, although the effective retirement age has begun to stabilize in most Organization for Economic Cooperation and Development (OECD) economies.

Many of the countries that we analyze in this study, especially the European economies, pay more generous public pensions than does the United States. The dilemma for policymakers in these countries is that any reform efforts that call for reducing benefits or increasing taxes are very unpopular politically. In Europe there have been demonstrations and even riots triggered by proposals to cut benefits or increase the age of retirement. Tax increases are not as unpopular in Europe as in the United States, but European policymakers are very aware of their already high levels of taxation and the possible incentive problems these may create, especially in a global economy where high-income, high-tax individuals have the option of moving to a country with lower tax rates.

The goal of the study that constitutes this book, commissioned by the Ford Foundation, was to identify lessons from the experiences of other countries that may be useful to the United States in reforming its Social Security program. When the study agenda was first formulated, establishing individual accounts as part of the public retirement program was at the forefront of the US policy debate, and the Ford Foundation asked us to look at the track record of such accounts in other countries.

The George W. Bush administration had made proposals that, if fully implemented, would have drastically changed the nature of the Social Security program. The Bush administration had suggested individual accounts, which would enable workers to divert a fraction of their Social Security tax contributions to a retirement fund with a portfolio of financial assets that would generate retirement income. In return these workers would receive a smaller benefit from the traditional Social Security program. But the individual accounts were not aimed at reducing the system's funding deficit; rather, the shortfall in Social Security funding would be addressed by varying the amount of indexing in the benefit formula depending on the level of recipients' income. Social Security benefits would gradually become a smaller portion of retirement support for middle-class Americans, who would instead be encouraged and expected to invest in individual accounts together with private retirement accounts, whereas low-income workers would continue to receive the same level of benefits as under the current system. Social Security would thus become an antipoverty program for the elderly, not the broad retirement program it is today.

Whatever its merits and flaws, the Bush plan for individual accounts is generally considered dead, as it achieved no political or popular acceptance. Because the lessons from foreign experiences of individual accounts may therefore seem less relevant, we broadened the scope of this study to consider a much wider set of pension policy issues in many countries, including statutory and actual retirement ages, distributional challenges, and the intersection between public and private retirement plans.

Importantly, however, despite the change in the United States policy debate, we retained an emphasis on individual accounts because we believe that the creation of such a program, as an addition to the current Social Security retirement plan, is important, perhaps even essential, for the future of older Americans of moderate income. The Bush administration's mistake was in trying to replace the current Social Security retirement program with such accounts. The existing Social Security program is broadly popular, and although it faces a significant fiscal challenge, this challenge could be overcome by modest adjustments on the revenue and benefit sides.

In fact, one of the key lessons from this international comparison is that the current US Social Security retirement program has substantial virtues. The fact that the benefit levels are modest carries the advantage that the program does not cause significant changes in private behavior, such as early retirement or the displacement of private saving for retirement. The small impact on employment decisions is reinforced by the adjustment of benefit levels depending on the age at which people first take benefits. The modest benefit levels also mean that the program's funding shortfall is not particularly sizable, in comparison with many countries where more generous public pension benefit levels have effectively displaced most private pension programs (which are much higher in the United States than in other countries). With a few exceptions, these countries have not accumulated trust funds for their public pension programs and must pay for future benefits from future payroll taxes, so their funding shortfalls are much larger.[3]

After reviewing public pensions in many countries, we concluded that the first problem to address in US retirement policy is that low-wage workers do not save and rely too heavily on Social Security benefits. A virtue of the US Social Security system—its modest scale—also means that workers who do not save end up with inadequate financial resources when they retire.[4] Any broad increase in the generosity of benefits is not going to happen in the United States, because it would exacerbate the system's funding problems. That means another solution is needed to the problem of inadequate income for the elderly: namely, a plan to increase saving among low- and moderate-income households. We believe that a program of individual accounts to supplement Social Security benefits would be a valuable contribution.

After comparing individual account programs around the world, we found that the Bush administration proposal for such accounts was well designed. It was based on the work of an expert commission[5] convened in 2001 to design a program of individual accounts that would avoid most of the problems of such plans in other countries. This design should form the template for a program that automatically enrolls US workers in supplementary individual retirement accounts.

The Social Security Administration would administer the program and the Internal Revenue Service (IRS) would collect the money, which would range from 2 to 5 percent of Social Security wages. These government agencies would be precluded from either investing or controlling how the funds are invested and how any equities holdings are voted; private managers, under the supervision of an independent board of trustees, would handle the investment of funds. Workers would be able to opt out of the program, but there would be incentives for them to participate. The administrative costs of the plan, except for a fee paid to the fund managers, would be covered by general tax revenues. Employers who did not offer a private retirement plan to their employees would be required to

---

3. As Peter Diamond reminded us in comments on this chapter, whether or not there is a trust fund does not indicate the underlying cost of supporting future retirees. With lower per capita income and labor force participation, however, the fiscal challenge facing many European economies is substantial. The US economy has the additional concerns of a much higher cost of health care and a large net foreign debt.

4. McKinsey Global Institute (2008) describes the lack of preparedness for retirement among the baby-boomer generation.

5. The President's Commission to Strengthen Social Security released its report on December 21, 2001. It is available at www.csss.gov/reports.

match the employee contributions.[6] In addition, the minimum age at which workers could start collecting Social Security benefits would be higher for workers that failed to participate in the retirement program, unless they had an adequate private retirement plan. This provision would prevent low-wage workers who retire at age 62 from becoming poor at later stages in life at age 85 or 90. Participants would be automatically enrolled in an age-adjusted default portfolio of bonds and stocks but could opt out after signing a waiver. Many higher-income employees enrolled in employer-sponsored retirement plans would likely opt out.

The second problem with the US Social Security program is its funding shortfall. As we have noted, the funding problems of the Social Security retirement fund are small relative to those in many other countries; however, they still need to be addressed. We also support a continued increase in the retirement age over time as life expectancy increases. The funding shortfall is a solvable problem.[7] However, our international study gave us a particular perspective on the issue. We were struck by the uniqueness of the United States in its reliance on tax preferences to support social insurance. Health insurance for those under 65 can be purchased with before-tax dollars. Home ownership (arguably a form of social insurance) can be financed with tax-deductible mortgage interest payments. And, of course, individuals can save for retirement out of before-tax dollars and employers can offer tax-preferred retirement benefit plans All of these provisions are advantageous primarily to upper-income households, and all are very popular politically and unlikely to be changed any time soon (in fact, the scope of retirement saving out of after-tax dollars has been significantly expanded in the last few years).

Another weakness of the US Social Security retirement plan is that it does not redistribute from high- to low-income participants.[8] The average retiree receives $1,000 to $1,500 a month, as we said earlier, but a married person who is a household's single wage earner and retires at 65 at the maximum level of Social Security benefits would receive over $3,000 a month. The lack of redistribution is not uncommon around the world, but some countries have retirement payments that are substantially more redistributive.

---

6. It is common for employers to have a vesting period for their retirement plans, such that short-term employees are not credited with anything in their retirement accounts when they leave. Such employers (including small businesses) would have to at least match their employees' contributions to the national plan.

7. There are several good proposals already on the table, notably the plan presented by Peter Diamond and Peter Orszag (2005).

8. Social Security overall is redistributive because of the disability and survivor benefits that disproportionately benefit lower-income recipients. On the other hand, the retirement program's spousal benefits favor husband-and-wife households with only one earner, and these are often the more affluent households.

Overall, therefore, the US Social Security retirement program and tax code provisions for private pensions provide significantly larger financial advantages to upper-income than to lower-income households. Retirement income has been likened to a three-legged stool, with public pensions, employer pensions, and individual saving as the three legs. Because two of these favor high-income households, we conclude that reducing the level of Social Security retirement benefits for higher-income workers is justifiable as part of an overall plan to address the funding shortfall. The approach is based on the principle of fairness: Those who benefit most from tax preferences as they build private retirement wealth receive somewhat less from the public retirement pension plan. We propose linking the size of that reduction to the amount of recipients' tax-advantaged saving during their working life. There is widespread support for both "fixing Social Security" and ensuring that Social Security benefit cuts affect only those who earn higher incomes.[9] We believe that the proposals presented in this book offer an intuitively fair and thus politically sound way to accomplish these goals.

Structure of the Book

The most common approach to comparative cross-country studies of pension systems is to assess each country's experiences and use them to draw broader conclusions. Typically, a native specialist author writes about his or her country, or a country specialist at an international institution like the OECD or the World Bank provides coverage. There are numerous recent studies and reports of this type.[10]

We have chosen to structure our comparative report differently, looking at specific challenges that affect pension systems in aging societies and that present obstacles to pension reform. We have made this choice for several reasons. First, we acknowledge that we could not provide the same level of country expertise available in many country-specific studies. Second, we feel that there is a risk of getting caught up in the details with country studies. Each country's pension system is complex and unique, with a particular history and political anchoring that offer abundant idiosyncratic details and data—so much so that there is a risk that the comparative value of such "pension system anthropologies" is drowned

---

9. The differential indexing proposal included in the Bush proposals for Social Security reform would have cut benefits for high-income families relative to the current system.

10. See, for instance, Gruber and Wise (1999), Holtzman et al. (2005), Penner (2007), Whitehouse (2007), and many others. The Gruber and Wise study is decentralized, in the sense that national experts made the calculations with an international set of terms of reference. The OECD and World Bank studies were centralized and then checked with national experts.

in historical minutiae and country-specific data. By focusing instead on challenges that affect all developed economies, we hope to avoid falling into this trap.

Third, we wish to take advantage of recent improvements in the collection and quality of pension-relevant cross-country data, particularly by the OECD. We use such data extensively throughout this report and believe that they provide a sound empirical basis for our cross-country analysis. We do, however, acknowledge that our cross-country data focus limits our analytical options—such that, for instance, we do engage in forward projections for individual countries—and data limitations has been a recurring issue in writing this book.

Fourth, we believe that by focusing on several challenges to the pension system, we avoid "silo'ing" our study: Too often, cross-country studies of pension systems focus on just one aspect (tier) of the total pension system, such as Social Security in the United States and government-run PAYGO schemes in other countries. In this study we extensively cover the challenges facing other parts of the pension system in the United States and elsewhere, most importantly the labor market and corporate pension schemes. Nicholas Barr and Peter Diamond (2008a, 2008b) also identify a comprehensive view of pension reform as a key reform principle. We look carefully at the sizable corporate pensions in America, as these, together with other non–Social Security sources of income, provide the largest share of retirement income for the top income quintile. We believe our broader focus enables us to draw a series of powerful conclusions and offer a reform proposal for the United States that integrates Social Security with other parts of the US retirement income security system.

Fifth, we acknowledge that our focus on challenges in some respects limits our pool of potential countries of interest to relatively "like units" at least somewhat similar to the United States in overall levels of economic development.[11] As a result, with few exceptions (notably Chile and Mexico), we do not venture beyond high-income OECD or EU member countries. However, this scope of analysis enables us to capture most of the international pension reform experiences and challenges relevant to US Social Security.

Last, we also acknowledge that our comparative cross-country methodology has inherent limitations. It is not possible to determine the details of a plan for US Social Security reform simply by looking at what has and has not worked in other countries. We are, therefore, reluctant to identify specific numeric target values for Social Security reform. We do not, for instance, believe that the experiences of other countries are helpful in determining specific revenue-raising measures for US policymakers in their efforts to reform Social Security. Rather, we believe the experiences of other countries are useful and informative in determining the broader

---

11. See Sartori (1996) on the selection of units for comparison.

policy areas and tools that have achieved results and thus would be suitable for inclusion in US Social Security reforms, given the particular circumstances found in the United States. Our aim is to provide US policymakers with advice about general directions for reforming Social Security, not to deliver a finely detailed and fully estimated reform proposal.

We begin in this chapter by highlighting the most important findings likely to be of interest to US policymakers, and we then discuss the policy implications of these findings. The following chapters cover most of the OECD economies and assess pensions on many dimensions. Chapter 2 deciphers the fiscal or budget challenge facing retirement programs and how it is affected by demographic change. Chapter 3 discusses the distributional challenge of retirement plans, in terms of both alleviation of elderly poverty and equity among generations and demographic groups. We include a section on the differences between public and private pensions. Then chapter 4 examines the labor markets and work incentive challenges and assesses the extent to which retirement programs alter economic incentives and resulting labor market participation. Chapter 5 looks at individual accounts in practice, with a focus on funded accounts and how the introduction of individual accounts has or has not responded to the challenges. Chapter 6 does the same for notional (nonfinancial) or unfunded individual accounts. Chapter 7 considers the relevance of private employer–sponsored retirement programs to reforms for Social Security and other public-sector programs. Chapter 8 presents our conclusions and integrated reform proposal for US Social Security.

Key Findings

On Fiscal and Demographic Challenges

The fiscal challenges facing the US Social Security retirement program are smaller than in most other OECD countries. The reasons for this finding are as follows. First, the generosity of Social Security benefits is lower than that of most European economies, and so the fiscal burden of future benefit payments is not nearly as large as for those economies. Japan and the United Kingdom are similar to the United States in providing only modest mandatory government pension benefits. Second, the age of withdrawal from the labor market is higher in the United States than in most other advanced economies (Japan is the main exception). In many European countries there is an "official" age of eligibility for a full public pension of around 65, but in practice many workers retire and begin receiving early retirement benefits before then. Third, until the early 1970s, the European economies had labor force participation rates and hours of work comparable to those in the United States; since then, however, unemployment has risen, labor force participation has fallen, and

Figure 1.1   Gross public pension expenditure, 2005 and 2050

percent of GDP

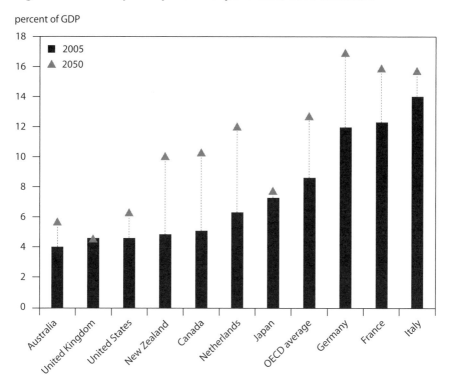

OECD = Organization for Economic Cooperation and Development

Source: Queisser and Whitehouse (2005).

hours of work per employee have declined substantially. Thus the amount of work done by the working age population in Europe is now much lower than in the United States. Fourth, birth rates have declined sharply in some European and North Asian countries, which means that the rate of population growth is low and in some countries there is even population decline; projected population declines in Northeast Asia and Eastern and Mediterranean Europe are very large. Taken together, these trends indicate that the retiree population is being supported by taxes paid on relatively few hours of work and that the challenge of public pension provision is going to get much worse in many countries. Figure 1.1 shows the percentage of GDP going to gross public pensions in 2005 (bars) and 2050 (arrowheads). The United States starts low and increases less than many countries.

We conclude that unlike in many other countries, where the problems in the public pension system are the principal driver of future fiscal trajectories and forces politicians' hands, this is not the case in the United States.

The US Social Security program is in much better shape than the retirement programs of most other advanced countries. But this does not mean there is no fiscal problem in America. For one thing, US government health care spending is growing rapidly and will continue to do so unless there are major reforms in Medicare. The federal budget overall will therefore be under great stress even though the Social Security fiscal problem is not that serious in international comparison. This is of additional concern because of the persistent substantial federal budget deficit (even recently, when the economy was basically at full employment). In short, the US Social Security program must restore its own solvency because there are a lot of other claims on general tax revenues, making the option of covering the Social Security shortfall with these revenues not viable.

The level of total prefunded assets toward pension provision is very high in the United States. Evaluations of countries' preparations for aging populations usually focus on the state of public finances, but this is only part of the picture, as substantial assets in many countries have been accumulated in the private sector. Surprising, perhaps, to some for such a "low savings economy," the level of prefunded assets for pension provision in the United States is among the highest in the OECD, at 136 percent of GDP in 2006. This substantially improves the comparative level of preparation for aging societies in the United States and emphasizes the scale of the challenges facing some OECD countries (particularly in Southern Europe).

Tax treatment of pension benefits differs widely across the OECD; US taxation of pension benefits is among the lowest. Total taxation levels (i.e., including both direct and indirect taxes) on pension benefits vary from 10 percent or less in Japan, Mexico, and the United States to 50 percent or more in the Scandinavian countries. This difference has a large, but frequently overlooked, impact on the sustainability of public pension systems in the OECD.

The value of tax breaks given to pensions is very high in the United States and a few other OECD countries. When computing the true net level of public pension expenditures, it is not sufficient to account only for the net effects of taxation of benefits; one must further account for the value of tax breaks for pension savings. In the United States these are very high, at more than 1 percent of GDP. This means that the net level of public pension expenditures in the United States is higher relative to many other countries—including Canada, the United Kingdom, and the Scandinavian countries—than many believe.

The adverse demographic outlook is concentrated in Eastern and Southern Europe and Northeast Asia; the United States has the most favorable outlook in the OECD. The United States will continue to experience a growing workforce (albeit at a much slower rate) in the first part of the 21st century. The US population will, therefore, merely grow older, whereas most countries in Northern Europe will experience stagnant or mildly declining growth in their working age populations, and their populations overall will age much faster than in the United States. In Southern and Eastern Europe, Germany, and Northeast Asia, the working age population, on the other hand, will shrink dramatically and their populations will not merely age but shrink in the decades ahead.

Immigration is not the answer to the funding shortfall. The fiscal problems of advanced-country pensions are partly the result of declines in population growth. Although it may appear that adding more people of working age could provide an important part of the solution, we found that this was not the reality. Under any realistic scenario of immigration, the fiscal problems will still be severe.

In many countries effective retirement ages matter more than demographics for labor supply. The effective retirement age[12] in the United States at about 63 years of age is only slightly below the age of full pension eligibility (65–67 years for Social Security). In other OECD countries, the difference between statutory and effective retirement ages may be as much as 6 to 7 years, leading to very low effective retirement ages (e.g., less than 60 in France). In contrast, the effective retirement age in Japan is close to 70, indicating a far more robust position than the country's demographic outlook alone would predict.

On the Distributive Challenge

Most developed-country pension programs derive from two historical models. Government retirement pension programs can be traced back to policies developed in Germany and the United Kingdom in the 19th and early 20th centuries. In Germany, Bismarck introduced welfare reforms in 1891, including a contributory pension plan in which workers would pay into the program during their working lives and draw out from it during retirement. And in 1908 the United Kingdom introduced a flat rate elderly pension, paid for out of general tax revenue and means-tested so that only those with low incomes received the pension. It was designed as an anti-poverty plan for the elderly.

In the United States, federal financial support for the elderly was not introduced until the Social Security Act of 1935. The first of the act's two parts provided for grants to states for assistance to the elderly who had

---

12. Throughout this book, we use the standard OECD definition of "effective retirement age": the average age at which persons 40 and older leave the labor force.

very low incomes. This program, similar in basic structure to the UK plan, was financed by general tax revenue, as it still is, having evolved into the Supplemental Security Income (SSI) program. The second part of the act called for the financing of federal old age benefits by employer and employee taxes; its design is close to the German model.

Until the postwar period the SSI program was far larger than the contributory Social Security plan, for the obvious reason that few retirees had contributed much. There was also no indexing of benefits until 1951, so that real benefit levels were seriously eroded by postwar inflation. Gradually, Social Security became the predominant vehicle for income support of the elderly and SSI is now small in comparison. In other words, in its early decades, the US Social Security system was far more redistributive than it is today.

The historical review helps to put government retirement programs around the world in context. The English-speaking countries often have plans that were designed initially to alleviate elderly poverty rather than as contributory programs. Some are means-tested, as with the minimum benefit in Australia, and some simply provide a low level of benefit to everyone, as in New Zealand. The programs of continental Europe, built more closely on the German model, provide more generous average retirement benefits, scaled to replace a significant proportion of each worker's income at the level achieved in the years before retirement. In practice, most countries have hybrid programs that balance the principle of giving more to those who have contributed more against the principle of redistribution and poverty alleviation. However, the originating principles are still evident; the most generous countries, measured by average benefit levels, are often the least redistributive because they are based on contribution levels.

US Social Security is less redistributive than the retirement benefits of other English-speaking countries. US Social Security is significantly less redistributive than mandatory pension systems in other English-speaking countries with which the United States is normally compared. However, there is no indication in other English-speaking countries (or elsewhere) that higher levels of redistribution in the mandatory pension systems undermines public support for it.

OECD poverty rates for the elderly differ substantially and are very high in some countries. The OECD has its own definition of poverty, based on *relative* income—persons receiving less than 50 percent of median income (after adjusting for household size). In the United States in 2000, this meant a poverty-level income of about $12,000 rather than $8,300, which was the official US poverty level for a single adult. Based on the OECD definition, the US old-age poverty rate is above average for the OECD membership, although this is in part because of the high median income of nonelderly US households. However, also according to the OECD definition, over 30 percent of persons over age 76 in the United States live in poverty.

In nearly all OECD countries, including the United States, most of the income of elderly families comes from government pensions (except for the highest income groups). The key similarity between the United States and other OECD countries is that retirees outside the top income quintile rely entirely or predominantly on Social Security and public payments for their income. Only among retirees in the top income quintile (except in Japan) does income from private capital or employment beyond retirement age constitute a substantial part of retirement income.

Time spent in retirement has substantially increased in recent decades. With the combination of rising life expectancies and declining effective retirement ages, retiring generations in the OECD can look forward to 5 to 10 years more in retirement than their parents' generation.

Directly linking life expectancies to retirement ages is increasingly popular in mandatory pension programs. Many countries have introduced prefixed increases in the eligibility ages for (both early retirement and) full pensions, as the United States did for Social Security in 1983. An increasing number of OECD countries are also linking eligibility ages in mandatory pension systems directly to changes in life expectancies, sometimes in addition to (i.e., coming into effect after) prefixed rises.

Life expectancy varies by income and education. Data from the OECD countries reveal a relationship between income level and life expectancy that contributes to a distributional challenge. On average, workers with low incomes or low education or both die younger than those at higher income or educational levels and thus receive government pension benefits for fewer years.

Many countries have instituted early retirement programs for manufacturing or other workers who do manual or physically demanding work because of the perception that it is difficult for such workers to continue beyond their mid-50s.

In addition, in Europe early retirement has often been a way to restructure industries with declining employment, and in the United States it has similarly been offered to unionized workers in industries such as auto manufacturing and steel, where the unions bargained for early retirement and health care.

Aside from unions, however, whose numbers have dwindled drastically, there are no such provisions in the United States. Social Security allows early retirement but only with a reduction in monthly benefits.

OECD public-sector employees generally enjoy better pensions and are older than those in the private sector. Partly as an intentional outcome of personnel management and human resource policies, government employees across the OECD typically enjoy lower retirement ages and higher replacement rates than available to the general public. Government workers are also typically older than the average workforce. This is especially true for state and local government employees in the United States.

Substantial underfunding of pension promises exists among some US state and local governments, and potentially even larger unfunded health care–related expenses will soon be added. The funding levels of US state and local government pension funds vary from extreme underfunding (funding ratios of less than 20 percent in 2006) to significant overfunding. Thus no general public pension funding crisis exists in the United States, but localized pain may be significant. With the implementation of Government Accounting Standards Board (GASB) Rule No. 45, state and local governments will have to estimate and reveal the extent of their unfunded "other postemployment benefits" (OPEBs), which are overwhelmingly in health care. Some estimates suggest that this may require funding of $500 billion to $1 trillion in additional liabilities for state and local governments. It also seems certain that the impact of the fall 2008 global economic crisis and declining asset prices will put significant additional financial stress on state and local government pension funds.

On the Labor-Market Incentives Challenge

Employment rates of older workers differ significantly by gender and between OECD countries. Employment rates for older male workers declined rapidly in most OECD countries after 1970 but started to rise slowly again in the mid-1990s. But there has been a constant rise in the employment rates of 55- to 64-year-old women, mirroring the rise in overall female labor force participation in the OECD. A few countries, noticeably Japan, did not experience any decline in male employment rates among older workers.

Retirement and tax policies significantly affect employment rates of older workers. This finding is illustrated by the following observations:

- Econometric analysis has found a strong relationship between labor force participation of the elderly and measures of economic incentives.

- There is very little variation across OECD countries in the employment rate of males 25 to 54 years old but large variations for men over 55. Employment rates have declined most in the countries that have increased the availability of early retirement benefits, notably the European economies.

- A policy change in New Zealand in the 1990s increased the retirement age in the public pension program and resulted in a large increase in the employment rate of older workers. There were no comparable changes for younger cohorts.

- Japan has high employment rates for older men matched by strong incentives to work. The basic government pension is very low, and workers over age 65 do not face a reduction of pension benefits as a result of continued earnings (although a 2004 reform introduced an earnings test for workers aged 65–69 to be phased in starting in 2013).[13]

- The average retirement age in the United States is higher than in most European countries. The US Social Security system is not especially generous, does not allow benefits to be drawn before age 62, and adjusts benefit levels so that the program is roughly incentive-neutral for retirement between 62 and 70.

- Evidence from Sweden indicated that take-up rates for "part-time pensions" were extremely sensitive to the replacement rate offered to beneficiaries.

Older workers in most OECD countries will be significantly better educated. As a direct outcome of rising educational attainment in recent decades, most OECD countries will experience a significant improvement in the educational attainment of their older workers (55–64) in coming decades. This will be less true in the United States, where educational attainment among the same age group is already high and will plateau.

On Individual Account Plans

Policymakers see individual accounts as a way to address the fiscal challenge of retirement plans, improve work incentives, and increase national saving. Policymakers facing budgetary shortfalls in public pension programs and declining rates of labor force participation have been attracted to individual account plans because they can be self-financing. If workers pay in while working and then collect back their contributions (plus interest) in retirement, then the government simply facilitates individual saving for retirement and does not face budget obligations.

Similarly, if workers see that the amounts deducted from their paychecks for retirement are actually going into an accumulating fund from which they will withdraw later, they may view these payments as deferred

---

13. Employment rates in Japan have been boosted by the fact that many of the elderly were agricultural and rural workers who received lower pension benefits than public and private employees. Cultural factors may also affect Japan's higher employment rates.

compensation rather than as taxes. When deciding whether or not to retire, workers will trade off the value of a longer retirement against the benefit of accumulating a larger pool of retirement funds to consume once they retire. For policymakers concerned about the impact of taxes in reducing labor supply, this is an advantage.

Increasing the rate of national saving is an objective for many policymakers, and compulsory funded individual accounts can be expected to increase private saving. There is a first-round impact on saving, as contributions to the program add to total saving. This could overstate the final impact as some contributors will reduce their voluntary saving in response to the required program, but the impact will still be positive as workers who would not have saved voluntarily are required to do so.[14] Some workers may add to their voluntary saving as they gain experience as owners of a retirement account.

Individual accounts are not redistributive, often leading policymakers to add provisions to reduce elderly poverty. In a pure individual account system where contributions are a percent of earnings, the distribution of earnings translates directly into a matching distribution of pension receipts. Workers that earn near-poverty-level wages will find that their retirement assets are too small to provide retirement income above the poverty line.

This distributional issue has led to the modification of some individual account systems to assist the poor. In Chile, for example, low-income participants in the individual account system receive the minimum benefit level rather than the amount based on their retirement assets. Many workers participate in the program only long enough to qualify for the minimum benefit or stay out of the program altogether. In the country's recent elections, both main parties promised to provide more support for the elderly poor—and in fact such provisions have now been enacted into law.

In Sweden, there are various provisions to assist those with low incomes, including subsidized benefits for those whose individual accounts are small, as well as housing, health, and transportation subsidies. The individual account proposal by the US administration in 2002 had a provision for low-income workers to continue to receive the level of Social Security benefits that they would have received under the current system.

In practice, therefore, the goals of policymakers in setting up individual accounts are not fully realized. There remains a fiscal burden from supporting low-wage workers. And work incentives are reduced if further contributions to the retirement plan have no impact on future benefits, which are set by the minimum level and not by contributions.

---

14. If a system of funded individual accounts replaces a PAYGO system, then any reduction of private saving is likely to be minimal, since some individuals may have already offset expected retirement benefits by reduced saving.

Unfunded plans, proposed as an alternative to the fiscal challenge of replacing a PAYGO pension program with an individual account plan, do not increase saving. Nearly all contributory public pension plans in the OECD have relied on the PAYGO structure. Shifting to individual accounts creates a huge budget challenge because of the obligations to existing retirees and workers who have made contributions. A few countries, such as Australia, have met this challenge by using general tax revenues to pay past obligations and funneling new contributions to individual accounts invested in private stocks and bonds. Others have opted for unfunded plans in which new contributions are credited to individual accounts but the money is actually used to pay past obligations (e.g., Latvia and Sweden, both of which also have small funded accounts).

Unfunded individual accounts can change the work incentive for beneficiaries, creating a tight link between contributions made while working and benefits received in retirement. These accounts also face the same distributional issue as funded accounts. And, since no funds are invested in real assets, there is no increase in saving from these programs.

Individual accounts are a way to frame the policy debate. Several countries found a sustainable solution to their pension funding shortfalls by introducing individual accounts. The best such example is Sweden, where the policy change (to unfunded individual accounts) was debated and widely understood, paving the way for adoption of a "balancing" formula that will adjust pensions in the event of funding shortfalls. Chile and Mexico also have replaced failing public pension plans with individual accounts and created sustainable retirement assets for the middle class. In Italy, on the other hand, the individual account plan was not understood, and implementation was de facto postponed well into the future.

Administrative costs for privately managed individual accounts are high. The experiences of Chile and Mexico show that the administrative costs of privately managed funded individual accounts have been very high, sharply reducing effective returns to contributors, particularly those with low wages and low contribution levels (the real rate of return on the largest fund asset in Chile averaged 10.2 percent per year in 1985–2002, while returns accruing to participants averaged 4.3 to 6.9 percent). There is a very strong case for pooling contributions before passing them on to private investment managers, as is done for the funded portion of the Swedish retirement program.[15] Chilean pension funds have also had high marketing expenses.

---

15. According to Turner (2005), administrative costs in Chile averaged 1.4 percent of account balances as of 1998, while those in Sweden averaged 0.95 percent as of 2000. Of the 0.95 percent in fees in Sweden, 0.3 percent goes to the central government agency that pools the individual contributions.

Competition among fund managers did not lower administrative costs in Chile or Mexico. The government of Chile wanted to use competition among different funds to lower both administrative and marketing costs of the public pension program, recognizing that high costs would substantially lower returns, especially for low-wage workers with small contributions. This did not happen. Instead, the funds competed against each other in their marketing efforts and costs remained very high. A similar experience occurred in Mexico.

We found no evidence of excessively risky investments by participants. We did not find examples where participants had made rash investment decisions and incurred losses on their accounts. In most plans the investment choices have been constrained, often to investments in safe bonds, although many plans (notably in Chile) are increasing the range of choices. The United Kingdom had individual accounts available to public pension participants during the technology bubble, but, after looking at the policy literature and press reports and contacting experts on the UK program, we found no evidence of people having lost a disproportional amount of money on speculative investments in the UK individual accounts program.[16]

Allowing retirees with individual accounts to withdraw the funds in a lump sum creates serious problems. Australia allows lump-sum withdrawals, and many participants take advantage of this option, generally to reduce their debts or finance living expenses for early retirement. Then, once they reach the official retirement age, having exhausted their personal retirement savings, they apply for the means-tested minimum public pension and get it because they have little or no other income at that point (Australia exempts the value of the primary residence from the means-testing). Effective regulation could avoid this problem by requiring the purchase of annuities, as is done in some countries.[17]

The distributional problem in individual account plans has been difficult to solve. In Chile, the distributional problem has resulted in a high dependence on the minimum pension provision, which is too low to prevent elderly poverty. Even though the individual account system is required of employees, many workers in Chile either do not participate or participate only long enough to qualify for its minimum pension and then move into

---

16. However, there was a scandal in the United Kingdom because financial institutions advised people to withdraw from the state PAYGO plan and create individual accounts when this was not in their best financial interests.

17. There are alternatives to annuities with similar results—programmed withdrawals, for example.

self-employment or the informal sector. Sweden prevents elderly poverty by providing low-wage workers with retirement support beyond the level justified by past contributions, although many retirees face a very high implicit tax rate (48 percent) on other income received in retirement.

Individual account plans do not solve or obviate problems created by political pressure groups. Individual accounts appear to be a politically feasible way to deal with failing pension plans and/or the funding crisis created by demographic change, but political pressures do not disappear. Public-sector employees in Latvia, for example, were able to negotiate a special retirement deal that has partly undercut the introduction of individual accounts, and pensions for the armed forces in Chile were exempt from the individual account plan.

Evidence on the question of whether funded accounts increase national saving is positive but thin. There is pretty solid evidence that the introduction of funded individual accounts in Chile, which has the longest-running funded plan, increased the national saving rate. But it would be nice to get corroborating evidence elsewhere. Australia, Canada, and the United Kingdom have not seen clear signs of increased saving, although their programs may be too small, have design problems, or not have been in place long enough.

There have been administrative problems in individual accounts in some countries, but not broadly. The introduction of individual accounts has generally been free of administrative problems, but there are a few exceptions (e.g., Hungary, Mexico, and Poland). Latvia is also an exception, but this is because of its transition economy and the loss of past employment records. It appears that individual accounts are feasible in most advanced economies with good record keeping and computerized systems.

On Corporate Pensions

Coverage rates for employer-funded private pensions in America have remained roughly stable since the 1970s, but coverage has shifted away from defined benefit plans. Private employer-sponsored pension programs were never a universal part of the labor market. These programs typically covered higher-wage white-collar workers and union workers, who were only a fraction of the workforce. Furthermore, the decline in coverage of such programs for males has been offset by an increase in coverage for females, so that the proportion of the US workforce covered by such plans has not fallen by much. About 25 percent of the workforce had company pension plans in 1960; this figure rose to slightly below 50 percent by the late 1970s and was still at about that level as of 2006. The decline in unionization has resulted in a decline in pension coverage for blue-collar workers, and there has also been a substantial shift to defined contribution plans and away from defined benefit plans.

Only a minority of those over 65 receive any private pension income. The fraction has been rising slowly but remains well below 50 percent. In 1975, in the bottom three quintiles of the income distribution for persons over 65, only about 2, 5, and 18 percent, respectively, received *any* income from private pensions. Even for the top income quintile the figure was only around 45 percent. By 2005, these figures had risen to around 5, 10, and 25 percent, respectively, for the lower three quintiles and about 55 percent for both of the top quintiles.

Private corporate pensions were often introduced as supplements to Social Security. Corporate pensions, introduced during and after World War II, were often closely tied to the provisions of Social Security. Many were "top-up" plans, in which the company agreed to ensure that the retiree had a certain level of income, based on Social Security and a company supplement if the government benefit fell below the agreed amount. Any increase in Social Security benefits would then be matched by a decrease in the employer contribution.

To a greater extent than in most other countries, the United States encourages tax-advantaged private retirement saving and has a larger stock of private pension wealth than any other economy. This finding may seem inconsistent with those above, but it is not, because the private retirement wealth is held mostly by higher-income workers, a small fraction of the US population. The OMB estimated that the tax revenue loss from private pension provisions in 2005 was over $100 billion.[18]

By 2006, US corporate defined benefit pension plans had returned to solid funding levels. By 2006 the so-called perfect pension fund storm of declining stock prices and record low interest rates in the early 2000s had passed. The overall funding level for the largest US corporate pension plans in S&P 500 had returned to full funding by then.[19] However, corporate pension plan funding levels remain volatile, and the impact of the fall 2008 global economic crisis on funding levels is likely to be dramatic. The OECD (2008) estimates that the total decline in OECD pension fund assets from December 2007 to October 2008 reached $3.3 trillion, of which $2.2 trillion occurred among US pension funds alone.

---

18. This is a tricky calculation because tax receipts are lower at the time income is sheltered but higher at the time it is withdrawn. See OMB (2007).

19. The adequacy of funding for pensions depends on the discount rate used, which can be volatile.

Nearly all US defined benefit plan terminations are voluntary, and only a very small number of very high–income Americans have lost any pension benefits as a result. Of the defined benefit plans terminated in the United States since 1974, 98 percent have been voluntary and without any loss of workers' pension benefits. Only a very small number of Americans (those with defined benefit pensions about four times the average Social Security benefit) have experienced any loss of benefits.

The financial situation of the Pension Benefit Guaranty Corporation (PBGC) is stabilizing, and the corporation has successfully sheltered covered American workers against pension benefit losses, but it is declining in importance. The level of "reasonably possible" liabilities for the PBGC fell by $46 billion to $62 billion from 2005 to 2007, reflecting the overall improvement in US corporate defined benefit plan finances. Combined with the reforms of the PBGC included in the 2006 Pension Protection Act (PPA), this puts the PBGC in a relatively good position to weather the impact of the 2008 global economic crisis on corporate pension plans. The share of US workers covered by the PBGC is declining rapidly as defined benefit plan provision becomes rarer.

Long-term trends, rather than short-term financial pain, explain the switch from corporate defined benefit pension plan provision in the United States. Rapidly rising administrative costs, longevity risk, shifts in accounting rules toward more transparency, asset-liability mismatches, and the advantages in a flexible work environment of defined contribution plans all explain the shift from corporate defined benefit pension plan provision in the United States. Also, many workers do not expect to remain with the same firm long enough to receive pensions from defined benefit plans.

The shift from corporate defined benefit plans is a global one, as financial troubles in such plans have been widespread among the major industrialized economies. Corporate defined benefit pension plans in Canada, Germany, Japan, and the United Kingdom have experienced many of the financial and funding problems seen among US corporations. The prolonged stagnation in Japan in the 1990s even necessitated a government rescue of the country's corporate defined benefit plans, which saw up to $120 billion of hitherto private corporate pension plan assets and an unknown (but significantly higher) level of corporate pension plan liabilities transferred to the Japanese government. In most industrialized countries corporations are shifting away from defined benefit pension plans for the same reasons as are US corporations.

Many OECD countries have had corporate pension plans based solely on defined contribution benefit provision for many years. Unlike in the United States, where corporate pension schemes were traditionally of the defined benefit type and have only relatively recently shifted toward defined contribution/hybrid schemes, several OECD countries with large-scale corporate pension schemes have relied solely on defined contribution pensions for decades.

US corporations have experienced no relative competitive disadvantage vis-à-vis companies in other major industrial nations from their pension commitments. As defined benefit plans and associated financial trouble have both been widespread across companies in major industrialized nations, pension liabilities in US corporations have not created any particular competitive disadvantage. Instead, any such disadvantage for US corporations is related primarily to health care.

Policy Implications

Lessons from Overseas Do Not Suggest a Need for Major Reform in the United States

There is always a good deal of stickiness in the policy environment, and it is rare that policymakers succeed in upending the policy cart and changing a system. For example, President Bill Clinton's attempt at major reforms in the US health care system went down to defeat in the 1990s. And the Bush administration's attempt to introduce individual Social Security accounts made no progress even though the proposal was for a voluntary program. Looking overseas we see similar resistance to change. The countries that have instituted major reforms (Australia, Chile, Italy, Latvia, Mexico, Poland, Sweden, and the United Kingdom), particularly those that have introduced individual accounts as replacements for PAYGO plans, have faced substantial budget problems in their pension programs and in many cases were undergoing major economic transformations. And even in these countries there has been a fair amount of backtracking from a purely contributory individual account plan as they face the problem of low-wage workers that drop out of the system and end up in poverty or on a minimum pension program.

Given the political difficulties involved, is it worthwhile to attempt a major overhaul of the US system? Several of our findings are relevant to the answer, specifically those that relate to the fiscal shortfall, labor force participation, the saving challenge, and the distributional challenge.

First, the fiscal problem with the US Social Security system is not very large, so major reforms are not necessary to deal with it. Instead, incremental changes to benefit levels, taxes, or retirement ages would restore solvency to the program. This contrasts with the situation for pension programs in other countries (and with the US Medicare program), where the projected funding shortfalls are huge.

Second, the structure of the Social Security program allows participants to retire before the normal eligibility age for a full pension at age 65, but it does not give them an economic incentive to do so. Participants are free to choose their retirement age beyond the minimum age of 62 but with benefit levels adjusted for age of first benefit receipt. This contrasts with many European countries, where public pension programs have often subsidized early retirement.

The third point is more nuanced. The current Social Security system does not add to national saving; indeed, it may reduce it to the extent that participants count on public benefits and fail to save on their own. In addition, the United States is generally a low saving economy (independent of retirement planning); in fact, the national saving rate is almost certainly too low. So, in principle, a major reform of Social Security that raised the national saving rate would have merit. But this is not a compelling argument for major reform because there is no feasible plan on the table for Social Security reform that would add to national saving. An unfunded system like that in Latvia, Poland, and Sweden does not increase saving. The Bush administration's proposal for individual accounts and increased government borrowing would not increase saving. A major reform that would increase saving would replace the current system of PAYGO benefits with individual accounts and increase taxes to fund obligations to workers who have paid into the old system. But there is (as yet) no widespread support for this approach. Thus, although policies that would increase national saving in the United States are desirable, major reform of Social Security is not a promising way to achieve this goal.[20]

Finally, there is the distributional issue. The US Social Security program leaves some retirees at or below the poverty line. The persons with the highest poverty incidence are widows, particularly those over 75. There is bipartisan agreement on the need for reforms that improve the situation of the elderly poor: Liberal reformers recognize the need for higher benefits for this group (e.g., the proposals in Diamond and Orszag 2005), and the Bush administration's plan also indicated the need to address the problem.

This problem is not unique to the United States but is not widespread among advanced countries. Most European countries provide

---

20. The only country that has used public pension reform as a way to increase national saving is Chile. Latvia, Poland, and Sweden introduced small funded individual accounts as add-ons to their unfunded account programs and these may have increased national saving. See the discussion below for the case for add-on individual accounts. Mexico may be another example like Chile. Increasing saving was not primary motivation for reform in Chile or Mexico. The United Kingdom under Margaret Thatcher introduced major reforms of its public pensions, making the program substantially less generous and creating optional individual accounts. This was part of a package of extensive economic reforms but has not resulted in a large increase in national saving (although it helped the overall budget).

more generous income support to the poor than the United States. However, Chile and the United Kingdom introduced pension reforms that leave too high an incidence of elderly poverty, indicating a need for modifications to the reform package. We saw no country with a major reform of public pensions whose principal goal was to make the program more redistributive. Realistically, that is not going to happen in the United States either, although a distributional improvement, as part of an incremental package dealing with the funding shortfall, should be possible.

The conclusion of this section is, therefore, that the experiences of other countries do not support an overhaul of the US Social Security program. The reason for most major reforms in other countries is that their pension programs were in severe budget crisis and/or labor force participation was low or declining. These arguments are not as compelling for the United States, where the funding shortfall is not great and employment incentives in the existing program are pretty good.

Variable Life Expectancy and Early Retirement

We report that life expectancy varies by income and education and that low-income and less educated (frequently manual) workers draw retirement benefits for fewer years. Does that mean these workers should be allowed to retire earlier or receive higher benefits when they retire?

Intuitively, it may seem sensible to say that workers who are likely to die younger than the average should be compensated by receiving higher monthly retirement benefits while they are alive. From the perspective of economic theory, however, this intuition is not valid. First, many characteristics influence life expectancy, including race and gender. Should women receive lower monthly benefits than men because they have a longer life expectancy? Should African-Americans receive higher monthly benefits than whites because their life expectancy is lower? Providing different benefit levels based on personal characteristics would open up many tough issues, such as who qualifies for favorable treatment and why.

More generally, in an economic model in which people's well-being or utility depends on their consumption, it is easy to conclude that social programs that protect against low consumption are a form of insurance against adverse outcomes and can make society better off. It is much more difficult to make the case that those likely to live longer should face lower consumption levels.

In our cross-country comparisons we did not find examples of mandatory pension programs for the general population that gave higher benefits to those expected to die early. Indeed, in the countries that do discriminate among recipients, women are given more favorable treatment, being allowed to retire at a younger age, even though they are expected to live longer. But retirement differences between men and women are being phased out.

In light of these observations we conclude that there is not a case for giving higher or lower benefits based on expected lifetime.

The question of allowing workers with physically demanding jobs to retire early is more difficult. It is not hard to create a model in which people whose jobs become harder to do as they age would choose to retire at a younger age, and an ideal pension program would take this into account. For example, someone who is skilled at moving heavy furniture would likely choose to retire younger than someone skilled at sitting at a computer and writing research reports like this one. Many European economies have created special early retirement programs geared loosely to those who work with their hands. As noted above, however, such programs have been in response to union resistance to restructuring or privatization.[21] Many European countries also have generous sickness and disability benefits that serve as early retirement programs for manual workers.

In the United States there are no government-sponsored early retirement plans,[22] although private companies do use buyouts to reduce employment. Much more so than in Europe, in the United States there is a view that an individual who is laid off from a job, or who cannot continue in a job because of its physical demands, is expected to take a different job, even if it is at a lower wage.

The experience of other countries does not provide compelling guidance about how to address this issue. European policymakers are generally trying to increase the retirement age and reduce the number of people collecting early retirement, and many countries are trying to rein in spending on disability programs. It is very difficult, indeed perhaps impossible, to determine objectively how fit people are to continue working as they age, and this means that workers with leverage or persistence or who find doctors willing to vouch for disabilities often get more generous treatment. The research in this project was not aimed at disability programs, but the conventional wisdom says that the US disability program gives benefits to some who are not really disabled and denies benefits to some who are. The feature of the US Social Security retirement program that allows people to retire "early" at 62, with a penalty, may be the best policy.

---

21. Renault, the French auto company, had to restructure in order to compete effectively when the European Union allowed open competition. The state-owned company was being prepared for privatization (with some remaining state ownership) and the government subsidized early retirement programs in order to reduce the workforce. Renault closed its plant in Belgium and gave employees early retirement, including workers as young as 48!

22. There is, however, a Social Security disability program, which generally makes payments to persons who have been in the lower-wage segment of the labor force.

Increases in Life Expectancy and Retirement Age

Every advanced country has experienced increases in average life expectancy, a boon that carries with it the penalty of higher pension obligations. Economic analysis does not speak unequivocally as to whether people should work longer if they live longer. Holding overall earnings constant, it is very likely that people who make rational saving and retirement decisions would respond to a longer expected lifetime by saving more while working and by working for more years. Offsetting this, however, is the fact that incomes and living standards are rising, and time spent in retirement becomes more affordable as incomes rise (retirement was not an option for many workers in the 19th and early 20th centuries).

Most of the OECD economies are only now starting to respond to pension budget pressures by pushing up official retirement ages, arguing that because people are living more years, they should also work more years so that they can sustain their income in retirement. Over the past 30 years, European countries have drastically reduced the number of hours per year worked by those who are employed and have greatly increased the number of workers given early retirement. The policy changes that made this possible were based partly on the illusion that such measures would lower unemployment rates among the general population. Today, this trend is gradually being reversed in Europe through the realization that there needs to be an increase in employment or hours to pay for all the benefits that have been granted. Almost all recent pension reforms have therefore included either prefixed increases in eligibility ages for early or full pensions or direct life expectancy links. As we describe in chapter 8, we believe that additional direct linkages to life expectances should be part of any reform of Social Security, too.

The Case for Add-On Individual Accounts

In our assessment of the Bush administration's plan for individual accounts, we find that the plan's design features dealt effectively with many of the problems seen in other countries. In particular, investors would be given the choice of a limited selection of funds modeled on the current federal retirement plan, the Thrift Savings Plan. This would mean that savers would not be tempted by rash or unsound investments and would be encouraged to develop safer portfolios as they came closer to retirement. Participants would be required to purchase annuities on retirement and not be allowed to withdraw their funds in a lump sum.

The administration plan did not define the extent to which the government would provide administrative services to individual accounts, although there was clearly an awareness that competition among providers might not result in low administrative costs. Based on the experience in the United States and other countries, we have argued here that a centralized governmental authority would have an advantage in lowering administrative costs. The Social Security Administration runs very efficiently, inasmuch as its total costs are a very small percentage of its benefit payout. It could provide a pooling service to individuals who chose to participate in an individual account plan in addition to Social Security. Much of the necessary record keeping would already be in place. By providing such services, a governmental authority could give an effective subsidy to low- and moderate-income participants, who would not be charged the full amount of the administrative costs that their accounts incurred.

There is traditionally in America considerable political concern about a governmental authority investing in private-sector assets. However, if the Social Security Administration were to operate the bookkeeping part of an individual account plan, it could still be precluded from making investment choices or holding stocks or bonds or voting on company decisions. The contributions of individual account holders would be assigned to the funds the holder had chosen and the money would then be pooled and sent to private investment managers to invest in the markets. An independent advisory board would be responsible for the selection of investment managers, who would be subject to careful rules.

We have explained why we believe that the lessons from other countries do *not* suggest that the US Social Security system should undergo a massive design change or overhaul. It works pretty well compared with other countries' retirement plans. Why, then, create an add-on plan of individual accounts? Because we found that countries that had adopted individual account plans had achieved a considerable measure of success with these plans. Individual accounts work. In the United States, almost all academics have individual account plans that provide, or will provide, the bulk of their retirement income and they are pretty happy with the results.[23] For those less confident of their ability to make investment choices, the plan could offer advice, limited choices, and a well-balanced default option.[24]

The four main flaws of the 2005 Bush Social Security plan were: (1) It was not expected to remain solvent, (2) it did not result in additional saving and may even reduce national saving, (3) it did not provide very generous retirement benefits to most recipients, and (4) it left too many recipients, notably elderly widows, in poverty. An add-on individual

---

23. Academics are not necessarily more knowledgeable than others when it comes to portfolio choice. The story has been told about two Nobel prize winners in economics who were asked for advice about allocating funds between stocks and bonds in the academic pension program TIAA-CREF. "Oh, 50–50 is a good rule" was the response.

24. Most participants in the Swedish individual account plan take the default option suggested by the program.

account plan would address two of these flaws—(2) and (3)—and it could be designed to address (4) by, for example, giving each child born in the United States an individual account of, say, $1,000. An individual account plan would not deal with the solvency problem, but it would add to national saving and result in more retirement money for low- and moderate-income participants.

Or there could be alternative policies to lower elderly poverty, by making the SSI program more generous, for example. How large? Compulsory or voluntary? Our research does not provide clear answers to these questions. Larger contributions—say, 5 percent of wages up to a dollar limit—would increase the size of accounts and lower the ratio of administrative costs relative to contributions. Thus there would be a meaningful increase in national saving and in the funds available at retirement; low- and moderate-income workers would have higher pension benefits; and workers who retire at 62 because of reduced physical or mental capacity would still have enough money for a basic retirement income.

On the other hand, a smaller or voluntary contribution would be more politically acceptable. Introducing a compulsory contribution of 5 percent of wages would be noticed as a drop in workers' take-home pay. There would be complaints about higher "taxes" even though this would not be a tax in the usual sense. This argument seems strong enough to make the case that initially an add-on program should be voluntary with contributions up to a limit. Over time, if it became popular, contributions could become compulsory, unless the individual already had an adequate employer-provided plan. Because the participation rate is much higher if contributory pensions are set up as "opt-out" rather than "opt-in," the national plan could be set up so that workers are automatically enrolled unless they choose to opt out.

Lessons from Other Countries for Dealing with the Solvency Issue

Two lessons stood out from this research. First, increasing the retirement age is a very powerful tool to restore solvency and is strongly suggested by the increase in life expectancy in all advanced countries. As it is, governments around the world have been dealing with their fiscal solvency issues by "selectively defaulting" on some of their liabilities toward younger retirees.

Second, the United States has a much wider distribution of income than other countries. The average income level of persons over 65 is pretty high in international comparison—82 percent of the national average (Förster and Mira d'Ercole 2005)—but there is much variation in the distribution of this income. A large group of low- to moderate-income retirees depends heavily on Social Security benefits that are not terribly generous, whereas higher-income taxpayers can shelter substantial amounts of money through 401(k) plans, employer-funded plans, and in some cases deferred income plans (in which executives are paid in options or restricted stock units that are not taxed until withdrawn). We have also found that the finances and funding of corporate pension plans are relatively secure, so this stream of income to high-income people looks set to continue. The capital gains tax is also very low in the United States, allowing high-wealth individuals to pay a low tax rate on an important component of their income; for example, the capital gain on a principal residence is exempted from tax up to $500,000 for a married couple, a tax break that can be taken repeatedly.[25]

Given these observations, we conclude that the main avenues to restore solvency to the Social Security program are to continue to gradually increase the retirement age and to reduce the level of Social Security benefits paid to high-income or high-wealth recipients.

Prefixed increases in the normal retirement age are already in effect until 2027. We propose that this gradual rise in the eligibility age for a full Social Security pension continue and be tied to rises in life expectancies beyond the legislated increases in retirement ages to 67 by 2027. This is most appropriately achieved by fixing the fraction of Americans' lifetime spent in retirement to total life time at historical levels.

In terms of lowering benefits for high-income individuals, we argue that taxpayers who have taken advantage of tax sheltering opportunities for their personal retirement savings should face an automatic markdown of their expected publicly provided Social Security benefits. We make the case for this policy in chapter 8, pointing out the large discrepancy in tax-sheltered wealth across income categories and the fact that the United States stands out from other OECD countries in its tax treatment. Critics of this proposal may argue that we are taxing savings and that this is a mistake in an economy that is short on saving. Our view is that the low saving rate is a problem primarily for lower-income families that typically do not have large private pension funds. In addition we do not propose completely eliminating the tax break for saving. Moreover, most taxpayers will take a "bird-in-the-hand" tax break now rather than worry about a modest reduction in future Social Security benefits. So the impact on private saving is likely to be modest.

The wide distribution of income before and after retirement in the United States compared to other countries further bolsters the case for reducing benefits to high-income retirees rather than across the board. Based on evidence from other countries, we do not believe that the increase in the progressivity of Social Security will lead to any decline in the broad political support for the program in the United States.

---

25. Capital gains on assets held in tax-preferred pension plans are tax exempt until withdrawal, when they are taxed as ordinary income.

References

Barr, Nicholas, and Peter A. Diamond. 2008a. *Reforming Pensions*. Working Paper 08-22. Cambridge, MA: Massachusetts Institute of Technology, Department of Economics.

Barr, Nicholas, and Peter A. Diamond. 2008b. *Reforming Pensions: Principles and Policy Choices*. New York and Oxford: Oxford University Press.

CBO (Congressional Budget Office). 2008. *Accounting for Sources of Projected Growth in Federal Spending on Medicare and Medicaid*. Washington. Available at www.cbo.gov.

Diamond, Peter A., and Peter R. Orszag. 2005. Saving Social Security. *Journal of Economic Perspectives* 19, no. 2 (Spring): 11–32.

Förster, M. F., and M. Mira d'Ercole. 2005. *Income Distribution and Poverty in OECD Countries in the Second Half of the 1990s*. OECD Social, Employment and Migration Working Paper 22. Paris: Organization for Economic Cooperation and Development.

Gruber, Jonathan, and David A. Wise, eds. 1999. *Social Security and Retirement Around the World*. Chicago: University of Chicago Press.

Holzmann, R. et al. 2005. *Old-Age Income Support in the 21st Century: An International Perspective on Pension Systems and Reform*. Washington: World Bank.

McKinsey Global Institute. 2008. *Talkin' 'Bout My Generation: The Economic Impact of Aging U.S. Baby Boomers*. San Francisco: McKinsey & Company.

OECD (Organization for Economic Cooperation and Development). 2008. *Pension Markets in Focus*, no. 5 (December). Paris.

OMB (Office of Management and Budget). 2007. *President's Budget 2008—Analytical Perspectives*. Washington: Executive Office of the President.

Penner, Rudolph G., ed. 2007. *International Perspectives on Social Security Reform*. Washington: Urban Institute Press.

Queisser, Monika, and Edward Whitehouse. 2005. Pensions at a Glance: Public Policies Across the OECD Countries. Presentation at the Organization for Economic Cooperation and Development, Washington, June 17. Available at www.oecdwash.org.

Sartori, Giovanni. 1996. Comparing and Miscomparing. In *Comparative Politics: Notes and Readings*, 8th ed., ed. Roy C. Macridis and Bernard E. Brown. Belmont, MA: Wadsworth Publishing Co.

Turner, John. 2005. *Administrative Costs for Social Security Private Accounts*. Research Report (June). Washington: AARP Public Policy Institute.

Whitehouse, Edward, OECD (Organization for Economic Cooperation and Development), and World Bank. 2007. *Pensions Panorama: Retirement-Income Systems in 53 Countries*. Washington: World Bank.

2

Fiscal and Demographic Challenges

I . . . place economy among the first and most important of republican virtues, and public debt as the greatest of the dangers to be feared.

—Thomas Jefferson

With the rich world's populations rapidly aging, all governments are, or very soon will be, facing tough policy choices forced on them by the fiscal implications of aging. This is the case irrespective of whether countries have pay-as-you-go (PAYGO) pension systems, funded systems, or hybrids of the two. The broad impact of pension-related expenses on government finances will be negative, even though there will be occasional relief in the form of increased tax receipts from pension withdrawals.[1] However, the exact scope of the pension challenge to countries' fiscal policies is clouded by vast cross-country differences both in the gravity of the demographic change and in the current "starting points" of government fiscal positions.

This chapter attempts to bring together the key concepts and data required to analyze the scope and impact of the future fiscal and demographic challenges. Focusing on cross-country comparisons of key concepts, we show comparatively that the challenge for numerous countries looks very different from what is frequently assumed, after accounting for such factors as net government debt levels, the existence of private pension assets, sovereign and public pension reserve funds (SPPRFs), the

---

1. Under the most prevalent tax-preferred treatment of private pension savings, where taxation is postponed until the time of withdrawal of savings, sudden large withdrawals may temporarily raise a government's tax income.

level of taxation applied to pension benefit payments, the value of tax breaks for pension provisions, and effective (rather than statutory) retirement ages. The comparative picture is summarized in appendix table 2A.1.

As mentioned in chapter 1, in order to avoid "getting lost in the weeds" of country-specific data and information, we focus in this chapter on the broad concepts mentioned above and on the cross-country lessons. We do not include a comprehensive listing and combined effects of small and large pension-related reforms in individual countries in recent decades.[2]

The chapter is organized in the following manner: First, in order to set the factual stage for the pension debate, we analyze the different fiscal starting points of governments in terms of debt, deficit levels, and nongovernment pension assets. Next we examine the actual net costs to governments of pension provision, with a special focus on the differences between countries in taxation of pension benefits and in the use of tax breaks with a social purpose. Last, we consider the principal driver of future fiscal trends in pensions. We present the diverse demographic outlook for the economies of Organization for Economic Cooperation and Development (OECD) and look at the scope for changes in fertility and immigration to change this picture under realistic scenarios. We pay particular attention to the difference between the future effect of aging by itself (i.e., demographics) and the impact today of already very low effective retirement ages (i.e., labor market outcomes). In several OECD countries, the impact of actual ages of withdrawal from the labor market on long-term sustainability is already larger than that projected from the demographic aging process until 2050.

Assessing Countries' "Fiscal Starting Point"

The ability of governments in the future to manage the effects of an aging population depends in part on how much debt they have on their books today—how large are the liabilities already incurred and thus already payable by future generations. The terms "debt" or "financial liabilities" are defined in many different ways, depending on the precise use and context. The most frequently used concept, that of gross general government financial liabilities, provides a measure of the total outstanding issuance of government paper of all kinds. Figure 2.1 shows gross liabilities by country for OECD participants in 2006 and reveals that the range of values is quite large—from 179 percent of GDP in Japan to just 10 percent in Luxembourg, with the United States and the large EU countries at

---

2. For this type of more comprehensive model-based approaches, see EPC and European Commission (2005), European Commission (2006), Carone et al. (2005), and OECD (2005a, 2007a).

Figure 2.1 General government fiscal positions, 2006

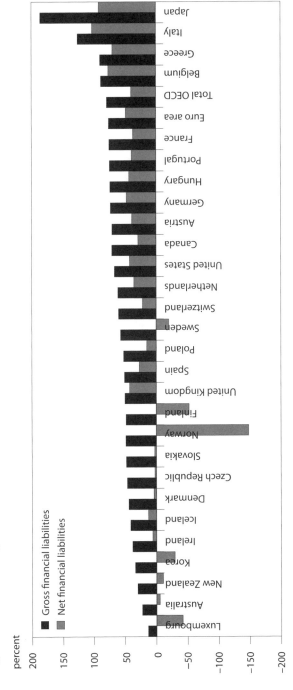

percent

Gross financial liabilities
Net financial liabilities

Japan
Italy
Greece
Belgium
Total OECD
Euro area
France
Portugal
Hungary
Germany
Austria
Canada
United States
Netherlands
Switzerland
Sweden
Poland
Spain
United Kingdom
Finland
Norway
Slovakia
Czech Republic
Denmark
Iceland
Ireland
Korea
New Zealand
Australia
Luxembourg

Note: Gross debt data are not always comparable across countries due to different definitions or treatment of debt components. Notably, they include the funded portion of government employee pension liabilities for some OECD countries, including Australia and the United States. The debt position of these countries is thus overstated relative to countries that have large unfunded liabilities for such pensions, which according to ESA95/SNA93 are not counted in the debt figures but rather as a memorandum item to the debt. Net debt measures are not always comparable across countries due to different definitions or treatment of debt (and asset) components. First, the treatment of government liabilities with respect to their employee pension plans may be different. Second, a range of items included as general government assets differs across countries. For example, equity holdings are excluded from government assets in some countries, whereas foreign exchange, gold, and special drawing rights holdings are considered assets in the United States and the United Kingdom. Germany includes the debt of the Inherited Debt Fund, and Japan includes the debt of the Japan Railway Settlement Corporation and the National Forest Special Account.

Source: OECD Economic Outlook, December 2007.

about 50 to 70 percent. (These data do *not* include government pension liabilities; see below. All levels of government—national, state, and local—are included, however).

This concept of gross liabilities is often used in discussions but is far from the most valid concept when discussing pension obligations and aging populations. Instead, *"net* general government financial liabilities" is a consolidated concept, netting out the financial assets of the general government sector, which may include such assets as cash, bank deposits, loans to the private sector, participation in private-sector companies, holdings in the central bank, and public corporations, or even in some countries foreign exchange reserves.[3] These net liabilities provide a better picture of the total debt service obligations of governments that will have to compete with pensions for resources. Governments may issue gross debt in the form of debt securities for several reasons apart from the need to raise funds. Specifically, a relatively large level of outstanding government bonds at different maturities is often instrumental in ensuring a liquid national risk-free debt benchmark against which private-sector debt may be priced in the financial markets. Some level of outstanding gross government debt is, therefore, independently beneficial to an economy and need not have a close relation to the overall government fiscal health.[4]

Figure 2.1 accordingly also shows net liabilities by country, and it is clear that the shift makes a very large difference for some countries. As a result of particularly large holdings of securities by the Bank of Japan, Japan drops nearly 100 percentage points to "just" 85 percent of GDP. The United States drops to 43 percent and Canada to 27 percent. Italy, with just below 100 percent of GDP in net liabilities, is now the country with the most wobbly looking general government finances, while governments in Australia, Finland, Korea, Norway, Luxembourg, New Zealand, and Sweden

---

3. See the footnote to OECD Sources and Methods for the *Economic Outlook* data, the source of the data in figure 2.1. This footnote states that, in general, some caution must be taken in interpreting these data, due to national institutional differences. It states further: "The figures for net financial liabilities measure the gross financial liabilities of the general government sector [gross data which are consolidated within and between the sub-sectors of the general government sector, national sources permitting] less the financial assets of the general government sector. For the United States, the data reported by the Federal Reserve and used by the OECD include only that portion of the liabilities that is funded (which amounted to 8.3 percent of GDP at the end of FY2003, including both pension and insurance reserves). Both government assets and liabilities exclude the Thrift Plan of Federal Employees Retirement system, which is classified outside the general government sector. Unfunded central government pension liabilities are excluded from the data (they amounted to 10.2 percent of GDP in 2001)." See methodological notes to sources of OECD (2007b) at www.oecd.org.

4. In 2000 there was concern in the United States about the disappearing government debt and its impact on financial markets (those were the days). Norway has continued to issue government bonds to create a benchmark for financial markets.

were actually net creditors as of 2006 (the figure shows the amounts of liabilities, so that countries with negative liabilities are in fact net creditors).

Governments that in the present stage of their population aging processes are in positions of generally sound government finances and post positive net government financial liabilities are further at a substantial advantage relative to countries that are already deep in the red. The former group will have far more policy options available to them in the years ahead, while potentially also needing to make only modest modifications to their pension systems to remain solvent and/or keep their investment grade credit rating.

One sign of the potential importance of this issue comes from Standard & Poor's (2006), which predicts that in a hypothetical "no policy change" option of simply continuing current general fiscal policies, only three members of the OECD or European Union (Austria, Canada, and Denmark) would be able to issue investment grade securities by 2040; the United States would drop into speculative territory between 2020 and 2030. Such a decline in credit rating for most of the OECD countries could be associated with a significant rise in government debt service costs, as investors demand a higher risk premium to own these (now perceived as) riskier assets. Although the highly liquid and varied super-AAA-rated dollar-denominated US Treasury bonds currently benefit from their status as the principal "safe haven" for global investors in times of financial uncertainty, that status may be threatened as the United States faces additional adverse impacts from a credit downgrade in a "no policy change" scenario.

The next important step in evaluating governments' "starting positions" is to look at current government fiscal balances—whether budgets have recently been in deficit or surplus. Countries with structural surpluses on their current budgets will, ceteris paribus, be better able to weather future deficits in their pension accounts, as they will typically need fewer reforms in other policy areas. At the same time it is the case that excessive tax cuts, overly generous unemployment benefits, too easy access to disability pension, or repeated loss-making government bailouts of national champions can undo the positive fiscal effects of even the most far-sighted pension reforms.

The inclusion of annual deficits to get a fuller picture is particularly relevant in countries such as the United States, which explicitly includes in its federal government deficit numbers the current surpluses (and by inference, therefore, future deficits) of its Social Security Trust Funds. Technically, these amounts are shown as "off-budget,"[5] but they are

---

5. The United States by law excludes the revenues and outlays of the Old-Age and Survivors Insurance Trust Fund and the Disability Insurance Trust Fund as well as the transactions of the Postal Service from the budget. The Old-Age and Survivors Insurance Trust Fund (i.e., the Social Security Trust Fund) is by far the largest of the three. See CBO (2007a).

nonetheless included as part of the headline deficit figures each year. In 2006 the US Social Security surplus amounted to $186 billion; without its inclusion the US federal deficit that year would have been not the official $248 billion but rather $434 billion.[6] However, as the cash flow in the Social Security Trust Funds turns negative (projected to occur in 2018–19), a rapidly rising "off-budget" deficit from Social Security will have to be included in the annual headline figures. This development will certainly (ought to at least) serve to raise the political tension surrounding the general annual spending priorities in the US federal budget.[7]

The last "starting point" feature to consider is what assets governments or other private actors may already have amassed (i.e., prefunded) to provide for future old age expenditures. Differing institutions, histories, and traditions across countries somewhat complicate this issue. Hitherto, the precise status and treatment of government-sector pension assets in funded pension schemes in the national accounts have frequently been arbitrary and occasionally subject to outright manipulation by governments.[8]

Currently (but soon to be revised)[9] the international System of National Accounts (SNA; guidelines for measuring GDP and government accounts) distinguishes between two types of funded pension plans[10]: autonomous and nonautonomous. The first, also known as government pension reserve funds, should be classified as outside the general government sector, which means that their assets and liabilities are not reflected in the general government debt data in figure 2.1. Nonautonomous pension plans should be classified as inside the general government sector and only the funded component reflected in the general government liabilities.[11]

As we explain below and in chapters 3 and 7, the accounting for future government pension spending is a particularly problematic aspect of

---

6. Data are from OMB (2007).

7. See, for instance, Nataraj and Shoven (2003) for an in-depth discussion of the distinction between the unified, on- and off-budget federal government balances.

8. See van den Noord and Koen (2005) for an inventory of such abusive government practices.

9. See OECD (2007c) for an overview of proposed changes in the System of National Accounts 93 rev. 1.

10. SNA Annex IV, The Treatment of Insurance, Social Insurance and Pensions; Entry 12: The Units Involved. Available at http://unstats.un.org/unsd/sna1993.

11. The SNA further recommends that the liability inherent in unfunded schemes be recorded as a memorandum item for the government sector. However, the online footnotes to the OECD *Economic Outlook* state diplomatically, "while some countries have produced some estimates of these implicit liabilities, few follow the 1993 SNA recommendation." Available at www.oecd.org.

liability assessment. At this point, though, the issue is limited to the asset side of the balance sheet and to the question of which prefunded assets to include in the starting point. The United States, with the Social Security Trust Funds, has for decades earmarked government pension reserve funds that have by now accumulated substantial assets. Some other countries, such as Canada in 1997 or France in 1999, only started accumulating SPPRFs much later, and their funds are, therefore, much smaller. According to the OECD (2007d), 16 OECD countries now have an SPPRF, up from 13 in 2005. Thus almost half of the OECD countries have no government SPPRF and continue to fund pensions directly out of contribution revenue and general tax revenue.[12]

Some countries, like the Netherlands, rely on mandatory employment-related schemes that accumulate pension assets in private plans that are administratively and legally separate from the government. The same is true for the many employer and union pension plans in the United States. Other, particularly European, countries rely overwhelmingly on unfunded pension systems.

Due to the large historical institutional differences and ambiguous accounting rules, the best approach (or perhaps, better put, the least misleading approach) to cross-country comparisons of the assets already available for a country's future pension provision is to include not only the general government net debt position above, which includes nonautonomous pension plan assets, but also private pension assets, which include autonomous pension plans. On the one hand, counting all private pension assets, which overwhelmingly are the legal property of private individuals, will overstate the value of assets immediately and directly available to governments for future pension provision. On the other hand, excluding private pension assets would make the analysis deeply flawed, as it would not include the influence on government pension policy actions of the presence (or absence) of significant private pension assets. Accordingly, we make a separate accounting for such private pension assets as we assess the sustainability of countries' pension systems. However, we caution that this analysis remains incomplete. The inclusion of formal private pension assets cannot account for the direct and indirect effects on government retirement income policy actions of people's potentially large savings toward retirement outside the formal pension system. Such savings are typically in the form of housing, informal assets, and other nonpension financial assets.[13]

---

12. See OECD (2006a, 2007d). Seven of the 16 OECD SPPRFs started in the last 10 years.

13. With house prices rising rapidly until 2005–06 in many countries, real estate—at least temporarily—took on a more prominent role in many older homeowners' total wealth. See Apgar and Di (2005).

In calculating the assets of designated private pension funds,[14] however, we have to account for the fact that in several countries most private assets for pension provision are held not in pension funds, as in the United States or United Kingdom, but rather as assets in the life insurance sector.[15] This is the result of either simply historical tradition or favorable tax treatment and it applies, for instance, to Sweden, which has few private pension assets (just 9 percent of GDP in 2006) but substantial private life insurance assets (43 percent of GDP in 2006).[16] Finally, private pension assets should also include (nonautonomous) book reserves—company pension promises to employees backed only by corporate productive assets (and not a legally separate pension fund), which for instance in Germany remain legal and popular as a means of financing corporate pension liabilities.[17]

Figure 2.2 illustrates the combination of the different pieces of information described so far that determine a country's starting point for pension assessment. These three elements are (1) the (stock) level of government net debt (as shown in figure 2.1); (2) the (flow) budget deficit (the average cyclically adjusted deficit for 2002–06, the most recent five-year period); and (3) the (stock) level of prefunded pension assets. The position of the diamonds in figure 2.2 indicates the first two of these and thus reflects each country's fiscal situation.[18] The figure's four quadrants

---

14. The OECD classifies pension fund assets in the following manner: "The pool of assets forming an independent legal entity that are bought with the contributions to a pension plan for the exclusive purpose of financing pension plan benefits. The plan/fund members have a legal or beneficial right or some other contractual claim against the assets of the pension fund. Pension funds take the form of either a special purpose entity with legal personality (such as a trust, foundation, or corporate entity) or a legally separated fund without legal personality managed by a dedicated provider (pension fund management company) or other financial institution on behalf of the plan/fund members" (OECD 2006a, 12).

15. The OECD classifies such assets as "An insurance contract that specifies pension plan contributions to an insurance undertaking in exchange for which the pension plan benefits will be paid when the member reaches a specified retirement age or on earlier exit of members from the plan" (OECD 2006a, 12).

16. From the OECD Global Pension Statistics database. In the United States 18 percent of GDP was in life insurance assets in 2005 and 74 percent in pension fund assets. Available at www.oecd.org/daf/pensions/gps.

17. The OECD defines (nonautonomous) book reserves as "sums entered in the balance sheet of the plan sponsor as reserves or provisions for pension benefits. Some assets may be held in separate accounts for the purpose of financing benefits, but are not legally or contractually pension plan assets" (OECD 2006a, 12).

18. The OECD data presented in figure 2.2 distinguish between four different taxes in the cyclical adjustment process: personal income tax, Social Security contributions, corporate income tax, and indirect taxes. Unemployment-related transfers are treated as cyclically sensitive. No adjustment for long-term pension-related liabilities is made, and US data do not include off-budget items. See Girouard and André (2005) for detailed methodology.

represent budget surpluses or deficits as percentages of GDP (vertical axis) and level of government net debt or net total assets (horizontal axis), also as a percentage of GDP.[19] Combining stock and flow for government finances (the position of the diamonds) reveals significant differences among OECD nations. The diamonds for countries such as Greece, Hungary, Italy, Japan, and the United States appear in the undesirable lower left corner because they have both significant levels of net general government liabilities and high recurring structural deficits, which will likely continue to add to their debt totals. The same is true to a lesser extent for the four large EU countries (France, Germany, Italy, and the United Kingdom) as well as Portugal. Moving toward the upper right, on the other hand, reveals that a number of countries—Australia, Canada, Ireland, the Scandinavians, Switzerland, and New Zealand—have significantly sounder current government fiscal positions with both structural surpluses and more modest total debt levels as of 2006.[20]

Even before considering pension liabilities and the costs of future adverse demographics, figure 2.2 illustrates that countries with diamonds in the lower left quadrant—especially Greece, Hungary, Italy, Japan, and the United States—will need to achieve some degree of broader fiscal consolidation to be able to afford any additional pension expenditures in the coming decades.[21] In contrast, the further countries are to the right and up in figure 2.2, the more additional future pension expenditure their governments in general will be able to afford. Politicians in Finland, New Zealand, and Sweden face a vastly more benign general fiscal outlook when considering their pension options than do their Japanese or Greek colleagues, and as a consequence, many more options will be available to them and less draconian measures perhaps needed.

Figure 2.2 also includes information about prefunded pension assets accumulated. These data come from the OECD Global Pension Statistics and cover the available consolidated data for what we, lacking a more inspiring terminology, will term total prefunded assets toward pension provision (TPATPP), which include autonomous sovereign and public pension reserve funds (SPPRFs for all levels of government), private pension fund assets, private life insurance assets, private nonautonomous book reserves, and other private assets (including all types of pension plans, whether occupational, personal, mandatory, or voluntary and in both the

---

19. The four quadrants do not themselves necessarily determine a country's overall fiscal and net asset position. A position toward the lower right in figure 2.2 merely means that a country has a *relatively* stronger total asset base and weaker government finances.

20. Norway is excluded from figure 2.2 for reasons of readability of the figure.

21. See also Standard and Poor's (2006) for an evaluation of which countries should focus on immediate budget consolidation and which countries on pension reforms in order to retain their credit ratings.

Figure 2.2   OECD countries' "starting point" in 2006 (percent of GDP)

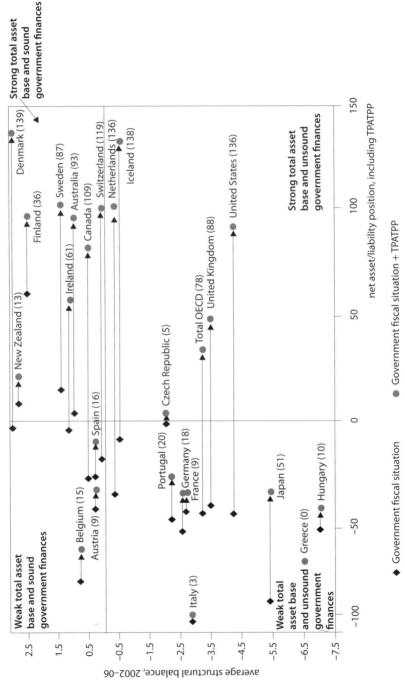

Note: For details on what is included in total prefunded assets toward pension provision (TPATPP), see appendix 2A. Numbers in parentheses are country's TPATPP in percent of GDP.

Sources: OECD *Economic Outlook*, December 2007; OECD Global Pension Statistics, 2007; authors' calculations.

public and private sectors). The detailed data for what is shown in figure 2.2 are explained in appendix 2A.[22] The lengths of the arrows in the figure show how each country's overall asset and pension financing situation is shifted by adding TPATPP to net general government assets, and the circles show the combined net government assets plus TPATPP in each country. The number in parentheses (indicating the distance between a country's diamond and circle in figure 2.2) shows the value of the country's TPATPP in percent of GDP.

Adding TPATPP to the picture makes a very large difference for some countries, but much less for others. In seven OECD countries—Canada, Denmark, Iceland, the Netherlands, Norway (not shown), Switzerland, and the United States—for which data are available, TPATPP exceed 100 percent of GDP. Of these, the United States (perhaps surprisingly to some) is among the most frugal pension savers, with fully 136 percent of GDP in government pension reserve funds, private pension fund assets, life insurance assets, or other pension assets, all of which improve the overall outlook for US pension sustainability. The comparison to France is illustrative, as the two countries are almost identical today in terms of the stock of net government debt and recurring structural deficits, but with the addition of private-sector and prefunded pension assets the United States pulls ahead of France in terms of the total availability of pension assets and moves substantially farther to the right in figure 2.2. Figure 2.2 thus illustrates that if the United States could achieve structural budget surpluses (which would probably require a substantial cost-reducing health care reform, government revenue increases, or a combination thereof), it would join the best-positioned and best-prepared OECD countries in the upper right quadrant.

It is noteworthy that, with the inclusion of TPATPP, the longer-term sustainability of Japan does not look nearly as bad as is frequently postulated, based solely on gross government debt levels. Again, as with the United States, this suggests that Japan should return fiscal policy to structural surpluses (Ito 2007) in order to promote the longer-term sustainability of pensions (subject to the caveat that fiscal policy should not drag the economy back into stagnation).

Most of the countries with government structural surpluses in the early years of the 2000s—notably Australia, Canada, Ireland, the Scandinavian countries, and New Zealand, all in the upper right corner of figure 2.2—also have substantial TPATPP at their disposal for future pension

22. A crucial item on the flow side (y-axis) that is missing from the TPATPP data series (grey circles) in figure 2.2 is the annual levels of earmarked member contributions, investment returns, and benefit payouts on private pension assets. However, no consistent cross-country data exist for this category. We also note that adding TPATPP assets to a country's government net financial liabilities means adding private assets that may be invested in many different ways and frequently outside the country.

provision. Thus, with both sound government fiscal balances and a strong broad asset base at present, these countries can with some justification claim a relatively nonthreatening starting point at the cusp of the era of more rapid population aging. In other words, for this group of countries— even without substantial further future pension reforms—alarmist predictions of pension-related fiscal doom seem unwarranted.

However, as is evident in the lower left corner of figure 2.2, the opposite is the case in some countries. For example, it is striking that a country such as Greece, with a government fiscal position broadly comparable to that of Japan, has no TPATPP of any magnitude and therefore is at a far worse starting point than Japan. Similarly, with a combination of poor government finances and a weak base of TPATPP, France, Germany, Hungary, and Italy also face considerable potential threats from their aging populations in the future.

In summary, figure 2.2 shows that long-term pension reforms in several countries will be best initiated by—and quite possibly require— improving the overall structural budget balance. This applies to Japan, the United States, and the four large eurozone members. Figure 2.2 also shows that in several countries—conspicuously Canada, Japan, the Netherlands, the United Kingdom, and the United States—the addition of TPATPP materially improves their starting points. Last, the other English-speaking countries and the Scandinavian countries are in far better starting positions than the rest of the OECD.

True Cost of Public Pensions Today

In the previous section we set the stage by looking at the overall fiscal starting point of OECD countries and the extent to which that position is affected by private pension assets. We turn now to the size of future government pension liabilities, starting with a deceptively simple question: How much do governments currently spend on pension provision?

One way to answer the question is to look at the amount paid out in pensions from gross public expenditure data. However, this measure is not accurate because public pension expenditures need to be adjusted for the impact of taxation—that is, how much the government takes back of the benefits it provides, a calculus that both reduces the generosity of pensions and the future fiscal challenge to governments as their populations age. At the same time, government tax provisions can also supplement retirement income. Thus we make two major adjustments to public gross pension expenditure data: We (1) assess the impact of direct and indirect taxation, which varies widely by country, and (2) include the costs to the public of tax benefits offered to pension savings. These adjustments dramatically alter the total as well as relative present public pension spending levels among OECD countries.

Figure 2.3 shows the total public gross cash benefit pension expenditures for selected OECD countries from 1990 to 2003.[23] Due to access to early retirement schemes in many countries, we include in figure 2.3 not only the total costs of public pensions but also the costs to treasuries of early retirement schemes.[24]

Wide differences exist in gross expenditures among generally high-spending continental European countries that were already allocating more than 10 percent of GDP in 2003 to public pension provision. At the same time, most of the English-speaking OECD countries spent about half that amount (US 6.2 percent), Korea and Mexico the least, and the remaining OECD members (many of which are not included in figure 2.3) 5 to 10 percent of GDP.[25]

For most countries, public pension expenditure levels have been relatively stable since 1990. Ireland even saw a drop in its expenditure for pension provision benefits. It experienced this decline in expenditure as a share of GDP, partly as a result of better demographics (a younger population than most of the rest of the OECD) and partly due to rapid economic growth over the period, once again illustrating that the rising tide of a growing economy may lift even the supertanker of increasing pension expenditures (Irish public pension expenditures actually more than doubled in real terms from 1990 to 2003[26]). Plain economic growth should

23. The data include direct public expenditure and mandatory private pension spending, which in countries such as the Netherlands may be substantial. For reasons of cross-country comparability and subsequent conversion to net expenditure status, only cash benefits are included. These make up the vast majority of pension expenditure and in a number of countries all pension expenditure. Some countries also spend public resources on "in-kind benefits" targeted to the elderly, such as residential care and home help services. However, these types of expenditures are outside the core "old age income provision" of cash benefits and are treated in an uneven accounting manner across OECD countries and are thus excluded from these data. In addition, for several countries, no data exist for private voluntary pension expenditure.

24. At least some of the expenses for disability pensions or long-term unemployment benefits constitute similar functional equivalents of old age pension spending, but these data are not immediately available. It is likely that the data on costs of public pensions presented in figure 2.3—equaling the sum of old age, early retirement, and survivor pension expenditure, but no spending on disability pensions or unemployment benefits—represent an underestimate of the true costs to the public of "primary income provision to older citizens."

25. Mexico's low pension spending reflects its far younger population compared with the other OECD countries. Korea's initially low public expenditure on pension provision is due to the broad program's relatively recent origin. Although civil servant pensions were established in 1960, the Korean National Pension Scheme (NPS) was not introduced until 1986 and became fully functional only in 1988. Initially, only a subset of Koreans was covered, although a series of reforms throughout the 1990s (mostly phased in as a result of the 1997 financial crisis) gradually expanded eligibility to near universality by 1999. See Walker (2004).

26. Cash benefit provisions rose from 1.6 billion to 5.1 billion Irish pounds in nominal terms, equaling approximately 130 percent in real (consumer price index [CPI]–deflated) terms over the period. Data are from OECD SOCX database, 2007, and the online CPI statistics database.

Figure 2.3 Total (old age + early retirement + survivor) public gross pension cash benefit expenditure, 1990–2003

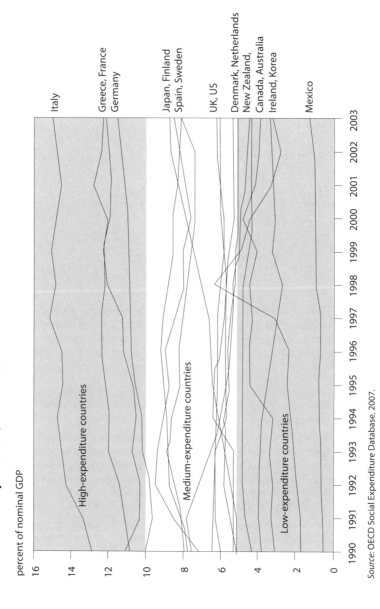

Source: OECD Social Expenditure Database, 2007.

therefore never be forgotten as one great aid in dealing with the costs of an aging population. Only Japan has seen large increases over the period,[27] while several other countries, such as Finland, the Netherlands, New Zealand, and Sweden, seem already to be benefiting from early reforms to their pension systems (see chapters 4 and 6).

Impact of Direct and Indirect Taxation on Benefits

Adjusting the gross pension expenditure data for the impact of taxation is obviously important from the perspective of the pension benefit recipient, as higher taxes on benefits mean a lower level of disposable income and a lower standard of living. It is, however, also of vital importance when considering the fiscal implications of public pension expenditure. If—as is the case in two OECD countries—governments claw back in direct and indirect taxes more than half of the gross benefits they pay out to retirees, this obviously will have a large positive impact on the fiscal sustainability of such pension benefit transfers. This remains the case even if, as a result of generally progressive direct tax systems and the typically lower income of older people relative to those of working age,[28] the elderly at an individual/family unit level face a lower direct tax burden than the average population. In addition to such built-in automatic redistribution toward the elderly in progressive direct tax systems, countries have also frequently implemented direct tax benefits targeted exclusively to the older population. Comprehensive analyses by Gordon Keenay and Edward Whitehouse (2003) indicate that such targeted tax breaks toward the elderly are quite prevalent among the OECD countries.

For the purposes and level of detail of this comparative analysis, we focus on how much the tax treatment of social benefits, and particularly pension benefits, differs across OECD countries. Table 2.1 presents the differences in tax treatment for 2003.[29]

Although child benefits, housing benefits, and social assistance are generally tax exempt in the OECD, member states generally levy some kind of taxation on pension benefits, and five countries—Denmark, Iceland, New Zealand, Spain, and Sweden—actually tax pension benefits as regular

---

27. This is also the case in Poland and Portugal over this period.

28. See Disney and Whitehouse (2001) and Keenay and Whitehouse (2003).

29. Table 2.1 provides an aggregate OECD-wide overview of a very complex policy area. It cannot convey the level of detailed analysis required to estimate the effective tax rates facing elderly people across the OECD. The detailed analysis in Keenay and Whitehouse (2003), which considers the effects of general income tax breaks targeted to the elderly as well as the differences in tax treatment of income from public and private pensions, indicates that the relative difference in effective tax rates facing retirees versus the working population differs quite a lot among OECD countries.

Table 2.1 Tax and Social Security treatment of benefits, 2003

Country	Pension transfers (old age, disability)	Child benefits	Unemployment	Housing	Social assistance
Australia	T(reduced)	N	T(n)S(n)	N	—
Austria	TS(reduced)	N	*	N	N
Belgium	T(n)	N	T(n)	—	N
Canada	T(reduced)	N	T	—	N
Czech Republic	T(reduced)	N	N	N	N
Denmark	T	N	TS(reduced)	N	TS(reduced)
Finland	TS(reduced)	N	TS(reduced)	N	N
France	TS(reduced)	S(reduced)	TS(reduced)	S(reduced)	N
Germany	TS(reduced)	tc	*	N	N
Iceland	T	N	TS	N	TS
Ireland	TS(reduced)	N	T(n)	N	N
Italy	T(reduced)	N	TS(reduced)	—	N
Japan	TS(reduced)	N	N	N	N
Korea	T(reduced)	—	N	—	N
Mexico	T(n)	N	—	—	—
Netherlands	T(reduced) S(reduced)	N	TS	N	*
New Zealand	T	N	—	N	—
Norway	T(reduced) S(reduced)	N	TS	N	N
Slovakia	T(n)	N	N	—	N
Spain	T	N	TS(reduced)	—	T(n)
Sweden	T	N	TS	N	N
United Kingdom	T(reduced)	N	T(n)S(n)	N	N
United States	T(reduced)	N	T	N	N

T = taxes are payable; S = Social Security contributions (SSC) are payable; N = neither taxes nor SSC are levied; T(n) or S(n) = (long-term) recipients will not pay the taxes or SSC as the credits, allowances, or zero rate bands exceed the benefit level; (reduced) = reduced rate is payable for beneficiaries; tc = nonwastable tax credit; — = no specific scheme or no information available; * = benefit is a proportion of after-tax income (and thus not taxable).

Source: OECD (2007a, table 5.1).

income. This stands in contrast to the United States, which taxes pension benefits at only a reduced rate. In 1984–93, up to 50 percent of individuals' Social Security (or disability) pensions were subject to federal income tax. In 1994 the level of Social Security pension benefits subject to direct federal taxation was raised to 85 percent.[30] Equally important, OECD

30. This increase was enacted only for recipients with incomes over certain thresholds. See SSA (2008). In 2007 total OASDI income from taxation of benefits was $18.6 billion, or 2.4 percent of total OASDI income.

countries have highly varying levels of indirect consumption taxes, rang-
ing from an across-the-board 25 percent in several Scandinavian countries
to as low as 5 to 10 percent in the United States (depending on the type of
product and the US state).

Figure 2.4 shows the differences in levels of direct and indirect taxation of consumption from benefit payments in the OECD countries in
2001.[31,32] Reflecting their generally lower tax burden (OECD 2006c),
OECD countries in North America and Asia have very low total levels of
taxation of pension benefits—about 10 percent in Australia, Japan, Mexico, and the United States. The United States has the lowest indirect taxation of benefits of any OECD country, but slightly higher direct taxation
of pension benefit income, splitting total proceeds about in half. At the
other end of the spectrum, Denmark levies a total tax of 58 percent on its
pension benefit payments, ahead of the other Scandinavian countries—

---

31. We note that figure 2.4 presents estimated average taxation rates and that significant uncertainty surrounds these estimates. Direct taxation data are from OECD (2007e, appendix 2)
and are, where available, in the form of estimated "average itemized tax rates" (AITR). AITR
equal the total taxes paid by those receiving a given benefit, divided by total income from all
sources of the person(s) receiving this benefit. Some benefits in some countries are tax-
exempt, yielding an assumed AITR of zero. Complications arise when households receive
income from several different sources/benefits, in which case total taxes paid are assumed
distributed across income components according to the weights of each. Furthermore, benefit income may be subject to progressive taxation, in which case income tax paid is calculated
using household tax rates for particular income levels. The data in figure 2.4 are, to the degree data availability allows, a weighted average of AITR for public and private pension income. This is necessary, as in many countries, like the United States, the AITR for public
pension income is lower than for private pension income when individual recipients receive
income from both public and private sources. This is because the national AITR estimate
equaling the total taxes paid on public pensions/total public pension income is lowered relative to the private estimate by the fact that many more lower-income people pay lower
taxes only on their public pensions in much lower-income brackets than many recipients of
private pension income. For instance, in the United States, up to one half of public Social Security pension benefits is taxable if income including one half of the pension exceeds
$25,000. This may increase to a maximum of 85 percent for higher-income pensioners if half
of the Social Security benefits plus other income exceeds $34,000. Meanwhile, US private
pension income is taxed at the capital gains tax rate of 15 percent. For a more detailed description of AITR, see OECD (2007e, especially Box 3), and for US Social Security taxation,
see OECD (2005a, 187ff.)

32. Indirect taxation data in figure 2.4 equal the ratio of general consumption taxes and ex-
cise duties from benefits over private consumption plus government consumption minus
government wages. It is the lowest of three from estimates of indirect taxation in OECD
(2007e, table 5.2). This estimator includes some government indirect taxation income that is
not paid by households and thus is likely a limited overestimate. This methodology further
implicitly assumes that benefit recipients do not save anything but rather consume all their
benefit income. However, as all savings are, especially among seniors, consumed at some
point and the marginal propensity to consume hence in all probability very close to 1, this is
a limited potential error.

Figure 2.4 Total taxation of pension benefits, 2003

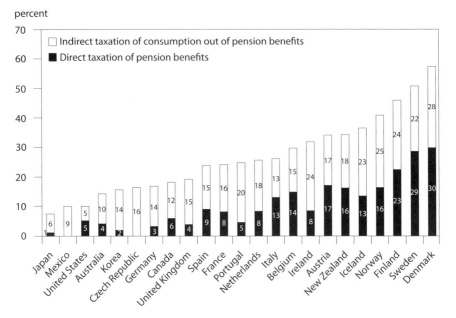

Source: OECD (2007d, table 5.2 and appendix 2); authors' calculations.

Sweden with 51 percent and Finland and Norway at 47 and 41 percent, respectively. What this means is that the net public expenditure on pension provision in the Scandinavian countries is close to half the gross levels presented in figure 2.4, while that of North American and Asian countries is significantly closer to their gross levels.[33]

---

33. The data in figure 2.4 present pension benefits from the perspective of the government and essentially asks "how much of these benefits does the government take back again," with an eye to contemplating the fiscal sustainability of such payments. As such, the implicit distinction between gross and net pension payments is somewhat different than in much of the other pension-related literature. Typically, a distinction is made here between the gross and net replacement rates, where the former (very simplified) equals the ratio of the gross pension payment to gross preretirement wage earnings and the latter (again very simplified) equals the ratio of the pension payment and the preretirement wage after personal income taxes and Social Security contributions paid by pensioners and workers. The difference between the two ratios is equal to the difference between the bottom part of the bar in figure 2.4 and the national average wage earner tax rate for the relevant income group (not shown). In general, therefore, in such comparisons of gross and net replacement rates, no adjustment is made for the fiscal impact of indirect taxation (the white part of the bar in figure 2.4), which in several countries is substantial.

Value of Government Tax Breaks for Pensions

In addition to generating revenue via taxation of benefits,[34] governments may also "spend resources" via the tax system. This occurs through so-called tax expenditures, which can take several different forms: tax exemptions (income excluded from the tax base), tax allowances (amounts deducted from gross income), tax credits (amounts deducted from tax liability), tax relief (tax rate reduction for specific groups, such as retirees), and tax deferrals (postponement, but not elimination, of a tax payment).

The value of tax breaks with a social purpose, for pensions in particular, can be calculated in several ways (OECD 1996). The two most commonly used, and the only ones used by the Office of Management and Budget (OMB) for US federal budget analysis,[35] are the "revenue forgone method," which ex post estimates the amount by which tax revenues were reduced due to a specific provision, and the "outlay equivalent method," which estimates the hypothetical costs to the government in terms of expenditure, were it to provide the same direct benefits as generated by the "tax breaks for pensions." The former method usually gives lower results but is preferred by most countries, according to Willem Adema and Maxime Ladaique (2005), due to its relative simplicity of calculation. We therefore use this method for the data in this book.

We note, however, that some uncertainty surrounds the techniques used today by the OMB to estimate the precise values of US tax expenditures. The last time these estimations were described in detail was in OMB (1985).[36] It is thus important to emphasize that US taxes are ultimately collected on tax-benefited pension contributions (from both employer and employee) and investment gains at the time of dispersion of pension benefits. Tax exemptions for contributions made today (and the cost thereof) are therefore conceptually offset by future tax collection (see box 7.1 for an elaboration).

The extent of provision of tax breaks for government pensions is related to the scope of private pension schemes. OECD (2007e) shows that

---

34. If both gross benefits and taxation levels are high, tax revenues from benefits may be substantial. In Sweden and Denmark, for instance, they made up 9 to 10 percent of all tax revenue in 2004. See Eurostat (2006).

35. Each year the OMB, in accordance with the Congressional Budget Act of 1974 (Public Law 93-344), publishes a list of tax expenditures in the "Analytical Perspectives" of the president's budget. See the most recent 2007 Analytical Perspectives (OMB 2007, chapter 19). No estimates exist of the value of tax breaks offered by US state and local governments, but their aggregate value for pensions is likely small, as this policy field generally is outside state jurisdiction.

36. We are grateful to Gary Burtless for pointing this out to us in his comments on this manuscript.

the value—or cost to the government budget—of this type of tax break is more than 1 percent of GDP in Australia, Canada, Ireland, the United Kingdom, and the United States.[37] But it is unclear just how strong the stimulative effect of this type of tax break is on the adoption by private citizens and employers of voluntary schemes (see also chapter 7 on private pensions).[38] Box 2.1 explains why the nonobserved economy is close to a nonissue for pension sustainability.

Bringing the Parts Together for the Actual Net Public Pension Expenditure

Figure 2.5 combines the information on direct and indirect taxation of pension benefits from figure 2.4 as well as the value of countries' tax benefits for pensions to generate the implied truer, actual full public net pension expenditures for the OECD countries for 2003. There are three components for each country. The black lever indicates the budget gross spending on pensions—the usual measure of the cost of pensions (from figure 2.3). The white segment of the bar measures the after-tax cost of pensions (it is the bar adjusted for the amount of tax paid on pension receipts from figure 2.4). The grey of the bar captures the value of tax expenditures for retirement saving. The combined height of the bar then reflects the total net cost of pension spending, net payments plus tax expenditures, and the countries are shown ranked by the amount of this total as a percent of GDP.[39]

It is surprising to note in figure 2.5 that the US government at a combined 6.8 percent of nominal GDP spends more than any of the Scandinavian so-called cradle-to-grave welfare states of Denmark, Finland, Iceland, Norway, or Sweden, as well as significantly more than other English-speaking countries—Australia, Canada, and Ireland.[40] It is also noteworthy that for most of the countries, the total net spending is often much lower than the budget outlays on pensions. Only in Australia, Canada, Ireland, and the United States is the total level of expenditure higher than the gross value of pension cash benefit. The concluding

---

37. OECD (2007e) cautions that at present there is no full comparable dataset of the value of these tax breaks with a social purpose and thus includes them only as a memorandum item.

38. See, for instance, Hubbard and Skinner (1996) and Engen, Gale, and Scholz (1994).

39. However, figure 2.5 brings together data for several different economic concepts and, despite their disparities, amalgamates them into a single chart. This treatment of the data does not fully do justice to the methodological difficulties inherent in their collection and estimation. For in-depth descriptions of the methodological caveats required, see Adema and Ladaique (2005) and OECD (2007e).

40. This ranking would be influenced by the missing data for tax breaks with a social purpose for Denmark, New Zealand, the Netherlands, and Korea, as the first three have very significant private pension schemes.

Box 2.1 The nonobserved economy: Close to a nonissue for pension sustainability

An occasional explanation for the recent lag in growth performance among Mediterranean countries, in particular behind the rest of the OECD countries, is the size of the nonobserved or shadow economy—in Greece, Italy, Portugal, and Spain, for instance, it is estimated at more than 20 percent of the total economy.[1] Could this nonobserved economy serve as a resource to help make pension systems more sustainable? Such an approach could be useful, especially to the countries mentioned above, which are among those with significant longer-term problems. However, for at least two reasons the nonobserved economy represents a broad negative for pension sustainability.

The first reason concerns the five broad areas that constitute the nonobserved economy[2]:

1. *Underground production*, which according to the 1993 System of National Accounts (SNA)[3] (paragraph 6.34) covers "certain activities that may be both productive in an economic sense and also quite legal (provided certain standards or regulations are complied with) but deliberately concealed from public authorities for the following reasons:
   a) avoid the payment of income, value-added or other taxes;
   b) avoid the payment of social security contributions;
   c) avoid having to meet certain legal standards, such as minimum wages, maximum hours, safety or health standards; or
   d) avoid complying with certain administrative procedures, such as completing statistical questionnaires or other administrative forms."

2. *Illegal production*, which according to the 1993 SNA (paragraph 3.54), if they fit "the characteristics of transactions—notably the characteristic that there is mutual agreement between the parties—are treated the same way as legal actions."

3. *Informal-sector production*, which according to the 15th International Conference of Labor Statisticians Resolution Paragraph 5(1), is described as follows: "The informal sector may be broadly characterized as consisting of units engaged in the production of goods or services with the primary objective of generating employment and incomes to the persons concerned. These units typically operate at a low level of organization, with little or no division between labor and capital as factors of production and on a small scale. Labor relations—where they exist—are based mostly on casual employment, kinship or personal and social relations rather than contractual arrangements with formal guarantees."

(box continues on next page)

4. *Household production for own use*, which includes production of crops, livestock, and other goods (such as cloth) for own use, construction of own houses, imputed rents of owner-occupiers, and services of paid domestic servants.
5. *Production missed due to deficiencies in data collection*, which covers data deficiencies arising from undercoverage of enterprises, nonresponse to surveys by enterprises, and underreporting by enterprises.

In developed economies (the focus of this book), only the first of these, underground production, has the potential size to be relevant to long-term concern regarding pensions. However, in the second reason (b) cited for such production, the SNA recognizes the explicit motivation "to avoid the payment of social security contributions." It seems straightforward to conclude that the higher such contributions generally are set, the more economic activities can be expected to migrate underground to escape them. Thus there is likely an inverse relationship between the size of the underground economy in developed economies and the size of contributions to, and subsequently the long-term sustainability of, a country's pension system. More importantly, though, any concerted effort to bring these activities into the official and fully legal economy seems destined to fail, as the underground existence is initially preferred precisely because of the extra costs of a fully legal existence. Rather than transfer seamlessly to the official legal economy, when confronted by concerted government action, most underground activities are likely to simply come to a halt. It might even be further argued that a hypothetical successful campaign that suddenly brought a lot of hitherto underground workers into an already underfunded official pension system would actually reduce its sustainability, unless there was a very close relationship in the official pension system between officially credited contributions made and benefits paid out.

A large underground production will also likely lead to suboptimal sizes of production units—producers forgo economies of scale in the attempt to remain out of sight of the authorities. Noncompetitive, noncompliant enterprises are similarly likely to remain in business longer than would be the case in a fully transparent and competitive market. Such enterprises lower overall productivity in the economy and therefore rob a country of one of the most important levers with which to ease its pension burdens.[4]

A less harmful type of "cheating the pension system," in terms of old age income security at least, occurs when retirees continue to work after retirement and thus receive salary income but do not report it to the relevant authorities to avoid government means-testing of pension benefits. In countries like Australia, this has proven a substantial pension policy problem. We return to this issue in chapters 4 and 5.

Finally, it is crucial to realize that governments' tendency to deal statistically and thereby also largely macroeconomically with their nonobserved economies by simply adjusting official GDP figures (e.g., with a top-up, which in Italy, for example, is a nontrivial 15 percent of GDP[5]) does not in any way redress the adverse effects on pension sustainability. To the degree that such accounting exercises imbue governments with a false sense of accomplishment, they probably aggravate the long-term outlook.

1. Estimates from Schneider (2002).

2. This breakdown is from Baily and Kirkegaard (2004). See chapter 3 of OECD, ILO, IMF, and CIS STAT (2002) for a detailed description of the nonobserved economy.

3. See UN Statistical Division at http://unstats.un.org for a description of the 1993 SNA classification system.

4. See "The Hidden Danger of the Informal Economy," *McKinsey Quarterly* 2004, no. 3, for an in-depth analysis of the adverse productivity impact of this issue, which may in some countries lower productivity by up to 50 percent.

5. Greece in September 2006 proposed to Eurostat to adjust its GDP upward by 25 percent. See the *Financial Times*, "Oldest Profession Boosts Greek Output," September 28, 2006.

statement of Adema and Ladaique (2005, 35) puts the implications of this succinctly:

> [I]t does show that observations of social expenditure levels across countries that do not account for private social benefits and the impact of the tax system are prone to be misleading. Care is needed when making statements of the form: "country X spends more than country Y"—all too often these statements are wrong.

Figure 2.5 also shows that in several countries with really high gross expenditure (Austria, Belgium, France, Italy, and Portugal), looking at the actual, full, net expenditure levels significantly diminishes the fiscal burden—by more than 2.5 percent of GDP in 2003. Hence the actual, net disparities in OECD countries' current public pension expenditures are not as large as suggested by the gross expenditure levels in figure 2.3.

Figure 2.5   Actual cost of public expenditures on pension cash benefits, 2003 (percent of nominal GDP)

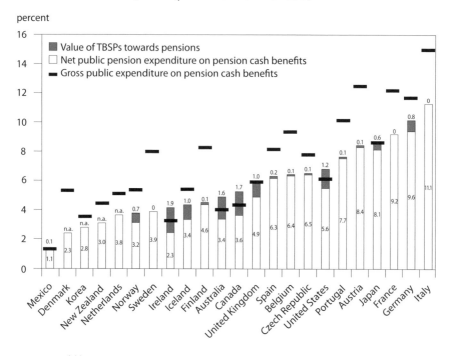

n.a. = not available

TBSP = tax breaks for social purposes

Source: Authors' calculations, based on OECD Social Expenditure Database.

The possibility of taxing or not taxing pension benefits provides policymakers with an additional potent policy lever with which to adjust pension systems to accommodate both fairness and fiscal sustainability. This lever has the political advantage of potentially being of a stealthy nature—it can be buried in arcane details and thus introduced below the political radar screen but has large effects in the longer term. This is something historically not lost on US lawmakers, as, for instance, they buried deep in the Omnibus Budget Recollection Act of 1993 (Public Law 103-66) a raise in the level of Old-Age, Survivors, and Disability Insurance (OASDI) benefits subject to federal taxation for income over certain thresholds (from 50 to 85 percent) and thus reduced the degree of tax exemption for these benefits. Moreover, US lawmakers at that time decided that the increase in tax revenue derived from this additional taxation of OASDI benefits should accrue not as with the first 50 percent to the OASDI Trust Fund but rather to the far more economically stressed Medicare Federal Hospital Insurance (HI) Trust Fund; in 2007 the HI Trust Fund received $10.6 billion in income (4.7 percent of its total income) from taxation of OASDI benefits.[41] Through the taxation of pension benefits, US lawmakers thus in 1993 devised a way to channel resources from pension provision toward the rapidly growing health care costs in the United States.

At the same time, of course, the current level of taxation in an economy plays a large role in determining the realistic size of a government's room for fiscal and taxation maneuvering. There are large differences in the total tax burden among OECD countries: As of 2003, total tax revenue in Sweden made up more than half of GDP, whereas in Japan, Korea, and the United States it was only a quarter and in Ireland and Switzerland less than 30 percent (OECD 2005b).[42] Although the public's acceptance of high levels of taxation seems significantly higher in Sweden than, for instance, in the United States, it nonetheless is highly improbable that an already high-taxation country such as Sweden or other Scandinavian countries could solve a hypothetical future pension crisis by further increasing taxation. On the other hand, before considering the domestic political climate, this seems far less true in the United States or Japan, which have far lower levels of taxation.

In summary, in this section we have illustrated that, with the adoption of a perhaps broader than usual pension sustainability focus and the inclusion of private pension assets and the tax treatment of pension benefits in the analysis, very large differences emerge among the OECD countries in terms of their respective fiscal "starting points"; adding TPATPP to general government balances improves pension sustainability in the United States more than in any other OECD country; and frequently ignored differences in the tax treatment of pension benefits among OECD countries has a very significant impact on true net government expenditures on pension benefits and tends to push up expenditures in some OECD countries (for example, in the United States) while reducing it in others.

Value of the "Pension Promise"

As we explain in chapter 3 about the distributional challenges related to pensions, the vast divergence in underpinning philosophies behind different countries' pension systems accounts for the largest part of these cross-country disparities in pension generosity. Each country's philosophy—whether the principal aim of the public pension system is to avoid abject

---

41. Boards of Trustees of the Federal Hospital Insurance and Federal Supplementary Medical Insurance Trust Funds (2008).

42. The OECD data include Social Security taxes.

old age poverty or to sustain into old age the same living standard that insured wage earners enjoyed before retirement—makes a huge difference in the level of financial liabilities the government is likely to incur.

Figure 2.6 captures these cross-country differences in generosity by showing how retirees' net retirement income from mandatory pensions differs substantially as they move up the income distribution.[43] Retirees in countries with flat rate (or close thereto) mandatory systems, such as Ireland, New Zealand, and the United Kingdom, have net retirement income essentially unchanged across the income range (the nearly horizontal lines in figure 2.6 indicate a rapidly declining net replacement rate with the level of preretirement income). At the other extreme, retirees in countries with generous mandatory insurance-based systems, such as Greece and Turkey, have net pension retirement incomes that essentially mirror their preretirement earnings across the income range (illustrated by the 45° line in figure 2.6). Italy, the Netherlands, Poland, and some of the Scandinavian countries also have relatively high mandated retirement incomes for higher-income groups, while France closely matches the OECD average, approximately midway between matching net retirement income systems and flat rate systems, and Australia, Canada, Germany, Japan, Korea, and the United States are much closer to the flat rate systems. Few countries—most noticeably Denmark (above the 45° line on the left side of figure 2.6)—have mandatory retirement income for low-wage earners significantly above their preretirement earnings.

Mandatory pension liabilities in countries with far higher net pension replacement rates for higher-income groups are invariably far higher than in countries with flat rate systems. Increased numbers of such high-level pension recipients (i.e., those with high income and consequently high levels of private contributions during their working life) are perhaps the greatest threat to the financial sustainability of PAYGO systems. With these systems paying benefits out of the contributions of today's workers, cash flow will come under severe pressure as the number of high-income

---

43. These data rely on new OECD estimates using the concept of the "average worker" (AW) rather than the earlier concept of the "average production worker" (APW). This latter group included adult full-time employees (on establishment payrolls), directly engaged in a production activity in the manufacturing sector (ISIC D—Manufacturing), including manual (nonsupervisory) workers and minor shop-floor supervisory workers. Excluded were nonmanual (supervisory) workers, part-timers, and all workers outside the manufacturing sector. The new category of AW is far broader than APW and includes all ISIC sectors from C though K (mining and quarrying, manufacturing, utilities, construction, wholesale/retail/ repair, hotels/restaurants, transportation, financial services, and real estate) as well as both manual and nonmanual workers. Included in both categories are all wages, cash supplements, bonuses, overtime pay, holiday pay, Christmas bonuses, and the like. This transition from APW to AW generally lowers US average wages by over 10 percent and Canadian wages by 5 percent, while boosting that of other G-7 countries by up to a third. See OECD (2003, 2004, 2005c, 2006c) for more information.

Figure 2.6 Net retirement income from mandatory pension programs, by preretirement net earnings in multiples of average wage (for men)

net retirement income = net replacement rate × preretirement earnings

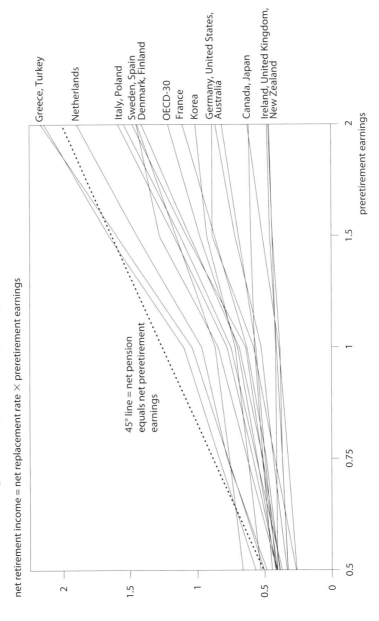

Source: OECD (2007a, 35).

retirees increases dramatically and, in some countries, the number of contributing workers declines.[44]

Net retirement income rates, however, matter most to individuals, as they may or may not have to adjust consumption levels to life in retirement. On the other hand, what matters to governments and their finances is not just the relative pension benefit level and retirement income measured against income in preretirement life but rather the absolute net (after-tax) level of pension benefits and the duration for which these have to be paid to individuals. In short, governments need to know the level of mandatory pensions promised to individuals.

To estimate this level, the OECD (2005a, 2007a) uses its impressive array of country pension benefit models (box 2.2) to compute a comparable number across countries for the value of the total average pension promise (diplomatically termed "pension wealth" by the OECD) to individuals in the OECD member states. These estimates are reproduced in terms of multiples of each country's average wage in figure 2.7, where the average pension promise estimate shown in figure 2.7 for each country equals the present value of the stream of pension benefit payments promised to the average future retiree, measured as a multiple of the national average earnings in 2004. (It reflects the individual promise embodied in the right to future pension receipts; it does not reflect national liabilities.) The figure shows clearly that the size of the mandatory pension promise payable to the individual differs substantially among OECD countries.

However, viewed through the lens of government finances, the estimated cross-country differences shown in figure 2.7 may, in fact, be too small. This is because the OECD, in order to produce comparable data from diverse national pension systems, had to rely on a series of simplifying assumptions, noticeably concerning the timing of withdrawal from the labor market. In its analysis, the OECD (2007a, 12) posits that people will remain in employment until the statutory full pension eligibility age—typically 65 among OECD countries.[45] But in a number of OECD countries, particularly in continental Europe, the effective age of retirement is very large (as discussed below), due to the presence of especially

---

44. This was the largest part of the explanation for the temporary freezing of German pension levels in October 2003, when Germany suddenly faced an estimated $11.6 billion shortfall in its PAYGO pension system. The shortfall was a result of an increasing number of retirees and—in the middle of a recession with German unemployment above 10 percent—a declining number of people contributing. We analyze this subject in more detail in chapter 3 on the distributional challenges of pensions.

45. All currently legislated rises in standard pension eligibilities are included in the OECD models. For the United States this includes the statutory rise in age from 65 to 67 for full pension eligibility.

Box 2.2 Pillars of pensions: Pension system typologies and terminology

A frequently used classification of different pension systems splits the individual national pension systems into several different subsectors, called "pillars" or "tiers." The OECD (2005a, 2007a) offers a purely descriptive pension system taxonomy, focusing on the objective for and actors in each part. The typology consists of three main tiers and a number of subtiers. The first tier is universal coverage for retirees aimed at providing a basic minimum standard of living—in the United States, this would be the means-tested Supplemental Security Income (SSI) program. The second tier consists of mandatory insurance-based programs, such as the old age provisions of Social Security. Some countries have mandatory programs that are privately administered, such as the individual account system in Chile. The third tier of retirement support includes voluntary contributory programs, such as private employer pension plans or 401(k) plans. The OECD typology is summarized in table 2B2.1. Although several additional pillar or tier-based typologies have emerged in recent years (see below), by far the largest share of relevant data concerning pensions today is structured according to the OECD typology; therefore we use this framework throughout our analyses, albeit with two caveats.

First, public pension expenditure as commonly defined includes direct government benefit expenditures, paid out under mandatory pension programs as shown in tiers 1 and 2 of table 2B2.1 (columns 1 to 4). But many governments also have significant "implicit pension expenditure" in the form of financial support (i.e., tax benefits) of other, typically privately administered, pension types.[1] As such, the distinction between the public and private segments of pension tiers is blurred. At the same time, it seems most plausible to assume that governments will ultimately be responsible for honoring the liabilities of all mandatory pension programs, even if—as is the case in, for instance, Australia, Chile, or the Netherlands—some of these are privately provided and managed. These mandatory programs make up such a large part of the pension system that a collapse due to government noninterference would be politically inconceivable, irrespective of public or private character and management. So in this book we use all mandatory programs (i.e., all of tiers 1 and 2[2]) as the base for analyzing future government pension liabilities (as is the case in OECD 2005a and 2007a).[3]

Second, several countries, such as Canada, Denmark, Germany, Japan, the United Kingdom, and the United States, have voluntary occupational schemes that cover large parts of their private workforce. This somewhat blurs the distinction between the second and third pension tiers shown in table 2B2.1

(box continues on next page)

Box 2.2   Pillars of pensions: Pension system typologies and terminology *(continued)*

(i.e., between mandatory and voluntary programs) in these countries, and determining where an individual country's system fits best may be a matter of judgment. In this book we attempt to follow the OECD typology and place voluntary programs in tier 3, but, for instance, Denmark's 90+ percent coverage of nominally voluntary programs places it in pillar 2. Pillar 3 will be the focus of chapter 7 on private and corporate pension systems.

As mentioned above, other pension plan frameworks have emerged. The World Bank in 1994 introduced its well-known prescriptive three-pillar typology, which differs from the OECD classification[4] and is briefly summarized below:

- First pillar: a publicly managed mandatory system, aimed principally at avoiding old age poverty and usually pay-as-you-go and defined benefit in character.
- Second pillar: a privately managed mandatory savings-based system, either defined benefit or defined contribution in character.
- Third pillar: a privately managed voluntary system, either individual or occupational in character.

---

1. The costs of occasional (and usually very expensive) ad hoc government bailouts of failing private pension plans are not included. Potential US government liabilities related to the deficit in the quasi-public Pension Benefit Guaranty Corporation (PBGC) are thus not counted as part of US public pension expenditure.

2. Column 5 in table 2B2.1 shows the private segments of the second tier.

3. Throughout this book, we provide information on the US SSI program and include it in the general analysis where relevant. However, the SSI program is materially different from the US Social Security (OASDI) program, and unless otherwise noted, the latter is the focus of our analyses.

4. The International Labor Office has also published a prescriptive three pillar–based pension system typology. See Gillion (2000).

early retirement programs.[46] At the same time, in other OECD countries—notably Japan and Korea—the effective age of withdrawal from the labor market is substantially above the official retirement age, indicating that the period during which individuals collect their pension is significantly

---

46. Effective retirement age refers to the average age at which persons at 40 and older left the labor force.

Table 2B2.1 OECD typology of pension systems

| | First tier: Universal (mandatory) coverage, aimed at redistribution and poverty alleviation | | | Second tier: Mandatory insurance-based programs | | Third tier: Voluntary insurance-based pension provision schemes | |
| | Public sector | | | Public sector | Private sector | Private sector | |
Resource/means tested	Basic pension	Minimum pension	Defined benefit/defined contribution	Defined benefit/defined contribution	Occupational	Individual
Systems that pay higher levels of benefits to poorer retirees and lower (or even no) benefits to well-off retirees. Depends on income sources and assets. An example is US Supplemental Security Income. Old age income security may also be achieved through similar programs available to entire population.	Flat rate pension systems (Ireland and New Zealand); pension benefit depends only on years of residency (not past earnings).	Systems that guarantee that retirees with few years of contributions to second tier insurance based systems receive a minimum pension. Usually benefit levels are determined based only on pension income and not on assets or other income. Example is the UK Pension Credit System.	Mandatory defined benefit, notional defined contribution, or points systems that provide benefits toward ensuring a sufficient living standard, based on number of years of contributions and a measure of individual earnings. Example is US Social Security.	Mandatory defined benefit schemes may also be private (as in the Netherlands), while defined contribution schemes provide each retiree with an individual account in which contributions are invested. Accumulated capital provides pension income. Example is Australia's Superannuation Scheme.	Voluntary occupational (or employer-provided) schemes may be either defined benefit or defined contribution. Examples are US auto-industry defined benefit plans or US 401(k) plans.	Voluntary individual retirement plans may be defined benefit or defined contribution, and in the United States include IRAs, Keogh, and Roth plans.

Sources: OECD (2005a, 2005b, 2007a); authors.

Figure 2.7 Average mandatory pension promise, as a multiple of average wage, 2004

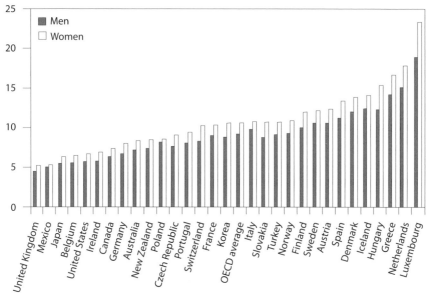

multiples of average wage

Source: OECD (2007a).

lower than the standard retirement age would indicate. Including in the estimation process these differences in effective retirement ages—which, while strictly outside the mandatory pension promise methodology, have direct implications for government finances—would undoubtedly raise promise levels substantially for many European countries (but decrease them dramatically for others, such as Japan)[47] and further amplify the cross-country differences in the full retirement income promise granted to individuals.

Even so, in figure 2.7 there are striking cross-country differences in the generosity of the mandatory pension promise, especially considering the relatively equal general wealth levels among the majority of OECD member states. Mandatory pension promises range from a total value of five

---

47. See chapter 4 on the labor market challenge for a discussion of the Japanese notion of the working retiree, where many workers continue to work while receiving a corporate pension.

times the average earnings in the United Kingdom to more than 20 times the average earnings in Luxembourg.[48]

Prominent in figure 2.7 is the fact that the United States, together with Belgium, Ireland, Japan, Mexico, and the United Kingdom, has a very low level of pension wealth relative to earnings. Other English-speaking countries, such as Australia, Canada, and New Zealand, are also relatively low, as are Germany and Poland. These countries have pension wealth in the range of 5 to 8 times earnings, compared with 10 to 15 for most of the European countries.

The figure shows that the pension promise made to women is higher than for men. This finding may seem surprising, as it has been frequently documented that women have lower pensions than men, due to their shorter periods in the labor force.[49] The results in figure 2.7 are predominantly driven by unisex assumptions. The methodology employed assumes wages between the sexes are equal and that all people remain in the labor market throughout their working lives until the effective age of retirement. In addition, there is no adjustment for women's prolonged periods of absence from the workforce in conjunction with childbirth or family care duties. The generally larger estimated pension promises made to women, as shown in figure 2.7, are overwhelmingly driven by the longer life expectancies of women.

But why are there such large differences across countries? The answer lies in the large differences in generosity of pensions for higher-earning groups (toward the upper right part of figure 2.6). Cross-country differences in life expectancy at age 65 are only a minor factor, as are those in the levels of pensions provided to lower-income groups. The left half of figure 2.6 shows that pension levels for lower-income ranges are much closer to one another across the OECD than at higher levels.[50]

Although the comparison here does not have a direct policy implication, it is nonetheless of considerable policy interest. Certainly, for the United States adding the length of time spent receiving benefits to estimate the total mandatory pension promise reinforces the conclusion that the US Social Security system is not particularly generous by international comparisons. Moreover, this section indicates that most countries, should they be compelled to improve the sustainability of their pension systems through benefit cuts, ought to focus on mandatory pensions paid to the higher-income groups.

---

48. Expressing pension wealth relative to earnings provides a more valid comparison of the magnitude of the public pension liabilities relative to the wealth level of a given country than would be the case for the absolute values of pension wealth.

49. See, for instance, IWPR (2007). Women are frequently also tied as dependents to their husband's plans. We elaborate on this issue in chapter 7 on private pensions.

50. See appendix 2B for an elaboration.

The Demographic Outlook

Whether you're a brother or whether you're a mother, You're stayin' alive, stayin' alive.
Feel the city breakin' and ev'rybody shakin' And we're stayin' alive, stayin' alive. . . .
—Bee Gees, *Stayin' Alive*, 1977

The megatrend that is probably most likely to shape the fiscal challenges to future pension systems is the rapidly growing size of aging populations in all developed countries. We have so far examined governments' fiscal starting points, the impact of taxation on pension expenditures, and the sizes of individual pension promises, which are all important components. However, many would probably argue that they pale in importance compared to changes both in the number of retirees and in the number of workers available to support them in the coming decades. Population aging and the higher ratio of retirees to workers affect every country examined in this book. As with other issues, though, not all countries are alike and the severity of the problem varies quite a bit: Some countries are facing the potentially far more serious issue of a future where the number of workers is not merely growing less rapidly, as in the United States, but instead will soon be declining outright in absolute terms.

In the final part of this chapter we argue that while population aging is obviously important, it is not the only factor determining the pension outlook. In fact, aging will be fiscally devastating only if it is combined with poor economic policies and unsustainably low actual retirement ages. To illustrate this important point, we explore the differences between old age support ratios that are purely demographic and old age support ratios that take into consideration also the age at which people actually retire and leave employment.

Three main long-term issues affect the quantity of a country's workforce: fertility, immigration, and effective retirement age. We analyze them in the next sections, following a discussion of the outlook for the working age population (i.e., potential maximum labor force) for the OECD countries shown in figure 2.8.

Outlook for the Size of the Workforce

Countries such as the United States and Canada are, based on recent levels of immigration,[51] projected to continue to experience labor force

---

51. All data in figure 2.8 are national statistical agencies' "medium projections," which typically rely on recent years' immigration levels to estimate future inflow. Given the current political discussions concerning immigration, particularly in the United States, there is some question as to whether historical levels of immigration will continue in the United States.

Figure 2.8 Working-age population (15–64 years) in selected OECD countries, 2006–50

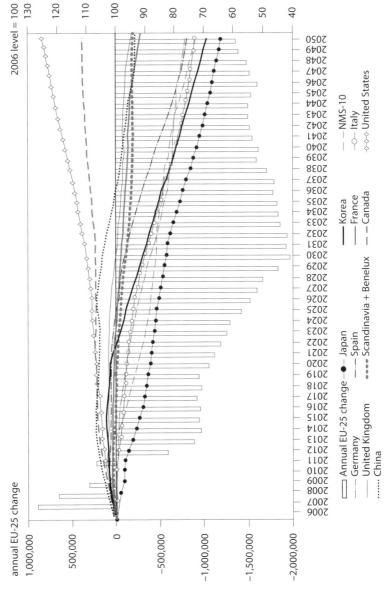

NMS = new EU member states

Sources: Eurostat 2004 Demographic Database; US Census Bureau; Statistics Canada; Japan National Institute of Population and Social Security Research (2002).

growth, although at reduced rates (indeed, Canada will stagnate completely toward the end of the projection period). North America (and other OECD countries like Australia or New Zealand with broadly similar projections) will therefore experience the aging process largely from increases in the number of retirees, not from labor force declines. Other countries, however, are less fortunate.

The bars in figure 2.8 indicate the annual absolute changes in the EU-25 potential labor force (i.e., ages 15–64) from 2006 projected to 2050. The labor force continues to grow for another few years until 2011, after which it drops precipitously by 1 million to 2 million workers a year from 2013 on for the duration of the projection period. As a comparison, the entire Irish potential workforce in 2006 was 2.8 million workers: In other words, the equivalent of that entire workforce will disappear from the EU-25 every two to three years.

However, figure 2.8 also illustrates the vast differences within the European Union. Indeed, the majority of the old members—the Benelux, France, Ireland[52] (not shown), the three Scandinavian EU countries (Denmark, Sweden, and Finland), and the United Kingdom—face only stagnating or modestly declining potential workforces aged 15–64, dropping by about 5 percent by 2050. Far more serious is the situation for Germany, the Mediterranean countries of Italy and Spain, and the new member states (NMS-10),[53] all of which can expect to see their potential workforces decline by 25 percent by 2050. These sharp differences indicate just how unevenly the demographic challenge is distributed even within the European Union. However, the North Asian economies of Japan and Korea face the biggest declines—up to fully 30 percent—in their workforce populations.

For comparison purposes, figure 2.8 includes China, where the working age population is projected to start declining by about 2020. China falls in about the middle of the pack of OECD countries.

Given the large diversity of projections among the OECD economies, and the significant implications of the future of the labor force for the sustainability of pensions, it is worth looking at the reasons for the diversity and whether government policies can or should try to change behavior. There are two main contributors to the diversity of projections: (1) fertility, which drives the size of the native-born population, and (2) immigration.

---

52. Ireland has a uniquely young age profile in the European Union, and, due to this and a current reversal of earlier periods' emigration from the country, its potential labor force growth is projected to be comparable to Canada's until 2050.

53. The ten new EU member states are Cyprus, the Czech Republic, Estonia, Hungary, Latvia, Lithuania, Malta, Poland, Slovakia, and Slovenia.

Fertility and Workforce Size

The general decline in total average fertility (i.e., the total number of children born, on average, per woman in her lifetime) in recent decades is half of the demographic pincer affecting developed economies (we examine the other—increasing life expectancies—in chapter 3). However, while total average fertility in all OECD countries has fallen below the replacement rate of 2.1,[54] both the trajectories of this decline and the levels today vary significantly.

As can be seen in figure 2.9, OECD countries fall into two main groups in terms of their total fertility since 1970.[55] One group of countries, including Germany, Greece, Italy, Japan, Korea, and Spain—call them "the constant decliners"—saw large declines in fertility in the 1970s and early 1980s and have since continued a steady decline to very low levels of 1.1 to 1.4 children per woman in 2004. Fertility in the other group—France, Ireland, the Netherlands, the Scandinavian countries, and the United States—also declined rapidly in the 1970s and early 1980s (the Netherlands and Denmark were the lowest-fertility countries in 1982) but then started to recover and by 2004 was between 1.7 and 2.04 children—the highest-fertility country being the United States. These are "the recoverers."

While figure 2.9 shows that declines in fertility are not irrevocable, it is useful to consider what types of government policies—in liberal democracies, at least—might feasibly be utilized to raise total fertility (see box 2.3). Moreover, for the purposes of this chapter, the more pertinent question is whether policies to raise fertility levels would really do much for the sustainability of public pensions.[56] Even if a silver bullet government policy for raising fertility levels were found tomorrow, it would take a quarter of a century—when additional workers would enter the labor force—for any impact, and even then the size of that impact is questionable. The example of South Korea is illustrative: It is the country in figure 2.9 with the lowest total fertility in 2004, at 1.19. Even if South Korea managed to reverse its decline in total fertility and in future decades approached what the UN Population Division estimates is the long-term

---

54. This is not just an OECD country phenomenon, as the United Nations lists more than a third of the world's countries (58 countries out of 172 with reported data in the *Human Development Report 2006*) as, on average, below this level during 2000–05. See UN Development Programme data at http://hdr.undp.org/statistics.

55. We have omitted several countries from figure 2.10 to make the chart readable. Those not included fall between the two groups described in the text in terms of their 2004 total fertility levels and as such represent intermediate observations, which can for purposes of illustration be ignored here.

56. See appendix 2C for a discussion of the infeasibility of offsetting rising pension costs with lower education expenses resulting from the reduction in population growth.

Figure 2.9 Total fertility in selected OECD countries, 1970–2004

children per woman

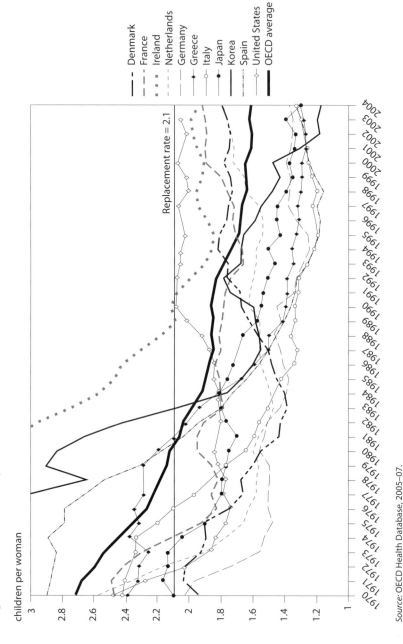

Legend:
- Denmark
- France
- Ireland
- Netherlands
- Germany
- Greece
- Italy
- Japan
- Korea
- Spain
- United States
- OECD average

Replacement rate = 2.1

Source: OECD Health Database, 2005–07.

Box 2.3 Government policies to raise total fertility levels: What seems to work

The 20th century has understandably made many uncomfortable with blatantly pronatalist government policies among the OECD countries. On the other hand, the decline in OECD fertility levels since 1970 had by 2003 convinced 11 OECD member states to adopt policies to raise their fertility levels.[1] It is clear that in the long term, fertility levels do matter.

It has long been established that in developing countries there is a very strong negative correlation between fertility levels and women's educational attainment and/or work-outside-the-home of women.[2] Unfortunately, this finding can lead to the conclusion that there is a policy-relevant trade-off involved between the two. While this may be the case for the developing world, the fact is that in the developed world, not only is there no trade-off but also the correlation is completely reversed. Indeed, as can be seen in figure 2B3.1, in the rich world OECD[3] mothers tend to both work and get a university degree!

Figure 2B3.1 plots for the early 2000s the average total fertility levels of women as a function of both the share of women with a university-level degree (left side) and the employment ratio for women in their child-bearing years (25–54). In both cases, the correlation is positive and statistically significant.[4]

We distinguish between inter- and intracountry differences in fertility levels. It is the case generally that more educated women have fewer children than those with less education (D'Addio and Mira d'Ercole 2005), but these intracountry differences are dwarfed by the cross-country differences, indicating that other country-specific circumstances (and possibly policies) play the biggest role in determining fertility levels.

One aspect of child bearing that has gone hand in hand with the decline in fertility rates is the rise in the age of first-time mothers. In the United States, this age has risen to over 25 (up from 21 in 1970), and it is over 28 in most of Europe and about 30 in Australia and New Zealand.[5] Policies aimed at boosting total fertility levels should, therefore, strive to ensure that postponement of childbirth does not become abandonment of it.[6] Clearly, governments should target such policies toward the needs of women close to or into their 30s.

Several empirical studies surveyed by D'Addio and Mira d'Ercole (2005) indicate that the availability and low cost to the user of child care facilities has a large and positive effect on fertility rates,[7] while high costs have a negative impact. Given the findings in Immervoll and Barber (2005) that the share of infants (age 0–2) in OECD countries who are in registered child care[8] varies from two-thirds

(box continues on next page)

Box 2.3 Government policies to raise total fertility levels: What seems to work (continued)

(in Denmark and Sweden) to about 5 percent (in Greece, Italy, and Spain), and that the total net costs of child care range from about 10 percent of average family income in Germany, Scandinavia, and (interestingly, given the low participation) Greece to more than half in Ireland, this seems to be an area of possible straightforward government policy intervention.

Other empirical work indicates that financial cash benefits are effective, although it is not always clear how much the effects result from changes in timing rather than overall family size.[9] Again, this could be a relatively easy government intervention without, presumably, any negative externalities.

A number of studies further show that higher unemployment rates and increased income uncertainty for women lower fertility rates.[10] This finding would seem verified by figure 2B3.1, which by using employment (rather than labor force participation) rates explicitly includes national differences in unemployment rates. A well-functioning labor market, in other words, seems to have a positive spillover effect in terms of fertility levels—something government policies obviously should strive to act on.

In summary, while policy options are clearly available to governments wishing to raise fertility levels, none of them seem to work in anything other than the (very) long term.

---

1. These are Austria, the Czech Republic, France, Greece, Hungary, Japan, Korea, Luxembourg, Poland, and Slovakia. Except France and Luxembourg, fertility levels in all these countries were below 1.5 in 2003, indicating limited results from such policies. In addition, the governments of Italy, Norway, Portugal, Spain, and Switzerland had the official view that their fertility levels were too low but did not implement policies to address the issue. Compiled from the UN World Population Policies, 2003 (D'Addio and Mira d'Arcole 2005). Since 2003, Australia has instituted a A$4,000/child bonus payment, which according to preliminary results has been quite effective in at least bringing forward childbirths in Australia. See AFP (Sydney), "Baby Bonus Boosts Australia's Birthrate: Government Data," September 16, 2006.

2. See, for instance, UN Population Division (1996, 2004).

3. The two lowest-income OECD members, Mexico and Turkey, are excluded from this figure.

4. The p-values shown are for a two-sided hypothesis test of no correlation between the two variables.

5. Data are from national statistical authorities.

6. The fertility data that we used are estimated by taking the ratio of the number of births in a given year and the average annual number of women of reproductive age (15–49). If there is indeed significant postponement of childbirth within an age cohort, there may also be cyclical swings in total fertility rates. Initially upon postponement, total fertility

Figure 2B3.1   Fertility, women's educational attainment, and employment, 2000–04

average annual total fertility rate (children per woman)

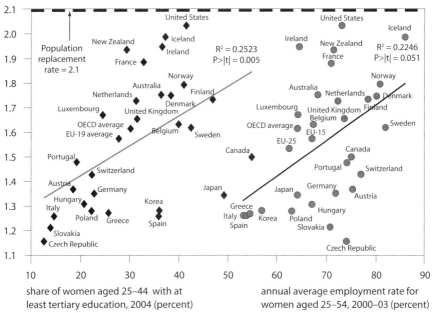

share of women aged 25–44 with at least tertiary education, 2004 (percent)

annual average employment rate for women aged 25–54, 2000–03 (percent)

Note: Age group 25–44 is weighted average of the 25–34 and 35–44 age groups.

Sources: OECD *Society at a Glance,* 2005; OECD (2006b); OECD Labor Market Database.

Figure 2.10   South Korea's workforce (15–64 years) under different fertility scenarios, 2005–50

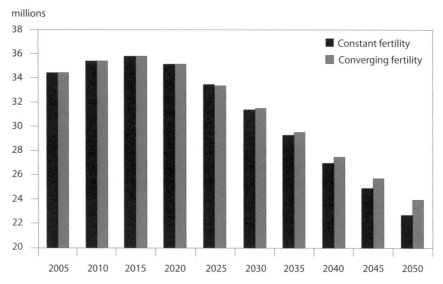

millions

Source: UN Population Division (2004).

convergence point—a total fertility level of 1.85 children per woman[57]—this convergence point would still be below the replacement rate of 2.1. The data illustrated for all the countries in figure 2.9 suggest that the world's population will go into decline in the medium to long term.

Figure 2.10 shows the trajectories of the working age population in South Korea from 2005 to 2050, with the fertility level either constant at the current low values[58] or rising gradually toward the global convergence point. As can be seen, there is no difference in the two until after 2025, and even at the furthest extension of these projections, in 2050, the difference is less than 1.2 million workers, or about 5 percent of the constant work-

---

57. See the assumptions for the UN *World Population Prospects* at http://esa.un.org/unpp. The value of 1.85 derives from the experience of all countries with declining fertility from 1950 to 2005. Due to the very low total fertility level in South Korea in 2004, according to the UN estimates, even with ongoing convergence, the country would not reach 1.85 by 2050 but only 1.77 children per woman in the period 2045–50.

58. The UN World Population Database's assumptions operate in five-year intervals and thus the fertility level, which is kept constant in the black bars in figure 2.10, is the average estimated fertility of the 2000–05 period of 1.23. See the assumptions for the UN *World Population Prospects* at http://esa.un.org/unpp.

force. Put another way, the realistic change[59] from rising total fertility levels in South Korea even by 2050, when estimating potential old age support ratios (i.e., the ratio of the total 15–64 and 65+ age cohorts), is an improvement from 1.47 with constant fertility until 2050 to 1.55 with converging fertility levels until 2050.[60] Thus the realistic gains for South Korea—the OECD country with the most to gain from rising total fertility levels in coming decades—amount to a mere second-decimal improvement in the straight population old age support ratio by 2050.

Put in perspective, this extremely limited potential impact of rising total fertility levels—and only after 2025—should be compared with, for instance, the Standard and Poor's (2006) projections, which estimate that (with unchanged policies) the vast majority of OECD countries will be speculative-grade credits already by 2040. Thus, for the OECD as a whole, the time is long past for policy options to influence the fiscal challenges of aging populations by raising the total fertility rate and policymakers should look to other areas for the necessary policy tools to deal with this issue.[61]

Immigration and Workforce Size

An obvious way to increase the size of a country's labor force is through immigration. Bringing in more and younger workers from outside the country and employing them productively in the domestic economy will have a direct and immediate positive effect on old age support ratios and on fiscal sustainability more broadly. There may be many reasons why it is beneficial for countries to facilitate immigration, but for our purposes it is important to point out the limitations of immigration as a solution to the problem of the long-term outlook for pensions.

While the impact of immigration on the fiscal challenge will likely be positive,[62] it will not generally have more than a small quantitative impact, except in the United States. A simple numerical exercise can illustrate this. How many new immigrants of working age would be required

---

59. "Realistic" here is defined as the trajectory of rising fertility estimated by the UN Population Division, based on historical data. This, of course, does not rule out historically unprecedented rises in South Korean fertility levels, due to possible new and innovative government policies.

60. All other assumptions for mortality, other vital events, and immigration levels are kept similar for the two scenarios. Only fertility levels differ.

61. This, of course, does not rule out that governments may for other good reasons wish to raise their fertility levels.

62. This positive outcome cannot be assured if, for instance, as in many European countries, immigrants exhibit far lower labor force participation and far higher unemployment rates than do native residents.

Figure 2.11 Cumulative number of new work permits/immigrants needed in the G-7 to stabilize old age support ratio at 2005 level, 2005–50

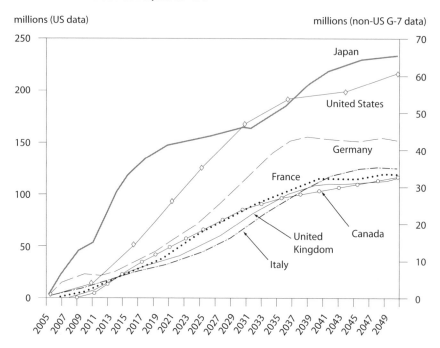

Sources: Eurostat Medium Population Forecast 2004 Base Year; US Census Bureau; Statistics Canada (scenario 2); Japan National Institute of Population and Social Security Research (medium variant); authors' calculations.

in a country to stabilize the old age support ratio at the 2005 level? "Prohibitively many" is the short answer. Figure 2.11 presents the estimates for just how many additional working age immigrants would be required cumulatively in the G-7 nations to stabilize the 15–64/65+ population ratios at 2005 levels until 2050.[63]

---

63. For the sake of the heuristic value of the longer-term results in figure 2.11, the assumption is that additional immigrants do not stay beyond their 64th year and, therefore, do not add to the denominator of the old age support ratio. Without this assumption, estimates quickly lose even their heuristic value. If, for instance, a realistic assumption of age distribution for new arrivals in the age category of 15–64 is adopted, and these arrivals are allowed in the projections to remain into their retirement and hence increase the number of retirees, the required number of new immigrants at working age to maintain the fixed ratio grows to absurd levels. Coleman (2006) provides estimates showing that the British population under such assumptions would grow to more than 300 million by 2050 and that the entire population of the world would need to move to South Korea to stabilize the South Korean old age support ratio at its (admittedly still high) 2000 level.

All the population projection scenarios used for figure 2.11[64] assume a positive level of net international immigration, thus the figure presents only the additional number of working age immigrants required. This is most important in the case of the US data, which—based on recent historical data for both legal and illegal immigration to the United States—assume net immigration rates of almost 1 million annually until 2025 and then rising to 1.1 million by 2050.[65]

Figure 2.11 shows that for the G-7 countries to have the same individual straight population old age support ratios by 2050 as in 2005—i.e., to effectively stop the aging process of G-7 populations—460 million additional immigrants would be needed, with the United States alone accounting for 217 million.[66] Immigration at this level is not going to happen. And it is not just in the long term that immigration is an untenable policy solution to aging populations; the number of new immigrants needed in the G-7 to stabilize the 2005 support ratios by 2010 is a staggering 37 million, most of whom would be needed in Japan.

One might argue that a requirement to stabilize the old age support ratio at present levels is far more than would, ceteris paribus, be required to guarantee the future sustainability of a pension system and thus sets far too high a bar for immigration to have the necessary positive effect. On the other hand, figure 2.11 illustrates "additional immigrants needed" in excess of the G-7 levels of recent years. We believe that any sustained numerical expansion in the total number of immigrants entering the G-7 above that of the early 2000s will prove politically problematic. Thus it is crucial to understand that increased immigration does not provide a policy answer to aging societies, at least in purely quantitative terms, as there may be room for governments to raise the average skill levels of immigrant populations and thus positively affect long-term economic growth and fiscal trends (Hanson 2005, Kirkegaard 2007).

The 2003 report of the Technical Panel on Assumptions and Methods to the Social Security Advisory Board (TPAM 2003) further illustrates the

---

64. US Census Interim Projections, based on 2000 Census; Eurostat Medium Population Projections; Statistics Canada Scenario 2 (www.statcan.ca); and Japan National Institute of Population and Social Security Research Medium Forecast.

65. See assumptions for Interim Projections of the US Population, based on the 2000 Census, at the US Census website, www.census.gov/ipc. The assumptions for net migration levels are different in US Census projections and the projections of the US Social Security Trustees (see below).

66. The United States and Canada are penalized by this type of estimate for not being so far into their aging process in 2005 as, say, Japan; their old age support ratio is, therefore, fixed at a considerably higher level—5.4 and 5.3 in the United States and Canada versus 3.3, 3.4, 3.6, 4.0, and 4.1 for Japan, Italy, Germany, France, and the United Kingdom, respectively. This, in turn, requires far more new immigrants to stabilize the US and Canadian support ratio levels.

relatively minor impact of immigration levels on long-term pension sustainability. The panel very sensibly recommended that the Social Security Trustees fundamentally change their assumptions regarding net migration levels for the long-term projected outlook for the Social Security Trust Fund. Rather than using current immigration law as the foundation for deriving a plausible assumption of a fixed level of future migration, the board recommends using a net migration rate based on US historical experience relative to the size of the US population.

Previously, the Social Security Trustees assumed, based on current US immigration laws, that net immigration levels would decline at a fixed rate from 2003 levels of 1.2 million to 900,000 by 2023 and remain flat thereafter for the remainder of the projection period. Instead, the Technical Panel recommended that the Trustees increase significantly their assumptions of future levels of net international migration so that the intermediate cost scenario includes increasing annual levels of net migration. The annual number of net immigrants would thus increase at half the rate of population growth until the net migration rate declined to its historical average value of 3.2 per 1000, after which, by holding the net migration rate constant, the level of net immigration would grow at the same rate as the total US population.

This is a sound suggested change of migration assumptions that would remove some of the probable downward bias in the migration figures used in the Trustees' current long-term estimates. It raises the assumed intermediate scenario US total population by 24 million by 2050 to 413 million.[67] Although this is a substantial change (about equal to the population of Texas in 2006), it has a very limited impact on the long-term sustainability of US Social Security. The Office of the Chief Actuary at the Social Security Administration estimated that implementing this change would cut the long-term Social Security deficit by just 5.7 percent and defer exhaustion of the Social Security Trust Fund by merely two years, to 2044.[68] Thus this reasonable suggestion to change the formula used to describe the future of the Social Security system would not greatly alter the estimates of the underlying fiscal problem.

Outlook for the Number of Older (65+) People

The fact that developed-country populations are getting older, on average, is a sign of progress and improved welfare but also a source of additional pressure on many public services in the years ahead. Thus the denomina-

---

67. And by 50 million, to 471 million, by 2080.

68. All data are from TPAM (2003).

Figure 2.12   Population aged 65+, selected OECD countries and regions, 2006–50

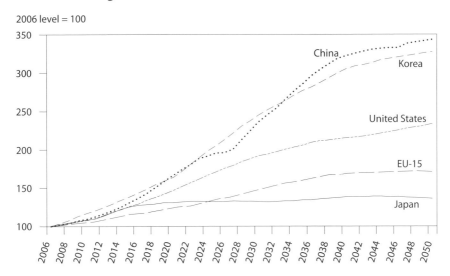

2006 level = 100

Sources: Eurostat 2004 Demographic Database; US Census Bureau; Statistics Canada; Japan National Institute of Population and Social Security Research (2002).

tor of the ratio of working age people to those over 65 is rising. Figure 2.12 shows the data for OECD countries' populations aged 65 and older. The lines show the sizes of the elderly populations as of 2006 (set equal to 100) and illustrate the growth of this population group up to 2050.

Japan is the country with the smallest projected increase in the number of residents 65 or older. This striking projection reflects the fact that the aging of Japan's population is already significantly progressed—the share of the elderly in the Japanese population is already above 20 percent, compared with only 12 percent in the United States and 17 percent in the EU-25. As a result the absolute number of elderly in Japan is projected to be roughly stable after 2020, whereas in the EU-25, elderly population growth will stabilize only in the 2040s. In terms of broader sustainability, this is again only a partial result—even a stable number of retirees may be unsustainable with a rapidly declining number of people to support them—but nonetheless gives an indication of the timing of the demographic pressure on other types of old age–related expenditures, most noticeably health and long-term care. The relatively stable number of old people in Japan after 2020 points to somewhat reduced expenditure pressures in this sector after that—a trend less likely to occur in the United States, which as a result of its generally rising population will continue to see its absolute number of elderly rise throughout the period.[69] On the other hand, even the United States will not experience anything like the increase in the absolute number of elderly that will occur in relatively late aging countries such as China and Korea, which are both projected to experience more than a tripling of their 2006 numbers by 2050.

Toward the end of the projection period, the number of people 65 and older in America will have more than doubled to about 85 million, while the number of elderly in Japan will rise only by about a third to approximately 35 million. The aggregate EU-15, the new member states, and most individual EU members will see growth of about 75 percent in the number of elderly residents by 2050.

In summary, we have illustrated in this section that changes in either fertility levels or immigration laws will not offer much respite against the accelerating aging of populations across the OECD. At the same time, however, we have shown the considerable dissimilarity among nations' projected intensity in the effects of aging; in terms of working age populations—for example, the United States and Canada will continue to experience increases, while European and Asian OECD members will see substantial declines. Simultaneously, Japan, already far into its aging process, will see substantially smaller increases in the absolute number of elderly than will European countries or the United States. Thus the extent and degree of determinism in the fiscal deterioration implied by demographic trends is very different across the OECD. Indeed, as we illustrate in the following section, in some OECD countries, the behavioral impact from differences in effective retirement ages will matter more to the likely overall fiscal impact than the aging process itself.

Understanding the Impact of Looking at Effective Retirement Ages

In the preceding section we showed the differences between the projected scenarios in the OECD for both working age labor forces (15–64 years old) and elderly populations (65 and older). As mentioned, the sizes of these two populations are frequently combined in the old age support ratio to yield an indicator of how many supporting workers a country has per

---

69. However, by far the largest share of future increases in US health care expenditure for the elderly (Medicare) is expected to result not from the rise in the absolute number of retirees but rather from the rapid above-GDP growth rate in increases in expenditures per individual beneficiary. See CBO (2007b). See also Kotlikoff and Hagist (2005) for estimates that show the United States facing the largest challenge in medical expenditure of 10 OECD countries surveyed.

benefit-receiving retiree. Projecting this ratio into the future is a useful tool when trying to highlight the future effects of population aging but does not provide a good basis for cross-country comparisons. The ratio can be misleading—because in some countries not everyone under 65 is working, while in other countries everyone over 65 is necessarily retired—and therefore does not provide a sound basis for policymaking or discussion. Thus population aging is not everything.

In this section we explore what happens when the focus is on when people actually withdraw from productive employment, i.e., on the OECD differences in effective retirement age and how they affect the "real" old age support ratios.

Statutory and Effective Retirement Ages in the OECD

As mentioned earlier, countries' potential workforces are typically defined as the age group between 15 and 64,[70] reflecting the OECD's current median statutory full pension eligibility retirement age of 65. Most countries base their retirement plans and regulations on this age (or something close to it). There are a few exceptions to the rule, such as France, Greece, Japan, Korea, and Turkey, where the standard retirement age is significantly lower. The United States is increasing its statutory retirement age above 65, and Iceland, Ireland, and Norway also already have retirement ages above 65 (see chapter 4).

As noted earlier, however, the *effective* age of retirement in many OECD countries is frequently very different from the *statutory* retirement age. Figure 2.13 shows both the standard retirement age by country and the actual retirement age for men and women from 1999 to 2004.[71] In three countries, Japan, Korea, and Mexico, the effective retirement age is much higher than the official age. In ten countries the effective age is close to the official age. But for about half of the OECD countries the effective retirement age is substantially lower than the official age. For the United States, the gap is small for men, but women retire about 2½ years

---

70. See, for instance, the OECD Labor Market Database (www1.oecd.org/scripts). This is not uniform, however. For instance, the US BLS Current Population Survey—thanks to US child labor laws—defines the labor force as those age 16 or older. These alternative definitions among countries frequently make a significant difference, given the relatively low participation among workers 65 and older. For example, the US labor force participation for the age group 16 and above in 2004 was 66 percent, while for the age group 15–64 it was 70.8 percent, or nearly 5 percentage points higher. Data are from OECD and BLS Current Population Survey (http://data.bls.gov).

71. Effective retirement age is defined as the average age at which a person over age 40 left the labor force in 1999–2004.

Figure 2.13 Effective and official retirement ages in the OECD, 2004

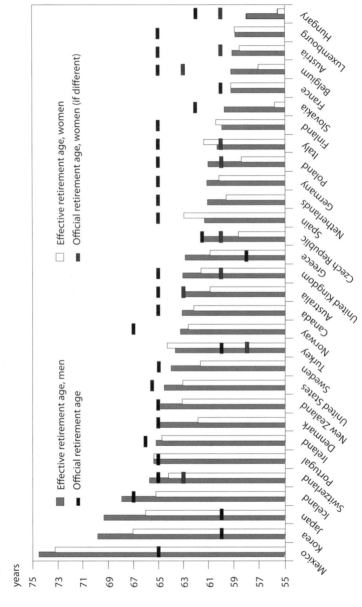

Note: Effective retirement age refers to the average age at which persons 40 and older left the labor force during 1999–2004. Official retirement age refers to the earliest age in 2004 at which workers are entitled to full old age pension irrespective of contributions and work history.

Source: OECD (2006d, figure 2.4).

earlier than the official age of 65–66 (the age for receipt of full Social Security benefits).

The diversity of official and actual retirement ages across countries tells us that comparing simple old age dependency ratios (the population aged 65 and over compared with the working age population aged 15–64) gives a misleading picture. For example, Japan is experiencing a large drop in the working age population over time, but because the Japanese retire roughly a decade later than, say, the French, this allays Japan's demographic problem.

Early retirement has an impact on the fiscal challenge facing countries because most people who leave the labor market after age 55 will be on government-supported programs of one kind or another (disability pensions, sickness payments, or unemployment benefits or similar programs).[72] In many OECD countries there are financial penalties on people that retire earlier than the statutory age for receipt of a full pension,[73] but from the perspective of government treasuries, these early retirees represent a fiscal liability similar to that of a regular full pension retiree above the statutory retirement age.[74]

An important exception applies to the United States with respect to the provision of health care. Because the US government, unlike all the other OECD governments with universal health care systems, does not provide health care benefits for the general population until age 65, combined with the reduced early retirement Social Security benefit (see chapter 3), the direct additional financial liability for the US government from early retirements is likely smaller than in many other OECD countries.

---

72. Large country differences exist, with fully 12 percent of all Swedes in their late 50s not working due to incapacities and a remarkable 43 percent of similarly aged Italian women not working due to family responsibilities (traditional family patterns apparently disappear very slowly). Similarly, several countries—most noticeably France and Germany—have no work-search requirement for older unemployed persons, meaning that from the perspective of the individual, there is probably no difference between being unemployed or retired.

73. These are typically similar to the US Social Security rules stipulating that Americans born before 1937 who retire at 62 rather than 65 suffer a permanent 20 percent reduction in their benefits, a penalty that rises to 30 percent for Americans born after 1967. See the Social Security Administration website, www.ssa.gov. Queisser and Whitehouse (2006) provide an overview of these benefit reductions for early retirement in the OECD.

74. In many countries with contribution-based systems, workers entering the labor market early can retire substantially earlier than age 65 with a full pension and with no financial penalties. This will serve to equate from the perspective of the government the cost levels of retirees above or below age 65. We elaborate in chapter 3 on the distributional challenge and in chapter 4 on the labor market challenge.

Impact of Effective Retirement Age

An increase in a country's effective retirement age has a double effect—it both raises the number of people paying into the pension system and simultaneously lowers the number of people drawing from the pension system. A quick illustration using data for France and Japan shows the dramatic extent of this. (For illustrative purposes, to highlight the differences between the sexes in terms of life expectancies and effective retirement ages, we discuss the impact for men and women separately, although this gender distinction does not make sense in terms of broader pension sustainability.)

The straight population ratio of 15–64/65+ for French men and women in 2006 was 4.9 and 3.4, respectively, while in Japan it was 4.1 for men and 2.9 for women.[75] Thus it may seem that France today is in a somewhat better position than Japan with respect to shouldering its pension burden. However, after adjusting the data to reflect the average effective retirement ages of a little over 59 for French men (59.3) and women (59.2), and of 69.3 for Japanese men and 66 for Japanese women, these results change materially. Now the true effective old age support ratio of roughly 15–59/60+[76] in France declines to 3.3 for men and 2.5 for women, while in Japan the approximately 15–69/70+ ratio for men rises to 6.1 and the 15–66/67+ ratio for women goes up to 3.2. The true effective old age support ratio for Japanese women is now almost equal to the corresponding ratio for French men, while that for Japanese men is roughly twice that for French men. Japan looks better able to support its elderly population than does France by this more economically relevant measure.[77]

To further illustrate the relative impact on sustainability ratios both from aging itself (i.e., what is expected to happen because of aging from now until 2050) and from current differences in effective retirement ages (i.e., how far the effective retirement age is from age 65), we now combine the two measures.

Figures 2.14a and 2.14b show, first, the standard old age support ratio (circles) in 2004 based on the 15- to 64-year-old population (numerator) and the 65+ population (denominator) and, second, the projection of this ratio in

---

75. The longer life expectancy of women depresses their old age support ratio.

76. Individual years are split proportionally between the groups, so that for the effective retirement age of 59.3, 30 percent of the French men aged 59 go into the ranks of workers and 70 percent are deemed retirees. A similar methodology is used for Japanese data.

77. With average US retirement ages for men of 64.6 and 63 for women, this corresponding adjustment does not yield nearly the same magnitude of difference between the old age population ratio and the effective ratio in the United States.

Figure 2.14a Standard old age support ratios, 2004 and 2050, and effective old age support ratio, 2004, men

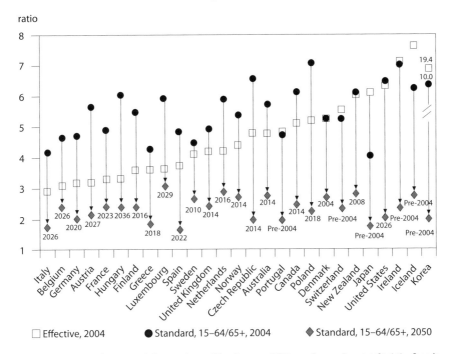

Sources: Organization for Economic Cooperation and Development; US Census Bureau; Eurostat; Statistics Canada (2005–51); authors' calculations.

2050 (diamonds). It then ranks countries by the effective old age support ratio in 2004 (squares).[78] In light of the large differences in effective retirement ages between the sexes, each is shown separately for illustrative purposes (figure 2.14a for men and figure 2.14b for women).[79] Finally, to show the relative importance of aging itself and of current low effective retirement ages, we indicate the year that each country, based on projected pure

78. The effective support ratio is calculated using the most detailed age group data available. Intra-interval values are estimated assuming uniform distribution within each interval, i.e., an effective retirement age of 62.5 means that the number of people aged 62 are split 50-50 between the numerator and the denominator. A similar procedure is used for the few countries for which only five-year age cohort data are available.

79. The straight population old age support ratio for women is lower than for men, especially in 2004, because of women's higher life expectancy. As life expectancy for men is expected to rise more than for women in coming decades, the difference between men and women is projected to be smaller in 2050 than it was in 2004.

Figure 2.14b   Standard old age support ratios, 2004 and 2050, and effective old age support ratio, 2004, women

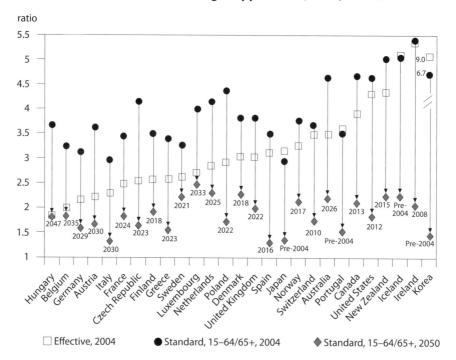

Sources: Organization for Economic Cooperation and Development; US Census Bureau; Eurostat; Statistics Canada (2005–51); authors' calculations.

demographic trends[80] from the 2004 starting point[81] of straight population ratios, should reach the same ratio as, in true effective terms, its current ratio.

The figure shows that a number of core continental European countries, such as France, Germany, and Italy, have effective ratios much lower than the pure population ratios. Indeed, they are in some cases already close to the level projected for their population ratios in 2050. They are

---

80. These trends differ substantially in terms of the speed, precise timing, and magnitude for the countries in question. Each country is estimated according to its own nonlinear (typically accelerating toward the end of the period) trajectory, and thus the relative graphic distances in figures 2.14a and 2.14b between the circles, squares, and diamonds are not representative of how far into the future the effective ratio is.

81. All 2004 population data used in this book are from actual census estimates of present-day country populations, rather than earlier population estimates including 2004 data or population estimates for longer periods. As individual countries' regular censuses frequently reveal unsuspected developments in population sizes and characteristics, this is an important distinction if one wishes to achieve a maximum of reliability and validity in the data used for analysis.

therefore—in real terms—already decades further into their aging process because of their current exceptionally low effective retirement ages. This issue is most pronounced for countries with very low retirement ages for women, such as Hungary and Belgium.

However, this process works in the other direction, too. Several countries frequently labeled demographic basket cases (most noticeably Japan) are in real terms not nearly as progressed in their aging process, thanks to their very high effective retirement ages, as their pure population old age support ratios would suggest.

Adjusting the support ratio does not make much of a difference for the position and outlook for the United States itself, which has an effective retirement age close to 65. However, as most of the other OECD countries look significantly worse in true effective terms, the relative US position on this important statistic is improved.

Accounting properly for effective retirement ages has a dramatic impact on the relative severity of the demographic challenge. In many respects, because raising the effective retirement age works on both sides of the equation (boosting the denominator while lowering the numerator), several European countries (such as France and Italy) face as much a current employment challenge—simply getting more people to remain in the labor market longer—as they do a future demographic challenge. Their demographic future has already arrived.

In contrast, countries with better current employment records for older workers, such as the United States and Japan, are at a substantial advantage and reap a clear advantage from their job-generating labor markets. Meeting the challenge of an aging population is much easier for countries with later effective retirement ages, so many countries should look to policies that reduce disincentives for employment (see chapter 4).

Synthesis of Fiscal and Demographic Challenges

This chapter has attempted to shed light on the most decisive aspects of the fiscal and demographic challenge facing (most) developed countries today. It has done so by looking at (1) starting points in terms of government finances and prefunded pension assets, (2) tax treatment of pension benefits, (3) actual net costs to governments of current pension provision, (4) the generosity of average individual pension promises, (5) the demographic outlook for the labor force, (6) the demographic outlook for the number of elderly, and (7) effective retirement ages across the OECD, which in many places alter the aging outlook substantially.

Table 2.2 amalgamates the information in this chapter for the main OECD countries analyzed and points out the most significant fiscal and

Table 2.2 Synthesis of selected OECD countries' fiscal and demographic challenges

Country	Fiscal starting point			Cost of pension provision		Labor-market effect: Effective retirement age	Demographic outlook			Overall impact level/most threatening aspects
	Net debt levels	Structural position	Overall	True costs of current public pension provision	Generosity of individual pension promise		Labor force	Elderly	Overall demographic outlook	
Australia	None	Surplus	Strong	Moderate	Moderate/low	Low	Rising	Rapid rise	Moderate pressure	Moderate impact/low retirement age
Austria	Moderate	Limited	Limited	High	High	Extremely low	Decline	Moderate rise	Moderate pressure	High impact/high pensions and low retirement age
Belgium	Severe	Surplus	Moderate	Moderate/high	Moderate	Extremely low	Stable	Moderate rise	Moderate pressure	High impact/poor fiscal starting point and low retirement age
Canada	Limited	Surplus	Strong	Low	Low/moderate	Low	Rising	Rapid rise	Moderate pressure	Moderate impact/low retirement age
Czech Republic	None	Severe	Moderate	Moderate	Moderate	Low	Severe decline	Moderate rise	High pressure	High impact/low retirement age and demographic outlook
Denmark	None	Surplus	Strong	Low	Moderate	Average	Stable	Moderate rise	Moderate pressure	Moderate impact/demographic outlook
Finland	None	Surplus	Strong	Moderate	High	Extremely low	Decline	Moderate rise	High pressure	High impact/low retirement age and demographic outlook

Country										
France	Moderate	Moderate	Moderate	High/moderate	Moderate	Extremely low	Stable	Moderate rise	Moderate pressure	High impact/low retirement age and cost of pensions
Germany	Moderate	Moderate	Moderate	High	Moderate	Low/extremely low	Severe decline	Moderate rise	High pressure	High impact/low retirement age and demographic outlook
Greece	Severe	Severe	Severe	n.a.	High	Low	Severe decline	Moderate rise	High pressure	Very high impact/low retirement age and demographic outlook
Hungary	Moderate	Severe	Severe	n.a.	High	Extremely low	Severe decline	Moderate rise	High pressure	Very high impact/low retirement age and demographic outlook
Iceland	None	Surplus	Strong	Moderate	Moderate	High	Stable	Moderate rise	Moderate pressure	Moderate impact/demographic outlook
Ireland	None	Surplus	Strong	Low/moderate	Low	Average	Rising	Rapid rise	Moderate pressure	Moderate impact/demographic outlook
Italy	Severe	Moderate	Severe	High	High/moderate	Extremely low	Severe decline	Moderate rise	High pressure	Very high impact/low retirement age and cost of pensions
Japan	Severe	Severe	Severe	High	Low	High	Severe decline	Limited rise	Moderate pressure	High impact/fiscal starting point
Korea	n.a.	n.a.	n.a.	Low	Low	High	Severe decline	Rapid rise	High pressure	High impact/demographic outlook

(table continues next page)

Table 2.2 Synthesis of selected OECD countries' fiscal and demographic challenges (*continued*)

| Country | Fiscal starting point | | | Cost of pension provision | | Labor-market effect: Effective retirement age | Demographic outlook | | | Overall impact level/most threatening aspects |
	Net debt levels	Structural position	Overall	True costs of current public pension provision	Generosity of individual pension promise		Labor force	Elderly	Overall demographic outlook	
Luxembourg	n.a.	n.a.	n.a.	n.a.	High/extreme	Extremely low	Rising	Moderate rise	Moderate pressure	Moderate impact/low retirement age
Netherlands	Moderate	Limited	Limited	Low/moderate	High	Low	Stable	Moderate rise	Moderate pressure	Moderate impact/low retirement age
New Zealand	None	Surplus	Strong	Low	Low	Average	Rising	Rapid rise	Moderate pressure	Moderate impact/demographic outlook
Norway	None	Surplus	Strong	Low	Moderate	Low/average	Stable	Moderate rise	Moderate pressure	Moderate impact/demographic outlook
Poland	n.a.	n.a.	n.a.	n.a.	Moderate	Extremely low/low	Severe decline	Moderate rise	High pressure	Very high impact/low retirement age and demographic outlook
Portugal	Moderate	Severe	Severe	n.a.	Moderate/high	Average	Severe decline	Moderate rise	High pressure	Very high impact/fiscal starting point and demographic outlook

Slovakia	n.a.	n.a.	n.a.	Moderate	Moderate	Extremely low	Severe decline	Rapid rise	High pressure	Very high impact/low retirement age and demographic outlook
Spain	Moderate	Limited	Limited	Moderate	High	Low	Severe decline	Rapid rise	High pressure	Very high impact/low retirement age and demographic outlook
Sweden	None	Surplus	Strong	Moderate	High	Average	Stable	Moderate rise	Moderate pressure	Moderate impact/demographic outlook
Switzerland	Limited	Surplus	Strong	n.a.	Moderate	Average/high	Stable	Moderate rise	Moderate pressure	Moderate impact/demographic outlook
Britain	Moderate	Moderate	Moderate	Moderate	Low	Low	Stable	Moderate rise	Moderate pressure	Moderate impact/low retirement age
United States	Moderate	Moderate	Moderate	Moderate	Low	Average	Rising fast	Rapid rise	Moderate pressure	Moderate impact/demographic outlook

n.a. = not available

Source: Authors' estimates, based on various sources.

demographic challenges to individual countries. Several main points are clear from table 2.2:

- The overall situation among OECD countries varies considerably, with the most severe impact focused on a minority of countries. In close to half (13) of the 28 OECD countries shown, the relative future impact of aging populations on pension systems is in the least severe "moderate impact" category, while eight countries face "high impact" and seven countries "very high impact" (Greece, Hungary, Italy, Poland, Portugal, Slovakia, and Spain).

- The United States—with only a moderately poor fiscal starting point, moderate current costs of pension provision, low levels of future pension promises, average retirement age, and only moderate demographic pressure (both a growing labor force and rising numbers of elderly)—is in the category of OECD countries that can expect to be only moderately affected. This is an important point when trying to filter the occasionally overly gloomy commentary regarding the outlook for the US economy and its future ability to provide for its retiring baby-boomers.[82] Most OECD countries face more immediate and severe future challenges to the sustainability of their pension systems than does the United States.[83] Awareness of these challenges has in recent years already led to a number of pension reforms in OECD countries (see chapter 4).

- In some countries, notably in Eastern Europe and the Mediterranean, pension liabilities pose the most severe threat, due to the combination of generous pension promises, low retirement age, and very adverse demographics.

- The eight countries facing the most severe impact of population aging do so more as a result of their extremely low effective retirement ages than their demographic outlook.

- The English-speaking countries (Australia, Canada, Ireland, New Zealand, the United Kingdom, and the United States), the Scandinavian countries (Denmark, Iceland, Norway, Sweden, and, less so, Finland), and the Netherlands generally face only a moderate impact on pension systems from future population aging.

---

82. This overall ability to potentially provide for the elderly may not prevent distributional problems from arising.

83. This is not the case in other policy areas affected by population aging, especially health care costs, where the United States probably faces the biggest cost challenge of any OECD country.

- The core continental economies (Austria, Belgium, the Czech Republic, France, and Germany) face a high impact of population aging on pension systems, and a very high impact is likely in Eastern and Southern Europe (Greece, Hungary, Italy, Poland, Portugal, Slovakia, and Spain).

- The very high effective retirement age in both Korea and Japan partly makes up for (in Japan) a very poor fiscal starting point and (in Korea) a poor demographic outlook. Northeast Asian OECD countries can expect significant future stress on their pension systems in the future, but not nearly as much as would be the case with a lower age of retirement.

References

Adema, Willem, and Maxine Ladaique. 2005. *Net Social Expenditure, 2005 Edition—More Comprehensive Measures of Social Support*. OECD Social, Employment and Migration Working Paper, no. 29. Paris: Organization for Economic Cooperation and Development.

Adsera, A. 2004. Changing Fertility Rates in Developed Markets. The Impact of Labor Market Institutions. *Journal of Population Economics* 17: 17–43.

Apgar, William D., and Zhu Xiao Di. 2005. *Housing Wealth and Retirement Savings: Enhancing Financial Security for Older Americans*. Harvard University Joint Center for Housing Studies, Working Paper 05-8. Available at www.jchs.harvard.edu.

Baily, Martin N., and Jacob F. Kirkegaard. 2004. *Transforming the European Economy*. Washington: Institute for International Economics.

Blau, D. M., and P. K. Robins. 1988. Child Care Costs and Family Labor Supply. *Review of Economics and Statistics* 70: 374–81.

Blau, D. M., and P. K. Robins. 1989. Fertility, Employment, and Child-Care Costs. *Demography* 26, no. 2: 287–99.

Boards of Trustees of the Federal Hospital Insurance and Federal Supplementary Medical Insurance Trust Funds. 2008. *2008 Annual Report of the Board of Trustees of the Federal Hospital Insurance and Federal Supplementary Medical Insurance Trust Funds*. Washington.

Carone, G., D. Costello, N. Diez Guardia, G. Mourre, B. Przywara, and A. Salomäki. 2005. *The Economic Impact of Ageing Populations in the EU-25 Member States*. European Commission Economic Paper no. 236. Brussels: European Commission.

Cigno, A. 1994. A Cost Function for Children: Theory and Some Evidence. In *Standards of Living and Families: Observation and Analysis*, ed. O. Ekert-Jaffe. Paris: John Libbey Eurotext.

Coleman, David. 2006. The Future of European Populations—Diversity and Divergence? Paper presented at Eurostat-UNECE Work Session on Demographic Projections, Oxford Centre for Population Research, Vienna, September 21.

College Board. 2006. *Trends in College Pricing 2005*. Available online at www.collegeboard.com.

CBO (Congressional Budget Office). 2007a. *The Budget and Economic Outlook: Fiscal Years from 2008–2017*. Washington. Available at www.cbo.gov.

CBO (Congressional Budget Office). 2007b. *The Long-Term Budget Outlook, December 2007*. Washington. Available at www.cbo.gov.

D'Addio, Anna Christina, and Marco Mira d'Ercole. 2005. *Trends and Determinants of Fertility Rates in the OECD Countries: The Role of Policies*. OECD Social, Employment and Migration Working Papers 27. Paris: Organization for Economic Cooperation and Development.

Del Boca, D., M. Locatelli, S. Pasqua, and C. Pronzato. 2003. *Analysing Women's Employment and Fertility Rates in Europe: Differences and Similarities in Northern and Southern Europe*. Turin: WP Child.

Disney, R. F., and E. R. Whitehouse. 2001. *Cross-Country Comparisons of Pensioners Incomes.* Research Report no. 142. London: Department of Work and Pensions.

EPC (Economic Policy Committee) and European Commission. 2005. *The 2005 EPC Projections of Age-Related Expenditure (2004–2050) for the EU-25 Member States.* Underlying Assumptions and Projection Methodologies in European Economic Reports and Studies, no. 4. Brussels.

Engen, Eric M., William G. Gale, and John Karl Scholz. 1994. Do Saving Incentives Work? *Brookings Papers on Economic Activity* 1: 85–151. Washington: Brookings Institution.

Ermisch, J. 1988a. Econometric Analysis of Birth Rate Dynamics in Britain. *Journal of Human Resources* 23: 563–76.

Ermisch, J. 1988b. Economic Influences on Birth Rate. *National Institute Economics Review* (November): 71–81.

Ermisch, J. 1989. Purchased Child Care, Optimal Family Size and Mother's Employment: Theory and Econometric Analysis. *Journal of Population Economics* 2: 79–102.

European Commission. 2006. *The Impact of Ageing on Public Expenditure: Projections for the EU25 Member States on Pensions, Health Care, Long-term Care, Education and Unemployment Transfers (2004–2050).* Brussels.

Eurostat. 2006. Structures of the Taxation Systems of the European Union Data 1995–2004. Luxembourg: European Commission.

Gauthier, A. H., and J. Hatzius. 1997. Family Benefits and Fertility: An Econometric Analysis. *Population Studies* 51: 13–37.

Gillion, C. 2000. The Development and Reform of Social Security Pensions: The Approach of the International Labour Office. *International Social Security Review* 53, part 1: 35–64. International Social Security Association, Geneva.

Girouard, N., and C. André. 2005. *Measuring Cyclically-Adjusted Budget Balances for OECD Countries.* OECD Economics Department Working Paper 434. Paris: Organization for Economic Cooperation and Development.

Hanson, Gordon H. 2005. *Why Does Immigration Divide America? Public Finance and Political Opposition to Open Borders.* Washington: Peterson Institute for International Economics.

Hubbard, Glenn R., and Jonathan S. Skinner. 1996. Assessing the Effectiveness of Savings Incentives. *Journal of Economic Perspectives* 10, no. 4: 73–90.

Immervoll, H., and D. Barber. 2005. *Can Parents Afford to Work? Childcare Costs, Benefits and Work Incentives.* OECD Social, Employment and Migration Working Paper 31. Paris: Organization for Economic Cooperation and Development.

IWPR (Institute for Women's Policy Research). 2007. *The Economic Security of Older Women and Men.* Available at www.iwpr.org.

Ito, Takatoshi. 2007. The Fiscal Consolidation Policies in Japan During the Koizumi Government. Presentation at the Peterson Institute for International Economics, March 2007.

Japan National Institute of Population and Social Security Research. 2002. *Population Projections for Japan 2001–2050.* Tokyo.

Keenay, G., and E. R. Whitehouse. 2003. *Financial Resources and Retirement in Nine OECD Countries: The Role of the Tax System.* OECD Social, Employment and Migration Working Paper no. 8. Paris: Organization for Economic Cooperation and Development.

Kirkegaard, J. F. 2007. *The Accelerating Decline in America's High-Skilled Workforce: Implications for Immigration Policy.* Policy Analyses in International Economics 84. Washington: Peterson Institute for International Economics.

Kotlikoff, L., and C. Hagist. 2005. *Who's Going Broke? Comparing Growth in Health-care Costs in Ten OECD Countries.* NBER Working Paper 11833. Cambridge, MA: National Bureau of Economic Research.

Kravdal, Ø. 2002. The Impact of Individual and Aggregate Unemployment on Fertility in Norway. *Demographic Research* 6/10.

Laroque, G., and B. Salanié. 2004. *Fertility and Financial Incentives in France.* CEPR Discussion Paper DP4064. London: Center for Economic Policy Research.

Nataraj, S., and J. B. Shoven, 2003. *Has the Unified Budget Undermined the Federal Government Trust Funds?* NBER Working Paper 10953. Cambridge, MA: National Bureau of Economic Research.

Ní Bhrolcháin, M., and L. Toulemon. 2002. *The Trend of Later Childbearing: Is There Evidence of Postponements?* SSRC Application and Policy Working Paper A03/10. New York: Social Science Research Council.

OECD (Organization for Economic Cooperation and Development), ILO (International Labor Organization), IMF (International Monetary Fund), and Statcommittee of the CIS (CIS STAT). 2002. *Measuring the Non-Observed Economy: A Handbook.* Paris: Organization for Economic Cooperation and Development.

OECD (Organization for Economic Cooperation and Development). 1996. *Social Expenditure Statistics of OECD Member Countries* (provisional version). Labor Market and Social Policy Occasional Papers, no. 17. Paris.

OECD (Organization for Economic Cooperation and Development). 2002. *Public Management Committee: Highlights of Public Sector Pay and Employment Trends*, 2002 Update. Paris.

OECD (Organization for Economic Cooperation and Development). 2003. *Taxing Wages 2003.* Paris.

OECD (Organization for Economic Cooperation and Development). 2004. *Taxing Wages 2004.* Paris.

OECD (Organization for Economic Cooperation and Development). 2005a. *Pensions at a Glance—Public Policies Across OECD Countries.* Paris.

OECD (Organization for Economic Cooperation and Development). 2005b. *OECD Tax Revenue Statistics 2005.* Paris.

OECD (Organization for Economic Cooperation and Development). 2005c. *Taxing Wages 2005.* Paris.

OECD (Organization for Economic Cooperation and Development). 2006a. *Pensions Markets in Focus* no. 3 (October). Paris.

OECD (Organization for Economic Cooperation and Development). 2006b. *Education at a Glance 2006.* Paris.

OECD (Organization for Economic Cooperation and Development). 2006c. *Taxing Wages 2006.* Paris.

OECD (Organization for Economic Cooperation and Development). 2006d. *Live Longer, Work Longer.* Paris.

OECD (Organization for Economic Cooperation and Development). 2007a. *Pensions at a Glance—Public Policies Across OECD Countries 2007.* Paris.

OECD (Organization for Economic Cooperation and Development). 2007b. *OECD Economic Outlook December 2007*, statistical annex. Paris.

OECD (Organization for Economic Cooperation and Development). 2007c. *The Revision of the 1993 System of National Accounts—What Does it Change?* OECD Statistical Brief no. 13. Paris.

OECD (Organization for Economic Cooperation and Development). 2007d. *Pensions Markets in Focus* 4 (November). Paris.

OECD (Organization for Economic Cooperation and Development). 2007e. *The Social Expenditure Database: An Interpretive Guide*, June version. Paris.

OMB (Office of Management and Budget). 1985. *Special Analyses, Budget of the United States Government, Fiscal Year 1985: Special Analysis G: Tax Expenditures.* Washington: Executive Office of the President.

OMB (Office of Management and Budget). 2007. *President's Budget 2008—Analytical Perspectives.* Washington: Executive Office of the President. Available at www.whitehouse.gov/omb/budget.

Queisser, M., and E. R. Whitehouse. 2006. *Neutral or Fair? Actuarial Concepts and Pension-System Design.* Social, Employment and Migration Working Paper no. 40. Paris: Organization for Economic Cooperation and Development.

Schneider, F. 2002. *The Size and Development of the Shadow Economies and Shadow Economy Labor Forces in 21 Countries: What Do We Really Know?* IZA Discussion Paper 514. Bonn: Institute for the Study of Labor.

SSA (Social Security Administration). 1994. *1994 Annual Report of the Board of Trustees of the Federal Old-Age and Survivors Insurance and Disability Insurance Trust Funds.* Washington.

SSA (Social Security Administration). 2008. *2008 Annual Report of the Board of Trustees of the Federal Old-Age and Survivors Insurance and Disability Insurance Trust Funds.* Washington.

Standard and Poor's. 2006. *Global Graying: Ageing Societies and Sovereign Ratings.* London.

TPAM (Technical Panel on Assumptions and Methods). 2003. *Report to the Social Security Advisory Board.* Washington.

Toulemon, L., and M. Mazuy. 2001. Les naissances sont retardées mais la fécondité est stable. *Population* 56, no. 4: 1–11.

UN Population Division. 1996. *Women's Education and Fertility Behavior: Recent Evidence from the Demographic and Health Surveys.* New York.

UN Population Division. 2004. *The 2004 Revision of World Population Prospects.* New York: Department of Economic and Social Affairs of the United Nations Secretariat.

van den Noord, Paul, and Vincent Koen. 2005. *Fiscal Gimmickry in Europe: One-off Measures and Creative Accounting.* OECD Economics Department Working Paper 417. Paris: Organization for Economic Cooperation and Development.

Walker, Alan. 2004. Evaluating the National Pension for Salary Earners and the Self-Employed. In *Modernizing the Korean Welfare State*, ed. R. Mishra, S. Kuhnle, N. Gilbert, and K. Chung. Seoul: Transactions Publishers.

Whitehouse, E. R. 2000. Administrative Charges for Funded Pensions: Measurement Concepts, International Comparison and Assessment. *Journal of Applied Social Science Studies* 120, no. 3: 311–61.

Whitehouse, E. R. 2001. Administrative Charges for Funded Pensions: Comparison and Assessment of 13 Countries. *Private Pension Systems: Administrative Costs and Reforms, Private Pensions Series* 3. Paris: Organization for Economic Cooperation and Development.

Whittington, L. A. 1992. Taxes and the Family: The Impact of the Tax Exemption for Dependents on Marital Fertility. *Demography* 29, no. 2: 215–26.

World Bank. 1994. *Averting the Old Age Crisis: Policies to Protect the Old and Promote Growth.* Washington: World Bank Press. Available at www-wds.worldbank.org.

Zhang, J., J. Quan, and P. Van Meerbergen. 1994. The Effect of Tax-Transfer Policies on Fertility in Canada, 1921–1988. *Journal of Human Resources* 29: 181–201.

Appendix 2A
Pension Data in Detail

This appendix lays out the details and numerous statistical caveats of the pension-related data presented in this chapter. We describe two data items: public pension expenditure (what is included in different country totals) and pension assets, public and private.

Public Pension Expenditure

The public expenditure data are from the OECD Social Expenditure (SOCX) database (available at www.oecd.org). As explained in the chapter, the public pension expenditure is the sum of expenditures for old age and survivor pensions, which the SOCX defines as follows.

Old Age Expenditure

Old age expenditures comprise all cash expenditures (including lump-sum payments) on old age pensions in the public sphere. Old age cash benefits provide an income for persons retired from the labor market or guarantee incomes when a person has reached a "standard" pensionable age or fulfilled the necessary contributory requirements. This category also includes early retirement pensions, paid before the beneficiary has reached the standard pensionable age relevant to the program. Excluded are programs concerning early retirement for labor market reasons, which are classified under unemployment. The SOCX database includes supplements for dependents paid to old age pensioners with dependents under old age cash benefits. Old age expenditures also include social expenditure on services for the elderly people—day care and rehabilitation services, home help services, and other benefits in kind. It also includes expenditure on the provision of residential care in an institution (e.g., the cost of operating homes for the elderly).

Survivor Pension Expenditure

Many countries have public-sector social expenditure programs that provide the spouse or dependent of a deceased person with a benefit (either in cash or in kind). Expenditure in this policy area has been grouped under survivors and includes allowances and supplements for dependent children of the recipient of a survivors' benefit.

Pension Asset Data

The data for pension assets in OECD and non-OECD countries presented in this chapter are primarily from the OECD Global Pension Statistics (available at www.oecd.org) unless otherwise explicitly noted below. The classification system used is that of the OECD Private Pension: OECD Classification and Glossary (available at the OECD website).

There are four types of financing vehicles for pension assets in the OECD classification:

- **Pension Funds (Autonomous).** The pool of assets forming an independent legal entity that are bought with the contributions to a pension plan for the exclusive purpose of financing pension plan benefits. The plan/fund members have a legal or beneficial right or some other contractual claim against the assets of the pension fund. Pension funds take the form of either a special-purpose entity with a legal personality (such as a trust, foundation, or corporate entity) or a legally separated fund without legal personality managed by a dedicated provider (pension fund management company) or other financial institution on behalf of the plan/fund members.

- **Book Reserves (Nonautonomous).** Book reserves are sums entered in the balance sheet of the plan sponsor as reserves or provisions for pension benefits. Some assets may be held in separate accounts for the purpose of financing benefits but are not legally or contractually pension plan assets.

- **Pension Insurance Contracts.** These contracts specify pension plan contributions to an insurance undertaking in exchange for which the pension plan benefits will be paid when the members reach a specified retirement age or on earlier exit of members from the plan.

- **Other.** Other types of financing vehicles not included in the above categories.

Five pension plan types are defined in the OECD Glossary:

- **Occupational Pension Plans.** Access to such plans is linked to an employment or professional relationship between the plan member and the entity that establishes the plan (the plan sponsor). Occupational plans may be established by employers or groups thereof (e.g., industry associations) and labor or professional associations, jointly or separately. The plan may be administered directly by the plan sponsor or by an independent entity (a pension fund or a financial institution acting as pension provider); in the latter case, the plan sponsor may still have oversight responsibilities over the operation of the plan.

- **Personal Pension Plans.** Access to these plans does not require an employment relationship. A pension fund or financial institution acting as pension provider establishes and administers the plan without any employer intervention. Individuals independently purchase and select material aspects of the arrangement. An employer may nonetheless make contributions to personal pension plans. Some personal plans may have restricted membership.

- **Defined Benefit (DB).** This term applies to occupational plans other than defined contribution plans. DB plans generally can be classified as one of three main types: traditional, mixed, and hybrid.

  - A traditional DB plan uses a formula to link benefits to the member's wages or salary, length of employment, or other factors.

  - In a hybrid DB plan, benefits depend on a rate of return credited to contributions, where this rate of return is either specified in the plan rules independent of the actual return on any supporting assets (e.g., fixed, indexed to a market benchmark, tied to salary or profit growth) or is calculated with reference to the actual return of any supporting assets and a minimum return guarantee specified in the plan rules.

  - A mixed DB plan has two separate DB and defined contribution components that are treated as part of the same plan.

- **Defined Contribution (Protected).** This category includes personal or occupational defined contribution pension plans other than unprotected pension plans. Guarantees or promises (e.g., deferred annuity, guaranteed rate of return) may be offered by the pension plan/fund itself or the plan provider.

- **Defined Contribution (Unprotected), Total.** This plan type covers personal or occupational defined contribution pension plans where the plan/fund itself or the pension provider does not offer any investment return or benefit guarantees or promises for the whole plan/fund.

There are numerous gaps in the international collection of data on the present magnitude of "hard assets" available for future pension provision in individual countries. Presently, this is subject of the OECD Task Force on Pension Statistics, a cooperative effort between the OECD, several national supervisory authorities, and a number of private-sector actors (for further information on the work of the task force, see the OECD website, www.oecd.org). We attempted in figure 2.2 to illustrate government-sector total prefunded assets toward pension provision (TPATPP) to get a fuller picture of each country's starting point; the detailed asset composition of what was included in the figure's representation of TPATPP is presented in table 2A.1. A special notice concerns Finland, which accord-

Table 2A.1 Breakdown of total prefunded assets toward pension provision in 2006 (millions of current US dollars)

Country	Pension funds (autonomous)	Book reserves (nonautonomous)	Pension insurance contracts	Other	Total all private funds	SPPRF name	SPPRF assets	Total prefunded assets toward pension provision	Total prefunded assets toward pension provision (percent of GDP)	GDP, 2006
Australia	687,265	n.a.	—	—	687,265	Future Fund	13,678	700,943	93	755,659
Austria	15,611	12,217	—	n.a.	27,828	n.a.		27,828	9	323,828
Belgium	16,769	n.a.	42,604	—	59,373	n.a.		59,373	15	394,507
Canada	678,952	143,982	59,027	424,162	1,306,124	Canadian Pension Fund	86,392	1,392,516	109	1,275,283
Czech Republic	6,462	n.a.	n.a.	n.a.	6,462	n.a.		6,462	5	142,517
Denmark	89,570	n.a.	237,715	57,618	384,902	Social Security Fund	659	385,561	139	276,400
Finland	149,497	—	13,588	n.a.	163,085	State Pension Fund	12,929	176,014	84	209,771
France	25,094	—	129,109	1,004	155,207	Fondo de Reserve des Retraites	39,140	194,347	9	2,252,213
Germany	122,764	329,186	59,971	—	511,921	n.a.		511,921	18	2,915,867
Greece	23	n.a.	—	n.a.	23	n.a.		23	0	308,720
Hungary	10,978	n.a.	n.a.	—	10,978	n.a.		10,978	10	112,899
Iceland	21,672	n.a.	—	797	22,469	n.a.		22,469	138	16,307
Ireland	110,093	n.a.	—	—	110,093	National Pension Reserve Fund	23,710	133,803	61	219,368
Italy	55,681	—	6,013	n.a.	61,693	n.a.		61,693	3	1,852,585
Japan	1,020,807	n.a.	n.a.	n.a.	1,020,807	National Reserve Funds	1,217,551	2,238,358	51	4,366,459

Country					Fund				
Korea	25,829	n.a.	30,622	11,771	68,222	National Pension Fund	190,842	259,064	29	888,267
Luxembourg	—	—	—	—	—	n.a.	—	—		41,505
Mexico	96,470	—	n.a.	1,243	97,714	IMSS Reserve	7,392	105,106	13	840,012
Netherlands	860,877	n.a.	53,154	n.a.	914,031	n.a.		914,031	136	670,929
New Zealand	13,120	n.a.	n.a.	—	13,120	n.a.		13,120	13	104,607
Norway	22,874	n.a.	—	n.a.	22,874	Government Pension Fund Global	278,124	300,998	90	335,856
Poland	37,964	n.a.	260	—	38,224	Demographic Reserve Fund	1,760	39,984	12	340,969
Portugal	26,581	n.a.	—	3,604	30,185	Social Security Financial Stabilization Fund	8,330	38,515	20	194,790
Slovakia	1,537	n.a.	n.a.	n.a.	1,537	n.a.		1,537	3	55,103
Spain	92,527	20,088	14,465	28,275	155,355	Fondo de Reserva de la Seguridad Social	44,875	200,230	16	1,231,733
Sweden	36,397	7,165	166,462	8,028	218,052	National Pension Funds (AP1-AP4 and AP6)	117,468	335,520	87	384,388
Switzerland	462,095	n.a.	—	—	462,095	n.a.		462,095	119	387,987
Turkey	3,965	n.a.	n.a.	n.a.	3,965	n.a.		3,965	1	401,763
United Kingdom	1,831,290	n.a.	285,906	n.a.	2,117,197	n.a.		2,117,197	88	2,398,946
United States	9,721,120	n.a.	2,356,445	3,808,000	15,885,565	Social Security Trust Funds	2,048,112	17,933,677	136	13,194,700
OECD total	16,243,885	512,637	3,455,341	4,344,502	24,556,367		4,090,962	28,647,329	78	36,893,938

n.a. = not applicable. This has been determined thanks to the metadata describing the countries' pension system.

— = not available.

SPPRF = sovereign and public pension reserve funds

Sources: OECD Global Pension Statistics; OECD *Economic Outlook*, December 2007; International Monetary Fund; authors' calculations.

ing to table 2A.1 should have approximately 84 percent of GDP in TPATPP. However, according to OECD (2006e, box 2.1), 47 percent of GDP in TPATPP is included in Finland's net government financial position, and so figure 2.2 shows that the country has only 36 percent of GDP in genuine TPATPP.

Appendix 2B
Methodological Assumptions for OECD
Pension Modeling

Figure 2.7 presents the data provided in OECD (2005a, 2007a) from the OECD pension models. While we cannot in this appendix in any way do justice to those extensive efforts, we reproduce here the principal assumptions for these estimates as set forth in the OECD *Pensions at a Glance* publications (OECD 2007a, 12–14).

Legislation: Current Law of 2004

The future pension entitlements that are compared are estimated using the legislation that is currently in place in OECD countries. Changes in rules that have already been legislated but are being phased in gradually are assumed to be fully in place from the start. Reforms that have been legislated since 2004 are included where sufficient information is available.

Coverage: All Mandatory Pensions for Private-Sector Workers

The pension models presented include all *mandatory* pension schemes for private-sector workers, regardless of whether they are public (i.e., they involve payments from government or from social security institutions, as defined in the System of National Accounts) or private. For each country, it is only the main national scheme for private-sector employees is modeled. Schemes for civil servants, public-sector workers, and special professional groups are excluded.

Systems with near-universal coverage are also included provided they cover at least 90 percent of employees. This applies to schemes such as the occupational plans in Denmark, the Netherlands, and Sweden.

Resource-tested benefits for which retired people may be eligible are also modeled, subject to the thresholds listed below. These can be means-tested, where both assets and income are taken into account, purely income-tested, or withdrawn only against pension income. The calculations assume that all entitled pensioners take up these benefits. Where there are broader means tests, taking account also of assets, the income test is taken as binding. It is assumed that the whole of income during retirement comes from the mandatory pension scheme (or from voluntary pension schemes in those countries where they are modeled).

Pension entitlements are compared for workers with earnings between 0.5 times and twice the economywide average. The 0.5 times the economywide average lower threshold for inclusion means that Supplemental Security Income in the United States are not included in these estimates.

Baseline Economic Assumptions

- Real earnings growth: 2 percent per year (given the assumption for price inflation, this implies nominal wage growth of 4.55 percent).

- Individual earnings: assumed to grow in line with the economy wide average; the individual is assumed to remain at the same point in the earnings distribution, earning the same percentage of average earnings in every year worked.

- Price inflation: 2.5 percent per year.

- Real rate of return after administrative charges on funded, defined-contribution pensions: 3.5 percent per year.

- Discount rate (for actuarial calculations): 2 percent per year (see Queisser and Whitehouse 2006 for a discussion of the discount rate).

- Mortality rates: The baseline modeling uses country-specific projections (made in 2002) from the United Nations/World Bank population database for the year 2040.

- Earnings distribution: Composite indicators use the OECD average earnings distribution (based on 18 countries), with country-specific data used where available.

The real rate of return on defined-contribution pensions is assumed to be net of administrative charges. In practice, this assumption might disguise genuine differences in administrative fees between countries (see Whitehouse 2000 and 2001 for an analysis).

The calculations assume the following for the pay-out of pension benefits: When defined contribution benefits are received upon retirement, they are paid in the form of a price-indexed life annuity at an actuarially fair price calculated from mortality data. Similarly, the notional annuity rate in notional accounts schemes is (in most cases) calculated from mortality data using the indexation rules and discounting the assumptions employed by a particular country.

Taxation

The modeling assumes that tax systems and social security contributions remain unchanged in the future. Therefore, "value" parameters, such as tax allowances or contribution ceilings, are adjusted annually in line with

Figure 2B.1   Net pension income at high wages and total pension promise, men, 2004

average mandatory pension promise, multiple of average wage

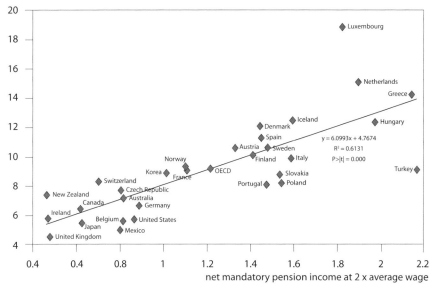

Source: OECD (2007a).

average earnings, while "rate" parameters, such as the personal income tax schedule and Social Security contribution rates, remain unchanged. General provisions and the tax treatment of workers for 2004 can be found in the OECD report *Taxing Wages* (OECD 2006c). We follow the conventions used in that report (for example, regarding which payments are considered taxes).

Career Length

The modeling assumes that a "full career" begins with entry into the labor market at age 20 and continues until the standard pension-eligibility age, which varies among countries.

To illustrate the essentially mathematically required close relationship between the value of the total average mandatory pension promise to the individual and the net retirement income at high wages, figure 2B.1 plots the net relative pension income at twice the average wage and the total pension promise for men. As can be seen, the high relative pension income at high wages explains most of the variation in the total average mandatory pension promise.

Appendix 2C
Why the Decline in the Number of Children Is Unlikely to Help Offset Public Expenditure Levels in Most OECD Countries

Some have argued that as a counterweight to rising pension expenditures, government expenditure on education can be expected to drop as a result of the declining number of children entering the educational system. This presumed cost saving, however, will be small for many countries for four reasons.[1]

First, in many OECD countries public spending on pensions is already substantially higher than expenditure on education (which makes up the bulk of public spending targeted to children; see figure 2C.1). So even substantial declines in the number of children will not offset future increases in pension expenditure.

Second, the number of young people is not expected to decline noticeably in all countries. Indeed, based on current projections, the number of Americans aged 0–16 (i.e., in the K–12 age group) is likely to increase by more than a third from 2006 to 2050,[2] while the total educationally active 5- to 25-year-old cohort will expand similarly. In Britain, France, the Scandinavian countries, and the Benelux, the declines in these age groups will be less than 15 percent by 2050.[3]

Third, many OECD countries face the challenge of putting a far higher share of their young people through the educational system. As can be seen in figure 2C.2, countries such as Germany, Greece, Italy, and the Eastern European member states lag significantly behind the OECD average of 32 percent of workforce entrants aged 25–34 with a tertiary education. Raising this level substantially in the coming years is likely to offset any quantitative decline in expenditure from declining youth demographics.

Finally and most importantly, OECD data for educational expenditure per student from 1995 and 2003 show a total real rate of increase in expenditure per student of, on average, 33 percent for nontertiary and 6 percent for tertiary education over the period.[4] Given that competition from developing countries in higher-skill occupations can be expected to intensify in the decades ahead as the tradability of services increases, it

---

1. This is also the conclusion of the European Commission (2006, 164), which states that "as the reductions in education expenditure are relatively minor, they can not be expected to offset the rise in old-age-related expenditure."

2. US Census interim projections, based on the 2000 Census. Available at www.census.gov/ipc.

3. See also OECD (2006b, indicator B2.4) for estimates that even very large swings in the student population in OECD countries will change expenditures by only 1 to 2 percent of GDP.

4. Data from OECD (2006b, indicator B1.7).

Figure 2C.1 Gross public expenditure in OECD countries on pensions and education, 2003

percent GDP

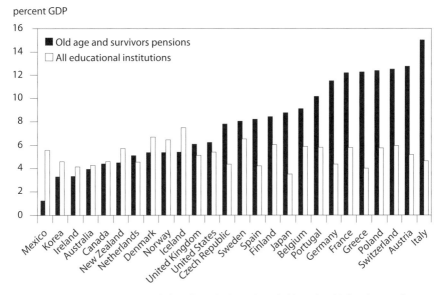

Note: Public education expenditure includes public subsidies to households attributable for educational institutions, as well as direct expenditure on educational institutions from international sources.

Sources: OECD Social Expenditure Database; OECD *Education at a Glance,* 2006.

Figure 2C.2 Share of population with tertiary education, age 25–34, 2005

percent of age group

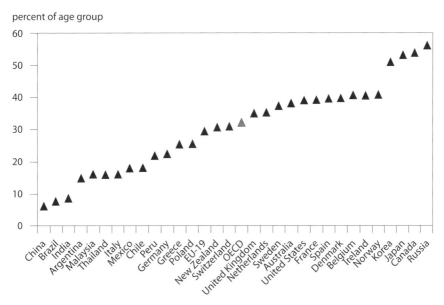

Note: Tertiary education means at least a college degree. 2005 or latest available from 2003/04.

Source: UNESCO/OECD *World Education Indicators*; OECD *Education at a Glance,* 2007; *China Statistical Yearbook 2005* for China; and the 61st National Sample Survey Round for India.

seems unlikely that the level of per-student expenditure in rich countries will not continue to rise substantially in real terms or above the rate of GDP growth.

We also note that US experiences with large-scale private provision of education indicate that such expenditure rises even faster than overall educational expenditure and so provides little if any scope for significant cost savings.[5]

Thus it is not from fewer children in school that future pensions will be financed.

---

5. The College Board (2006), for instance, shows that total charges for a private four-year college rose in real terms by more than $16,000 from 1975 to 2005, whereas those for a public four-year college rose only $6,200.

3

The Distributional Challenge

We can never insure one hundred percent of the population against one hundred percent of the hazards and vicissitudes of life, but we have tried to frame a law which will give some measure of protection to the average citizen and to his family against the loss of a job and against poverty-ridden old age.

—Franklin Delano Roosevelt, Presidential Statement
Signing the Social Security Act, August 14, 1935

Public pension income is such an integral part of the livelihood of so many people in developed economies today that any discussion of the subject—whether focusing on benefit levels, duration, access, or longer-term sustainability—invariably ends with the classic political question: "Who gets what, when, and how much?"[1] However, as we saw in the previous chapter, pension expenditures in several OECD countries may, if left unreformed, soon reach levels that will cause severe problems for overall government finances. Many retirees risk losing the pensions and income levels they thought they had been promised, while others—the younger members of society—risk exorbitant taxation levels to pay for those promises. The questions then become "How do we determine a fair outcome for retirees and other groups?" and "How do we judge pension systems on their ability to distribute wealth across generations and among different social and economic groups within any given generation?" In this chapter we try to answer these questions by presenting data

---

1. Adapted from Lasswell (1990).

on the crucial challenges to the distribution of resources as pension systems are under increasing demographic pressure.

We look at distributional challenges in six sections. First, we explain the historical roots of the two principal approaches to pension provision—insurance and universal means testing—and show that the OECD insurance-based systems are generally far more generous than universal systems. The US Social Security program falls in the middle among OECD members in terms of the progressivity of its pension benefit payments, although it is substantially less progressive than other English-speaking countries.

Second, we analyze the extent of poverty among the elderly (those age 65 and older) and show that it is substantially greater than for the working age population and that all but the top income quintile of elderly in the United States and most other OECD countries receive most of their income from public pensions. Both issues suggest limited possibilities for significant across-the-board pension benefit cuts in the United States and many other OECD countries to salvage fiscal sustainability; any such cuts will instead have to be targeted to selected groups to avoid large increases in old age poverty.

Third, we discuss intergenerational transfers, particularly the fact that current retiring generations can look forward to considerably longer "leisure shares" of their life in retirement than could previous generations. We then present an approach to link retirement ages with rising life expectancies to achieve pension reforms that more fairly reflect the fraction of life spent at paid work.

Fourth, we consider whether the use of national average retirement ages in the face of widely diverging life expectancies among subgroups of developed countries' populations is a policy issue. Some countries still have provisions allowing women to retire earlier than men; we argue that these should be phased out as women live longer than men, on average. More generally, the case for specifying different retirement ages for different social groups raises many impenetrable issues—particularly surrounding estimations of the causes of longer life expectancies for certain groups—and the practice should be avoided.

Fifth, we look at the distributional issues of pension systems for public-sector workers. In all OECD countries, these employees have more generous pension systems than the general population, although they also face more adverse demographics. In the final section of the chapter we focus on the characteristics, financial outlook, and accounting rules concerning US state and local government employees' pension systems, and emphasize the prospects for a pension crisis among some state and local governments in the coming years.

We conclude that a financial solution similar to that implemented for private-sector employee pensions in recent years—which have seen substantial cutbacks in future benefit levels—is likely.

The Two Philosophies of Pension Provision: Universality versus Insurance

Pension systems tend to be long-lived beasts, politically nearly impossible to reform in the absence of definitive political events (such as in Eastern Europe after the collapse of the Berlin Wall in 1989). Once national pension systems have come into being, they usually develop incrementally and expand in cost and coverage. Given this degree of permanency, it makes sense, when considering what particular distributional challenges pension systems face at the outset, to briefly define the two historical ideal type pension systems.

Whether a public pension program is termed "social security" or "social insurance" may seem innocuous, but the distinction frequently reveals an important difference in the pension system's goals. Most countries' current pension systems are hybrids that evolved from two main historical models: the British universal means-tested model and the German contributory insurance model.[2]

- **The British Universal Means-Tested Model.** This model originated with the Old Age Pension Act of 1908, which granted a universal old age flat rate pension for certain persons over the age of 70 of initially five shillings a week for singles and seven shillings and sixpence for a married couple.[3] This flat rate pension was paid out of the general funds of the UK Treasury and required no prior contributions from workers or employers. But the pension was means-tested, and only relatively poor people with an annual income of less than 31pounds 10shillings were eligible (Brabrook 1908). Recipients had to have been a British citizen for at least ten years and have resided in the United Kingdom for no fewer than 12 years since attaining the age of 50 (if a national-born citizen) and no fewer than 20 years since attaining the age of 50 (if a naturalized citizen; thus naturalized citizens had to have resided permanently in the United Kingdom for the 20 years prior to be eligible for a pension at age 70). Applicants lost their pension eligibility if they had been detained in an insane asylum or imprisoned, or

2. We note that both Denmark (from 1891) and New Zealand (from 1898) had universal means-tested programs that predated the British program from 1908. However, both the Danish and New Zealand programs were more akin to "general (noncontributory) poverty alleviation programs" available to all, with a few special additional provisions for the elderly. As such, in our opinion they do not constitute independent old age only, universalist means-tested programs.

3. Notionally, the Old Age Pension Act of 1908 instituted a pension benefit that was graded by income. However, as described by Halsey (1934), the reality was that 99 percent of eligible retirees received the maximum benefit of five shillings for singles and seven shillings and sixpence for married couples.

if they had failed to work to their "full potential." This latter requirement penalized any persons who had been unemployed during their working age lives.[4] The explicit aim of this type of pension is to provide a minimum old age income security or, in the words of its principal author, British Chancellor of the Exchequer David Lloyd George, "to banish the poorhouse from the horizon of every [aging] workman in the country"(Grigg 1978). It is highly income redistributive, as it does not require direct personal participation in pension provision and is not available to the highest income earners.

- **The German Contributory Insurance Model.** This model originated in 1891 with Bismarck's welfare reforms,[5] which introduced a pension system for most German wage earners over the age of 70.[6] The system's finances were based predominantly on the (initially equal) contributions of workers and employers, with the German government at the start contributing a flat rate supplement of 50 marks per year per retiree.[7] Contributors were separated into four income categories, so that higher-wage workers contributed more and could look forward to a higher pension.[8] The aim of this model is, like the British model, to achieve income security in old age, but also to ensure that in the insurance quid pro quo, benefits paid out are directly related to contributions paid in; thus the model evens out living standards over periods of unemployment or lower wage earnings. This quid pro quo model is less income redistributive, as it requires individual participation in personal old age retirement provision and pension benefit levels are linked to levels of contributions.

A country's choice of pension model—whether to emphasize insurance or universality—has direct implications for the degree of redistribution built into a pension system. A universal pure flat rate pension system would be entirely redistributive, whereas a pure insurance-based system

---

4. See Gazeley (2003). It is evident that in the absence of the contributory financing requirement, the British government made substantial legal efforts to restrict eligibility to only those people who could reasonably be expected to have had *productive* lives. Given the lack of direct contributory financing, this is an obvious consequence of the otherwise large immediate demand on general government tax-based resources that such a retirement pension program entails.

5. In addition to pensions, contributory invalidity insurance was also introduced in 1891 (Sakmann 1934).

6. Bismarck's program excluded high-wage earners above a certain threshold and certain high-skilled professions (such as doctors and lawyers).

7. According to Sakmann (1934), this meant that, on average, the German government paid roughly one-third of costs on pensions.

8. See Brabrook (1908) and Hogarth (1896) for details of the Bismarckian old age pensions.

would imply no income redistribution at all among similarly aged participants (pure insurance-based pensions do not rule out large income redistribution between age cohorts and other subgroups).

To facilitate cross-country comparison of the degree of redistribution inherent in the pension benefit formulae, the OECD has estimated a 0–100 "index of progressivity,"[9] where 100 equals pure flat rate pensions and zero pure insurance-based provision.[10] In figure 3.1, this index is combined with the estimated average targeted gross pension level for men,[11] expressed as a percentage of average economywide earnings,[12] to give a combined expression of both the generosity of mandatory pension levels and their degree of redistribution. Figure 3.1 does not include voluntary (mostly occupational) pension systems, similar to those found in the United States, but does include the programs of three OECD countries— Denmark, the Netherlands, and Sweden—with nominally voluntary but de facto mandatory private-sector pension systems with a coverage rate of more than 90 percent.

Figure 3.1 shows a clear relation between the average level of generosity of mandatory pension levels and the degree of redistribution: In general, the higher the degree of redistribution, the lower the generosity of mandatory pension levels.[13] It is noteworthy that, in terms of the relative level of redistribution in pension benefits paid out (scoring about 50 on the y-axis), the mandatory US Social Security insurance system (including Supplemental Security Income [SSI]) is significantly less redistributive than similar systems in other English-speaking countries (clustered in the upper-left corner of figure 3.1) and only slightly more progressive than the OECD average. This suggests some room for additional redistribution in the US Social Security system.

The income distribution–weighted average replacement level of US Social Security pensions, compared with other nations' mandatory pension programs, is clearly at the less generous end of the spectrum (left side

---

9. The index is formally calculated as 100 minus the ratio of the Gini coefficient of pension entitlements divided by the Gini coefficient of earnings (expressed as percentages). In each case the Gini coefficients are calculated using the earnings distribution as the weight. See OECD (2005, annex I.3) for details.

10. Only old age pensions are included in these comparative data.

11. Only the targeted level for men is available in the source of these data.

12. This relative pension level is the weighted average of replacement rates for incomes between 0.3 and 3.0 percent of average economywide earnings, with the corresponding earnings-distribution groups as weights. We also used this measure in chapter 2 to estimate the total present value of the pension promise to retirees (OECD 2007a, 49).

13. Figure 3.1 presents data from OECD (2007a, 45), which, where data are available (18 member states), uses national earnings distributions to estimate inequality in pension entitlements; for the remaining 12 countries, the average OECD distributions of earnings are used.

Figure 3.1 Mandatory pension progressivity and the weighted average mandatory pension replacement level (men), 2004

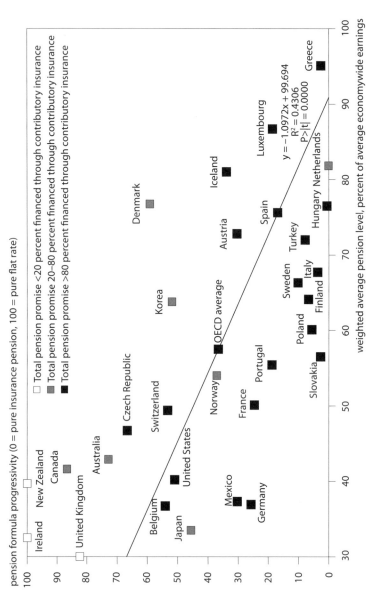

Source: OECD (2007a).

of figure 3.1) but comparable to other English-speaking countries and more generous than both Japan and Germany.[14] Continental European countries with more generous insurance-oriented mandatory pension systems cluster in the lower right corner of figure 3.1.

Another way to illustrate the degree of progressivity in US Social Security benefits is to estimate the inflation-adjusted internal rates of return for different earnings groups in a given age cohort. Duggan and colleagues (1993) estimated that for the US 1895–1922 age cohort, the internal rate of return for low-income participants was nearly double that of high earners—13.8 to 7.6 percent. The Congressional Budget Office (CBO 2006) estimates that including Social Security's three main benefits—old age, disability, and auxiliary—for all 10-year cohorts born after 1940, the net benefit, or benefit-to-tax ratio, for the lowest-income quintile is above 150 percent, while the middle quintile is close to 100 percent and the top quintile significantly below 100 percent. Moreover, CBO (2006) shows that the differences in net benefits between the recent age cohorts are relatively small compared to the differences between earnings groups.[15]

However, the relative progressivity of the entire US old age income security system is driven overwhelmingly by the progressivity of disability pensions, which go disproportionately to people with lower lifetime earnings. Old age Social Security pensions, viewed separately, are less progressive. It is important when discussing the progressivity of US Social Security to recall Liebman's (2001) report that most intracohort redistribution in Social Security originates in factors unrelated to income, primarily between people with low life expectancies and people with high life expectancies and between singles and dual-income/married single-income households.

Looking back at figure 3.1, it is perhaps counterintuitive that the most redistributive pension systems are at the same time the least generous, but the reason is cost. Universal pensions of the original British model, financed out of general tax revenue, could easily become prohibitively expensive for governments if they were not able to limit costs through means testing and relatively low promised benefit levels. Indeed, Halsey (1934), in her preparatory report on the experiences of other countries' pension provision, observes that the English experiences from 1908 onward indicate an inability to control costs due to the fact that "benefit provisions tend to become more liberal and qualifying conditions less exacting." The

---

14. The finding that Germany, despite its high public pension expenditure (as discussed in chapter 2), has a relatively ungenerous weighted average pension level, at 36.9 percent of average German wages (lower than the US average of 40.2 percent), is surprising. But, as we discuss in chapter 4, it is related to the country's extensive use of generous early retirement options, which significantly increase public pension expenditure.

15. CBO (2006) assumes that all benefits will be paid as scheduled and hence that no benefit cuts will occur after a Trust Fund exhaustion.

original writers of the US Social Security Act rejected limitations on costs through means testing in the longer term but, partly because of the UK experience, decided to implement the US Social Security Act as an insurance-based system.

Highly redistributive means-tested programs risk inducing moral hazard problems by creating extremely high implicit tax rates on employment for low-wage workers. But this work incentive problem evidently diminishes as people age, and low-wage workers are not likely to continue to work beyond the normal eligibility age for a full pension. Thus the main moral hazard lies in the availability of highly redistributive programs at an early age. Contributory insurance financing has the benefit of partly avoiding the problem by encouraging participants to work so that they can contribute to their own retirement. However, unless properly structured, contributory insurance financing risks creating other types of "labor input hazards" by incentivizing relatively early (i.e., premature from the perspective of sustainability) retirement, as might occur if the contributor/recipient reaches a very high level of pension benefits relatively early in his or her career, with a correspondingly reduced incentive to continue working. We revisit this topic in chapter 4.

From the short-term perspective of governments, contributory insurance can be largely self-financing through payments from an increasing number of contributors. In fact most of the insurance-based systems in the OECD were set up in periods of both young and rapidly rising populations.[16] Essentially by demographic determination, they initially generated large surpluses of contributions compared with the amounts paid out in benefits, allowing policymakers to provide generous benefits from the beginning of the program without running into immediate financing constraints. The OECD's pension models (described in chapter 2 and OECD 2007a) show that countries with mandatory pension systems targeting an average pension level of more than two-thirds[17] of average economywide earnings for full-career workers are overwhelmingly contributory insurance–based systems. This is illustrated in figure 3.1, too; it is clear that the three countries (Ireland, New Zealand, and the United Kingdom) with the least contributory insurance–based financing in their total pension promises have at once the most progressive and least generous mandatory pension systems in the OECD. At the same time, countries to the lower right in figure 3.1 have overwhelmingly insurance-financed, relatively nonprogressive, and, on average, quite generous mandatory pension plans. As

---

16. With the exceptions of Korea, Turkey, and Switzerland, which did not have a limited pension provision laws until 1973, 1949, and 1946, respectively, all OECD countries had pension provision laws in place by the end of World War II, when working-age populations were not only very young but also expanding relatively rapidly. See SSA (2006b, 2007).

17. The US Social Security target by the same metric in figure 3.1 is just below 40 percent.

we saw in chapter 2, many countries in this group are among those facing the largest sustainability problems from adverse demographics.

US Social Security has historically (box 3.1) been a hybrid pension program with both universal and contributory insurance aspects. In addition, although the program is overwhelmingly contribution funded,[18] it falls almost precisely halfway (with a score of 51 on the OECD's 0–100 scale; figure 3.1) between a flat rate pension and a completely mechanical link between contributions paid and benefits received. Its insurance-based funding principle notwithstanding, the progressivity of the Social Security benefit formula—which deviates from the pure insurance principle on which its funding relies—makes it a fairly redistributive pension system compared to other insurance-based pension systems similarly funded through direct contributions. Figure 3.1 shows that US Social Security is among the most progressive of the predominantly contribution-financed mandatory pension systems.

Progressivity and redistribution in insurance-based pension systems come through two main channels and typically from a combination of both. The benefit formula either restricts the benefits for the highest earners/highest contributors or boosts the benefits available to the lowest-income/lowest-contributing groups. Either way, the formula violates the implicit quid pro quo principle of contributory insurance–based pension systems. However, viewed from the perspective of long-term sustainability, *how* a contributory pension system becomes more progressive matters profoundly. Governments that make a pension system more progressive by capping benefit levels at the top increase progressivity through cost savings, whereas boosting benefit levels at the bottom increases progressivity through higher expenditures. In box 3.2 we explain that the Social Security benefit formula, as in most pension systems, does both. At the same time, figure 2.7 in the previous chapter showed that OECD countries differ substantially in the net retirement income rates offered to high earners and that the United States was among the OECD countries with a relatively low net retirement income for high earners. One of the main reasons why Social Security faces only modest long-term sustainability issues is that it has targeted a relatively modest average pension benefit level (in figure 3.1, about 40 percent of average earnings), achieved by restricting the scope of Social Security by limiting the overall participation of high-income Americans (i.e., both their contributions and guaranteed benefits).

---

18. In addition to contributions from payroll taxation, the OASDI Trust Funds also generate parts of their income through interest payments from the US Treasury on their holdings of Treasury bills, as well as parts of the tax revenue withheld from paid-out benefits. SSI, as noted in box 3.1, is also paid out of general government tax revenues. See chapter 2 and below.

Box 3.1   Historical overview of US Social Security

Most mandatory national pension systems today are hybrids—part noncontributory, part insurance.[1] Thus when the Social Security Act established the US public pension system in 1935, it distinguished between Federal Grants to States for Old-Age Assistance (Title I) and Federal Old-Age Benefits (Title II). The former were basically noncontributory, as it was left to the states to define their own criteria for eligibility. In 1972 the state-level programs became part of the Supplemental Security Income (SSI) program, run since its inception by the Social Security Administration (SSA).[2] However, unlike Social Security benefits, SSI is not paid by either the Social Security taxes or trust funds but through US Treasury general funds. SSI is means-tested and based on recipients' incomes, living conditions, and resources, and is thus broadly redistributive and closely related to the British Universal Means-Tested Model.

Federal Old-Age Benefits (Social Security as it is known today) have always been entirely funded by employer and employee contributions paid into the Social Security Trust Funds and so, despite the name, are an example of the German insurance model. The pure insurance model of pension benefits, however, was available to contributing workers only until 1940, when two new recipient categories were created: dependent benefits (for the spouse and minor children of a retired contributing worker) and survivor benefits (for the family in case of the premature death of the covered worker). This transition from an insurance system based on only the contributing worker to a family-based plan made the system more redistributive, as more people now had access to benefits from the same number of contributors. Today more than 7 million Americans draw dependent and survivor benefits.

From 1937 to 1940 (when monthly payments were initiated), Social Security benefits were paid out in a single lump sum. When the monthly payments began, their levels were fixed irrespective of cost of living. Combined with the relatively limited number of eligible Americans (only 222,000 in 1940, up to less than 3.5 million in 1950), the fixed-amount payments meant that by 1950 the value of Social Security's retirement benefits was frequently significantly below that of the means-tested state-level old age assistance (the precursor to SSI), which more Americans received than the Social Security benefits. In the early days, therefore, effective old age assistance in America was far more redistributive than today's Social Security. Yet this early redistributive character did not seem to seriously erode political support for the system at the time.

In 1951, the first cost of living allowance (COLA) of Social Security benefits was introduced, immediately raising benefits by 77 percent, followed by frequent additional legislative increases (only by 1975 did COLAs become automatic annual increases based on the US consumer price index).

Thus by the early 1950s America had effectively switched from relying predominantly on a British universal means-tested pension model to the German insurance-based model. Insurance-based Social Security is now the only public pension system that touches the vast majority of Americans. In 2006 it had almost seven times as many beneficiaries as the means-tested SSI, paying out approximately 11 times as much in benefits—roughly $460 billion, as against the $42 billion in SSI.

1. This box is based on, and all data are from, the official SSA history, available at www.ssa .gov/history.

2. President Franklin D. Roosevelt originally envisioned SSI as a temporary relief, to be phased out as more people were covered by Social Security in their old age.

The contributory insurance–based financing model of America's mandatory pension system has probably facilitated its relative progressivity, which goes to the heart of whether Americans perceive their payroll tax payments to the Social Security Trust Funds as "just another tax" or as "personal contributions."[19] The more progressive and redistributive a pension system is, the more the quid pro quo principle of contributing to one's own retirement is violated, and the more payroll tax payments start to look like just another tax rather than a personal contribution. And the more something is viewed as a tax, the more public hostility it is likely to engender. This matters particularly in the United States, as Americans are substantially more politically hostile to paying taxes than elsewhere in the OECD. It is, therefore, unlikely that a mandatory pension system could have achieved a relative progressivity similar to that of Social Security had it been financed directly through general tax revenues rather than through a contributory insurance–based system.

In summary, the US mandatory pension system in Social Security (plus SSI) is, partly as a result of its relatively modest scope at high incomes, quite progressive when compared with other OECD countries with higher mandatory contributory pensions for high-income groups. Yet it is

19. See discussion in chapter 8.

Box 3.2 Pension benefit calculation: Detail is a necessary evil to align conflicting policy goals

As with most public affairs, the level of any pension benefit is the outcome of a plethora of mostly conflicting public policy goals, usually old age poverty alleviation and progressivity, on the one hand, and fiscal sustainability and desired direct benefit-earnings linkages, on the other. The operational tool for estimating any given pensioner's benefit level—the mathematical benefit estimation formula—becomes a highly complex entity. A brief walk through how Social Security benefits are estimated in the United States in 2007 will be illustrative.[1]

Social Security is financed by direct contributions (taxes) from employers and employees, and the tax base for the plan rises every year with the average wage index. In 2007 the maximum tax base for Social Security contributions was 12.4 percent of $97,500, or up to $6,045 payable by both the employer and employee. An increase in the tax base to improve the long-term solvency of Social Security, without altering the benefit formula, would represent a move toward increased progressivity and fiscal sustainability, as Americans[2] with incomes over $97,500 would pay higher taxes without receiving a higher benefit in retirement. If the tax base threshold in 2007 had been $150,000, people earning that income would have paid $9,300 in Social Security taxes rather than the $6,045 they actually paid—a more than 50 percent increase in the contributions for this high-income group of Americans.

Social Security benefits are computed using the average of the highest earnings over up to 35 years. The 35-year average is far longer than is typically used in defined-benefit final salary-based pensions (see appendix 3A), for which the usual reference is the average of only the three to five highest income years. The longer the period over which average wages are calculated, the lower the resulting pension benefit. Thus estimation of Social Security benefits over all lifetime earnings, rather than "just" 35 years, without other changes to the benefit formula, would likely result in significantly lower benefits as it would include additional (early) years of low earnings.

The 35-year contribution history for Social Security benefit estimation raises the importance of what the Social Security Administration terms the average indexed monthly earnings (AIME) estimation (also sometimes referred to as valorization or preretirement indexation).[3] The AIME estimation covers years worked until the recipient turns 60 to protect the value of past earnings and account for changes in living standards between the time Social Security contributions were first made and the time at which benefits are claimed (this period could be more than 35 years in the United States).[4] The SSA, for benefit computation purposes, indexes earlier periods' earnings by the growth in national average wages,[5] a method that captures rising living standards over a worker's contribution period. However, if Social Security were indexed for valorization purposes according to increases in inflation rather than wages (i.e., excluding real wage increases), the difference in benefit levels would be substantial and negative, due to the cumulative effects of interest compounding over long periods of time.[6]

The logic of the AIME estimation is similar to that of the more well-known automatic cost of living allowance (COLA) to Social Security benefits after the age of earliest eligibility (age 62) according to changes in the US consumer price index (CPI).[7] If COLAs were based on wage growth (similar to wage indexation) rather than the CPI for valorization purposes, the effect on (future) benefit levels would also be substantial, but positive. Wage or price indexation (or hybrids of the two) of both pension contributions (valorization) and benefits (COLAs) are the subject of some of the most important long-term policy decisions on pension benefit levels and pension sustainability.

Following estimation of the AIME, Social Security benefit levels are derived from the primary insurance amount (PIA), which is estimated from the AIME using a formula that relies on two formula bending points. In 2007 these points were $680 and $4,100[8]: For all AIME at or below $680, the Social Security recipient receives 90 cents on the dollar in monthly benefits; for all AIME between $680 and $4,100, the retiree receives 32 cents on the dollar; and for all AIME above $4,100, just 15 cents on the dollar. Thus the PIA formula is clearly the main progressive element of Social Security benefit regulations, as it ensures that the system redistributes in favor of lower-income retirees. Tweaking the PIA formula in either direction would easily amplify or reduce the level of progressivity in benefit estimation. If, for instance, benefits for AIME below $680 were raised relative to AIME above $680, Social Security progressivity would increase, and if the benefits were decreased, so would the progressivity.

Finally, in order to encourage Americans to retire at a later age, the PIA is adjusted for an early or delayed retirement age to arrive at the final level of initial Social Security benefits (subject to subsequent COLAs). The standard retirement age for full pension eligibility for Americans born in 1942 is 65 years and 10 months, while for those born in 1943–54 (i.e., between ages 53 and 64 in 2007), it is 66 years.[9] For those in the latter group—which includes many of the baby-boomers who retire at the earliest possible age (62) instead of 66—the PIA would be adjusted downward to 75 percent of what benefits would have been

(box continues on next page)

at retirement at age 66. Similarly, the PIA would rise by 8 percent annually (on top of COLA) for each year of postponed retirement until age 70. Hence, this retirement age adjustment formula is another complication for estimating Social Security benefits. The world is rarely simple, and pension benefit estimation never is.

1. All data in this box are from the Social Security Administration website, www.ssa.gov.
2. It is important to note that immigrants on temporary employment visas, such as H1-B or L-1 visas, are not eligible for Social Security, despite the fact that they, via contributions, pay into the OASDI Trust Fund while working in the United States. As such, a numerical expansion of these groups would represent a strengthening of the finances of Social Security.
3. AIME equals the sum of the highest 35 years of contributions after valorization divided by the number of months in contribution years.
4. If pension benefits were based on just the final year of salary, obviously no valorization would be required.
5. OECD (2007a) notes that wage indexation is used for valorization in the overwhelming majority of OECD member states.
6. As Social Security earnings for benefit valorization purposes are always indexed to wages two years before the first year of eligibility (age 62), all recipients *lose at least two years of wage growth* in the valorization process. In other words, the indexing factor for valorization after age 60 is always 1. Extending this period of no valorization of earnings to more than two years would lower total benefits.
7. There is, therefore, a two-year gap from age 60 to 62 where no inflation protection indexation to either wages or prices is offered.
8. PIA formula bending points are themselves indexed to earnings. This indexation is relatively more generous in terms of benefit levels than price indexation of PIA formula bending points would have been.
9. This will rise gradually to 67 by 2027 for Americans born in 1960 or later.

far less progressive than mandatory pension systems in other English-speaking countries. Given that this section ignores the effects of private and voluntary pension schemes (which, as we shall see below and in chapter 7, are in the United States almost exclusively for high-income groups), this comparative analysis suggests that there is likely some political room for making Social Security more progressive. We base this conclusion on two insights. First, Social Security, regardless of its degree of progressivity, is based on the contributory insurance principle, which, ceteris paribus—with its implied link between contributions and benefits preventing it from being viewed as a government handout—ought to blunt some of the political hostility toward increased progressivity in the benefit formula. Second, other English-speaking countries—Ireland, New Zealand, and the United Kingdom—have in place universalist, means-tested mandatory pension systems much more transparently progressive than US Social Security, yet there is nothing to indicate that this additional progressivity has undermined broad political support for redistribution in their pension systems. Comparative analysis, therefore, suggests that a more progressive Social Security system would not undermine broad political support in the United States.

How Well Do Different Pension Systems Alleviate Old Age Poverty?

One of the central aims of all mandatory pension systems, public and private alike, is to reduce old age poverty among retirees. This goal distinguishes them from private voluntary pension systems, which use the provision of a future pension as an alternative to cash wages to attract and retain talented employees.[20] In addition to these differing goals, in practice it is mostly public pensions that stand between lower-income elderly and poverty. Ideally, therefore, it would be useful to have data that separate public and private pension income. Unfortunately, however, such income data are not, to our knowledge, collected on a consistent basis across countries. As a result, the income data we use include the total income from all pensions, whether mandatory (public) or voluntary (private).[21]

Further data concerns include very big differences between income and consumption measures of poverty. Theoretically, the measure of individual comfort and welfare is derived from consumption. However, due to collection costs and the burden on respondents, total household-level consumption is rarely surveyed, and instead efforts to gauge the extent of poverty rely overwhelmingly on income-based measures. This approach raises problems, particularly in measures of poverty among older households/heads of households and individuals, who draw down wealth and savings toward the end of their lives. Elderly families or individuals with assets can consume in excess of their income and so may thus on the

---

20. This has certainly been the case in the United States, where many corporate pension systems originated with the wage controls put in place during World War II, which forced companies to offer employees noncash incentives. We explore this subject in detail in chapter 7.

21. The comparability of cross-country income data for the older cohorts is reduced by the presence in some countries, like the United States, of substantial voluntary private pension schemes. Because the aim of such schemes is not to reduce poverty, their presence increases intracohort income inequality.

broader total consumption basis be less likely to experience poverty than those with only income,[22] as is particularly the case among the oldest individuals, who are typically widowed women.

Most of the data that we present below are from the OECD and are based on the concept of equivalent disposable household income.[23] This term includes all gross earnings, gross capital income, self-employment income, financial gains, real estate rents, occupational pensions, all other private transfers, and all types of cash transfers from public sources. The sum is adjusted for direct (but not indirect) taxation and employee Social Security contributions (if any). In accordance with the literature listed in footnote 22, this means that all household assets may not be included in these poverty data, which may therefore be substantially deflated relative to a consumption-based poverty indicator. For instance, Michael Hurd and Susann Rohwedder (2006) find that, based on longitudinal data from the Health and Retirement Study (HRS), US consumption-based poverty rates in 2001 were almost 30 percent lower for the oldest group of single men in America (75+ in their study) and 20 percent lower for single women in this category than was the case using the official Current Population Survey (CPS)–based poverty data.[24] The differences among the 65- to 74-year-olds are substantially smaller. The authors attribute this to the significantly negative post-tax savings rate among the 75+ age cohort but not among the younger group. The negative savings rate among the oldest cohort points to a substantial drawdown of assets, which will lift some of this cohort out of poverty despite their low incomes.

We caution that the data presented below concern only monetary income and taxes and do not take into account lower work-related expenditures (e.g., little or no commuting to work) and lower housing costs in retirement. This may exaggerate poverty risks among the elderly in these data, especially in countries where in-kind support is available through, for instance, subsidized rents.[25] The data in this section must therefore be approached with some skepticism about the precise numerical values and the focus on cross-country comparable data. Nonetheless, they offer valuable

---

22. A large number of studies have argued for the superiority of consumption as a better measure than income for measuring material welfare. See, for instance, Hurd and Rohwedder (2006), Cutler and Katz (1991), Jorgenson and Slesnick (1987), Slesnick (1993, 2001), Johnson, Smeeding, and Torrey (2005), and Meyer and Sullivan (2003).

23. See Förster and Pearson (2002) for a more detailed description.

24. Hurd and Rohwedder (2006) find that for couples, the differences are smaller, with the CPS data indicating a poverty rate only 0.5 percentage point higher at 4.5 percent.

25. Förster and Mira d'Ercole (2005) cite Ritakallio (2003) for estimates from Finland and Australia showing that when accounting for expenditures for utilities, mortgages, and interest costs, "after-housing poverty rates" are indeed lower for the elderly than for younger working-age cohorts. Other types of excluded "nonmonetary income" include food stamps, health benefits, and goods produced and consumed on farms.

insights into cross-border differences, and it is unlikely that an upward bias in the poverty data will materially change our policy conclusions.[26]

With these qualifications in mind, we use two main parameters to evaluate the effectiveness of mandatory pension systems in combating old age poverty: (1) How many retirees live in poverty, both absolutely and relatively to the working population—i.e., is it more likely or not that old people slip through the social safety net, as compared with the working age population? And (2) where do retirees get their income from—i.e., do they depend primarily on public benefits or do they have other sources of income?

How Many Old People Live in Poverty?

When determining the number of elderly people living in poverty, the most important piece of information is the threshold of poverty used for measurement. The politically explosive nature of poverty data, large cross-country differences, and the data issues discussed above present obstacles for the determination of an objectively acceptable poverty threshold. The threshold used in the OECD data presented here is 50 percent of the median equivalent disposable income of the entire population, a measure widely used in international comparative studies (Antolín, Dang, and Oxley 1999). This threshold eliminates the impact of most differences in overall country income levels. It is, however, significantly above the (very low) official US poverty threshold, published annually by the US Census. In 2000, the year of the comparative OECD data, the US definition of poverty—less than 50 percent of the median income that year—was $11,977 for a single adult and $20,745 for two adults with one child. This corresponds to the Census Bureau official US pretax poverty threshold in 2000 of $8,259 for singles (over 65) and $11,824 for two adults with one child (under 18 and the householder above 65). As such, the poverty threshold used here is substantially higher (45 and 75 percent, respectively, for singles or families with one child) than the official US poverty threshold.[27]

Any poverty threshold is exactly that—a threshold—and derived dichotomous above-or-below data provide no information about the income

---

26. It is not possible to easily discern the extent of cross-border differences—for example, in the fact that US retirees may have far more private assets to draw down than, say, retirees in Italy—between consumption and income-based poverty indicators.

27. See US Census Bureau's webpage on poverty at www.census.gov/hhes/www/poverty. The US Census poverty threshold includes the following income: earnings, unemployment compensation, workers' compensation, Social Security, Supplemental Security Income, public assistance, veterans' payments, survivor benefits, pension or retirement income, interest, dividends, rents, royalties, income from estates, trusts, educational assistance, alimony, child support, assistance from outside the household, and other miscellaneous sources. Capital gains or losses are excluded. See appendix 3A for the implied poverty thresholds for all countries included.

distribution of the elderly. As a result, a country may look good in terms of its poverty threshold but have a very large population just above that threshold. One would thus predict that countries with mandatory universal flat rate pension systems would, if benefit levels were at appropriate levels, have low levels of absolute poverty but a lot of elderly just above the threshold. As we shall see below, this is the case for universalist New Zealand, which has very low old age poverty rates but a large elderly population just above the poverty threshold.[28]

Before the introduction of public old age pension systems, old people generally depended either on their families for support (at least one reason for having many children was as a retirement insurance policy) or on their own ability to continue working "until the end." Although such dependence has disappeared in the developed world, the two means of support still play a role in analyses of the income levels of old people. According to OECD data from household surveys,[29] roughly a third of all people living in "households with an elderly head" live alone (the "single elderly"). Furthermore, most elderly people, having retired, obviously do not work. Single people not working, regardless of age, are at a higher risk of poverty than other groups in society, and data from Michael Förster and Marco Mira d'Ercole (2005, 43) confirm that the overwhelming share of elderly poor are either unemployed or living alone or both.[30] One should therefore expect that these old people—irrespective of the pension system that provides their benefits—would have higher poverty rates than the average population. But this is not necessarily the case, as can be seen in figure 3.2.

In seven OECD countries—Canada, the Czech Republic, Germany, Hungary, the Netherlands, New Zealand, and Poland—the poverty rates for those over 65 are lower (to the left of the 45° line in figure 3.2) than for the working age population,[31] evidence that it is quite possible to construct a pension system that protects the elderly—if not entirely, then certainly more than the average population—against poverty. Eight continental European OECD countries—Austria, Denmark, Finland, France, Luxembourg, Norway, Sweden, and Switzerland—have slightly higher poverty rates for the elderly but still below the OECD-25 average for this age group and about the average of 10.2 percent for the total population.

Moving to the right in figure 3.2 we see that the situation for the elderly in other OECD countries is far less benign. In Australia, Greece, Ireland,

---

28. See old age income distribution data for New Zealand in OECD (2007c).

29. Förster and Mira d'Ercole (2005), based on member state–submitted data.

30. Dang and colleagues (2006) show that in all OECD countries covered by their survey, the share of elderly women in poverty far exceeds that of men, indicating the "widow problem."

31. Note that due to the assumption of parental support until legal age 18, the "working age population" for poverty issues is assumed here to be 18–64, not 15–64.

Figure 3.2   OECD poverty rates by age group, 2000

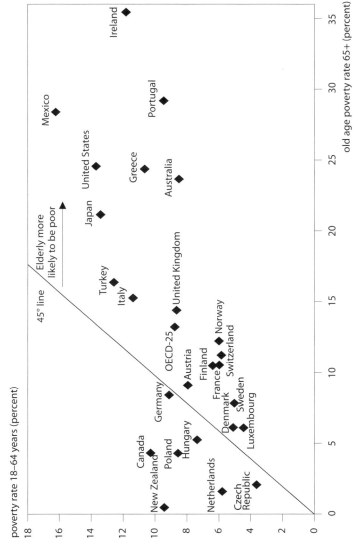

Note: Poverty rates are measured as the proportion of individuals with equivalized disposable income less than 50 percent of the median income of the entire population. 2000 data for all countries except 1999 for Australia, Austria, and Germany.

Source: OECD Equity Indicators 2006.

Japan, Mexico, and Portugal, poverty rates for those 65 and older by the relative to median income definition used here all exceed 20 percent—twice the OECD population average—and in the United States the rate is nearly 25 percent. With the exception of Japan, the poverty rate for the elderly in these countries is more than 10 percent higher than for the working age population, indicating that the elderly in these countries are, on average, significantly worse off than the average working age population.[32] Ireland's old age poverty rate of more than one-third indicates that, as of 2000, the Irish universal flat rate pension system had not yet caught up with the country's recently created wealth and that significant expansions of its pension system, aimed at providing a higher basic old age income security, are likely in the near future.[33]

When considering poverty rates among the elderly, it is important to take into consideration the heterogeneity of the 65+ age cohort. As shown in figure 3.3, in all the OECD countries (except Hungary, Spain, and Turkey) for which data are available, poverty rates for the oldest age cohort, those 76 and older, are higher than for the 66- to 75-year-old cohort, and in some countries, the difference is substantial. Similarly, in all four Scandinavian countries the poverty rates for the oldest residents are more than double those of the age group 66–75. Poverty rates rise to nearly 30 percent for Americans 76 or older, and in Ireland, Mexico, and Portugal, they top 35 percent.

The poverty rates for those 76 and older are rather sobering, considering that in all OECD countries (except the Czech Republic, Hungary, Mexico, Poland, Slovakia, and Turkey) life expectancy at birth is more than 76 years (OECD Health Indicators 2006).[34] By this measure it could be argued that nearly 30 percent of all Americans will die in poverty[35]—about three times the share of Germans and French and more than five times the share of Canadians.

Figure 3.3 illustrates a substantial distributional problem, as old age poverty rates—especially for the very old and thus especially for women—

---

32. Dang and colleagues (2006) surveyed nine OECD countries (Finland, France, Germany, Italy, Luxembourg, Norway, Sweden, the United Kingdom, and the United States) relying on national household microdata and found that only in the United States is the income inequality among the elderly larger than in the population as a whole.

33. OECD (2008) indicates that this has indeed been occurring in Ireland, which since the late 1990s has seen sustained and large increases in mandatory pension levels and accompanying declines in old age poverty rates.

34. In Turkey the average is lower than 70.

35. Strictly, one cannot, however, methodologically draw the conclusion that the combination of a 30 percent poverty rate for those 76 and older and an average life expectancy of 76 or older means that 30 percent will die in poverty. Life expectancy at birth is a projected average lifespan for a population in a given year, not an absolute indicator for the age at which a person will die.

Figure 3.3 Old age poverty rates by elderly subcohorts

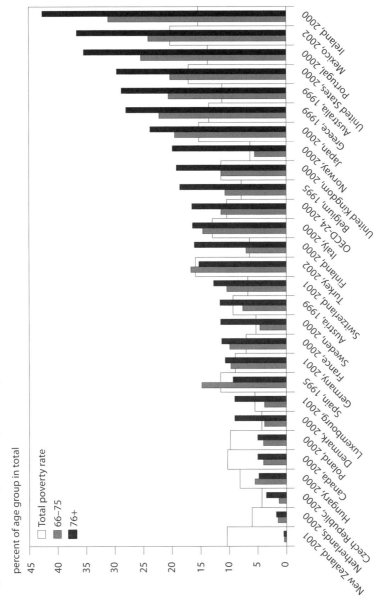

percent of age group in total

Legend:
- ☐ Total poverty rate
- (grey) 66–75
- (black) 76+

Countries (axis labels):
Ireland, 2000
Mexico, 2002
Portugal, 2000
United States, 2000
Australia, 1999
Greece, 1999
Japan, 2000
Norway, 2000
United Kingdom, 2000
Belgium, 1995
OECD-24, 2000
Italy, 2000
Finland, 2000
Turkey, 2002
Switzerland, 2001
Austria, 1999
Sweden, 2000
France, 2000
Germany, 2001
Spain, 1995
Luxembourg, 2001
Denmark, 2000
Canada, 2000
Hungary, 2000
Czech Republic, 2000
Netherlands, 2000
New Zealand, 2001

Note: Poverty rates are measured as the proportion of individuals with equivalized disposable income less than 50 percent of the income of the entire population. 2000 data for all countries except 1999 for Australia, Austria, and Germany.

Source: Förster and Mira d'Ercole (2005).

127

are much higher than for the average population[36] in many countries. And, as discussed in chapter 2 and shown in figure 3.3, for many countries, including the United States, the potential for shoring up the financial sustainability of pension systems in the future—predominantly through across-the-board reductions in the real and relative levels of benefits—may be more limited than many believe. These countries will need to pursue other options for achieving the long-term fiscal sustainability of their pension systems.

Finally, these poverty rates indicate that longevity risk—i.e., the risk, from the retirees' perspective, that they have not saved enough for the duration of their old age—poses a significant problem for the oldest retirees in most of the OECD countries (see box 3.3 for more on Americans' retirement savings).

The Income of the Elderly: From What Source(s)?

For analyses of old age poverty it is important to determine the main income source of the elderly. Are they primarily dependent on public pension benefits, do they receive income from assets and capital, or do they rely on earnings from work? For those in the first group, reducing public benefits would be particularly harmful to poverty prevention, whereas this would not be the case should most elderly in fact rely overwhelmingly on capital income or earnings for their income.

Due to large national differences in data collection methodology, the comparative data presented below are subject to a number of caveats.[37] Figures 3.4 and 3.5 distinguish between earnings (income from work[38]), capital income (private/individual pensions, rents, dividends, and interest[39]), and public transfers.[40] For the 23 other OECD countries data are reported using disposable income as the denominator: For 17 of the reporting countries the data are on a gross income basis so total effective tax rates are also reported,[41] and for six countries income shares are net of

---

36. Figure 3.3 also includes 0- to 17-year-olds in the comparative total population.

37. These are further elaborated in appendix 3A.

38. Includes wages, salaries, and nonfarm and farm self-employment.

39. For the United States, this includes private company/union/non–Social Security general government pensions (i.e., pensions to retired public-sector workers in addition to Social Security), IRAs, Keogh, 401(k) plans, interest, and dividend income.

40. For the United States, this includes Social Security, SSI, family support, and other public assistance.

41. Adema and Ladaique (2005) and OECD (2007b) indicate that there are substantial differences in the tax rates of many OECD countries on different types of income, depending on whether it is from a public or private source. The tax data presented are, therefore, approximate. See appendix 2B for details.

Box 3.3 Americans' (lack of) savings for retirement

Probably the most comprehensive survey coverage of the perceptions of and preparations for retirement in America is the annual Employee Benefit Research Institute (EBRI) Retirement Confidence Survey (RCS), published since 1991.[1] This makes the RCS a natural source of information about the severity of any possible misperceptions that Americans may have concerning their retirement. Its findings generally make sobering reading about retirement preparations among Americans today: The RCS finds widespread misperceptions of basic retirement circumstances.[2]

While over 60 percent of workers expect to receive benefits from an employer-based defined benefit pension plan in retirement, just 40 percent report that they (or their spouse) are enrolled in a defined benefit plan. And with US employers rapidly scaling back such plans, this misperception is likely to grow in the future. Half of Americans (51 percent) do not know the correct age at which they will be fully eligible for Social Security benefits and mistakenly believe that they will be eligible for full benefits sooner than is the case, even though the Social Security Administration has mailed annual individual benefit statements to the entire US population since the late 1990s. Table 3B3.1 summarizes several key findings in the most recent RCS.

Table 3B3.1 shows that from 1994 to 2007 the share of Americans who have tried to estimate their financial needs in retirement has remained relatively stable at around 40 percent, while roughly one-third of Americans have not saved anything toward retirement, and about 40 percent do not do so now. These findings clearly indicate that a very, very large group of Americans is not making any personal financial preparations for retirement. This is highly unlikely to be a well-informed choice.

The RCS report's authors further find several serious misperceptions among Americans who do save toward their retirement. First, most Americans seem to believe that only relatively modest savings will be needed for retirement. Table 3B3.1 shows that almost half think that $500,000 or less will be sufficient. This might be a serious underestimate, at least for most high-income Americans or people with high expenses in retirement, as the share of required savings for retirement is highly dependent on one's standard of living while working (assuming a desire for lifetime income smoothing), and high-income people, therefore, need higher savings to sustain them.

(box continues on next page)

Box 3.3   Americans' (lack of) savings for retirement *(continued)*

Second, there are relatively high fixed costs of continuing to live, especially for people without health care insurance, so low-income workers will need to save more as a multiple of income. VanDerhei (2006) stochastically estimates that high- and low-income groups will need savings multiples of 12 to 13 and 42 to 54 times current income in retirement, respectively.[3] Hence, it is worrying that the RCS finds that 57 percent of Americans expect to need only a savings multiple of 10 or less of their current wages, and only 8 percent believe they will need more than a multiple of 40.

Third, alas, the belief that they need less savings in retirement than seems plausible is not the most pressing misperception facing those Americans with any savings. Rather, it is the fact, as seen in the lower right corner of table 3B3.1, that they fail to reach even their own deflated saving goals. Half of saving Americans close to retirement age (55+) have less than $100,000 in total savings. In the face of such findings, it is cold comfort to discover that 47 percent of American workers somewhat or strongly agree that they (and their spouse) "aren't likely to live long enough to use up all their savings."

Helman, VanDerhei, and Copeland (2007) in their end-remarks diplomatically discuss the risk of "overconfidence" among many Americans concerning their "financial retirement security." However, the RCS findings at least pose the question as to whether—given the level of misperceptions—individual choice and responsibility will continue to be preferred avenues for retirement savings and income security in the future or perhaps more compulsion should be required.

---

1. All data in this box are from the 2007 RCS, published by the EBRI in April 2007 (Helman, VanDerhei, and Copeland 2007).

2. Other types of economic research indicate that Americans are better financially prepared for retirement. See, for instance, the augmented stochastic life cycle model in Scholtz, Seshadri, and Khitatrakun (2006).

3. A Monte Carlo estimate for obtaining a 90 percent chance of having adequate retirement income to cover basic living expenses, plus noncovered health care costs. The low end of the value ranges apply for men and the high end values to women. The estimates apply best for older workers, as no assumptions are made for wage growth.

Table 3B3.1   Selected Retirement Confidence Survey findings on retirement preparations among Americans, 1994–2007

Year	Workers who have tried to calculate how much money they need in retirement	Workers who have saved no money for retirement	Workers who are currently saving
1994	31	43	n.a.
1995	32	42	n.a.
1996	29	40	n.a.
1997	33	34	n.a.
1998[a]	42	41	n.a.
1999	48	27	n.a.
2000	53	22	n.a.
2001	44	31	61
2002	38	28	61
2003	43	29	62
2004	42	32	58
2005	42	31	62
2006	42	30	64
2007	43	34	60

Amount of savings American workers think they need for retirement, 2007

Dollar amount	All workers
<250,000	26
250,000–499,999	18
500,000–999,999	20
1 million–1.49 million	7
1.5 million–1.99 million	3
2 million+	8
Don't know	18

Reported total savings and investments among those responding, 2007[b]

Dollar amount	All workers	Age 55+	Current retirees
<10,000	35	26	32
10,000–24,999	13	5	13
25,000–49,999	10	9	10
50,000–99,999	13	11	12
100,000–149,999	8	11	8
150,000–249,999	7	9	12
250,000–499,999	7	11	5
500,000+	7	17	9

n.a. = not available

a. The phrase "and/or your spouse" was added to the question in 1999, accounting for some of the difference between 1998 and 1999.

b. Does not include the value of primary residence or defined benefit plans.

Source: Helman, VanDerhei, and Copeland (2007).

Figure 3.4   Sources of income for the 65+ population, circa 2000

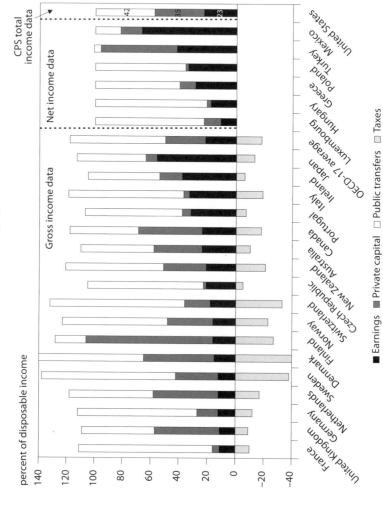

percent of disposable income

CPS total income data

Net income data

Gross income data

■ Earnings   ■ Private capital   □ Public transfers   □ Taxes

CPS = Current Population Survey

Sources: Förster and Mira d'Ercole (2005); US data are from SSA (2002, table 7.1).

Figure 3.5 Sources of income for 65+ population, by income group, circa 2000

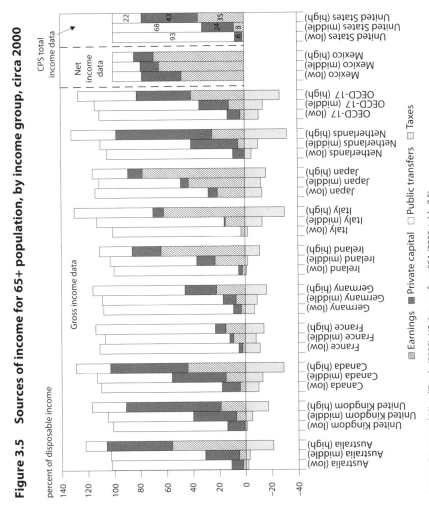

Sources: Förster and Mira d'Ercole (2005); US data are from SSA (2002, table 7.5).

taxation. Unfortunately, comparable data are not available for the United States; however, as the focus here is the relative importance of different sources of income, it is feasible to compare the OECD data with US data from the CPS, which are based on pretax total personal income. US data are on the right in figures 3.4 and 3.5.[42]

These disclaimers notwithstanding, the data indicate large country differences in the sources of income for the elderly.[43] For example, looking at the share of income from earnings, the high shares in Mexico, Turkey, and (less so) Poland reflect the fact that a large number of elderly continue to work (especially in the agricultural sector) past age 65 (see also the very high effective retirement ages in Mexico shown in figure 2.14). The same is likely true in Japan and Ireland. In other continental European countries, Scandinavia, and the United Kingdom, the income share from work is less than 20 percent, and the US share is 23 percent, roughly equal to the OECD-17 average (22 percent). It is, in other words, the case, in terms of the share of income derived from continuing employment, that the US 65+ population do not work more than in other countries; in fact they work pretty much the same as the OECD average. They derive a share of their old age income from work, similar to other English-speaking countries (Australia, Canada, and New Zealand), but far less than in Italy, Ireland, or Japan.

The share of income from capital is somewhat distorted by accounting issues (see appendix 2A for an elaboration on the special case of Finland, for instance). Still, there is a clear pattern in which, for example, Canada, the Netherlands, the Scandinavian countries, the United Kingdom, and the United States have above average shares of income from capital: These are the countries shown in figure 2.2 with substantial total prefunded as-

---

42. The US Census Bureau describes its personal income data as follows: "Data on consumer income collected in the CPS by the Census Bureau cover money income received (exclusive of certain money receipts such as capital gains) before payments for personal income taxes, Social Security, union dues, Medicare deductions, etc. Therefore, *money income does not reflect the fact that some families receive part of their income in the form of non-cash benefits, such as food stamps, health benefits, rent-free housing, and goods produced and consumed on the farm* [emphasis added]. In addition, money income does not reflect the fact that noncash benefits are also received by some non-farm residents, which often take the form of the use of business transportation and facilities, full or partial payments by business for retirement programs, medical and educational expenses, etc. Data users should consider these elements when comparing income levels. Moreover, readers should be aware that for many different reasons, there is a tendency in household surveys for respondents to underreport their income. Based on an analysis of independently derived income estimates, the Census Bureau determined that respondents report income earned from wages or salaries much better than other sources of income and that the reported wage and salary income is nearly equal to independent estimates of aggregate income" (see www.census.gov/population).

43. Due to limited data availability, it is not possible to adjust these data from the 65+ cutoff point to the effective retirement ages, so there may be some distortion of data between countries, especially for the earnings share.

sets toward pension provision (TPATPP). In contrast, France, Germany, and the Mediterranean countries have a very limited share of income from private capital, making these countries far more reliant on public pension provision only.[44] Public transfers are the largest individual income item in all OECD countries (except Turkey and Mexico), underlining the crucial reliance of the elderly on government pension promises. Finally, the data in figures 3.4 and 3.5 reveal substantial differences between countries in the level of taxation of pension benefits.

All the data in figure 3.4, however, are national averages across all income classes. As both earnings potential and capital income differ widely among income classes (quintiles) for the 65+ age group, it is useful to attempt to break down income sources by income class. The results of this breakdown are illustrated in figure 3.5, which shows the sources of income for three different groups age 65 and older: the lowest quintile (0 to 20 percent), the three mid-quintiles (20 to 80 percent), and the top quintile (80 to 100 percent).[45]

Several important issues are illuminated in figure 3.5. First, the share of income (from both earnings and capital) rises dramatically in the highest-income quintile, whereas for the lowest-income quintile (with the exception of Mexico and, less so, Japan), income from earnings plays virtually no role after age 65. Evidently, this is not a group for whom employment beyond the statutory retirement age is an immediately appealing opportunity.

This is perhaps not too surprising for the lowest-income quintile, considering that many jobs held by this group are physically stressful and/or repetitive, making it probable that a large share will be physically worn down by age 65.

Second, the fact that the share of income from earnings is extremely modest (again, Mexico and Japan excluded) for the "middle classes" (i.e., the three middle-income quintiles) as well raises the question of just how much even this group is willing—incentivized—to work beyond age 65. In the United States, just 8 percent of this group's income comes from earnings, suggesting that the frequently mentioned notion that "baby-boomers will revolutionize retirement and broadly retire at will later" may indeed be quite revolutionary. It seems more likely that worker earnings past age 65 will continue to be concentrated in the highest-income quintile[46] and thus that a large majority of the population—80 percent—

---

44. We saw in chapter 2 that in some countries, such as France and Germany, insurance-based assets accounted for a substantial amount of private retirement savings. The income data presented in this section make no distinction between income from private pension fund savings and insurance-based assets.

45. Data for all reporting countries are presented in appendix 3A.

46. This would further be consistent with the findings in Kuhn and Lozano (2005) of a substantial rise in working hours in recent decades among the highest-earning groups in the United States.

will not continue to work much beyond age 65. As a substantial fraction of OECD employment today is in services, it seems implausible that the limited role of old age earnings is rooted in concerns about declining health. It may be that the institutional incentive structures for those 65 and older in OECD countries need to be fundamentally changed—for instance, through higher statutory retirement ages; we elaborate on this subject in chapter 4.

Third, the share of income from capital (including private pensions) is, like earnings, of marginal importance to the lowest-income quintile in all the OECD countries (except Mexico). For this group—irrespective of the large differences in institutional setup and organization between their pension systems—public pension benefits provide essentially all income. This is true even in countries such as the Netherlands, where the main part of the mandatory funded insurance-based scheme falls in this capital category. Any distortion of the findings caused by omitting the drawdown of assets will be very small for this low-income group.[47] Hence for the lowest-income quintile of the elderly, public pensions are the predominant—or only—source of retirement income.

Fourth, looking at the share of income from capital among the middle classes in the OECD, it is somewhat surprising that only in Canada, the Netherlands, and the United Kingdom does this source of income reach one-third of the total (the United States is at just under one-quarter). These findings are especially unexpected, as the level of private pension fund assets in the United States is on par with the Netherlands and substantially above the levels in Canada and the United Kingdom.[48] The explanation for this discrepancy may lie in the fact that US pension fund assets are concentrated more among the highest-income group than is the case in the other three countries. Given that private pensions in this category are mandatory for all in the Netherlands, it is predictable that they would play a larger role in income provision for the middle classes there than in the United States, where voluntary private pensions cover only about 50 percent of wage earners,[49] a figure that is nonetheless higher than the roughly one-third in Canada and the less than half in the United Kingdom (OECD 2005). In earlier periods there was extensive private pension coverage of US middle-class workers in traditional sectors (e.g., steel and auto production), but today this is of less significance for middle-class families in the United States and is essentially nonexistent for the

---

47. Assets in the form of housing are a potential exception to this.

48. These were in percent of GDP, excluding life insurance assets, in 2001: 102.6 in the Netherlands, 96.2 in the United States, 72.5 in the United Kingdom, and 53.3 in Canada.

49. When measured as a share of the total elderly population, the coverage drops substantially. Wu (2006) lists only 31.5 percent of all those 65 and older as recipients of any non–Social Security pension income. AARP (2008) shows how this dropped to 30.7 percent in 2006.

middle classes in the three major continental European economies and Japan. Thus for France, Germany, and Italy, the public sector is basically the only provider of middle-class retirement income, whereas in Japan earnings contribute more than 40 percent.

This breakdown by income reveals that it is only the top quintile of elderly income earners in the OECD that do not rely heavily on the public sector for pension income. Thus we now see that the national averages of the distribution of income sources for the elderly (figure 3.4) paint an overly flattering "average picture" of the importance of both earnings and capital for pension income. In reality, this importance does not reach beyond the top income quintile.

Based on the data illustrated in figure 3.5, it is clear that public pension reforms in the OECD and certainly in the United States would face serious political obstacles as they may threaten the retirement income of essentially the entire middle class. A high degree of political consensus for change would be necessary to implement major pension reforms, consensus that would be very hard to reach in the absence of an imminent crisis. This explains why Social Security reform is the third rail of American politics. See box 3.4 on who gets what, from where, and when in life.

Intergenerational Transfers

We now shift our focus from traditional intragenerational poverty and income issues to longer-term intergenerational transfers and the related distributional issues.

Generational Accounting

As illustrated above, there is quite a large difference between how many resources pension systems in different countries transfer intragenerationally (i.e., within a given age cohort). Yet in this era of aging populations, with more retirees and fewer workers to come, a more pertinent concern is the level of current and future intergenerational transfers (i.e., between age cohorts of different age, typically from younger to older generations). This concern is at the core of the concept of "generational accounting," originally proposed by Alan Auerbach, Jagadeesh Gokhale, and Laurence Kotlikoff in a series of papers in the early 1990s (Auerbach, Gokhale, and Kotlikoff 1991, 1992, 1994).[50] Generational accounting

50. Generational accounting as originally presented by the authors is completely silent on intragenerational transfers and simply assumes that any burden is distributed evenly across all members of a given age cohort. It further assumes that any future burden is distributed evenly across all future generations.

Box 3.4   Who gets what, from where, and when in life?

Individual benefits accruing from social spending, whether public or private, are usually closely associated with age. Income assessments using cross-sectional analyses combining household microdata and tax-benefit simulations have shown that social benefit expenditures, net of taxes, remain very low until the age of retirement.[1] The explanation for this bias in favor of retirees is clear: Public spending is typically intentionally redistributive across the life cycle, especially targeting this older group, and retirees, in the case of an insurance-based pension system, receive their previously paid-in contributions in retirement, usually in their 60s. By and large, in terms of expenditures, "social protection" means "old age protection."

It is instructive to compare the scope of this intentional life cycle redistribution across different countries and income groups. This is done in figure 3B4.1, based on data from Dang and colleagues (2006). (The discussion in this box also draws extensively on their insights.) The three components of the figure show, for selected OECD countries, the age distribution of total social spending net of taxation, excluding health care but including public and private pension benefits, sickness and invalid benefits, unemployment benefits, housing benefits, social assistance, and in-work benefits as a percentage of average spending for the total population (figure 3B4.1a) and for the bottom (figure 3B4.1b) and top (figure 3B4.1c) quintiles. A reading above 100 percent indicates that the values of benefits paid to individuals in a given age group exceed those of the population as a whole, or in other words that redistribution favors this group. It is important to note that this figure illustrates only the relative internal redistribution of each country's social expenditure and cannot be used to compare levels of gross social spending between countries, on which continental European countries spend far more as a share of GDP than does the United States.

Figure 3B4.1a shows that US social spending is significantly higher for older age groups than in other OECD countries, reflecting the fact that Social Security is the largest nationally comprehensive social protection program in America.[2] In contrast, social spending for working age populations in other OECD countries, with more comprehensive unemployment benefit systems, is more evenly distributed than in the United States. In figure 3B4.1b, this is particularly evident for the lowest-income quintile, where US social spending is far more redistributive toward older age groups than elsewhere in the OECD. Figure 3B4.1c shows, however, that this is not the case among the top income quintiles, as social spending on the highest-earning elderly in France is on par with that in the United States. It is further noteworthy that the earlier statutory and effective retirement ages in

Box 3.4   Who gets what, from where, and when in life? *(continued)*

France and Italy are reflected in a spike in social spending for those over 50, earlier than in other countries.

In the United States, the top income quintile receives a higher relative share of social spending in old age than the bottom income quintile: 440 percent of the average from age 65+ versus 310 percent. This in all likelihood reflects the contributory insurance aspects of Social Security. As a comparison, more universal, redistributive social spending, as in the United Kingdom or the Scandinavian countries, results in the top-income elderly receiving only 170 and 280 percent, respectively, of average social spending.

The broad-based social spending measure in figures 3B4.1a to 3B4.1c illustrates the emphasis on old age social protection in the United States when measured against beneficiaries in other age groups. High-income Americans over age 65 benefit relatively more from redistribution of social spending not only than elderly cohorts in most other OECD countries but also Americans in the bottom income quintile. These findings suggest that any cuts in US social expenditure would be most equitably targeted toward this group.

---

1. See, for instance, Gottshalk and Smeeding (2000) and Förster and Mira d'Ercole (2005).

2. Social Security is run by the federal government (through the Social Security Administration), whereas other US social assistance programs (e.g., Medicare/Medicaid and Unemployment Insurance) are national in scope but administered locally by state governments (with federal grants for funding).

provides an approach to overcome the deficiencies of the traditional definition of government deficit by illuminating the intergenerational transfers in unfunded pay-as-you-go pension promises.[51]

Funded pension systems and promises do not generally entail any generational transfer worth mentioning,[52] an evident financial advantage

---

51. Other policy areas, such as revenue-neutral changes to the tax system and government-induced adjustments to the market valuations of real and financial assets, may also involve intergenerational transfers not captured by the traditional deficit measures. For an elaboration, see Auerbach, Gokhale, and Kotlikoff (1994).

52. Issues concerning differences in tax treatment of contributions to funded pension systems muddy this picture a little, as ultimately any tax breaks for such contributions will have to be paid by someone! Frequently, however, tax advantages for contributions are paid by the same generation upon retrieval, yielding a very limited net gain. See chapter 7 for an elaboration of this issue.

Figure 3B4.1a   Net public benefit expenditures, total population, by age group, late 1990s

net benefit expenditure, percent of total population average

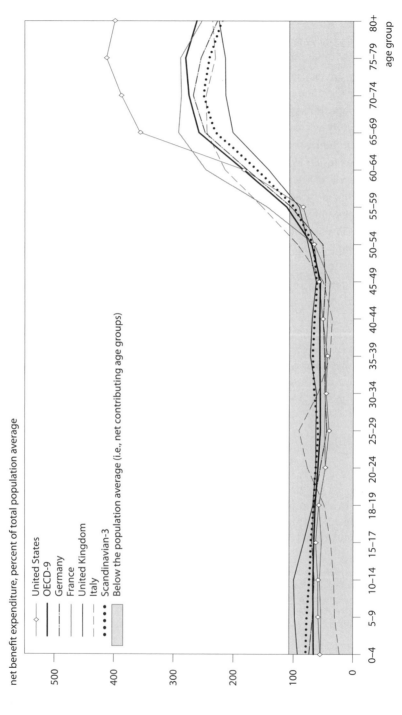

Source: Dang et al. (2006).

Figure 3B4.1b Net public benefit expenditures, bottom income quintile, by age group, late 1990s

net benefit expenditure, percent of total population average

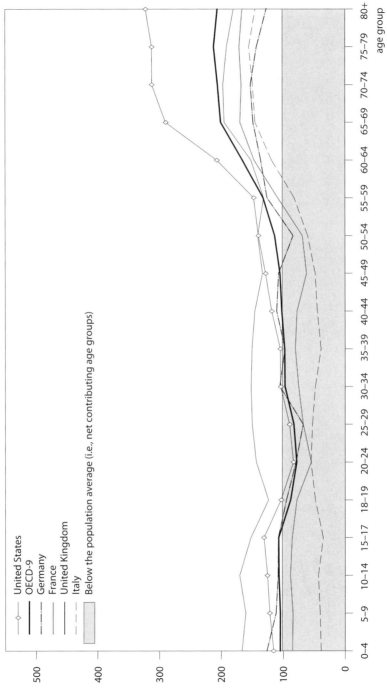

Legend:
- United States
- OECD-9
- Germany
- France
- United Kingdom
- Italy
- Below the population average (i.e., net contributing age groups)

Source: Dang et al. (2006).

Figure 3B4.1c Net public benefit expenditures, top income quintile, by age group, late 1990s

net benefit expenditure, percent of total population average

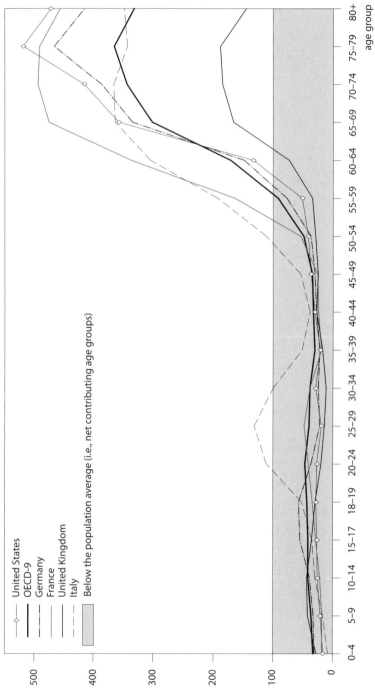

Legend:
- United States
- OECD-9
- Germany
- France
- United Kingdom
- Italy
- Below the population average (i.e., net contributing age groups)

age group: 0–4, 5–9, 10–14, 15–17, 18–19, 20–24, 25–29, 30–34, 35–39, 40–44, 45–49, 50–54, 55–59, 60–64, 65–69, 70–74, 75–79, 80+

Source: Dang et al. (2006).

of such systems. Instead, generational accounts estimate the value of what the average member of each age cohort can expect (on a net basis) to receive from/pay to the government (including state and local levels) over their remaining lifetime, as well as what future generations will receive/pay. It thus becomes possible to compare what newborns today will receive from/pay to the government with the benefits/payments of future newborns. Estimating the net future burden of government for both living and future generations is done through the "government's intertemporal budget constraint," which posits that the government's spending on goods and services cannot surpass the sum of three items: (1) current government net wealth, (2) the present value of net payments of current generations, and (3) the present value of net payments of future generations. In other words, the government must eventually pay for its spending through either the resources it already commands (#1) or those it plans to extract from current (#2) or future generations (#3).[53]

Like any exercise in long-term government financial projections, generational accounting is sensitive to assumptions concerning government expenditure growth, discount rates, economic growth rates, and demographic developments. However, one particularly crucial issue is the treatment of government education expenditures: Are they treated as consumption or as a transfer to a particular age cohort (like Social Security benefits, for example)?[54] The answer matters because it affects the treatment of PAYGO pension system first generations.

As a matter of simple mathematical reasoning, generations that retire soon after the foundation of a PAYGO pension system—say, Americans retiring in the first decades after Social Security was set up in 1935 (see box 3.1)—receive a large transfer simply due to fortuitous timing, as they are entitled to benefits until death after paying in only a few years (rather

---

53. This extremely superficial walk-through of the central assumptions of generational accounting hardly does justice to its methodology. See Auerbach, Gokhale, and Kotlikoff (1991, 1992, 1994) for in-depth methodological descriptions.

54. In their original description of generational accounting, Auerbach, Gokhale, and Kotlikoff (1991) treated only OASDI, Hospital Insurance, Welfare, Unemployment Insurance, and food stamps as transfers or receipts from the government and thus almost invariably had Americans remaining net contributors to the government until approximately the age of retirement at 60–65. In later estimations (e.g., Kotlikoff and Raffelhüschen 1999), several versions of generational accounts treated education expenditures as either consumption or a transfer. The European Commission (1999), which estimated generational accounts for 12 EU members in 1995, included educational expenditures as a transfer and reached estimates showing that net transfers to Europeans peak at around age 25, when they have enjoyed the full benefits of government education expenditures and not yet, on average, begun to pay full taxes. Thereafter their net transfers for their remaining lifetime declines, with tax payments exceeding benefits received until approximately age 60, after which pension benefits cause the net balance to rise again toward (but not reaching) zero at the end of their lives.

than their entire working life). This is also the origin of the "legacy debt" described by Peter Diamond and Peter Orszag (2005).[55] An illustrative, if extreme, example is the case of Ida May Fuller, the first American to receive a monthly Social Security check, in January 1940. Ms. Fuller worked for three years under the Social Security program and paid total accumulated taxes during that time of $24.75. She went on to live until the age of 100, and during her last 35 years received a total of $22,888.92 in Social Security benefits, yielding her a lifetime return from her three-year participation in Social Security of nearly thousand-fold![56]

On the other hand, as pointed out by Antoine Bommier and colleagues (2004), the same American generations that thus received a large windfall from participation in the upward transfers (i.e., from young to old) of Social Security (and later Medicare) incurred substantial lifetime losses by not being able to reap the benefits of public education (a downward transfer from old to young), which only really took off in America in the 20th century, even as later in their lives these same generations (who had grown up without public education) helped finance it through their general tax payments.[57] Given the relatively simultaneous expansion of both public education and old age pensions in many OECD countries during the first half of the 20th century, this is not a uniquely US situation.

Generational accounting, therefore, is open to criticism on a number of accounts (Haveman 1994, Diamond 1996, Buiter 1997), and its specific assumptions are crucial. Yet it has prompted numerous countries (26 in 2000, according to Gokhale et al. 2000) to use the methodology to estimate the burden of future generations relative to those alive today. Briefly summarized, comparative studies indicate that the vast majority of OECD countries run sizable generational imbalances, with future generations facing either significantly higher taxes or lower government benefits. For instance, Kotlikoff and Bernd Raffelhüschen (1999) present results from 22 developed countries (of which 19 are also members of the OECD) and find that only three do not exhibit generational imbalances.[58] Undoubtedly, these research efforts have helped to raise public and political awareness of these otherwise largely hidden transfers between generations.

---

55. Diamond and Orszag (2005) estimate this legacy debt at $11.5 trillion. Leimer (1994) estimates that all Americans born between 1876 and 1937 will receive more than $8.1 trillion more from Social Security than they paid in. See also CBO (2006).

56. See SSA, Historical Background and Development of Social Security, at www.ssa.gov/history for more details.

57. Becker and Murphy (1988) hypothesize that, introduced separately, neither public education nor Social Security may be Pareto-improving reforms but that they may be if deliberated together.

58. Auerbach, Kotlikoff, and Leibfritz (1999) find a similar overwhelming share of imbalances for a smaller (overlapping) sample of countries. See also European Commission (1999).

Time Spent in Retirement—A Transfer of Leisure to Current Generations?

A comprehensive measure of intergenerational transfers like the generational accounts above depends on the assumptions built into the model used to make the estimations. Other, more straightforward measures can illustrate the differences among generations in the transfers they can expect to enjoy during their lifetimes. One such is time spent in retirement. Economic theory assumes that rational actors will choose preferred levels of work and leisure and thus attach a value to leisure. Traditional labor economics shows that the labor supply curve may be backward bending as the lure of higher wages encouraging more hours of work is offset by the fact that higher wages mean higher incomes with which to buy more leisure time.[59] Furthermore, rising life expectancies grant workers more total time. How might rational workers respond to the additional years of life and how should governments and societies respond in terms of retirement pension policies? Should pension programs be designed to allow workers to retire at the same age regardless of their life expectancy? Or should workers be expected to work more years?[60] Bluntly put, which groups get to enjoy the benefits of rising life expectancies?

To address this question we start with changes in life expectancy across the OECD countries. Life expectancy at birth has lengthened dramatically in the last generation (1970 to 2004), rising 8.1 years for men and 5.7 years for women in the United States. For the OECD as a whole, the increase is slightly larger (the straight average of 30 members), at 8.3 and 7.9 years of additional life, respectively. Life expectancy at birth is not the measure most relevant to pension analysis, however, because quite a bit of the increase has been the result of reduced infant mortality and lower death rates for young people. Life expectancy at age 65 is the more relevant measure for pension considerations. The rise in this category has been smaller, only 4 and 3 years, respectively, for men and women in the United States, while the OECD, on average, saw a corresponding lengthening of 3.5 and 4 years over the period. As with other data in this book, the range of variation across the OECD is quite wide. As shown in figure 3.6, for example, from 1970 to 2004 the expected life of a Japanese woman at age 65 rose by 8 years, about 2.5 times more than the increase for an

---

59. Different economic choices among countries are frequently explained by differences in the "preference for leisure." The most notorious explanation is that today's Europeans work so much less than Americans because they put a higher emphasis on leisure than do Americans. See Blanchard (2004) for this explanation of differences in labor input between Europe and the United States.

60. In chapter 4 we discuss in detail the economic incentives that the elderly face when deciding their age of retirement.

Figure 3.6 Increase in life expectancy at age 65, 1970–2004 (years)

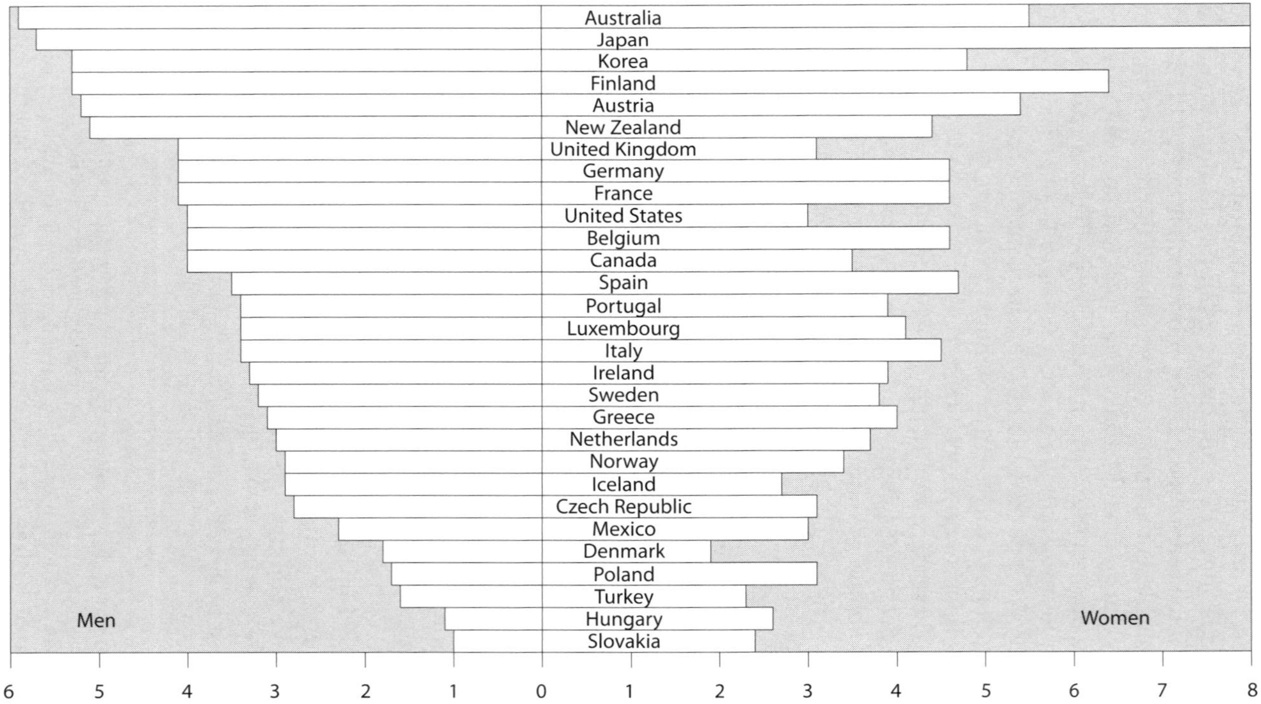
Australia
Japan
Korea
Finland
Austria
New Zealand
United Kingdom
Germany
France
United States
Belgium
Canada
Spain
Portugal
Luxembourg
Italy
Ireland
Sweden
Greece
Netherlands
Norway
Iceland
Czech Republic
Mexico
Denmark
Poland
Turkey
Hungary
Slovakia
Men
Women
6
5
4
3
2
1
0
1
2
3
4
5
6
7
8

Note: Data from 1970, 2004, or nearest available year.

Source: OECD Health Indicators, 2006.

American woman and over four times more than for a Danish woman. During the same period, an Australian man around retirement age experienced an expected increase of 6 years of life, one-half more than that of American men and six times that of a Slovak man.

Even the smaller numerical increases in life expectancies for the 65-year-olds translate into hefty rates of change. The six extra years of life for Australian men, for instance, equal a 50 percent increase over the period, or almost double the rate of change for American men. Thus in terms of future pension liabilities, the rate of increases in life expectancies is the best indicator of the rate of increases in pension-related liabilities.

Because of differences in the effective age of retirement illustrated in figure 2.13, however, the spread across countries of years in retirement is much greater than the spread of life expectancy. This is illustrated in figure 3.7, which shows for 2004 a rough estimation of the years from the age when a person, on average, leaves the labor market to expected death.[61]

Differences are sizable—Belgian women can expect to live almost 27 years in retirement, about a decade longer than Korean women. French men, meanwhile, can look forward to just over 21 years in retirement, four years longer than American men, nearly seven years more than Japanese men, and more than a decade longer than Korean men.

Not only are these differences in time spent in retirement considerable between the sexes (women typically both retire earlier and live longer) and between countries (Austrians, Belgians, and the French spend more time in retirement than do Americans or almost anyone else, while the Japanese, Irish, and Portuguese spend noticeably less), they also give rise to politically important additional distributional challenges both between generations and between different groups in society.

Even as life expectancy has been rising, the effective age of retirement in nearly all OECD countries has declined. In the United States, for instance, the effective retirement age for men has declined by three to four years, from over 68 around 1970 (figure 3.8) to about 64 today. And the decline in effective retirement ages over the same period in continental Europe was generally larger than in the United States. The absolute decline has been less pronounced for women who, in earlier decades, tended to leave the labor market significantly earlier than men; they still do, but the gap is smaller.

Figure 3.9 combines the data in figure 3.7 with similar estimates for 1970 to show the increase—from both rising life expectancy and declining

---

61. The OECD source notes the following concerning these data: "These estimates of the average number of years that workers can expect to spend in retirement are likely to be underestimates. They are based on "period" estimates of life expectancy, which do not take into account future declines in mortality rates but only contemporaneous mortality rates by age and gender. Cohort estimates of life expectancy are consistently higher when these declines are taken into account" (OECD 2006, chapter 2, footnote 3).

Figure 3.7　Estimated years spent in retirement, 2004

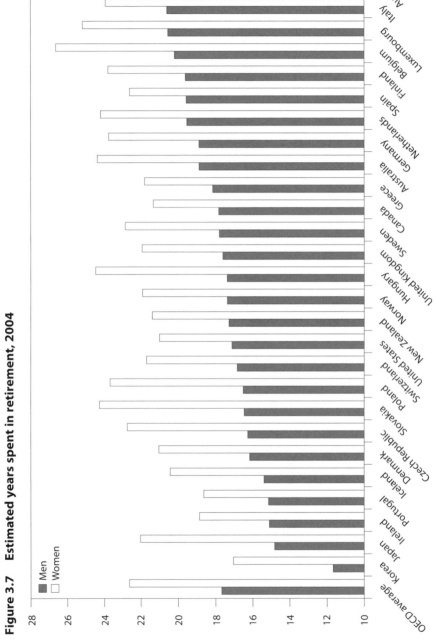

Source: OECD (2006).

Figure 3.8 Average effective retirement age, selected OECD countries, 1965–2005

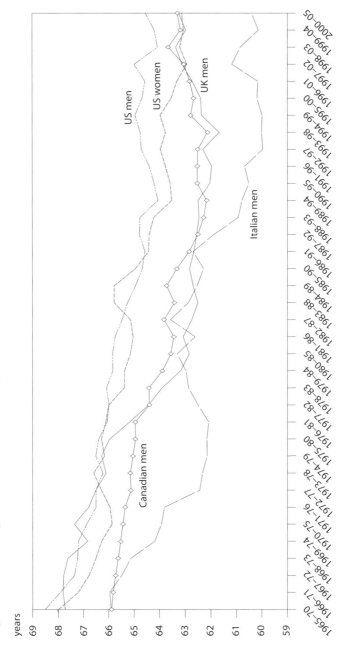

Notes: The average effective age of retirement is calculated as a weighted average of (net) withdrawals from the labor market at different ages over a 5-year period for workers initially aged 40 and over. In order to abstract from compositional effects in the age structure of the population, labor force withdrawals are estimated based on changes in labor force participation rates rather than labor force levels. These changes are calculated for each (synthetic) cohort divided into 5-year age groups. The estimates for US women are less reliable as they have been derived from interpolations of census data rather than from annual labor force surveys.

Source: OECD estimates, available at www.oecd.org.

Figure 3.9   Increase in expected years in retirement, 1970–2004

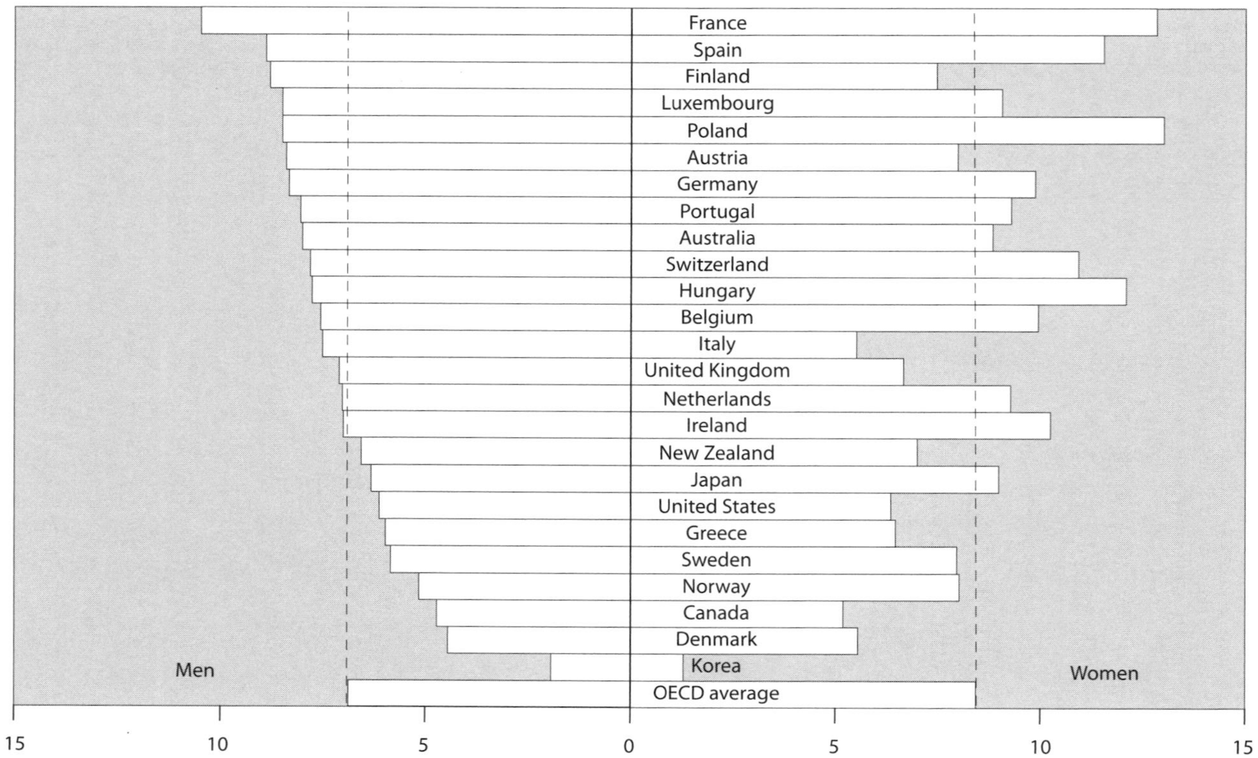

Source: OECD (2006).

age of retirement—between 1970 and 2004 in the average amount of time spent in retirement across countries. Substantial changes took place in most countries, especially for women.[62]

The rise in life expectancy is, of course, a benefit to society, but the fact that French men who retired in 2004 can look forward to more than a decade of additional time in retirement than their countrymen in 1970 indicates a very large increase in the number of years of life spent outside the labor market for the currently retiring generation, relative to earlier ones. And women in six countries have an additional decade or more in retirement. In some countries (e.g., Canada, Denmark, Greece, and the United States), the additional expected years of leisure for today's retirees are not as large—about 4 to 6 years for both sexes. Only Korea has seen a relatively marginal increase in the number of years spent in retirement. Overall, the increase in life expectancy in the OECD countries has been passed on in the form of longer retirements. This is evident in figure 3.10, which breaks down the total increase in years in retirement from 1970 to 2004 for men based on the rise in life expectancy and the decline in effective retirement age.[63]

Figure 3.10 shows that the composition of the increase in years spent in retirement varies substantially among OECD countries. On average, the split is close to 50-50 between the rise in life expectancy and decline in effective retirement age. In countries like France, Hungary, Poland, and Spain, the decline in effective retirement age makes up the bulk of the total rise, whereas increases in life expectancy dominate in Australia, Canada, Japan, and the United States. Only Korea—with the smallest increase in years spent in retirement over the period—has in recent decades seen healthy financially sustainable development, as an increase in the effective retirement age after 1970 (illustrated by the *negative decrease* in figure 3.10) acted as a partial offset to the large increase in life expectancy. Many other OECD countries are now trying to emulate this Korean experience.

The fiscal impact of this increase in years of retirement adds impetus to OECD country efforts to raise retirement ages. It is important to

---

62. If estimates of the decline in "work performed" from one generation to the next were carried out on the basis of total lifetime hours worked, rather than simply by effective age of retirement, currently retiring generations in many countries would invariably be shown to be in an even more advantageous relative position. This is because of the decline in average annual work hours from 1970 to 2004, as well as the later entry into the workforce due to more time spent in education, of more recent retirees. As such, the relative generational transfer of leisure time to currently retiring generations presented here, which concerns itself with only the part related to the retirement decision, is an underestimate of the total magnitude of the transfer.

63. Figure 3.10 is an approximation, as it subtracts a country's rise in life expectancy at age 65 from the total increase in years spent in retirement from the age of withdrawal from the labor market. As this age is typically lower than 65, the increases in life expectancies illustrated in 3.10 are likely biased downward.

Figure 3.10 Components of increase in years in retirement for men, 1970–2004

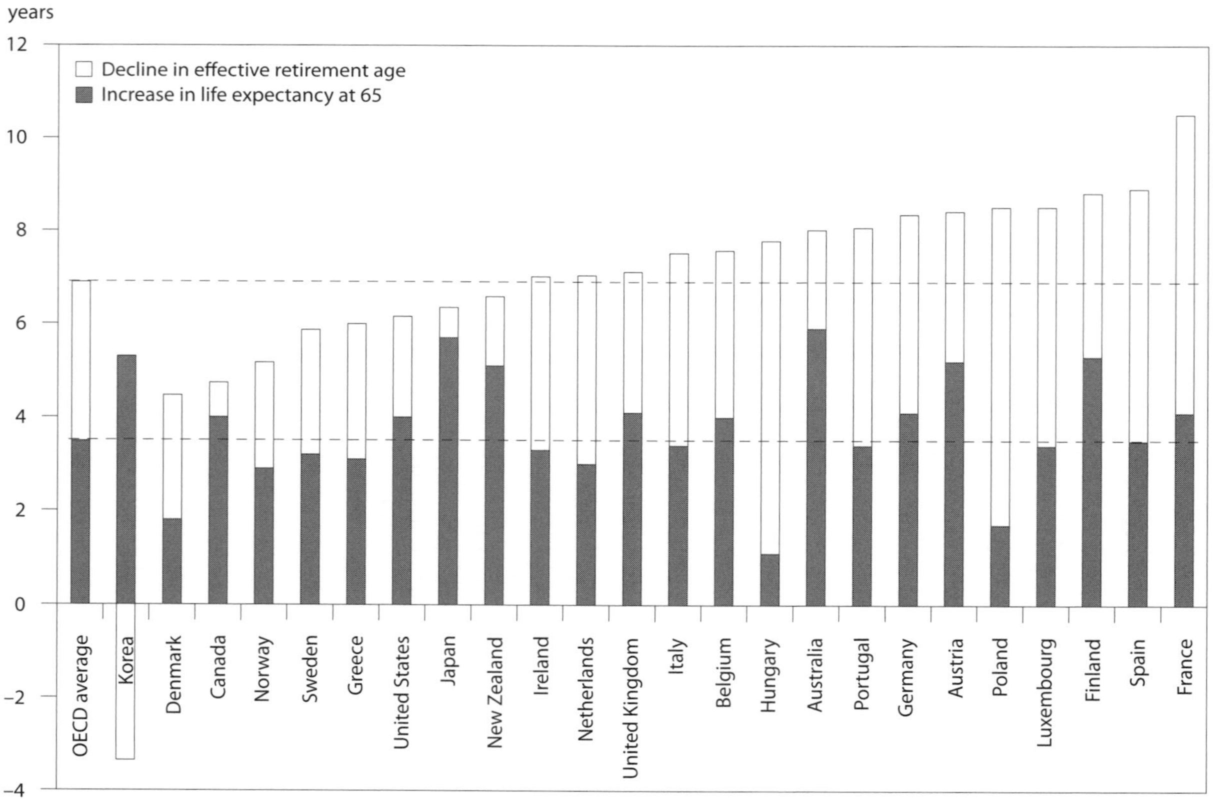
years
12
10
8
6
4
2
0
−2
−4
Decline in effective retirement age
Increase in life expectancy at 65
OECD average
Korea
Denmark
Canada
Norway
Sweden
Greece
United States
Japan
New Zealand
Ireland
Netherlands
United Kingdom
Italy
Belgium
Hungary
Australia
Portugal
Germany
Austria
Poland
Luxembourg
Finland
Spain
France

Sources: OECD (2006); OECD Health Database, 2007.

distinguish between (1) *prefixed gradual rises* in the age at which an individual is entitled to a full (or reduced early) pension, such as those initiated in the US Social Security system by President Ronald Reagan in 1983, which will see this eligibility age rise in the United States from 65 in 2000 to 67 in 2027,[64] and (2) *explicit life expectancy links to retirement ages*. While the former obviously cuts the amount of time in retirement future retirees can expect, these predetermined rises in retirement ages rarely account for sudden unexpected increases in life expectancies and are usually capped at politically determined levels of minimum voter pain. They may, therefore, not provide any long-term guarantees of fiscal sustainability. Thus even as the retirement age in US Social Security is scheduled to rise a total of two years from 2000 to 2027, average life expectancy at 65 for Americans rose more than two years over the past 27 years (although the rise is unevenly distributed between men and women).[65]

Many OECD countries have in recent years scheduled rises in their earliest and full eligibility ages of the former prefixed gradual rises type. As such, they have implemented this aspect of the 1983 Social Security reform, too. However, these types of reforms have a relatively limited ambition, as they lack the direct link to life expectancies; they merely attempt to reverse the practice of current generations that retire prematurely (as early as their mid-50s) by raising retirement ages. Many reforms as a result will not provide much more than a first step toward a long-term fiscally sustainable pension system, and many countries may need to further increase their retirement ages in the future. Table 3.1 provides a nonexhaustive listing of such recent reforms in OECD countries.

It is clear from table 3.1 that the phasing in of later retirement ages is for political reasons generally set far in the future. This mirrors the 17-year US preannouncement of rises in the full Social Security eligibility age in 1983. Given their later decision to raise retirement ages, it is evident from table 3.1 that only a few countries have, similar to the United States in 2000, actually started to raise the retirement age already. But the large size of baby-boomer generations entering retirement in many countries means the timing of retirement age increases matters materially for the sustainability impact of these reforms. If, through excessively long phase-in

---

64. The Social Security phase-in works such that those born in 1937 or earlier may retire at the age of 65. This rises by two months per earlier year of birth between birth years 1938 and 1943, so that for those born in 1942, the age of retirement with a full Social Security pension is 65 years and 10 months. For birth years 1943–54, the age of retirement with a full pension is fixed at 66, before rising again by two months per birth year, so that people born in 1960 or later will face a retirement age of 67 (i.e., be able to retire with a full pension only in 2027). See Social Security Administration's website, www.ssa.gov/retirechartred.

65. The most recent data for the period 1976–2003 show a rise from 13.8 to 16.8 for men and from 18.1 to 19.8 for women. See OECD Health Division, October 2006 Update, www.ecosante.org.

Table 3.1   Recent phased-in raises of the retirement age in selected OECD countries

Country	Reform type	Affected group	Period of phase-in
Australia	Full eligibility age: From 60 to 65	Women	1995–2014
	Earliest age: From 55 to 60 (for mandatory occupational pensions)	All	2015–25
Austria	Full eligibility age: From 60 to 65	Women	2023–33
	Earliest age: From 60 to 62	Men	2000–05
	Earliest age: From 55 to 62	Women	2000–27
Belgium	Full eligibility age: From 60 to 65	Women in private sector	1997–2009
Czech Republic	Full eligibility age: From 60 to 63	Men	1996–2012
	Full eligibility age: From 53–57 to 59–63	Women	1996–2012
Denmark	Earliest age: From 60 to 62	All	2019–22
	Full eligibility age: From 65 to 67	All	2024–27
Germany	Earliest age: Reduced from 63 to 62	Men	By 2010
	Earliest age: From 60 to 62	Women	2011–16
	Full eligibility age: From 65–67	All	2012–29
Italy	Full eligibility age: From 58 to 60	All	2008–11
Japan	Full eligibility age: From 60 to 65 for flat rate pension	Men	2001–13
	Full eligibility age: From 60 to 65 for flat rate pension	Women	2006–18
	Full eligibility age: From 60 to 65 for earnings-related pension	Men	2013–25
	Full eligibility age: From 60 to 65 for earnings-related pension	Women	2018–30
Korea	Full eligibility age: From 60 to 65	All	2013–33
	Earliest age: From 55 to 60	All	2013–33
Switzerland	Full eligibility age: From 62 to 64	Women	2000–05
United Kingdom	Full eligibility age: From 60 to 65	Women	2010–20
	Earliest age: From 60 to 65 (pension credit)	Men	2010–20
	Full eligibility age for state pension: From 65 to 68	All	2024–46
United States	Full eligibility age: From 65 to 67	All	2000–27

Note: In countries with insurance-based systems, it is possible to de facto raise the official retirement age for full pension eligibility by simply raising the number of years in which individuals need to have been contributing to the system. Such changes do not concern retirement ages explicitly and are thus excluded from this table. An example would be the rise in the number of contribution years for French public servants to (the private sector level of) 40 years, up from 37.5, for full pension eligibility in 2003.

Sources: OECD (2006); BBC News, http://news.bbc.co.uk; IPE News, www.ipe.com.

periods, decision makers let the large generations retire at an early age, at least part of the fiscal impact of the reform will be lost, as large generations will "slip through" into retirement.[66] Thus the fact that US increases in the full pension eligibility age will have been fully phased in relatively early is a fiscal advantage for the country.

Delays in phasing in increases in retirement ages have had spectacular intergenerational distributional effects. If OECD policymakers had made the decision as early as 1970 to link life expectancies and retirement ages, the effects would already have been dramatic. Life expectancies and retirement ages can be linked in several ways (see below). If, for instance, there had been a decision to freeze the 1970 ratio of "time in retirement" to "time not in retirement," a measure that correlates rises in life expectancy and in retirement age, then the average retirement age in the OECD would have had to rise substantially from the lower 60s to age 70 by 2004, as illustrated in figure 3.11.[67]

The political feasibility of having maintained such a stable ratio since 1970 is probably quite low. Certainly no American administration would have contemplated overseeing the gradual rise of US retirement ages to almost 72 years of age for men and 69 for women today, and French presidents would probably have had a challenging time persuading their countrymen that they would have to work more than a decade longer in 2004 than was actually the case! On the other hand, we do feel that the implications of figure 3.11—namely, that earlier generations spent a much smaller proportion of their lives in retirement than today—ought to feature more prominently among the public arguments in favor of raising retirement ages in many OECD countries.

This discussion is part of our assessment of fairness, because we are looking at how societies allocate the benefits of additional years of life among generations. In the OECD, the benefit has been given in full to current retirees, who are relying on current workers to pay the cost of additional years of pension benefits. This has occurred with little if any thought of fiscal sustainability because it has been the politically attractive option. However, this trend is starting to change. Edward Whitehouse (2007) notes that a growing number of OECD countries (13 out of 30) have begun to directly and indirectly link mandatory pensions to life expectancy, over

66. See box 3.5 for a blatant example of this type of "reform timing" in Denmark.

67. Figure 3.11 is created by first taking the ratio of expected years in retirement in 1970 (from figure 3.10) over the full life expectancy for people who reached age 65 in 1970. The full life expectancy at 65 is used as the denominator, as full life expectancies at the effective age of retirement in 1970 are not available. However, as the effective retirement ages in 1970 were close to age 65, this data inaccuracy is unlikely to affect the results substantially. Second, the full life expectancy for people who reached age 65 in 2004 is multiplied by (1 − the ratio from the first step) to yield the effective retirement age in 2004 had the ratio of time in retirement been the same as in 1970.

Figure 3.11a Observed and implied effective retirement ages for men, 2004

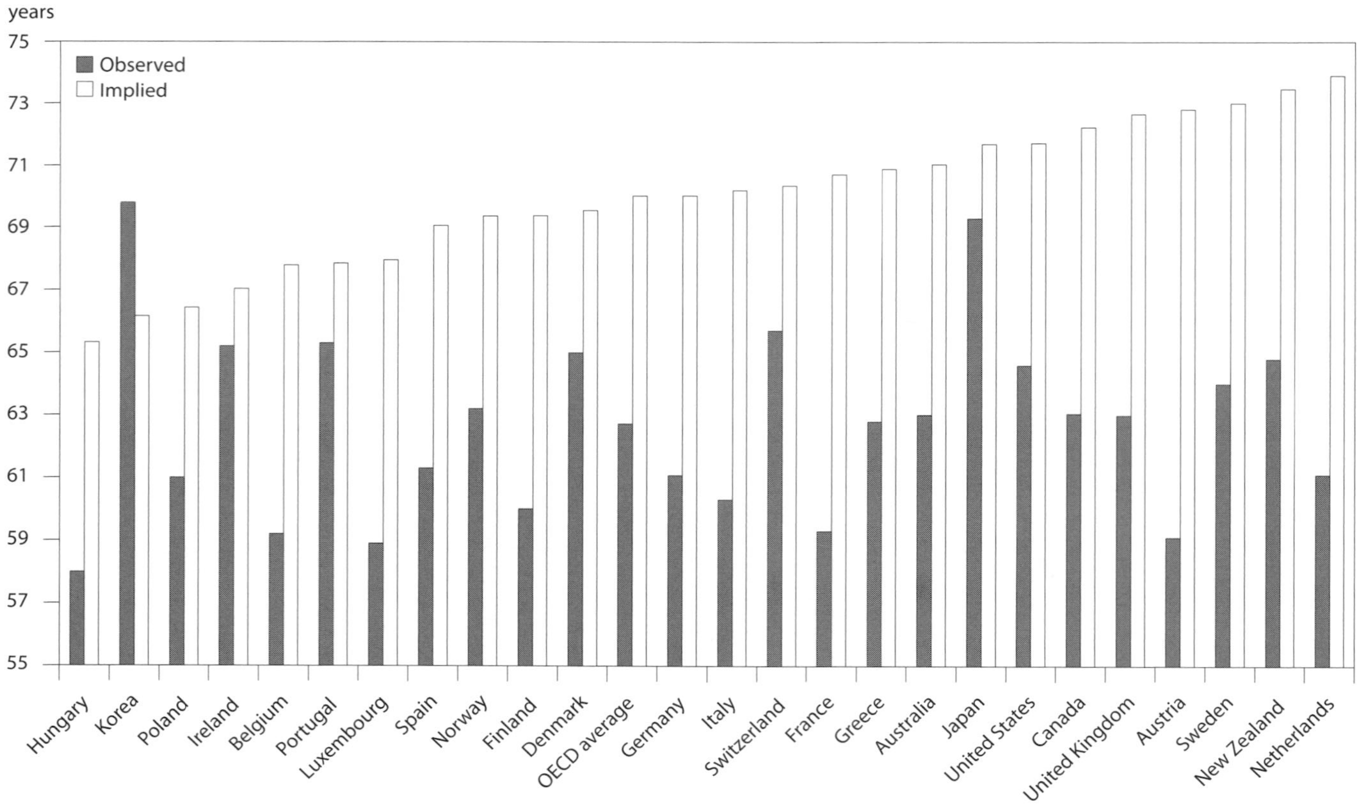
years
75
73
71
69
67
65
63
61
59
57
55
Observed
Implied
Hungary
Korea
Poland
Ireland
Belgium
Portugal
Luxembourg
Spain
Norway
Finland
Denmark
OECD average
Germany
Italy
Switzerland
France
Greece
Australia
Japan
United States
Canada
United Kingdom
Austria
Sweden
New Zealand
Netherlands

Sources: OECD (2006); authors' calculations.

Figure 3.11b Observed and implied effective retirement ages for women, 2004

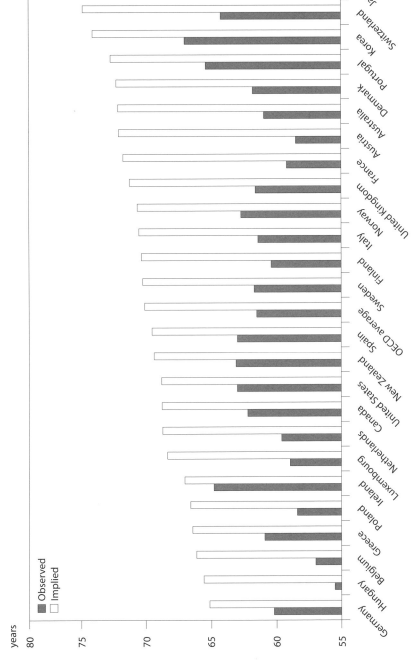

years

- Observed
- Implied

Sources: OECD (2006); authors' calculations.

and above the prefixed increases listed in table 3.1. He describes four ways to link life expectancies to mandatory pensions (Whitehouse 2007):

- *Defined Contribution (DC) Plans.* Countries can introduce mandatory DC systems as a substitute for earlier defined benefit (DB) pensions. As DC benefits are directly related to the available capital at the time of retirement, the link between life expectancy in retirement and benefits is clear. Seven OECD countries have in recent years introduced this type of life expectancy link to their mandatory pension system.[68]

- *Notional DC Plans.* Three OECD countries (Italy, Poland, and Sweden) have introduced these types of systems, which link payouts to life expectancy in the same way as funded DC plans, even though there is no actual funding created by worker contributions (see chapter 6).

- *Links to Benefit Levels.* Finland, Germany, and Portugal have introduced automatic adjustment mechanisms, predominantly driven by changes in life expectancies, to the benefit levels of their mandatory pension systems (see also the discussion below).

- *Direct Eligibility Age Qualifications.* The systems in Denmark (see box 3.5) and France (box 3.6) feature the most intuitive link between life expectancy and retirement ages. Denmark will explicitly raise the earliest and full pension eligibility ages in accordance with life expectancies, once prefixed increases are fully phased in by 2027. Functionally similar, France will link to life expectancy the number of quarters of contributions required to be eligible for a full pension. As in Denmark, this linking will occur once prefixed increases in the number of quarters of contributions (up to 164 quarters, or 41 years) have been implemented in 2012. After 2012, required contributions for a full pension will rise in such a way that the ratio of expected time in retirement and required period of contributions for full pension eligibility (i.e., working life) will remain constant at approximately 0.5.[69] The long-term target in France will be that recipients of a full pension must have worked roughly twice as long as they are projected to live in retirement.[70] In other words, one might superficially say that the long-term target for the French mandatory pension system is an individual old age support ratio of 2.

---

68. Whitehouse (2007) identifies Australia, Denmark, Hungary, Mexico, Norway, Poland, Slovakia, and Sweden. We return to this subject in chapter 5.

69. The projected life expectancy at age 61 for France in 2012 is 21.8 years, equaling 53 percent of the required 41-year contribution period for a full pension (Whitehouse 2007, 34).

70. See also Jeger and Lelievre (2005).

Box 3.5   The 2006 Danish pension reform and the future retirement age

In June 2006, an overwhelming majority (80+ percent) in the Danish parliament passed a series of reforms to the Danish pension system to raise the average retirement age and keep people in the labor market longer.[1]

Until this reform, Denmark had a dual public pension system: an early retirement system, allowing people to retire at age 60,[2] and a universal tax–financed old age pension system with a statutory retirement age of 65.[3] The reform maintains the dual system but raises the ages both for access to early retirement (by six months each year from 2019–22 to 62 years of age) and for universal old age pension (by six months per year from 2024–27 to 67 years of age). These prefixed scheduled rises are similar to other such reforms (shown in table 3.1) that reverse unsustainably low retirement ages (including a reduction in Denmark as recently as 2004 from 67 to 65 years of age in the universal old age pension).

Nonetheless, the 2006 reform created a loophole that undermines the attempt to restore generational fairness. More than a quarter of the entire Danish population will be able to retire during the 65–window in place from 2004–24.[4] This policy change illustrates how the political process of pension reform necessitates providing special advantages for powerful voting constituencies—in Denmark nearly all of the large baby-boomer generation will be able to retire at age 65, rather than at 67, like preceding and subsequent generations.

However, the more interesting aspect of this reform is the explicit link to life expectancies it provides in the period after these predetermined and scheduled rises in retirement ages in the mid-2020s. The law explicitly states the aim to ensure that the period in early/universal retirement remains at approximately 19.5 years measured at age 60, irrespective of further rises in life expectancies. As such, this reform is based on a target number of years in retirement that distributes all benefits of future rises in life expectancy to contributing society at large and grants none to future retirees. Moreover, the gap between the time of the earliest retirement (62 by 2022) and the normal retirement age (67 by 2027) is foreseen to remain five years, such that the availability of early retirement is also directly linked to life expectancies.[5]

The reform includes efforts to ensure that the public receives ample notice of any changes in the retirement eligibility age to allow individuals to plan accordingly. Any increase in the retirement age must be published 10 years in advance, which means that the formulae for determining such increases will contain some uncertainty from having to use 10-year projections of life expectancy at 60. The

(box continues on next page)

Box 3.5   The 2006 Danish pension reform and the future retirement age *(continued)*

target number of 19.5 years is the historical average of years in retirement (from early and universal retirement) since the introduction of early retirement in Denmark in 1979 until 1995, when life expectancy from age 60 began rising. A distributionally important issue is that the reform formula uses a simple average of the life expectancies for both men and women at 60. But expected lifetimes at age 60 are significantly higher for women than for men in Denmark (23 years to 19.7 years, respectively, in the most recent data, 2004–05[6]), implying a longer period in retirement for women than men.

Surprisingly perhaps, the 2006 reform was approved at a time of no immediate economic crisis in Denmark. At the same time, the reform (excluding the baby-boomer loophole) is austere in the long term, as it allocates all future increases in life expectancies after the mid-2020s to society as a whole rather than to retirees, while simultaneously linking early retirement options to life expectancy. The 2006 reform thus implies a gradually declining ratio of expected-time-in-retirement to time-not-in-retirement after the mid-2020s and makes no allowance for the potential desire of future wealthier generations to consume more leisure. The rise in age for early retirement also may affect people with physically demanding jobs and generate political discontent in the future.

It seems likely that the generally extensive nonretirement-related welfare state in Denmark facilitated this austere outcome. Nonetheless, the large political majority behind it in 2006 notwithstanding, any pension reform is only as strong as present-day political will and leadership.

---

1. The information in this box is from the final agreement of June 2006 (Danish Ministry of Finance 2006).
2. A number of additional conditions must be fulfilled in order to get early retirement. The three most important are: (1) residency in an EEC country; (2) early retirement contributions for 25 of the preceding 30 years; and (3) full participation in the labor force up until retirement (i.e., seeking employment in case of unemployment). Several of these conditions were implemented in a 1998 reform.
3. Denmark further has a very extensive quasi-voluntary occupational pension system, covering about 85 percent of workers.
4. This group consists of those aged 45–65 in 2004, which amounted to 27 percent of the entire population (National Danish Statistical Authority Population Database, available at www.dst.dk).
5. This follows the emphasis of Barr (2006), who suggests that the principal problem of pension systems is the time of the earliest available retirement option. See also chapter 4.
6. Data are from the National Danish Statistical Authority, www.dst.dk.

Box 3.6 Public and private pensions in France: Toward egalité

Recent developments in public and private pensions in France elegantly exemplify many of the issues described in this section. When the French universal pension scheme (now known as the Régime général d'assurance vieillesse des travailleurs salaries, RGAVTS) was set up in 1945, many French working either directly in the public sector or in (then) state-owned industries and utility monopolies had no financial interest in participating, as they were already covered by more generous separate public schemes and succeeded for decades in maintaining their separate and privileged status. Thus there existed a pension system duality between the RGAVTS and the (occasionally far) more generous "special schemes" (the 19 régimes spéciaux[1]) from the beginning of public pensions for the broader French population. In effect, the "universal system" was intended for the private sector only.

In 1993 the government of Prime Minister Edouard Balladur implemented a set of remarkably far-reaching reforms of private-sector pensions.[2] For the RGATVS basic pension, the necessary period of contributions for a full pension was raised from 150 to 160 quarters (37.5 to 40 years, scheduled to rise to 41 by 2012), the period of reference wage for pension estimation was gradually raised from 10 to 25 best years by 2008, and all upward valorization of the 25 annual salaries and all pensions were to be indexed to the consumer price index rather than wages. When fully phased in, these reforms will, by some estimates, reduce gross replacement rates by 22–43 percent, depending on particular career paths—some private-sector retirees will see their total pension cut almost in half (Benallah, Concialdi, and Math 2003).

Thus France showed that the reform of pensions *is* possible. Indeed, very deep and far-reaching pension reforms were carried out in the early 1990s—at least for some.

By so dramatically reducing the value of private pensions in France, the "Balladur reform" not only did much to maintain the financial sustainability of the private pension system; it also exacerbated the distributional unfairness relative to the unreformed public pension system. These increasingly large differences in generosity levels between the French private and public systems opened a political reform strategy for the public pension system. Interest grew in restoring fairness by subjecting the approximately 25 percent of the workforce covered by public-sector schemes to the reforms implemented for the far larger private workforce.

The French public bestows high levels of legitimacy on their pension systems as an embodiment of their social rights. When the government of Prime Minister

(box continues on next page)

Box 3.6   Public and private pensions in France: Toward egalité
(continued)

Alain Juppé tried in 1995 to extend the major parts of the "Balladur reform" to public-sector pension plans, it had to withdraw the proposals after large-scale street demonstrations. It was only by 2003 that the government of Jean-Pierre Raffarin managed, after facing down massive demonstrations, to implement more limited reforms of French public pensions. For example, as for private-sector pensions, the number of years of contributions for a full public pension increases from 37.5 to 40 (by 2008, rising to 41 in 2012), and pensions are indexed to the consumer price index rather than to wages.[3]

However, the 2003 reform excluded most of the smaller "special schemes" in the French public sector. Although it included the main civil servant pension schemes, the reform did not apply to public-sector workers in the state utility monopolies and quasi-monopolies—SNCF (state railways), RATP (greater Paris public transportation network), EDF (former state power monopoly), GDF (former state natural gas monopoly), and la Poste (state postal monopoly)—or to special schemes for the Bank of France, seamen, and miners. These groups represent roughly half a million French workers, not counting dependents.[4]

Two factors account for the exclusion of these groups from the 2003 reforms: First, all of the (former) state monopolies are heavily unionized,[5] and second, they command significant disruptive force, as striking SNCF, RATP, EDF, and postal workers can largely cripple French public infrastructure—and have, as in 1995, 2003, 2007, and 2008.

Hence it was only in late 2007 that the newly elected President Nicolas Sarkozy acted to extend the 2003 public pension reform to the *régimes spéciaux*, ending the most blatant inequalities in pension coverage between French workers in the private and most of the public sectors and a small subset of public-sector employees. The stated intentions of the reform were fairness and "bringing the special schemes in line with the standard public scheme."[6]

Thus the politics of fairness and *égalité* overcame decades of entrenched opposition to the reform of generous public pensions even in France[7]—a lesson that should not be lost on either US policymakers at the state and local levels or public employees.

---

1. The *régimes spéciaux* is a series of—as the name implies—special pension schemes in place only for workers at (previously) state-owned companies and public utility monopolies in France. See below.

2. At the time, these comprised the RGAVTS (basic pension), the ARRCO (compulsory supplemental occupational pensions for all private-sector wage earners), the AGIRC (compulsorysupplemental occupational pensions for managerial and professional workers), and IRCANTEC (similar to the ARRCO for employees in the public sector without civil servant status). See ADECRI (2005) for details.

3. Some elements in the 2003 reform concerned both private- and public-sector employees, but the latter were by far the most affected. However, substantial distributional inequalities persisted between public and private workers. Although the 2003 reform lengthened the calculation period for public-sector pensions from a reference rate of the last six career months to the last three career years, this remains relative to the 25 best years for the private sector. Similarly, the contribution levels for public-sector employees at 7.85 percent of wages are substantially lower than for private-sector employees, whose combined pension contributions (RGAVTS plus compulsory supplemental pension contributions) typically start at 9.5 percent of wages. See EIRO (2003b, 2003c) for a complete overview of the 2003 reform.

4. The number in the late 1990s—523,191—is cited in Rothenbacher (2004) based on data from Charpin (1999).

5. The CGT (Confédération générale du travail), generally considered the most militant among France's five national unions, is the majority union in most of the former national utility monopolies. See EIRO (2003d).

6. See Sarkozy's speech to the Senate, "Nicolas Sarkozy announces plans for a new social contract," September 18, 2007, available at www.premier-ministre.gouv.fr.

7. The details of the 2007–08 extension of the 2003 reforms are not yet clear. The government accepted extensive transitional agreements for affected workers, so the total financial savings from this final piece of reform for the French government are unclear and may not be particularly significant.

Whitehouse (2007) explains that the precise distribution of the gains from increases in life expectancies (or, from the perspective of financial costs, life expectancy risk) differs materially depending on the specifications of the four life expectancy linkages. One important general aspect to note here is the shift from a pure DB (like Social Security) to a pure DC system transfers all gains from increased life expectancies to society as a whole and none to retirees, irrespective of when in life mortally declines; in contrast, direct age eligibility qualifications, which use changes in life expectancies for ages at or close to retirement as a reference age, do not. This is because an individual's retirement decision cannot be undone, and laws are not—in liberal democracies at least—enacted retroactively, so any increases in life expectancies that occur at ages above the reference age after an individual has retired will accrue completely to the retiree.[71] Hence any direct age eligibility qualifications will inherently entail some distribution of increases in life expectancies between workers and retirees.

US Social Security has no link to life expectancies and instead relies only on prefixed gradual rises to be fully implemented by 2027. After that, American retirees will reap all benefits from any increase in US life expectancies (and the US government will correspondingly carry the financial risk). With Social Security needing long-term financial reform, we believe this is a mistake and that US lawmakers as part of this reform process ought to legislate an explicit life expectancy link to both the earliest age of eligibility (currently 62) and the age of full eligibility for Social Security, for implementation by 2027.[72] As we believe system-changing reforms of Social Security are unwarranted, and that lowering benefit levels for all recipients will be untenable, we suggest that this link be instituted via a direct eligibility age link, similar to the approaches in Denmark and France.

The question is how to implement such a direct age link. We saw in box 3.5 that Denmark after the mid-2020s will target a fixed number of years in retirement and raise retirement eligibility ages with rises in life expectancy at age 60. Assuming simplistically (and likely erroneously for most people concerned) that additional years of employment bestow no benefit to the individual, this will transfer all post-2020 benefits from increases in life expectancy below age 60 to society and none to retirees.[73] We believe this type of direct life expectancy link will be not only unsuitable for the highly heterogeneous US workforce but also very politically challenging to implement.

Instead, we propose to link life expectancy and Social Security eligibility ages in a way that would keep constant the relationship between years spent in retirement and the rest of an individual's lifetime—that is, to adopt a ratio of expected time in retirement (ETR) to time not in retirement (TNR). Another possibility would be the ETR to working life ratio, to be implemented in France after 2012. This ratio links extra time in retirement to extra time spent working and thus is more rigorous than the ETR-TNR ratio. We believe that our suggested ratio is superior, as it does

---

71. The lower this reference age, the larger the share of life expectancy increases that will be transferred to retirees.

72. Whitehouse (2007, 39) notes that given the relatively limited scope of Social Security, such a life expectancy link will have less of a fiscal impact in the United States than similar measures in other OECD countries.

73. Given that the reference age of changes in retirement ages in Denmark will be 60 (i.e., below the country's current retirement ages of 62 and 67), the link will be further uncertain, as changes in life expectancies at 60 may differ from changes in life expectancies at 62 or 67. If, hypothetically, mortality risk declines occurred only between ages 60 and 67, then life expectancy at age 60 would not change, Danish retirement ages would not be raised, and retirees would still enjoy longer retirements.

not penalize individuals for late entry into the workforce (e.g., due to long periods in tertiary education). In contrast, the proposed French ratio—if combined with increasing educational attainment—will have a double impact on raising eligibility ages for a full pension. We believe this could be an unfortunate disincentive to engage in especially the longest tertiary education courses.

For the sake of argument, assume that it is reasonable to spend 18 percent of expected lifetime in retirement (the midpoint between the ratio in the OECD countries for 1970 and the ratio for 2004 is 18.7 percent[74]) and that the reference age for changes in life expectancies is 65.[75] A life expectancy of 80 for people who reach age 65 implies a retirement age of 65.6 years. Were life expectancy for people who reach the age of 65 to rise to 90, this would raise the retirement age to 73.8 years. In both cases, retiring generations who reach the age of 65 would look forward to spending 18 percent of their expected lifetime in retirement. Moreover, the benefit of the ten years of expected lifespan from 80 to 90 would be distributed with 1.8 years of additional leisure to the retirees and 8.2 years of additional labor force participation to contribute to paying for that extra retirement.

A fair pension system in terms of the distribution of retirees' leisure years among generations would target a fixed share of expected lifetime in retirement, so that each generation—irrespective of life expectancy at the reference age—might enjoy the same amount of lifetime in retirement.[76] Adopting a target ETR-TNR ratio also has the political advantage that it "gives something to everyone," as both retirees and younger generations benefit from a rise in life expectancy at any age.[77] Any future such pension reform would thus be "leisure-fair" rather than laissez-faire.

However, such a constant ETR-TNR ratio may overlook important welfare economic implications. The labor supply curve bends backward as income rises and people choose to consume more leisure. If we assume that real wages rise over time, this is also true across long intergenerational time spans, such that one might expect future and thus wealthier generations to "consume" more leisure in retirement than a constant ratio would imply. This would indicate that the ETR-TNR ratio should gradually decline over time as richer generations choose a longer retirement. At the same time, a constant ETR-TNR ratio would, given the power of

---

74. Choosing such a historical average for a target ETR-TNR ratio stretching over several generations has the distributional fairness advantage and therefore likely political appeal of smoothing out any large intergenerational differences.

75. Age 65 remains the most common age of eligibility for a full pension in OECD countries.

76. See Andersen (2005) for a theoretical discussion of a similar proposal.

77. As mentioned above, increases in life expectancies above the reference age after retirement invariably benefit the retiree.

compound interest rates, imply a constant lowering of the implicit rate of return on pension contributions.

But such welfare theoretical considerations do not take into consideration the starting point of any potential reform. Present-day retirees in the OECD enjoy vastly longer periods in retirement than did their parents so, even before considering the need to maintain a fiscally sustainable retirement system (of the PAYGO variety), there is a case for "adjusting the pendulum" by increasing normal retirement ages. Indeed, from figures 3.10 and 3.11 it is clear that in many OECD countries, retirement ages will for a period have to rise faster than life expectancies. A target ETR-TNR ratio should be adopted only after a period of scheduled rises in retirement age in excess of the rises in life expectancy in order to "make up" for the disproportional allocation of additional years of life expectancy to retirees in recent decades.

Average National Retirement Ages and Differing Life Expectancies—A Distributional Issue in National Pension Systems?

Life expectancies differ substantially across different groups, giving rise to vastly different retirement lengths and thus directly affecting each group's pension generosity, as people may have contributed the same amount to a national PAYGO or DB system. Does this imply that retirement age should be varied across different groups? On theoretical grounds, at least, Baily (1987) found, based on an intertemporal utility model, that policymakers should not attempt such stratification, as it would violate the principle of consumption smoothing.

The single most important and immediately observable subnational determinant of life expectancy is gender—women live significantly longer than men, irrespective of estimated life expectancies. In the OECD, women's life expectancy at birth in 2004 was 81½ years, which is almost 6 years longer than men. At age 65, OECD women in 2004 with 19½ years remaining still had an almost 3½ year advantage over men.[78] Figure 2.13 in the previous chapter showed that 10 OECD countries (Australia, Austria, Belgium, the Czech Republic, Hungary, Italy, Poland, Switzerland,

---

78. See OECD Health Database, 2007. Although life expectancies for both men and women in the OECD continue to rise, they do so at very different rates depending on the age at which they are measured. For instance, life expectancy for American men at birth has risen by more than eight years from 1960 to 2004, whereas at age 65, it has risen by only about four years. The 2003 Technical Panel to the Social Security Board of Trustees discusses the two tales of declining US mortality rates in the 20th century, with very rapid declines at young ages in the first half and rapid declines at older ages from 1950 on. See TPAM (2003).

Turkey, and the United Kingdom) already have different legal retirement ages for men and women. However, in all 10 the statutory retirement age for women is two to five years lower than for men. So, ironically, the existing stratification of retirement ages by gender makes these countries' pension systems even more skewed in favor of women than life expectancies alone would imply. This is certainly a holdover from an earlier era, when in overwhelmingly single-earner households women's retirement ages from the labor force were of mostly symbolic importance and mattered little in fiscal terms as women retired earlier to care for their typically older spouse. The ongoing reform efforts we saw in table 3.1 (e.g., in Australia, Austria, Belgium, the Czech Republic, Italy, Switzerland, and the United Kingdom) to eliminate such differences and align the official retirement ages of men and women (by raising that of women closer, if not equal, to the level of men) should therefore be welcomed.

Erasing distributional differences in retirement ages seems an intuitively fair policy reform. However, using differences in life expectancies to regulate new distributional differences is fraught with danger.

Estimates of life expectancies and derived approximations of distributional fairness based on them are invariably ex ante in nature and therefore rely (merely) on the best estimates of the future available at a particular time.[79] As government transfers and pension systems provide the majority of income for most retirees, exceptionally high validity requirements would have to be attached to any such estimates that might be used—in the name of distributional fairness—to discriminate in favor of a single group in terms of retirement age. Indeed, in the United Kingdom the government considered uncertainties concerning life expectancies so great that it rejected the original proposals from Lord Turner's Pension Commission suggesting an explicit life expectancy link for all retirees. Instead, with the stated desire to provide ample notice to UK retirees about changes in retirement ages, the government implemented a fixed schedule, pushing the retirement age to 68 by 2044.[80]

Who Wants to Live Forever? The Disputed Future of Life Expectancies

How long we will live is a question that most people ponder at some stage in life. Some Americans may find it comforting to look at the World Health Organization's annual World Health Report (WHO 2006) and discover that US life expectancy at birth in 2004 was 75 for men and 80 for women. However, like most single number answers to complex questions, this one conveys what Gigerenzer (2002) has called the "illusion of

---

79. See Queisser and Whitehouse (2006) for a discussion of this issue in relation to actuarial concepts.

80. See Whitehouse (2007) and UK Department of Works and Pensions (2006).

certainty," as estimating average life expectancies is both complex and highly assumption driven.

Life expectancy estimates are based on age-specific death rates for a given population (e.g., all residents of a country). An age-specific death rate of 5 percent at age 75 indicates that 5 percent of everyone in that population alive on their 75th birthday will die before the 76th. When age-specific death rates are known for all of a given population cohort (usually everyone born in a given calendar year), it is possible to compile an accurate cohort life table (also known as a generational life table) and calculate life expectancies at all ages.

Constructing a cohort life table requires continuous data collection over a very long time, as actuaries need to wait for everyone in the cohort to die before the data input is complete. Invariably, therefore, the tables are ex post and out of date as they reflect the circumstances of a group of people in the past whose historical conditions of life are unlikely to be the same for future generations.

To be both economically feasible and relevant, it is useful to estimate (rather than calculate) a different type of life table, the period (or current) life table. Instead of relying on long-term historical data to map the life spans of an actual age cohort, a period life table estimates how a hypothetical cohort would fare if its members throughout their lives suffered the mortality conditions experienced by all ages during a specific period. Data collection thus switches from the longitudinal (covering the entire lifetime of people born in year x) to the cross-sectional (covering all age groups alive in a given year), producing a snapshot of prevailing mortality conditions in period x.

For illustrative purposes, a recent period life table for the entire US population is presented in abbreviated form in table 3.2.[81] The calculations in the table are based on a snapshot of data, signaling the broad circumstances of life in the United States in 2003. No allowances have

---

81. Data for $q_{(x)}$ are derived from final numbers of deaths in the United States during 2003 and represent the only direct data input to the life table. $l_{(x)}$ is the number of people from the hypothetical cohort (originally set at 100,000 live births) who survive to the beginning of each age interval: 99,116 get to celebrate their 10th birthday, while 2,363 become centenarians. $d_{(x)}$ is the number of deaths in each age interval from the original 100,000. For instance, 687 will die during their first year, or 1,240 when they are 65. $L_{(x)}$ shows the number of person-years lived by the hypothetical cohort in each age interval from x to $x + 1$. Hence 99,290 represents the number of years the 99,313 who celebrated their 1st birthday live before their 2nd birthday. $T_{(x)}$ represents the total number of years that will be lived after the beginning of age interval x to $x + 1$ by the hypothetical cohort. Hereby, 6,756,754 equals the total number of years to be lived after their 10th birthday by the 99,116 who celebrated it. Finally, $e_{(x)}$ represents the average number of years to be lived by those still surviving in the hypothetical cohort, based on the estimated age-specific values of $q_{(x)}$. It is derived by dividing $T_{(x)}$ by $l_{(x)}$, so that, for instance, the average remaining life expectancy for the hypothetical cohort between their 65th and 66th birthday would be 1,524,128 ÷ 82,668, or 18.4 years.

Table 3.2 US total population life table, 2003

x – age	$q(_x)$ – probability of dying between ages x and $x+1$	$l(_x)$ – number surviving to age x	$d(_x)$ – number dying between ages x and $x+1$	$L(_x)$ – person-year (years lived between ages x to $x+1$)	$T(_x)$ – total number of person-years lived over age x	$e(_x)$ – expectation of life at age x
0–1	0.00687	100,000	687	99,394	7,748,865	77.5
1–2	0.00047	99,313	46	99,290	7,649,471	77.0
10–11	0.00017	99,116	16	99,108	6,756,754	68.2
65–66	0.01501	82,668	1,240	82,048	1,524,128	18.4
100+	1.00000	2,363	2,363	6,044	6,044	2.6

Source: Abbreviated version of table in CDC (2006).

been made for changes in these circumstances in the future; thus the assumption is that the newborns in table 3.2 will in 50 years face the same medical technology, prevalence of smoking, cancer risks, murder rates, vehicle safety levels, obesity rates, and anything else that will affect their probability of death as those aged 50 in this table. This assumption of a status quo is, of course, highly questionable, and it lies at the heart of all notions of uncertainty concerning life expectancies.[82] What should we assume about age-specific death rates in the future? Maybe a new electronic toddler alarm will be created, so that infant mortality drops (i.e., the 687 deaths before the 1st birthday in table 3.2 decline), or maybe a cure for lung cancer is discovered, dramatically reducing death rates among the elderly (i.e., the 1,240 deaths at age 65 in table 3.2 drops)?

Medical and demographic experts are split on the question of how to refine such estimates for future changes in lifestyle or medical technology. One school of thought (the historical optimists) espouses the view that future decreases in mortality rates (increases in life expectancies), evolving from a complex interaction of behavioral and social factors and the continuing emergence of new medical technologies, will continue at the constant pace seen in the last more than 150 years.[83] This would entail a continued rise in life expectancies at birth of up to 2½ years per decade for the foreseeable future. The other school of thought (the worried empiricists) reject the continued projection of historical trends and instead focus on current trends that they contend will slow or even reverse life expectancy increases in many

---

82. It further determines the magnitude of longevity risk, a topic we analyze in chapter 7.

83. See Watson Wyatt (2005), Vaupel and Kistowski (2005), Vaupel and Jeune (1995), Oeppen and Vaupel (2002), Kannisto (1994), Kannisto et al. (1994), Riley (2001), Jeune (1995), and Wilmoth (1995) for representatives of this line of thinking.

developed countries.[84] This school of thought worries about the impact of rapidly rising obesity levels,[85] diabetes, infectious diseases, and antibiotic-resistant pathogens on the mortality rates of older people, in particular.

The debate is ongoing. For instance, the 2003 Technical Panel advising the US Social Security Advisory Board[86] recommended that the SSA change its assumptions guiding the predicted declines in US mortality rates and thus by extension in US life expectancies. In its intermediate scenario, the panel recommended raising the average life expectancy at birth for Americans in 2078 from the current Social Security Trustee estimate of 82.9 to 84.4 years of age,[87] in either case a significant increase over the latest life expectancy of 77.5 years (table 3.2).[88] And even the recommendations of the technical panel came with significant uncertainties. Cheng and colleagues (2004) estimated that the standard 95 percent confidence interval for the panel's predictions for life expectancy at age 65 for men in 2078 would equal ranges of 17.2–24.8 years and 19.4–28.1 years for women. Indeed, most long-term projections of life expectancies now come in the form of probabilistic fan charts, sketching a range of possible scenarios and outcomes.[89] Antolín (2007), after a review of different approaches to predicting changes in mortality rates,[90] attempts to quantify the degree of uncertainty by suggesting a Monte Carlo–based stochastic approach for attaching probabilities to different mortality outcomes.

---

84. See Watson Wyatt (2005), Olshansky et al. (2005), Olshansky, Carnes, and Désesquelles (2001), and McNeill (1976) for representatives of this school.

85. Olshansky et al. (2005) estimate that current obesity levels in the United States have lowered life expectancy by up to a full year for some groups of Americans. Reynolds et al. (2005) find a significantly higher risk of disability among the obese.

86. One member of the technical panel, J. R. Wilmoth, is a recognized member of the school of historical optimists.

87. The panel recommended several additional technical changes to how the Social Security Trustees estimate future changes in mortality rates. See TPAM (2003) and Cheng et al. (2004). However, as with the Panel's recommendations on fertility, the recommended changes in mortality assumptions have a quite limited impact on the long-term financial situation of Social Security. The Office of the Chief Actuary estimates that implementing the advisory panel's mortality recommendations of an increase in life expectancies raises the unfunded 75-year obligation by "only" $500 billion and brings forward the exhaustion year for the trust fund by just one year (to 2041).

88. The 2003 Panel's recommendation represented a decrease from the previous 1999 advisory panel, which had recommended an end-of-projection period life expectancy at birth of 85.2 years.

89. Such charts are increasingly common in many types of even short-term predictions. See, for instance, the Bank of England's inflation and GDP projection charts, available at www.bankofengland.co.uk.

90. Antolín (2007) surveys process-based biomedical forecasts, causal econometric forecasting, and historically based extrapolative forecasts.

Inevitably, predictions of life expectancies fall into the category of inherent uncertainties that, unlike risks, according to Knight (1921), cannot be directly quantified. This reality should discourage rules that discriminate against individual groups based on such estimates.

Other Possible Stratifications of Retirement Ages

Gender is the most obvious of factors that cause differences in life expectancies among population subgroups. But socioeconomic variables such as education, family income, marital status, homeownership, employment/labor force participation, geographic address, and race are also consistently correlated in the medical literature with large differentials in life expectancies in the OECD and many other countries. However, there is no scholarly consensus about the extent of the impact of any individual socioeconomic factor because of the complex impact on health of many of these variables, correlations between them as explanatory variables (for instance, education and income are almost invariably highly correlated), concerns about the direction of causality,[91] and issues of data validity.[92] Nonetheless, the evidence is clear: A substantial international literature points to a large positive impact of education/socioeconomic status/income on mortality risk for all age groups, irrespective of whether free universal government-provided health care is available (as in Europe) or not.[93] Thus those who are highly educated and/or have

91. The classic chicken-and-egg issue: Does limited time in school cause poor health and increased mortality or might some people already be ill and, therefore, drop out of school? Some studies, like Lleras-Muney (2005), suggest that lack of schooling causes increased mortality later in life. See also the *New York Times*, "A Surprising Secret to a Long Life: Stay in School," January 3, 2007. Similar issues haunt the relationship between increased mortality and unemployment or sudden drops in income.

92. Lynch et al. (2005) show the significant difference the choice of time period and the choice between US Census inequality data and IRS tax revenue–based inequality data makes for the magnitude of the impact of inequality. Further, it is a frequently mentioned worry concerning especially older death certificates, where race was identified overwhelmingly based on the visual impression of the body by a certifying physician, funeral director, or the family, which may differ from the corresponding race identification in US Census data, containing socioeconomic input.

93. See, for instance, von dem Knesebeck, Verde, and Dragano (2006) for evidence from 22 European countries; De Vogli et al. (2005) for Italy and 21 other countries; Huisman et al. (2004) for 11 OECD countries; Mackenbach, Huisman, and Kunst (2003) for six European countries; Brønnum-Hansen (2006) and Brønnum-Hansen et al. (2004) for Denmark; Bopp et al. (2003) for Switzerland; McLeod et al. (2003) for Canada; Davey Smith et al. (1998) for the United Kingdom, and Sundquist and Johansson (1997) for Sweden. A number of other studies report that in the former Communist countries in Europe, a very large gap in mortality rates has opened between different socioeconomic groups since the fall of the Berlin Wall in 1989. See Shkolnikov et al. (2006); Kalediene and Petrauskiene (2004); and Leinsalu, Vågerö, and Kunst (2003).

a high income and/or are married and/or are employed generally live (in some places much) longer than their countrymen less fortunate in these regards.[94]

America occupies a special place in the literature on the effect of socioeconomic factors on health. First, US income and health care access differentials are larger than in all other OECD countries. Second, for obvious historical reasons, US society is uniquely race conscious and has produced a very large scholarly literature on the impact of race on mortality rates. In this area, America represents arguably not only the best but also the worst in the world. Murray and colleagues (2006) found that in 2001 life expectancy at birth for Asian women in America was 86.7 years, more than two years longer than the highest national average (Japan) in the world that year. The same was found for Asian men in America, who with a life expectancy of more than 81 had three years more than the world's next highest male life expectancy (78.2 in Iceland). However, for urban black American men, life expectancy was 15.4 years lower than for Asian men, roughly equal to that of men in Albania, Egypt, and Peru (WHO 2002). Such differences in life expectancies have significant independent distributional policy consequences. For example, Woolf and colleagues (2004) find that all the improvements in medical technology in America between 1991 and 2000 saved only one-fifth of the lives lost to the excess mortality rates among African-Americans over the same period. In other words, bringing African-American mortality rates down to the US average would have saved five times more lives than all technological medical improvements achieved during the 1990s.

Other socioeconomic variables are intertwined with the impact of race on mortality rates. Both education and race may affect the mortality rate, but the outcome is blurred when, as Hillary Waldron (2002) points out, for the most recent cohorts, a higher share of white males drops out of high school than black males, even as a larger share of white men goes to college.[95] Richard Rogers and colleagues (1996) estimate that blacks have a higher mortality rate than whites from diabetes, homicide, and in-

---

94. A specialized strand of the medical literature considers whether rising income inequality has an independent adverse impact on mortality rates. Proponents of the "social capital thesis" argue that rising income inequality reduces the level of social capital (as defined by, for instance, Putnam 1993 and 2000) via "psychosocial interpretation effects" of increasing levels of frustration over relative deprivation and the adverse health effects of social conflict. See, for instance, Kaplan et al. (1996) and Lynch et al. (2000). Other authors (e.g., Pearce and Davey Smith 2003) contest this theory, arguing for the primacy of absolute (rather than relative) levels of deprivation and of macroeconomically and politically determined underinvestment in human, physical, and health infrastructure.

95. One possible explanation is that in terms of mortality, it is irrelevant whether one drops out of or completes high school; rather, only higher levels of education confer beneficial impacts on earnings and the ability to learn and implement healthy behavior.

fectious diseases (HIV/AIDS) but a lower mortality rate from accidents, respiratory diseases, and suicide. Some studies emphasize the effect of early-life deprivation for many blacks (see, for instance, Warner and Hayward 2006), while others conclude that, when controlling for socioeconomic variables, the effect of race on US mortality rates disappears entirely, especially at higher ages.[96]

The socioeconomic stratification of mortality rates in America seems to be widening, with educational attainment or income becoming more important in recent years. Gopal Singh and Mohammad Siahpush (2006) find that life expectancy disparities between two groups of Americans differentiated by socioeconomic deprivation rose from 2.8 years in the early 1980s to 4.5 years in the late 1990s.[97] This widening in life expectancies by socioeconomic status cuts across racial barriers, as several studies show that high-income blacks have experienced the same declines in mortality as other high-income groups, while low-income blacks have not (Barnett, Armstrong, and Casper 1999).

In summary, while socioeconomic variables and (in America) race play substantial roles in determining mortality rates and life expectancies, the complexity of their impact and uncertainties in projected life expectancy estimates ought to, as with gender, caution against using these parameters in pension legislation to implement different retirement ages for different socioeconomic groups. The inherent measurement uncertainties are very daunting. Even if it were judged desirable to pay higher monthly Social Security pensions to, say, African-Americans than to Caucasian Americans, the practical problems of implementing such a measure would be horrendous, and any regulations to this effect would likely be declared unconstitutional.

There may, however, be a case for providing different pensions for workers based on the types of job they perform. Several countries already have such programs in place that would seem to mirror such intent. Italy's legislation offers retirement up to five years earlier than the standard retirement age to Italians with "arduous work" (*lavoro usurante*), defined as "a particularly intensive and continuous mental or physical effort, caused by factors that cannot be prevented by taking appropriate measures."[98] Similarly, France's provisions for people with "long working lives" allow citizens to retire with a full pension as early as age 56. However, the eligibility criteria are strict: Participants must have paid social insurance contributions for 42 years—from the age of 14 to retire at 56! Thus this option is essentially open only to people with low educational

---

96. See, for instance, Rogers (1992), Menchik (1993), and Sorlie, Backland, and Keller (1995).

97. See also McDonough et al. (1997), Schalick et al. (2000), Crimmins and Saito (2001), and Lin et al. (2003).

98. As defined in Legislative Decree No. 374/1993, available at www.eurofound.eu.int.

skills.[99] French civil servants in "active services" also have access to full pensions as early as 50 (police officers) and 55 (nurses). Similar options for a relatively low retirement age are available for many US firemen and police officers, based on municipal or state pension rules.

Such rules create more problems than they solve. Who decides what is a hard job? Where do the funds come from to support the early retirement? From the employers that generate the hard jobs? From the workers employed in them? From general tax revenue? There is a general consensus that many workers who do physically demanding jobs do not receive particularly high wages and are also forced to retire early because they cannot perform these jobs beyond age 55 or so. This is part of a broader issue of the widening of the wage and income distribution in the United States, and it is not clear that public pension policy is necessarily the place to tackle it.

One of the big differences between the labor market in the United States and that in many countries in Europe is that Americans are required to work in order to receive income, except for short-term assistance such as Unemployment Insurance. This suggests that workers may be expected to take different jobs rather than early retirement if they can no longer perform the tasks they have been performing. So while it is unreasonable to expect aging workers to continue to carry heavy furniture or move heavy boxes, there may be many other tasks they can perform.

A Closer Look at the Distributional Effects of Public Pensions

A particular distributional pension issue is whether public-sector pensions are more generous than those available to the general population and, if so, what impact this may have on government finances and other issues. We believe this issue is particularly pertinent in the United States, as several state and local government employee pension schemes will soon face significant economic stress, a challenge that seems bound to raise some distributional concerns between US private-sector workers and state and local employees. In this section we analyze (1) OECD data on the differences in retirement ages and benefit generosity between public-sector pension schemes and those universally available and (2) the age profile of the sector's workers. We also begin the discussion of government pension accounting issues.

---

99. Participants must have paid contributions for 41 years to retire at age 58 and 40 years to retire at age 59 and also have had at least five quarters of contributions before the end of the calendar year in which their 16th birthday fell. Certain other criteria also apply. See EIRO (2003a).

Public Pension Schemes—Generosity Levels and Consequences

Powerful organizations can over time be expected to "look after their own," and governments, being among the oldest and certainly most powerful organizations around, are no exception. So it is little surprise that civil servants and other public-sector employees—soldiers, police officials, teachers, state-owned enterprise employees, and others—were frequently covered by government pensions well before the public at large. In the United States, the federal government in 1789 accepted the responsibility of providing pensions for disabled war veterans from the Revolutionary War; in 1857 New York City started a pension fund for the city's police; and in Chicago and New Jersey, teachers acquired coverage during the 1890s.[100] Older countries in Europe started even earlier: Austrian state civil servants became eligible for public pensions as early as 1750, central government officials in France in 1790 (evidently the revolution there looked after its own, too—at least initially) and all French civil servants in 1853 (Benallah, Concialdi, and Math 2003), British civil servants in 1810 were granted a noncontributory pension by parliament,[101] and the first German *beamte* in Bavaria become eligible in 1805. Rothenbacher (2004) cites the average year of introduction of civil servants' public pensions in 18 surveyed countries as approximately 1850, 60 to 70 years before the introduction of public pensions for other workers, employees, and/or the general public.[102]

Of course, there were many good reasons for granting public pensions to civil servants. One imperative was to ensure the loyalty of the country's armed forces—it is easier to make soldiers stay and fight if they know it earns them a future pension. It was also considered important to (try to) guarantee the financial independence of public servants and to make careers in the public services appealing through pension provision.[103] Using future pension benefits as a substitute for cash in hand today pushes the financial costs of attracting and maintaining a competent civil service well into the future—a tax burden that future politicians will have to deal with.

---

100. See the Social Security Administration website for an in-depth time line of social insurance in the United States until the 20th century (www.ssa.gov/history). See also Hewitt Associates (2005).

101. Raphael (1964), cited in Palacios and Whitehouse (2006).

102. According to Rothenbacher (2004), only in Ireland did civil servants and the general public get access to public pensions simultaneously in 1909. However, this is due to the fact that Ireland, at the time a British colony, did not have a separate indigenous administrative class of civil servants, and hence all Irish residents, irrespective of occupational sector, participated in the first British universal pensions from 1909.

103. This argument is, of course, even more important concerning public legislators, government ministers, and judges. Typically, these small groups have pension schemes far more generous than any other group, or, in the case of judges, lifetime appointments.

The fact that public-sector workers are among the groups most likely to vote may amplify the moral hazard risk for political leaders.[104]

When for largely electoral political reasons mandatory public pension systems were expanded in the 20th century to cover the general population, governments often did not include public-sector employees (who were typically already covered). As Robert Palacios and Edward Whitehouse (2006) describe, this "dualism of public pension systems" frequently emerged and persisted due to the powerful ability of civil servants to protect their pecuniary interests through their own special systems, which were and remain, on average, significantly more generous than those to which the general public has access (see below).

According to survey data collected by Palacios and Whitehouse (2006), 14 OECD countries in 2004 had civil service pension schemes completely or partially integrated with the national scheme but with separate "top-up" benefits. This is similar to the current system for US federal government employees, who, if hired since 1984, have been covered by Social Security but in addition have had a top-up benefit in the form of the defined contribution Federal Thrift Savings Plan.[105] Nine countries (seven in the euro zone as well as Korea and Turkey) have kept their civil service schemes completely separate from the general national schemes; it is only in Finland and the Netherlands that civil servants may be on separate programs but enjoy the same benefits as all other resident participants.[106]

Such differences matter in terms of pension distribution. Public employment is nontrivial in all OECD countries: In the United States it accounted in 2005 for 16.3 percent of total CPS employment, or almost 22 million (excluding the armed forces), and more than 15 percent in all major OECD countries in 2001.[107] In their survey of civil servant pension schemes, Palacios and Whitehouse (2006) found that statutory retirement ages in half of the countries for which data are available are significantly

---

104. The same moral hazard issue also affects corporate pension decision makers; see chapter 7.

105. The Federal Thrift Savings Plan is in many ways similar to a regular private tax-deferred 401(k) plan. It also covers the US armed forces. Apart from employee contributions, it consists of a 1 percent automatic agency contribution as well as matching contributions of 100 percent of up to 3 percent of salary and 50 percent of the next 2 percent (FRTIB 2005). Federal employees hired before 1983 have access to additional vested pension rights under the previous federal government–defined benefit scheme. The other 11 fully integrated countries are Canada, Denmark, Iceland, Ireland, Italy, Japan, Norway, New Zealand, Spain, Sweden, and Switzerland, while the United Kingdom and Australia have partially integrated systems (Palacios and Whitehouse 2006, appendix table 1).

106. Both Finland and the Netherlands rely extensively on privately (the Netherlands) or quasi-governmentally (Finland) managed mandatory occupational pension funds.

107. Data from the BLS CPS (www.bls.gov/cps) and OECD (2002).

below those for general national pension schemes—typically by five years but in Mexico until recently a staggering full decade (55 instead of 65).[108] They also found that maximum replacement rates for full-career civil servants are substantially higher than for similar workers in the general national schemes. Their findings are summarized in table 3.3.

These significantly more generous civil service pension schemes[109] constitute an additional problem for government finances, as they are almost exclusively funded on a PAYGO basis, and less than one in four had accumulated any type of prefunding (Palacios and Whitehouse 2006). We also note that even when there are public employee contributions, as in the case of the US Federal Employee Thrift Pension System, these are accompanied by matching employer contributions and thus represent an additional budgetary pension outlay for governments.

One way to further illustrate this difference in pension levels among private and public employees in America is to study the SSA's sources of income data for people over 65 (SSA 2006a). These are broken down by government employees (including federal and military pension recipients) and private employees[110] as well as by size of the employment-based pension income (i.e., excluding Social Security benefits; figure 3.12).

As can been seen in the distributions of employment-based pension income for government and private employees, the former clearly have a relatively more generous employment-based pension income. In fact the government-sector median employment-based pension income is, at $15,600, fully 130 percent higher than the corresponding private-sector median at just $6,720. And—perhaps surprisingly, given the attention bestowed on the pension income of US corporate executives—far higher shares of retired public-sector workers in America have annual employment-based pension income above $15,000 as well as in the highest ($50,000+) category than is the case for private-sector workers.

Perhaps more worrisome, public sectors across the OECD are faced with a worse demographic outlook than the rest of the economy. Due to the rapid expansion of the government sector in many countries around the time of the baby-boomer generation's entry into the workforce and traditionally long public-sector career paths, a very large share of public workers

---

108. This mismatch in Mexico has been partly reversed by an increase in the public-sector retirement age to 60, following reforms enacted by the Calderón government in 2007.

109. Civil service schemes are far more likely than general national schemes to be indexed to earnings rather than prices.

110. "Government sector" here refers to recipients of federal, state, local, and military employment-based pensions. "Private sector" refers to recipients of any (i.e., DB, DC, hybrid, or other) private employer-based pensions and annuities (SSA 2006a, chapter 5). See also appendix 3A and SSA (2002) for additional information on the underlying data and the precise definition of "included units," of which there are 3.8 million in the government sector and 8.4 million in the private sector.

Table 3.3 Civil service and general national pension schemes, retirement ages and replacements rates

Country	Normal statutory retirement age: Civil service scheme	Normal statutory retirement age: General national scheme	Maximum replacement rate: Civil service scheme	Maximum replacement rate: General national scheme
Australia	55–60	65 (5–10 years higher)	66–88	52
Austria	60	60 (f)/65 (m) (five years higher for men)	80	80
Belgium	60	65 (five years higher)	75	60
Canada[a]	65	65 (same)	90	56
Czech Republic	n.a.	65	n.a.	n.a.
Denmark	65	65 (same)	n.a.	n.a.
Finland	63–65	65 (up to two years higher)	60	60
France	60	60 (same low age)	75	71
Germany	65	65 (same)	75	46
Greece	60	65 (five years higher)	69	n.a.
Hungary	n.a.	60 (f)/62 (m)	n.a.	n.a.
Iceland	65	67 (two years higher)	76	73
Ireland	n.a.	66	n.a.	n.a.
Italy	n.a.	60 (f)/65 (m)	80	66
Japan[a]	65	60 (five years lower!)	n.a.	n.a.
Korea	n.a.	60	n.a.	n.a.
Luxembourg	n.a.	60	83	71
Mexico[a,b]	55	65 (10 years higher)	n.a.	n.a.
Netherlands	65	65 (same)	n.a.	n.a.
Norway	67	67 (same)	66	53
Portugal[a]	60	65 (five years higher)	80	n.a.
Spain[a]	60	65 (five years higher)	95	88
Sweden	65	65 (same)	73	76
Switzerland	62	64 (f)/65 (m) (3/2 years higher for f/m)	65	58
Turkey	n.a.	58 (f)/60 (m)	n.a.	n.a.
United Kingdom	60	65 (five years higher)	67	37
United States	n.a.	65+	n.a.	n.a.

n.a. = not applicable

a. Years of service: 15 in Mexico, 25 in Canada and Japan, 30 in Spain, and 36 in Portugal.

b. 2007 reforms by the Calderon government will gradually lower the Mexican difference to five years by raising the public retirement age to 60.

Note: Female (f)/male (m), where difference in retirement age exists.

Source: Palacios and Whitehouse (2006).

today are from these generations and are fast approaching retirement age. Indeed, detailed studies by the US Office of Personnel Management and the Government Accountability Office (GAO) suggest that up to one-third of all US federal government employees will be eligible for retirement by 2012, including at such high-profile agencies as the US Treasury,

Figure 3.12 US annual employment-based pension income distribution in 2004, by sector

percent share of total

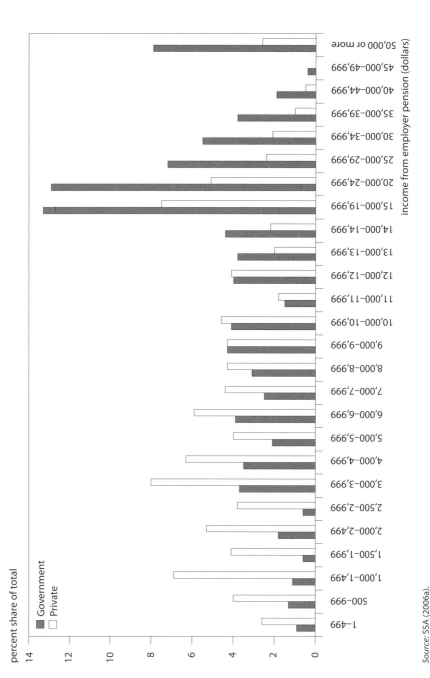

Source: SSA (2006a).

Department of Defense, Department of State, and—not without irony—the Social Security Administration (GAO 2008).

The situation is similar in many OECD countries, as up to one-third of all government employees were, in 2007, less than 10 years from a retirement at the relatively high (for public servants, according to table 3.3) age of 65.[111] In all countries except Australia, Japan, Korea, Portugal, and Turkey,[112] this share is substantially larger than for the economies as a whole, clearly indicating that expenditure on civil service pensions can be expected to rise rapidly in the near future (figure 3.13; see below for data on US state and local governments).

Yet, viewed in strictly financial terms, the facts that public pensions are more generous than the national average and that public-sector employee pension expenditure will correspondingly soon make up a larger share of total public expenditure, hardly constitute an overwhelming problem in OECD countries, as these generally have reasonably well-functioning public sectors and a broad tax base to support them. Certainly, no OECD countries have permitted the exceptionally generous and macroeconomically distorting public-sector pension benefits (i.e., government liabilities) of several developing countries (such as Brazil and India).[113] Rather, the core concerns are those of labor market distortions, public-sector human resources management, and the politics of pension fairness.

As mentioned above, pensions usually and rationally make up an important share of the total lifetime compensation package used to lure human capital to the public sector.[114] However, a detrimental issue arises when public-sector pension promises hinder job mobility between the public and private sectors and if, in attempting to hold on to prized employees, governments penalize people who do not spend their entire career in public service. There are two commonly used forms of such penalties. First, employers impose long vesting periods (periods of service required to receive any public-sector pension) that strongly incentivize employees to continue working in the public sector for up to 15 years in

---

111. Americans born in 1943–54 can retire at 66 with a full Social Security pension. These comparative data are from 2001. CPS data for the United States only showed that in 2005 29 percent of all government workers were aged 45–54, 17 percent aged 55–65, and 3 percent 65+. The corresponding figures for total nonfarm employment were 22, 12, and 3 percent, respectively.

112. In these four countries, the likely reason for their relatively youthful workforce is not (Turkey partly excepted) that they have a great number of very young employees but rather that many more of the older (55 or 60+) public-sector employees have already retired, thus lowering the relative share of older employees.

113. See Palacios and Whitehouse (2006), OECD (2005), and 2006 IMF Article IV consultations with both Brazil and India.

114. See Schiavo-Campo, de Tommaso, and Mukherjee (2003) for examples of other, less important, nonwage benefits used for this purpose.

Figure 3.13 Share of employed 50+, selected OECD countries, 2001 or most recent

percent

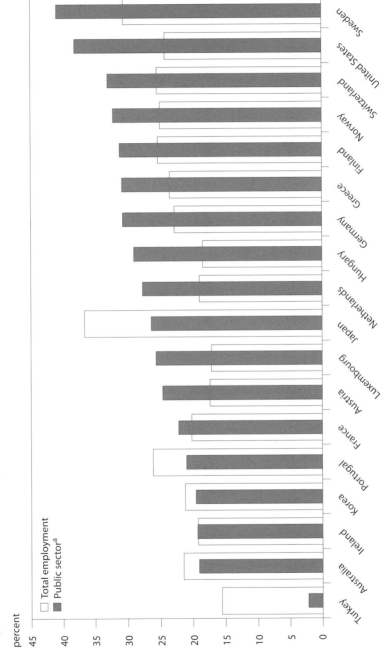

□ Total employment
■ Public sector[a]

a. Total public sector, except Australia, Austria, and Switzerland (federal administration) and Ireland, Greece, and Sweden (central government).

Sources: OECD (2002); OECD Labor Force Statistics; Eurostat.

some OECD countries[115] if they want to accrue any pension benefits from their employment. Second, early departees from public-sector pension schemes may receive a much lower value of their accrued pension than what it would have been worth had they remained in the public sector for their entire career. A similar situation faces many private-sector workers who leave a job with an occupational DB pension plan for other employment. We further discuss pension portability in chapter 7.

Public pension schemes, typically more generous than the average national schemes, may further amount to significant obstacles for the privatization of former state-owned enterprises (SOEs) or other parts of the public sector (see chapter 7 for an example from France). Potential private-sector buyers usually are not willing to take over the running of such entities in competitive markets if they are saddled with pension liabilities owed to past and present retirees significantly in excess of the national average. And public-sector/SOE employees will, of course, oppose privatization if it entails substantial reductions in their pensions. In most ways, this is not dissimilar to the likely unwillingness of a potential buyer to take over General Motors, for example, including GM's pension (and health care) liabilities, and the equally likely opposition of the workforce to any such sale excluding them. However, given the probable improvements in productivity and other beneficial spillover effects from privatization of government assets (such as the introduction of competition in former government monopoly service areas), the blocking of privatizations due to conflicts over pensions for (soon to be formerly) public servants frequently means forgoing even very large efficiency gains for an economy.

US Government Pension Accounting—Time to Empty the Augean Stables?

By far the most potent distributional issues concerning public-sector pensions are transparency and fairness. All pension accounting, even on the best of days, can be a rather murky business of opaque rules, complicated formulae, and far-reaching assumptions. In addition to these factors, public pension accounting has been largely (although rapidly becoming less so) outside the watchful eye of financial markets, and so until recently the true extent of government pension liabilities has had very little real-life impact. At least at the federal government level, this is partly due to the reluctance of sovereign governments to acknowledge that their pension liabilities may constitute tangible, legally binding promises;

---

115. Palacios and Whitehouse (2006) list Austria, France, Portugal, and Spain for this requirement.

otherwise, it would likely become more legally and legislatively difficult to reform these systems. The 2006 proposal by the US Federal Accounting Standards Advisory Board (FASAB)[116] to change a crucial assumption concerning government Social Security pension liabilities elegantly illustrates this issue.

The federal government recognizes a liability for its pension promises to both public servants and the population at large only when the pension benefit is due and payable (i.e., at the time of cash payment). This is essentially in keeping with the follow-the-money principle of cash-flow accounting, according to which promises of future pension benefit payments are conveniently not counted on the government balance sheet so that legally and politically they remain, in effect, just promises. Instead, the FASAB in October 2006 suggested that the US federal government starts incurring expenses (and liabilities thus emerge) "when participants substantially meet eligibility requirements during their working lives." For Social Security,[117] this change to accrual accounting principles would mean that liabilities related to pension promises would be put on the government books after 10 years (40 quarters) or the equivalent period of covered employment. By changing the accounting assumptions, the net costs of providing Social Security benefits for everyone with more than 10 years of contributions (and therefore substantially eligible) would suddenly be put on the government record today, rather than only when these Americans actually retire.[118] Given the large number of people in this category—including the overwhelming majority of baby-boomers—this would lead to an immediate and sizable deterioration in the long-term financial position of the SSA and, by extension, the US federal government budget, relative to how both are presented today.

---

116. The Treasury, Office of Management and Budget (OMB), and Comptroller General established the FASAB in October 1990, which is responsible for promulgating accounting standards for the US government. These standards are Generally Accepted Accounting Principles (GAAP) for the federal government. For details on this proposal, see the FASAB press release from October 23, 2006, "FASAB Issues Preliminary Views Regarding Accounting for Social Insurance," and the exposure draft at www.fasab.gov. See also public comments on the FASAB preliminary views in FASAB Memorandum on Social Insurance, July 12, 2007, at www.fasab.gov.

117. As well as railway retirement programs.

118. In detail, the FASAB would require that these "new" liabilities—(1) the present value of future benefits from work in covered employment; (2) interest on the liability; (3) prior service costs; and (4) actuarial gains—be included as a net cost in the Statement of Social Insurance (SOSI). The SOSI presents the actuarial present value for the 75-year projection period of the Old-Age and Survivors Insurance (OASI) and Disability Insurance (DI) future income and cost expected to arise from the legally specified formulae for current and future program participants. The SOSI in its present form is in the SSA annual financial statements. For the 2006 data, see www.ssa.gov/finance/2006/Financial_Statements.pdf.

Yet the inclusion in government budget publications of long-term cost estimates for Social Security–based accrual accounting is not tantamount to turning these future pension promises into inviolable guarantees. Rather, as expressed by former Federal Reserve Chairman Alan Greenspan in 2003 testimony before the Senate Committee on Banking, Housing, and Urban Affairs, "accrual-based accounts would lay out more clearly the true costs and benefits of changes to various taxes and outlay programs and facilitate the development of a broad budget strategy."[119] For instance, under current accounting rules, reform proposals involving an increase in government debt (a recognized liability) and offsetting decreases in future (unrecognized) pension liabilities would erroneously show up as simply a deterioration in the government fiscal position. Accrual-based accounts might thus increase awareness of the broader spending priorities of the federal budget. It seems plausible that putting the accrual accounting–based costs of future pension promises on the books would help minimize the risk of ill-informed Social Security reform decisions.

Similarly, the use of cash-flow accounting in the early years of Social Security assisted in masking the buildup up of sizable legacy debt in the form of underfinanced benefit payments to early Social Security recipients. Peter Diamond and Peter Orszag (2005) estimate this debt at $11.5 trillion, and its ongoing amortization is the principal reason for the long-term financial problems of Social Security.

At the same time the financial situation of the Social Security system and the OASDI Trust Funds is, in fact, very transparent and regularly made public—in excruciating detail and with all long-term assumptions laid bare—in the annual reports of the OASDI Trustees.[120] As such, contrary to the situation in many US private and certainly other US public (see below) pension schemes, the financial outlook for Social Security is very well illuminated and understood. Unfortunately, current government accounting rules, by not stipulating required remedial action, have facilitated that this knowledge be consistently ignored by policymakers.

However, even the most translucent accounting rules will not compel or constrain sovereign democratically elected decision makers: Only voters can do that. The most that can be expected to emerge from rewriting the government accounting rules is improved clarity about the current state of affairs and about viable reform options. Even much-needed improvement in the transparency of the accounting rules cannot substitute for the political will to own up to the future liabilities of current pension promises.

---

119. Federal Reserve Board's semiannual monetary policy report to the Congress, US Senate, February 11, 2003. Diamond and Orszag (2004) present a similar view of support for the informative effects of accrual accounting.

120. Available at SSA's website, www.ssa.gov/OACT.

State and Local Government Accounting and Retirement Finances

Among US state and local governments,[121] it is clear that transparency, brought to bear where there was previously little or none (such as in the area of accounting for state and local government employee pension liabilities), can have a substantial independent effect.

Unlike in most other countries, US public-sector employee pension liabilities are not solely the responsibility of the central (federal) government. Instead, given that almost one-quarter and two-thirds of all public-sector employees work at the state and local levels, respectively,[122] these two levels of government hold the vast majority of public-sector pension liabilities.

As mentioned above, US federal government employees hired after 1984 have been on the regular Social Security system plus the defined contribution Federal Thrift Savings Plan. However, when looking at the 80 percent of US public employees that work in state and local government, it becomes clear that a similar move toward DC plans and Social Security participation among this group has failed to materialize. A relatively stable 80 percent of state and local government employees remain on DB plans, according to the most recent data available from the Bureau of Labor Statistics.[123] As can be seen in figure 3.14, this is four times the share of private industry workers. This difference in DB coverage ratios is also evident in the employer costs of benefit provision. According to BLS data, in 2007 state and local governments spent, on average, over six times as much on DB compensation as did private-sector employers—$2.59 (and rising) per hour versus just $0.42 per hour.

At the same time, though, state and local governments spend less on DC pension compensation than do private-sector employers.[124] This is illustrated in figure 3.15, which also shows that while private-sector

---

121. The situation is not unique to the United States but is also present in other countries with powerful local governments. See, for instance, Japanese Ministry of Internal Affairs and Communications, White Paper on Local Public Finance (2005) for recent efforts in Japan to gather balance sheets reflecting the frequently dire financial situation for prefectures and municipalities. See also Robaschik and Yoshino (2001, 2004) for a discussion of Japanese local government finances and attempts to improve transparency.

122. In 2005, US state governments employed just over 5 million Americans, and local governments had more than 14 million on their payrolls. In contrast, the federal government (excluding the armed forces) accounted for only 2.7 million. Data from the BLS Current Employment Survey (CES) at www.bls.gov/ces/home.htm

123. See BLS National Compensation Survey (NCS) at www.bls.gov/ncs/ebs.

124. McDonnell and EBRI (2005) found that part of the reason for the disparate cost of benefits between public- and private-sector employees is the fact that many public-sector workers are concentrated in relatively better-educated and thus higher-income brackets and have longer careers under single plans than private-sector workers.

Figure 3.14   Pension coverage for US state and local government and private industry employees, most recent year available

share of workers covered, percent

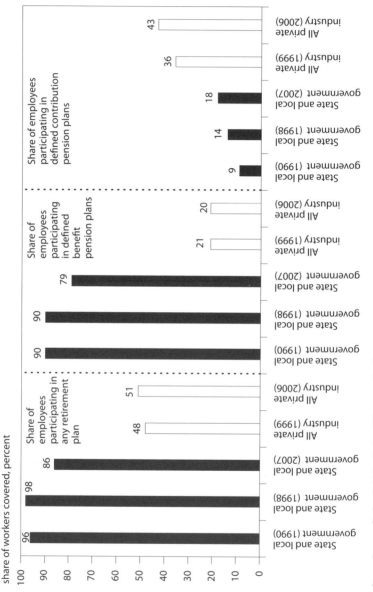

Source: Bureau of Labor Statistics, National Compensation Survey.

Figure 3.15   US employer cost of benefits per hour worked, all employees in sector

dollars per hour worked

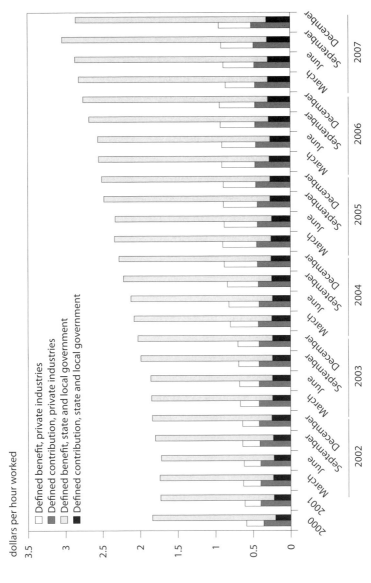

Legend:
- ☐ Defined benefit, private industries
- ▨ Defined contribution, private industries
- ☐ Defined benefit, state and local government
- ■ Defined contribution, state and local government

Note: SIC-based data until 2003; NAICS-based data 2004 onwards.

Source: BLS ECEC Survey, www.bls.gov/ncs.

employer expenditure in 2007 on pension benefit provision was split roughly half and half between DB and DC plans (54 percent DC and 46 percent DB), fully 90 percent of state and local government expenditure went toward DB pensions. On average, therefore, US state and local government workers carry far less financial risk into retirement than do their private-sector compatriots.

Surveys from NASRA (2007), the Wisconsin Legislative Council (2007), and Bovbjerg (2008) found that in 2006 approximately a quarter of all state and local government workers did not participate in Social Security, rising to almost half among public school teachers.[125] However, that same year, non–Social Security–eligible state and local workers were, on average, covered by retirement plans with median contribution rates substantially (44 percent) above those of their Social Security–eligible peers.[126] For about three-quarters of state and local workers, DB pension plans are thus only one component of their total pension eligibility, which might also include a DC plan with employer contributions, not dissimilar to the Federal Thrift Savings Plan.

It is reasonable to state, therefore, that the overwhelming majority of US state and local employees have significantly more generous pension coverage than do employees in either the federal government or the private sector. And this can be by quite some margin (appendix table 3B.1 describes the details of the DB pension plans that cover about 80 percent of state and local workers). Consider state employees in New Mexico: In addition to Social Security, they receive a DB plan offering a guaranteed pension of 3 percent of the highest three consecutive years of salary per year of service, available after 25 years. So a New Mexico state employee who retires at the earliest age for Social Security coverage could retire at age 62—even if he or she was a "wayward youngster" and started working at the late age of 37—after working for 25 years, with reduced Social Security and a guaranteed DB pension worth 75 percent of the average of the three highest consecutive income years of work.[127] Not a bad deal, most Americans would likely agree! Indeed, as table 3B.1 shows, on average the DB component alone for state and local employees is typically worth over half of their highest income years' salary. Considering that three-quarters of US state and local employees also have access to either Social Security and/or DC pension plans, this compares them very favor-

---

125. NASRA (2007) shows that most state and local workers in Alaska, Colorado, Louisiana, Maine, Massachusetts, Ohio, and Nevada did not participate in Social Security.

126. Median employer and employee contribution rates were 8.5 and 5 percent, respectively, for Social Security–eligible state and local workers and 11.5 and 8 percent, respectively, for non–Social Security–eligible state and local workers (NASRA 2007, figure M).

127. New Mexico DB pension accrues at 3 percent per service year but is capped at 80 percent of the average of the three highest earnings years. See appendix table 3B.1 for selected details of 85 state and local pension plans for all 50 states.

ably indeed with "spoiled" French civil servants. French *fonctionnaires* have "only" their government DB pension, worth approximately three-quarters of their highest years of salary, to fall back on if they retire at age 62 after 34 years of service.[128]

The flip side of generous pension benefits to state and local employees is invariably large and rapidly rising pension contributions and liabilities for those governments. Indeed, as shown in figure 3.16, the level of annual contributions by state and local governments to their pension funds has risen by more than 80 percent from 2000 to $63 billion in 2007. At the same time, total payments from the same pension funds have risen by 90 percent to $153 billion in 2007.[129]

Given the highly adverse demographic outlook for the government sector in general, as highlighted above, it seems certain that both these trends will rise steeply in the years ahead as baby-boomers retire. This is a major worry for some state and local governments, given that NASRA (2007) shows that actuarial funding levels of state and local pension funds have continued to decline every year, albeit at a declining rate from 101 percent of actuarial liabilities in FY2001 to 86 percent in FY2006, despite a strong performance by financial markets after 2002.[130]

NASRA (2007) further shows that the combined underfunding of 127 surveyed state and local pension funds was approximately $385 billion in 2006.[131] However, some industry specialists have calculated that such approximate levels of underfunding may be a serious underestimate, derived by using more generous accounting assumptions than are available to private pension plans. Had state pension plans in 2004 used the same accounting assumptions demanded by private-sector DB plans, estimates indicate that their total funding deficit would have more than doubled, from about $300 billion to almost $700 billion.[132]

---

128. French civil servants accrue 2 percent of their three highest years of income for every year of service and get a 3 percent bonus for each year worked after age 60. Thus for 34 years of service at age 62, they are eligible for a DB pension worth 74 percent of the highest three years of income. See EIRO (2003a, 2004).

129. Total income for public pension funds over the 2000–07 period was made up roughly of two-thirds investment income, just over 20 percent government contributions, and the remainder employee contributions.

130. See also Wilshire Consulting (2006, 2007) and Standard and Poor's (2006a).

131. NASRA (2007) surveys about 85 percent of all employees covered by state and local government pension funds. Taking these numbers as an average, this suggests that the total underfunding in US state and local pension funds might be as high as $450 billion. The NASRA (2007) survey is more comprehensive than the more detailed data presented in appendix table 3B.1.

132. See estimates from Barclays Global Investors, described in *Business Week*, "Sinkhole," June 13, 2005. For an elaboration on how elastic accounting assumptions may inflate or deflate pension liabilities, see chapter 7.

Figure 3.16   Quarterly US government contributions to and total payments from state and local pension funds, 2000–07 (billions of dollars)

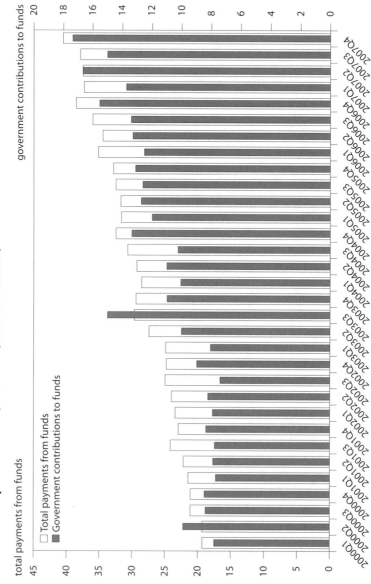

total payments from funds

government contributions to funds

☐ Total payments from funds
■ Government contributions to funds

Source: US Census Bureau, Finances of Selected State and Local Government Employee Retirement Systems, table 2, http://ftp2.census.gov/govs/qpr/table2.txt.

These large numbers notwithstanding, it is, on the other hand, erroneous to allege that a general state or local government pension crisis exists—or may even be in the works—in the United States. When compared to fully sovereign borrowers, even the total of state-level debt and unfunded pension liabilities is nowhere near many countries' central government debt. Only in Connecticut, Hawaii, Mississippi, Rhode Island, and West Virginia does this share climb to the low teens compared with state-level GDP.[133] The low level of US state debt is partly due to the frequently difficult political process of authorizing borrowing in state capital, where frequently direct voter approval and at least legislative approval are required. This is unlike debt at the federal level, where legislative approval is only periodically required for raising the federal government debt ceilings.[134]

US subgovernmental pension funding levels vary tremendously, too—several states have financially healthy pension systems, while others are in various degrees of financial trouble. Appendix table 3B.1 shows that public pension funds in Delaware, Florida, North Carolina, and Oregon were actually overfunded as of 2006, and funds in Georgia, Nebraska, and New York were close to fully funded. On the other hand, about a dozen of the 85 plans shown had funding ratios of less than two-thirds of liabilities, and the West Virginia Teachers Retirement System had a worrisome 19.1 percent of projected liabilities. Given the demographic trends illustrated above, it thus seems certain that there will be serious financial problems in some state and local pension funds even in the short term.

However, given that pension liabilities are very long term in nature, that there are several trillions of dollars of prefunded assets in pension funds available to draw upon, and that benefits pay out relatively slowly—does any of this really matter? It may start to very soon, due to an unfolding change in the accounting rules for state and local governments.

Since June 1997, the Government Accounting Standards Board (GASB)[135] has required that state and local governments measure and

---

133. 2004 data from Standard and Poor's (2006a).

134. Snell (2004) surveys indicate that 16 states require direct voter approval, and five state constitutions forbid the incurring of general obligation debt.

135. The Government Accounting Standards Board (GASB; www.gasb.org) was organized in 1984 to establish standards of financial accounting and reporting for state and local government entities. Although GASB has no authority to enforce any of its standards, rating agencies in case of bond issuances do consider whether state and local government reporting adheres to the GASB standards (GAO 2007).

disclose annual DB pension costs on an accrual accounting basis.[136] However, the pension promises to retiring state and local workers—for which over $2.9 trillion in assets were available at the end of fiscal year 2005–06[137]—do not constitute the entirety of retirement promises to this group. There is another category, blandly known as other postemployment benefits (OPEBs). This essentially residual category consists of nonpension benefits—primarily health care and life insurance—promised to state and public retirees. Until now, OPEB expenses have been included in governments' general expenditures and merely laid out in a footnote to the audited accounts, while being expensed on a cash-flow pay-as-you-go basis. However, in its Statement No. 45 issued in mid-2004, the GASB required pension plan sponsors to start accounting for their OPEB expenses, based on the accrual accounting that also governs the reporting of pension liabilities.[138] Yet very few governmental entities have set aside any assets to fund these obligations. Unlike pension promises, which as stated above have approximately $2.9 trillion in the bank already and are only about 15 percent *underfunded*, OPEB promises are almost wholly *unfunded*. This unfunded status constitutes a potentially serious issue for many state and local governments, due to the requirement in Statement 45 for governments to start to prefund these costs of OPEBs.[139] The Statement requires governments to report an annual OPEB cost, consisting of "the normal accrual accounting OPEB costs for the year" plus a "component for amortization of the total unfunded actuarial accrued liabilities over a period not exceeding 30 years," the total of which equals the annual required contribution (ARC). Hereby state and local governments, if they have made very generous OPEB promises to their employees and, as is most

---

136. See GASB Statement No. 27 (available at www.gasb.org), which was issued in November 1994 and came into force in June 1997. State and local governments that participate in DC pension schemes are also required to estimate their net liabilities on an accrual accounting basis. However, a relatively wide range of accounting assumptions were made available to public plan sponsors, leading some members of GASB in 1994 to criticize the new rules as failing to meet the test of responsibility, as they allowed "an extraordinary number of accounting options," evidently making it possible for some plan sponsors to artificially prop up finances. See the *New York Times*, "Public Pension Plans Face Billions in Shortages," August 8, 2006.

137. Data from US Census Bureau, Table 1: National Summary of State and Local Government Employee-Retirement System Finances Fiscal 2005–06, available at www.census.gov/govs/retire.

138. GASB took the position that OPEBs, like pension benefits, are part of public employees' total compensation and so should be included in the costs of providing these services. See Standard and Poor's (2005).

139. The statement becomes effective gradually, beginning after December 15, 2006, for phase 1 governments (those with total annual revenues of $100 million or more); after December 15, 2007, for phase 2 governments (those with total annual revenues of $10 million or more but less than $100 million); and after December 15, 2008, for phase 3 governments (those with total annual revenues of less than $10 million).

common, until now made no prefunding arrangements, may suddenly be faced with substantial additional liabilities to finance arising from promises to retiring public-sector employees.

The extra bill to taxpayers may in some places be substantial. Standard and Poor's (2005, 2006b, 2007) estimates that the extent of OPEB promises varies among government entities far more than other pension plans and may in some cases constitute up to 50 percent of the total pension liability.[140] Standard and Poor's (2007) most recent partial estimate, covering 40 of the 50 state governments, is $394 billion—about as much as the total underfunding of state and local government pension funds. However, actuarial OPEB liabilities are likely to be even more volatile and to increase more rapidly than actuarial pension liabilities, as estimating them requires taking into account future health care cost inflation. State and local government finances are thus affected by the same crushing effects of health care costs as are the federal Medicare and Medicaid programs (but unlike the federal government, the state and local governments are now obliged to put these costs on their books).[141]

The effects of these multiple developments—an aging workforce, continued generous pension provisions, a history of underfunding retirement promises, and new accounting rules for state and local governments' health care obligations—are not yet clear. There are several possible scenarios. While a broad state and local level government pension crisis is unlikely, several, if not numerous, pension entities at these levels of government will face substantial financial challenges in the years immediately ahead.

This will soon matter politically. State and local government pension plans, unlike their private-sector counterparts, are not covered by the Employee Retirement Income Security Act of 1974 (ERISA) or the insurance operation run by the Pension Benefit Guaranty Corporation (PBGC).[142] Hence there is no federal guarantee for these pension promises. States will have to pay for them themselves.

On the other hand, and likely as a direct result, the GAO (2007, 19) reports that 31 states have a total of 93 constitutional provisions—the strongest form of legal protection a state can provide—protecting public-

---

140. Some state and local governments have offered their employees very generous health care coverage for dependents, whereas others have made no such commitments.

141. As a result, other industry estimates of state-level OPEB obligations are significantly higher than Standard and Poor's (2007). Credit Suisse analysts Zion and Varshney (2007) indicate that unfunded health care liabilities may be as high as $1.5 trillion, while Aon Consulting in late 2006 estimated the total state and local government retiree health care bill at approximately $1.1 trillion (*New York Times*, "Paying Health Care From Pensions Proves Costly," December 19, 2006). Edwards and Gokhale (2006) estimate that OPEBs relating to health care could be $1.4 trillion.

142. Public pension funds must still, however, comply with IRS requirements for tax-exempt treatment (GAO 2007).

sector pension provisions. The overwhelming majority of state and local pensions, negotiated by unions in collective bargaining, have this additional protection. Pension promises are thus very hard to renege on for state and local governments.

However, given that these future promises are, on average, substantially more generous than those available to employees in the private sector, and that they will ultimately have to be paid by all taxpayers, continuing to honor them in the face of rapidly rising costs seems likely to cause future political fissures. This is especially so as most state and local governments maintain balanced budget requirements[143] that generally restrict the financing of (general fund) activities and PAYGO pension payments through more debt.[144] Instead of simple debt financing, state and local governments will have to rely to a larger extent on either direct tax increases or cuts in other expenditure items to finance rising pension expenditures. With the limited political appetite in America in recent years for the former and the largest other expenditure item being education,[145] it is easy to identify the contours of upcoming state and local clashes of interest in what will be close to a zero-sum game between the traditional low tax/limited government constituency, families with children, and public-sector retirees. Simply relying on one-off budget fudges in the form of sales of earmarked "pension bonds"[146] or public assets or raising

---

143. Snell (2004) carried out a survey for the National Conference of State Legislators, showing that all states except Vermont had such rules in place of constitutional or statutory rules, or those derived by judicial decision from constitutional provisions about state indebtedness. As states typically follow fund accounting (in which all revenues and expenditures are designated a particular fund), they must distinguish in their state balanced-budget requirements between the general fund and other funds (typically for such items as highways or general transportation). Balanced-budget requirements for states usually concern the general funds, which account for the vast majority of state spending.

144. The federal government debt held by the public rose from $3.5 trillion to $5.1 trillion, or more than 45 percent, from 2002 to March 2007, according to the June 2007 Treasury Bulletin (www.fms.treas.gov/bulletin); the total outstanding federal debt reached $8.9 trillion in March 2007. Furthermore, the assets of the Social Security Trust Fund are entirely made up of Treasury bills, and as such are a government IOU to benefit recipients.

145. In FY2003–04, state and local governments spent $655 billion, or 34 percent of all direct general expenditure, on education, with three-quarters at the local level (US Census Bureau, State and Local Government Finances, www.census.gov).

146. Several states, such as New Jersey, have tried to issue pension obligation bonds (POBs), where the proceeds of the bond sale go not to funding the general state government but to the state pension fund(s). Essentially, POBs are a bet that the market return of pension fund investments will surpass the interest paid on the bond. Standard and Poor's estimates that in 1995–2005 state and local governments raised approximately $30 billion through POB issuance. However, given volatile market returns since 2000, POBs have not always paid off for the issuing entity. See *Business Week* Special Report—Public Pensions, "Online Extra: How the Garden State Dug a Hole," June 13, 2005. POBs, and the related practice of "reverse compounding," are highly relevant for private-sector pensions, too, and are discussed in detail in chapter 7.

fees for other public services seems highly unlikely to financially suffice, even if such options were (improbably) politically passable.

State and local governments may instead choose, in the face of overwhelming financial challenges, to renege on the pension promises to retirees. Choosing such approach would represent a novel development in the area of public pensions in America, as, for instance, not even the default of New York City in the late 1970s resulted in changes to any of the city's promised public worker pensions. Yet there are signs that it is beginning to happen. Several states have in recent years opted to cut public worker pensions rather than take any of the unpalatable options mentioned above,[147] although strong legal protections (in either state laws or union contracts) for public pensions seem destined to lead states that choose this option into costly litigation.

Whatever option state and local governments choose, massive pension-related inequalities cannot politically persist. Given the generosity of state and local public-sector pensions relative to those for private-sector workers and the increasing exposure of the true costs to governments of these promises (thanks to the new GASB accounting rules), the public sector may elect to follow the example of the private sector, where increased accounting transparency and rising financial stress led to a dramatic scaling back of pension promises (see chapter 7). Such a trend seems plausible given the political difficulty, once the distributional unfairness becomes known to the wider voting public, of having to defend public-sector pension promises that are much more generous than those available to the average public. If there is a large-scale reduction in public-sector pension benefits, a decline among state and local workers (especially in the most financially strained state and local governments) seems possible, if not likely. This is another lesson from the decade-long pension-related conflicts in France, which ended in 2007–08 only with the curtailment of generous "special pensions" for some public employees (see box 3.6).

Concluding Remarks

This chapter has focused on the distributional aspects and concerns of pension provision. We have shown how the fundamental organizing principles—universal means-tested or contributory insurance—of pension systems largely shape distributional outcomes and also play a big role in the outlook for countries' pension sustainability. US Social Security is relatively modest (especially at high incomes), falling approximately in the middle in terms of progressivity in the OECD, and is considerably less

---

147. *New York Times*, "Once Safe, Public Pensions Are Now Facing Cuts," November 6, 2006, lists Oregon, Rhode Island, Milwaukee County, and the city of Houston as such examples.

redistributive than mandatory pension programs in other English-speaking countries. We therefore conclude that there is political room to make Social Security a more progressive contributory insurance system.

We find that poverty is more prevalent among old people in the OECD than among working age populations, particularly among the very old (those 75 and older), who are overwhelmingly women. In fact, the United States is among the OECD countries with the highest levels of old age poverty. Looking at the sources of income for people over age 65, we find both for the United States and most OECD countries that only in the top income quintile do public transfers not make up the overwhelming majority of income (for the top income quintile, earnings account for a substantial share of income). As a result, we conclude that pension reforms aimed at improving the solvency of Social Security are not tenable if they include across-the-board cuts in benefits. Instead, we propose that benefit cuts be targeted only to the highest-income quintile in the United States.

Currently, retiring generations across the OECD can look forward to substantially larger shares of their lifetime spent in retirement, relative to both earlier generations and—if anything like current benefit levels are maintained—future generations as well. OECD countries are, therefore, increasingly taking measures to link retirement to life expectancies. While the United States has legislated a prefixed gradual increase in the full Social Security eligibility age from 65 to 67, it is not among the countries to have legislated a direct link to life expectancies. We believe that is a mistake and propose that after 2027, both the early and full age of Social Security eligibility be linked directly to Americans' life expectancy. We believe this is best done in a manner that maintains the fraction of Americans' lifetime spent in retirement to total lifetime fixed at historical levels. As we describe elsewhere, this gradual increase in the normal retirement age should be accompanied by measures to encourage saving for workers wishing to retire early and to ensure that disabled workers are not pushed into poverty.

However, predictions of life expectancies are uncertain and contested. Direct links to life expectancies must therefore tread a fine line between the necessary "early warning" to allow the public to plan accordingly for changes and the risk of increasing uncertainty by premature announcements. While disparities in life expectancies for different population subgroups are rapidly increasing in the United States, we conclude that the uncertainties of life expectancy estimation are too great to permit differentiation of retirement ages in mandatory pension systems.

Public employee pensions across the OECD and in the United States are significantly more generous than average mandatory pensions available to the general public. In the United States, given recent cuts to private-sector pension benefits, political resistance to tax increases, and the scale of retirement-related funding problems among some state and local governments, it seems likely that any long-term financial problems in state and local government pension plans will be addressed largely through cuts in pension benefits. This is particularly likely as public pension accounting is undergoing the same transition to accrual accounting as previously experienced in the private sector, where a scaling back of pension promises quickly followed. Recent hotly contested reductions in the generosity of public-sector pensions in France also point to the fact that in periods of intense fiscal stress, it is politically untenable to maintain significantly more generous retirement programs for public-sector workers relative to other workers.

References

AARP (American Association of Retired People) 2008. *Sources of Income for Older Persons in 2006*. AARP Fact Sheet. Available at http://assets.aarp.org.

ADECRI (Agence de Coopération Internationale en Sécurité Sociale). 2005. *The French Social Protection System*. Paris.

Adema, Willem, and Maxime Ladaique. 2005. *Net Social Expenditure, 2005 Edition—More Comprehensive Measures of Social Support*. OECD Social, Employment and Migration Working Paper 29. Paris: Organization for Economic Cooperation and Development.

Andersen, T. M. 2005. *Social Security and Longevity*. Working Paper no. 1577. Munich: CESIfo.

Antolín, Pablo. 2007. *Longevity Risk and Private Pensions*. OECD Working Paper on Insurance and Private Pensions no. 3. Paris: Organization for Economic Cooperation and Development.

Antolín, Pablo, Thai-Thanh Dang, and Howard Oxley. 1999. *Poverty Dynamics in Four OECD Countries*. OECD Economics Department Working Paper 212 (April). Paris: Organization for Economic Cooperation and Development.

Auerbach, Alan J., Jagadeesh Gokhale, and Laurence J. Kotlikoff. 1991. Generational Accounts: A Meaningful Alternative to Deficit Accounting. In *Tax Policy and the Economy* 5: 55–110. Cambridge, MA: MIT Press.

Auerbach, Alan J., Jagadeesh Gokhale, and Laurence J. Kotlikoff. 1992. Generational Accounting: A New Approach to Understanding the Effects of Fiscal Policy on Savings. *Scandinavian Journal of Economics* 94, no. 2: 303–18.

Auerbach, Alan J., Jagadeesh Gokhale, and Laurence J. Kotlikoff. 1994. Generational Accounting: A Meaningful Way to Assess Generational Policy. *Journal of Economic Perspectives* 8, no. 1: 73–94.

Auerbach, Alan J., Laurence J. Kotlikoff, and Willie Leibfritz, eds. 1999. *Generational Accounting around the World*. Chicago: University of Chicago Press.

Baily, Martin N. 1987. Aging and the Ability to Work: Policy Issues and Recent Trends. In *Work, Health, and Income Among the Elderly*, ed. Gary Burtless. Washington: Brookings Institution.

Barnett, E., D. L. Armstrong, and M. L. Casper. 1999. Evidence of Increasing Coronary Heart Disease Mortality Among Black Men of Lower Social Class. *Annals of Epidemiology* 9, no. 8: 464–71.

Barr, Nicholas. 2006. Non-Financial Defined Contribution Pensions: Mapping the Terrain. In *Pension Reform: Issues and Prospects for Non-Financial Defined Contribution Schemes*, ed. Robet Holtzmann and Edward Palmer. Washington: World Bank Publications.

Becker, Gary S., and Kevin M. Murphy. 1988. The Family and the State. *Journal of Law and Economics* 31 (April): 1–18.

Benallah, Samia, Pierre Concialdi, and Antoine Math. 2003. The French Experience of Pension Reforms. Paper presented at the European Network for Research on Supplementary Pensions (ENRSP) seminar, London, September 19–21.

Blanchard, Olivier. 2004. *The Economic Future of Europe.* NBER Working Paper 10310. Cambridge, MA: National Bureau of Economic Research.

Bommier, Antoine, Ronald Lee, Timothy Miller, and Stephane Zuber. 2004. *Who Wins and Who Loses? Public Transfer Accounts for US Generations Born 1850 to 2090.* NBER Working Paper 10969. Cambridge, MA: National Bureau of Economic Research.

Bopp, M., and C. E. Minder. 2003. Mortality by Education in German-Speaking Switzerland, 1990–1997: Results from the Swiss National Cohort. *International Journal of Epidemiology* 32, no. 3: 346–54.

Bovbjerg, Barbara D. 2008. *State and Local Government Pension Plans: Current Structure and Funded Status. Testimony before the Joint Economic Committee.* GAO Document 08-983T. Washington: Government Accountability Office. Available at www.gao.gov.

Brabrook, Edward. 1908. Social Insurances. *Journal of the Royal Statistical Society* 71, no. 4: 601–12.

Brønnum-Hansen, H., O. Andersen, M. Kjøller, and N. K. Rasmussen. 2004. Social Gradient in Life Expectancy and Health Expectancy in Denmark. *Soz Praventivmed* 49, no. 1: 36–41.

Brønnum-Hansen, H. 2006. Social Differences in Mortality Trends in Denmark (in Danish). *Ugeskr Laeger* 168, no. 21: 2066–69.

Buiter, Willem H. 1997. Generational Accounts, Aggregate Saving and Intergenerational Distribution. *Economica* 64: 605–26.

CBO (Congressional Budget Office). 2006. *Is Social Security Progressive?* Economic and Budget Issue Brief (December). Washington.

CDC (Centers for Disease Control and Prevention). 2006. United States Life Tables, 2003. *National Vital Statistics Reports* 54, no. 14. Washington: National Vital Statistics System.

Charpin, Jean-Michel. 1999. *L'Avenir de nos Retraites: Rapport au Premier Ministre.* La Documentation Française. Paris: Commissariat Général du Plan.

Cheng, A. W., M. L. Miller, M. Morris, J. P. Schultz, J. P. Skirvin, and D. P. Walder. 2004. *A Stochastic Model of the Long Range Financial Status of the OASDI Program, 2004.* Actuarial Study no. 117. SSA Publication no. 11-11543. Washington: Social Security Administration.

Crimmins, E. M., and Y. Saito. 2001. Trends in Health Life Expectancy in the United States, 1970-1990: Gender, Racial, and Educational Differences. *Social Science & Medicine* 52: 1629–41.

Cutler, D., and L. Katz. 1991. Macroeconomic Performance and the Disadvantaged. *Brookings Papers on Economic Activity*, no. 2. Washington: Brookings Institution.

Dang, Thai-Thanh, Herwig Immervoll, Daniela Mantovani, Kristian Orsini, and Holly Sutherland. 2006. *An Age Perspective on Economic Well-Being and Social Protection in Nine OECD Countries.* OECD Social, Employment and Migration Working Paper 34. OECD Directorate for Employment, Labor and Social Affairs. Paris: Organization for Economic Cooperation and Development.

Danish Ministry of Finance. 2006. *Aftale om fremtidens velstand og velfærd og investeringer i fremtiden—Aftale om fremtidig indvandring.* Copenhagen.

Davey, Smith G., P. J. Marang-van de Mheen, C. L. Hart, and L. J. Gunning-Schepers. 1998. Socioeconomic Differentials in Mortality among Men within Great Britain: Time Trends and Contributory Causes. *Journal of Epidemiol Community Health* 52, no. 4: 214–18.

De Vogli R., R. Mistry, R. Gnesotto, and G. A. Cornia. 2005. Has the Relation between Income Inequality and Life Expectancy Disappeared? Evidence from Italy and Top Industrialised Countries. *Journal of Epidemiol Community Health* 59, no. 2: 158–62.

Diamond, Peter A. 1996. Generational Accounts and Generational Balance: An Assessment. *National Tax Journal* 49: 597–607.

Diamond, Peter A., and Peter R. Orszag. 2004. Accrual Accounting for Social Security. *Harvard Journal on Legislation* 41, no. 173.

Diamond, Peter A., and Peter R. Orszag. 2005. Saving Social Security. *Journal of Economic Perspectives* 19, no. 2 (Spring): 11–32.

Duggan, James E., Robert Gillingham, and John S. Greenlees.1993. *The Returns Paid to Early Social Security Cohorts.* Department of the Treasury Research Paper 9302 (April). Washington: US Treasury.

Edwards, Chris, and Jagadeesh Gokhale. 2006. Unfunded State and Local Health Costs: $1.4 Trillion. *Cato Institute Tax and Budget Bulletin*, no. 40 (October). Washington: Cato Institute.

European Commission. 1999. *Generational Accounting in Europe*. European Economy, Reports and Studies, no. 9. Brussels.

EIRO (European Industrial Relations Observatory). 2003a. *Retirement before 60 Introduced for People with Long Working Lives*. Available at http://eiro.eurofound.europa.eu.

EIRO (European Industrial Relations Observatory). 2003b. *Pension Reform Adopted*. Available at www.eurofound.europa.eu.

EIRO (European Industrial Relations Observatory). 2003c. *Government's Pension Reform Adopted*. Available at www.eurofound.europa.eu.

EIRO (European Industrial Relations Observatory). 2003d. *Electricity and Gas Workers Reject Agreement on Pension Reform*. Available at www.eurofound.europa.eu.

EIRO (European Industrial Relations Observatory). 2004. *EDF Pension System Incorporated Into General System*. Available at www.eurofound.europa.eu.

FRTIB (Federal Retirement Thrift Investment Board). 2005. *Summary of the Thrift Savings Plan—August 2005*. Washington.

Fisher, T. Lynn. 2005. *Measurement of Reliance on Social Security Benefits*. Washington: Social Security Administration. Available at www.fcsm.gov.

Förster, M. F., and Mark Pearson. 2002. Income Distribution and Poverty in the OECD Area: Trends and Driving Forces. *OECD Economic Studies*, no. 34. Paris: Organization for Economic Cooperation and Development.

Förster, M. F., and M. Mira d'Ercole. 2005. *Income Distribution and Poverty in OECD Countries in the Second Half of the 1990s*. OECD Social, Employment and Migration Working Paper 22. Paris: Organization for Economic Cooperation and Development.

GAO (General Accounting Office). 1999. *State Pension Plans—Similarities and Differences Between Federal and State Design*. GAO GGD 99-45. Washington.

GAO (Government Accountability Office). 2007. *State and Local Government Retiree Benefits: Current Status of Benefit Structures, Protections, and Fiscal Outlook for Funding Future Costs*. GAO Report 07-1156. Washington.

GAO (Government Accountability Office). 2008. Federal Agencies Face Challenges but Have Opportunities to Hire and Retain Experienced Employees. Statement by Barbara D. Bovbjerg, director of education, workforce, and income security issues, and Robert N. Goldenkoff, director of strategic issues, before the Senate Special Committee on Aging, Washington, April 30.

Gazeley, Ian. 2003. *Poverty in Britain 1900-1965*. London: Palgrave-Macmillan.

Gigerenzer, Gerd. 2002. *Adaptive Thinking: Rationality in the Real World*. Oxford: Oxford University Press.

Gokhale, Jagadeesh, Benjamin Page, Joan Potter, and John Sturrock. 2000. Generational Accounts for the United States: An Update. *American Economic Review* 90, no. 2: 293–96.

Gottshalk, P., and T. Smeeding. 2000. Empirical Evidence on Income Inequality in Industrial Countries. In *Handbook of Income Distribution*, ed. A. Atkinson and F. Bourguignon. Elsevier.

Grigg, John. 1978. *Lloyd George: The People's Champion, 1902–1911*. Berkeley and Los Angeles: University of California Press.

Halsey, Olga S. 1934. *British Old Age Pensions and Old Age Insurance*. Washington: Social Security Administration Committee on Economic Security. Available at www.ssa.gov.

Haveman, Robert. 1994. Should Generational Accounts Replace Public Budgets and Deficits? *Journal of Economic Perspectives* 8: 95–112.

Helman, Ruth, Jack VanDerhei, and Craig Copeland. 2007. *The Retirement System in Transition: The 2007 Retirement Confidence Survey*. EBRI Issue Brief 304 (April). Washington: Employee Benefit Research Institute.

Hewitt Associates LLC. 2005. *Micro-History of Employee Benefits and Compensation 1794–2005*. Lincolnshire, IL. Available at www.hewittassociates.com.

Hogarth, Janet. 1896. The German Insurance Laws. *Economic Journal* 6, no. 22: 283–94. London: Royal Economic Society.

Huisman, M., A. E. Kunst, O. Andersen, M. Bopp, J. K. Borgan, C. Borrell, G. Costa, P. Deboosere, G. Desplanques, A. Donkin, S. Gadeyne, C. Minder, E. Regidor, T. Spadea, T. Valkonen, and J. P. Mackenbach. 2004. Socioeconomic Inequalities in Mortality among Elderly People in 11 European Populations. *Journal of Epidemiol Community Health* 58, no. 6: 468–75.

Hurd, Michael, and Susann Rohwedder. 2006. *Consumption and Economic Well-Being at Older Ages: Income- and Consumption-Based Poverty Measures in the HRS*. Working Papers 110. Michigan Retirement Research Center, University of Michigan.

Japanese Ministry of Ministry of Internal Affairs and Communications. 2005. *White Paper on Local Public Finance—2005*. Tokyo: Government of Japan.

Jeger, Francois, and Michel Lelievre. 2005. The French Pension System and 2003 Reform. *Japanese Journal of Social Security Policy* 4, no. 2 (December): 76–84.

Jeune, B. 1995. In Search for the First Centenarians. In *Exceptional Longevity*, ed. B. Jeune and J. W. Vaupel. Odense, Denmark: Odense University Press.

Jorgenson, D., and D. Slesnick. 1987. Aggregate Consumer Behavior and Household Equivalence Scales. *Journal of Business and Economic Statistics* 5, no. 2: 219–32.

Johnson, D., T. Smeeding, and B. Torrey. 2005. Economic Inequality Through the Prisms of Income and Consumption. *Monthly Labor Review* (April): 11–24.

Kalediene, R., and J. Petrauskiene. 2004. Socio-Economic Transition, Inequality, and Mortality in Lithuania. *Economic & Human Biology* 2, no. 1: 87–95.

Kaplan, G. A., E. R. Pamuk, J. R. Lynch, R. D. Cohen, and J. L. Balfour. 1996. Inequality in Income and Mortality in the United States—Analysis of Mortality and Potential Pathways. *BMJ (British Medical Journal)* 312, no. 7037: 999–1003.

Kannisto, V. 1994. *Development of the Oldest-Old Mortality, 1950–1990*. Odense, Denmark: Odense University Press.

Kannisto V., J. Lauritsen, A. R. Thatcher, and J. W. Vaupel. 1994. Reductions in Mortality at Advanced Ages: Several Decades of Evidence from 27 Countries. *Population Development Review* 20, no. 4: 793–830.

Knight, Frank H. 1921. *Risk, Uncertainty, and Profit*. Hart, Schaffner, and Marx Prize Essays, no. 31. Boston and New York: Houghton Mifflin.

Kotlikoff, Laurence J., and Bernd Raffelhüschen. 1999. Generational Accounting Around the World. *American Economic Review* 89, no. 2: 161–66.

Kotlikoff, Laurence J., Ben Marx, and Pietro Rizza. 2006. *Americans' Dependency on Social Security*. NBER Working Paper 12696. Cambridge, MA: National Bureau of Economic Research.

Kuhn, Peter, and Fernando Lozano. 2005. *The Expanding Workweek? Understanding Trends in Long Work Hours Among U.S. Men, 1979-2004*. NBER Working Paper 11895. Cambridge, MA: National Bureau of Economic Research.

Lasswell, Harold D. 1990. *Politics: Who Gets What, When and How?* New York: Peter Smith Publishing.

Leimer, Dean R. 1994. *Cohort Specific Measures of Lifetime Net Social Security Transfers*. ORS Working Paper no. 59 (February). Washington: Office of Research and Statistics, Social Security Administration.

Leinsalu, M., D. Vågerö, and A. E. Kunst. 2003. Estonia 1989–2000: Enormous Increase in Mortality Differences by Education. *International Journal of Epidemiology* 32, no. 6: 1081–87.

Liebman, Jeffrey B. 2001. *Redistribution in the Current U.S. Social Security System*. NBER Working Paper 8625. Cambridge, MA: National Bureau of Economic Research.

Lin, C. C., E. Rogot, N. J. Johnson, P. D. Sorlie, and E. Aries. 2003. A Further Study of Life Expectancy by Socio-Economic Factors in the National Longitudinal Mortality Study. *Ethnicity and Disease* 13, no. 2 (Spring): 240–47.

Lleras-Muney, Adriana. 2005. The Relationship Between Education and Adult Mortality in the United States. *Review of Economic Studies* 72, no. 1: 189–221.

Lynch, J., P. Due, C. Muntaner, and G. Davey Smith. 2000. Social Capital—Is It a Good Investment Strategy for Public Health? *Journal of Epidemiol Community Health* 54: 404–408.

Lynch, John, Sam Harper, George A. Kaplan, and George Davey Smith. 2005. Associations Between Income Inequality and Mortality Among US States: The Importance of Time Period and Source of Income Data. *American Journal of Public Health* 95, no. 8: 1424–30.

Mackenbach, J. P., M. Huisman, and A. E. Kunst. 2003. Socioeconomic Inequalities in Morbidity among the Elderly: A European Overview. *Social Science & Medicine* 57, no. 5: 861–73.

Manton, K. G., and X. Gu. 2001. Changes in the Prevalence of Chronic Disability in the United States Black and Nonblack Population above Age 65 from 1982 to 1999. *Proceedings of the National Academy of Sciences* 98: 6354–59.

Mathers, C. D., C. J. L. Murray, A. D. Lopez, J. A. Salomon, R. Sadana, A. Tandon, T. Bedirhan Ustun, and S. Chatterji. 2001. *Estimates of Healthy Life Expectancy for 191 Countries in the Year 2000: Methods and Results.* World Health Organization Global Health Programme on Evidence for Health Policy Discussion Paper no. 38. Geneva: World Health Organization.

McDonnell, Ken, and EBRI (Employee Benefit Research Institute). 2005. *Benefit Cost Comparisons Between State and Local Governments and Private-Sector Employers.* EBRI Notes 26, no. 4 (April). Washington: Employee Benefit Research Institute.

McDonough P., G. J. Duncan, D. Williams, and J. House. 1997. Income Dynamics and Adult Mortality in the United States, 1972 through 1989. *American Journal of Public Health* 87, no. 9: 1467–83.

McLeod, C. B., J. N. Lavis, C. A. Mustard, and G. L. Stoddart. 2003. Income Inequality, Household Income, and Health Status in Canada: A Prospective Cohort Study. *American Journal of Public Health* 93, no. 8: 1287–93.

McNeill, W. H. 1976. *Plagues and Peoples.* Garden City, NY: Anchor Press/Double Day.

Menchik, Paul L. 1993. Economic Status as a Determinant of Mortality among Black and White Older Men: Does Poverty Kill? *Population Studies* 47, no. 3: 427–36.

Meyer, Bruce D., and James X. Sullivan. 2003. Measuring the Well-Being of the Poor Using Income and Consumption. *Journal of Human Resources* 38: 1180–220.

Murray, Christopher J. L., Sandeep Kulkarni, Catherine Michaud, Niels Tomijima, Maria T. Bulzaccchelli, Terrell J. Iandiorio, and Majid Ezzati. 2006. Eight Americas: Investigating Mortality Disparities Across Races, Counties, and Race-Counties in the United States. *PLoS Medicine* 3, no. 9: e260.

NASRA (National Association of State Retirement Administrators). 2007. *Public Fund Survey Summary of Findings for FY 2006.* Available at www.publicfundsurvey.org.

OECD (Organization for Economic Cooperation and Development). 2002. *Public Management Committee: Highlights of Public Sector Pay and Employment Trends: 2002 Update.* Paris.

OECD (Organization for Economic Cooperation and Development). 2005. *Pensions at a Glance—Public Policies Across OECD Countries.* Paris.

OECD (Organization for Economic Cooperation and Development). 2006. *Live Longer, Work Longer.* Paris.

OECD (Organization for Economic Cooperation and Development). 2007a. *Pensions at a Glance—Public Policies Across OECD Countries.* Paris.

OECD (Organization for Economic Cooperation and Development). 2007b. *The Social Expenditure Database: An Interpretive Guide, OECD SOCX 1980-2003,* June version. Paris.

OECD (Organization for Economic Cooperation and Development). 2007c. *Economic Survey of New Zealand.* Paris.

OECD (Organization for Economic Cooperation and Development). 2008. *Economic Survey of Ireland.* Paris.

Olshansky, S. Jay, Bruce A. Carnes, and Aline Désesquelles. 2001. Prospects for Longevity. *Science* 291, no. 5508: 1491–92.

Olshansky S. Jay, Douglas J. Passaro, Ronald C. Hershow, Jennifer Layden, Bruce A. Carnes, Jacob Brody, Leonard Hayflick,, Robert N. Butler, David B. Allison, and David S. Ludwig.

2005. A Potential Decline in Life Expectancy in the United States in the 21st Century. *New England Journal of Medicine* 352, no. 11: 1138–45.

Oeppen, Jim, and James W. Vaupel. 2002. Broken Limits to Life Expectancy. *Science* 10 (May): 1029–31.

Palacios, P., and E. Whitehouse. 2006. *Civil-Service Pensions around the World*. Washington: World Bank.

Pearce, N., and G. Davey Smith. 2003. Is Social Capital the Key to Inequalities in Health? *American Journal of Public Health* 93, no. 1: 122–29.

Putnam, Robert D. 1993. *Making Democracy Work: Civic Traditions in Modern Italy*. Princeton: Princeton University Press.

Putnam, Robert D. 2000. *Bowling Alone: The Collapse and Revival of American Community*. New York: Simon & Schuster.

Queisser, M., and E. R. Whitehouse. 2006. *Neutral or Fair? Actuarial Concepts and Pension-System Design*. Social, Employment and Migration Working Paper no. 40. Paris: Organization for Economic Cooperation and Development.

Raphael, M. 1964. *Pensions and Public Servants: A Study of the Origins of the British System*. Paris: Mouton.

Reynolds, S. L., Y. Saito, and E. M. Crimmins. 2005. The Impact of Obesity on Active Life Expectancy in Older American Men and Women. *The Gerontologist* 45: 438–44.

Riley J. 2001. *Rising Life Expectancy: A Global History*. Cambridge: Cambridge University Press.

Ritakallio, T. M. 2003. *The Importance of Housing Costs in Cross-National Comparisons of Welfare (State) Outcomes*. Turku: Department of Social Policy, University of Turku.

Robaschik, Frank, and Naoyuki Yoshino. 2001. Comparative Analysis of the Public Banking Systems of Germany and Japan. *Japanstudien*, Band 13: 343–72.

Robaschik, Frank, and Naoyuki Yoshino. 2004. *Local Government Finance in Japan: Can Irresponsible Borrowing Be Avoided?* Duisberg Working Papers on East Asian Economic Studies 72/204. Duisberg: University of Duisburg-Essen.

Roemer, Marc. 2000. *Assessing the Quality of the March Current Population Survey and the Survey of Income and Program Participation Income Estimates, 1990-1996*. Washington: US Census Bureau.

Rogers, R. G. 1992. Living and Dying in the USA: Socio-Demographic Determinants of Death Among Blacks and Whites. *Demography* 29, no. 2: 287–303.

Rogers, R. G., R. A. Hummer, C. B. Nam, and K. Peters. 1996. Demographic, Socioeconomic, and Behavioral Factors Affecting Ethnic Mortality by Cause. *Social Forces* 74, no. 4: 1419–38.

Rothenbacher, Franz. 2004. *The Welfare States of the Civil Servants in Europe: A Comparison of the Pension Systems for Civil Servants in France, Great Britain and Germany*. MZES Working Papers no. 74/2004. Mannheim: Mannheim Centre for European Social Research.

Sakmann, Marianne. 1934. *Financial History of Workers' Invalidity, Old Age and Survivors' Insurance of Germany*. Washington: Social Security Administration Committee on Economic Security. Available at www.ssa.gov.

Schalick, Lisa Miller, Wilbur C. Hadden, Elsie Pamuk, Vicente Navarro, and Gregory Pappas. 2000. The Widening Gap in Death Rates Among Income Groups in the United States From 1967 to 1986. *International Journal of Health Services* 30, no.1: 13–26.

Scherer, Peter. 2001. *Age of Withdrawal From the Labor Force in OECD Countries*. OECD Labor Market and Social Policy Occasional Papers 49. Paris: Organization for Economic Cooperation and Development. Available at www.oecd.org.

Schiavo-Campo, Salvatore, Giulio de Tommaso, and Amitabha Mukherjee. 2003. *An International Statistical Survey of Government Employment and Wages*. World Bank Policy Research Working Paper 1806. Washington: World Bank.

Schoeni, R. F., L. G. Martin, P. M. Andreski, and V. A. Freedman. 2005. Persistent and Growing Socio-Economic Disparities in Disability Among the Elderly: 1982–2002. *American Journal of Public Health* 95, no. 11: 2065–70.

Shkolnikov, V. M., E. M. Andreev, D. Jasilionis, M. Leinsalu, O. I. Antonova, and M. McKee. 2006. The Changing Relation between Education and Life Expectancy in Central and Eastern Europe in the 1990s. *Journal of Epidemiol Community Health* 60, no. 10: 875–81.

Scholz, John Karl, Ananth Seshadri, and Surachai Khitatrakun. 2006. Are Americans Saving "Optimally" for Retirement? *Journal of Political Economy* 114, no. 4: 607–43.

Singh G. K., and S. Siahpush. 2006. Widening Socio-Economic Inequalities in US Life Expectancies, 1980–2000. *International Journal of Epidemiology* 9 (May).

Slesnick, D. 1993. Gaining Ground: Poverty in the Postwar United States. *Journal of Political Economy* 101.

Slesnick, D. 2001. *Consumption and Social Welfare.* Cambridge: Cambridge University Press.

Snell, Ronald K. 2004. *State Balanced Budget Requirements: Provisions and Practice—Updated.* National Conference of State Legislatures. Available at www.ncsl.org.

SSA (Social Security Administration). 2002. *Income of the Population 55 or Older, 2000.* Washington. Available at www.ssa.gov.

SSA (Social Security Administration). 2006a. *Income of the Population 55 or Older, 2004. Washington.* Available at www.ssa.gov.

SSA (Social Security Administration). 2006b. *Social Security Programs Throughout the World—Europe, 2006.* Washington.

SSA (Social Security Administration). 2007. *Social Security Programs Throughout the World—Asia and the Pacific, 2006.* Washington.

Sorlie, P. D., E. Backland, and J. B. Keller. 1995. U.S. Mortality by Economic, Demographic, and Social Characteristics: The National Longitudinal Mortality Study. *American Journal of Public Health* 85, no. 7: 949–56.

Standard and Poor's. 2005. *Funding OPEB Liabilities: Assessing the Options.* Standard and Poor's Ratings Direct (December 15).

Standard and Poor's. 2006a. *CreditWeek—Special Issue: Pension Storm Clouds Gather* (June 7).

Standard and Poor's. 2006b. *Accounting for OPEB Liabilities: Can State and Local Governments Cope?* Standard and Poor's Ratings Direct (June 15).

Standard and Poor's. 2007. *US States are Quantifying OPEB Liabilities and Developing Funding Strategies as the GASB Deadline Nears.* Standard and Poor's Ratings Direct (November 12).

Sundquist, J., and S. E. Johansson. 1997. Indicators of Socio-Economic Position and their Relation to Mortality in Sweden. *Social Science & Medicine* 45, no. 12: 1757–66.

TPAM (Technical Panel on Assumptions and Methods). 2003. *Report to the Social Security Advisory Board.* Washington.

UK Department of Work and Pensions. 2006. *Security in Retirement: Towards a New Pensions System.* London: The Stationery Office.

US Census Bureau. 2005. *65+ in the United States.* Current Population Report Special Studies P23-209. Washington.

VanDerhei, Jack. 2006. *Measuring Retirement Income Adequacy: Calculating Realistic Income Replacement Rates.* EBRI Issue Brief 297 (September). Washington: Employment Benefit Research Institute.

Vaupel, J. W., and B. Jeune. 1995. The Emergence and Proliferation of Centenarians. In *Exceptional Longevity,* ed. B. Jeune and J. W. Vaupel. Odense, Denmark: Odense University Press.

Vaupel, James W., and Kristin G. V. Kistowski. 2005. *Broken Limits to Life Expectancy.* Rostock, Germany: Max Planck Institute for Demographic Research.

von dem Knesebeck O., P. E. Verde, and N. Dragano. 2006. Education and Health in 22 European Countries. *Social Science & Medicine* 63, no. 5:1344–51.

Waldron, Hillary. 2002. *Mortality Differentials by Race.* ORES Working Paper no. 99 (December). Washington: Office of Policy, Social Security Administration.

Warner, D. F., and M. D. Hayward. 2006. Early-Life Origins of the Race Gap in Men's Mortality. *Journal of Social Behavior* 47, no. 3: 209–26.

Watson, Wyatt. 2005. *The Uncertain Future of Longevity.* London: WatsonWyatt/Cass School of Business.

Whitehouse, Edward. 2007. *Life-Expectancy Risk and Pensions: Who Bears the Burden?* OECD Social, Employment and Migration Working Papers no. 60. Paris: Organization for Economic Cooperation and Development.

Wilmoth, J. R. 1995. The Earliest Centenarians: A Statistical Analysis. In *Exceptional Longevity*, ed. B. Jeune and J. W. Vaupel. Odense, Denmark: Odense University Press.

Wilshire Consulting. 2006. *2006 Report on City & County Retirement Systems: Funding Levels and Asset Allocation*. Santa Monica, CA.

Wilshire Consulting. 2007. *2007 Wilshire Report on State Retirement Systems: Funding Levels and Asset Allocation*. Santa Monica, CA.

Wisconsin Legislative Council. 2007. *2006 Comparative Study of Major Public Employee Retirement Systems*. Madison, WI.

Woolf, Steven H., Robert E. Johnson, George E. Fryer, Jr., George Rust, and David Satcher. 2004. The Health Impact of Resolving Racial Disparities: An Analysis of US Mortality Data. *American Journal of Public Health* 94, no. 12: 2078–81.

WHO (World Health Organization). 2002. *World Health Report 2002*. Geneva. Available at www.who.int.

WHO (World Health Organization). 2006. *World Health Report 2006*. Geneva. Available at www.who.int.

Wu, Ke Bin 2006. *Sources of Income for Older Persons in 2004*. AARP Data Digest 148. Washington: American Association of Retired People.

Zion, David, and Amit Varshney. 2007. *You Dropped a Bomb on Me, GASB*. Credit Suisse Americas/United States Equity Research Accounting & Tax (March 22). Available at http://online.wsj.com.

Appendix 3A
Data and Definitions

Poverty Thresholds

The poverty thresholds (using the definition of 50 percent of median disposable income) of selected OECD countries are shown in table 3A.1. The thresholds include national currencies, in US dollars, as a share of the US threshold (in only three countries is it higher) and as a share of take-home pay of the average production worker.

Old Age Income Data

All income data presented in this chapter are from Förster and Mira d'Ercole (2005) and based on answers to OECD country questionnaires. The only exception is the data for the United States, which are from the Social Security Administration (SSA 2002). We discuss the data from Förster and Mira d'Ercole (2005) first.

This section relies extensively on appendix 1 in Förster and Mira d'Ercole (2005). The authors attempted to maximize country coverage by drawing on different data sources, primarily household surveys but also, for Belgium, Denmark, and Sweden, a combination of survey and administrative data.

However, the surveys in different countries use different methodologies, so the precise definition of a household may vary. For example, do adult children living with their parents constitute a separate household? The more the definition reduces the size of the household, the more likely it is to relatively depress income and thus increase poverty. As mentioned in the chapter, 17 OECD countries report data on a gross basis (before direct taxation and, where applicable, payroll taxation), whereas Austria, the Czech Republic, Greece, Hungary, Mexico, Poland, Spain, and Turkey report on a net tax basis. Due, however, to differences in the way gross taxes are estimated—relying on taxpayer-respondent answers, administrative data, or microsimulations—direct and literal cross-country comparisons should be approached with caution.

Income components are split into three categories. "Earnings" covers wages, salaries, and self-employment income. "Capital, private" includes rents, dividends, and interest paid in cash (but Denmark, Germany, and Turkey also include imputed rents of homeowners). "Public transfers" cover cash transfers paid by the government to households and individuals but exclude in-kind transfers such as subsidized rents, an exception that may distort results.

The classification of "private pensions" is surrounded by large differences, particularly concerning their income category classification. In the

Table 3A.1 Values of poverty thresholds for single adults used to measure relative poverty at half of median disposable income

| Country | Latest year | 50 percent of nominal equivalized disposable household income | | Share of US poverty threshold (percent) | Poverty threshold for a single adult relative to take-home pay of an average production worker (percent) |
		National currency	US dollars		
Australia	1999	10,617	6,852	57	36
Austria	1999	104,972	8,127	68	47
Canada	2000	13,019	8,764	73	49
Czech Republic	2000	63,025	1,631	14	46
Denmark	2000	83,391	10,301	86	53
Finland	2000	49,733	7,722	64	49
France	2000	48,284	6,796	57	48
Germany	2001	14,998	7,079	59	40
Greece	1999	1,359,057	4,437	37	49
Hungary	2000	361,892	1,282	11	63
Ireland	2000	6,668	7,816	65	48
Italy	2000	11,601,000	5,531	46	41
Japan	2000	1,380,000	12,801	107	38
Luxembourg	2001	552,877	12,269	102	60
Mexico	2002	13,050	1,351	11	23
Netherlands	2000	20,325	8,515	71	51
New Zealand	2001	10,208	4,289	36	33
Norway	2000	99,701	11,313	94	52
Poland	2000	5,740	1,322	11	37
Portugal	2000	718,005	3,306	28	57
Sweden	2000	78,833	8,594	72	52
Switzerland	2001	22,384	13,252	111	45
Turkey	2002	1,468,727	970	8	21
United Kingdom	2000	5,981	9,065	76	43
United States	2000	11,977	11,977	100	52

Notes: Data refer to annual disposable income. Values, as reported in country questionnaires, for the most recent year are expressed in prices of the base year. For the purpose of this table, these values have been adjusted in line with changes in the consumer price index. "Equivalized" disposable income is household disposable income divided by household size at the power 0.5. National currency data are converted at annual Federal Reserve average market rates (GSA releases) and the original euro conversion rates. Currency data for the Czech Republic, Hungary, Poland, and Turkey are from the Pacific Exchange Rate Service.

Source: Förster and Mira d'Ercole (2005).

data presented in this chapter, they are all classified as "capital, private" with the exception of Austria, the Czech Republic, Hungary, Italy, and Mexico, where they are included as part of "public transfers." However, in Hungary, Italy, and Mexico, the scope of private pensions is negligible, making this an issue of minor importance for these countries.

Finally, the extraordinarily large share of elderly income in Finland from "capital, private" is due to the classification of the entire mandatory Finnish insurance-based pension system in this category. As such, the "public transfer" category includes only non-directly-pension-related transfers from the government.

The income distribution data for all reporting countries in Förster and Mira d'Ercole (2005) are reported in table 3A.2.

The source of the US data presented in this chapter is the SSA's biannual report on "Income of the Population 55 or Older" for 2000, which in turn draws on the US Census Bureau's data from the Current Population Survey (CPS). The SSA made several adjustments to the CPS data for the purposes of their biannual publication. The main difference lies in the SSA's unit of analysis, which is based on age and not a construct of families and unrelated individuals, as used by the Census Bureau. In the data presented in this chapter, the age cutoff is 65, and "aged units" are married couples living together, at least one of whom is 65 or older, and nonmarried persons 65 or older (married persons not living with a spouse are counted as nonmarried). Unlike the Census Bureau, the SSA does not classify a younger relative living with an older relative as a member of a "nonaged family." As this distinction increases the size of households, it has the broad impact of reducing poverty measures. The 2000 SSA report (www.ssa.gov/policy) comments as follows on the direct quantitative comparison of the two measures: "Census data show that the number of households with a householder aged 65 or older in 2000 was 21,828,000. In comparison, SSA data show 25,230,000 such households. The SSA count generally includes the Census Bureau's aged households plus some aged units living in nonaged households or living with other aged units in the same household. The number of aged households was 87 percent of the number of aged units."

The income measure used is total money income, which is the sum of all income received by the aged unit before any deductions such as those for taxes, union dues, or Medicare premiums. As such, although the US data are listed under "net tax income," they are pretax. However, as we saw in chapter 2, figure 2.5, the direct taxation on pension benefits is limited at 5 percent. Other sources of retirement income for the vast majority of Americans can equally be assumed to be lightly taxed, with the exception of earnings income in high tax brackets. However, the differences in income shares when accounting for taxes can be assumed to have an immaterial impact on the conclusions derived from these data.

Table 3A.2   65+ income distribution, by source and income group, circa 2000 (percent)

Country	Earnings	Private capital	Public transfers	Taxes
Australia				
Low	2	9	91	−2
Middle	5	26	72	−3
High	56	50	16	−21
United Kingdom				
Low	1	13	87	−1
Middle	7	33	65	−5
High	19	72	26	−17
Canada				
Low	4	14	92	−10
Middle	15	41	57	−13
High	44	59	26	−29
Czech Republic				
Low	0	0	99	0
Middle	4	1	99	−1
High	60	4	49	−13
Denmark				
Low	1	10	120	−31
Middle	6	36	92	−33
High	35	87	33	−55
Finland				
Low	1	59	49	−9
Middle	6	93	24	−23
High	35	96	9	−40
France				
Low	2	3	106	−11
Middle	9	3	95	−8
High	15	8	91	−14
Germany				
Low	3	6	99	−7
Middle	7	10	92	−9
High	22	24	70	−16
Ireland				
Low	2	3	95	−1
Middle	23	14	66	−2
High	64	22	25	−11
Italy				
Low	3	0	98	−2
Middle	15	1	97	−13
High	62	8	60	−30

Table 3A.2   65+ income distribution, by source and income group, circa 2000 (percent) *(continued)*

Country	Earnings	Private capital	Public transfers	Taxes
Japan				
Low	21	7	86	−13
Middle	43	6	62	−12
High	78	11	27	−16
Netherlands				
Low	0	9	96	−5
Middle	5	36	69	−10
High	25	73	34	−32
New Zealand				
Low	0	4	116	−20
Middle	10	18	89	−18
High	40	53	33	−25
Norway				
Low	1	12	95	−8
Middle	7	27	86	−20
High	38	48	48	−33
Portugal				
Low	3	2	95	0
Middle	28	5	72	−4
High	40	9	63	−12
Sweden				
Low	1	11	107	−18
Middle	4	22	109	−35
High	28	50	72	−50
Switzerland				
Low	8	9	126	−43
Middle	11	11	105	−27
High	32	29	77	−38
OECD-17 average				
Low	19	25	73	−16
Middle	12	23	79	−14
High	41	41	45	−27
Greece				
Low	9	6	85	n.a.
Middle	22	7	71	n.a.
High	39	16	44	n.a.
Hungary				
Low	3	1	96	n.a.
Middle	8	3	89	n.a.
High	41	5	54	n.a.

(table continues next page)

Table 3A.2 65+ income distribution, by source and income group, circa 2000 (percent) *(continued)*

Country	Earnings	Private capital	Public transfers	Taxes
Luxembourg				
Low	0	1	98	n.a.
Middle	8	6	86	n.a.
High	19	25	56	n.a.
Mexico				
Low	48	30	22	n.a.
Middle	65	14	21	n.a.
High	69	15	17	n.a.
Poland				
Low	6	2	92	n.a.
Middle	17	3	80	n.a.
High	61	1	38	n.a.
Turkey				
Low	56	33	11	n.a.
Middle	49	45	7	n.a.
High	35	62	3	n.a.

n.a. = not applicable

Note: Low = lowest income quintile; Middle = 2nd to 4th income quintile; High = highest income quintile.

Source: Förster and Mira d'Ercole (2005).

"Total money income" includes wages and salaries, self-employment income (including losses), Social Security, Supplemental Security Income, public assistance, interest, dividends, rent, royalties, estates or trusts, veterans' payments, unemployment compensation, workers' compensation, private and government retirement and disability pensions, alimony, and child support. Importantly, however, capital gains (or losses) and lump-sum or one-time payments such as life insurance settlements are excluded. Furthermore, the measure does not reflect in-kind transfers such as food stamps, health benefits, subsidized housing, payments in kind, or fringe benefits from one's employment (SSA 2002).

Several authors have attempted to estimate potential biases in the CPS measurement of both poverty and income sources. These estimates do not address the question of consumption versus income discussed in the text but concern themselves merely with any methodological biases in the income-based approach. Marc Roemer (2000) compares CPS data with an adjusted national income and product account (NIPA)–based estimate of old age income and estimates that the CPS in 1996 captured 96 percent of earnings, 70.9 percent of capital income, 88.3 percent of public transfers, and 76.6 percent of private and non–Social Security–related public pensions. In total, the CPS captured 92.6 percent of the NIPA-based old age income. Roemer attributes this underestimate (of capital income, in particular) to respondent difficulties and possible unwillingness to answer the CPS survey questions about assets and capital income. Lynn Fisher (2005) focuses on CPS respondents' underreporting of asset ownership, which presumably occurred as financial asset ownership rates rose during the 1990s. She finds that, in aggregate, "the evidence suggests that the CPS underestimates whether or not a source of [asset-based] income was received, but estimates higher amounts for those receiving it" (Fisher 2005, 6).

Laurence Kotlikoff and colleagues (2006) use a different data source and report comparable data for some of the income sourcing reported in this chapter. Using the 2004 Federal Reserve Survey of Consumer Finance, they estimate that in the event of a reduction of 100 percent of Social Security benefits, one-third of the 65+ singles would experience a 90+ percent reduction in living standards, while the corresponding percentage for married couples is 41 percent. There is no immediate way to verify that these people who rely overwhelmingly on Social Security for their old age income are in the low-income bracket, but the results suggest that there is a large group of low-income people with few if any other sources of old age income in the United States. The results from Kotlikoff and colleagues (2006) thus seem to at least partly support this chapter's central conclusions about old age income sources.

SSA (2002) also reports a number of relevant supporting data for the broad conclusions of this chapter. According to the report's table 6.A.1, 78 percent of those 65 and older report having no earnings income, split between 65 percent for 65- to 74-year-olds and 91 percent for those over 75. In addition, 52 percent of those over 65 have no asset income of any kind, with virtually no difference between that group and the oldest (75+). The report found that 71 percent of Americans age 65 or older have no income from private pensions or annuities, clearly illustrating the limited coverage of such voluntary pensions in the United States.

In its table 6.A.2, SSA (2002) presents data by income quintile. With regards to income from private pensions or annuities, the share reporting no income is 94, 83, 65, 54, and 60 percent, respectively, for the five income quintiles (in rising order). Concerning earnings, 96, 94, 85, 71, and 46 percent, respectively, report no income. Asset-based income is zero for 80, 66, 51, 39, and 27 percent, respectively. Thus public pension benefits provide the overwhelming share of old age income for most Americans other than those in the top quintile.

Appendix 3B

Table 3B.1 Comparative details of 85 major public employee retirement funds in 2006

	State	Fund name	Employee coverage[a]	Active employees	Beneficiaries and annuitants	Fund "support ratio"	Participants covered by Social Security	Normal retirement (age/years)	Early retirement (age/years)	Reduction for early retirement
1	Alabama	Alabama Employees Retirement System	S, L	82,830	33,266	2.49	Yes	60/10; any/25	None	
2		Alabama Teachers Retirement System	T	135,126	64,362	2.10	Yes	60/10; any/25	None	
3	Alaska	Alaska Public Employees Retirement System	S, L	34,660	21,852	1.59	No	60/5; any/30	55/5	6% a year
4		Alaska Teachers Retirement System	T	9,835	9,349	1.05	No	60/8; any/20	55/8	Table
5	Arizona	Arizona State Retirement System	S, L, T	217,893	78,392	2.78	Yes	65; 62/10; R80	50/5	Table
6	Arkansas	Arkansas Public Employees Retirement System	S, L	43,453	22,234	1.95	Yes	65/5; any/28	55/5; any/25	6% a year
7		Arkansas Teachers Retirement System	T	85,916	30,014	2.86	Yes	60/5; any/28	Any/25	Lesser of 5% for each year less than 28 yrs. of service or 5% for each year prior to age 60
8	California	California Public Employees Retirement System	S, L	809,690	443,341	1.83	Yes	55/5	50/5	Multiplier varies
9		California State Teachers Retirement System	T	453,365	207,846	2.18	No	60/5	55/5; 50/30	3% to 6% a year
10	Colorado	Colorado Public Employees Retirement Association	S, L, T	180,360	69,416	2.60	No	65/5; 50/30; 55/R80	50/25; 55/20; 60/5	6%; 3%; 4%
11	Connecticut	Connecticut State Employees Retirement System	S	50,605	36,964	1.37	Yes	62/10; 60/25	55/10	3% a year
12		Connecticut Teachers Retirement Board	T	51,015	26,695	1.91	No	60/20; any/35	Any/25; 55/20; 60/10	3% a year
13	Delaware	Delaware Public Employees Retirement System	S, T	34,313	19,108	1.80	Yes	62/5; 60/15; any/30	55/15; any/25	2.4% a year
14	Florida	Florida Retirement System	S, L, T	643,379	252,060	2.55	Yes	62/6; any/30	Any/6	5% a year
15	Georgia	Georgia Employees Retirement System	S	72,716	31,355	2.32	Yes	60/10; any/30	Any/25	7% a year; max. 35%
16		Georgia Teachers Retirement System	T	209,349	70,239	2.98	Yes	60/10; any/25	Any/25	7% a year
17	Hawaii	Hawaii Employees Retirement System	S, L, T	64,069	34,304	1.87	Yes	62/5; 55/30	55/20	6% a year
18	Idaho	Idaho Public Employee Retirement System	S, L, T	64,762	26,438	2.45	Yes	65/5; R90	55/5	3% a yr. for 1st 5 yrs.; 5.75% a yr. thereafter
19	Illinois	Illinois State Employees Retirement System	S	68,075	54,868	1.24	Yes	60/8; R85	55/25	6% a year
20		Illinois Teachers Retirement System	T	159,272	85,103	1.87	No	62/5; 60/10; 55/35	55/20	6% a year
21		Illinois Municipal Retirement Fund	L	174,008	84,704	2.05	Yes	60/8; 55/35	55/8	3% a year
22	Indiana	Indiana Public Employees Retirement Fund	S, L	153,664	62,248	2.47	Yes	65/10; 60/15; 55/R85	50/15	Table
23		Indiana State Teachers Retirement Fund	T	73,350	39,849	1.84	Yes	65/10; 60/15; 55/R85	50/15	5% a year
24	Iowa	Iowa Public Employees Retirement System	S, L, T	163,091	82,204	1.98	Yes	65; 62/20; R88	55/4	3% a year

Employee contribution	Employer contribution	Vesting period (years)	Final average salary period[b]	Formula multiplier	Limitation	Annual postretirement COLAs	Investment return assumption (percent)	Wage inflation assumption (percent)	Real rate of return assumption (percent)	Fund funding ratio (percent)
5%	7.78%	10	3 H/10	2.01%	None	Ad hoc only	8	4.50	3.50	89.6
5%	9.36%	10	3 H/10	2.01%	None	Ad hoc only	8	4.50	3.50	84.0
6.75%	16.77%	5	5 HC	2% (1st 10 yrs.); 2.25% (2nd 10); 2.5% (added yrs.)	None	75% of CPI if 65, 9% cap; 50% of CPI if 60 or retired 5 yrs. - 6% cap	8.25	3.50	4.75	65.7
8.65%	13.76%	8	3 H	2% (1st 20 yrs.); 2.5% (added yrs.)	None	75% of CPI if age 65, 9% cap; 50% of CPI if 60 or retired 8 yrs.	8.25	3.50	4.75	60.9
9.10%	9.10%	Immediate	3 HC	2.1% (1st 20 yrs.); 2.15% (next 5 yrs.); 2.2% (next 5 yrs.); 2.3% over 30	None	Excess earnings - 4% cap	8	4.50	3.50	83.7
5%	12.54%	5	3 H	2%	None	3%	8	4	4	83.0
6%	13.26%	5	3 H	2.15%	None	3%	8	4	4	80.3
6%	10.36%	5	1 H	2% at 55; 2.5% at 63 or older	65 yrs. max.	2%	7.75	3	4.75	87.3
8%	8.25%	5	1 H	2% at 60; 2.4% at 63	100% FAS	2%	8	3.25	4.75	86.0
8%	10.15%	5	3 H	2.50%	100% FAS	3.50%	8.50	3.50	5	73.3
2%		5	3 H (cap)	1.33% + 0.5% over $43,400; 1.625% yrs. over 35	None	60% of CPI up to 6%, 2.5% minimum	8.50	5	3.50	53.2
6%	3.01%	10	3 H	2%	75% FAS	Excess earnings: 1.5% or 6% cap	8.50	4	4.50	68.4
3% above $6,000	6.10%	5	3 H	1.85%	None	Ad hoc only	8	3.75	4.25	101.7
Non-contributory	6.72%	6	5 H	1.6% to 1.68% (age & yrs. of service)	100% FAS	3%	7.75	4	3.75	105.6
1.25%	10.41%	10	2 HC	0.0	90% high yr.	CPI - 1.5% semi-annual cap	7.50	3.50	4	94.5
5%	9.24%	10	2 HC (cap)	2%	40 yrs. max.	CPI - 1.5% semi-annual cap	7.50	3.75	3.75	98.0
6%	13.75%	5	3 H	2%	None	2.50%	8	4	4	65.0
6.23%	10.39%	5	3 1/2 HC	2%	100% FAS	CPI - 1% minimum to 6% max. (conditional)	7.25	4.50	3.25	95.2
4%	$210.5 million	8	4 HC/10	1.67%	75% FAS	3%	8.50	3	5.50	52.2
9.40%	7.64%	5	4 HC/10 (cap)	2.20%	75% FAS	3%	8.50	3.50	5	62.0
4.50%	10.04%	8	4 HC/10 (cap)	1.67% (1st 15 yrs.); 2% (added yrs.)	75% FAS	3%	7.50	4	3.50	100.1
3%	4.70%	10	5 H	1.1% + money purchase annuity	None	Ad hoc only	7.25	N.D.	N.D.	96.8
3%	19.25%	10	5 H	1.1% + money purchase annuity	None	Ad hoc only	7.50	4.50	3	43.4
3.70%	5.75%	4	3 H	2% (1st 30 yrs.); 1% (next 5 yrs.)	65% FAS	Excess earnings - 3% cap	7.50	4	3.50	88.4

(table continues next page)

Table 3B.1 Comparative details of 85 major public employee retirement funds in 2006 *(continued)*

	State	Fund name	Employee coverage[a]	Active employees	Beneficiaries and annuitants	Fund "support ratio"	Participants covered by Social Security	Normal retirement (age/years)	Early retirement (age/years)	Reduction for early retirement
25	Kansas	Kansas Public Employees Retirement System	S, L, T	149,073	63,348	2.35	Yes	65; 62/10; R85	55/10	2.4%/7.20% a year
26	Kentucky	Kentucky Retirement Systems	S, L	145,384	73,000	1.99	Yes	65/4; any/27	55/5; any/25	5%/4% a year
27		Kentucky Teachers Retirement System	T	73,740	38,497	1.92	No	60/5; any/27	55/5	5% a year
28	Louisiana	Louisiana State Employees Retirement System	S	57,811	40,624	1.42	No	60/10; 55/25; any/30	50/10; any/20	Table
29		Louisiana Teachers Retirement System	T	81,347	61,554	1.32	No	60/5; 55/25; any/30	Any/20	Multiplier varies
30	Maine	Maine State Retirement System	S, L, T	52,282	32,918	1.59	No	60/5	Any/25	2.25% a year
31	Maryland	Maryland State Retirement and Pension System	S, L, T	191,273	103,831	1.84	Yes	60/5; any/30	Any/25	6% a year; max. 30%
32	Massachusetts	Massachusetts State Employees' Retirement System	S	83,178	50,593	1.64	No	55/10; any/20	None	
33		Massachusetts Teachers Retirement Board	T	88,788	44,452	2.00	No	55/10; any/20	None	
34	Michigan	Michigan State Employees Retirement System	S	32,575	45,980	0.71	Yes	60/10; 55/30	55/15	6% a year
35		Municipal Employees' Retirement System of Michigan	L	37,826	21,505	1.76	Yes	Varies by plan	Varies by plan	Varies by plan
36		Michigan Public School Employees Retirement System	T	305,445	157,163	1.94	Yes	60/5; any/30	55/15	6% a year
37	Minnesota	Minnesota State Retirement System	S	48,000	24,204	1.98	Yes	Soc. Sec. normal*	55/3	Table
38		Minnesota Public Employees Retirement Association	L	158,366	66,102	2.40	Yes	Soc. Sec. normal*	55/3	Table
39		Minnesota Teachers Retirement Association	T	79,164	44,683	1.77	Yes	Soc. Sec. normal*	55/3	Table
40	Mississippi	Mississippi Public Employees Retirement System	S, L, T	158,893	69,729	2.28	Yes	60/4; any/25	None	
41	Missouri	Missouri State Employees Retirement System	S	54,493	27,052	2.01	Yes	65/5; 65/4 Active; 60/15	57/5	6% a year
42		Missouri Local Government Employees Retirement System	L	29,940	11,787	2.54	Yes	60/5; R80 option	55/5	6% a year
43		Missouri Public Schools Retirement System	T	75,539	38,110	1.98	No	60/5; R80; any/30	55/5; any/25	Table
44	Montana	Montana Public Employees Retirement Board	S, L	27,962	15,654	1.79	Yes	65/any; 60/5; any/30	50/5; any/25	Table
45		Montana Teachers Retirement System	T	18,099	11,019	1.64	Yes	60/5; any/25	50/5	6%; 3.6% a year
46	Nebraska	Nebraska Public Employees Retirement Systems	S, L	62,245	14,604	4.26	Yes	55		Money purchase
47		Nebraska Schools Public Pensions	T	36,042	13,052	2.76	Yes	65; 55/R85	60/5; any/35; 55/R85	3% a year
48	Nevada	Nevada Public Employees Retirement System	S, L, T	98,187	33,262	2.95	No	65/5; 60/10; any/30	Any/5	4% a year
49	New Hampshire	New Hampshire Retirement System	S, L, T	51,738	19,711	2.62	Yes	60/any	50/10; R70/20	1.5%; 3%; 4%; 6.67% a year
50	New Jersey	New Jersey Public Employees Retirement System	S, L	310,392	121,166	2.56	Yes	60/any	Any/25	3% a year
51		New Jersey Teachers, Police and Firemen	T	151,873	65,445	2.32	Yes	60/any	Any/25	3% a year
52	New Mexico	New Mexico Public Employees Retirement Association	S, L	51,699	22,699	2.28	Yes	65/5 to 60/20; any/25	None	

Employee contribution	Employer contribution	Vesting period (years)	Final average salary period[b]	Formula multiplier	Limitation	Annual postretirement COLAs	Investment return assumption (percent)	Wage inflation assumption (percent)	Real rate of return assumption (percent)	Fund funding ratio (percent)
4%	5.27%	10	3 H	1.75%	None	Ad hoc only	8	4	4	68.8
5%	5.89%	5	5 H	1.97%	None	CPI	7.75	4	3.75	61.3
9.86%	13.11%	5	3 H	2.50%	100% FAS	1.50%	7.50	4	3.50	73.1
7.69%	19.10%	10	3 HC	3.33%	100% FAS	Excess earnings; CPI - 3% cap	8.25	N.D.	N.D.	63.9
8%	15.90%	5	3 HC + (cap)	2.50%	100% FAS	CPI - 3% cap	8.25	3.20	5.05	67.5
7.65%	15.09%	5	3 H	2%	None	CPI - 4% cap	7.75	4.75	3	77.1
2%	9.18%	5	3 HC	1.80%	100% FAS	CPI - 3% cap	7.75	4	3.75	93.8
8.30%	2.90%	10	3 HC	0.5% to 2.5% (age-related)	80% FAS	CPI - on 1st $12,000- conditional, 3% cap	8.25	N.D.	N.D.	81.5
11%	15.40%	10	3 HC	0.1% to 2.5% (age-related) + 2% for each yr. over 24	80% FAS	CPI - on 1st $12,000- conditional, 3% cap	8.25	N.D.	N.D.	67.2
Non-contributory	13.60%	10	3 HC	1.50%	None	3% ($300 annual cap)	8	3.50	4.50	79.8
Varies by plan	Varies by plan	6, 8, or 10	5/3 HC	1.3% to 2.5% (employer option)	80% FAS for multipliers over 2.25%	3 plans - depending on employer agreement	8	4.50	3.50	76.0
3 to 4.3%	7.60%	10	3 HC	1.50%	None	3%	8	3.50	4.50	79.3
4%	4%	3	5 HC	1.70%	None	CPI - 2.5% cap plus investment surplus	8.50	N.D.	N.D.	96.2
5.50%	6%	3	5 HC	1.70%	None	CPI - 2.5% cap plus investment surplus	8.50	6	2.50	74.7
5%	9.05%	3	5 HC	1.70%	None	CPI - 2.5% cap plus investment surplus	8.50	5	3.50	92.1
7.25%	10.75%	4	4 HC (cap)	2% (1st 25 yrs.); 2.5% (added yrs.)	100% FAS	3%	8	4	4	72.0
Non-contributory	12.59%	5	3 HC	1.7% (and .8% to age 62 if R80 met)	None	80% CPI: 5% cap	8.50	3.50	5	85.3
0% to 4%	Varies by plan	5	5/3 HC	1% to 2% (employer option)	None	CPI - 4% cap	7.50	4	3.50	95.0
5.50%	5.50%	5	3 HC	2.5%; 2.55% with 31 or more yrs. service	100% FAS	CPI - 80% of original benefits lifetime cap	8	N.D.	N.D.	82.6
6.90%	6.90%	5	3 HC	1.785%; 2% with at least 25 yrs. of service	None	3%	8	4.25	3.75	88.0
0.072	7.58%	5	3 HC	1.67%	None	1.50%	7.75	4.50	3.25	76.1
4.80%	156% of EE rate	3		Money purchase	None	Money purchase	7.60	3.50	4.10	104.0
7.98%	101% of EE rate + .7%	5	3 HC	2%	None	CPI - 2.5% cap	8	3.50	4.50	93.4
10.50%	10.50%	5	3 HC	2.67%	75% FAS	2% to 5% (varies) with number of years retired	8	3.50	4.50	74.9
6.30%	6.70%	10	3 H (cap)	1.67% to 65; 1.515% after 65	None	Ad hoc	9	3.50	5.50	68.0
5%	$7.97 million	10	3 H	1.82%	None	60% of CPI	8.25	4	4.25	89.9
5%	$93.83 million	10	3 H	1.82%	None	60% of CPI	8.25	4	4.25	81.5
7.42%	16.59%	5	3 HC	3%	80% FAS	3%	8	4.50	3.50	92.1

(table continues next page)

	State	Fund name	Employee coverage[a]	Active employees	Beneficiaries and annuitants	Fund "support ratio"	Participants covered by Social Security	Normal retirement (age/years)	Early retirement (age/years)	Reduction for early retirement
53	New Mexico (continued)	New Mexico Educational Retirement Board	T	63,362	26,100	2.43	Yes	65/5; any/25; 60/R75	R75	2.4%/7.2% a year
54	New York	New York State and Local Retirement Systems	S, L	561,951	306,531	1.83	Yes	62/5; 55/30	55/5	6%/3% a year
55		New York State Teachers Retirement System	T	260,041	129,587	2.01	Yes	62/5; 55/30	55/5	6%/3% a year
56	North Carolina	North Carolina Teachers and State Employees	S, T	375,516	134,719	2.79	Yes	65/5; 60/25; any/30	60/5; 50/20	3% a year
57		North Carolina Local Government Employees Retirement System	L	141,255	38,488	3.67	Yes	65/5; 60/25; any/30	60/5; 50/20	3% a year
58	North Dakota	North Dakota Public Employees Retirement System	S, L	18,102	6,187	2.93	Yes	65/any; R85	55/3	6% a year
59		North Dakota Teachers Fund for Retirement	T	9,585	5,893	1.63	Yes	65/3; R85	55/3	6% a year
60	Ohio	Ohio Public Employees Retirement System	S, L	381,464	156,747	2.43	No	60/5; any/30	55/25	3% a year
61		Ohio State Teachers Retirement System	T	175,065	119,184	1.47	No	65; any/30	60/5; 55/25	3% a year
62	Oklahoma	Oklahoma Public Employees Retirement System	S, L	45,472	24,372	1.87	Yes	62/6; R90	55/10	Table
63		Oklahoma Teachers Retirement System	T	87,194	41,782	2.09	Yes	62/5; R90	55/5	Table
64	Oregon	Oregon Employees Retirement System	S, L, T	187,704	101,519	1.85	Yes	65/any; 58/30	55	Actuarial reduction
65	Pennsylvania	Pennsylvania State Employees Retirement System	S	110,972	102,060	1.09	Yes	60/3; any/35	Any/5	Table
66		Pennsylvania Public School Employees Retirement System	T	255,000	157,000	1.62	Yes	62; 60/30; any/35	55/25	3% a year
67	Rhode Island	Rhode Island Employees Retirement System	S, T	32,000	19,000	1.68	Yes	60/10; any/28	None	
68	South Carolina	South Carolina Retirement Systems	S, L, T	181,022	94,667	1.91	Yes	65/any; any/28	60; 55/25	Table
69	South Dakota	South Dakota Retirement System	S, L, T	36,074	18,076	2.00	Yes	65/3; 55/R85	55/3	Table
70	Tennessee	Tennessee Consolidated Retirement System	S, L, T	204,735	89,772	2.28	Yes	60/5; any/30	55/10; any/25	4.8% a year
71	Texas	Texas Employees Retirement System	S	132,411	67,596	1.96	Yes	60/5; R80	None	
72		Teacher Retirement System of Texas	T	874,369	257,144	3.40	No	65/5; R80	55/5; any/30	Table
73		Texas Municipal Retirement System	L	95,583	32,175	2.97	Yes	60/5; any/20 or 25 option		Money purchase
74	Utah	Utah Retirement Systems	S, L, T	99,589	38,509	2.59	Yes	65/4; any/30	Any/25; 60/20; 62/10	3% a year; 7% for each year before age 60
75	Vermont	Vermont State Employees Retirement System	S	8,288	4,173	1.99	Yes	62/any; any/30	55/5	6% a year
76		Vermont Teachers Retirement System	T	10,696	4,789	2.23	Yes	62/any; any/30	55/5	6% a year
77	Virginia	Virginia Retirement System	S, L, T	332,916	124,639	2.67	Yes	65/5; 50/30	50/10; 55/5	6%; 4.8% a year
78	Washington	Washington Public Employees Retirement System	S, L	222,854	80,402	2.77	Yes	65/5	55/20	Table

Employee contribution	Employer contribution	Vesting period (years)	Final average salary period[b]	Formula multiplier	Limitation	Annual postretirement COLAs	Investment return assumption (percent)	Wage inflation assumption (percent)	Real rate of return assumption (percent)	Fund funding ratio (percent)
7.83%	10.90%	5	5 HC	2.35%	None	50% of CPI - 4% cap	8	3	5	70.4
3%	8%	5	3 HC (cap)	1.67% (under 20 yrs.); 2% (over 20 yrs.); 3.5% (over 30 yrs.)	None	If age 62 + retired 5 yrs.: 50% of CPI, max. 3% on 1st $18,000	8	3	5	N.D.
3%	7.97%	5	3 HC (cap)	Same as New York's ERS	None	If age 62 + retired 5 yrs.: 50% of CPI, max. 3% on 1st $18,000	8	3	5	98.8
6%	2.66%	5	4 HC	1.82%	None	Ad hoc	7.25	N.D.	N.D.	106.5
6%	4.80%	5	4 HC	1.85%	None	Ad hoc	7.25	N.D.	N.D.	99.4
4%	4.12%	3	3 H/10	2%	None	Ad hoc	8	3.50	4.50	88.8
7.75%	7.75%	3	3 H	2%	None	Ad hoc	8	3	5	75.4
9%	13.70%	5	3 H	2.2% (1st 30 yrs.); 2.5% (added yrs.)	100% FAS	3% cap	6.50	4	2.50	93.0
9%	13.70%	5	3 H	2.2% (1st 30 yrs.); 2.5% (added yrs.)	100% FAS	3% cap	8	3.50	4.50	75.0
3% to 3.5%	11.50%	8	3 H/10	2%	None	Ad hoc	7.50	2.50	5	74.1
7%	13.43%	5	5 HC	2%	None	Ad hoc	8	3	5	49.3
6%	8.04%	5	3 H	1.5% + money purchase annuity	None	CPI - 2% cap	8	3.75	4.25	104.2
6.25%	3.52%	5	3 H	2.50%	100% high yr.	Ad hoc	8.50	3	5.50	92.7
7.16%	4%	5	3 H	2.50%	None	Ad hoc	8.50	3.25	5	83.6
8.75% (9.5% teachers)	14.84%	10	3 HC	1.7% (1st 10 yrs.); 1.9% (2nd 10 yrs.); 3% (21–34 yrs.); 2% (35+)	80% FAS	3%	8.25	3	5.25	59.6
6.25%	7.55%	5	3 HC	1.82%	None	CPI - 4% cap	7.25	3	4.25	71.6
6%	6%	3	3 HC/10	1.625% (service before 7/1/02); 1.55% service after 7/1/02	None	3.10%	7.75	N.D.	N.D.	96.7
Non-contributory	7.30%	5	5 HC	1.5% + .25% FAS over SSIL	94.5% FAS	CPI - 3% cap	7.50	N.D.	N.D.	99.8
6%	6.45%	5	3 H	2.30%	100% FAS	Ad hoc	8	4	4	95.2
6%	6.40%	5	3 H	2.30%	None	Ad hoc	8	3	5	87.3
3, 5, 6, or 7%	3% to 14%	5		Money purchase options	None	Up to 70% of CPI (employer option)	7	N.D.	N.D.	82.1
Non-contributory	11.59% to 14.52%	4	3 H	2%	None	CPI - 4% cap	8	4.75	3.25	93.2
3.35%	6.26%	5	3 HC	1.67%	50% FAS	50% of CPI - 5% cap	8	N.D.	N.D.	99.3
3.40%	5.09%	5	3 HC	1.67%	50% FAS	50% of CPI - 5% cap	8.25	N.D.	N.D.	84.6
5%	6.62%	5	3 HC	1.70%	100% FAS	CPI - 5% cap	7.50	3	5	81.3
6%	2.25%	5	5 HC	2%	None	CPI - 3% cap	8	4.50	3.50	N.D.

(table continues next page)

Table 3B.1 Comparative details of 85 major public employee retirement funds in 2006 *(continued)*

	State	Fund name	Employee coverage[a]	Active employees	Beneficiaries and annuitants	Fund "support ratio"	Participants covered by Social Security	Normal retirement (age/years)	Early retirement (age/years)	Reduction for early retirement
79	Washington *(continued)*	Washington Teachers Retirement System	T	67,270	37,321	1.80	Yes	65/5	55/20	Table
80	West Virginia	West Virginia Public Employees Retirement System	S, L	36,000	18,900	1.90	Yes	60/5; 55/R80	55/10	6% a year
81		West Virginia Teachers Retirement System	T	22,500	24,600	0.91	Yes	60/5; 55/30; any/35	Any/30	Actuarial reduction
82	Wyoming	Wyoming Retirement System	S, L, T	39,619	18,788	2.11	Yes	60/any; R85	50/4; any/25	5% a year
83	Milwaukee	Milwaukee City Retirement System	L	12,015	10,787	1.11	Yes	60/any; 55/30	55/15	Table
84		Milwaukee County Retirement System	L	5,056	7,275	0.69	Yes	60/any; 55/30	55/15	5% a year
85	Wisconsin	Wisconsin Retirement System	S, L, T	260,302	129,289	2.01	Yes	65/any; 57/30	55	Varies by amount of service
	Total/average			12,092,132	5,646,026	2.14				

a. Coverage: S = state; L = local; T = teachers

b. H = highest; HC = highest consecutive

* and N.D. = not determined

COLA = cost of living allowance

CPI = consumer price index

FAS = financial accounting standard

SSIL = Social Security integration level

[shaded] = State does not participate in Social Security.

Source: Wisconsin Legislative Council (2007).

Employee contribution	Employer contribution	Vesting period (years)	Final average salary period[b]	Formula multiplier	Limitation	Annual postretirement COLAs	Investment return assumption (percent)	Wage inflation assumption (percent)	Real rate of return assumption (percent)	Fund funding ratio (percent)
5% to 15%	2.92%	5	5 HC	1% + money purchase	None	CPI - 3% cap	8	4.50	3.50	N.D.
4.50%	10.50%	5	3 HC/10	2%	None	Ad hoc	7.50	3.50	4	73.2
6%	15%	5	5 H/15	2%	None	Ad hoc	8	3.50	4.50	19.1
5.57%	5.68%	4	3 HC	2.125% (1st 15 yrs.); 2.25% (added yrs.)	None	CPI - 3% cap	8	4	3	95.1
5.50%	0	4	3 H	2%	70% FAS	2% after 5 yrs. retired	8.50	3	5.50	122.9
Non-contributory	$46,929,347	5	3 HC	2%	80% FAS	2%	8	3.50	3	76.2
5%	4.50%	Immediate	3 H	1.60%	70% FAS	Investment earnings; reductions possible	7.80	4.10	3.70	99.6
							7.9	3.8	4.2	82.0

4

The Employment Incentive Challenge for Aging Populations

Growing old is no more than a bad habit, which a busy man has no time to form.
—André Maurois (1885–1967)[1]

As we have shown in earlier chapters, life expectancies and retirement ages are increasing in most OECD countries—although the latter are rising very slowly after falling sharply since 1970. In the United States, the eligibility age for full Social Security benefits is also rising, posing the economic policy challenge of how to employ an aging workforce. Without employment opportunities for aging populations, merely raising retirement ages may lead to little increase in the actual number of years spent working.

An individual's decision to remain in the workforce or not depends on a complex interaction between a number of factors. Employer age discrimination may play a role if older workers earn higher wages than younger workers or if there is a perception among employers that older workers are less productive in a labor market characterized by the rapid adoption of new technologies.[2] Or a lack of training opportunities or of job search assistance for older workers may discourage their labor force participation.

In its recent multiyear Aging and Employment Policies Project and the resulting series of in-depth country reviews on the topic, the OECD documented the multifaceted aspects of individual old age employment

---

1. André Maurois, *The Art of Living*, translated by James Whitall, chapter 8: 282–83 (1940).

2. See, for instance, Carone et al. (2006) for estimations of the impact of aging on productivity. We revisit this issue in chapter 7.

decisions at a level of detail we cannot hope to match.[3] Rather, we argue along classical economic lines—relying on the underlying data and conclusions from the OECD project—that the most important decision factor for individuals is straightforward financial incentives. If it pays to remain employed, most people will do so, whereas if people have access to generous retirement benefits, they will choose to retire. Governments will thus fail in attempts to increase the employment of older workers—irrespective of employer attitudes, active labor market policies targeted at older workers, and any other factors—unless they present them with financial incentives to continue working. Fortunately, as we illustrate in this chapter, there have recently been significant improvements in the incentive structures for older workers across the OECD. Most governments are gradually rising to the employment incentives challenge.

Economic Dependency Ratios Going Forward— Some Countries Will Have to Act

In chapter 2 we showed that differences in countries' effective retirement ages correlate with the impact of the aging population on pension programs. But the raw ratios of different population age groups are useful only in illustrating the pure demographic aspects of the challenges from aging populations. Without considering the degree to which different age groups are officially employed—and hence pay taxes and/or participate in an individual pension—old age ratios yield little direct information about the economic impact of population aging.

A more enlightening ratio is the economic dependency ratio, which shows in the numerator the share of a population that is not employed (inactive) and in the denominator the share of people employed (active), thus conveying in a single number the relationship between a country's economically contributing and economically dependent individuals. By focusing in the denominator only on the number of people in actual employment, the economic dependency ratio captures the full economic impact of changes in the rates of both labor force participation and unemployment.[4]

Figure 4.1 shows the economic dependency ratios for a number of OECD countries for 2005. Then, freezing the separate gender and five-

---

3. See the multiyear OECD Project on Aging and Employment Policies and resulting series of in-depth country reviews on the OECD website at www.oecd.org/els/employment/older workers). OECD (2006) is the concluding report of this project.

4. The total ratio includes all age groups and thus captures the effects of policies not related to older workers. It serves here as a general illustration of the cross-country differences in the intensity of the "support burden" rather than as an illustration of the specific burden from inactive older workers.

Figure 4.1 OECD economic dependency ratios (inactive/active), 2005–51

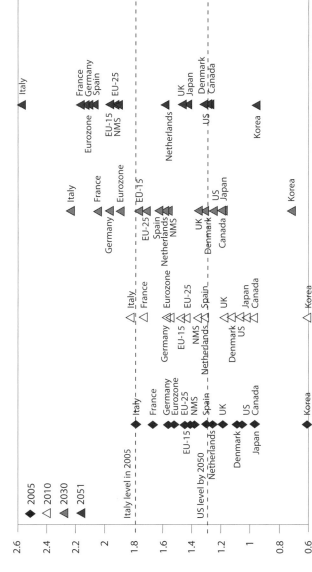

NMS = EU new member states

Notes: Data refer to 2004 employment rates for Canada, Japan, Korea, and the United States. EU aggregates are estimated using the member countries' employment-weighted average annual hours worked.

Sources: Eurostat online database, http://www.epp.eurostat.ec.europa.eu; Organization for Economic Cooperation and Development; US Census Bureau International Database, www.census.gov; Bureau of Labor Statistics, Foreign Labor Statistics Database, www.bls.gov; The Conference Board and Groningen Growth and Development Centre, Total Economy Database; authors' calculations.

year categories of age-specific employment rates for that year, the corresponding ratios are estimated for 2010, 2030, and 2051.[5] To improve the cross-country comparative validity of the data in terms of actual labor input, we adjust the employment data for the large differences among countries in the average annual number of hours worked in a full-time job.[6] We did this by deflating with the 2006 ratio of annual average hours worked in the country in question and the number of hours worked in the United States[7]. This allows us to capture the risks to pension sustainability if increased employment involves merely redistributing work through more part-time jobs rather than generating new full-time employment.[8]

For figure 4.1 the countries are normalized relative to the United States. In the 2005 column Korea is clearly the best performer in terms of relative labor input to inactive population, thanks to its combination of very high employment rates for both younger and older workers and very high annual average hours worked in 2006 (fully one-third higher than in the United States). Canada and Japan also do better than the United States on this measure, due to both high employment rates and high annual hours worked, while Denmark is roughly on par with America, due to higher employment rates but lower annual average hours worked. Other European countries are located further up the 2005 column, at a significantly less sustainable position than that of the United States, with France, Germany, and Italy all suffering from both very low employment rates (especially for women) and low annual average hours worked.[9]

The columns labeled 2010, 2030, and 2051 describe what will happen if age-specific employment rates and annual hours worked are both frozen at 2005 levels as demographic projections unfold over the next 45 years. Of course, holding constant these labor market parameters during a period of

---

5. In order to facilitate cross-country comparisons, 2005 gender-specific employment rates for only the following age categories are included: 15–19, 20–24, 25–29, 30–34, 35–39, 40–44, 45–49, 50–54, 55–59, 60–64, 65–69, and 70–74. It is assumed that no employment exists above age 74. No assumptions are made concerning labor productivity. The final projection year of 2051 is chosen as this is the last year of available projected data.

6. Data are from the Conference Board and Groningen Growth and Development Centre, Total Economy Database, January 2008, www.conference-board.org/economics.

7. We chose to deflate all data and projections by 2006 data, as these were the latest available data at the time of writing.

8. Note that the focus in figure 4.1 is the relative position of countries and not the value on the y-axis. This value, given that it is a country-specific inactive/active ratio expressed relative to US annual hours worked, is not itself a meaningful number.

9. Workers in the three big eurozone countries (France, Germany, and Italy) had just 87, 80, and 88 percent, respectively, of the average annual hours of US workers in 2006.

rapid population aging would be quite a challenge. For example, maintaining the 2005 employment rate for the 55- to 59-year-old age group in 2050, when this group will be far more numerous and make up a larger share of the total population, would represent a pretty good outcome. Thus the "freeze assumption" in figure 4.1 is intrinsically optimistic.

Not much will change by 2010, but by 2030 all countries will feel the effects of aging populations (all values in that column are significantly higher than those for 2005). Moreover, the big three continental European countries have now clearly separated themselves with work-time-adjusted economic dependency ratios significantly higher than all the other countries. This trajectory continues to 2051, when Italy will face especially severe labor input sustainability issues, and Spain and Poland will have joined France and Germany at the top of the column. Japan will be worse off than the United States, which will be on par with Canada and Denmark. Korea will continue to enjoy its superior position under these frozen parameters.

Another way to look at figure 4.1 is to compare each country intertemporally, and here several perhaps surprising results emerge. In the event of "business as usual" and no labor input changes until 2050, the demographic aging of the US population will have pushed the productively employed share of Americans to a position of supporting a burden smaller than that of the EU-15 in 2005. In other words, purely in terms of labor input, if nothing changes in 45 years, aging will not have turned the United States into what "old Europe" is today! Even by 2050, US workers will only have to support an inactivity burden significantly smaller than that faced today by productively employed Germans, French or Italians. Figure 4.1 further illustrates that with frozen labor input parameters, projected aging will by 2030 have moved the economic dependency ratio in the EU population to be about the same as for Italy today. But fortunately for the workers in question here, most northern European and non-European OECD countries will not, even in 2050, approach Italy's present level.

While in no way allowing the US government to escape hard political choices in the coming decades, it is evident from figure 4.1 that the United States in labor input terms is relatively well positioned, due to its current high employment rates and high annual hours worked, and will, if the present status could be sustained, face only a relatively limited employment challenge in the coming years. This, however, is decisively not the case in most eurozone, Southern, and Eastern European countries in the upper right corner of figure 4.1. To keep the dependency ratio from becoming extremely high, this group will have to do much better than simply maintaining 2005 labor input parameters. These countries should aim to increase employment rates and hours worked per employee, a significant policy challenge for this group of countries (and for Italy in particular; see box 4.1).

Box 4.1   What must greying Europe do?

Continental Europe's acute labor input challenge in the face of aging popula-tions[1] raises the question of what type of policy reforms might succeed and what reforms will not be sufficient. The method used for figure 4.1 is also convenient for exploring the relative merits of several policy options.

The starting point is again the "freeze concept" of gender- and age category–specific employment rates in 2005, adjusted for differences in countries' annual average hours worked. For this discussion, the benchmark is annual average hours worked in the EU-15 (not the United States, as in figure 4.1). In figure 4.1, the aging process played out with fixed or frozen labor market parameters. To in-vestigate the effects of several policy options, the labor market parameters are here selectively unfrozen, simulating specific labor market development scenar-ios. For the sake of simplicity, we assume that each policy option is phased in gradually during the five-year period between the starting point in 2005 and 2010 and that the policy option parameters are maintained for the duration of the scenario. To retain the focus on the different outcomes of individual policy scenarios rather than the accelerating underlying population aging, the scenario duration is limited to the 2005–30 period.

We explore three policy options:

1. *The Lisbon Agenda's Employment Targets Are Reached by 2010.* As part of the Lisbon Agenda, EU leaders in 2002–03 established high-profile employment targets, several of which concerned elderly workers[2]: employment rates of older workers (age 55–64) should be at least 55 percent and at least 60 per-cent for women, and total employment rates should be 70 percent. It is as-sumed that by 2010 all countries will have met these target values.[3] A country whose employment rates in 2005 already surpassed the Lisbon Agenda goals is expected to maintain those rates (in keeping with the "freeze assumption").

2. *OECD "Best Practice" in Place by 2010.* This scenario assumes that all countries from 2005 to 2010 reach the gender- and age group–specific 2005 employ-ment rates of the OECD's major "best practice" country: Switzerland (we ignore tiny Iceland), with an overall employment rate of 82.9 percent that year. Swiss 2005 employment rates are assumed apply for the duration of the scenario.

3. *Imagine No Early Retirement.* This policy option attempts to explore what would happen to future support burdens if suddenly tough-nosed European politicians had decided in 2005 to phase out early retirement options for older workers (55–64) by 2010. This assumes that in 2010, gender- and age group–specific employment rates for the 55- to 64-year-olds equal those of the 50- to 54-year-old age group in 2005.[4]

Box 4.1   What must greying Europe do? *(continued)*

The outcome of each policy scenario, as well as the 2005 starting point and the status quo option of no policy action (i.e., as shown in figure 4.1), is illustrated in figure 4B1.1.[5]

As in figure 4.1, if 2005 employment rates remain in effect to 2030, economic dependency rates rise will substantially by then, and the eurozone, dominated by the three big continental European countries, will reach unsustainable support burdens for the working population.[6]

Next it can be seen that even in the event that the Lisbon Agenda's employment targets are successfully met by 2010, this will only really have an effect on the support burdens in the worst relative performers in the European Union, namely France, Germany, and Italy. As hugely beneficial as a successful Lisbon Agenda in employment terms would be in the three large EU laggards, this finding certainly illustrates the rather modest level of ambition in the Lisbon Agenda employment targets. The quantitative EU employment targets (included in the Lisbon Agenda) were watered down so all members could support them; even if these targets were achieved, it would make no difference to EU member states except to those with the lowest present employment rates. The Lisbon Agenda employment targets alone will not be sufficient to seriously dent the future support burden for productively employed workers in the European Union.

If, however, EU member states by 2010 achieved the "best practice" standard of Switzerland, figure 4B1.1 shows that this would substantially reduce the support burden on working populations by 2030, when a number of EU countries would find themselves below the best 2005 ratio in Denmark. Indeed, all countries in 2030 would be below the 2005 average support burden for the EU-15. The fact that the relative improvement (downward movement) in each scenario is proportional to the extent of the employment reforms required to achieve the scenario goals is evident in the "best practice" column, where 2005 bottom-placed Italy improves dramatically to a position in the middle of the pack, whereas best-placed Denmark moves little from 2005 to 2030. This reflects the fact that Danish employment rates would need to rise only slightly to reach best practice employment rates by 2010, whereas nothing short of a revolution in the Italian and several other labor markets would be required to reach this target.

Finally, the data in the far right column reveal that terminating early retirement options in the European Union and assuming that everyone employed at age 50–54 would continue to work for another decade would make a huge

(box continues on next page)

Box 4.1   What must greying Europe do? *(continued)*

difference. Eliminating early retirement options by 2010 would essentially annul the effects of the aging process on labor input until 2030. In several countries, particularly Italy and France, this policy option will even lead to lower support burdens in 2030 than those of 2005.[7]

In summary, we have shown here that the EU Lisbon Agenda's employment targets are inadequate for the challenge of dealing with rising support burdens in the European Union. Instead, EU countries must aim for OECD best practice targets to make significant inroads in their present support burden, and the place to begin must be to reduce early retirement options for the 55- to 64-year-old age group.

---

1. The decline in the number of inactive young people due to declining fertility rates in the countries in question will be dwarfed by the rise in the number of inactive elderly.

2. See http://ec.europa.eu for details on EU Lisbon Agenda employment targets.

3. No explicit target exists for male employment, but it is simplistically assumed that with a female target of 60 percent and an overall target of 70 percent, 80 percent is a symmetric overall target for male employment.

4. Given that a certain level of "frictional departures" must be expected during ages 55–64, fixing employment rates at the 50–54 level will invariably be an overly optimistic assumption.

5. For ease of reading, figure 4B1.1 does not show all EU countries. Poland, due to its size and broad similarities to the other new member states, represents them here.

6. The counterintuitive finding that the 10 new EU member states (NMS) fall below the EU-15 aggregate, which itself places below the EU-25 and the eurozone, is due to several methodological impacts. The NMS get a relative boost from the annual-hours-worked adjustment, due to significantly higher annual hours than for the EU-15. However, the employment-weighting of the EU-25 aggregate category obscures the NMS-specific benefit. The euro zone does much worse than the EU-15 due to the exclusion of the three opt-out countries (Denmark, Sweden, and the United Kingdom), each with high labor input.

7. To be effective, however, early retirement cannot simply be replaced by increased income support programs of other kinds.

A Closer Look at Employment Rates for Older Workers

One of the main drivers of the variation in labor input in figure 4.1 is large cross-country differences in the employment rates of older workers. Recalling that the most common statutory retirement age in the OECD today is 65, and that most earlier retirement options in the OECD become available after age 55 (OECD 2006, table 3.2), it is sensible to define "older

Figure 4B1.1 OECD economic dependency ratios in 2030 under different policy scenarios

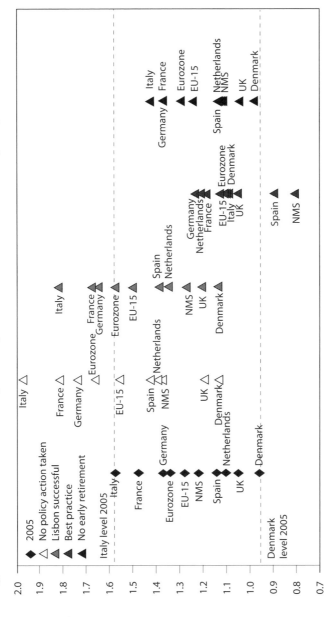

NMS = EU new member states

Note: EU aggregates are estimated using countries' employment-weighted average annual hours worked.

Sources: Eurostat online database, http://www.eurostat.ec.europa.eu; Organization for Economic Cooperation and Development; US Census Bureau International Database, www.census.gov; Bureau of Labor Statistics, Foreign Labor Statistics Database, www.bls.gov; The Conference Board and Groningen Growth and Development Centre, Total Economy Database; authors' calculations.

workers" as those aged 55 to 64 years.[10] Figure 4.2 shows the 2004 OECD employment rates of prime age (25–54) and older (55–64) men and women.

According to figure 4.2, the employment rates of prime age men are relatively uniform across the OECD in a narrow band (the grey band across the top of the figure)—between 80 and 95 percent; only Poland at 74 percent fell outside this range.[11] Unsurprisingly, prime age males have strong ties to the labor market and by and large are productively employed across the OECD. However, looking at the employment of male "older workers," only Japan, Korea, Mexico, New Zealand, the Scandinavian countries, and Switzerland have employment rates of 70 percent or more. Elderly US men were slightly less likely to be in employment, at 66 percent in 2004. On average, OECD employment rates for older men were just over 60 percent, or fully 25 percent lower than for prime age men. Several countries, though, have far lower employment rates for older men. In the EU-15, it is barely half (51 percent), in Germany just 49 percent, France 45 percent, Italy 42 percent, and Poland 36 percent. Many OECD countries appear to face a significant challenge in retaining older males in employment.

The employment rates of prime age women are substantially lower than for men, breaching the lower range of male prime age employment rates of 80 percent in only four Scandinavian countries.[12] And prime age women in the OECD are, at 65 percent, only slightly more likely to be employed than older male workers aged 55–64. The dispersion among OECD countries in female prime age employment rates is noticeably larger than for men, probably indicating the legacy influence of widely diverging traditional social institutions and practices concerning female employment. These issues appear to be at play in Greece, Italy, and Spain as well as in Korea, which all hover at a 58 percent prime age female employment rate. The lowest female prime age labor force participation is in the two poorest OECD members, Turkey and Mexico, at merely 26 and 48 percent, respectively.

It is less surprising that only in New Zealand, the Scandinavian countries, Switzerland, and the United States are the employment rates of older women above 50 percent. The United States thus does better at

---

10. Disability pensions are generally available at any age, subject to medical examinations. Some literature uses a broader definition of "older workers" as the age group 50–64; see, for instance, OECD (2006).

11. Poland in 2004 (together with Slovakia) had the highest unemployment rate in the OECD at 19 percent. Unemployment has since come down dramatically due to large waves of labor migration from Poland and relatively high economic growth after 2004, so that in 2008–09 employment rates of male Poles (inside or outside Poland) age 25–54 will surely be in the 80–95 percent range found elsewhere in the OECD.

12. See also box 2.3 for an overview of policies that enable women of child-rearing age to remain in employment.

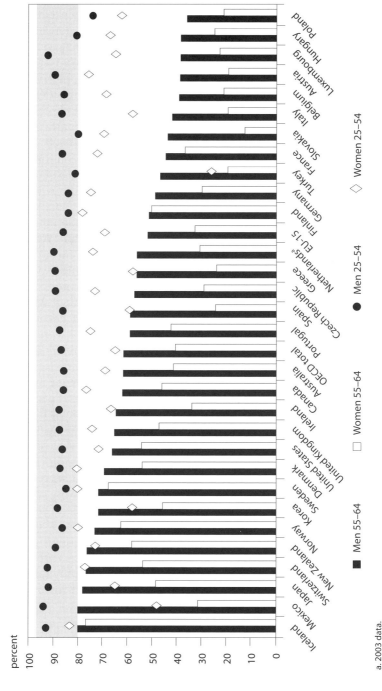

Figure 4.2 OECD employment rates, by age group and gender, 2004

percent

■ Men 55–64   □ Women 55–64   ● Men 25–54   ◇ Women 25–54

a. 2003 data.

Note: The narrow gray band indicates that employment rates of prime age men (25–54) are relatively uniform across the OECD.

Source: OECD, Labor Force Statistics Database, http://stats.oecd.org.

keeping older women employed than older men. The absolute decline in employment rates between prime age and older women is, at 24 percent, about the same as for men (25 percent). However, the fact that the employment rate for older women is less than 25 percent in no fewer than ten OECD countries illustrates the scale of the challenge for this group. In addition to the challenge of retaining male workers into old age, many OECD countries, noticeably in Eastern and Southern Europe and Northeast Asia, face the additional challenge of not only retaining older women in the workforce but also providing them with more employment opportunities and making sure policy does not discourage their participation at any age. In these countries, raising the employment prospects for older workers cannot be separated from improving both the general functioning of the labor market and the employment rate of women in particular.[13]

The gender differences in employment rates among older workers become even clearer when looking at their trends over time. OECD employment rates for older men and women have since 1960 been almost mirror opposites. Figure 4.3a shows that older male workers after 1960 experienced a dramatic decline in employment rates, lasting in most countries until the early to mid-1990s, after which a limited rebound is visible in 2004.[14] Nonetheless, employment rates for older male workers in most OECD countries today remain significantly below what they were until the early 1970s. Contrastingly, the employment rates of older women (figure 4.3b) have been rising since the mid-1980s, and in 2004 were at an all time high, albeit, as illustrated in figure 4.2, at levels significantly below those of older men.

Figures 4.3a and 4.3b illustrate several trends. First, older men seem to have benefited disproportionately from the introduction of early retirement options in the OECD in the early 1970s (more on this below), whereas women have increased their employment at higher ages, reflecting the general increase in female labor force participation since the 1960s. Second, the general upward trend across the OECD in employment for older workers of both sexes since the mid-1990s should serve as a reminder that country-specific explanations (such as the collapse of the dot-com bubble and subsequent decline in equity-based pension savings in the United States) should probably be viewed with some skepticism. Third, there is tremendous diversity among country experiences. For instance, Japan, which (wisely) never instituted early retirement options, did not experience as dramatic a decline in older male employment in the 1970s and 1980s as elsewhere; the country's employment rates of older

---

13. See appendix 4A for a discussion of the impact of early retirement on employment rates for younger workers.

14. Based on the general economic performance and labor market trends since 2004, it seems likely that the rising employment trend among older male workers continues.

Figure 4.3a   OECD employment rates for men aged 55–64, 1960–2004

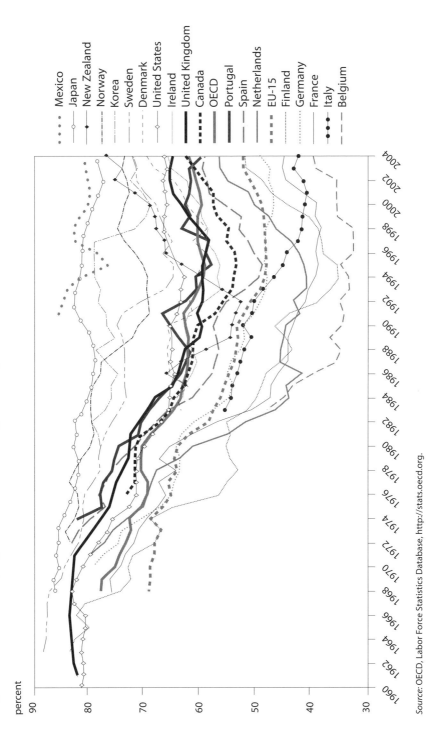

Source: OECD, Labor Force Statistics Database, http://stats.oecd.org.

Figure 4.3b   OECD employment rates for women aged 55–64, 1960–2004

percent

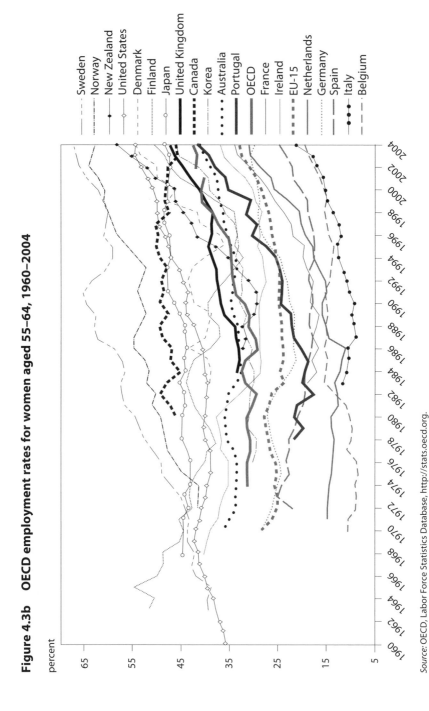

Source: OECD, Labor Force Statistics Database, http://stats.oecd.org.

men have held steady at about 80 percent. France and Germany had roughly similar male employment rates around 1970, but these fell to less than 50 percent by the 1990s. Another striking example is New Zealand, which during the 1990s experienced a remarkable growth in employment of both older men and women, propelling these to record levels by 2004, a trend that bears a closer look.

New Zealand: The Impact of Pension Reform

As seen in figures 4.3a and 4.3b, New Zealand witnessed an unprecedented increase in the employment of its older workforce during the 1990s. Figure 4.4 plots the employment rates of New Zealanders from 1986 to 2004 by sex and age in the context of the country's real GDP growth rate. Employment rates for prime age workers (25–54) remained relatively stable at between 75 and 85 percent during this period.

Beginning in 1992 economic growth in New Zealand improved markedly (apart from a mild recession in 1998) over poor performances in the late 1980s. Employment rates among men ages 55–59, like those for prime age workers, remained relatively stable over this period, at 75–85 percent. However, employment rates among men ages 60–64 more than doubled, from 32 percent in 1992 to 67 percent just 12 years later in 2004. At the same time, employment rates among women ages 55–59 grew by more than 20 percentage points, from 46 to 68 percent, while employment among women ages 60–64 positively exploded, tripling from a mere 15 percent in 1992 to 45 percent by 2004.[15]

It is evident from figure 4.4's juxtaposition of the relatively stable employment rates among prime age workers (and men ages 55–59) and the dramatic rise in employment rates among older workers that factors beyond higher economic growth rates were at work in New Zealand from 1992 onward. The increase in the country's retirement age from 60 to 65, phased in from 1992 to 2001, clearly raised employment rates among older New Zealanders. It is noteworthy that men ages 55–59 did not see any significant change in employment rates, while the rates for women of the same age improved in line with the international upward trends illustrated in figure 4.3.

Figure 4.4 shows that older New Zealanders responded immediately to the change in economic incentives in their pension system and that the year of pension eligibility serves as a powerful implicit tax on work. It is further noteworthy that, although the country's economic slowdown in

---

15. Furthermore, the New Zealand Department of Labor (2002, 2007) notes that the rapid increase in participation rates of older workers has not been accompanied by an increased proportion of older part-time or self-employed workers, making the rise in participation rates that much more beneficial to the economy.

Figure 4.4   New Zealand's real GDP growth and employment rates, by gender and age group, 1986–2004 (percent)

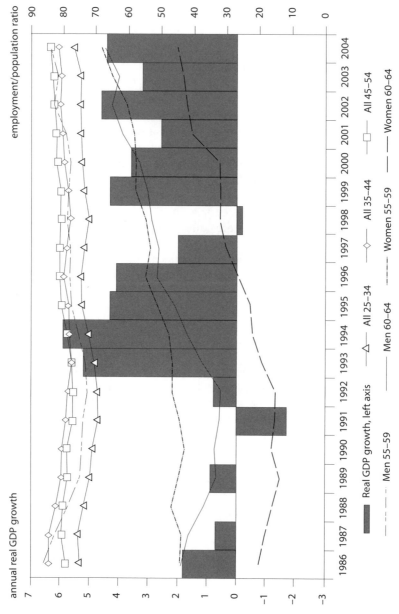

Sources: OECD, Labor Force Statistics Database, http://stats.oecd.org; IMF, *World Economic Outlook* database, www.imf.org.

1997–98 caused a slight dip in the employment rates of prime age workers, it did not affect those of older workers beyond a brief and slight slowdown in the generally rising employment trend.

The New Zealand pension system, a flat rate, taxable, superannuation defined benefit scheme, has been described as "simple, egalitarian, and unique."[16] New Zealand is one of only two OECD countries (together with Ireland) with no mandatory second-tier pension scheme (chapter 2; OECD 2007b). Moreover, Kwang-Yeol Yoo and Alain de Serres (2004) estimated that New Zealand effectively offered no tax subsidy for private pension savings; in other words, such savings receive neutral tax treatment compared to other forms of saving. As a result, participation in private pension plans in New Zealand is low and has, unlike in most OECD countries, been in gradual decline: As of 2004, only 14.1 percent of all individuals over 65 had any retirement income from an occupational pension, a decline from 22.6 percent in 1990 (OECD 2007a, 2007b). And as we saw in chapter 2, private prefunded retirement asset levels in New Zealand remain very low at less than 15 percent of GDP.

The extremely small use of occupational or private pensions in New Zealand helps explain why the delay in retirement age had such a dramatic labor market effect during the 1990s. In other countries, like the United States, retirement income for retirees is (increasingly) a mixture of private savings, occupational pensions (defined benefit or 401(k)), and public pensions. With more savings instruments from which to draw assets, the financial incentive of a delay in the eligibility age for public pension benefits would be less important to potential retirees in a country like the United States. Rather than having to work longer until they can claim public pension benefits, they have the option to retire earlier and draw on their alternate retirement income until they become eligible for the public pension, too. In New Zealand, on the other hand, where public pension benefits account for almost all retirement income, most workers have no option but to remain employed until they are eligible for public benefits. Thus, the effects of the delay in the age of first eligibility in New Zealand were particularly large, and are not likely with similar reforms in countries where retirees have other financial resources. But the findings from New Zealand may be highly relevant for low-income segments of the US population who have little or no other financial resources to draw on in retirement (as discussed in chapters 3 and 7).

The uniqueness of New Zealand's pension system is, however, gradually disappearing, as in 2007 the New Zealand government introduced

---

16. Susan St. John, New Zealand's Unique Approach to Retirement Income, speech to the 6th Asia/Oceania Regional Congress of the International Association of Gerontology, Seoul, June 7–11, 1999.

tax-benefited status for most private pension schemes[17] and thus partly reversed its policies of tax nondiscrimination among different means of saving. Moreover, the new KiwiSaver program of defined contribution individual accounts, introduced in 2007 (see chapter 5), also operates with a significant tax benefit for this type of pension saving. It is too early to determine whether these new reforms of New Zealand's pension system will lead to an increase in private pension savings or merely a substitution of existing private savings to these new tax-benefited means of saving.[18]

Japan: Why Older Workers Remain Employed

The employment situation for older workers in Japan provides another intriguing case study for the labor market challenge.[19] As can be seen in figure 4.3, the country has persistently enjoyed higher employment rates for older male workers than most other OECD countries.[20] Japan is one of few OECD countries whose effective retirement age is higher than its official age—the effective retirement age of Japanese men is about 69 and that of women 66—and it has the largest gap between official and effective retirement ages.

Nonetheless, over the past few decades, the effective retirement age for men in Japan has declined (albeit less than in the rest of the OECD), as shown in figure 4.5. Yoshio Higuchi and Isamu Yamamoto (2002) point to the deep recession in the 1990s and a lower share of self-employment in the workforce as the principal reasons for the decline (this latter reason deserves special attention and is discussed below). However, over the same period Japanese public pension benefit levels have increased significantly in real terms: From 1970 to 1993, employee pension levels increased four times faster than the consumer price index (Tajika 2002). As we have discussed, such an upward trend would equate to an increase in implicit taxes on continued work. A brief analysis of the Japanese pension situation suggests that, in addition to their traditional strong

---

17. Employer contributions to all registered occupational pension schemes, up to 4 percent of an employee's gross salary, became tax free. A related elimination of capital gains taxation on shares held by portfolio investors (i.e., also private pension funds) in New Zealand and Australian companies should further push New Zealand toward a tax treatment of pension savings similar to the OECD norm. Yoo and de Serres (2004) identify this as the exempt-exempt-taxed (EET) treatment of private pensions; we discuss this issue in-depth in chapter 7.

18. See Börsch-Supan (2005) and Attanasio et al. (2005), and the discussion in chapter 8.

19. This section draws on OECD (2004).

20. A strong work ethic inherent in Japanese culture is often cited as the driving force behind this prolonged working life; for example, see Takayama (1999) and Heller and Ruiz-Quintanilla (1995).

Figure 4.5   Average effective retirement age in Japan, 1960–2005

years

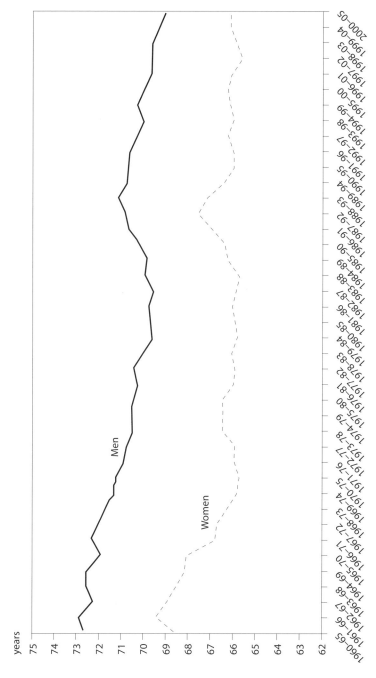

Men

Women

Note: Estimated average age at which individuals older than 40 left the labor force during any given five-year period. The estimates are derived using pseudo cohorts by five-year age groups for persons initially aged 40 and over. They are calculated by weighting the average age of each cohort over a given five-year period by its share of the total decline in participation rates for all cohorts between the beginning and end of the period.

Sources: Japan Ministry of Internal Affairs and Communication, Labor Force Survey, 2007, www.sta.go.jp; OECD (2004).

work ethic, older Japanese workers are responding rationally to economic incentives[21]; also central to this trend, as we will see, is the shift in the composition of the older workforce from self-employed agricultural to nonagricultural workers.

While average retirement ages have declined somewhat over the last few decades, Japanese workers continue to work longer than almost all their counterparts in the rest of the OECD. What drives them to remain in the labor force for so long? Despite the significant increase in pension benefit levels, the replacement rate of the Japanese pension remains low compared to most other OECD countries. As estimated by the OECD (using the methods discussed in chapter 2), the average net replacement rate among OECD countries for an average wage earner was 70.1 percent in 2007, while in Japan it was 39.2 percent (down from 46.5 percent before reforms; OECD 2007a).[22] However, several countries with lower retirement ages (Ireland, Mexico, New Zealand, the United Kingdom, and the United States) all have low replacement rates as well, so there are evidently other factors at play. To understand this behavior, we must understand the incentives in the Japanese pension system.

The Japanese Pension System: Structure and Incentives

The public pension system in Japan is a two-tiered defined benefit, pay-as-you-go scheme. The first tier, called the national pension, is a flat rate basic pension set at the low level of ¥66,208 per month in 2004 (equal to just under $500 a month at the PPP exchange rate for that year). Primarily meant as an income security scheme for the self-employed (including agricultural workers) and unpaid family workers (housewives), it is completely unrelated to earnings and thus has only a small incentive effect on retirement decisions for most (and an increasing share) of the Japanese population. A 1994 reform raised the eligibility age for national pension benefits from 60 to 65, to be phased in from 2001 to 2013.

The second tier, called employees' pension insurance, is a defined benefit system based on average lifetime earnings with a fixed contribution rate (shared equally between employer and employee) of 14 percent of annual wages as of October 2004, set to increase incrementally every

---

21. See also Seike (2001, 2003) for this argument.

22. The net replacement rate is typically defined as the "individual pension entitlement net of taxes and contributions as a percentage of individual pre-retirement earnings net of taxes and contributions. The upward trend in benefits ceased in 1994, when the Liberal Democratic Party (LDP) fell from power. Reform by the new non-LDP government in 1994 indexed future benefits to net rather than gross wages. Furthermore, the 2000 reform reduced the accrual rate from 0.75 to 0.7125 and indexed benefits to the CPI rather than net wages. The gap in increases between the CPI and future wages is estimated to be 1 percent, thereby having a substantially negative effect on benefits. For more information, see Takayama (2005).

year until 2017 to 18.3 percent of annual wages (see also chapters 7 and 8). The 2004 reform of the pension system anchored the future pension system by a fixed contribution rate rather than a fixed benefit rate, a relatively new approach, as many pension systems are based on a set benefit rate and adjust contribution rates accordingly. But the traditional approach is problematic, given current demographic trends toward aging populations that may necessitate continual increases in contribution rates to ensure a degree of fiscal solvency.

The 2004 reform also introduced an "adjustment indexation," which gives the government the flexibility to adjust future benefit levels to adapt to economic and social change. While the new system will require future cutbacks in benefit levels, it addresses one aspect of intergenerational equity by ensuring no future increases in contribution rates. These "automatic stabilizing measures" are in some respects similar to provisions put in place in Germany in 2003, the so-called sustainability factor (discussed in chapters 6 and 8). The pension pays roughly ¥233,300 (about $1,750 a month) for a hypothetical worker earning the average national salary for 40 years (Kabe 2006). A 2000 reform raised the age of eligibility for employees' pension insurance benefits from 60 to 65, which will be phased in from 2013 to 2025 for men and starting in 2018 for women.

Until this reform is phased in, Japanese workers 65 or older can receive their full pension with no earnings test and are exempt from paying contributions even if they work full-time. An individual aged 60–64 who continues to work, on the other hand, may receive only a reduced employees' pension insurance, subject to the *zaishoku* pension earnings test.[23] If a person earns even a small wage, employees' pension insurance benefits are reduced by 20 percent under the *zaishoku*, and by a proportionally higher amount as wages increase.[24] A 2004 reform abolished the unconditional 20 percent suspension but kept the rest of the earnings test in place.[25] Although intended to improve the government's financial solvency by preventing unneeded benefit payments, this earnings test effectively penalizes higher earnings and at the same time effectively encourages workers to scale back their hours (i.e., to change to part-time work

---

23. The *zaishoku* test on workers aged 60–64 was not changed by the 2000 reform to increase the age of eligibility for employees' pension insurance benefits to 65. The reform reintroduced an earnings test for workers 65–69, overturning a 1984 rule that abolished it.

24. Before the 2004 reform, the employees' pension insurance benefit was suspended under the *zaishoku* test as follows: (1) if the sum of the monthly wage and the "monthly base amount" of the pension was less than ¥220,000, 20 percent of the monthly pension was suspended; (2) if the sum exceeded ¥220,000 and the wage was less than ¥370,000, the pension amount equivalent to half of the amount in excess is suspended; and (3) if the wage exceeded ¥370,000, the pension amount equivalent to the wage above this level is suspended (OECD 2004).

25. See Sakamoto (2005) for this and further details on the 2004 pension reform.

instead of remaining in full-time employment) and earn lower wages in order to minimize the *zaishoku* penalty. OECD (2004) cites a survey that asked whether the *zaishoku* earnings test influenced the respondent's decision to work; the results indicated that 20–25 percent of those entitled to employees' pension insurance benefits reduced their working hours or retired altogether because of the payment suspension rule. The quantitative effect of the test on labor input, however, is difficult to measure. According to a 2007 Labor Force Survey conducted by Japan's Ministry of Internal Affairs and Communication, male workers after age 60 reduce their weekly hours by roughly 11 percent, from about 46 to 41 hours a week, until they reach age 64, after which they reduce their hours by another 12 percent, down to 36 hours a week.

While the *zaishoku* discourages work after age 60, before that age there are virtually no financially viable pathways to early retirement in Japan through either social insurance or the pension system. Relative to most other OECD countries, Japan has maintained a pretty meager welfare state. One of the benefits of this tradition in labor input terms is that Japan in the 1970s resisted the political urge to institute the early retirement schemes popular in continental Europe. As the same time, the government has limited access to disability pensions through strict medical eligibility rules. Instead, far ahead of any other OECD nation, Japan started to put in place the legal and institutional framework to promote high employment rates for older workers as early as 1971 with the Law for Stabilization of Employment of Older Workers (OECD 2006). This led to the rise of the "working pensioner" that would become central to the Japanese pension system.

Another key aspect of the Japanese retirement system is the company practice of mandatory retirement around age 60. It is customary for employers, private or public, to lay off employees once they reach age 60 (the law prohibits mandatory retirement ages of less than 60). One might have thought that employers eager for additional labor input would do away with such a relatively early mandatory retirement age. However, due to Japan's traditional wage system based on seniority, as well as rigid employment protection legislation (EPL) making layoffs of long-tenured staff very expensive, Japanese businesses usually are reluctant to give up mandatory retirement at 60, as it is a useful tool for managing labor costs.

Japanese workers receive, at the time of termination, a lump-sum severance payment that, for a typical college graduate who has worked for the same firm for 35 years, is roughly equal to 48 months' wages (Oshio and Yashiro 1997; also see chapter 7). This severance payment is available only to workers who stay in their job until age 60. Thus, in the absence of early retirement schemes in Japan, no rational individual will retire before the mandatory retirement age so as not to lose the employer severance payment.

Figure 4.6 Pension distribution among Japanese men, by age group, 1992, 1996, and 2000

percent of total male population

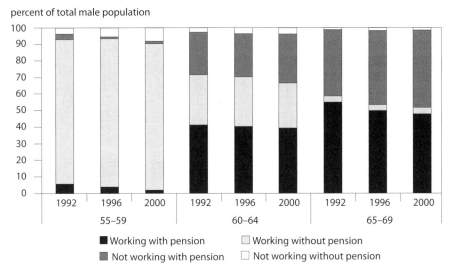

Source: OECD (2004).

While far from actuarially neutral, the employees' pension insurance benefit system does encourage workers to continue working after age 60. Employees' pension insurance benefits are based on average lifetime as opposed to final salary, which means benefit recipients do not incur much of a penalty from lower earnings after age 60. Moreover, as the number of years of contributions is not capped, continuing to work and pay contributions after age 60 increases eventual pension levels (Oshio and Yashiro 1997). With such a low replacement rate to begin with, the ability to incrementally increase benefit levels even slightly through continued work is surely a strong incentive to remain in the labor force. Many workers return to their previous employer but in a different position (frequently as an independent contractor), or they seek new jobs that pay less and are less strenuous. In other cases, employers often play an active role in helping the "mandatorily retired worker" find a new job, increasing the likelihood of employment for older workers.

These variables give rise to a unique Japanese labor market situation for older workers, many of whom remain employed throughout their 60s even as they draw a pension (or have received a lump-sum severance payment). As can been seen in figure 4.6, the vast majority of Japanese men work without a pension from age 55 to 59. However, fully 40 percent of Japanese men ages 60–64 during 1992–2000 remained in the workforce but with a pension (or previously received lump-sum payment). At the same time, about 30 percent (slightly declining in 1996–2000) of Japanese men ages 60–64 worked without access to a pension. Among the oldest male workers (ages 65–69), a remarkable roughly 50 percent (but slightly declining from 1992–2000) were still employed but with a pension (or earlier lump-sum payment), while only a small percentage of such men were employed without access to a pension. Thus over half of workers aged 60–64 who continue to work do so with a (reduced) pension. After 65, when a "working pensioner" is no longer subject to the *zaishoku* earnings test, almost all those employed work with a pension.[26] Thus Japan's continued high effective retirement age could not be sustained without the many "working pensioners."

Recent Positive Developments and Potential Causes for Future Concern

In part to counteract the potentially negative effect of the *zaishoku* earnings test on work, the earnings continuation benefit (ECB) was introduced in 1995 as a wage subsidy for 60- to 64-year-old workers who incur a reduction in their wages after mandatory retirement. It is meant to boost the incentive for them to continue working rather than retire or take unemployment benefits. As of 2003, workers aged 60–64 who incur a reduction of 25 percent or more from their wages at age 60 are eligible to receive the benefit of 15 percent of their current wages (marked down from a 25 percent benefit pre-2003). The benefit level is reduced if the worker earns 61–75 percent of his wages at 60, which (similar to the *zaishoku* test) effectively penalizes higher wages.

This penalty notwithstanding, the ECB in theory offers a substantial incentive to continue working after mandatory retirement and should decrease the implicit tax on work for the 60- to 64-year-old age cohort. However, in 2001 only 3 percent of this working group took advantage of the ECB. Indeed, Higuchi and Yamamoto (2002) found that the ECB increased full-time employment, but the increase was not statistically significant.

While any impact of the ECB thus remains uncertain, recent labor market developments nonetheless suggest that the downward trend in the labor force participation of older workers has halted and perhaps even inched upward. Looking at data from the most recent Japanese Labor Force Survey, from 2004 to 2006, labor force participation rates of workers aged 60–69 increased over a two-year period for the first time since the late 1980s, when a three-year increase in labor force participation rates of older workers was the result of a cyclical temporary surge in labor demand (Oshio and Yashiro 1997). While the recent upward trend is relatively small (from 70.7 to 70.9 percent and from 45.6 to 47.6 percent for workers aged 60–64 and 65–69, respectively), it suggests recent pension

---

26. This huge jump at age 65 will almost certainly be narrowed once the 2000 reform is phased in and the earnings test is reintroduced for those aged 65–69.

reforms may have had some impact.[27] The 1994 reform, which raised the age of eligibility for national pension benefits to be phased in starting in 2001, may be a factor, at least for the 60- to 64-year-old cohort. Another reason could be the 2004 reform that did away with the unconditional 20 percent *zaishoku* reduction for earning even a slight income after age 60, perhaps encouraging more people to remain in the labor force after mandatory retirement. For the 65- to 69-year-old cohort, the cause behind the recent upturn is more difficult to identify. At least until 2013, when the employees' pension insurance eligibility age is raised, those over age 65 remain unaffected by the changes in the pension system, as they are exempt from both contributions and the earnings test. Time will tell if this recent upturn signals a positive effect of labor market reform or just a cyclical response to recovery from the burst of the bubble economy in the 1990s.

It is also important to note the influence of agricultural workers in the very high numbers of older workers in Japan. As self-employed workers, they are unaffected by the pension system when they retire, as their employment status makes them ineligible to receive the earnings-related employees' pension insurance benefits. They instead receive only the limited flat rate national pension benefit and therefore face much stronger incentives to continue working than do nonagricultural workers. Most likely as a result, agricultural workers have historically higher labor force participation rates among older workers. The share of agricultural workers in Japan's working population has steadily and significantly dropped in the last five decades: In 1953 agricultural workers accounted for 38 percent of the working population; by 2002, that number had fallen to just over 4 percent.[28] As of 1995, while the share of agricultural workers in the entire population was roughly 5 percent, the share among workers over age 60 was 50 percent.[29] Thus, in that year 50 percent of the workers continuing to work after age 60 were unaffected by the employees' pension insurance, the *zaishoku*, the ECB, or any other incentive variables in the pension system. Any analysis, then, that does not differentiate between agricultural and nonagricultural workers will be biased.

A resumption of the trend toward earlier retirement would be alarming for Japan. Charles Yuji Horioka, Wataru Suzuki, and Tatsuo Hatta

27. See Japan Ministry of Internal Affairs and Communication, Labor Force Survey, 2007, table on "Labor force and labor force participation rate by age (five-year group)," available at www.stat.go.jp.

28. Oshio and Yashiro (1997); Japan Ministry of Internal Affairs and Communication, Labor Force Survey, 2007, tables on "Employed persons by agri-/non-agriculture, status in employment (employee in non-agricultural industries by number of persons engaged in enterprise), weekly hours of work (10 classes)" and "Employed persons by industry, status in employment (employee by number of persons engaged in enterprise)," available at www.stat.go.jp.

29. Ibid.

(2007) point out that Japan, having had the lowest percentage of its population considered elderly in 1975, has since become the greyest country in the OECD. This distinction means that retirement incentives are critical to future economic performance in Japan—potential retirees simply make up too large a percent of the population to be allowed to withdraw from employment. Japan cannot afford to rest on its high retirement age laurels.

Most OECD Older Workers Will Be Better Educated in the Future

The most important factor determining the employment opportunities of any age group is educational attainment: More education raises the likelihood of employment at any age. Thus, as US baby-boomers are by and large the best-educated baby-boomer generation in the world, it is easier for them to imagine continuing to work longer than in countries where the majority of this age segment has only a primary education. This is generally true across the OECD for workers aged 55–64, as is evident in figures 4.7a and 4.7b, which show that the share of the older workforce consists of far more highly skilled people than their share of the similar-aged population would predict. At the same time, low-skilled workers (both men and women) are significantly underrepresented in the older workforce. People with an intermediate level of education (upper secondary but no tertiary education) fall somewhere in between, with workforce participation roughly similar to their share of the older population. OECD women in this group tend to be underrepresented in the workforce, but this is likely related to the general underrepresentation of women at any age in the workforces of many OECD countries rather than to gender-specific skill effects.

These data indicate that rising educational attainment in the OECD countries, where far larger shares of the younger population have a tertiary education, will eventually provide a significant boost to efforts aimed at increasing employment among older workers.[30] However, the degree of educational improvement in the OECD's older workforces will be very dissimilar among member countries. Some countries will see dramatic increases in the share of older workers with tertiary education and equally dramatic declines in the share of low-skilled workers, while others will see no changes. It goes without saying that the latter group faces additional difficulties in the decades ahead in raising old age employment rates from today's levels.

The dissimilar cross-country trends are illustrated in figures 4.8a to 4.8d for low- and high-skilled men and women. These figures must be

---

30. See also OECD (2006) for a discussion of this issue.

Figure 4.7a Employment and educational attainment among OECD older male workers aged 55–64, 2003 (percent)

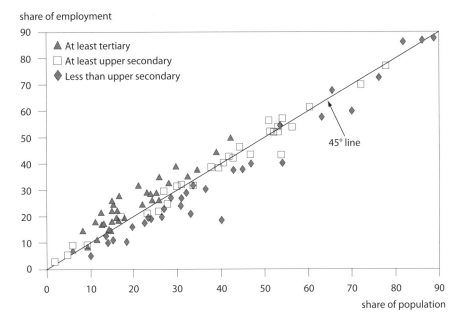

share of employment

- ▲ At least tertiary
- ☐ At least upper secondary
- ◆ Less than upper secondary

45° line

share of population

Note: Data are for 30 OECD countries and Israel. Data for Iceland, Italy, and the Netherlands are from 2002. Positions above the 45 degree line indicate higher share of employment than share of population would predict.

Source: OECD, Labor Force Statistics Database, http://stats.oecd.org.

read as a time series, with the difference in each country value indicating the extent of improvement or deterioration in educational attainment among older workers.[31] Most of the OECD countries will see a substantial increase in the share of older workers of both sexes with tertiary education (figures 4.8a and 4.8c). This rising educational attainment will be most prevalent among women, so that in about 15–20 years older female workers will generally be better educated than their male peers. This is

---

31. We derived the data in figure 4.8 by considering a "snapshot" of the educational attainment of different population age groups (25–34, 35–44, 45–54, and 55–64) in 2003 and then assuming that these remain fixed in the future. We assume that all people have ended their formal education by age 34 and do not include any effects of lifelong learning or immigration after 2003; thus some uncertainty surrounds these projections. Note, though, that people must only have concluded their bachelor's degree equivalent by age 34 to be included in the high-skilled category, meaning that later acquisitions of master's and doctoral degrees do not add to the absolute number of the high-skilled. Other issues, such as differences in mortality between educational groups (discussed in chapter 3), further affect the assumptions here.

Figure 4.7b   Employment and educational attainment among OECD older female workers aged 55–64, 2003 (percent)

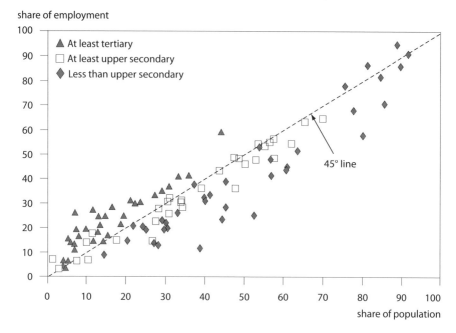

Note: Data are for 30 OECD countries and Israel. Data for Iceland, Italy, and the Netherlands are from 2002. Positions above the 45 degree line indicate higher share of employment than share of population would predict.

Source: OECD, Labor Force Statistics Database, http://stats.oecd.org.

encouraging news, since we saw in figures 4.2 and 4.3 that current employment rates for women aged 55–64 are far lower than those for men. But this educational trend also emphasizes the challenge many countries face in efforts to increase female labor force participation.

A corresponding significant decline in the number of older workers, and especially older women, with only low skills is evident in figures 4.8b and 4.8d. This future decline in the number of low-skilled older workers ought to reduce the rate of early retirement due to disability and/or physical wear-down from a long life of manual labor.

On the whole these trends are good news for the employment opportunities of older workers. Yet, as can be seen in figures 4.8a to 4.8d, the benefits will be very unevenly distributed across the OECD. Leaving aside non-OECD-member Israel, which is a special case due to its unique level of high-skilled immigration from the former Soviet Union in the late 20th century, the United States and Germany stand out among OECD countries in terms of educational improvement among older male workers: Only in these two countries, as a direct result of stagnating national educational

Figure 4.8a   Current and projected share of OECD population aged 55–64 with at least tertiary education, men

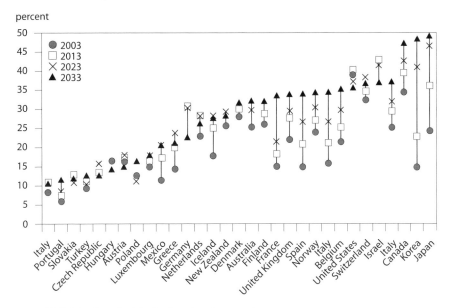

Source: OECD, Labor Force Statistics Database, http://stats.oecd.org.

Figure 4.8b   Current and projected share of OECD population aged 55–64 with less than upper secondary education, men

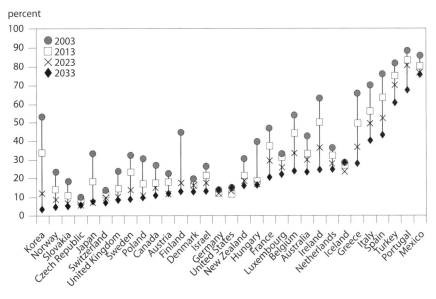

Source: OECD, Labor Force Statistics Database, http://stats.oecd.org.

Figure 4.8c   Current and projected share of OECD population aged 55–64 with at least tertiary education, women

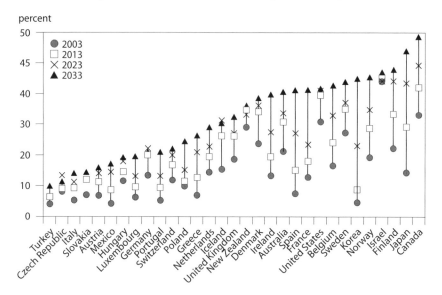

Source: OECD, Labor Force Statistics Database, http://stats.oecd.org.

Figure 4.8d   Current and projected share of OECD population aged 55–64 with less than upper secondary education, women

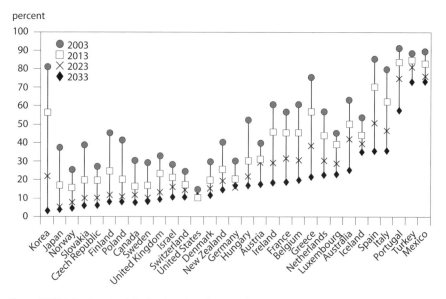

Source: OECD, Labor Force Statistics Database, http://stats.oecd.org.

standards in recent decades, will older men actually experience a decline in the share of those with a tertiary education in the coming 30 years. Thus, for Germany and the United States, there will be no future "educational dividend" in terms of improved prospects for boosting the employment of older men. On the other hand, this "male dividend" will be very large in Canada, France, Ireland, Japan, Korea, Spain, and the United Kingdom.

These distributional findings are broadly mirrored among older women. In both the United States and Germany, the share of older women with at least a tertiary education will stop increasing in the coming 10 years, but the majority of OECD countries will reap in some cases substantial female educational dividends from improving standards over the next 30 years. The share of older female workers with a tertiary education in Spain and Korea, for instance, will rise from less than 10 percent today to over 40 percent in the early 2030s. Ironically, Spain, Korea, and other countries with the biggest projected improvement in educational attainment among older female workers have the lowest current employment rates for this group, reemphasizing the need for these countries to become better at using the talents of women in their workforces. Otherwise, the rapidly rising female skill pool among older workers will be largely and unsustainably wasted.

Finally, it is important to distinguish between the level of educational attainment and its rate of change. Figures 4.8a to 4.8d make clear that older workers in the United States will retain their current comparatively high level of educational attainment into the 2030s and, as such, should retain relatively good employment prospects. But the figure also shows that this educational level among older US workers (ages 55–64) will stop improving and that they will soon cease to be the best-educated older workforce in the world. This development should be a source of significant concern for US policymakers independently of any retirement-related issues.

Why Do People Withdraw Early from the Workforce?

With older OECD workers increasingly well educated in the future, it should be easier for them to work longer years. However, pension systems impose implicit taxes on older workers by offering retirement benefits as a substitute for wage income, which may make continued employment an unfavorable financial choice. The reported reasons for choosing not to work among the 55- to 64-year-old age group differ across the OECD, reflecting the differences in retirement choices available to them.

Figure 4.9 illustrates the rates and reasons for low employment among older workers; countries at the top of the figure have lower employment rates for these workers. There is in all cases a significant difference between

Figure 4.9 Main reasons why older people leave the labor force, 2004
(share of total age group)

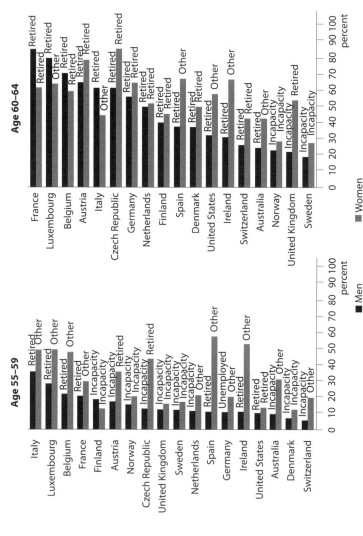

Note: "Other" includes family care duties and other non-health-related circumstances.

Sources: European Union Labor Force Survey for European countries; national labor force surveys for the other countries. Reported in OECD (2006).

the rates for men and women, as women generally retire earlier and for different reasons than do men. For example, the category "other" includes family care duties and features prominently for women in many countries, as they are usually younger than their male spouses, earn less income, and frequently assume a caretaking role in an aging household. It may not be good policy to discourage decisions to leave the labor force to care for relatives—the alternative, institutional long-term care, is usually much more expensive. It may, however, be good policy to provide some form of assistance that does not involve institutionalized care but that frees women to continue to work if they wish to do so. As the population ages, the burden on family members to provide care for elderly relatives will be greater than it is today. Because this burden often falls on daughters, it is important that policymakers ensure that decisions concerning long-term care provision by individual family members be as flexible and conducive to individual choices as possible. The personal decision to care for an elderly family member at home should not be based on financial need nor at the expense of (especially) women's careers.

The prominence of "incapacity" as a reason for retirement in many countries, particularly for those aged 55–59, illustrates the physical difficulties that many older workers face. However, it also suggests that in some OECD countries, the medical access criteria to disability pensions have probably been too lax.[32] Tightening of medical eligibility rules in some OECD countries, coupled with rising educational attainment among older workers, should reduce the prominence of "incapacity" among older retirees in the future.

The fact that actual retirement is the most common reason for inactivity in most countries, especially for those aged 60–64, illustrates the wide access to official early retirement options before age 65 in many countries. We return to this topic below.

One data point in figure 4.9, however, deserves special attention as it illustrates the risk of "leakage" among withdrawal options for older workers. The most common reason for inactivity among German men aged 55–59 in 2004 was unemployment. This is because unemployed Germans 58 or older who receive unemployment benefits can opt out of the obligation to either look for work or accept job offers (OECD 2006, box 3.2). The

---

32. See Baily and Kirkegaard (2004) for examples of this and subsequent "access retrenchment" in Sweden and the Netherlands. Autor and Duggan (2006) find a very limited effect of population aging on disability pension enrollment and instead offer three reasons for the rapid rise since 1985 in the number of US disability pension beneficiaries. First, Congressional policy reforms to disability screening in 1984 enabled workers with non-life-threatening disorders (such as back pain, arthritis, and mental illness) to more readily qualify for benefits. Second, a rise in the after-tax disability insurance income replacement rate strengthened the incentives for workers to seek disability benefits. Third, the rapid increase in female labor force participation increased the pool of eligible workers.

unemployment benefits are open-ended and without attached obligations, thus becoming de facto early retirement schemes. This is particularly unfortunate, as cyclical downturns in the economy may cause older workers to exit the labor market and miss out on improved reemployment opportunities during the next upturn. In March 2004, 75 percent of unemployed German men age 58 or older had opted out, likely influencing the slower reported decline in German unemployment among older workers after the country's remarkable labor market rebound began in early 2005.[33]

Germany is not alone in presenting its older unemployed with this "back door" to early retirement. A 2006 list from the OECD shows that eight other member countries either have, or until recently had, similar exemptions from requirements normally attached to unemployment benefit eligibility for older workers.[34] The effects of such loopholes can be dramatic, as examples from Belgium and France show (figure 4.10). In Belgium in 1985, workers age 55 or older who had been unemployed for more than 2 years became exempt from work search requirements, and in 1996 the thresholds were lowered to 50 years of age and unemployment spells of more than 1 year. The Belgian government initiated a gradual reversal of these options in 2002. In France in 1984, workers age 55 and older who received social assistance were exempted from work search requirements; in 1985 the age was raised to 57½, and in 1999 the 55-year-old minimum was reinstated but with the requirement of 40 years of contributions. In both countries, the number of those who accepted open-ended unemployment benefits leaked into the total number of early retirees and surpassed the number of people in official early retirement programs, reaching 150,000 in Belgium around 2000 and 400,000 in France by 2004.

It is evident that any pension reform aimed at raising retirement ages and/or reducing official early retirement programs will not achieve its full potential if such alternative options for labor force withdrawal continue. Indeed, there seems to be little justification for such early retirement loopholes to exist at all. Policymakers can alleviate hardship for older segments of the population through access to official early retirement programs rather than providing "under the radar" opportunities for such workers to exit the labor force. In this way they can ensure that

---

33. German total unemployment declined 30 percent from its peak of 5.3 million in February 2005 to 3.7 million in August 2007. Unemployment among German workers age 55 and older during the same time period was 23 percent (Bundesagentur für Arbeit [Federal Agency for Employment] online database, www.arbeitsagentur.de).

34. The countries in question are Australia, Austria, Belgium, Finland, France, Ireland, the Netherlands, and the United Kingdom (OECD 2006), and according to the European Commission's Labor Market Reforms (LABREF) Database, similar measures are in place in the Czech Republic and Portugal. No data are available for such rules at the state level in the United States.

Figure 4.10   Persons in early retirement schemes or on unemployment benefits without work search requirements, Belgium and France, 1981–2004

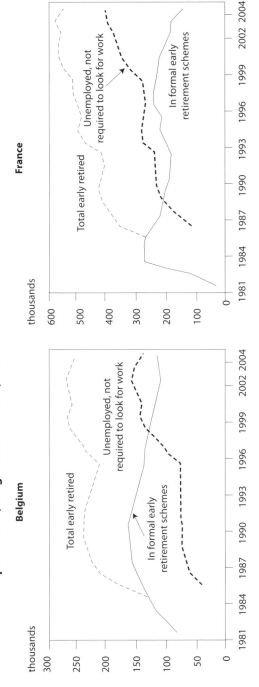

Note: The number of early retired refers to all persons on state-subsidized early retirement schemes. A small number of persons in some special schemes are excluded from the Belgium data.

Source: OECD (2006).

potentially costly policies—that are likely to be politically difficult to scale back once in place—are implemented only after a broad and open debate about their cost and desirability.

The Retirement Decision

Cross-country studies cannot fully account for all aspects of an individual's decision to retire—such as wanting to spend time with grandchildren or the risk of *karoshi* in Japan[35]—but the economics profession has developed a set of powerful analytical tools for analyzing the reasons behind this decision.

Jonathan Gruber and David Wise (1999) explain that the level of implicit Social Security tax/subsidy shapes older workers' choice to remain in or retire from the workforce. The implicit tax/subsidy rate can be roughly defined as the change in net Social Security wealth (SSW) that results from remaining in the workforce beyond the age of initial retirement pension eligibility.[36] Conceptually, SSW is closely related to the value of the "pension promise" estimated in chapter 2 and equals the total real value of the future stream of benefits for which an individual is eligible upon reaching relevant age thresholds. The difference between the SSW at time t and at time $t + 1$ equals the SSW accrual. If the SSW accrual is positive, delaying retirement to time $t + 1$ results in an increase in the present value (PV) of an individual's total future benefit stream (i.e., an implicit subsidy); and if it is negative, delaying retirement to time $t + 1$ results in a decrease (i.e., an implicit tax, or the "opportunity cost" of continuing to work). Naturally, for an economically rational worker to decide to continue working beyond the age of initial pension eligibility, the SSW accrual must be positive. In addition to the effect on the accrual rate, such opportunity cost may take the form of forgone leisure, which economic theory assumes an individual values more than work.

As can be seen in figure 4.11 (from Gruber and Wise 1999), the cumulative effects of implicit taxes have a powerful influence on the retirement

---

35. *Karoshi* loosely translates as "death from overwork" and refers to the extreme dedication of some Japanese to their workplace, resulting in their working unpaid overtime until they literally drop dead. *Karoshi* legally applies to a deceased employee who worked "over 80 hours overtime per month from two to six months prior to death" and experienced physical symptoms of illness in that period. For a recent example, see BBC News, "Overwork Kills Toyota Employee," July 10, 2008, http://news.bbc.co.uk.

36. Some debate exists in the economics profession about whether to include employer contributions in the implicit tax on continued work. The argument is that such contributions are ultimately borne by the employee through decreased wage growth. See Steuerle et al. (2006). Gruber and Wise (1999) do not include employer contributions.

Figure 4.11 Tax forces and risk of labor-market exit in the OECD

share of men aged 55–64 outside labor force

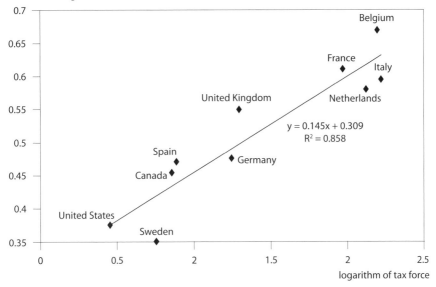

Source: Gruber and Wise (1999).

decisions. Figure 4.11 plots the log "tax force" against the proportion of men aged 55–64 outside the labor force (i.e., unused potential labor input) for a number of OECD countries. Using the implicit tax measurement defined above, the tax force is defined as the sum of the implicit tax rate for each year from age 55 to age 69. The summation begins at age 55 because, although the official retirement age is usually 60, most countries offer substantial incentives for early retirement. Figure 4.11 illustrates the good fit between a country's pension tax on work and exit from the labor force, implying that OECD workers respond to economic incentives in considering their decision to retire.

Gruber and Wise (1999, 2002) have described a series of ways that an implicit tax molds economic incentives for workers to retire at an earlier age.

Age of Initial Eligibility for Full Pension

Gruber and Wise (2002) refer to the relationship between retirement rates and the age of initial full eligibility as an "empirical regularity," showing that the propensity to retire tends to spike at the age when workers are first eligible to receive full pension benefits.[37] Retirement rates are negligible at earlier ages, as most workers typically do not, in the absence of other non-age-related annuity payment streams,[38] have enough assets to live comfortably without access to either wage earnings or old age pension benefits. Thus once an individual reaches the initial age of pension eligibility, s/he encounters the first and most obvious implicit tax on continued work. Before reaching the age of initial pension eligibility, there are no opportunity costs of continuing to work in terms of an individual's pension, as claiming pension benefits is simply not an available option. But as an individual reaches the threshold of eligibility, s/he must weigh the marginal benefit from continued wage earnings against the cost of withholding both pension benefits and the appeal of increased leisure. Gruber and Wise (2002) show how across countries this tradeoff at the age of first eligibility manifests itself in significant spikes in retirement propensity rates at the age of initial eligibility across the countries they study.

The strong empirical importance, in terms of the retirement decision, of the age threshold for initial pension benefit eligibility illustrates why raising these age thresholds could be a powerful and effective way to counter the effects of population aging on the fiscal shortfall in pension programs. And as table 3.1 showed, the United States and other OECD countries have been raising these age thresholds.

In a cross-country simulation with twelve OECD countries, Gruber and Wise (2002) use an option-value[39] model to estimate the effect on retirement rates of a three-year delay in the first age of eligibility for all retirement benefit programs. They find that such a delay would decrease the proportion of men entering retirement during the period by 28 to 47 percent. Moreover, the outcomes are fairly similar across all countries included, implying that a three-year delay can have a considerable effect in any country, regardless of pension scheme.

Early Retirement Schemes

As we have noted, there is a big difference between statutory and effective retirement ages. In many countries, this is due to the implicit taxation

---

37. Most countries do not actuarially adjust (see below) retirement benefits to the age of retirement, so the emphasis here on "full benefits" is largely superfluous, as the retirement decision is an either-or issue between "no eligibility" or "full benefits eligibility."

38. These could include a disability pension or open-ended sickness benefits.

39. The option-value model evaluates the expected present discounted value of incomes for all possible retirement ages and then compares the "value" of retiring at the optimal date with the "value" of retiring today at time t. If continuing to work suggests future gains, the person is more likely to stay in the labor force, as can be shown in a simple equation: $OVr^* =$ (discounted future wages through age r^*) + [(discounted benefits if retiring at r^*) − (discounted benefits if retiring at r)].

Figure 4.12 Pathways to retirement for German men, 1958–95

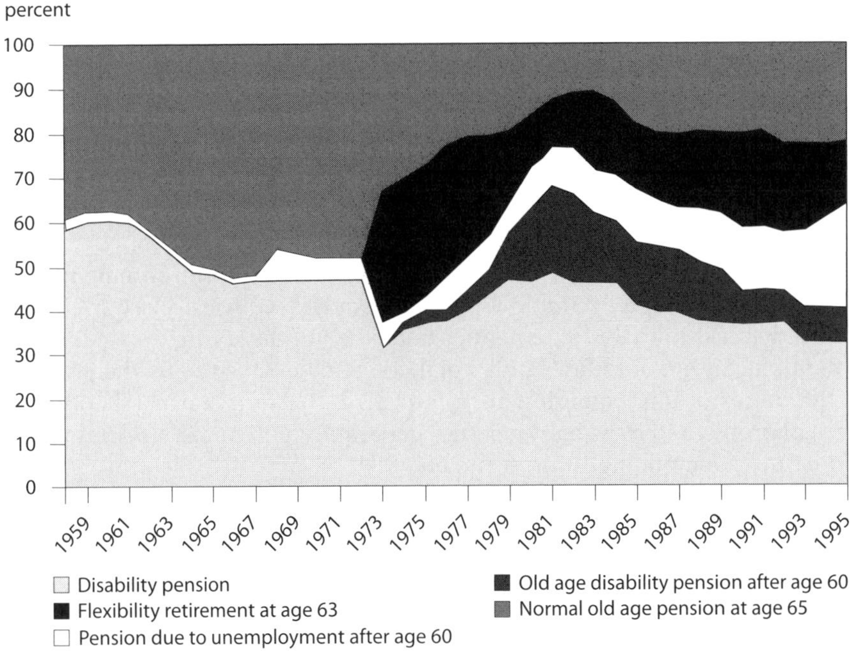

percent

Source: Börsh-Supan, Kohnz, and Schnabel (2002).

on continued work through access to alternate sources of social benefits before the statutory retirement age threshold. Such social benefits may be available through official early retirement programs, disability pension programs, open-ended sickness benefits, or exemptions from normal work search requirements during unemployment. Romain Duval (2003, 39) suggests that "closing early pathways into retirement is the most straightforward step towards reducing implicit tax rates."

Again, Germany provides an illustrative example. The German statutory retirement age has been 65, and a disability pension has been available since the late 19th century. In 1972 the country's pension system was reformed—seemingly under the politically opportunist but erroneous influence of the lump-of-labor fallacy—to introduce paths to early retirement, including a disability pension for people over 60 with 35 years of work experience, unemployment benefits starting at age 60, and a "flexible" early retirement option at age 63. The effects of these 1972 reforms are clearly visible in figure 4.12, which depicts the paths to retirement for German men from 1958 to 1995. Until the early 1970s, German men retired almost exclusively under the regular disability pension or at the normal eligibility age of 65. However, soon after the 1972 reform, nearly

50 percent of them were taking advantage of the new retirement options, and men working until the "normal" retirement age fell from roughly 50 percent in the 1960s to less than 30 percent by the 1990s. Indeed, by 1995 fewer than 29 percent of German men worked until age 65. This decline is also evident in figure 4.3 for Germany and numerous other, particularly continental European, countries.

As a result of experiences like those in Germany, several OECD countries have begun to scale back early retirement options to reduce the extent of premature labor market exits. Table 4.1 presents a nonexhaustive list of such recent reform efforts in OECD and other countries.

It is noteworthy that, as with the raising of statutory retirement ages discussed in chapter 3 (table 3.1), a number of countries phase in the reduced access to early retirement options well in the future, likely beyond the political life of today's policymakers. Such delays reflect the political difficulties of implementing such reforms but also risk exacerbating the fiscal problems, as the baby-boomer generation will already be retired by the time policy changes come into effect.[40]

Actuarial Neutrality

People generally respond to economic incentives in deciding when to retire in a rational, individually advantageous manner, so "actuarial neutrality" is important in pension systems. According to Monika Queisser and Edward Whitehouse (2006, 8), with actuarial neutrality "the present value of accrued pension benefits for working an additional year is the same as in the year before (meaning that benefits increase only by the additional entitlement earned in that year). Conversely, retiring a year earlier should reduce the pension benefit both by the entitlement that would have been earned during the year and by an amount to reflect the longer duration for which the pension must be paid." Thus "implicit taxes" on pension systems must be zero. This was attempted for US Social Security by reducing benefit levels for those who retire early (between ages 62 and 65–67) and increasing benefit levels for those who postpone retirement closer to age 70 (see box 3.1 for an explanation of how Social Security benefits are estimated). Unfortunately, as described by Queisser and Whitehouse (2006, 29), most pension systems in the OECD are not actuarially neutral, and "as a result they subsidize early retirement and penalize late retirement."

It is beyond the scope of this book to provide details of the assumptions concerning discount rates, level of the risk-free rate, or investment returns required for empirically estimating when or to what degree a pension system is actuarially neutral. For a detailed discussion, see the studies by Queisser and Whitehouse (2006) or Raphael Desmet and Alain

---

40. See box 3.5 for the Danish example of this political logic of *postponing pain*.

Table 4.1 **Examples of country reforms of early retirement options**

Country	Reform type	Affected group	Period of phase-in
Australia	Age threshold for "early retirement" raised from 55 to 60 (for mandatory occupational pensions)	All	2015–25
Austria	Age threshold for "early retirement" raised from 60 to 62; general eligibility tightened	Men	2000–2005
	Age threshold for "early retirement" raised from 55 to 62; general eligibility tightened	Women	2000–2027
Belgium	Require 35 rather than 30 years of contributions for access to early retirement at 60	All	1997–2005
Czech Republic	Reduce early retirement benefits in an actuarially fair manner for those who retire three years before retirement age	All	2001
	Restrict possibility to retire early: abolition of the temporarily reduced early retirement scheme (eligibility: two years prior to the statutory retirement age, having been registered with the district labor office for at least 180 days)	All	2003
Denmark	Tighten access to disability pensions. New disability pension granted on a full-time basis only to people with a permanently reduced working capacity who are neither able to work part-time nor in a publicly subsidized job	All	2003
	Age threshold for early retirement raised from 60 to 62	All	2019–22
Finland	Unemployment pension scheme available at 60 to be phased out; early retirement scheme available at age 60 abolished, but medical criteria for disability pensions relaxed	All	2009–14
	Minimum age of eligibility for individual early retirement raised from 58 to 60 years	All	2000
	Unemployment pension discontinued as a separate type of pension for employees born in 1950 or after	All	2004

(table continues next page)

Table 4.1   Examples of country reforms of early retirement options
(continued)

Country	Reform type	Affected group	Period of phase-in
France	Phasing out of the "end of career leave" (*congé de fin d'activité,* CFA) scheme for civil servants. Created in 1996, this scheme enabled civil servants to retire as early as 56 on an income equivalent to their future pension provided they had 40 years of contributions and 15 years of civil service	Civil servants	2002
	(1) Reduction in preretirement schemes by limiting fiscal incentives to physically demanding jobs and restructuring firms in financial distress; (2) elimination of progressive early retirement (*préretraite progressive*); (3) increased cost of company early retirement schemes, where employer now has to contribute at a special dissuasive rate (23.85 percent); (4) restrictions on state-financed early retirement schemes	All	2003
Germany	Age threshold for early retirement lowered from 63 to 62	Men	By 2010
	Age threshold for early retirement raised from 60 to 62	Women	2011–16
Italy	Access to disability benefits severely tightened, focusing solely on particular physical and psychological conditions (against the international trend, the expenditure on disability pensions fell during the 1990s)	All	1980s onwards
Korea	Age threshold for early retirement raised from 55 to 60	All	2013–33
Latvia	Persons with an insurance record of at least 30 years entitled to request early retirement pension two years before the official retirement age	All	2005
Netherlands	Intensive screening of new disability entrants and recertification requirement for all existing recipients of disability pensions, to reduce inflows into disabilty pension schemes; planned abolition of early retirement program	All	Ongoing since late 1990s

Table 4.1   Examples of country reforms of early retirement options
(continued)

Country	Reform type	Affected group	Period of phase-in
Norway	Previously open-ended sickness benefits replaced with temporary disability pensions of one to four years	All	2004
Poland	Withdrawal of early retirement availability for some categories of workers	All	Post-1990
	Eligibility to preretirement programmes limited to individuals living in areas with a high unemployment rate; elimination of the possibility to combine income from work with a preretirement benefit and allowance	All	2000
Portugal	Suspension and abrogation of some existing early retirement schemes: Private-sector workers may no longer retire early from Portugal's pay-as-you-go retirement system (previously, workers could qualify for early retirement benefits either at age 55 with 30 years of contributions or at age 58 if they were unemployed)	All	2005
Slovakia	Early retirement pensions are allowed but full pension benefits are reduced by 0.5 percent for each month by which retirement precedes the regular pensionable age	All	2003
Spain	Partial early retirement allowed only for workers at least 61 years old, with more than six years of service in the company and more than 30 years of contributions	New entrants	2006
Sweden	Restriction of the availability of disability pensions and open-ended sickness benefits	All	Ongoing since late 1990s
	Introduction of the possibility for early retirees to return to work	All	2000
United Kingdom	Age threshold for "early retirement" raised from 60 to 65 (pension credit)	Men	2010–20
	Stricter activation measures for disabled claimants, with prospective plans to require up to 80 percent of beneficiaries to seek work have benefits reduced	All	Ongoing since 2006

Sources: OECD (2006, 2007a); European Commission, Labour Market Reforms (LABREF) database, available at http://ec.europa.eu.

Jousten (2003). However, although actuarial neutrality is a useful technical concept, it does not indicate the overall best level of pensions, which take into account issues such as the reduction of old age poverty or the need to restore sustainability in financing.

Several OECD countries have started to move toward actuarially more neutral pension systems by linking benefit level adjustments to retirement age, measures not unlike those implemented for Social Security. A brief description of some recent reforms of this type is provided in table 4.2.

Replacement Rates

The replacement rate in a pension scheme (i.e., the ratio of pension benefits over wage earnings before retirement) can represent an implicit tax on continued work. As noted by Duval (2003), countries with high replacement rates typically have high implicit tax rates. A high replacement rate creates a substantial "income effect" in favor of retirement by increasing an individual's net SSW, making retirement a financially more attractive option.

The incentive effects of replacement rates can actually increase labor force participation, as Eskil Wadensjö (2006) found in an analysis of the impact of replacement rates on participation in Sweden's erstwhile part-time pension program, initiated in 1976 but phased out in 2001 on the grounds of fiscal unsustainability. In the spirit of keeping older workers in the workforce longer, it gave them the opportunity to postpone full-time retirement by switching to part-time work and receiving a reduced pension. The system subsidized older people who opted for this switch with a certain "replacement rate" of their corresponding loss of earnings.

The replacement rate was first set at 65 percent, then lowered to 50 percent in 1981, and then raised to 65 percent again in 1987. Wadensjö (2006) shows that the number of part-time pensioners who enrolled in a given year was extremely sensitive to changes in the replacement rate: The number decreased dramatically in 1981 (from 33,000 in 1980 to 12,500 in 1981), when the replacement rate was reduced to 50 percent, and continued to fall until 1987, when the rate was increased back to 65 percent (and enrollment rose from 8,000 in 1986 to 15,000 in 1987).

Wadensjö goes on to simulate the effect of the part-time pension system on total hours worked, and he estimates that the average part-time pensioner worked 4 to 5 hours per week more than in the absence of the scheme. Basically, the number of retirees who switched from full-time retirement to part-time work, thus increasing labor input, was greater than the number of people who switched from full-time to part-time work, decreasing labor input. According to the simulation, the option of part-time work for older people resulted in more hours worked in the Swedish economy than in its absence, and if the average older

Table 4.2   Recent OECD reforms toward actuarial neutrality in pension systems

Country	Reform type	Implementation
Australia	Lump-sum bonus for deferring retirement up to five years	1998
Austria	Increasing financial penalty for retiring early from 2 to 4.2 percent of benefits per year	1997
Belgium	Higher pension for deferring retirement after age 60 (statutory public-sector threshold) in public sector, up to 9 percent by age 65	2001
Denmark	Reduction in pension benefits by about 10 percent for retiring early (age 60 to 62). Lump-sum bonuses for continuing to work at ages 62 to 65. Higher pensions for deferring retirement after age 65 (statutory threshold), e.g., 7 percent extra for age 66	1999/2004
Finland	Flexible retirement age (62 to 68); 7.2 percent bonus for deferring retirement to age 63 and 4.5 percent from age 63 to 68	2005
France	A 3 percent bonus for each year of deferment of retirement after age 60 for people who have made sufficient contributions to a full pension; option for workers to access a fraction of the pension while continuing to work under a "progressive retirement" scheme	2004/2005
Germany	Pension reduction of 3.6 percent if retirement at age 63 to 64; 6 percent pension bonus per year after age 65	1997–2004
Italy	Actuarially equivalent reductions if retirement prior to age 57 through notional defined contribution system	2015–2033
Spain	2 percent bonus per year for deferring retirement until after age 65, no upper limit; for people with at least 35 years of contributions	2002
Sweden	Notional defined contribution system with flexible retirement ages after 61 with actuarially based rewards/penalties for all individuals with 35 years of contributions	1999
United Kingdom	Pension bonus of 10.4 percent for each year of deferred pension between ages 65 and 70, with a lump-sum option	2005

Source: OECD (2006).

person is working more hours, that person is choosing to delay retirement in favor of working longer.

These results show that the level of the replacement rate in a pension system affects a person's decision to retire and that people are drawn to a pension with a higher replacement rate. If a full pension is available only to retirees, eligible workers will be more likely to retire and claim benefits. If, on the other hand, it is available only to older workers who continue working, guaranteeing a certain level of wage income (a type of subsidized employment similar to "wage insurance schemes" in the United States), a high replacement rate can increase the labor force participation rates of older workers by enticing them back into the workforce.

Tax Treatment of Pensions and other Allowances

As discussed in chapter 2, the manner and extent of taxation on pension benefits differ widely across the OECD, and policy decisions about such taxation have a big effect on retirement incentives. In table 2.1 we showed that only five countries in the OECD do not tax retirement benefits at a reduced level. In addition, most income tax systems are progressive, taxing higher incomes at higher rates. The combination of these two factors effectively widens the gap between SSW and wage earnings, affecting an individual's decision whether to retire.

Retirees also receive other benefits. Once Americans reach age 65 they are eligible for Medicare, and this eliminates an important reason many workers remain employed—to receive employer-sponsored health care. In Europe health care coverage is universal, but many countries provide additional benefits for older people above a certain age threshold, including free or low-cost public transportation, subsidized housing, and other benefits that all influence an individual's retirement decision.

Final Salary versus Average Salary Pension Schemes

As described in chapter 3, the formula to determine defined benefit pension levels in many plans is based on a worker's salary over the last few years before retirement rather than on average salary over an entire working career. Perhaps surprisingly, this sort of "final salary" scheme creates a substantial incentive to retire earlier rather than later, constituting another implicit tax on continued work. Final salary schemes effectively encourage workers to retire at the age of their peak earnings, in their late 50s,[41] well before the typical statutory retirement age of 65. Continued work after the peak earning age likely results in a high implicit tax

---

41. See OECD (2006, figure 3.4), for OECD country wage profiles by age cohort.

through negative accrual rates and penalties via reductions in the future annuity (Disney and Whitehouse 1999, Murphy and Welch 1990).

Schemes based on lifetime average salaries rather than on the final few years can mitigate this disincentive for continued work. First, with their longer "averaging period" (including lower-earning career years) for pension benefit determination, such schemes tend to result in lower levels of defined benefit pension benefits and thus provide an incentive to continue working. Second, if a worker enrolled in a lifetime earnings scheme remains in the workforce for an additional few years beyond the earnings peak and therefore receives lower wages during the final years of employment, the lifetime average salary will decrease by only a small fraction, while the same additional work will significantly lower average wages over just the last few years. The minimal negative effect of lower wages on pension payments in a lifetime earnings scheme tends to be offset by the longer duration of contributions, resulting almost invariably in a positive accrual rate. A company that wishes to reward employees who stay with the company could base its pension on the last few years, but at a relatively small percentage of the final salary.

Several countries have initiated reforms along these lines (OECD 2006). Austria in 2003 started extending the period of estimation for benefits in the public defined benefit system from the best 15 years to the best 40 (i.e., essentially a lifetime earnings average). As described in chapter 3, France extended its average estimation period from 10 to 25 years, first in the private sector and subsequently the public sector, beginning in 1993; and the introduction of Sweden's notional defined contribution (NDC) system in 1999 meant a switch from a 15-year estimation period to a lifetime earnings basis.

Minimum Pension Guarantees

Most developed countries offer a minimum pension guarantee comparable to the US Supplemental Security Income (SSI)[42] as a redistributive element of their pension system, whether as minimum guaranteed benefits in earnings-related pension schemes or as a basic pension in flat rate benefit programs. These minimum guarantees serve as social insurance programs to ensure a degree of income security for low-income workers once they retire. But the presence of such a guarantee may heavily distort the retirement decision for low-income workers, placing a significant implicit tax on continued work for this group after the first age of eligibility for benefits.

Sergi Jímenez-Martín and Alfonso Sánchez-Martín (2005), using a large sample of records from the Spanish Social Security Administration, estimate that abolishing Spain's minimum pension would reduce the

---

42. See *What You Need To Know When You Get Supplemental Security Income (SSI)*, SSA Publication no. 05-11011, March 2008, available at www.ssa.gov.

incidence of early retirement by 20 percent (from 75 to 60 percent). Such a move would be both politically infeasible and socially undesirable, but the impact on retirement rates of guaranteed pensions highlights the need to avoid adverse work incentives for lower-wage workers. Minimum pensions should not be so high that they discourage work. And there may even be a case for measures to encourage employment for older workers, particularly in European countries that are trying to change social norms about when people expect to retire.

Phased Retirement Option

One option for increasing the labor input from older workers is for them to remain in the workforce longer while working fewer hours, avoiding casting the decision to retire as a Manichean choice between full-time work and full-time retirement. Many surveys and commentators have suggested that retiring baby-boomers will choose to remain in the workforce if offered part-time work, or phased retirement (Penner, Perun, and Steuerle 2002; Brown 2005; Chen and Scott 2006). As we discussed above, such opportunities to retire gradually must be facilitated by pension systems that do not impose a high implicit tax on part-time work nor penalize elderly part-time workers by cutting their retirement benefits because of their earnings.

The current US Social Security program penalizes beneficiaries who receive labor income above a pretty low minimum until they reach age 70, and most OECD countries impose implicit taxes on part-time workers (Even and Macpherson 2004). But even if these were reduced or eliminated, there is a question of how much extra labor input there is to be had through phased retirement. The Swedish experience in 1976–2001 showed that phased retirement options are effective at encouraging employment if they heavily subsidize employment for older workers. However, that approach can be very expensive and may not be the best outcome. Simply raising the eligibility age for receipt of benefits may be the most effective way to increase the participation of older workers.

It is clear that in countries like the United States (and for men in general throughout the OECD), where the share of part-timers is very low among older workers, phased retirement options offer substantial potential for keeping more people in the workforce. Older workers should have the option of continuing to work, whether part- or full-time, and should not face discrimination by employers. And public pensions should not discourage work, whether full- or part-time. On the other hand, as illustrated in figure 4.13, which shows the increase in part-time work from workers aged 45–54 to those 55–64, phased retirement options in the form of part-time work at high ages are already available and widely used in many OECD countries. It is thus doubtful whether coun-

Figure 4.13   Incidence of part-time employment, by gender and age groups, 2006

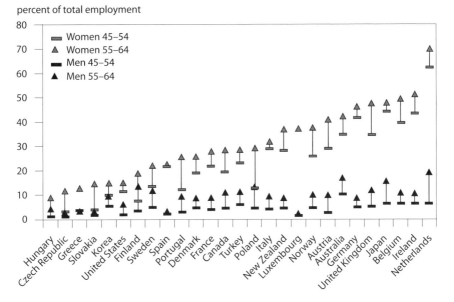

percent of total employment

Note: Part-time employment defined as a usual work-week of less than 30 hours.

Source: OECD, Labor Force Statistics Database, http://stats.oecd.org.

tries such as, for instance, the Netherlands can realistically hope to achieve much additional labor input from older women by relying on part-time work.

Concluding Remarks

Incentives matter, and mandatory pension programs in OECD countries, along with other tax and benefit programs, have reduced labor force participation and hours of work. This does not mean the policies involved are inherently wrong; providing income support and insurance for the elderly is very worthwhile, even if it affects labor force decisions.

But many OECD countries, especially in Europe, have overdone the subsidies for early retirement, and as a result they are facing large budget problems and very low rates of labor force participation among older workers. Despite strong social opposition, several countries have therefore scaled back their pensions and implemented significant reforms. Indeed, we find evidence of an accelerating trend among OECD countries toward scaling back early retirement options. We also find an almost uninterrupted increase in the employment of older female workers, suggesting that the scaling back of early retirement options has an important emancipating effect, as historically more male than female workers have taken advantage of these options.

One sign of the need for change is that dependency ratios are expected to rise to levels that look unsustainable. We adjust these ratios across countries for differences in labor force participation and in hours worked per year per employee. This adjustment reveals the seriousness of the problem of rising dependency in many countries, but it shows that the United States is in comparatively good shape, even though its ratio will rise substantially.

We find that most OECD countries can, as their average educational levels improve, expect to reap a substantial future "educational dividend" among older workers: Better-educated workers will be more likely to remain in employment until the normal age of eligibility for a full pension (i.e., they will have less physical need to enter into early retirement or disability pension schemes). This long-term trend should assist many countries in raising the employment levels of older workers, especially among women.[43]

Cultural differences across countries or individual preferences for leisure versus income may play a role in the decision to retire, but both the country-specific and cross-country evidence suggests that economic incentives are the key driver of retirement age differences. Countries with low average effective ages of retirement had much higher average ages in earlier periods, when incentives were different and early retirement options not yet available.

The option of part-time work may provide a valuable transition from full-time work to retirement. Public pensions should, therefore, not discourage part-time work by reducing retirement benefits for those who wish to work part-time.

References

Attanasio, O., J. Banks, and M. Wakefield. 2005. *Effectiveness of Tax Incentives to Boost (Retirement) Saving: Theoretical Motivation and Empirical Evidence.* OECD Economic Studies, no. 39, 2004/2. Paris: Organization for Economic Cooperation and Development.

Autor, David H., and Mark G. Duggan. 2006. The Growth in the Social Security Disability Roles: A Fiscal Crisis Unfolding. *Journal of Economic Perspectives* 20, no. 3 (Summer): 71–96.

Baily, Martin, and Jacob Kirkegaard. 2004. *Transforming the European Economy.* Washington: Institute for International Economics.

Börsch-Supan, Axel, Simone Kohnz, and Reinhold Schnabel. 2002. *Micro Modeling of Retirement Decisions in Germany.* University of Mannheim Working Paper 20. Mannheim, Germany.

---

43. The "educational dividend" will be largely absent in the United States and Germany, given their current relatively high level of average educational attainment.

Börsch-Supan, Axel. 2005. *Mind the Gap: The Effectiveness of Incentives to Boost Retirement Saving in Europe*. OECD Economic Studies, no. 39, 2004/2. Paris: Organization for Economic Cooperation and Development.

Brown, S. K. 2005. *Attitudes of Individuals 50 and Older Toward Phased Retirement*. Washington: AARP Knowledge Management.

Carone, G., C. Denis, K. McMorrow, G. Mourre, and W. Röger. 2006. *Long-Term Labour Productivity and GDP Projections for the EU-25 Member States: A Production Function Approach*. European Commission Economic Paper 253 (June). Brussels: European Commission.

Chen, Y. P., and J. Scott. 2006. *Phased Retirement: Who Opts for It and Towards What End?* Washington: AARP Public Policy Institute.

Desmet, Raphael, and Alain Jousten. 2003. *The Decision to Retire: Individual Heterogeneity and Actuarial Neutrality*. Washington: Center for Economic and Policy Research.

Disney, Richard, and Edward Whitehouse. 1999. *Pension Plans and Retirement Incentives*. Social Protection Discussion Paper Series no. 9924. World Bank: Human Development Network/Social Protection Unit.

Duval, Romain. 2003. *Retirement Behavior in OECD Countries: Impact of Old-Age Pension Schemes and Other Social Transfer Programmes*. OECD Economic Studies, no. 37. Paris: Organization for Economic Cooperation and Development.

Even, William E., and David A. Macpherson. 2004. *Do Pensions Impede Phased Retirement?* IZA Discussion Paper no. 1353. Bonn: Institute for the Study of Labor.

Gruber, Jonathan, and David Wise. 1999. *Social Security, Retirement Incentives, and Retirement Behavior: An International Perspective*. EBRI Issue Brief 209. Washington: Employee Benefit Research Institute.

Gruber, Jonathan, and David Wise. 2002. *Social Security Programs and Retirement Around the World: Micro Estimation*. NBER Working Paper 9407. Cambridge, MA: National Bureau of Economic Research.

Heller, Frank, and S. Antonio Ruiz-Quintanilla. 1995. *The Work Ethic*. Center for Advanced Human Resource Studies Working Papers Series. Ithaca, NY: Cornell University.

Higuchi, K., and I. Yamamoto. 2002. Employment of Older Workers in Japan—Analysis on the Effectiveness of Employment Management, Employment Policies, and Pension Systems. Paper presented at the Ninth EU-Japan Symposium, Brussels, March 21–22.

Horioka, Charles Yuji, Wataru Suzuki, and Tatsuo Hatta. 2007. *Aging, Savings, and Public Pensions in Japan*. NBER Working Paper 13273. Cambridge, MA: National Bureau of Economic Research.

Jiménez-Martín, Sergi, and Alfonso R. Sánchez-Martín. 2005. *An Evaluation of the Life-Cycle Effects of Minimum Pensions on Retirement Behavior*. Economics Working Paper 715. Barcelona, Spain: Department of Economics and Business, Universitat Pompeu Fabra.

Kabe, Tetsuo. 2006. Japan's Public Pension Reforms. Paper presented at the International Conference on Social Security Reform, Urban Institute, Washington, February 24.

Murphy, Kevin M., and Finis Welch. 1990. Empirical Age-Earnings Profiles. *Journal of Labor Economics* 8, no. 2. Chicago: University of Chicago Press.

New Zealand Department of Labor. 2002. *Globalisation of Labour Flows and Its Impacts on New Zealand* (October). Available at www.dol.govt.nz.

New Zealand Department of Labor. 2007. *Older Workers Labor Market Outcomes* (March). Available at www.dol.govt.nz.

OECD (Organization for Economic Cooperation and Development). 2004. *Ageing and Employment Policies: Japan*. Paris.

OECD (Organization for Economic Cooperation and Development). 2006. *Live Longer, Work Longer*. Paris.

OECD (Organization for Economic Cooperation and Development). 2007a. *Pensions at a Glance—Public Policies Across OECD Countries 2007*. Paris.

OECD (Organization for Economic Cooperation and Development). 2007b. *Economic Survey of New Zealand 2007*. Paris.

Oshio, Takashi, and Naohiro Yashiro. 1997. *Social Security and Retirement in Japan*. NBER Working Paper 6156. Cambridge, MA: National Bureau of Economic Research.

Penner, Rudolph G., Pamela Perun, and Eugene Steuerle. 2002. *Legal and Institutional Impediments to Partial Retirement and Part-Time Work By Older Workers*. Washington: Urban Institute.

Queisser, Monika, and Edward Whitehouse. 2006. *Neutral or Fair? Actuarial Concepts and Pension-System Design*. OECD Social, Employment and Migration Working Paper 40. Paris: Organization for Economic Cooperation and Development.

Sakamoto, Junichi. 2005. *Japan's Pension Reform*. Social Protection Discussion Paper no. 0541. Washington/Tokyo: World Bank/Nomura Research Institute.

Seike, Atsushi. 2001. An Economic Analysis of Age Discrimination—The Impact of Mandatory Retirement and Age Limitations in Hiring on the Utilization of Human Resources in an Aging Society. Paper presented at Global Aging Initiative conference on Managing the Global Ageing Transition, sponsored by the Center for Strategic and International Studies, Zurich, Switzerland, January 22–24.

Seike, Atsushi. 2003. Pension Reform Towards and Aging Society. *Japanese Journal of Social Security Policy* 2, no.1.

Steuerle, Eugene C., Barbara A. Butrica, Richard W. Johnson, and Karen E. Smith. 2006. The Implicit Tax on Work at Older Ages. *National Tax Journal* 59 (June): 211–34. Washington: National Tax Association.

Takayama, Noriyuki. 1999. *Financial Balancing Between Work and Retirement: The Japan Case*. Japan: Institute of Economic Research, Hitotsubashi University.

Takayama, Noriyuki. 2005. Pension Reform in Japan. Paper presented at the Korean Development Institute international conference on Population Aging, Seoul, Korea, March 17–18.

Tajika, Eiji. 2002. *The Public Pension System in Japan: The Consequence of Rapid Expansion*. Washington: International Bank for Reconstruction and Development/World Bank.

Wadensjö, Eskil. 2006. *Part-time Pensions and Part-time Work in Sweden*. IZA Discussion Paper no. 2273 (August). Bonn: Institute for the Study of Labor (IZA).

Yoo, K., and A. de Serres. 2004. *Tax Treatment of Private Pension Savings in OECD Countries and the Net Tax Cost Per Unit of Contribution to Tax-Favoured Schemes*. OECD Economics Department Working Paper 406. Paris: Organization for Economic Cooperation and Development.

Appendix 4A
Exorcising the "Lump-of-Labor" Ghost One More (Last?) Time

It is useful to briefly address one frequent justification for early retirement options, especially in Europe after 1970: that opportunities for older workers to exit the labor market generate more jobs for young people. If this argument carried any empirical merit, one should have seen large rises in male youth employment rates[1] after 1970 when employment rates for older men declined across most of the OECD (figure 4.3a).

Figure 4A.1 shows the change in employment rates for older (55–64) and younger (15–24) men over three decades: mid-1970s to mid-1980s, mid-1980s to mid-1990s, and mid-1990s to 2004.[2] According to the "lump-of-labor" hypothesis, the change in employment rates for young workers should be positive throughout the two decades from the 1970s to the mid-1990s, as employment rates among older workers fell dramatically during that time. Similarly, the rise in employment among older men beginning in the mid-1990s should have come at the expense younger workers. In figure 4A.1, this would mean that most countries should be in the upper-left quadrant from the 1970s to 1990s and in the lower-right quadrant during the more recent time period.

However, figure 4A.1 shows very different results from those predicted by the lump-of-labor hypothesis. During the period of rapidly declining employment for older men from the mid-1970s to the mid-1990s, employment rates of younger men did not rise but rather declined along with those of older workers across the OECD.[3] Thus the result of early retirement options seems to have been a general reduction

---

1. Given the generally rising trend in female employment rates, this analysis applies to men only.

2. Mid-1970s refers to the 1974–76 three-year average, mid-1980s the 1984–86 three-year average, and mid-1990s the 1994–96 three-year average.

3. The one case of the predicted tradeoff from the mid-1970s to the mid-1980s was in Norway. However, the Norwegian employment rate for older workers declined by only 3 percentage points to a still high 79 percent in the mid-1980s. Norway, therefore, provides limited support for the old-young worker employment tradeoff argument. During the 1980s to 1990s, the Netherlands saw a small 2 percentage point decline to 41 percent employment among older male workers but a large rise of 19 percentage points in male youth employment. This rise, however, is related to a series of youth employment reforms in the Netherlands over this period, which among other things saw the legal minimum wages for young workers decline dramatically. In addition, the survey method in the Netherlands' labor force survey was changed in the early 1980s to count more part-time jobs (popular among youth). See Baily and Kirkegaard (2004) for details. Thus the Netherlands also provides limited support for the tradeoff hypothesis.

Figure 4A.1   Changes in employment rates for older and younger men, 1970s to present
(percent)

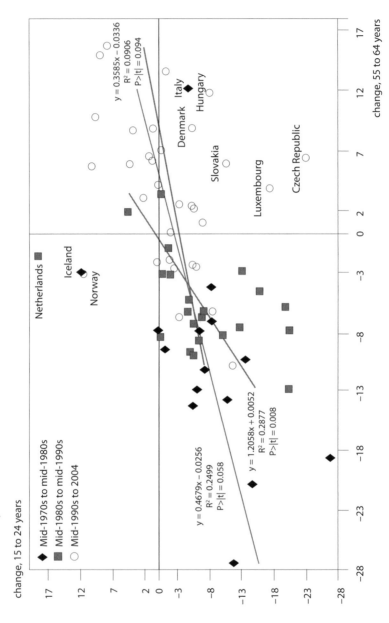

change, 15 to 24 years

- ◆ Mid-1970s to mid-1980s
- ■ Mid-1980s to mid-1990s
- ○ Mid-1990s to 2004

Netherlands ■

Iceland ○

Norway ◆

$y = 0.3585x - 0.0336$
$R^2 = 0.0906$
$P>|t| = 0.094$

Denmark

Italy ◆

Hungary ◆

Slovakia ○

Luxembourg ○

Czech Republic ○

$y = 0.4679x - 0.0256$
$R^2 = 0.2499$
$P>|t| = 0.058$

$y = 1.2058x + 0.0052$
$R^2 = 0.2877$
$P>|t| = 0.008$

change, 55 to 64 years

Source: OECD, Labor Force Statistics Database, http://stats.oecd.org; authors' calculations.

in all male labor input rather than an improvement in the employment rates of young men.[4]

There is, superficially, more support for the lump-of-labor hypothesis from the mid-1990s onwards. The presence of several OECD countries in the lower right quadrant of figure 4A.1 for this period indicates a decline in young male employment as employment rose among older workers. However, the light grey trend line for all countries is still upward sloping. The cross-country relationship between employment rates for older and younger men remained positive from the mid-1990s on.[5] We conclude that the lump-of-labor hypothesis is a fallacy. There is no case for providing early retirement programs as a way of opening jobs for young workers.[6]

---

4. The positive correlation is statistically significant for both periods. Furthermore, given the assumption of a negative correlation, one ought to use a one-sided hypothesis test, rather than the two-sided test presented in figure 4A.1. This is done by dividing the probability score by 2, yielding a statistical significance at the 95 percent confidence level for both time periods.

5. The one-sided hypothesis test of a positive correlation from the mid-1990s to 2004 is statistically significant at the 95 percent confidence level.

6. The finding is robust to different age groups of younger workers and reveals a similar pattern as shown in figure 4A.1 for the 25- to 34-year-old category.

5

Individual Accounts

It means your money would grow faster than that which the government can make it grow. And that's important.
> —George W. Bush, speech at Falls Church, Virginia, April 29, 2005

The use of individual defined contribution accounts in public pension programs is appealing to many policymakers because it addresses two of the challenges we have described above.[1] First, if individuals see the tax contributions they make to a Social Security plan accumulating in an account and earning a return, they may regard them as deferred saving rather than taxes. And when they see that by working more and contributing more they can add to the retirement income they will receive later, this perception reduces the work disincentive intrinsic to many public pension plans and alleviates the labor market challenge. Second, the investment of workers' contributions in real economic assets creates a fully funded pension program that can add to national saving and will not go bankrupt or require increased taxation in the future because of demographic changes. Individual accounts thus address the savings challenge and the fiscal challenge head on.

The importance of the first of these two points will increase over time. Because of demographic changes, greater longevity, and steadily rising medical costs, demands on the federal budget will increase significantly in the future and put upward pressure on tax rates. Economic analysis indicates that the impact of taxes in altering individual behavior rises as marginal tax rates increase (roughly as the square of the tax rate). Thus

---

1. The discussion in this chapter focuses on individual accounts in public pension schemes, in particular as a possible replacement for government-run pay-as-you-go (PAYGO) systems. In chapter 7 we analyze private accounts in corporate-sponsored schemes and their challenges, which are similar to many of the issues covered in this chapter.

workers' perception of taxes as contributions that provide a future benefit will be an advantage of rising value.

The Context in Support of Individual Accounts

Concern about the impact of rising payroll taxes on work incentives is understandable given work patterns in many European countries. The OECD calculates a "tax wedge" for its members showing the relation between employers' compensation cost per hour in each country and employees' net wage per hour. The difference between the two is created by payroll taxes and income taxes, so that, for example, a 40 percent tax wedge means that employers pay 40 percent more than workers receive.

The OECD also calculates the hours worked in each country, based on total employment times the average number of hours worked per year relative to the working age population (16–64). They report this in relation to the same figure for the United States. The cross-country results reveal differences in labor force participation, unemployment, the fraction of part-time work, and the number of hours worked per year by full-time employees.

Figure 5.1 shows that there are large variations among countries in both hours worked and tax wedges. Belgium, France, and Germany, for example, have tax wedges close to or over 50 percent, meaning an employer has to pay in labor costs about twice what a worker actually receives. Furthermore, in terms of hours worked, people in these countries (and the Netherlands) work, on average, almost 300 hours a year less than in the United States, whereas the difference is about 100 hours per year in Denmark and Finland. The figure also shows a very strong negative relation between these two variables: There is an inverse correlation between the number of hours worked and a country's tax wedge. It is dangerous to infer causation from correlation, but it is obvious why policymakers in high-tax countries are reluctant to see payroll taxes rise to finance an increased burden of pensions and retiree health care costs: Increasing the tax wedge may push people out of the (official) labor force or reduce the number of hours they work. A causal relation would indicate that each increase of 10 percentage points on the tax wedge would reduce hours worked by 108 per year, on average.[2] To the extent that individual ac-

---

2. There are exceptions, however. Several countries lie well off the line. Austria is able to sustain nearly the same number of hours worked per year as the United States with a much higher tax wedge. France has labor market restrictions, including the 35-hour workweek, that likely reduce labor input below the level suggested by tax rates alone. Moreover, countries that have seen changes in their tax wedge since 2000 have not seen a corresponding change in hours worked; the United States, for example, has reduced its tax wedge since 2000 but has also reduced hours worked per person of working age.

Figure 5.1   OECD average tax wedge and average annual hours worked, 2006

adjusted annual hours worked relative to US

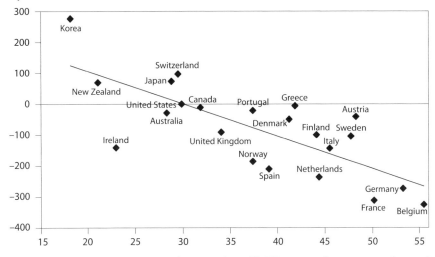

average tax wedge on workers with 100 percent of average wage (percent)

Note: For reasons of OECD country compatibility, ultra-small states (Luxembourg and Iceland) and the poorest OECD countries (the Czech Republic, Hungary, Mexico, Poland, Slovakia, and Turkey) have been excluded. Adjusted annual hours worked are estimated as total hours worked in a country, divided by the working age population.

Sources: OECD Tax Database and Labor Force Statistics Database, 2007.

counts reduce the disincentive effects of payroll taxes, they can alleviate this potential problem.

Individual accounts also have a related advantage in terms of political decision making. When voters are asked whether they think Social Security benefits should be cut, they say no. When voters are asked whether they think taxes should be raised to cover the budget shortfall in the program, they generally say they oppose tax increases. People want the services that government provides, but they do not want to pay the bill, evidenced by the fact that the US federal government has run deficits in all but a handful of years since 1945, despite strong economic growth and full employment. Individual pension accounts force people to see the direct connection between what is put in and what is taken out.

Disadvantages of Individual Accounts

But there are also some significant disadvantages or problems with individual account plans. First, they do not deal with the old age poverty challenge; indeed they will likely worsen it compared to typical public pay-as-you-go (PAYGO) plans. Workers that have low lifetime incomes will contribute small amounts to individual pension accounts and will receive low, perhaps below-subsistence, payments in retirement. Indeed, to the extent that contributions to individual pension accounts are given tax-preferred status, this will provide a larger subsidy to high-income contributors than to low-income contributors. (In the United States, the employer contributions to Social Security are tax preferred but most individual contributions are not.)

Secondly, we said above that individual accounts have a political advantage in forcing people to see the connection between contributions and benefits. Depending on one's perspective there may also be a corresponding distributional disadvantage. One reason traditional public pensions have been able to include redistribution is precisely that people do not see the connection between Social Security taxes and benefits received. If there is a minimum benefit level (as is the case with Social Security), people do not perceive that its payment depends on reducing the level of benefits that they themselves receive relative to their contributions. If a system of individual accounts were established in the United States by diverting, say, 10 percent of contributions to a fund for people whose own contributions were too low to provide a decent retirement, this could provoke opposition. This behavior pattern does not make poverty reduction among the elderly in a system of individual accounts impossible, but it certainly makes it more difficult.

Third, even for workers who make adequate contributions, the returns from the pension assets of individual accounts are subject to market volatility and therefore uncertain. PAYGO public pension plans, on the other hand, can provide workers with the assurance that when they retire they will receive an income that replaces a reasonable fraction of income and whose value during retirement is protected against inflation. The US Social Security system is set up to provide this assurance because initial benefits are indexed to wages (providing a fairly stable replacement rate), and subsequent benefits are indexed to inflation (providing a stable real value of the benefit during retirement). With a system of individual accounts, the average worker would face considerable uncertainty around their income when retired.

The importance of the indexation provision was illustrated by *Newsweek*'s Allan Sloan,[3] who figured out what it would cost to purchase an indexed annuity comparable to a Social Security benefit using quotes from Vanguard and AIG (which have combined to offer indexed annuities). The average monthly benefit (indexed for inflation) for a single per-

---

3. Allan Sloan, "The Big Value of Small Increases," November 6, 2006, www.msnbc.msn.com (accessed on March 1, 2007).

son retiring on full Social Security on January 1, 2007, was $1,361. Buying that same annuity would cost $263,000 in the market with indexing, or $192,000 without, so the indexing adds about a 37 percent premium to the market price. A married couple on full benefits would get $3,181 a month, and an indexed annuity at this level would cost $738,000 in the market[4]; the same level of initial benefit that is not indexed would cost only $539,000. The Vanguard-AIG inflation-indexed annuities build in a rate of inflation of 3.7 percent a year, which is pretty high compared with the rate for the past 10 years (2½ percent a year), but low compared with earlier periods (over 7 percent a year in 1973–85). Sloan's figures illustrate that an indexed asset in the private market is "really expensive to buy." He notes that only a small fraction of people that buy annuities from Vanguard-AIG actually take the indexed version.[5] His figures also illustrate just how valuable the Social Security pension is to recipients.

Fourth, most workers are not informed or skilled investors—many do not even know the difference between a bond and a stock.[6] We describe below the UK experience with individual accounts (dubbed the pension "mis-selling" scandal), which have been a bad deal for many workers: Financial institutions had an interest in workers' choosing individual accounts and persuaded many to do so although they would have been better off remaining in the state pension system (see, for example, Turner 2005b).

Fifth, there is disagreement about the impact of individual accounts in a public pension program when the private sector is moving rapidly to defined contribution pension plans. Some argue that the public sector should follow the lead of the private sector. Others suggest that with guaranteed pensions disappearing in the private sector, it becomes even more important to give workers a basic pension that yields a defined benefit. We look in depth at the issue of integrating public and private pensions in chapters 7 and 8.

Finally, there is a serious transition problem associated with individual accounts for any country with a PAYGO public pension. Contributions from current workers pay the benefits of current retirees. If these contributions are diverted to an individual account plan, there is no money to pay current retirees, or if there is a trust fund, it becomes depleted quickly. The solution to the problem is to use general tax revenue

---

4. Sloan points out that the Social Security benefit drops when one spouse dies. The figure of $738,000 is based on the assumption of maintaining an indexed benefit at $3,181, so the market value of the Social Security pension is somewhat less than this figure. We thank Patricia Colby of Vanguard Insurance and Annuity Services for providing comparable data (email communication, March 7, 2007).

5. The quote is from his column, op. cit.

6. See also the discussion of this issue in box 3.3 and chapter 7.

or raise new taxes to pay the current retirees. Canada has used this strategy (Stone 2004).

Before looking at the use of individual accounts in practice, it is important to clarify the pros and cons of individual accounts. In principle, a PAYGO public pension plan can address its fiscal challenges and eliminate work disincentives. For example, the US Social Security system allows participants to begin receiving benefits as early as age 62 or to postpone receipt until age 70 (and thus receive larger benefit payments).[7] And in principle, a program of individual accounts could address the elderly poverty problem, for example, by subsidizing the contributions of low-wage workers or by having a backstop income support program (Orszag and Stiglitz 2001, Diamond 2001). In practice, however, these principles are more difficult to achieve. The shift to individual accounts is often a social or policy device whose main objective is to generate greater work incentives or accommodate changing demographics. Individual accounts give workers greater personal responsibility for ensuring adequate resources for their retirement—and elderly poverty continues to plague some countries that have introduced them. While indeed a source of political strife, proposals for individual accounts should not be classified on a left-right political spectrum. In the United States, such accounts are favored much more by Republicans than Democrats, but Sweden is often seen as having a welfare state and it has introduced individual accounts.

To look at how individual accounts have played out in practice, we provide a brief history of their implementation in Australia, Chile, Mexico, and the United Kingdom, followed by an analysis of each country's treatment of four key issues: participation rates, administrative costs, elderly poverty and replacement rates, and the financing of the transition from a PAYGO system.

Structures and Brief Histories of Selected Countries' Individual Accounts

Australia

Australia has a flat rate means-tested pension plan for which men become eligible at age 65 and women at age 60. As of January 2004 the minimum pension benefit provided AU$11,772 annually to a single retiree and AU$19,656 to a married couple. The purchasing power parity exchange rate relative to the US dollar that year was 1.36, so these amounts translate

---

7. The increase in benefits is actuarially fair assuming the person lives to collect benefits. The fiscal situation of the Social Security system improves when people postpone retirement, because a fraction of them die before receiving benefits.

to US$8,656 and US$14,453. This amount has been indexed to rise with either the CPI or an index for average weekly earnings, whichever is larger. It has also been adjusted to about 25 percent, or the weekly earnings of a full-time male employee. The minimum pension receives favorable tax treatment.

Single retirees with an income of less than $2,294 (AU$3,120) receive the full minimum benefit, and the corresponding figure for a married couple is $4,053 (AU$5,512). For increments in income above these levels, the traditional retirement benefit is taxed at 40 percent. Retirees with an annual income of $24,213 (AU$32,929) or more receive nothing from the traditional system (the married couple figure is $40,463 or AU$55,029). In practice, 54 percent of retirees receive a full traditional benefit, 28 percent partial benefits, and 18 percent no benefit. Only 2.3 percent of recipients have labor income. The traditional pension system thus provides most of the cash income of Australian retirees.

In the 1980s, concerned about low national saving, a current account deficit of 6 percent of GDP, and low labor force participation among workers over 50, the government introduced a compulsory superannuation system.[8] This compulsory defined contribution retirement plan is designed to cover all employees who earn more than AU$450 a month; in 2003 it covered 90 percent of full-time employees, over 70 percent of part-time employees, and 67 percent of owners or managers of unincorporated businesses. Workers with qualifying defined benefit retirement plans from their employers could opt out of the plan. Overall, 78 percent of Australian workers had defined contribution retirement plans that year, while 21 percent had hybrid plans (defined benefit and contribution), and just 1 percent had only a defined benefit plan. The breakdown varies substantially between public and private employees: 84 percent of private employees have only a defined contribution plan, whereas the same is true of only 27 percent of public employees.

The retirement funds are privately managed, and until a few years ago the fund managers were chosen by either the employer or a union (individuals can now choose their own manager). Retirees may access the money at age 55 (being increased to 60) or older, and so early retirement is common in Australia as public-sector employees have a financial incentive to retire at age 55. A very important provision of the plan allows retirees to withdraw the full amount of their accumulated pension in a lump sum without major penalties, and 63 percent of recipients did this in 2006–07 (Australian Bureau of Statistics 2008). Of those that took a lump-sum payment, 42 percent used the funds to pay debts, including to reduce their mortgage.

In addition to the required pension plan, workers can contribute voluntarily to a supplemental superannuation plan, and in 2000 about a third of workers aged 15–64 made such contributions—46 percent of those aged

---

8. For an overview of the Australian system, see Edey and Simon (1996) or Sass (2004).

45–54 and 42 percent of those aged 55–64. Workers are more likely to contribute to the voluntary plan if employers match or partially match their contributions.

Chile

Chile, one of the first countries to introduce individual accounts in its social security system, reformed its PAYGO public pension system in 1981,[9] replacing an inefficient, increasingly inequitable, and unsustainable system with a privately administered contribution scheme that, proponents argued, would curb explosive fiscal costs, address the inequalities of the old pension scheme, and rectify that scheme's distortions of the country's labor market (Edwards 1998). Almost 25 years after the reforms were introduced, pension funds had accumulated assets of almost $70 billion, or 75 percent of Chile's nominal GDP, as of October 2005 (SAFP 2006).

For much of the late 1980s and early 1990s, Chile's pension reform attracted the attention of other countries pondering reform of their pension systems. The World Bank has based many of its recommendations on Chile's reform, and in 2004 and 2005, American lawmakers debating the sustainability of the US Social Security system reexamined the Chilean system's merits and faults (Orenstein 2008).

Chile's 1980 reform sought to connect workers' pension benefits and their contributions to the pension system, as any such connection had been utterly lacking in the old system. In the mid-1970s total contributions (from both employees and employers) to the public pension system varied from 16 to 26 percent of wages (Edwards 1998). The reform eliminated employers' contributions, and employees now pay 10 percent of their wages, to a maximum of US$2,000 per month (for workers switching to the new system, this represented a steep cut in the contribution rate and a substantial increase in take-home pay), into pension funds administered by highly regulated private financial managers called *administradores de fondos de pensiones* (AFPs). The value of an individual pension is determined by the level of the worker's lifetime wages, by the AFP's rate of return on the worker's contributions minus commissions, and by the frequency and amounts of the worker's contributions. Most of the country's workers convert their accumulated pension assets into annuities upon retirement. Chile also allows programmed withdrawals (which have the advantage of inheritability). Annuities are indexed for inflation and counted as *unidades de fomento* (UF), Chile's real unit of account.

The workers who participate in the plan contribute 10 percent of their wages (to a maximum of US$2,000 per month) to their retirement funds,

---

9. For a detailed account of the 1981 reform, see Diamond (1993).

which are privately managed by asset management companies that are highly regulated. At the outset, only the "C fund" portfolio type was available for most participants, and it held government bonds and bonds issued by financial institutions. Over time, the management companies were allowed to diversify somewhat, and by early 2002 the C fund also held domestic stocks and international securities (SSA 2003). The fund earned a real return of 10.2 percent a year from June 1981 to December 2006 (SAFP 2006). Starting in August 2002, Chilean pension funds had to offer four funds—B, C, D, and E—with varying degrees of risk; the first three own 60, 40, and 20 percent equities, respectively. Funds can also offer a fund A, with a maximum of 80 percent equities.

Chilean reformers hoped that the overhaul of the pension system would remove inefficiencies in the country's labor market and significantly reduce the cost of labor to employers, and indeed Sebastian Edwards (1998) finds that the reform greatly improved the functioning of Chile's labor market. In particular, he cites the reduction in payroll taxes as having led to significant job creation (the unemployment rate fell from 25 percent to 6 percent in less than 15 years, although that is not attributable solely to the pension reform). The transparency of the new system's linking of pension benefits and a worker's monthly contribution also improved official workforce participation. The rate of labor force participation does show a turnaround at the time the new pension system was introduced: It fell sharply from 1975 to 1982, but rose pretty steadily after that until it leveled off in the mid-1990s (PACPR 2006, figure III.1). Peter Diamond (1994) speculates that the switch to a defined contribution scheme made workers more aware of the actual costs and benefits of a pension system and thus reduced disincentives to join the official labor force. Edwards similarly asserts that with the reform in place, "most workers see their contributions as a deferred compensation, rather than as a tax" (Edwards 1998, 30).

Although Chile has indeed achieved significant accomplishments, its move to individual accounts has been plagued by continued elderly poverty and high administrative costs, which we discuss below.

Mexico

Before introducing individual accounts, Mexico's social security system, managed by the Instituto Mexicano del Seguro Social (IMSS), was a partially funded defined benefit PAYGO scheme. In an effort to bolster and supplement the basic retirement plan, the government introduced the SAR (retirement savings system) reform in May 1992 as a mandatory, fully funded saving scheme based on individual accounts. The reform called for, first, a new mandatory 2 percent employer contribution, based on private- and public-sector wages, to individual retirement subaccounts.

Table 5.1   Replacement rates under Mexico's social security system (percent)

Salary at retirement	Years in the system	
	Ten	Thirty
1 × minimum salary	100	100
6.5 × minimum salary	23	25
10 × minimum salary	14	16

Sources: Espinosa-Vega and Sinha (2000); Serrano (1999).

These funds were channeled to the Central Bank through the commercial banking system, and the Bank guaranteed a real rate of return of at least 2 percent on the subaccounts, which by end-1995 totaled about US$2.9 billion invested in government securities. Second, the reform implemented administrative changes to a specialized housing subaccount managed by the Instituto del Fondo Nacional de la Vivienda de los Trabajadores (INFONAVIT), to which employers since 1972 had contributed 5 percent of eligible wages for accounts that workers could use to finance the purchase of a home. The 1992 reform integrated the INFONAVIT program with the IMSS retirement plan so that the latter now operates both.

The basic state pension in Mexico does little to encourage extended labor force participation and effectively discourages participation by older workers. To illustrate this point, table 5.1 shows the replacement rates for the basic state pension after the 1992 reform for different wage levels and years of contributions. As table 5.1 makes evident, the incentive to contribute to the basic state pension beyond 10 years is minimal and, as of 1999, 86 percent of recipients were receiving only a minimum salary as their retirement benefit (Espinosa-Vega and Sinha 2000). The government also relaxed the age of retirement conditions over time, well before 1992, and made it easier for workers to retire on disability benefits (table 5.2). Given these disincentives to continue working into old age, the addition of mandatory individual accounts offered the potential to encourage additional work and increase private saving.

1997 Reform

Through legislation passed in December 1995 and April 1996, Mexico approved the operation of investment management companies (*administradoras de fondos de para el retiro*, or AFOREs) to manage individual retirement accounts for workers in the formal private sector.[10] A separate govern-

---

10. For greater detail on the 1997 reform in Mexico, see Grandolini and Cerda (1998) or Espinosa-Vega and Sinha (2000).

Table 5.2 IMSS-IVCM disbursements by old age retirement and disability categories (percent)

Year	Old age	Disability
1981	64.95	35.05
1985	58.86	41.14
1990	56.47	43.53
1994	57.01	42.99

IMSS = Instituto Mexicano del Seguro Social (Mexico's Institute of Social Security)

IVCM = Seguro de Invalidez, Vejez, Cesantía en edad avanzada y Muerte (Disability, Old Age, and Survivors)

Sources: Espinosa-Vega and Sinha (2000); IMSS (1997).

ment division, the Comisión Nacional del Sistema de Ahorro para el Retiro (CONSAR), was set up to oversee the activities of the AFOREs. The first contributions to the new system were collected in February 1997, and beginning in June 2005 some 12 million self-employed workers became eligible to set up individual accounts with an AFORE of their choice. A law passed in March 2007 allows public employees to switch to individual accounts beginning in 2008 (SSA 2007).

Contribution Structure in the Reformed System

Individual workers pay a compulsory 6.5 percent of their wages into an individual retirement account, and the government contributes a "social quota" of 5.5 percent of the prevailing minimum wage, funded from general revenue. Employers must contribute 5 percent to a housing subaccount (the INFONAVIT), but these accounts are consolidated with the AFORE account upon retirement unless used for the purchase of housing before retirement. Four percent of wages go to IMSS for disability and survivors insurance, and workers can make additional voluntary retirement contributions. If a worker had not chosen an AFORE by June 2001, the government assigned that account to an AFORE for the worker. The AFOREs are allowed to charge management fees as a percentage of the contribution, of the accumulated value, of the real return, or any combination of these; most charge fees as a percentage of the contribution. If an AFORE goes bankrupt, the workers' savings are protected by public insurance (Rodríguez 1999, 5–6). Table 5.3 summarizes the differences between the old system and the reformed system.

AFORE Funds

Workers can choose any AFORE for contribution but may not change it for one year. Fund hopping has therefore been low in Mexico: 0.01 percent

Table 5.3 Comparison of Mexico's pay-as-you-go and reformed old age security systems

Area	Pay-as-you-go	Reformed
Institutional responsibility		
Old age and severance	IMSS	New entrant picks AFORES or IMSS retirement (transition generation only)
Disability and life insurance	IMSS	IMSS
Contributions (percent of wage)[a]		
Contribution by employer and employee	10.075	10.075
Government contribution	0.425	2.425
Eligibility requirements		
Old age	500 weeks' (10 years') contribution; 65 years old	25 years' contribution; 65 years old (or able to finance an annuity of 1.3 × minimum wage)[b]
Severance	500 weeks' contribution; 60 years old	25 years' contribution; 60 years old
Old age: Withdrawals		Gradual withdrawals from individual account in AFORES[c] or annuity bought from an insurance company
Minimum pension guarantee (MPG)	Equivalent to one Mexico City minimum-wage level indexed to actual minimum wage	Equivalent to one Mexico City minimum wage on July 1, 1997 indexed to the consumer price index[d]

AFORES = administradoras de fondos para el retiro (private financial institutions in charge of the administration and investment of retirement savings)

IMSS = Instituto Mexicano del Seguro Social (Mexico's Institute of Social Security)

IVCM = Seguro de Invalidez, Vejez, Cesantía en edad avanzada y Muerte (Disability, Old age, and Survivors)

a. Does not include INFONAVIT housing account. Under IVCM, contributions could not exceed 10 times the minimum wage, and under the new system the limit is 25 times. The column listing the after-reform structure includes life and disability insurance.

b. Lump-sum withdrawal at retirement permitted only for balances in excess of 130 percent of the cost of an annuity equal to the MPG.

c. Only gradual withdrawals are allowed in order to reduce the risk that recipients will outlive their accumulated balances.

d. Current average wage for IMSS affiliates is 2.6 × minimum wage; thus MPG is approximately 38 percent of average wage.

Sources: Grandolini and Cerda (1998); Sales-Sarrapy, Solís-Soberón, and Villagómez-Amezcua (1998).

of workers changed funds in 1999, in contrast with Chile, where fund hopping has exceeded 25 percent per year. By the end of 1997, CONSAR had licensed 17 AFOREs, some of them fully owned by Mexican companies, others partly owned by foreign companies. No single AFORE can hold more than 17 percent of market share in terms of the number of participating workers, but there is no restriction on market share in terms of total value of assets in portfolios.

When the new system went into effect in 1997, the regulatory authority, CONSAR, stipulated that a minimum of 51 percent of an AFORE portfolio must be held in inflation-indexed bonds and at least 65 percent in assets with a maturity of no more than 183 days. These requirements were meant to establish trust and avoid the volatility that might come without indexing or with longer maturity bonds. The AFOREs were allowed to hold private debt but had to maintain a very high credit rating on the portfolios; this requirement prevented managers from making private debt a large part of any of the AFORE portfolios, which were thus heavily concentrated in government bonds (Espinosa-Vega and Sinha 2000).

The regulations have been eased over time, and in 2004 AFOREs were allowed to invest in stocks; that year, up to 10 percent of assets could be held in foreign securities. Since December 2004, workers under the age of 56 can choose between a fund that invests mainly in fixed-income securities and one that invests up to 15 percent of assets in approved equity indexes. Both types of funds may hold 20 percent of assets in foreign debt. The allocation of funds to the different AFOREs is fairly concentrated—6 of the 17 available funds held 77 percent of market share in terms of investment as of April 2000; after that, the number of funds fell to 12 before increasing again. There are 21 funds currently available.[11]

United Kingdom

The United Kingdom is one of the only Western European countries not haunted by the specter of an imminent budgetary crisis in its pension system. This position is due partly to the fact that the UK population is not aging as quickly as is most of continental Europe. More importantly, the government began to take steps as early as 1980, with reforms continuing into 2007, to reduce government liabilities to the pension system and to shift the burden of pension benefits to the private sector. But although the system is on sound fiscal footing, it is plagued by inequality, high rates of elderly poverty, and replacement rates that are among the lowest in the OECD.

---

11. See the online database available at the website of the Comisión Nacional del Sistema de Ahorro para el Retiro (CONSAR), Mexico, www.consar.gob.mx.

All retirees in the United Kingdom pay into the basic state pension (BSP),[12] which, as of July 2008, paid £90.70 (US$171) a week to individuals and £145.05 (US$273) to a married couple. The payment is means-tested, and most retirees do not qualify for the entire pension. In 2005 the weekly average pension for men and women was £76.10 (US$138) and £62.87 (US$114), respectively. Employees earning a wage income above a threshold level are required to pay into a National Insurance Contribution fund, which contributes to an additional pension plan to supplement the BSP and so offers a retirement income more in line with a person's lifelong earnings. This earnings threshold was set in 2005 at £82 (US$149) weekly, £356 (US$647) monthly, and £4,264 (US$7,750) annually; a person earning less than the threshold amount does not have access to the additional pension. The share of Britain's working population whose earnings were below the earnings threshold was 17.6 percent in the 1990s (Disney, Emmerson, and Wakefield 2001, 70–94).

Workers above the income threshold have three options for additional National Insurance Contributions:

- The first is to contribute to the second tier of the UK public pension system (originally called the State Earnings-Related Pension Scheme, or SERPS, and since 2002 called the State Second Pension, or S2P). S2P benefits were initially linked to earnings, but since April 2007 the pension has become a flat rate benefit, which is meant to encourage middle- and high-income savers to switch to one of the two other options.

- The second option is an occupational pension. Since the inception in 1975 of the second tier, employees with an employer-provided defined benefit plan have been able to opt out of the public system and receive rebates of their National Insurance Contributions in return. As of 2004, about half of Britain's pensioners were receiving a pension from a private occupational retirement scheme.

- The third option was made available starting in 1988, when employees were first allowed to opt out of the other two and could instead deposit their national insurance rebates in private personal retirement accounts. In 2004 11 percent of employees had accumulated pension savings in a personal account.

Proponents of the multitiered UK system point to the freedom it offers employees in choosing their retirement provision; they also note that

---

12. For more detail on the British pension system, see Blake (2003) or Disney, Emmerson, and Wakefield (2001).

by allowing employees to leave the state system, the government limits its future liabilities.[13]

The ability to opt out of both public and employee-sponsored plans, however, has also drawn a lot of criticism. Skeptics argue that women are at a disadvantage in pension accrual, and they also point to low saving and contribution rates as signs that the system is not working. Furthermore, a 2000 study by Colin Gillion and colleagues found that many workers who would have been better off in the public PAYGO system were persuaded to move to private accounts by financial institutions that wanted to manage their money. Two insurance companies began telling participants to move back to the state system, and in 2004 500,000 people actually did that (Cohen 2005).

Participation/Contribution Density

The issue of participation rates in a system of individual accounts is on both the extensive and intensive margins, as it is important to ensure not only that workers participate in the system but also that they contribute enough to have adequate income upon retirement. Focusing on participation brings up issues such as the effect of a large "shadow economy" and inequality among men and women, as well as administrative costs and elderly poverty, which we discuss in subsequent sections.

Australia

Participation in the Australian defined contribution individual accounts, as described above, is mandatory unless a worker has a qualifying occupational defined benefit scheme instead. Participation rates appear to be on track, as over one-third of Australian workers make voluntary contributions to a supplementary account. However, early retirement and low labor force participation among those over 50 are critical problems for Australia's retirement system. Pension reform has not solved these problems and in fact may have aggravated them by funding early retirement. In an attempt to deal with these issues, the government has introduced a bonus scheme to encourage people to postpone retirement, providing up to AU$34,000 to a couple that remains in the workforce an additional five years.

The biggest flaw in the Australian retirement plan is the provision that allows workers to withdraw all of their contributions in a lump sum

---

13. Others counter that it was mostly the cut in benefits that has kept government liabilities below the OECD average and that the partial privatization of the second tier will have little impact on the government's balance sheets (Disney, Emmerson, and Wakefield 2001, 90).

once they reach age 55. The incentive to do this is great because people can pay off debts or finance early retirement and then apply for the minimum government pension benefit once they reach the official retirement age.[14] The minimum benefit is not especially generous but is likely supplemented with casual unreported work, together with the imputed rent from an owner-occupied residence.[15]

The problems in the Australian public pension plan and the individual retirement account scheme are major. The goals of the plan were to move retirees off the traditional retirement program, increase national saving, and discourage early retirement. None of these goals appear to have been achieved. The Australian experience illustrates the importance of design features of retirement programs that seem minor when introduced but have very large effects on the outcome. As long as there is a minimum income guarantee for the elderly, it is vital to make sure that retirees cannot pull their retirement funds out in a lump sum.

Chile

In the years following the 1981 reforms, Chile's new pension system achieved relatively high participation rates, fluctuating between 65 and 76 percent over the next 10 years (figure 5.2).[16] In 1991 and every year thereafter, however, participation dropped markedly, averaging 56 percent (SAFP 2003, 215; authors' calculations). This low compliance rate raises the question of why so many are avoiding their yearly contributions to a supposedly obligatory system. Self-employed workers, seasonal workers, and the unemployed may opt not to contribute to an AFP, but participation is compulsory for all other wage earners who entered the system after the reforms went into effect. As the latter make up the majority of the Chilean workforce (about 67 percent in 1992), one would expect participation to increase, not decrease, as younger workers enter the labor market and join the system (Uthoff 1998). Furthermore, a significant number of contributors underreported their yearly earnings and thus were able to pay less into their funds—one-quarter of them at or below the minimum wage level in 1991 (Mesa-Lago 1994, 119).

---

14. Recall that 12 to 14 percent of men also receive sickness or disability payments upon retirement.

15. About 80 percent of Australians over 64 own their homes outright, and the wealth accumulated in a primary residence is not counted in assessing eligibility for the traditional pension or the benefit level.

16. Active participants are members of the new pension system who make a contribution to their pension fund in December of a given year.

Figure 5.2   Pension participation in Chile, 1981–March 2002

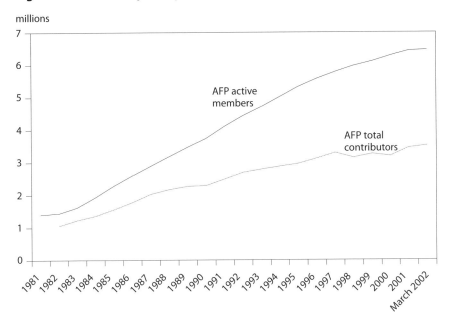

AFP = administradores de fondos de pensiones

Source: SAFP (2003, statistical appendix).

Reasons for Noncompliance

A major problem is the infrequency of workers' contributions throughout their working lives. The system's designers had estimated that workers would contribute to their pension funds for at least two-thirds of their working lives; instead, this contribution density has been only about 52 percent (OECD 2005).

A survey in the early 1990s sought to explain noncompliance among AFP members who were behind in payments for more than one year. Of those surveyed, 26 percent (mostly women) had voluntarily left the workforce, 13 percent were unemployed, 37 percent were self-employed—and 22 percent were simply "delinquent in their payments" (Marcel and Arenas 1992, 19).

There have been several explanations for the noncompliance. Under the new system, workers must contribute to their pension funds for 20 years in order to become eligible for the minimum pension. Dimitri Vittas and Estelle James (1994) suggest that many workers make payments for 20 years in order to qualify and then evade their obligations for the remainder of their working lives. Some workers underreport their income so as to qualify for the minimum pension. These strategies are widespread enough that an estimated 30 to 40 percent of workers in the new system may become eligible for the minimum pension upon retirement. Another factor is very low-income workers who pay no income tax; their delinquency stems not from a calculated scheme but because the favorable tax treatment toward saving provides no incentive for them to participate. Family support also plays a role. Truman Packard (2002) finds that child care and child education expenditures significantly decrease the likelihood of contributions to the new social security system. He also suggests that many Chileans are simply diversifying their investments by saving outside the formal pension system, often in the form of housing. Mesa-Lago and Arenas de Mesa (1998, 118) cite a "lack of adequate controls, a high contribution for the insured . . . and cheaper alternatives in public assistance" as reasons for noncompliance.

In addition to the impact of employee noncompliance, high inflation in the early 1990s provided employers with an incentive to delay the transfer of salary deductions, with the result that many have been delinquent in depositing employees' contributions with their AFPs (in the amount of US$200 million in 1991 [Kritzer 1996, 49; Mesa-Lago 1994, 118–19]).[17] In 1996 the Superintendencia de Administradores de Fondos de Pensiones (SAFP) had 150,000 such cases of negligence to resolve (Economist Intelligence Unit 1996). Furthermore, a number of AFP members have registered in the pension system more than once (Uthoff 1998; Mesa-Lago 1994, 119).

Efforts to Increase Participation and Enforce Compliance

A special advisory council on pension reform, appointed in 2006 to determine how to increase mandatory coverage to the entire population, predicted that "Without changes to the system, it is estimated that within 20 years only half of Chile's senior citizens will receive more than the minimum pension, less than five percent will have access to the minimum income guaranteed by the state, and the rest will scrape by on less than the minimum, a poverty pension, or nothing."[18] Since the Chilean government is responsible for making up the difference between the minimum pension guarantee and the payout of funds that do not meet that guarantee, it is in the government's interest to promote a higher participation rate. The Bachelet government therefore enacted a reform in 2007 to provide more incentives for participation. The reform addresses the four primary barriers to or disincentives for participation: self-employed workers' freedom not to enter the pension system, the disproportionate burden

---

17. Workers may contribute to the AFPs personally or delegate that responsibility to their employers.

18. Daniela Estrada, "Chile: Pension Reform to Combat Systemic Poverty," InterPress Service, September 15, 2007.

of domestic and child-rearing responsibilities on women, lack of competition among AFPs for lower-income customers, and the minimum pension guarantee. We discuss the first two barriers below, and the last two in following sections.

Self-employed workers—who, according to Chile's National Statistics Institute, make up 27 percent of the working population—are not obligated to join the new pension system and, indeed, only 4 percent of them participate in the pension program.[19] Following the suggestions of the advisory council, the 2007 reform required self-employed workers to join the pension system and make regular contributions. As such a sizable share of Chile's population is self-employed, this move should help to significantly boost participation rates.

The reform also targeted young low-income workers not subject to income taxes and thus unaffected by the favorable tax treatment of saving. Workers aged 19–35 whose income is less than 1½ times the minimum wage now receive a subsidy to encourage participation in the pension program.

In addition, the reform addressed the low participation among women. Because of economic and social pressures related to child rearing, women make up the majority of workers who voluntarily leave the labor market. To encourage them to remain at work and continue contributing to their individual pension funds, the 2007 reform heeded the pension reform advisory council's recommendation of "including child care in the rights of the working woman in the same way as other social security benefits, thereby making it easier for women to engage in paid work" (Presidential Advisory Council 2006). As an incentive to participate, the 2007 reform allocates a "bonus," equivalent to roughly a year's worth of contribution, to a woman's account for each of her children.

Mexico

Mexico, like Chile, faces problems in participation rates in its new system of individual accounts. The most common approach to tracking participation, by density of contributions, entails dividing the number of actual contributions by the number possible since the inception of private accounts. The density of contributions in Mexico from July 1997 to February 2007 was 44.25 percent.[20] Figure 5.3 represents participation in a different way: It shows the number of accounts registered along with the number of active and inactive accounts (accounts that have or have not had

---

19. Business News Americas, "Assn: 32 percent of Independent Workers Unhappy with Contributions," November 14, 2007.

20. The authors thank Juan Mateo Lartigue Mendoza of CONSAR for this information.

Figure 5.3 AFORES activity, Mexico, 1998–2007

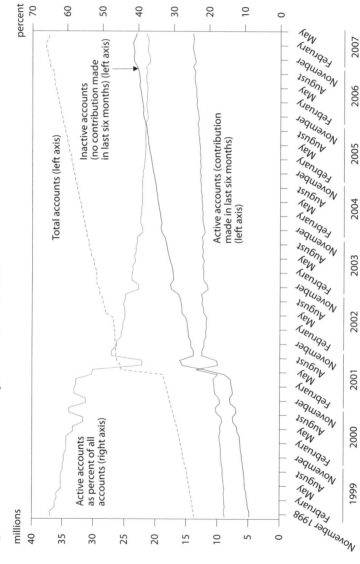

AFORES = administradoras de fondos para el retiro (private financial institutions in charge of the administration and investment of retirement savings)

Source: Juan Mateo Lartigue Mendoza of the National Commission for the Pension System (Comisión Nacional del Sistema de Ahorro para el Retiro, or CONSAR). On file with authors.

contributions in the previous six months). As in Chile, the number is inflated by duplicate accounts. The sudden jump in the number of accounts in June 2001 occurred because in that month the government assigned an account to all eligible workers who had not yet registered with an AFORE.

One of the problems with Mexico's social insurance program is that only a fraction of the workforce actually participates. The 1997 reforms did not address this but rather affected only those covered under the IMSS: the economically active population working in the formal private sector (equal to less than one-third of the economically active population and only a little more than half of formal-sector employment). As noted above, though, public employees may open their own private accounts on a voluntary basis. This follows the reform of the public pension system in March 2007, implemented by President Felipe Calderón, raising the retirement age for government workers gradually from 50 to 60. In many ways this public-sector reform mirrored that of the private sector in 1997.

United Kingdom

Inequality, especially between men and women retirees, has been a constant feature in discussions of UK pension system reform and is central to the country's focus on participation and contributions. Inequality prevents adequate returns for many low-income workers and discourages participation in the private saving plans, creating a feedback loop between low returns and low participation. Because both public and occupational defined benefit schemes are based on years of contributions during which a worker accrues rights to future pension payments, women, who often leave the labor force for long periods to care for children, or who work part-time to honor family obligations, have always been at a disadvantage (like their peers in Chile). Several reforms to the UK system have tried to correct this situation. The Home Responsibilities Protection introduced in 1976 allowed women to stay at home and care for a child without forgoing the full basic state pension benefits. The reform to the second-tier system in 2002 made similar allowances in SERPS (subsequently S2P) for women who provide child and eldercare. The Turner pension report of 2005 (Pensions Commission 2005), however, considered these adjustments insufficient and called for even greater allowances for those who assume family caretaking responsibilities.

Economists are quite concerned about UK workers who have opted out of both state and private occupational plans in order to contribute to personal pension accounts. Without a mandatory floor on contribution rates, the contribution density of most workers will not be high enough to provide enough retirement income. Indeed, most of these private savers, observers warn, do not save nearly enough to ensure adequate living standards in old age. Given the recent and projected rise in longevity, many investment advisors suggest to those relying on personal accounts that they contribute around 10 percent of their earnings to private plans (Disney, Emmerson, and Wakefield 2001, 86). But few workers who opted for private plans do so. In fact, as of the late 1990s, more than half of all members of private pension accounts contributed 4 percent or less of their national insurance rebate, which is likely to leave them with inadequate resources in retirement (Disney, Emmerson, and Wakefield 2001, 76).

The 2007 reform made some significant strides in addressing the issue of low participation and inadequate contribution densities brought on by the partial privatization of the system. Most significantly, and following the suggestions of the 2005 Turner report, starting in 2012, eligible workers will be automatically enrolled in an occupational pension and will have to choose *not* to participate, a move that aims to avoid the problem of myopic private saving and improve both participation rates and contribution densities. The 2007 pension plan estimates that this "opt-out" plan will generate 4 million to 8 million new savers in the workplace. These personal accounts will be aimed primarily at low- and middle-income workers, giving them the option to contribute a minimum of 4 percent of their gross earnings. And the state will match these contributions by a minimum of 3 percent of the employer's gross earnings and 1 percent in the form of tax relief.

Absent from the 2007 reform, though, was the enactment of a more far-reaching suggestion from the Turner report that everyone become a member of a plan called a National Pension Savings Scheme (NPSS). Under Turner's proposal in the report, the NPSS would be privately managed but centrally administered by a government agency, which would allow the government to buy pension plans in bulk and thus significantly reduce administrative fees. Although this potentially substantial cost-saving measure could indirectly have encouraged greater participation among low- and middle-income workers, it was scrapped in the reform. The 2007 Pension Act did, however, include a provision to begin constructing a low-cost, voluntary saving account targeted to low-income workers. While similar to Turner's proposal, this provision is not nearly as large in scope and will not be as far-reaching (see discussion below).[21]

Administrative Costs and Fees

Administrative costs and participation rates are intrinsically linked, especially for low-income workers, for whom high administrative costs can drastically reduce net replacement rates and discourage participation.

---

21. See the UK Department for Work and Pensions website at www.dwp.gov.uk/pensions reform.

Furthermore, it is less profitable for a private fund manager to manage contributions from a low-wage worker relative to a high-wage worker due to issues of scale. This fact can create an inherent disadvantage for lower-income workers in a privatized system unless steps are taken to address the scale issue, such as creating an agency to pool the contributions of low-wage workers.

Chile

Chilean law requires *administradores de fondos de pensiones*, the private fund managers, to charge their customers a single commission rate based on their wage income. This pricing scheme makes it more profitable to target customers with high, steady incomes and, conversely, much more costly to take on low-income customers. Additionally, because of the complexity of the product that AFPs offer, many clients neither understand nor seek to find out the difference in commissions between AFPs. Because of this undiscriminating pool of customers, AFPs cannot attract more business by lowering commissions.

The strict requirement that AFPs charge the same commission rate to all customers based on income creates a disadvantage for lower-income workers, as fund managers would rather seek customers with higher incomes to increase profitability. Chile's Presidential Advisory Council (2006) addressed this inequity by suggesting that AFPs be allowed to relax the uniform commission fees and pursue measures that would foster competition among AFPs based on commission rates. These recommendations have merit, but they also pose some risks. Many of the costs of administering an account—record keeping, for example—are fixed overhead costs. As a proportion of contributions, it is costlier for an AFP to manage the account of a low-wage worker than a high-wage worker. Because under the current system the fees are fixed by law, AFPs protect their profit margin by avoiding the low-wage workers—effectively "discriminating" against them. But if the regulation of fees were relaxed, the AFPs would likely charge higher fees (relative to contributions) for low-wage workers than for high-wage workers. The competitive outcome would involve a pricing schedule that reflects the underlying costs of the different accounts, and the resulting hike in fees would discourage low-wage workers from joining the system, just as the past discrimination discouraged them. One solution would be for some agency to collect and administer the small accounts and pool the money before passing it to the AFPs. A government agency, for example, could effectively subsidize the contributions of the low-wage workers, making their participation in the program more attractive. The 2005 Turner report proposed this idea for the United Kingdom (see below), and Sweden has actually implemented it.

There is general agreement that the administration of pension funds in Chile has been inefficient. As mentioned above, each AFP was initially allowed to offer only one fund, and investment options were highly regulated by a supervisory government institution, the Superintendencia de AFP (SAFP). A fund's return had to fall within a band of 2 percent above and below the market's average rate of return, so all management companies essentially offered workers the same portfolio. High administrative fees financed heavy advertising and lavish sales pitches, since managers could not distinguish themselves through adept investments or higher returns than other funds.

In addition, every AFP in Chile is responsible for collecting its clients' contributions directly. Observers note that such an operation is subject to increasing returns to scale and that administrative costs would have been lower if a single government agency had been responsible for the collection of contributions, as mentioned above. A CBO (2004) report points out that the US Thrift Saving Plan, for example, has administrative costs of 0.07 percent of total assets, whereas Chile's funds' administrative costs have been as high as 15 percent of total assets (or, in 1984, 9 percent of wages and 90 percent of contributions), although they have declined to 2.5 percent of wages and 0.7 percent of total assets in recent years.

Recent reforms have attempted to increase both competition and efficiency in the industry. In 2002 the government introduced significant reforms to the system to contain its horrendous costs (OECD 2005). Now each AFP can offer five different funds catering to investors' tolerance for risk; the most recent reform in 2007 also allowed AFPs to increase the share of their funds in foreign equities from 40 to 80 percent and lifted restrictions on more risky equity investment and investment in real estate. The reform also attempted to address the growing concentration among AFPs (their number fell from a peak of 21 managers in 1994 to 6 in 2007), for the first time allowing private banks and insurance carriers to act as fund managers in an effort to increase competition and lower commission fees.

Mexico

At the outset of Mexico's 1997 reform, administrative costs appeared to be relatively well contained. For example, worker contributions were funded through a payroll tax, collected and pooled by a central tax agency and then sent to the private AFOREs for investment (Mitchell 1999). The scale achieved by this measure is more efficient than that in Chile, where no such central agency exists and private fund managers must collect contributions from individual workers. This difference would imply that administrative costs in Mexico should be lower than they are in Chile.

Since the reform, however, there have been complaints that management fees are high, that they are lumped with insurance premiums for the life insurance component of the pension plans, that they are obfuscated because they are usually presented as a fraction of the worker's salary, and that it is not always clear whether the commissions are based on a proportion of yearly flows into the fund or a proportion of the balance in the fund at a given point or some combination of the two. For example, a participant may be charged 1.7 percent of wages, but someone contributing the mandatory 6.5 percent will effectively pay a 26.15 percent commission charge.[22] The complicated fee structure makes it hard to compare across funds.

United Kingdom

Analysts forecasted in a report nearly a decade ago that high administrative costs would plague the decentralized approach to the UK system of individual accounts (Murthi, Orszag, and Orszag 1999). The authors estimated that the administrative fees charged by fund managers would reduce the value of an average individual account by about 45 percent relative to its value with no fees. One of the main reasons for the extraordinarily high administrative costs is the fact that no central agency existed to pool individual contributions.

In the 2007 pension reform, while Turner's proposal to automatically enroll workers in individual retirement accounts was passed, his NPSS proposal to pool together individual accounts, so as to reduce high administrative costs, was rejected. Thus while the 2007 reform addressed issues of outright participation, it did not address this important issue, which could both significantly reduce administrative costs and, indirectly, encourage greater contribution densities by increasing real rates of return for low- and middle-income workers. While the far-reaching Turner proposal was shot down, the 2007 reform did enact a new measure to develop separate low-cost voluntary accounts coordinated by a central agency, which is discussed in the next section.

Elderly Poverty and Replacement Rates

One of the biggest sources of political resistance to proposals to replace a public pension system with individual accounts is that the latter can lead to severe poverty among low-income workers who do not save enough on their own, whether because they make too little, or do not contribute throughout their working lives (i.e., women with child-rearing responsibilities), or for any other reason.

---

22. However, AFOREs are allowed to give customers a "loyalty discount," reducing charges for those that remain with the same fund (SSA 2004).

Chile

We noted earlier that the largest pension fund in Chile returned 10.2 percent after adjusting for inflation. However, participating workers have not captured the full 10.2 percent return because of high administrative costs (see above). In addition to the 10 percent of their wages, workers are required to contribute 1 to 1.5 percent of wages plus administrative fees, depending on the AFP, so real net rates of return have been in the range of 4.4 to 6.9 percent, depending on income level and time of entry into the system (PACPR 2006, Table A.3.2). In addition, rates of return have declined over time; the high real rates of return in the 1980s and early 1990s reflected very high real rates of interest in Chile during this period (the C fund was invested primarily in government bonds), but more recently, real rates have been coming down worldwide.

Given the high past returns, the Chilean pension funds have performed well, on average, for those who have been with the system a number of years, with retirement incomes guaranteeing a replacement rate of 60 to 65 percent of the average wage in 2002 (OECD 2005).[23] But the average numbers hide a high degree of economic and gender inequality in the system. The OECD report finds that well-off workers have greater contribution densities than low-income employees and thus achieve replacement rates as high as 80 percent. In contrast, the pension incomes of as many as one-third of Chileans will replace only 10 to 30 percent of previously earned wages. Women have faced a particularly difficult time achieving adequate retirement income. Companies selling annuities to retirees are not required to use unisex life expectancy tables in Chile, so women end up with significantly lower retirement incomes than men. Most recently, husbands have been forced to buy joint annuities for themselves and their wives (James 2005), a requirement that has somewhat improved women's old age income. Women also have had much more difficulty completing the 20 years of contribution to a pension fund necessary to qualify for the government's minimum pension guarantee (MPG; see below). Advocates of the individual account system initially predicted that it would ease inequalities in Chilean society, but in practice it is the higher-wage workers that have been able to take advantage of the plan, so the problem of elderly poverty remains.

Elderly Poverty

In Chile's pension system there are at least three main determinants of old age poverty: employment history, dependence on one's children or others for support in retirement, and qualification for cash transfer pro-

---

23. The reformers had promised replacement rates of 80 percent at the outset of reforms.

grams. Because affiliates can contribute to their accounts only while formally employed, a significant amount of time away from the formal work sector can have a negative impact on one's retirement saving within the system. Indeed, the presence of a large informal economy in Chile has severely hurt the effectiveness of the privatized system in addressing elderly poverty; roughly 1.2 million Chileans work in the informal "shadow" economy and thus do not make regular contributions to their individual accounts. Furthermore, Truman Packard's 2002 study shows that expectations that one's children will provide care tend to significantly reduce one's contribution density, a practice that is not problematic only if one's children can provide care above the poverty threshold. Last, qualification for old age cash transfer programs—like the minimum pension guarantee, assistance pension, and part of the Chile Solidario program—has a positive fiscal effect on one's retirement resources. Armando Barrientos (2006) argues that the existence of assistance programs that target the elderly poor has greatly reduced the incidence of old age poverty in Chile, and at a relatively low cost (0.38 percent of GDP).

Effects of the 1981 Pension Reform on Old Age Poverty

Pension income is a significant factor in preventing old age poverty in Chile. Table 5.4 shows real poverty rates in Chilean households as well as simulated rates that calculate the incidence of poverty if older adults receive no retirement or pension income. Lack of a pension increases the poverty rate among households with at least one older adult and has a particularly deleterious effect on households with only elderly inhabitants.

The proper counterfactual to consider is whether individual accounts have been more effective than the former PAYGO system in combating poverty, but it is difficult to determine whether this is the case. Elderly poverty rates have come down since the reform but at about the same rate as the decrease in poverty in the overall population. From 1990 (when private accounts had been active for nine years and could have had a significant impact on pension benefits) to 2006, the poverty rate of those aged 65 and older dropped from 20 percent to about 7 percent, but this 64 percent decrease is about the same as the average of 65 percent across all age groups.[24] Cash transfer programs seem to be responsible for much of the reduction in elderly poverty but, as outlined above, they retain some drawbacks and are liable to invite workers to abuse the system.

---

24. Data are from Encuesta CASEN (National Characterization Socio-Economic Survey), 1990, 1992, 1994, 1996, 1998, 2000, and 2003, Ministerio de Planificación y Cooperación (Chile), available at www.mideplan.cl.

Table 5.4   Impact of retirement and pension income on total poverty in Chile, 1997 (percent)

Household/poverty rate	Urban areas	Rural areas
Households with older adults only		
Real poverty rate	6	5
Simulated poverty rate	39	35
Households that include older adults		
Real poverty rate	13	19
Simulated poverty rate	24	33
Total households with older adults		
Real poverty rate	11	16
Simulated poverty rate	29	33
Total urban households		
Real poverty rate	19	26
Simulated poverty rate	24	33

Note: Simulated poverty rate excludes retirement and pension income from total household income.

Source: Economic Commission for Latin America and the Caribbean (ECLAC) Database, www.eclac.org.

Programs and Reform to Combat Old Age Poverty

The framers of the 1981 pension reform aimed to reduce elderly poverty by creating a minimum pension guarantee (it was replaced in the 2007 reform). The aim of the MPG was to provide a decent standard of living to those who reached retirement age and had no other source of income and an inadequate balance in their private accounts. The MPG was available to those who had contributed to the system for at least 20 years, and the government set the level of the benefit on a consistent basis. In 1996 the MPG benefit was equivalent to 80 percent of the legal minimum wage and 40 percent of average earnings (Barrientos 1996, 312). An assistance pension (PASIS, legislated before the 1981 reform) was also available, but the requirements were more stringent and the benefits much lower than those of the MPG (Valdés-Prieto 2004).

The MPG and PASIS left gaps in pension coverage among the elderly and so were judged inadequate by the time of the 2008 reform. The MPG especially discriminated against women, whose domestic responsibilities more frequently cause them to leave the workforce and for longer periods than is true for men, preventing them from making the minimum 20 years of contributions. Also disadvantaged were those who frequently switch between the formal and informal work sectors and those who remain unemployed for long periods. PASIS was meant in part to catch those who slip through the cracks, but a 1994 government survey found that a number of people who met the requirements for PASIS did not receive it (Valdés-Prieto 2004, 44–45). While there were signs that its targeting was improving after 1994, its scope was just not far-reaching enough to adequately address the dire problem of elderly poverty in Chile. The lack of MPG and PASIS coverage, especially for those in the informal sector and for women, was central to the 2007 reform. As mentioned above, the 2007 reforms, signed by the Bachelet government and passed through Congress, attempted to help bridge the coverage gaps with, among other things, a subsidy for child-bearing women and required participation among independent-self employed workers.

A more groundbreaking measure to combat old age poverty replaced the MPG with the New Solidarity Pension System (SPS), a two-tiered benefit plan for those with incomes in the lowest 60 percent. The first tier is the Basic Solidarity Pension (PBS), a flat rate, noncontributory pension equivalent to roughly 60,000 pesos (about $115) a month, scheduled to rise by 2017 to 75,000 pesos ($143). The PBS, which somewhat ominously is reported to be funded by volatile profits from copper mining, will represent a significant boost in the replacement rate for low-income workers, as, on average, it will rise to 70 percent, up from 44 percent. Under the second tier, called the Solidarity Pension Contribution (APS), low-income workers who save will receive a gradually declining complement to their own saving starting in 2012, up to a maximum of 200,000 pesos ($383). Government economists say the plan will cost $2 billion a year; another calculation estimates it will cost roughly 1 percent of GDP annually (Errázuriz 2007). While criticized by some as inadequate to combat poverty among its recipients, the PBS must tread carefully so as not to discourage private savings by the poor in Chile; the second-tier APS hopefully has the potential to not only preserve but also strengthen the incentive to save among the poorer population. The 2008 reform in Chile is thus a recognition that a fully privatized system is not adequate to address elderly poverty among those who have not made regular contributions to their own accounts, especially in a country with a large informal economy and a system that has discriminated against women.

Mexico

Mexico's annual real rate of return on the pension system from 1997 to March 2006 was 3.23 percent. This rate takes into account the funds generated by workers' accounts, discounted by AFORE commissions, and adjusted for withdrawals and the effects of inflation. The real rates of return from 2001 to 2004 for the main AFORES are shown in table 5.5. The average for the funds was 5.43 percent for the three-year period, but the rates of return varied from over 6 percent (Actinver) to less than 4 percent (Inbursa).

Table 5.5 Real rates of return on Mexican SIEFOREs, 2001–04 (percent)

SIEFORE	Rate of return
Actinver	6.13
Azteca	4.75
Banamex	5.76
Bancomer	5.62
HSBC	5.30
Inbursa	3.90
ING	5.70
IXE	5.39
Principal	5.51
Profuturo	5.52
Banorte	5.72
XXI	5.67
Santander	5.38
Average	5.43

SIEFORE = Sociedad de Inversión Especializada en Fondos para el Retiro (specialized mutual funds for pensions).

Source: Sandoval (2004).

For workers at the minimum wage, the replacement rate is about 77 percent and varies little, with different rates of return because the government pledges to provide a minimum pension equal to 100 percent of the minimum wage, contributing more or less depending on the rate of return on contributions. For workers at higher-income levels, the replacement rate varies with the rate of return to the individual accounts. For a worker making 25 times the minimum wage, for example, the replacement rate could be as high as 27 percent or as low as 12 percent, depending on the rate of return on AFORE and INFONAVIT contributions.

United Kingdom

The inequality of the UK pension system and its effect on elderly poverty were cited in Adear Turner's 2006 report, in which he noted that today's pensioners in the United Kingdom are the most affluent retirees the country has ever seen. Still, he stresses, with the discontinuation of many generous occupational defined benefit schemes and with stock market returns well below the record levels of the mid- and late 1990s, divides in income level among UK pensioners will widen. Other authors have pointed out that it was especially the well-to-do workers at larger companies who had the fortune of being enrolled in well-funded and generous occupational defined benefit plans (Disney, Emmerson, and Wakefield 2001, 75).[25] Today, saddled with serious funding problems, many of these generous occupational plans are winding down or are closed to new hires. Occupational defined contribution schemes or private pension plans may initially have offered more lucrative rates of return than the state system or companies' defined benefit schemes, but since the stock market collapse in 2001, they have been considered riskier for employees and their benefit payouts have been substantially less than those of defined benefit plans.[26]

Lower-income workers who do not have access to historically generous company-sponsored defined benefit plans and who lack the financial savvy to invest in private retirement accounts are the ones most likely to stick with the public earnings-related system.[27] The high administrative costs of private schemes (which, as discussed, were only partially addressed by recent reforms) have also made private retirement provision for these workers quite unattractive, as they drastically reduce net rates of return (Williamson 2002, 415–30). The gross replacement rate for an average earner in the mandatory UK public system is currently 31 percent—the lowest among all OECD countries (Martin and Whitehouse 2008). Thus the gap is growing between a class of relatively wealthy pensioners who receive incomes from either generous defined benefit plans or well-invested personal accounts and a sizable group of pensioners who remain in the less generous public system and are more vulnerable to future public cuts and political tinkering with the system.

Furthermore, as discussed in the section on participation rates, many workers who opt out of both the public and occupational pension plans and instead contribute to a private account are not faring much better. The absence of a mandatory contribution rate for individual accounts is leading to low saving rates and will eventually result in high levels of poverty among many UK pensioners.

The 2002 reforms to the second tier of the public scheme, which replaced SERPS with the State Second Pension (S2P), increased the accrual rates for workers at the lower end of the earnings spectrum but also made the S2P a second flat rate system as of April 2007, making the second tier redistributive rather than earnings-related. The 2007 Pensions Act passed

---

25. Until very recently, these private defined benefit schemes also offered attractive early retirement packages.

26. Mean (median) weekly earnings from occupational defined benefit plans were £129 (£76) in 2004; in contrast, mean (median) earnings from personal pension plans were £76 (£31) (Pensions Policy Institute 2005).

27. Private pension funds find that it is uneconomical to provide advice to low-income savers (Davis 2004, 361).

by the UK parliament took a few more steps to address the poverty issue by linking the annual cost-of-living increases in the basic state pension (BSP) to earnings rather than to prices.[28]

In an effort to reduce the particularly high poverty rates among elderly women, the reform replaces the Home Responsibilities Protection with a system of weekly credits for those who care for children up to the age of 12 (as well as for those who spend 20 hours a week caring for severely disabled people).[29] It also lowers the minimum number of years of contributions from 39 for women and 44 for men to 30 for both sexes, which will increase the number of eligible women who interrupt their working lives for child care. Additionally, the age of eligibility for state pension benefits will gradually increase from 65 to 68 over the years 2024–46.

The 2007 Pension Act also includes plans to develop new low-cost, personal saving vehicles for low- and moderate-income workers who may not have access to occupational accounts or are self-employed. Furthermore, these accounts will allow workers to contribute to their savings when they are not working, such as between jobs or during child-rearing. Although the plan is still in its initial stage, according to the Act, these funds will be collected and pooled by a central agency but privately managed. By pooling the individual contributions, the plan could benefit from economies of scale and low administrative costs. The UK Department for Work and Pensions (DWP) ambitiously estimates that between 4 million and 7 million workers will be enrolled in this saving plan once it is completely set up (although it is unclear what share of this number will be *new* savers; see UK DWP 2008). It is also important that these voluntary saving vehicles both target lower-income workers and complement, rather than replace, occupational plans. This goal can be accomplished by, for example, imposing a cap on annual contributions below that of a higher-income worker.

Personal saving vehicles could have a significant positive impact on saving behavior as long as they are low-cost and well targeted. If enacted, the plan stands to benefit from economies of scale and low administrative costs if it can effectively pool the individual contributions. The vehicles must also be well targeted—since they are voluntary vehicles, enrolling first-time savers will not come automatically, especially among people out of work and those who frequently switch jobs and are thus not typically exposed to the opt-out occupational plans.

These voluntary saving accounts are promising, but it is not clear whether they are adequate to the daunting task of significantly improving

---

28. The UK government had resisted making this link in the hope that by linking the BSP to prices it would gradually decline as a source of income for pensioners whose retirement income would increasingly come from private saving, thus reducing government liabilities.

29. From the DWP website, www.dwp.gov.uk/pensionsreform (accessed on August 24, 2008).

the elderly poverty that plagues the UK system. To bring gross replacement rates in line with the OECD average for the average worker on the public benefit scheme, voluntary private saving would need to deliver a replacement rate of 28 percent. The contribution rates to achieve this goal would have to be quite high—average workers would have to maintain a voluntary private account contribution rate of 6.9 percent of their wages throughout their working life. And workers who missed, say, 10 years of contributions (for example, to raise children, or while between jobs) would need to maintain a contribution rate of roughly 10 percent during the rest of their working life (Martin and Whitehouse 2008).

Financing the Transition and Effects on National Saving

Any proposal to introduce individual private accounts must address the issue of how to finance the transition from the public system. Without a safety net, the introduction of individual accounts will leave imminent retirees, who have spent their working lives paying into the public system, with nothing. In any case, the government will need to incur some expense to pay these older workers as they would under the old system, at least until the point is reached where a retiree has been under the new system his entire working life. Furthermore, if social security is an entitlement, as it is in the United States (and most countries), then the government must partly compensate workers who have paid any amount into the old system but are now part of the new system.[30] How to pay for these costs is an important question for any proposal for individual accounts. Of course, one way to get around this problem is to introduce notional accounts, which we discuss in the next chapter.

The effect of individual accounts on national saving is linked to the fiscal cost of the transition from a PAYGO system. The terms on which a government finances the transition to individual accounts affects the deficit, which directly affects national saving. (We discussed the question of whether individual accounts increase household saving at the microeconomic level in the section on participation rates.) Taking these lessons into account, we now look at the macroeconomic effects on private, public, and national saving. The relationship between individual accounts and national saving is far from concrete; while the incentives in theory should align to create new saving among workers who had not previously saved, and while this new saving should outweigh any "dissaving" taken on by the government, many are still skeptical as to whether this plays out in practice (see Orszag and Stiglitz 2001, for instance).

---

30. A minimum pension guarantee is another expense, not only during the transition but throughout the life of the system.

Australia

The effect of individual accounts in Australia on national saving—the country's stated goal—has been mixed at best. Although it is hard to separate the determinants of private saving in Australia (or anywhere, for that matter), there is little macroeconomic evidence that such saving has materially increased since the introduction in the late 1980s of the mandatory defined contribution retirement plan. The current account deficit in 2005 was 5.9 percent of GDP, and as of March 2008 it had deteriorated to 6.5 percent of GDP. The system is not yet fully mature and so it is possible later experience will result in a higher estimate of the saving impact, but so far the results on boosting saving do not appear encouraging. However, a paper by Mariangela Bonasia and Oreste Napolitano (2006) does find evidence through a series of econometric tests that the introduction of mandatory personal saving has increased national saving, despite the worsening current account deficit. The varying results on this issue make clear that the empirical relationship between national saving and individual accounts is largely unclear.

Chile

In 1980, when Chile's military government contemplated reforms, its pension liabilities exceeded 100 percent of GDP, and the central government was contributing 4 percent of GDP to the pension system every year. One of the reform's objectives was to keep future costs in check (given the country's challenging demographic trends) (Edwards 1998). Although raising national savings had not been one of the Pinochet government's explicit goals, hopes for improving Chile's meager saving rate were high.

The Chilean government prepared to finance the transition in three ways: by raising taxes, selling government assets, and reducing spending. Importantly, because these three measures were forms of fiscal tightening rather than increased borrowing, the government did not take on a high level of "dissaving." At first, the transition increased costs to the central government: The public sector was still responsible for the pensions of all workers who had decided to remain in the old system, and it would eventually have to redeem the recognition bonds[31] of workers retiring under the new scheme. Edwards (1998) finds that government costs related to

---

31. Workers who paid into the old system but wanted to switch to the new system had the option of taking out "recognition bonds," i.e., receiving special bonds recognizing previous contributions to compensate them for those paid into the old system. Only workers who had at least 12 monthly contributions over the previous five years were eligible. The bonds were credited to the worker's personal account upon retirement. See CBO (1999) for how the government calculates the value of the recognition bonds.

the transition peaked in 1983 at 4.58 percent of GDP.[32] The liabilities related to the old system are shrinking every year, as most Chilean retirees today receive pensions under the new plan. The costs connected to recognition bonds, in turn, increase as a growing number of retirees redeem them. But according to Edwards, the value of maturing recognition bonds would peak in 2005, with public outlays thereafter decreasing.

Edwards calls the increase in Chile's savings "phenomenal," citing the rise in the saving rate from 7 percent to 25 percent of GDP between 1979 and 1995, but notes that it is unclear how much of this was plan-related. Based on data from 1960 to 1994, Felipe Morandé (1998) concluded that the reform of the pension system had a highly significant effect on private saving. He found that for every dollar put into a pension fund, Chileans withdrew only 50 cents from their voluntary savings, so that overall national savings grew. Morandé says that the reform has made Chileans less myopic about saving for retirement.

A study commissioned by the AFPs and carried out by economists Vittorio Corbo and Klaus Schmidt-Hebbel (2002) noted that the saving rate in Chile averaged 11.5 percent of GDP from 1960 to 1980 and that this increased to 16.4 percent in 1981–2001. Their model found that 2.3 percent of this increase was attributable to the plan and that this, in turn, added about 0.5 percent a year to growth in Chile, or about 10 percent of the total over the period.

Others have been more skeptical. Alberto Arenas de Mesa and Fabio Bertranou (1997) argued that Chile's decision to "frontload" the costs of the transition made the reform especially expensive: The government, they say, dramatically increased its implicit liabilities by handing out recognition bonds with attractive rates of return. This may have negatively affected private saving. Also, there were capital market reforms and a deepening of Chile's capital markets, which may explain much of the increase in the saving rate.

On balance, the case that the new pension plan contributed both to saving and (modestly) to economic growth in Chile seems fairly robust. Even though the Corbo and Schmidt-Hebbel study was commissioned by the AFPs, its methodology was good and the results of sensible magnitude. Also, since the burden of financing the transition was met more through fiscal tightening than government borrowing, the boost to private saving was not canceled out by high government dissaving, which makes a stronger case for positive national savings.

Among workers affiliated with the old pension scheme at the time of reform, only about 10 percent stayed in the old system (Kollmann 2002, 2). These workers had five years to decide whether to switch to the defined

---

32. Alternatively, CBO (1999) uses the data from Edwards (1998) and finds that costs peaked in 1987 at 4.84 percent of GDP.

contribution scheme. If they decided to switch, they received "recognition bonds" with a value based on the length and amount of their past contributions at an interest rate of 3.5 to 4 percent. These bonds were placed into the newly created AFPs and are redeemable upon retirement. During the first few years of the new system's operation, the funds' record rates of return induced many workers to switch. Further inducement to switch came from a government-mandated 11 percent net increase in wages, which made up for employees' increase in contributions after the elimination of the employer's contribution (Kay and Kritzer 2001, 43).

Mexico

There are three elements to the fiscal cost of Mexico's new pension system.[33] The first is the costs of providing the minimum guaranteed pension. As noted earlier, the closer workers' salaries are to the minimum wage, the more costly this benefit. It is likely the government will have to find other ways to cover the fiscal cost for most current workers by increasing the retirement age (more contributions) or by improving rates of return. However, these approaches are not easy to implement because the labor unions in Mexico will not allow an increase in the retirement age without any extra benefit. Furthermore, Mexico's economy is not as stable as that of a developed country, so any variation in macroeconomic factors affects the rates of return, which are not likely to remain fixed over the long term.

The second element of cost comes from the social quota, for which the government contributes to the system from general revenue. The amount of the contribution depends on the number of workers covered under the system and on the growth of the economy. These contributions are currently equivalent to 0.17 percent of the GDP, and this percentage would increase by only 0.01 percent of GDP with future GDP growth of 3 percent. But in a weak growth scenario, the amount could increase by up to, 0.32 percent of GDP.

The third element of cost comes from the provision of benefits to affiliated workers who are transition workers, those who contributed to the old pension system before 1997. These workers have the right to choose the higher benefit between the old and new systems, and estimates indicate that most will choose the old system, as it is likely to be much more generous. The fiscal costs of providing benefits to transition workers will depend, in part, on the rate of return on the AFOREs, as it will affect the replacement rate and whether more workers will elect benefits based on the old system. The age group that will have the highest impact on fiscal costs are workers who are now between ages 35 and 39, earn a salary of four times the minimum wage, and have 11 years of contributions to the IMSS.

---

33. This section draws on Sandoval (2004).

Calculating the overall transition costs for the Mexican system has proven difficult, but estimates put the figure at about 1 percent of GDP for the next 20 years (Grandolini and Cerda 1998). Some economists consider this estimate unrealistic, however. Jacobo Rodríguez (1999, 7–10) points out that various factors—"the social contribution, the government part of the mandatory contribution, the 'life-switch' option for transition workers, and the existence of a minimum pension guarantee"—create difficulties in calculating an accurate estimate of the transition's fiscal costs.

United Kingdom

As discussed above, workers in the United Kingdom may opt out of both the state pension and occupational pension and contribute instead to a personal private account. This option appears to have had a mixed to negative effect on household and national saving, largely because there is no mandatory contribution rate for these accounts: Although workers may need to regularly contribute 10 percent of earnings to ensure adequate retirement income, they may in fact contribute only 4 percent.

Richard Disney, Carl Emmerson, and Matthew Wakefield (2001, 87–88) find that even though the availability of new saving instruments should initially boost private savings, the possibility of opting out of the state and occupational system (and receiving national insurance rebates) in order to contribute to a private account was accompanied by such strong wealth effects that many UK consumers actually reduced savings in favor of greater consumption expenditures. The authors estimate that the gains to private saving throughout the 1990s were around 0.2 percent of GDP. In an empirical study, Brigitte Granville and Sushanta Mallick (2004, 123–36) find that the interest rate is negatively correlated to pension savings, indicating further evidence of a substantial wealth effect. They estimate that the partial privatization of the UK pension system has had no (or a negligible) effect on the country's private saving rate.

On the other hand, by allowing workers to switch from the public system to a private one, the government has reduced its own future liabilities.[34] Thus the reduction in government liabilities can have a positive effect on the public side of national saving.

Overall Conclusions

- In order to be truly effective—ensure adequate participation rates and contribution densities, prevent elderly poverty, and increase

---

34. In addition, the age of eligibility for state pension benefits will gradually increase from 65 to 68 over the years 2024–46.

national saving—it is imperative that any pension system of individual accounts address groups that "slip through the cracks": women, self-employed workers, and those who work in the informal or shadow economy. This is especially a concern for Chile and Mexico, where a large shadow economy allows many workers to evade contributions.

◆ Inequality for women (particularly with respect to periods of child rearing or care giving) pervades most systems but is beginning to be addressed in recent reforms across countries.

◆ A large shadow economy means many workers can evade mandatory contributions. This is a bigger problem in Chile and other Latin American countries that have a sizable informal sector. The 2007 reform in Chile extended mandatory contributions to self-employed workers, which is a good step to address this issue.

■ High administrative costs are a serious concern for an individual accounts system, as they affect real rates of return and have a large impact on low-income workers whose contributions are small.

◆ A central agency that pools individual saving contributions appears to be an important measure to lower administrative costs and encourage participation, especially among low-income workers. Such an agency can benefit from economies of scale and, by transferring the pooled contributions to private funds, can correct for market failure that makes it unprofitable for private savings fund managers to serve low-income customers.

◆ Competition among private funds to attract contributions does not work as a way of lowering costs—as Chile learned, the funds spend heavily on advertising and end up with high costs.

◆ The scale achieved by the pooling of contributions could significantly reduce administrative costs and increase real rates of return for participating individuals, thus both addressing elderly poverty and indirectly encouraging greater participation rates.

■ A system of individual accounts may fail to reduce elderly poverty among low-wage workers, workers who spend time out of the labor force, women, and family caregivers who do not accrue adequate contributions during their working lives. A minimum guaranteed pension is essential to provide adequate income for retirees without sufficient personal savings, but it also can discourage personal saving among low-income workers if it is too generous or too easily accessible.

◆ The 2007 Chile reform, which both increased the guaranteed minimum pension (PBS) and created a second tier that subsidized personal saving for low-income workers (the APS), is a promising approach to address this tradeoff.

♦ The success of an individual account system depends in part on the savings it generates among workers who previously had saved nothing. Low- and middle-wage workers are a natural target, as many have no prior voluntary savings. An inherent trade-off to a minimum guaranteed pension is that if it is too high, it can dull the incentives of low-wage workers to contribute to the system, thus erasing a potential source of new savings and increasing the fiscal burden to the government.

♦ Pension credits for periods of long-term care (as the United Kingdom and Chile have recently enacted) are a good step to address elderly poverty, as is the possibility for a third party to contribute to an individual's account.

■ Participants in individual retirement funds should be required to take annuities rather than lump-sum payouts at the time of retirement so that they don't spend the lump sum and then apply for the minimum payment for low-income retirees.

♦ Australia is an example of a country where many participants took early retirement, supported themselves with the lump-sum payment from their contributory pension, and then applied for the basic or minimum public pension when the money ran out.

■ Most workers do not have the experience and knowledge required to make good financial and retirement decisions, and private investment advice may be colored by the self-interest of those offering it. For example, in the United Kingdom, private financial institutions advised workers to shift to the individual account system even though this was not in the workers' best interests. There should be regulations that require, or at least encourage, investment in a diversified portfolio that is adjusted for risk as people approach retirement.

■ The issue of how to finance the transition from a PAYGO system to a fully funded individual account system will require governments to either raise taxes or borrow money to provide benefits to retirees who have paid into the old system. The fiscal burden of an individual account system is dependent on how national saving is affected and the size of the government's minimum guaranteed pension liabilities.

♦ The effect of the introduction of an individual account system on national saving is ambiguous, although in Chile it appears that the new system had a positive effect on saving.

◆ Australia, on the other hand, has not realized its goal of increasing national saving. The ability to withdraw one's fund as a lump sum upon retirement and then apply for the state minimum pension, is a strong disincentive to adequately save and a greater fiscal burden on the government in the form of more pension payments.

References

Arenas de Mesa, Alberto, and Fabio Bertranou. 1997. Learning from Social Security Reforms: Two Different Cases, Argentina and Chile. *World Development* 25, no. 3 (March): 329–48.

Australian Bureau of Statistics. 2008. *Retirement and Retirement Intentions.* ABS Issue no. 6238.0 (November).

Barrientos, Armando. 1996. Pension Reform and Pension Coverage in Chile: Lessons for Other Countries. *Bulletin of Latin American Research* 15, no. 3.

Barrientos, Armando. 2006. Poverty Reduction: The Missing Piece of Pension Reform in Latin America. *Social Policy & Administration* 40, no. 4: 369–84.

Blake, David. 2003. The United Kingdom Pension System: Key Issues. Pension Institute, Birkbeck College, University of London, London. Photocopy (May).

Bonasia, Mariangela, and Oreste Napolitano. 2006. The Impact of Privatisation of Pension System on National Saving: The Case of Australia and Iceland. University of Naples, Italy. Photocopy.

Cohen, Norma. 2005. A Bloody Mess. *American Prospect Online* (January 11). Available at www.cep.cl.

CBO (Congressional Budget Office). 1999. *Social Security Privatization: Experiences Abroad.* Washington: Government Printing Office.

CBO (Congressional Budget Office). 2004. *Administrative Costs of Private Accounts in Social Security.* Report 52–77 (March). Washington: Government Printing Office.

Corbo, Vittorio, and Klaus Schmidt-Hebbel. 2002. Macroeconomic Effects of Pension Reform in Chile. In *Pension Reforms: Results and Challenges,* ed. International Federation of Pension Fund Administrators. Santiago, Chile: International Federation of Pension Fund Administrators.

Davis, E. Philip. 2004. Is there a Pensions Crisis in the U.K.? *The Geneva Papers on Risk and Insurance—Issues and Practice* 29, no. 3: 343–70 (July). London: Palgrave Macmillan Journals.

Diamond, Peter. 1993. *Privatization of Social Security: Lessons from Chile.* NBER Working Paper 4510. Cambridge, MA: National Bureau of Economic Research.

Diamond, Peter. 1994. Pension Reform in a Transition Economy: Notes on Poland and Chile. In *The Transition in Eastern Europe,* ed. Olivier J. Blanchard, Kenneth Froot, and Jeffrey Sachs. Chicago: University of Chicago Press.

Diamond, Peter. 2001. Issues in Social Security Reform. In *LERA 2001 Research Volume: The Future of the Safety Net—Social Insurance and Employee Benefits,* ed. Sheldon Friedman and David Jacobs. Ithaca, NY: Cornell University Press.

Disney, Richard, Carl Emmerson, and Matthew Wakefield. 2001. Pension Reform and Saving in Britain. *Oxford Review of Economic Policy* 17: 70–94.

Economist Intelligence Unit. 1996. *Investing and Trading—Chile* (February 1).

Edey, Malcolm, and John Simon. 1996. *Australia's Retirement Income System: Implications for Saving and Capital Markets.* NBER Working Paper 5799. Cambridge, MA: National Bureau of Economic Research.

Edwards, Sebastian. 1998. The Chilean Pension Reform: A Pioneering Orogram. In *Privatizing Social Security,* ed. Martin Feldstein. Chicago: University of Chicago Press.

Errázuriz, Guillermo Arturo. 2007. *Chilean System under Reform* (October). Available at www.globalpensions.com.

Espinosa-Vega, Marco A., and Tapen Sinha. 2000. A Primer and Assessment of Social Security Reform in Mexico. In *Federal Reserve Bank of Atlanta Economic Review* (First Quarter). Atlanta, GA: Federal Reserve Bank of Atlanta.

Gillion, Colin, John Turner, Clive Bailey, and Denis Latulippe, eds. 2000. *Social Security Pensions: Development and Reform.* Geneva: International Labor Office.

Grandolini, Gloria, and Luis Cerda. 1998. *The 1997 Pension Reform in Mexico.* World Bank Publication no. WPS1933. Washington: World Bank.

Granville, Brigitte, and Sushanta Mallick. 2004. Pension Reforms and Saving Gains in the United Kingdom. *Journal of Economic Policy Reform* 7, no. 2 (June): 123–36. London: Routledge.

IMSS (Instituto Mexicano del Seguro Social). 1997. *La Seguridad Social ante el Futuro.* Mexico.

James, Estelle. 2005. *Reforming Social Security: Lessons from Thirty Countries.* NCPA Policy Report no. 277 (June). Dallas, TX: National Center for Policy Analysis.

Kay, Stephen J., and Barbara E. Kritzer. 2001. Social Security in Latin America: Recent Reforms and Challenges. In *Federal Reserve Bank of Atlanta Economic Review* (First Quarter). Atlanta, GA: Federal Reserve Bank of Atlanta.

Kollmann, Geoffrey. 2002. *Social Security: The Chilean Example.* CRS Report 95-839 (June 26). Washington: Congressional Research Service.

Kritzer, Barbara. 1996. Privatizing Social Security: The Chilean Experience. *Social Security Bulletin* 59, no. 3. Washington: Social Security Administration

Marcel, Mario, and Alberto Arenas. 1992. *Social Security Reform in Chile.* Occasional Paper no. 5. Washington: Inter-American Development Bank.

Martin, John P., and Edward Whitehouse. 2008. *Reforming Retirement-Income Systems: Lessons from the Recent Experiences of OECD Countries.* OECD Social, Employment and Migration Working Paper no. 66. Paris: Organization for Economic Cooperation and Development.

Mesa-Lago, Carmelo. 1994. *Changing Social Security in Latin America: Toward Alleviating the Costs of Economic Reform.* Boulder, CO: Lynne Reinner Press.

Mesa-Lago, Carmelo, and Alberto Arenas de Mesa. 1998. The Chilean Pension System: Evaluation, Lessons, and Challenges. In *Do Options Exist? The Reform of Pension and Health Care in Latin America*, ed. Cruz-Saco and Mesa-Lago. Pittsburgh: University of Pittsburgh Press.

Mitchell, Olivia S. 1999. *Evaluating Administrative Costs in Mexico's AFORES System* (January). Philadelphia: Pension Research Council, Wharton School, University of Pennsylvania

Morandé, Felipe G. 1998. Savings in Chile: What Went Right? *Journal of Development Economics* 57, no. 1 (October): 201–28.

Murthi, Mamta, J. Michael Orszag, and Peter R. Orszag. 1999. Administrative Costs under a Decentralized Approach to Individual Accounts: Lessons from the United Kingdom. Paper presented at the conference on New Ideas About Old Age Security, World Bank, Washington, September.

OECD (Organization for Economic Cooperation and Development). 2005. *Economic Surveys: Chile 2005.* Paris

Orenstein, Mitchell A., ed. 2008 (forthcoming). *Pensions, Social Security, and the Privatization of Risk.* New York: Columbia University Press.

Orszag, Peter, and Joseph E. Stiglitz. 2001. Rethinking Pension Reform: 10 Myths about Social Security Systems. In *New Ideas About Old Age Security*, ed. R. Holman and J. Stiglitz. Washington: World Bank.

Packard, Truman G. 2002. *Pooling, Savings and Prevention: Mitigating the Risk of Old Age Poverty in Chile.* World Bank Policy Research Working Paper no. 2849 (May). Washington: World Bank.

PACPR (Presidential Advisory Council on Pension Reform). 2006. PACPR Report, volumes I and II (in Spanish). Santiago, Chile: Secretaría de Comunicaciones, Ministerio Secretaría General de Gobierno (July).

Pensions Commission (chaired by Adear Turner). 2005. *Second Report of the Pensions Commission.* London. Available at http://news.bbc.co.uk.

Pensions Policy Institute (United Kingdom). 2005. Pension Facts (November). Available at www.pensionspolicyinstitute.org.uk.

Pensions Policy Institute (United Kingdom). 2007. Pension Facts (January). Available at www.pensionspolicyinstitute.org.uk.

Presidential Advisory Council (Chile). 2006. *El Derecho a una Vida Digna en la Vejez: Hacia un Contrato Social con la Previsión en Chile*. Santiago. Available at www.consejoreformapre visional.cl.

Rodríguez, L. Jacobo. 1999. In Praise and Criticism of Mexico's Pension Reform. *Cato Institute Policy Analysis*, no. 340 (April 14). Washington: Cato Institute.

SAFP (Superintendencia de Administradores de Fondos de Pensiones, Chile). 2003. *The Chilean Pension System*, 4th ed., ed. Alejandro Ferreiro Yazigi. Santiago.

SAFP (Superintendencia de Administradores de Fondos de Pensiones, Chile). 2006. *Boletín Estadístico*, no. 195 (December). Santiago.

Sales-Sarrapy, C., F. Solís-Soberón, and A. Villagómez-Amezcua. 1998. Pension System Reform: The Mexican Case. In *Privatizing Social Security*, ed. M. Feldstein. Chicago: University of Chicago Press.

Sandoval, Héctor. 2004. *Analysis of the Pension Reform in Mexico*. Waterloo, Canada: University of Waterloo.

Sass, Stephen A. 2004. *Reforming the Australian Retirement System: Mandating Individual Accounts*. Issues in Brief (April). Boston: Center for Retirement Research, Boston College.

Serrano, Carlos. 1999. Social Security Reform: How Much Will It Cost And Who Will Pay For It, the Mexican Case. World Bank, Washington. Photocopy.

SSA (Social Security Administration). 2000. *Social Security International Update. Recent Developments in Foreign Public and Private Pensions* (December), ed. Susan A. Carleson. Washington: Office of Policy, Social Security Administration.

SSA (Social Security Administration). 2003. *Social Security International Update. Recent Developments in Foreign Public and Private Pensions* (October), ed. Susan A. Carleson. Washington: Office of Policy, Social Security Administration.

SSA (Social Security Administration). 2004. *Social Security International Update. Recent Developments in Foreign Public and Private Pensions* (June), ed. Susan A. Carleson. Washington: Office of Policy, Social Security Administration.

SSA (Social Security Administration). 2007. *Social Security International Update. Recent Developments in Foreign Public and Private Pensions* (May), ed. Denise Lamaute. Washington: Office of Policy, Social Security Administration.

Stone, Leroy O., ed. 2004. *New Frontier on Research in Retirement*. Catalogue no. 75-511-XIE. Ottawa: Statistics Canada.

Turner, John. 2005a. *Administrative Costs for Social Security Private Accounts*. Research Report (June). Washington: AARP Public Policy Institute.

Turner, John. 2005b. *Problems Encountered with Private Accounts in the United Kingdom*. Fact Sheet (February). Washington: AARP Public Policy Institute.

UK DWP (United Kingdom Department for Work and Pensions). 2006. *Security in Retirement: Towards a New Pension Scheme*. Report presented to Parliament by the Secretary of State for Work and Pensions by Command of Her Majesty, May.

UK DWP (United Kingdom Department for Work and Pensions). 2008. *Pension Bill: Impact Assessment. Chapter 2: Making it Easier and More Attractive to Save* (April 24). Available at www.dwp.gov.uk.

Uthoff, Andras. 1998. Pension Funds, the Financing of Transition Costs and Financial Markets Development: Lessons from the Chilean Privatization Reform. Paper prepared for the conference on Pension Funds and Financial Markets, University of Paris, March 23.

Valdés-Prieto, Salvador. 2004. Social Security Coverage in Chile, 1990–2001. Background paper in *Keeping the Promise of Old-Age Income Security in Latin America*. Washington: World Bank.

Vittas, Dimitri, and Estelle James. 1994. Mandatory Saving Schemes: Are They an Answer to the Old Age Security Problem? Paper presented at the 1994 Pension Research Council Symposium, Securing Employer-Based Pensions: An International Perspective, Wharton School, University of Pennsylvania, May 5–6.

Williamson, John B. 2002. Privatization of Social Security in the United Kingdom: Warning or Exemplar? *Journal of Aging Studies* 16: 415–30. Amsterdam: Elsevier.

6

Notional or Nonfinancial Individual Accounts

For the United States, as for other developed economies, history constrains the choice of public pension design. These countries have had public pension systems for many years and have substantial obligations to current retirees and to those who have been paying into the system and expect to receive benefits; the US Social Security system, for example, has unfunded liabilities of $4 trillion over the next 75 years (Hassett and MacGuineas 2005). These large obligations are a barrier for policymakers who want to introduce individual accounts: If young workers' contributions to the public pension program go to individual accounts, there will not be enough money to finance benefit payments to current and upcoming retirees. This is the problem of the transition to an individual account system.

One way out of this dilemma is to increase taxes and use the additional revenue to pay off the benefit obligation to workers and retirees who have contributed to the old defined benefit system. Government saving would thus remain unchanged by the transition to the new pension plan, as the increase in taxes would offset the greater expenditure on retirement benefits. Private saving would rise on the first round because pension contributions/taxes would go into individual accounts that would buy financial assets in the market. National saving would be increased unless individuals were to fully offset their individual account contributions by reducing other saving. In practice, some offsetting reduction of private saving would likely occur, but the overall result would almost certainly be an increase in national saving, particularly since most low- and moderate-income families save very little at present. This growth in national saving would translate into either more domestic investment (and an increased capital stock over time) or more net foreign investment (for the United States, a reduction in the current account deficit and a smaller stock of net foreign obligations), or both. In all cases, national wealth and the level of future income would increase.

We described this alternative, and its implementation in Australia, Chile, and other countries, in chapter 5, and noted that economists had concluded that Chile's transition to the new public pension program had been accompanied by an increase in national saving that contributed to the country's economic growth. Australia and Canada[1] have also used general tax revenue to finance obligations to current retirees, although evidence of net increases in saving is weak or nonexistent for these countries.

The problem with using tax revenue to finance obligations to current retirees is that it involves the politically unpopular policy of increasing taxes. In the United States, voters tend to punish policymakers who increase taxes and reward those who cut them. In Sweden taxes were already very high and policymakers did not want to increase them further.[2] So both countries turned to an alternative approach to the transition problem. The George W. Bush administration proposed to divert a fraction of Social Security contributions to individual accounts and borrow the funds needed to fund current and upcoming obligations to retirees and workers who had paid taxes into the fund. Latvia, Poland, and Sweden, on the other hand, established nonfinancial or notional accounts: Of the taxes that workers or their employers pay into the public pension program, a notional amount is credited to an individual retirement account. However, the money does not finance purchases of stocks or bonds in the capital market; instead, the notional value of the contributions accumulates in the account while the money itself pays the benefits of current retirees.

Although these two approaches to the transition problem differ—the US approach would create actual accounts backed by stocks and bonds—their economic implications are the same: In both cases the individual accounts are not matched by any increase in national saving. In Sweden and Latvia, the individual accounts are bookkeeping entries and are not backed by an increment to business-sector assets. In the US proposal there are real accounts, but their impact on national saving is offset by the increased borrowing ("dissaving") of the federal government. There is no

---

1. While Canada still has a predominantly PAYGO system, it used general tax revenue to finance the transition of a small segment of its pension system to a fully funded program.

2. The Swedish tax reform of 1991, which combined drastic cuts to top marginal income tax rates with measures to broaden the tax base, caused a total revenue loss for the Swedish government of 6 percent of GDP. In comparison, the 1986 US tax reform and the Bush tax cuts lowered revenues by only about 2 percent of GDP (Agell, Englund, and Södersten 1999). Despite this, though, Sweden still has one of the highest tax rates in the world, and its government has been reluctant to add to this burden.

net saving increase in either case and hence no increment to income and wealth for the economy.[3]

To evaluate notional defined contribution (NDC) accounts, we look at the experiences of Sweden, which pioneered in the development of such plans, Poland, and Latvia, which was the first country to set up notional individual accounts. Although the NDC system is not without problems, its introduction was a necessary reform in these countries because of their particular economic and historic circumstances: Sweden was something of a welfare state with high average and marginal tax rates, and Poland and Latvia were transition economies looking to shed communism and usher in a free-market approach to work incentives. The analyses thus illustrate two distinctly different situations in which the switch to an NDC system made sense. But neither situation applies to the United States. We look at the Bush administration proposal for individual accounts; although it called for funded individual accounts rather than NDC accounts, it had the same macroeconomic implications as an NDC system. As we said in chapter 1, while this plan was not implemented, the proposal provides very useful lessons for how individual accounts might operate in the United States and thus merits closer analysis.

Notional Accounts in Sweden

Starting around 1992 the Swedish government began a debate about the country's pension program, a defined benefit pay-as-you-go (PAYGO) plan in which current workers' contributions financed benefits to retirees, as in the United States and most other rich countries. Projections of contributions and pension liabilities revealed that the plan was not fiscally sound: Because of demographic trends and increases in longevity, there would not be enough revenue to pay benefits—again, a situation faced by the United States and other OECD economies. At the same time, there was concern in Sweden about the very high rate of taxation on citizens, with the accompanying risk of adverse effects on labor supply. Concerns about the viability of the pension program were exacerbated in the 1990s when the economy went into a deep recession. The unemployment rate had hovered around 2.5 percent for many years, but in 1991 it started rising, held at over 8 percent from 1993 to 1998, and hit a peak of 10.1 percent in 1997. In 2006 the rate remained at 7.0 percent.[4]

---

3. In the case of the Bush plan, a full shift to individual accounts would generate net saving over the long term as the growth of the economy would eventually produce growth in individual saving, which would more than offset the present value of government borrowing to finance the transition.

4. Data are from the Bureau of Labor Statistics, Foreign Labor Statistics, available at http://stats.bls.gov.

New pension legislation was passed in 1994 after grueling political debate, and phase-in of the new system began in 1999. Persons born between 1938 and 1953 and after receive pensions that are partly determined by the new program, while those born in 1954 and after will receive their pensions entirely from the new system.[5] (See box 6.1 on transition in Italy.) The new system sets up a defined contribution plan that requires workers to contribute 18.5 percent of their taxable payroll (workers and employers split the cost in bookkeeping terms). Of this 18.5 percent, 16 percent is credited to a nonfinancial or notional account for the individual. The money does not buy financial assets but instead pays the pension benefits of current retirees, just like a standard PAYGO system. But the accumulated account values are important to individual workers because they determine the amount of income the individual will receive at retirement (subject to qualifications discussed below). The remaining 2.5 percent of payroll, also credited to the worker's individual account, goes to the purchase of financial assets. On retirement, workers' notional balances plus their financial balances determine the amount of their pension income from the system.[6]

Emphasis on Sustainability and Fairness

The priorities of policymakers in devising the reform plan were to create a program that would be sustainable as well as fair to individuals both within and across generations. Just as important, the reform had to be politically acceptable and supported by a majority of political parties in the Swedish parliament to forestall adjustments by successive governments.[7] The purpose of the shift to individual accounts was not to create an optimal retirement plan based on ideal welfare economics but rather to create

---

5. This meant that only Swedes age 61 or older at the time of the implementation of the reform were untouched by its provisions. All workers age 45 or younger at the time of implementation would be completely under the new system, while the intermediate age groups would be on a proportional mix of the two systems. The Swedish transition period to notional accounts is remarkably rapid compared with that in Italy, for instance (see box 6.1).

6. The 1994 reform also changed the quasi-mandatory occupational benefits that affected roughly 90 percent of workers, which had been meant to supplement public pension income, to a fully funded plan. Contribution rates vary around 3.5 percent, putting the fully funded returns to workers at roughly 6 percent (when included with the mandatory 2.5 percent from the public system) (Könberg, Palmer, and Sundén 2005).

7. Following the defeat of the Swedish Social Democrats in 1991, a new center-right, four-party coalition government came to power and formed a broad Parliamentary Working Group on Pensions together with the (now) opposition Social Democrats. The political negotiations leading to the Swedish NDC reform were thus effectively depoliticized and spurred on by the economic crisis in Sweden in the early 1990s. More than 85 percent of the Swedish parliament adopted the Working Group's proposals in 1994 after a purely symbolic parliamentary debate. See Könberg, Palmer, and Sundén (2005) for details.

Box 6.1   Italy: A case study in how not to implement a notional defined contribution system

As we have seen, Italy has among the lowest effective retirement ages in the OECD, even as it carries a huge government debt, has one of the highest current pension expenditure levels, and faces a very adverse demographic outlook. Not surprisingly, pension reform has been a recurring political topic in Italy, which has implemented several reforms in recent years.[1] First, in 1992, under acute financial pressure after that year's exchange rate crisis, a series of rises in the retirement age and extensions of required contribution periods—both from unsustainably low or short levels—erased perhaps a quarter of the total unfunded pension liabilities for privately employed workers. These nonetheless remained close to 300 percent of GDP after this reform (Beltrametti 1996).

Therefore, in 1995 the Italian government introduced a further reform of the still unsustainable pension system. The choice fell on the introduction of a notional defined contribution (NDC) system. On the face of it, this was a sensible idea, as Italy's labor market sorely needed the potential incentive for people to remain in the workforce longer that NDC systems provide through their direct links between worklife contributions and pension benefit levels.

However, at least three issues conspired to render Italy's 1995 NDC reform effort largely futile. First, the Berlusconi government introduced it almost overnight and without any kind of public debate over its strengths and weaknesses. The lack of prereform debate meant that the Italian public was entirely unprepared for the new individual provisions. This lack of preparation undoubtedly weakened the possible microeconomic behavioral impact of the NDC system on individuals' retirement decisions.

Second, and more importantly, the Italian government exempted essentially everyone except future workers from the reform. The excessively long transition period to the NDC system meant that all workers in 1995 with more than 18 years of contributions (i.e., those of about age 40, assuming an average working career starting in the early 20s) would be unaffected by the reform, and their pensions would be calculated entirely under the pre-1995 pension scheme. Only people who started to work after 1995 would be entirely under the new NDC scheme, and those in between would depend on each system proportionally according to their years of contributions. Needless to say, the exclusion of such a large part of the Italian workforce from the 1995 reform and the prolonged phasing-in period (likely stretching into the 2030s or 2040s) mean that the fiscal improvements from implementing the NDC system will be far lower in Italy than, for instance, Sweden.

(box continues on next page)

a good-enough plan that dealt with the large and looming budget short-fall. The Swedes did, however, understand the underlying economics of retirement reform when they set up the plan.

Economic theory posits that the rate of return in a PAYGO system is determined by the economy's rate of growth, or the rate of growth of the real wage bill for a payroll-financed plan (Orszag and Stiglitz 2001). An economy with population growth of even 1 percent a year can, for a given rate of contributions, afford to pay higher retirement pensions than an economy with a stationary population because the number of workers paying into the plan exceeds the number receiving benefits. Similarly, increases in real wages make each successive generation richer and raise the level of contributions without increasing the proportion of wages paid in contributions. This feature is not just a theoretical result; it has played out in practice, allowing PAYGO pension plans to be generous to past retirees by taking advantage of economic growth, whereas in recent years declines in both labor force and real wage growth rates have caused financial difficulties for the public pension plans of many countries.

Recognizing that a notional contribution plan shares this same feature with standard PAYGO systems, the Swedish planners initially thought to tie the rate of return on the nominal account balances to the growth rate of the wage bill—reflecting the growth in the contribution base and ensuring the sustainability of the program in the face of demographic shifts. However, after debate, they decided to use a modified system that tied the rate of return on the notional individual accounts to per capita rather than aggregate wage growth. The modification was to address concerns about shortchanging recipients who had contributed to the program throughout their working lives but who would be penalized if they were part of a large generation followed by a smaller generation. The policymakers were trying to balance the need for sustainability with the desire to avoid unfair treatment of an "unlucky" generation. However, the modification compromised sustainability, so the policymakers introduced a fallback provision—an "automatic balancing mechanism"—that would reduce the rate of return if projections indicated that the system would become fiscally unsound.[8]

The automatic balancing mechanism guarantees the financial sustainability of the NDC system by activating when the balance ratio of pension system assets and vested liabilities falls below unity.[9] Pension assets are defined as the capitalized value of pension contributions—that is, essentially equal to the pension liability that these annual contributions can finance in the long term, plus the value of the Swedish NDC system's so-called "buffer funds."[10] If the balance ratio drops below 1, per capita wage indexation of pension benefits is temporarily abandoned until the ratio rises back to at least 1. In American terms, such a measure would be the rough equivalent of stopping the automatic COLA rises in annual Social Security benefits when contributions to the Social Security Trust Fund fell below payments—a drop that is projected to happen in 2017 (SSA 2007).

It is obvious that pension system designs akin to "automatic stabilizers," which function by temporarily abandoning automatic indexing of pension benefits, shift the entire cost of achieving pension sustainability onto existing retirees (see box 6.2). However, there is equally little doubt that having such legal statutes for automation on the books that explicitly identifies "those who will suffer" from nonsustainability serves to, in a way, depoliticize future changes to keep the pension system fiscally sustainable by somewhat insulating it from the risk of manipulation for short-term political gain.

In Sweden workers can choose when to retire, and their benefits are adjusted accordingly. Because the amount of their annuity or monthly benefit payment is also adjusted based on life expectancy, recipients will have to accommodate the trend toward longer lifetimes, if it continues, by accepting lower benefits, working longer, or saving beyond the required contributions. Indeed, many in Sweden have enrolled in occupational

---

8. See box 6.2 and chapter 8 for more analysis of the effects of automatic balancing mechanisms (ABMs).

9. See Könberg, Palmer, and Sundén (2005) for details.

10. "Buffer funds" emerged in the Swedish system as the disability and survivor pension schemes were part of the reform split from the main new NDC pension system and subsequently financed through general government revenues. This created extra funds from employer payroll taxes, previously used to finance these two programs that were channeled into the buffer funds.

Box 6.2 Automatic balancing mechanisms in public pension systems in Sweden, Germany, Japan, and the United States

Automatic balancing mechanisms in the Swedish, German, and Japanese public pension system function via a mechanism that leads to the abandonment of pension benefit indexing either in the event that the total liabilities of the pension systems surpass assets (Sweden's notional defined contribution or "turnover duration" approach) or in the event that the ratio of contributing workers to retirees decline (Germany and Japan's "dependency ratio" approach). In Germany, this approach has arguably already been used in 2003–04 and led to the abandonment of cost of living allowance (COLA) increases in old age pensions and a subsequent cut in real benefit levels to German retirees.[1]

The use of such automatic stabilizers that freeze COLA increases puts the entire restructuring burden on current retirees. Fiscal balancing of the program is thus achieved through a cost-cutting strategy.[2] But apart from the political advantage of identifying in advance who will suffer from an unsustainable pension system (imagine, for instance, the difference in the AARP approach to Social Security reform if, by sometime before 2020, when the trust fund cash-flow turns negative, COLAs were automatically abandoned!), the economic advantage of automatic stabilizers is that the required burden is spread over many more people than if pension deficits accumulate over decades. An approach that maintains the status quo until right before the crisis hits will lead to far more drastic changes in either benefit levels or tax rates to restore sustainability than a gradual phase-in of the necessary changes (see also chapter 8).

Unfortunately, the current legal environment of US Social Security "rolls the snowball into the future." If the US Social Security Old-Age, Survivors, and Disability Insurance (OASDI) Trust Fund is not reformed and runs out of money, as is scheduled to occur in the early 2040s, there will be an uncertain legal situation. As laid out by Kathleen Romig (2007), the Social Security Act specifies that benefit payments shall be made *only* from the trust funds (42 U.S.C.§401(f)), and the Antideficiency Act prohibits government spending in excess of available funds (31 U.S.C. §1341). On the other hand, the Social Security Act also stipulates that Social Security is an *entitlement program*, which means that the US government is legally obligated to provide full Social Security benefits to all, as described in the text of the Act. The subsequent legal battle would have to be resolved by the courts and/or Congress.

The Social Security Trustees' 1982 Annual Report, which was issued prior to the 1983 Social Security Reform and, therefore, predicted that the Old Age and

Box 6.2   Automatic balancing mechanisms in public pension
        systems in Sweden, Germany, Japan, and the United States
        (continued)

Survivors Insurance (OASI)[3] Trust Fund would be insolvent by July 1983, indicates on page 2 that the immediate outcome of a trust fund insolvency would be the "inability to pay some benefits *on time*" [emphasis added], as the trust fund would be able to pay benefits only as tax receipts were credited to it.[4] This would mean that recipients would receive their full Social Security checks only about 9 months every year, indicating an automatic benefit cut of about 25 percent sometime in the 2040s (rising to about 30 percent by 2080).

This mechanism is essentially the same as the Swedish, German, and Japanese "automatic balancing mechanisms," only applied some 30 years from now, when the problem will have grown much bigger. The approaches in Sweden, Germany, and Japan are thus superior to the current US situation, as it tackles the possibility of underfunding earlier (instead of pushing the day of reckoning into the future) and spreads the problem over many more people.

One reason it is so difficult to reform US Social Security is that the voting group of the baby-boomers is so large. They are unwilling to accept cuts or to support those who suggest them. The difference in approach of equally politically powerful baby-boomer generations in Sweden, Germany, and Japan is noteworthy. To address pension system underfunding, voters in these countries have legislated immediate cuts in pension benefits for themselves, not just their children, and hence have espoused a degree of intergenerational fairness not evident in the US political system.

---

1. See Deutsche Welle (2003). Without this freeze in pension benefits, contributions to the German pension system would have had to rise in excess of 19.5 percent of wage income. In addition to the benefit freeze, German retirees also were made to pay full costs of nursing insurance, adding to the decline in the real level of old age income in Germany.

2. Automatic tax increases could also cover any underfunding, although they would put the burden of the cost of rescuing the underfunded pension system on workers rather than retirees.

3. The OASI Trust Fund is a separate legal entity. However, as old age and survivor pensions and disability pensions are intertwined and the OASI Trust Fund is far larger than the disability insurance trust fund, usually when discussing the fiscal status of Social Security, the two trust funds are presented together as the OASDI Trust Funds. See financial data for each at the Social Security Administration's website, www.ssa.gov.

(box continues on next page)

retirement plans that pay benefits in addition to the required government program.

For the 2.5 percent of payroll invested in financial assets, individuals receive market returns on their chosen asset portfolios (choices are limited to avoid unsafe investments) and government administration of the program minimizes administrative costs. Most participants did not choose an investment strategy but allowed their contributions to be placed in the default portfolio, which invests fairly conservatively, especially as people approach retirement age. Annika Sundén (2004) presents data showing that more than 90 percent of participants choose the default fund, a clear indication of the power of pension scheme design.[11]

The Minimum Pension Provision

As we found with the individual account systems in Chile and elsewhere, there is a potential poverty problem with such plans. Low-wage workers do not contribute much to their individual accounts and so do not build up very large balances at retirement. Their implied annuity payment is then low and they fall below the poverty line. Given the Swedish government's concern with fairness, it is not surprising that it's program addresses this issue squarely.

The minimum guarantee is available starting at age 65 to those who do not reach a threshold level of income from their retirement benefits; as

---

11. The Swedish government prevents the "default fund" from investing in certain companies, due to social policy considerations. See www.aarp.org.

of 2005, 30 percent of new retirees claimed at least some income from the minimum guarantee (Könberg, Palmer, and Sundén 2005). In 2005 the monthly minimum pension income was 6,993 Swedish kronor (SEK) for an individual and SEK12,476 for a married couple. It is tricky to put that in US terms because of exchange rate fluctuations and differences in the cost of living. But based on the OECD 2005 purchasing power parity exchange rate for the krona (SEK9.21 to the dollar), these amounts are about $760 a month for a single person and $1,355 for a couple—comparable to, but a bit less generous than, the typical US Social Security benefit.[12] However, Sweden also has other subsidies (e.g., for rent and transportation) for low-income elderly.[13]

On balance, the minimum living standard provided to the elderly in Sweden compares favorably with that in the United States. Sweden guarantees a solid minimum standard of living for its elderly regardless of their contributions to the individual account plan. That is a very important and valuable attribute of their system, but it carries a potential downside: It can reduce or even eliminate the favorable incentives created by a contributory pension plan by weakening the link between the amount paid in and the amount received. Furthermore, for some low-wage workers, there is absolutely no link between contributions to and receipts from the pension plan: In 2005 single persons eligible for a monthly earnings-related pension benefit of $450 (SEK4,137) or less received no financial benefit from their own contributions. As of 2005, 30 percent of new retirees claimed at least some income from the minimum guarantee (Könberg, Palmer, and Sundén 2005).

For retirees eligible for monthly pension benefits in the range of $450 to $1,094 (SEK4,137 to SEK10,080), the minimum guarantee is reduced by 48 cents for every dollar they received from the earnings-related pension program (Scherman 1999).[14] This means their retirement income is higher the more they have paid into the system, but the effective (implicit) marginal tax rate is 48 percent on the minimum guarantee, a figure high enough to dull the incentive to work longer or at a better-paid job. Retirees who reach the top of this range (above roughly $1,094) are unaffected by the minimum benefit and simply receive their earnings-related pension. These retirees can fully appreciate the full incentive impact of a contributory pension plan.

---

12. This comparison is intended to give a sense of the generosity of the minimum payment in Sweden. Clearly, a minimum payment and an earnings-related pension are different from each other.

13. At the same time, however, out-of-pocket health care costs are slightly lower in the United States (at 13.1 percent of total health care expenditure in 2005) than in the Scandinavian countries (OECD Health Database 2007).

14. Sweden is one of only five OECD countries that fully tax pension benefits. See table 2.1 for an overview of how Sweden and other OECD countries tax social benefits.

Provisions such as these in Sweden that reduce the work incentive provisions of public retirement plans are not unusual in other countries. For example, in the United States a spouse who has stayed out of the workforce for a number of years to raise children may find that the Social Security benefit he or she would receive based on his or her own income and Social Security contributions is lower than the benefit he or she would receive based on his or her spouse's contributions—which is equal to 50 percent of the spouse's benefit. For someone in such a situation, Social Security taxes on labor income are pure taxes with no influence on future retirement income and could have an impact on the decision whether or not to return to work or how long to work before retiring.

Making Up for Missed Contributions

The minimum pension guarantee is one way of making sure that persons who do not contribute much to their individual accounts do not end up in poverty. Sweden has other provisions to protect workers without a full work and contribution history (e.g., because of unemployment or leaving the workforce to care for children or a sick relative): The government uses general tax revenue to make contributions to the person's individual retirement account. The idea is to avoid penalizing workers who are unable to work; however, the incentive effects of these provisions are hard to determine. On the one hand, such provisions may encourage some individuals to remain unemployed rather than accept an available job, or to report that they are caring for children or relatives when, in fact, they could work and choose not to. On the other hand, these provisions may help avoid the problem of workers forced to leave employment for an extended period who then end up with the minimum pension, regardless of their work choices, as they approach retirement age.

Conclusions on the Swedish Plan

Sweden faced a serious fiscal shortfall in its public pension program at a time when the government was trying to reduce the very high average and marginal tax rates faced by its citizens. Policymakers did not want to raise taxes to deal with the projected pension funding shortfall, which left the alternative of finding a way to cut benefits while avoiding a divisive political debate. They succeeded in this goal and were able to gain the support of the political parties and the labor movement for the pension reform plan, which still has broad support—a remarkable achievement. In addition, they have created important protections against old age poverty by providing a minimum benefit and other support for the elderly, including health care.

One criticism of the Swedish plan is that, by indexing benefits to per capita rather than aggregate wage growth, it does not address the fact that with a PAYGO system, an increase in the proportion of the population receiving benefits will either impose an increased burden on the working population or result in reduced retirement benefits, or some combination of the two. There is no costless way to deal with this problem. If it is anticipated, then there can be an increase in saving that increases the capital stock and thus the size of the economic pie available in the future. But this is costly because it involves a reduction in consumption as the counterpart to the increased saving. In the Swedish plan, however, there is no increase in saving and hence no increase in future income to deal with the demographic shift and resulting larger retirement burden.

On the other hand, the reform plan with individual accounts was a way of making benefit cuts that were politically acceptable, while using the minimum benefit provision to avoid elderly poverty, even if that solution comes at the price of higher taxes on the working population. The cuts in benefits will affect higher-income retirees, who are required to contribute 16 percent of their taxable payroll to individual accounts that will yield pretty low rates of return, especially if the balancing provision is invoked. It is important in this context, though, to note that higher-income retirees may also receive benefits from any tax-favored contributory occupational retirement plans in which they might participate (although Swedish expenditures on such tax breaks are very limited).

The Swedish reform plan was something of a "smoke and mirrors" solution because it sets up bookkeeping notional individual accounts rather than real ones (in fact, some Swedes regard the system as a fraud). But it is difficult to have a realistic debate about the tradeoffs involved in pension reform in any country, so the Swedish approach may have been a necessary evil. The plan did get a number of things right, avoiding a fiscal collapse and strengthening the individual-level (microeconomic) link between the decision to retire or postpone retirement and the size of the retirement benefit. Furthermore, the Swedish model has a built-in automatic balancing mechanism, meaning that if political leaders allow the pension system to slip into deficit, the entire adjustment burden will automatically be borne by current retirees through temporary abandonment of pension benefit indexation—likely a very powerful incentive for political leaders to ensure that such a deficit does not arise.

The Swedish model is biased in favor of pension reforms earlier rather than later, undoubtedly a very positive feature in an otherwise traditionally hostile political economy of pension reforms. Aside from the relatively small contribution of 2.5 percent of payroll into financial accounts, the pension benefits in the Swedish system are not subject to investment risk and thus avoid the problems that some other countries have faced in this area.

Notional Accounts in Other Countries

The example of the Swedish plan has been an important one for other countries seeking to reform their public pensions. In particular, the countries of the former Soviet bloc have faced the necessity of pension reform as their economies made the transition to a market orientation.

Poland

Under the communist regime, Poland had a Bismarckian public pension program that was financed by a social tax. In January of 1999 this program was replaced by a new system of individual accounts both financial and nonfinancial. Workers' social security contributions were split, with 12.22 percent of payroll sent to the nonfinancial plan and the revenues used to pay the pension costs of the legacy workers and retirees inherited from the old plan; an additional 7.3 percent of payroll was allocated to a financial plan and the revenues invested in financial assets managed by private-sector agents. The rate of return in the financial part of the program reflects the market outcome and depends on the choices of the individual participants. For bookkeeping purposes, the contributions are split 50-50 between employers and employees and the amounts paid to the NDC plan cumulated in individual accounts, credited with an administered rate of return.

The rate of return for the nonfinancial accounts was set equal to the rate of growth of the total wage bill, that is to say, the rate of return intrinsic to a PAYGO system. Unlike the Swedish plan, Poland did not modify this formula to protect any given generation against possible adverse demographic shifts, making its NDC plan resistant to the budgetary effects of such shifts. It was easier to follow the intrinsic return in Poland because it is a transition economy that has the potential for rapid economic growth, and so the likely intrinsic rate of return is higher in Poland than in Sweden. The rate of return in the financial part of the program reflects the market outcome and, of course, ultimately depends upon the choices made by the individual participants.

The transition from the old public pension plan to the new one was rather easy from a political viewpoint: The policy choices were debated, and the public was made aware that the old system was bankrupt and needed reform; with the economic upheaval in Eastern Europe since the fall of the Soviet Union, there was a willingness to accept change. Workers born before 1948 kept their pensions under the old system, and the new plan was phased in for other workers (similar to Sweden's phase-in). Since the greater part of the new system is the NDC plan, this allows contributions from younger workers to pay for those born before 1948.[15]

---

15. It was not possible to apply the new plan to older workers because employment records from before 1980 had been destroyed with the change in economic system.

From an administrative viewpoint, however, the transition to the new plan was not smooth at all, with serious IT problems and employer reporting issues, and it took more than four years—until the end of 2003—to develop accurate administrative records. Given the long-term record keeping of the US Social Security Administration, such problems would be unlikely in a US reform, but it is a worthwhile lesson that the practical implementation of public pension reform can be a challenge.

Latvia

In common with other transition economies, Latvia was hard hit by the collapse of the Soviet system and saw a 40 percent decline in its GDP. The government's pension obligations went from 5.5 percent of GDP in 1985 to 10.5 percent in 1995 (Palmer et al. 2006), putting the program in budgetary crisis. There was also concern about the absence of a link between pension payments and contributions made while working. Given the very large obligations to existing pensioners, a fully funded contributory individual account system was seen as impractical, so Latvia decided on a notional or nonfinancial plan with a small additional funded program of individual accounts.

Latvia got the idea of an NDC pension program from the policy debate in Sweden, but it was actually the first country to implement such a plan, through legislation in 1995,[16] so Latvia is the country with the longest track record of such a program. Initially, the plan set a contribution rate of 20 percent of payroll for the NDC plan with a gradual transition, so that by 2010 the contributions will be split 50-50 between the NDC part to pay current retirees and a financial contribution plan with individual accounts backed by financial assets. Participation in the funded financial plan is compulsory for workers born after 1971, and the goal is to transition to a scheme with funded individual accounts as the main source of pension benefits.[17]

Being at the leading edge of innovation can be an uncomfortable place, and there were some tough adjustment problems in Latvia, such as the determination of pension rights for legacy workers, the age of retirement, and how to deal with persons who had already been given special early retirement rights. These issues all had to be resolved in an economy experiencing a lot of turmoil as it made the transition to a market economy.

---

16. Italy passed its legislation for individual accounts in the same year.

17. A successful transition to a fully funded individual account system could, over time, increase national savings as a growing share of contributions is invested in financial assets rather than funneled to retirees. Any increase in saving would be conditional on factors laid out in chapter 5, such as provisions to catch those who "slip through the cracks" as well as a minimum guarantee that does not effectively offset the incentive for low-income workers to contribute to the system.

There is understandable pride in the fact that the country has sustained the new plan despite the difficulties and that it remains broadly popular.

One reason for its popularity, however, would be hard to replicate elsewhere and is ultimately unsustainable. Latvia decided to credit the nonfinancial accounts with a rate of return equal to the growth rate of the wage bill, in keeping with theory and in line with what Poland did subsequently. Like other transition economies, Latvia suffered a severe downturn with the collapse of the Soviet Union but after a few years began to recover. It achieved a growth rate in real wages of 5.5 percent over the period 1997–2003 and an additional growth of 1.1 percent in the number of employees contributing to the program. Thus participants in the plan enjoyed a rate of return of 6.6 percent a year in 1997–2003, after inflation—a pretty attractive outcome but one that would be hard to duplicate elsewhere and will be hard to sustain in Latvia over the long run. While a positive development at the time, the large growth in real wages creates unsustainable growth in liabilities for the pension system down the line, especially since the Latvian system has no automatic stabilizing mechanism.

Under the reformed pension plan, recipients receive benefits in the form of annuity payments, but the Latvian program does not provide fully price-indexed benefits. The government determined that creating a financial or funded program of individual accounts, in addition to the NDC plan, was a higher priority and that trying to provide price-indexed benefits as well would not be practical for budget reasons. There is partial indexation of benefits, and the level of benefits upon retirement is based on the accumulated amounts in the notional and financial parts of the plan and on life expectancy applied uniformly to all participants. This means that workers' pensions will depend specifically on the wages they earned in formal or reported employment. Indeed, a significant component of the reform plan was to encourage greater participation in the formal labor force. After the breakdown of the Soviet-era system, many workers moved into informal positions to avoid taxes, and the pension reform was designed to lure them back to the formal sector. The chaotic beginnings to the system because of the economic collapse complicated this task. Because of reporting failures, it was hard to distinguish between people who had worked in the old system and those who had moved into the unreported sector to escape taxation.

The Latvian program has succumbed to the same political pressures that raised pension levels in many advanced economies in periods when funding was available. The parliament granted extra indexation of benefits in 1997 and 1998 and then in 1999 introduced a special pension right that allows workers who were part of the old pension system to recalculate their benefits, a measure that followed intense lobbying by a group representing older professional workers (Palmer et al. 2006). Even though, in principle, workers' benefits increase the longer they work, in practice these benefit enhancements seem to have encouraged or facilitated early retirement. This may be a temporary outcome triggered by the drastic changes in the economy that have altered the nature of the labor market and the work environment—older workers in many transition economies have had a hard time adjusting to the changes and have made use of early retirement provisions when they are available.

Lessons from Poland and Latvia

Poland and Latvia, two transition economies with nascent capitalist systems, decided to establish individual account retirement systems and were able to convince the public that individual accounts were a good way to deal with the budget problems of the old public pension plan. Moreover, both were able to "solve" the transition problem by using nonfinancial individual accounts, keeping in mind the fact that this approach does not, by itself, add to national saving. In both cases, the government put in place a fairly extensive program of individual financial accounts on top of the NDC plan, which can be expected to increase saving. Because these economies are much poorer than Sweden, they had a greater need for saving and made it a bigger part of the program.

The Latvian case is particularly interesting because not only are individual accounts a bigger share of its program but its NDC system is meant to serve as a transition to a fully funded individual accounts system; the share of contributions allocated to financial assets, rather than to existing retiree benefits, will grow over time until it reaches 100 percent. An NDC system is a useful transition, as it is a hybrid of the distributive structure of a PAYGO system (contributions fund existing retiree benefits) with the incentive structure of an individual accounts system (benefits are dependent on participants' contributions). However, the issue of funding the transition is still unresolved because the funding structure of an NDC system is analogous to that of a PAYGO system, as the benefits of legacy workers who paid into the old system still must be funded somehow, for example, by raising taxes or borrowing. Alternatively, if the country grew at a sufficiently high rate during the transition period, and contributions accumulated faster than benefit payments to legacy workers, and these payments decreased in proportion to the increasing share of contributions to funded individual accounts, then such a transition plan could theoretically fund itself. Or it could at least offset some of the government's liabilities. This approach would be far more effective in a transition country like Latvia than, say, the United States, as high growth in the wage bill would offer more slack against negative shocks to the system. The coming years in Latvia will be a testament to the efficacy of such a transition.

The Latvian case is also interesting because of the way the political system worked to alter the tight link between contributions and benefits. One of the advantages of individual account systems is that, as we have discussed, they compel participants to connect contributions to benefits. In Latvia many workers had been part of the old pension plan, so their level of benefits was not easily determined on the basis of past contributions, a situation that opened the door to political bargaining over what they would receive. After intense lobbying, they were allowed to add to their benefits using the NDC formula rather than that of the old system. Going forward, we will see whether future benefit levels will depend on political pressures from lobbying groups, or whether the system's "virginity" can be restored.[18]

It might be similarly difficult to insulate individual accounts in the United States from political pressure if a particular cohort of workers (or retirees) was seen to have had a bad deal from such accounts. In particular, the cohort that is part of the transition to the new system may be in a position to exercise political leverage to improve their position at the expense of creating a trust fund. Latvia has no trust fund, despite the fact that impending demographic changes suggest the need for one. The resources that would have gone into a trust fund were given instead to persons in or near retirement, a group that made up a fifth of voters.

US Proposals to Establish Private Accounts

President Bush appointed the President's Commission to Strengthen Social Security soon after he took office, and the commission issued its report in December 2001 (President's Commission to Strengthen Social Security 2001). The bipartisan commission was co-chaired by former Senator Daniel Patrick Moynihan and Time Warner CEO Richard Parsons, and its members included respected economic experts on Social Security. The mandate of the commission was to examine the use of voluntary individual accounts in Social Security and to look for reforms that would improve the fiscal sustainability of the program without raising payroll taxes and without changing benefits for those who receive them or are close to retirement. This was a tough assignment.

Price Indexing

The commission came up with three alternative plans to accomplish these goals, but the real meat of the report was in Reform Model 2, which "enables future retirees to receive Social Security benefits that are at least

---

18. Oscar Levant famously remarked: "I knew Doris Day before she was a virgin."

as great as those of today's retirees, even after adjusting for inflation, and increases Social Security benefits paid to low-income workers. Model 2 establishes a voluntary personal account without raising taxes or requiring additional worker contributions. It achieves solvency and balances Social Security revenues and costs" (President's Commission to Strengthen Social Security 2001, 15).

How did the commission propose to achieve this? The key element of the plan that improves the fiscal solvency of Social Security involves a change in indexing procedure. Under current law, Social Security benefit levels at retirement are linked to the growth of wages. Upon retirement, beneficiaries stand to receive an amount linked both to the level of wages in the economy and to their own employment and wage record.[19] Once they retire, future monthly benefits are indexed to the consumer price index (CPI). These provisions mean that the replacement rate (the ratio of the benefit level to the wage received immediately before retirement) remains roughly constant over time. For example, those born in 1950 who are in the lowest earning quintile when they retire will have a replacement rate of 69.5 percent; if current law remains in place, those born in 2000 who are in the lowest quintile will have a replacement rate of 69.7 percent. That constancy does not apply for those in the highest quintile, as their replacement rates fall from 27.8 to 22.8 percent over the same time period (CBO 2004). Still, the current system is designed to maintain Social Security benefits as a significant fraction of retirement income for all but the highest-income recipients.

The President's Commission recommended that Social Security stop indexing initial benefit levels to wages and start indexing to the CPI. This would mean that the inflation-adjusted benefits of future retirees would be similar to today's levels but well below the levels they would have received under current law. Instead of rising with the general increase in real wages over time, benefit levels would remain constant in real terms. Absent any offsetting adjustments, the replacement rate for Social Security would thus decline over time, making these benefits a smaller and smaller component of retirement income over the very long run for most Americans.

In terms of addressing the solvency problem of the system, the commission greatly overdid it. The proposal would lead to surpluses by the middle of the century, and after 100 years, the revenues would be twice the outlays (CBO 2004, Figure 1B), as tax receipts would rise over time with wages but benefits would rise with prices. Assuming that real wages increase, the revenues would grow faster than the outlays.

---

19. This "initial benefit level" means that the value of pension benefits earned prior to retirement are until the actual time of retirement linked to national wage growth. See box 3.2 for a detailed description of how Social Security benefits are estimated.

Antipoverty Provisions

The commission, recognizing that its plan would reduce benefits for low-income workers to unacceptably low levels, proposed two ways to deal with elderly poverty. First, a floor under benefits would ensure that recipients had at least 120 percent of the poverty level of income. Second, benefits for elderly widows would increase immediately, as this group has a high incidence of poverty under the current system.

President Bush's Proposal

In February 2005 the White House issued *Strengthening Social Security for the 21st Century* (White House 2005). This 13-page document summarized the fiscal problems of the current Social Security system and proposed a voluntary system of private individual savings accounts for workers born after 1950. Participants could opt to devote 4 percent of their taxable payroll to personal retirement accounts, up to $1,000 a year, an amount that would rise over time. If they made this choice, their contributions to the regular Social Security fund would be reduced dollar for dollar. The SSA would aggregate the contributions from individual workers and put them into a small number of funds for private management—equities, bonds, and so on. The plan would work in the same way that the Thrift Savings Plan operates for federal employees, and it was estimated that administrative fees for the managed funds would be kept at around 30 basis points, well below the level of most private plans.

Although workers could choose which fund or combination of funds they would prefer, there would be restrictions and protections on the individual accounts. Participants would be strongly encouraged to move to more conservative portfolios as they neared retirement, in order to protect against sudden market swings. They could not withdraw funds before reaching full retirement age, and upon retirement they would receive an annuity benefit and not a lump-sum payout.

The argument in favor of the president's proposal was that the privatization plan would not add to the total costs of Social Security—that is, it would not worsen the fiscal imbalance. However, it did not claim to solve that imbalance. It argues that individual accounts would make Social Security a better deal than the current system, implying that future benefits would actually be higher than those currently promised. The proposal calls for transition financing (borrowing) in the amount of $664 billion ($754 billion including interest) over the next 10 years to make up for payroll tax revenues no longer available for current and near-term retirees.

Although the February 2005 paper does not address the issue of the solvency of the system, in subsequent speeches the president discussed progressive indexing as an approach to this problem.[20] It is not easy, however, to determine precisely what was meant by progressive indexing; the White House website (accessed April 19, 2007) has only two references to this concept, including an explanation that consists of three paragraphs in the 2006 *Economic Report of the President* (Council of Economic Advisers 2006, 80–83). The idea is that low-income workers would receive benefits based on the current indexing scheme, which indexes initial benefits by wages and subsequent benefits by prices. Initial benefits for higher-income beneficiaries would be a mix of price and wage indexing, and for top income beneficiaries, only price indexing would be used. The progressive indexing could be structured to ensure the viability of the system for the long run.

Despite the relatively brief analysis, progressive indexing is the key part of the administration plan that solves the financing problem of Social Security. It preserves benefit levels for low-income workers but cuts them for higher-income workers. The progressive indexing could be structured so as to ensure the viability of the system for the long run. And middle- and upper-income workers who concluded that they were not likely to get a good deal out of Social Security benefits could move about a third of their contributions to individual accounts.

Strengths of the Bush Proposal

The Bush proposal deals well with a number of the problems in individual account plans instituted overseas, such as those of Chile or the United Kingdom (discussed in chapter 5). It puts the government in charge of consolidating small contributions and possibly of record keeping as well, measures that would help keep down administrative costs. Private-sector asset managers would be responsible for the aggregated funds, avoiding the problem of government ownership of or influence on private-sector corporations. The goal of the White House was to limit the fees earned by financial institutions to 30 basis points of assets, but based on our conversations with financial institutions, that goal would be difficult to reach; something in the range of 60 to 90 basis points would be more feasible.

The plan would reduce rash investments by participants, limiting choice to a small selection of funds with reputable entities and no undue risk. Such an approach could not avoid the problem of a sustained downturn in the broad equity market, but it would at least prevent speculation in very risky stocks.

The plan also addresses the problem that has plagued Australia, where individuals withdraw their retirement funds in a lump sum, use the money

---

20. For example, in speeches on June 2, 2005, at the Hopkinsville Christian County Conference and Convention Center in Hopkinsville, Kentucky and on June 8, 2005, at the Capitol Hilton in Washington. Available at www.whitehouse.gov.

to pay off debts and mortgages, and then apply for the minimum retirement pension. Under the administration proposal, retirees would be required to purchase annuities, thus improving the US annuity market. At present only a small proportion of retirees purchase annuities with their private retirement funds. This may be because people are reluctant to surrender control of their assets, but it is also because annuities are a bad deal for many people. Just as there is a problem of "moral hazard" with life insurance, with annuities there is a similar but inverse problem. With life insurance, persons who know they have a life-threatening condition or do not expect to live long have an incentive to buy a policy, and so insurance companies insist on medical exams and ask a lot of personal questions. Conversely, individuals who expect to live for a long time have an incentive to buy annuities, but it is difficult for financial institutions to make an accurate assessment of lifespan for an individual, and so they base their calculations on the life expectancy patterns of those who apply for annuities and not on the average life expectancy of a broader population.[21] An average person, therefore, gets a lower annuity payment than is actuarially warranted. A legal provision requiring retirees who participate in the government individual account plan to buy annuities would reduce the market distortion and make the annuity market more efficient. The widespread use of annuities would also increase their familiarity and perhaps voluntary purchases as well.

Another advantage of the administration plan is that it links individuals' work history more closely to their pension receipts. Instead of paying Social Security taxes into an anonymous fund, workers participating in the private account program would see how their contributions were adding up and would be likely to view payments as contributions to their own saving rather than as taxes. This might provide greater political support for the program and could bring work incentives more in line with efficient market incentives.

Concerns about the Bush Proposal

The biggest concern about the privatization plan parallels a problem with the Swedish reform: It would not add to net saving, and without that, there would be no addition to US capital formation.[22] In effect, the size of the economic pie would be unchanged by this program. So if, as is claimed,

---

21. The life expectancy of someone conditional on their having applied for an annuity is greater than the life expectancy of someone conditional on their not applying, controlling for other observable characteristics of the individual.

22. In the long run, it is not entirely correct that the plan would add no net saving. Once the net present value of government dissaving (borrowing to finance the transition) equaled the net present value in the stock of private savings, then any incremental growth in private savings after that could add to national savings (assuming positive economic growth).

participants in the plan would be better off than under the current Social Security system, the improvement in their future income would come at the expense of other Americans, in higher taxes to service the government debt incurred to finance the transition.

The second concern is the progressive indexing proposal. Although the impact on current retirees would be zero, and very small for those retiring in the near future, the impact over the long run would be profound. The progressive indexing would eventually convert the traditional Social Security benefit structure from a universal retirement program to an antipoverty program for the elderly. It is a matter of judgment whether that is a good or bad idea. Those who believe that a universal retirement program is a good feature are against this move; those who think that a government retirement program should provide a minimum benefit to avoid elderly poverty will consider this a good move.

One of the advantages of the plan may also be a disadvantage, namely the closer linking of benefit receipts to contributions. Low-wage workers who contribute only small amounts to the pension program would receive only small annuity payments after retiring. Unless there is an adequate separate antipoverty program for the elderly, any shift to individual accounts will increase poverty.

To address this concern, the administration plan suggests 120 percent of the poverty level as the minimum benefit level. But over time, many low-wage workers would find that the amount they were to receive from the revised Social Security program was lower than this minimum benefit, so that any additional contributions to Social Security, and indeed any additional taxes they would pay by participating in the labor force, would not add to their retirement income. Such workers would have a strong incentive to avoid additional contributions or taxes by retiring early or by working in the informal economy for cash and not reporting this income. This problem echoes concerns in Chile, where a high fraction of the workforce does not participate in the retirement plan, particularly once they have qualified for the minimum benefit. Working in the informal sector is more common and probably easier in Chile than in the United States, but plenty of Americans work in jobs where part or all of their income is in cash (or tips) and unrecorded—in babysitting, gardening, hair salons, and restaurants, for example. The presence of millions of unrecorded immigrants in the US labor market indicates the potential for working and avoiding regulatory requirements.

A core of supporters of US Social Security strongly opposes reforms that they believe will convert the program into a welfare plan for the elderly. They view the program as a great success of the New Deal and fear that its transformation to a welfare program will eventually undermine it because Americans do not like welfare programs. Keeping a universal retirement plan is a priority for this group, which considers the progressive indexing proposal combined with privatized individual accounts a first step toward dismantling the traditional Social Security retirement program.

It is hard to make a clear judgment on this view because it involves political factors and a view about the sustainability of a Social Security if it has a more progressive system of support for the elderly. However, unless the political climate changes drastically, there will have to be some benefit cuts, as it seems unlikely that the Social Security funding shortfall will be solved purely through higher taxes. Given the choice, it would be better to cut benefits for high-income than for low-income retirees. Any resulting flattening of the benefit schedule will make the program more progressive and thus more like a welfare program, it is true, but we do not believe it is inevitable that this would automatically lead to the program's disappearance. Other countries—New Zealand, for example—have very flat (i.e., highly progressive) benefit schedules and have maintained their programs intact. Indeed, the cross-country evidence on progressivity of pension systems (chapter 3) suggests that a number of OECD countries have maintained significantly more progressive government pension systems than US Social Security without any discernible loss of broad political support. Although Americans do not like welfare, they also do not like pushing the elderly into poverty. And it is easier to make the case for supporting elderly retirees than for supporting single mothers (the main recipients of the traditional welfare system).

Conclusions

Based on the experience of other countries, it is very hard to see that notional individual accounts or NDCs have any decisive advantage over the current US Social Security system. They do not increase national saving or provide a solution to the budget shortfall. Their big advantage is that they (might) have microeconomic effects on human behavior via their direct link between work history and benefits received, providing greater encouragement for employment—thus avoiding the disincentive to work that public pensions otherwise create. But this is not any great advantage for the US system, which already provides a benefit adjustment that makes any retirement age between 62 and 70 more or less actuarially neutral. If the United States wanted to link retirement benefits more closely to work history, it could do so through reforms to the current system—by making benefit levels depend on all years of employment, for example, or by reducing spousal benefits.

An NDC plan may have been a good selection for countries that are in transition, have seen the impact of over 50 years of communism, and wish to move aggressively to develop greater individual incentives; in Latvia, for example, the plan was useful in the transition to a fully funded individual accounts system. And it may have been a good selection for countries such as Sweden that have had a long tradition of a welfare state that weakened work incentives. But the United States does not fall into either category.

It is worth noting, also, that Sweden does not really have an individual account system for low-income workers, whose labor force participation is most likely to be affected. There are such strong subsidies for low-income retirees in the Swedish system that their standard of living is only marginally affected by their work history and retirement age. This balancing act for low-wage workers highlights the tradeoff in public pensions. The virtue of linking work history to pension benefits is also the vice of generating elderly poverty or of perpetuating an unequal wage distribution in an unequal retirement income. Sweden has a hybrid system, and the transition economies will likely gradually move to a hybrid system also. The US Social Security system is already there.

The Bush administration proposal for individual accounts, while different in structure from an NDC system, had nearly identical macroeconomic implications in that it would generate no net change in national saving in the short run. Unlike an NDC system, the proposed system would use funded individual accounts, and the costs of transition to the new system would be entirely financed through borrowing. The increase in private saving in individual accounts would be entirely offset for many years by the "dissaving" to finance the cuts from contributions to the Social Security fund. The Bush proposal, drawing on the report of the Moynihan-Parsons commission, had strengths. It recognized many of the problems that had surfaced with financial or nonfinancial accounts in other countries. It called for the pooling of contributions for allocation to private fund managers. It limited the choices of participants so that they would not make risky investments and pushed people to more conservative portfolios as they neared retirement. It would have given new impetus to the annuity market. And it would have made it possible to build on those strengths with a system of individual accounts in addition to the existing Social Security system.

References

Agell, Jonas, Peter Englund, and Jan Södersten. 1999. Tax Reform of the Century—The Swedish Experiment. In *Tax Policy in the Real World*, ed. Joel Slemrod. Cambridge: Cambridge University Press.

Beltrametti, L. 1996. Il Debito Pensionistico in Italia. *Il Mulino*. Bologna, Italy.

CBO (Congressional Budget Office). 2004. *Long-Term Analysis of Plan 2 of the President's Commission to Strengthen Social Security*. Analysis requested by the Honorable Larry E. Craig, Chairman, Special Committee on Aging, United States Senate, Washington, July 21.

Council of Economic Advisers. 2006. *Economic Report of the President*. Washington.

Deutsche Welle. 2003. *German Parliament Freezes Pensions* (June 13). Bonn, Germany.

Franco, Daniele, and Nicola Sartor. 2006. NDCs in Italy: Unsatisfactory Present, Uncertain Future. In *Pension Reform: Issues and Prospects for Nonfinancial Defined Contribution (NDC) Schemes*, ed. Robert Holtzmann and Edward Palmer. Washington: World Bank.

Hassett, Kevin A., and Maya MacGuineas. 2005. Promises, Promises. *National Review Online.* Available at www.nationalreview.com (accessed on August 30, 2008).

Könberg, Bo, Edward Palmer, and Annika Sundén. 2005. The NDC Reform in Sweden: The 1994 Legislation to the Present. In *Pension Reform: Issues and Prospects for Nonfinancial Defined Contribution (NDC) Schemes,* ed. Robert Holtzmann and Edward Palmer. Washington: World Bank.

Orszag, Peter, and Joseph E. Stiglitz. 2001. Rethinking Pension Reform: 10 Myths about Social Security Systems. In *New Ideas About Old Age Security,* ed. R. Holman and J. Stiglitz. Washington: World Bank.

Palmer, Edward, Sandra Stabina, Ingemar Svensson, and Inta Vanovska. 2006. NDC Strategy in Latvia: Implementation and Prospects for the Future. In *Pension Reform: Issues and Prospects for Nonfinancial Defined Contribution (NDC) Schemes,* ed. Robert Holtzmann and Edward Palmer. Washington: World Bank.

President's Commission to Strengthen Social Security. 2001. *Strengthening Social Security and Creating Personal Wealth for All Americans* (December 21). Washington.

Romig, Kathleen. 2007. *Social Security: What Would Happen if the Trust Fund Ran Out?* Congressional Research Service Report for Congress (June 14). Washington: Congressional Research Service.

Scherman, Karl Gustaf. 1999. *The Swedish Pension Reform.* Issues in Social Protection: Discussion Paper. Geneva: Social Security Department, International Labor Office.

SSA (Social Security Administration). 2007. The 2007 *Annual Report of the Board of Trustees of the Federal Old-Age and Survivors Insurance and Federal Disability Insurance Trust Funds.* Washington. Available at www.ssa.gov (accessed on August 30, 2008).

Sundén, Annika. 2004. How Do Individual Accounts Work in the Swedish Pension System? Paper presented at Annual Conference of Retirement Research Consortium on the Future of Social Security, Washington, August 12–13.

Turner, John. 2005. *Private Accounts in Sweden.* Research Report (March). Washington: American Association of Retired Persons.

White House. 2005. *Strengthening Social Security for the 21st Century* (February). Washington. Available at www.whitehouse.gov.

7

Challenges to Corporate Pension Provision

We think that all industry, in the absence of adequate government programs, owes an obligation to workers to provide for maintenance of the human body in the form of medical and similar benefits and full depreciation in the form of old-age retirement—in the same way as it does now for plant and machinery.

—Steel Industry Board (1949)[1]

In many OECD countries, private-sector social spending and pension provision has for decades constituted a crucial element of the social safety net. Therefore, any comprehensive analysis of pension systems must include a discussion of the particular challenges facing this sector.[2] In this chapter we describe the extent and status of corporate pensions in selected OECD countries, focusing on the situation in the United States, where, according to some commentators (e.g., Morris 2006), corporate pension provision is in terminal decline and many pension-sponsoring companies are unable to compete in global markets under the burden of "legacy" pension obligations.

---

1. Cited in McGill et al. (2005, 16).

2. This section follows the social spending classification from Adema and Ladaique (2005, 10) and where applicable includes pension benefits from mandatory employer contributions, as well as tax-benefited voluntary employer-provided pension benefits, i.e., both occupational pensions and individual retirement accounts (both defined benefit and defined contribution). We do not include pension benefits from insurance plans bought at market prices by individuals according to their own preferences. We use the terms "employer-based pensions" and "corporate pensions" interchangeably.

We argue differently. First, the "golden age of US corporate pension provision" is largely a myth, and the decline in corporate pension provision is less pronounced than alleged and affects a relatively small set of hitherto quite privileged American workers. We show that corporate pensions have always disproportionally benefited the highest-income groups in America and that the scope of employer-based schemes has, in fact, been largely stable as, in the rapidly growing workforce, millions have gotten access for the first time in the last decade. Furthermore, there has been a move away from defined benefit to defined contribution and hybrid plans among employers. This is the key trend in US corporate pension provision.

We further argue that unlike the scenario that has played out in several high-profile pension plan collapses in the US steel and airline industries,[3] the US trend away from defined benefit plan provision has occurred without any direct losses for workers and with full financing of vested pension benefits. Through the Pension Benefit Guaranty Corporation (PBGC), 98 percent of all terminated defined benefit plans have caused no direct economic losses for American workers. However, we will show that most corporate defined benefit pensions in America are probably far less generous than many believe, while as of 2006 the financial health of US corporate pension funds had improved dramatically with a return to a broad-based full funding.

We find that any improved financial situation for corporate pension plans will have no impact on the changes in plan type. Rather than resulting from short-term financial stress, the shift from defined benefit plan provision among employers in the United States and other major industrialized nations is rooted in long-term trends related to administrative costs, longevity, accounting changes, and increased risk of earnings volatility.

Last, we show that the stress on corporate finances from pensions is widespread among companies in major industrialized nations and that retirement promises, therefore, do not adversely affect the relative global competitiveness of US businesses (health care costs are a different story).

"Good Old Days" Revisited—How Extensive Was the US Corporate Welfare State?

The first US corporate pension plan was introduced as early as 1875 in the railway sector by American Express (Hewitt and Associates 2005) and in

---

3. In the case of established US airline companies, which are protected from foreign competition by US law, the issue was not only foreign competition but also new low-cost carriers, such as Southwest Airlines, that emerged after deregulation of the domestic US airline industry in the late 1970s, as well as generally bloated cost structures.

1882 by the Alfred Dodge Company in manufacturing.[4] By 1929 approximately 400 corporate pension plans existed in sectors like railways, utilities, iron and steel, and oil,[5] although coverage did not rise above approximately 5 percent of the private workforce until the introduction of Social Security in 1935.[6] Figure 7.1, based on several historical sources, shows that the coverage rate of employer-based pensions (of all types) hovered at or below 5 percent of the private workforce from the beginning of the 20th century to the late 1930s.

Moreover, until the 1930s US corporate pension provision was often the sole purview of the so-called American welfare capitalists, who provided limited pension benefits to their workforces, frequently as an expression of discretionary "corporate benevolence" (Hacker 2002, Clark et al. 2003). Indeed, one of the most generous plans of the time, that of the General Electric Company, offered after 20 years of employment just 1.5 percent of the average pay over the last 10 years of service.[7]

Larger US companies early on used their pension plans to cull older workers from their payrolls and to attract high-skilled, white-collar personnel. The former was spearheaded by US railway companies, which experienced increasing risks of serious accidents (with correspondingly large monetary and reputational costs) among their elderly workers: The companies learned that "pensioning off" older workers was more profitable than reassigning them to less perilous positions (e.g., in maintenance, administration, or night supervision), where they were dubbed "hidden pensioners." Businesses' elimination of these older workers was codified in the "efficiency cycle of the typical employee,"

---

4. The Alfred Dodge Company built pianos and organs, and its corporate pension plan was decidedly modest in scope: 1 percent of employees' wages were withheld and placed in a separate pension fund to which the company added 6 percent interest every year. In other words, even when allowing for compounding, the company's direct expenditures were only slightly above .06 percent of wages every year. This meant that for employees to have any meaningful benefit in retirement from this plan, they would need to spend a very long time employed at the company. Regrettably, the company went bankrupt just a few years after the plan's initiation. See Social Security Administration (SSA), History of Social Security, available at www.ssa.gov.

5. Sass (1997, 54), cited in Hacker (2002). McGill and colleagues, citing Latimer (1933), state that around 1900 there were about a dozen private pension plans in the United States, rising to 60 by 1910, 270 by 1920, and 420 by 1930. Clark and colleagues (2003) cite Conyngton (1926) for similar numbers—117 by 1916 and approximately 200 in 1926.

6. At the time of federal Social Security introduction, coverage by state government retirement plans was even lower, with just 3 percent of the elderly (although this is, of course, a larger group than private employees) receiving benefits. See SSA, History of Social Security, available at www.ssa.gov.

7. Meaning, under usual circumstances of rising salaries with tenure, a pension of less than 30 percent of a worker's final pay (Clark et al. 2003, 6ff).

Figure 7.1   Coverage of US corporate pensions, 1905–95

percent share of civilian labor force

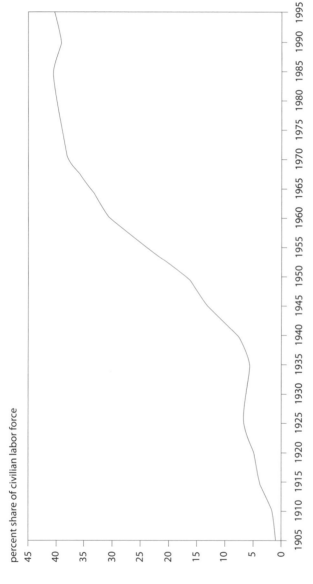

Note: Other historical sources indicate early levels of US corporate pension coverage slightly above the reproduced data here from Hacker (2002). Beller and Lawrence (1992) and unpublished Bureau of Labor Statistics data for 1940–2005 indicate that private pension plan participation rates were between 15 and 20 percent of private-sector workers in 1940–45, rising to about 50 percent in 1970, where they remained roughly stable until 2005. Schieber and George (1981, table III-1) show that worker participation in private pensions among "Wage and Salary Workers in Private, Non-Agricultural Establishments" rose from 25 percent in 1950 to about 45 percent in 1970 and 47.6 percent in 1979. The small differences in levels are probably due to different definitions of the employee groups included in the data. As all data show very much the same general trend—rapid growth from a low level during the period from 1945 to 1970, followed by stagnation until the present—these minor differences in data levels do not materially affect the conclusions of this chapter.

Source: Hacker (2002, figure 2.1).

according to which the value of an employee's services usually surpassed the employee's compensation in the years before age 50 and fell below compensation levels thereafter.[8] This management theory thus concluded that companies should shed their workers around the time they turn 50.[9] This blatantly age-discriminating practice was outlawed in 1967,[10] but job generation for and retention of an elderly workforce remains crucial for any country's solution to pension-related policy challenges.

As shown in figure 7.1, the rapid growth years (1940–70) of corporate pensions in America saw coverage levels rise from the single digits to about 40 percent of the private workforce, which is where they remain. Corporate pensions thus emerged as a supplement to the already existing and publicly provided Social Security benefits introduced in 1935. Unlike supplementary corporate pensions, US corporate health care provision thus always has occurred as a direct substitute/alternative to public health care provision rather than as a supplement. The situation concerning corporate health care provision in America was and remains starkly different, as there is no publicly provided and administered program in the health care sector available to the average US worker.[11]

This historical chronology of corporate pension provision shows that corporate pensions developed almost exclusively in the shadow of the incentives provided by the Social Security program, not least of all thanks to their tax-benefited status enjoyed since the mid-1920s, when the US Treasury implemented three crucial taxation policies that still guide corporate pension provision (see box 7.1): deferred taxation of pension trusts until their payment to retired workers (1926), tax exemption of investment gains and interest from pension trusts (1921 and 1926),

---

8. Such an outcome would, of course, be accentuated by a pay scale based predominantly on seniority. This is precisely the issue today in many Japanese companies, where the mandatory retirement age is 60, mostly as a way to get rid of expensive older staff. See chapter 4 for details.

9. See McGill et al. (2005) and Wyatt et al. (1945) for details on "efficiency cycle theory." See also the Watson Wyatt website, www.watsonwyatt.com.

10. The first passage of the Age Discrimination in Employment Act of 1967. Similar laws are now in place in most of the OECD.

11. Access to the federal Medicare program, set up in 1965, begins only at age 65, and coverage under Medicaid, also initiated in 1965, is means-tested and available only to the poorest Americans. Some states (e.g., Massachusetts in 2006) initiated reforms to make health insurance available and mandatory for all residents. See details of the Massachusetts health care reform, which explicitly aims to subsidize and expand corporate health care provision, at the Henry J. Kaiser Family Foundation website, www.kff.org/uninsured. Hawaii is the only state since 1974 to require that private-sector employers provide health insurance for their employees.

Box 7.1 Tax treatment of corporate and personal pension plans in the OECD

Private pension provision has received preferential tax treatment in most OECD countries to provide incentives both for employers to establish such benefits and for employees to participate in them. However, these are not the only objectives of such tax treatment, which differs widely among OECD countries.

Since 1928 American employers have been able to deduct their contributions to employees' retirement plans as a business expense (subject to certain eligibility conditions in the tax code). Today, tax-benefited status for company pension plans requires adherence to a number of criteria.[1] One important requirement is that companies adequately fund their defined benefit pension plans, although at the same time regulation prevents companies from using their pension plans purely for tax-minimization purposes.

US pension funding rules changed significantly with the 2006 Pension Protection Act (PPA), which called for tightening of the funding requirements for underfunded US corporate pension plans. Among many things (the complete bill is 393 pages long![2]), the PPA

- gradually raises defined benefit plan funding targets from 90 percent to 100 percent of liabilities;
- reduces the period over which the fair value of plan assets/interest rates can be smoothed from five/four to two years (with the shorter period of averaging plan values, plan sponsors will see more volatility in the value of their plans and will, therefore, be likely to maintain a larger cushion in their funding);
- narrows the corridor within which asset fair value may fluctuate from 80–120 percent to 90–110 percent of market value;
- requires any shortfall in funding to be amortized over seven years (except for US airline companies, which have 17 years);
- establishes requirements for at-risk (less than 80 percent funded) plans to return to full funding[3]; and
- restricts a company's ability to set aside assets to fund deferred compensation for the top five executive officers if the company's pension plan is deemed at risk.[4]

Less well known, perhaps, the PPA also liberalizes the IRS limits on the size of annual corporate tax deductions, which may now be for up to 150 percent of a plan's unfunded liability (this is up from 100 percent, which precluded tax-benefited status for plan overfunding). This measure is to encourage companies to establish a tax-benefited funding cushion for their pension plans and thus limit the risk of a repeat of the situation that emerged after 2001, when many companies, due to declining interest rates and falling stock markets, suddenly found their pension plans massively underfunded, after having been discouraged from overfunding their pension plans thanks to rising stock markets and limits on the tax deductibility of contributions to overfunded plans. The PPA is thus clearly an attempt to balance the competing social goals of the tax treatment of corporate pensions. With the dramatic decline in asset prices in the fall of 2008, it seems clear that the new plan funding provisions included in the PPA, especially the additional requirements placed on "at-risk plans" with less than 80 percent funding levels, will for the first time be tested in a US economic downturn. We hope that the PPA will stand this test of the "political congressional marketplace" better than previous incarnations of US corporate pension plan regulations.

To understand preferential tax treatments aimed at encouraging individuals to participate in private corporate pension plans, it is useful to distinguish among three transactional points[5]:

1. when a contribution is made to a pension saving instrument[6];
2. when investment income and capital gains accrue to the saving vehicle; and
3. when funds are withdrawn.

Preferential individual pension participation refers to a tax treatment of contributions that deviate from the benchmark of a comprehensive income tax regime, which would treat all sources of income equally. Such a benchmark would entail that pension savings be made from taxed earnings and that accrued investment income and capital gains also be subject to income taxation, but that upon withdrawal, assets be exempted from taxation. This is the taxed-taxed-exempt (TTE) treatment of individual pension savings. There are also several alternatives to the TTE benchmark. Legislators may exempt from taxation the portion of individual income that is saved as future pension income (also known as the expenditure tax regime). In this approach both the funds contributed and the reinvested accrued income are tax exempt until the time of withdrawal. In progressive tax systems, individual marginal income tax rates at the time of withdrawal in retirement are substantially lower than at the time of contribution; this tax deferral, or exempt-exempt-taxed (EET) system, usually entails substantial tax savings for the individual. Alternatively, taxes can be prepaid at the time of contribution in a taxed-exempt-exempt (TEE) system.

(box continues on next page)

Box 7.1 Tax treatment of corporate and personal pension plans in the OECD (continued)

Table 7B1.1 shows the differences in tax treatment of individuals' private pension participation in 2003 in the OECD member states. Most (18) of the OECD countries in 2003 applied a tax treatment roughly similar to the US EET treatment of individual contributions, accrued income, and benefits, and taxed benefits only at the time of payment. Half of these 18 countries even did so at a tax-benefited rate rather than treating pension benefits as regular income. Denmark, Italy, and Sweden applied an ETT treatment closer to the "benchmark comprehensive treatment" by also taxing accrued income, but only New Zealand actually applied a TTE treatment.[7] The remaining seven OECD countries applied TEE, TET, or TTT treatment. It is noteworthy that only Belgium had an annual "asset value tax" of 0.17 percent.[8] Such treatment is not dissimilar from a regular "wealth tax," and invariably, despite its seemingly low level, it is a major disincentive to saving for retirement.

Whether a country chooses to apply an EET or, like Australia,[9] a TTT treatment is not necessarily indicative of the magnitude of the tax subsidy. Any level of tax subsidy is, in theory, possible with any of the illustrated tax treatments.[10] By varying (or completely eliminating) the rates of taxation at any of the three transactional points, policymakers can achieve any net after-tax pension benefit desired for similar levels of contributions and pretax rates of investment return.

---

1. See McGill et al. (2005, chapter 5) for an exhaustive treatment of these criteria.

2. The PPA is available at the Department of Labor website at www.dol.gov.

3. This concerns single-employer plans, while for multiemployer plans, special funding rules for "endangered" and "critical" plans exist. For an overview of the provisions in the PPA, see Deloitte (2006).

4. If such funds are set aside in violation of these provisions, executives will be fully taxed on this income.

5. This follows the theoretical outline in Yoo and de Serres (2004).

6. These may be both defined benefit or defined contribution or any combination thereof. In most OECD countries, purely private benefits accruing from insurance plans bought at market prices according to individual preferences do not qualify for tax-benefited status.

7. In New Zealand, employer contributions on behalf of low-income employees were taxed at 21 percent (as of April 2004), while interest income from asset holdings (bank deposits and government bonds) are subject to a 19.5 percent resident withholding tax, but interest income is included in global income, and taxes paid are credited against total tax liability. Shareholders were taxed on dividend income but get an imputation tax credit so that double taxation is avoided (occurs when shareholders are taxed on distributed dividends paid from a company's after-tax profits (Yoo and de Serres 2004, 95). As noted in

and instant company deductibility of pension contributions as business expenses (1928).[12]

The combination of Social Security regulations and the tax status of US corporate pension expenditure after 1935 did much to ensure that these voluntary pension schemes were available primarily to higher-income employees. Social Security was from the beginning (1937–50) a compulsory contributory insurance-based retirement scheme that called for both employer and employee contributions of 1 percent[13] on the first $3,000 of income.[14] This wage contribution threshold meant that people making $3,000 or less got the highest replacement rates, while higher-earning people received a disproportionally lower pension benefit relative to their wage income. However, the higher-earning workers are those whom companies have a particular interest in attracting and retaining

---

12. For further details on the introduction of preferential tax treatment in America, see Hubbard (1993) and McGill et al. (2005, chapters 4–9). It is indicative of the attraction of these types of incentives that the first tax code–based encouragement to corporate pension provision—the elimination of taxation for corporate income contributed to employer-based stock bonuses or for profit-sharing plan purposes—was introduced as early as 1921, a mere eight years after the establishment of a federal income tax in 1913.

13. In 1950 the contributions were raised to 1.5 percent. It was 3.625 percent in 1966, when the Hospital Insurance (Medicare) tax was added, and the combined tax has been 7.65 percent since 1990. See the SSA website at www.ssa.gov/oact/progdata for historical levels of Social Security contributions.

14. The $3,000 contribution and benefit base was gradually raised after 1950 and in 2007 was $97,500. See the SSA website at www.ssa.gov/oact/cola for historical levels of Old-Age, Survivors, and Disability Insurance (OASDI) contribution and benefit bases.

Table 7B1.1 OECD tax treatment of individual private pensions, 2003

Category	Country	Tax treatment of individual mandatory and voluntary funded private managed pension schemes				
		Contributions[b]	Fund — Income	Fund — Asset value	Pension payments — Annuities	Pension payments — Lump sums
Exempt-exempt-partially taxed	France	Exempt	Exempt	Exempt	Taxed/PE	Taxed/PE
	Germany	Exempt	Exempt	Exempt	Taxed/PE	Taxed
	Ireland	Exempt	Exempt	Exempt	Taxed/PE	Taxed/PE
	Japan	Exempt	Exempt	Exempt	Taxed/PE	Taxed/PE
	Korea	Exempt	Exempt	Exempt	Taxed/PE	Taxed/PE
	Mexico	Exempt/S	Exempt	Exempt	Taxed/PE	Taxed/PE
	Slovakia	Exempt	Exempt	Exempt	Taxed	15 percent
	Spain	Exempt	Exempt	Exempt	Taxed	Taxed/PE
	Turkey	Exempt	Exempt	Exempt	Exempt	5 percent/PE
	United Kingdom	Exempt	Exempt	Exempt	Taxed	Taxed/PE
Exempt-exempt-taxed	Canada	Exempt	Exempt	Exempt	Taxed	Taxed
	Finland	Exempt	Exempt	Exempt	Taxed	Taxed
	Greece	Exempt	Exempt	Exempt	Taxed	Taxed
	Iceland	Exempt	Exempt	Exempt	Taxed	Taxed
	Netherlands	Exempt	Exempt	Exempt	Taxed	Not allowed
	Norway	Exempt	Exempt	Exempt	Taxed	Taxed
	Poland	Exempt	Exempt	Exempt	Taxed	Taxed
	Switzerland	Exempt	Exempt	Exempt	Taxed	Taxed
	United States	Exempt	Exempt	Exempt	Taxed	Taxed
Taxed-exempt-exempt	Hungary	Taxed	Exempt	Exempt	Exempt	Exempt
Exempt-taxed-taxed	Denmark	Exempt	15 percent	Exempt	Taxed	40 percent
	Italy	Exempt	12.5 percent	Exempt	Taxed/PE	Taxed/PE
	Sweden	Exempt	15 percent	Exempt	Taxed	Taxed
Taxed-exempt-taxed	Austria[a]	Taxed/PE	Exempt	Exempt	Taxed/PE	Taxed/PE
	Czech Republic	Taxed/PE/S	Exempt	Exempt	15 percent/PE	15 percent/PE
	Luxembourg	Exempt	Exempt	Exempt	Taxed	Taxed/PE
	Belgium[a]	Taxed/PC	Exempt	0.17 percent	Taxed/PC	10 percent
	Portugal[a]	Taxed/PC	Exempt	Exempt	20 percent/PE	Taxed/PE
Taxed-taxed-exempt	New Zealand[d]	Taxed	33 percent	Exempt	Exempt	Exempt
Taxed-taxed-taxed	Australia	Taxed	7.1 percent[c]	Exempt	Taxed/PC	PE/16.5 percent

PC = partial tax credit; PE = partial exemption or deduction from taxation; S = state subsidy

a. Pension taxation differs between employers' and employees' contributions. Only employees' portion is partially taxed.
b. Tax-deductible contributions are subject to certain limits in most countries.
c. The effective tax rate assuming a portfolio with 60 percent interest-bearing assets and 40 percent equities.
d. As discussed in chapter 4, New Zealand's tax treatment of pension contributions changed dramatically in 2006 and 2007.

Source: Yoo and de Serres (2004).

with pension benefit incentives. Because higher-income groups are more likely to demand additional pension coverage from Social Security, cost-conscious companies, generally seeking to limit their pension expenses, decided that their voluntary pensions should concentrate on these personnel. This preference was espoused by US business leaders, as is evident in the following 1942 congressional testimony from a representative of the 37,500-employee National Dairy Products Corporation:

> [t]he first thing that came to our attention was that only 1,200 of our total number of employees received over $3,000. Among those 1,200 were practically every employee that had a real influence on how the company went ahead, how it achieved success over its competitors. . . . So we decided . . . we will have nothing paid into the [voluntary corporate pension] plan by either employer or employee on salaries below $3,000, and we will let the social-security-tax program take care of the salaries under $3,000. (Gordon 1942; also cited in Hacker 2002, 119)

The establishment of Social Security thus likely unintentionally spurred the creation of voluntary supplementary corporate pensions, which not only provided higher-income workers with additional retirement income but also enabled businesses to target their pensions to high-value staff, as Social Security addressed the social considerations of poverty alleviation for the broader workforce.

Concerns about this practice led Congress to deny in the 1942 Revenue Act tax-benefited status for corporate pension plans that discriminated in favor of "officers, shareholders, supervisory, or highly compensated employees";[15] the measure disallowed both higher benefit accrual rates and higher employer contributions for these groups. But because corporate pensions were supplementary to Social Security, the new regulation allowed decisions regarding whether pension plans be granted tax-benefited status or not to be based on the total level of employer-sponsored retirement benefits, that is, both employer-based pensions and the share of Social Security benefits financed by the employer.[16] A corporate pension plan would therefore be eligible for tax-benefited status if (1) "it excludes employees the whole of whose remuneration consists of taxable wages under Social Security [$3,000]" and/or (2) "the contributions or benefits based on remuneration excluded from the Social Security tax base [$3,000] differ from contributions or benefits with this base."[17] In other words, it would be perfectly legal for US companies to discriminate against low-wage workers in their pension plans if they did so against all recipients of Social Security (i.e., people earning $3,000 or less).

---

15. Cited in Schultz and Leavitt (1983, 21); this section draws on the detailed description of US pension integration in their chapter 1.

16. See also sources cited in footnote 12.

17. 1942 Revenue Act, cited in Schultz and Leavitt (1983, 21).

Pension Plan Integration

As a follow-up to the 1942 Revenue Act, the Internal Revenue Service (IRS) in 1943 issued a ruling (Mimeograph 5539[18]) specifying the acceptable level of discrimination for tax-benefited status by laying down the rules for what became known as "pension plan integration" between Social Security benefits and private corporate pension plans. The ruling stated that (1) employees could have up to 150 percent (!) of the company's contributions to the Social Security Trust Fund subtracted, or offset, from their calculated normal private corporate retirement benefit; and (2) corporate plans could provide pension benefits equaling up to 25 percent of the share of an employee's wages in excess of the Social Security tax base of $3,000.

Few data exist on the share of US corporate pension plans that were integrated in the early decades, but given the savings to companies that engaged in these practices, it is not surprising that data from the early 1970s indicate that by then up to two-thirds of US corporate pension plans were integrated.[19] Moreover, these data likely underestimate the level of integration in earlier periods, as beginning in 1943 Congress and the IRS only gradually curtailed the economic benefits of pension integration by scaling back the permissible levels of regressive discrimination inherent in this type of pension integration. For instance, the permissible limit for offsets of corporate Social Security contributions was gradually lowered to less than 100 percent by 1969, and in 1971 the practice of allowing the subtraction of contributions for spouse, dependent, disability, or health insurance from an employee's corporate pension benefit, which lay behind the earlier 100+ percent offsets, was outlawed.[20]

The actual impact of pension integration on retirement benefit levels can be estimated only with the data for the actual level to which companies chose to integrate their plans with Social Security. A reasonable assumption is that profit-oriented companies would integrate their corporate pension plans with Social Security to the greatest extent possible, while remaining eligible for tax-exempt status, in order to reap the greatest

---

18. Ibid.

19. Data from Schultz and Leavitt (1983, table I-8). The authors cite eight studies from 1974–82 showing a weak correlation between pension plan integration and plan size (number of participants). However, at the time very few state and local government pension plans were integrated with Social Security.

20. IRS Revenue Ruling 71-446, described in Schultz and Leavitt (1983). The rules for pension integration were comprehensively revamped with the 1986 tax reform and the possibilities for integration further curbed. See Employee Benefit Research Institute (EBRI) Pension Fundamentals, chapter 13, available at www.ebri.org, for an overview of their present status.

cost savings. Richard Schreitmueller (1979) reports that early US corporate pension plans did just this and aggressively sought to "eliminate all duplication" with Social Security.[21] However, companies that sought too aggressively to cut costs through pension plan integration might do so at the expense of human resource incentives and motivational aspects. Companies taking "intermediate positions" in their level of pension integration—for instance, offsetting only 75 percent of an employee's Social Security benefits from the corporate-sponsored plan, when it would be legal to offset 150 percent—may therefore be quite numerous. Regrettably, a dearth of data on the most popular integration formulas prevents a detailed investigation of the subject (Schreitmueller 1979).

Major reform of the US tax system in 1986 did much to eliminate the economic benefits to corporations of pension integration. The Bureau of Labor Statistics (BLS 2007, table 45) presents data from the National Compensation Survey suggesting that pension integration with Social Security benefits today is relatively limited—only 9 percent of US workers with defined benefit coverage in 2005 had an offset integration with their Social Security benefits, although another 20 percent of defined benefit recipients were subject to other types of pension integration.[22]

Pension integration (i.e., the integration of both private corporate pension benefits and Social Security pension) can be described as an attempt to achieve a reasonable correlation between workers' total pension income (Social Security and private corporate pension) and their preretirement earnings and thus achieve the same pre and postretirement standard of living, regardless of the level of income. A laudable goal perhaps, but as described above, its pursuit allowed tax-benefited US corporate pension plans to offset the progressivity of Social Security benefits and discriminate in favor of high-income employees.[23]

---

21. Schreitmueller (1979). As described in Schultz and Leavitt (1983, 31), "eliminating duplication" must be inferred to mean that all possible Social Security benefits are offset from corporate pension benefits.

22. Pension integration between Social Security and private pension plans is a complex matter and can occur through several plan types, depending on the design of the private plan. Defined benefit plans can be integrated using so-called offset, excess, or step-rate excess formulas. Offset plans reduce employees' private pension benefits by a certain percentage of their Social Security benefits. Excess plans exclude a certain portion of employees' earnings below the integration level from the pension benefit or contribution calculation; the maximum acceptable to IRS integration level is the Social Security tax base. Step-wise excess plans work in a similar manner. Defined contribution plans (guaranteeing the contribution rather than the benefit level) may be integrated using excess and step-wise excess integration plans, both of which may also use a so-called integration percentage, under which the corporate pension plans pay the integration percentage in additional benefits for wages above the integration level. For a detailed treatment of pension integration and Social Security, see Schultz and Leavitt (1983, 1–34) and EBRI Pension Fundamentals, chapter 13, available at www.ebri.org.

23. See chapter 3 concerning the extent of Social Security progressiveness.

In all probability pension integration regulations led to the expansion of corporate pension provision beyond the extent that such plans would otherwise have been offered.[24] However, the extended coverage materialized only as a result of legal opportunities to skew corporate pension plans against lower-income groups. We emphasize that pension integration is evidence that corporate pension provision in the United States was likely never intended for the average worker.

Role of Unions in Expanding Corporate Pension Coverage

Several World War II–related issues provided additional incentives for targeted corporate pension provision. First, rising personal federal income tax levels to finance the war effort meant that tax-exempt remuneration in the form of pension benefits became more valuable to many workers, and disproportionally so for those in the highest tax brackets.[25] Second, US businesses also, with the 1942 Excess Profits Tax of 90 percent on affected companies, faced significantly higher tax rates; with the expectation that this tax was temporary and would be annulled once peace arrived, they established pension trusts as temporary tax shelters. Third, the 1942 wage freeze, which exempted pensions and other fringe benefits, further encouraged employers to offer voluntary private corporate pension benefits in their efforts to attract scarce workers.

Thus the early incentives to provide voluntary company pensions in America favored high-income groups, and this bias did not change after World War II as higher income tax levels persisted. However, supplementary voluntary corporate pensions in America became one of several frontlines in the collective bargaining struggle between workers, represented by labor unions, and US businesses. Two main factors drove this development. First, American unions reached the peak of their power in the years immediately after World War II, with as much as 35 percent of

---

24. Hacker (2002, 137ff) states that the opportunities to integrate private pensions with Social Security were crucially decisive in persuading American businesses to provide corporate pension plans.

25. Tax rates for the bottom tax bracket rose from an already historical high (excluding a 6 percent World War I special tax in 1918) of 4.4 percent in 1940 to 23 percent in 1944–45, while the threshold for payment of this tax was halved from $4,000 to $2,000. With a progressive taxation system, this lowering of the tax brackets in itself indicates a rise in the level of taxation, as income between $2,000 and $4,000 was taxed at a higher rate than the bottom tax bracket. Similarly, the top tax bracket tax level was raised from 81.1 percent to a maximum rate in 1944–45 of 90 percent, while the top income tax bracket threshold was slashed from $5 million to $200,000. As a result, even with the US economy strongly stimulated by the wartime effort, federal taxes as a share of GDP grew from 7.6 percent in 1941 to 20.4 percent in 1945 (US Treasury, www.ustreas.gov; Joint Committee on Taxation 2001).

the workforce enrolled by 1945–46.[26] Second, the same relatively high inflation period (1940–50), when Social Security benefits were fixed at $22.54 per month, saw the real value of these benefits decline dramatically,[27] indicating that Americans retiring in the late 1940s with only their Social Security benefits would face considerable economic hardship. (Only in 1950 did Congress enact the first—and at 77 percent, considerable—upward inflation adjustment of Social Security benefits.[28])

American unions sought to address this widespread and urgent social problem among their membership by pursuing additional retirement benefits for their members immediately after World War II. This urgency, combined with the fact that unions, which were heavily concentrated in sectors like mining, manufacturing, and transportation,[29] had a strong hand in negotiating with individual US businesses, explains union strategy at the time. Unions saw that they could get faster and better results for their members by extracting additional retirement benefits from corporate employers rather than pushing for and having to wait for new federal initiatives to expand the generosity of Social Security coverage. And US employers were acquiescent negotiators, as at the time they were at the peak of their global dominance—in 1950 the United States accounted for the largest share of world GDP in its history, larger than any other country or region.[30]

This period saw a significant expansion of corporate pension coverage from white- to blue-collar workers. But the expansion to union members limited coverage for nonunion workers, as the extent and generosity of pensions for the former were a direct result of their coercive power at the negotiating table; there was otherwise no real intention to expand the coverage of corporate pensions to the almost two-thirds of the private US

---

26. Union density reached 35 percent again in 1954 but has since declined every year to less than 15 percent of workers today. This means that US union membership is at levels last seen in the early 1930s. See Census Bureau—Historical Statistics of the United States, Colonial Times to 1970, available online at www.census.gov/population.

27. The consumer price index for all US urban consumers (CPI–U) rose from 14 to 24.1 (100 = 1982–84) from 1940 to 1950, a 72 percent increase (US Bureau of Labor Statistics).

28. Automatic cost of living allowances (COLAs) for Social Security were initiated only in 1975. Until then each individual rise in benefits had required an act of Congress (see SSA website at www.ssa.gov/history).

29. See Hacker (2002, 126ff) for the history of how private pension provision became the center of the bargaining drive for the United Mine Workers (UMW), United Auto Workers (UAW), and United Steel Workers (USW) in the late 1940s.

30. According to Maddison (2003, table 8b), the United States in 1950 accounted for more than one-quarter of world output in purchasing power parity terms and a far larger share in business and export-relevant market exchange rate terms. This dominant position even represented a decline from as much as 35 percent immediately after the end of World War II.

workforce who were not unionized. Indeed, in the words of Jacob Hacker (2002, 133), the access to corporate pensions that American unions negotiated for their members "undercut the common constituency for public social insurance and weakened labor support for more expansive government action. . . . Slowly but unmistakably, the spread of private plans undermined the notoriously weak solidarity of American workers and undercut support for the expansion or creation of public social programs."[31] And covered union workers might actually oppose broader coverage under government-sponsored pension benefits for fear that funding for them would require new taxes (Root 1982, Lowenstein 2008).

Furthermore, collectively bargained corporate pensions largely benefited white male workers, who dominated payrolls in large corporations and in the industries with heavily unionized workforces from the late 1940s through the 1960s. Although women's overall labor force participation rose dramatically during World War II and in 1948 was a nontrivial 32.7 percent (Bird 2006),[32] their share of unionized positions eligible for supplementary pension coverage was surely much lower.[33] The fact that most corporate pensions in this period were of the defined benefit type, which rewarded long-term employees,[34] further set back women, who, as discussed in previous chapters, were more likely to leave the workforce because of pregnancy, child rearing, and other family commitments.[35] In many ways, the assumption for corporate pensions in America was and is of a single-earner nuclear family, where the male breadwinner earns pension rights, which are shared with and sustain his wife in old age.[36] Exclusion from corporate pensions also affected most African-Americans and

---

31. A large literature has explored the absence of "class consciousness" among the American working class. See, for instance, Lipset and Marks (2000).

32. Women's labor force participation rose to 33.9 percent in 1950, 37.7 percent in 1960, and 43.3 percent in 1970 (Fullerton 1999).

33. We have found no empirical data to verify this but would argue—an intuitively valid claim—that very few women indeed were eligible for unionized supplementary pensions at the time.

34. See chapter 3 on public defined benefit pensions for details of how benefit formulas are typically crafted.

35. The introduction of PAYGO pension benefit schemes is most advantageous to the oldest workers, who will get the full benefits but pay contributions for a relatively limited time. Corporate defined benefit pensions were no exception and, therefore, disproportionally benefited the oldest workers with the longest tenure at the time of introduction. Among this group, due to the ongoing rise in female labor force participation, male overrepresentation was even larger than in the whole labor force itself, even in the 1940s.

36. The degree to which female divorcees shared their husband's corporate pensions is unclear, but presumably such pension benefits (together with other assets) would be split 50-50. See also PBGC on the Qualified Domestic Relations Order (www.pbgc.gov/docs) for how divorcees are treated by PBGC-administered plans.

other minority groups, who at the time (i.e., in pre–civil rights America) were overrepresented in seasonal, agricultural, and low-wage work, where corporate pensions were largely nonexistent.

In summary, then, the "golden age" of the US corporate-sponsored "welfare state" from the late 1940s to the 1970s, in terms of pension provision, is largely a myth. The decline of corporate defined benefit pension plans will affect primarily the "insider groups" (and their dependents) much more than the broader US workforce, the vast majority of whom will not lose what they never had. Indeed, one might argue that a gradual disappearance of US corporate defined benefit plans, financially painful as it will be for many workers, signals the demise of an aspect of the US labor market that has clear parallels to the insider-outsider problems that have haunted European labor markets, especially in France and Italy.[37]

Recent and Current Corporate Pension Provision

Decline in US Private Worker Participation Is Not as Great as Believed

Analysis of the recent and present state of US corporate pension provision is hindered by data scarcity.[38] Data for recent decades on corporate pension coverage, generosity, and funding are frequently from incongruent sources and inconsistently collected over time (as is evident in figure 7.2). A very large decline—from over 80 to 33 percent—in defined benefit plan participation rates among US private-sector workers is visible from 1980 to the present. However, over the same period the coverage rate of defined contribution plans rose from about 40 percent in the mid-1980s to 54 percent today, thus far outstripping present-day defined benefit coverage.[39]

---

37. See Lindbeck and Snower (1986) for a discussion of the insider-outsider problem.

38. This section focuses exclusively on data available for US active worker participation in retirement plans. These data are distinct from those for workers at businesses that offer a retirement plan. The share of the private US workforce at such businesses is roughly 10 percentage points higher than annual data for actual US worker plan participation. For instance, the most recent data from March 2006 indicate that 60 percent US private industry workers had access to a corporate pension plan but that only 51 percent participated (BLS National Compensation Survey data (available at www.bls.gov/ncs). This difference has been reasonably stable over recent decades, and Munnell and Perun (2006, figure 5) present data suggesting that it can largely be accounted for by rules pertaining to pension plan vesting (i.e., rules concerning eligibility requirements for retirement plan participation). Most nonparticipating workers do not do so because they do not meet age, service, working time, or job type requirements (Munnell and Perun 2006).

39. Meanwhile, by this data source, participation in any (defined benefit, defined contribution, or both) pension plan has declined from 90 percent to just two-thirds in the last two decades.

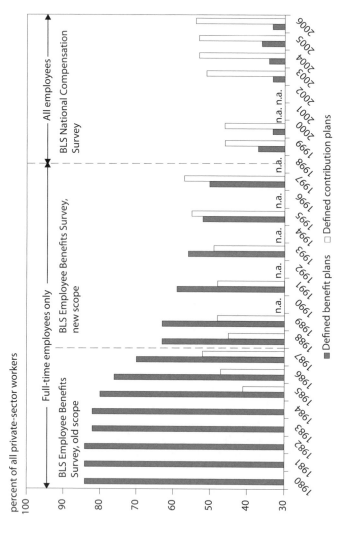

Figure 7.2   Participation of US private-sector workers in retirement plans, medium/large companies, 1980–2006

percent of all private-sector workers

n.a. = not available, as BLS surveys are not conducted annually

Sources: Employee Benefit Research Institute (EBRI) *Databook on Employee Benefits*, chapter 4; Bureau of Labor Statistics (BLS) National Compensation Survey, www.bls.gov/ncs/ebs.

Because a switch from a defined benefit to defined contribution pension plan entails the transfer of investment risk from the plan sponsor to the plan participant, there seems to have been a significant decline in the pension security of private American workers. However, a closer look at the BLS data in figure 7.2 may brighten this gloomy picture somewhat. The composite time-series BLS data shown in figure 7.2 come from three different surveys, each covering different scopes of the US labor market. The first segment of the BLS Employee Benefit Survey (EBS) from 1980 to 1988 included as few as 20 percent of US private-sector workers, concentrated among full-time employees in medium and large companies in the manufacturing sectors. In 1988 coverage expanded to 35 percent to include service sectors.[40] Only in 1999 did the BLS National Compensation Survey (NCS) include annual benefit data for the entire US private-sector workforce—at establishments of all sizes, in all sectors, and in all geographic locations. That year's survey thus represents the first comprehensive coverage of private US employer provision of benefits. As a result, we must turn to other sources for longer-term comprehensive data for US corporate pensions.

Figure 7.3 combines data from surveys of employers about their workers' pension plan participation from the 1981 Report of the President (pre-1980 data) reprinted in Schieber and George (1981), tabulations of early NCS trial data (Wiatrowski 2004), and NCS data for 1999–2006, covering all US private establishments (defined benefit and defined contribution plan data). Several trends are evident in figure 7.3. First, looking at the overall participation of US workers in any type of corporate pension plan, we see that coverage reached 45 to 50 percent in the late 1970s and has remained roughly stable at this level ever since. Second, there was a steep decline in the participation of US workers in defined benefit plans over the 1990s, from 35 to 20 percent, where it more or less stabilized from 2000 on. And third, during the same period defined contribution plan participation increased, from about 33 percent in 1989 to 43 percent in 2006. Thus, looking at the entire US private workforce, the data from employer-based surveys indicate that total participation in private plans has been roughly stable since 1980, but with a marked shift in enrollment from defined benefit to defined contribution plans in the 1990s.

Employer-based surveys are, however, only one of several sources of information about the participation of US private-sector workers in employer-sponsored pension plans. For example, rather than ask employers what plans they provide their employees, one might ask employees

---

40. This EBS survey was derived from the annual BLS Survey of Professional, Administrative, Technical, and Clerical Pay (the PATC), which was originally intended to look only for wage developments in companies most like the US federal government and included only medium and large companies mostly in manufacturing. Note, on the other hand, that, reflecting the increased costs of a more comprehensive survey after 1988, the survey was only carried out every other year. See Frumkin and Wiatrowski (1982), Morton (1987), Burke and Morton (1990), and Wiatrowski (2004) for details.

Figure 7.3 Participation in US corporate pension plans, 1950–2006

percent of all US private-sector workers

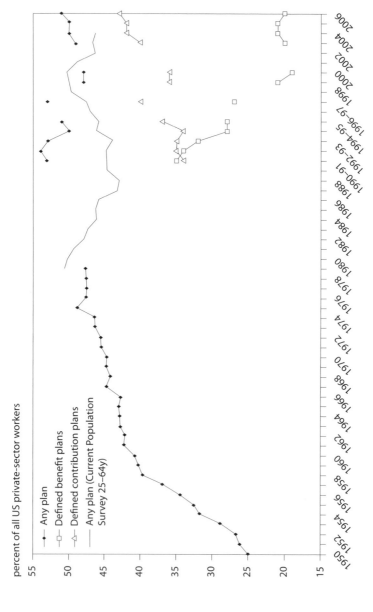

Note: Lines in the figure are broken due to missing data.

Sources: 1950–79: Schieber and George (1981); 1990–91 to 1996–97: Wiatrowski (2004); 1999–2006: Bureau of Labor Statistics, National Compensation Survey; Bureau of Labor Statistics, Current Population Survey data; Purcell (2005).

whether they are offered and participate in a plan. This is the approach of the annual March supplement to the BLS/US Census Bureau Current Population Survey (CPS), which covers the entire US working population since 1979;[41] figure 7.3 shows results from the most relevant CPS subpopulation (aged 25 to 64, 1979–2004).[42] These data reveal that US workers' participation in corporate pension plans is about 50 percent, roughly corresponding to the levels indicated by the BLS employer surveys.[43]

In fact, the 50 percent corporate pension participation level has been remarkably stable, as numerous scholars noted as early as the mid-1970s.[44] But even a stable rate translates, in periods of rapid employment growth, into significant gains in absolute numbers of participants in corporate pension plans. From 1950 to 1960, when private nonfarm employment rose from 40 million to 46 million,[45] the rising participation rates shown in figure 7.3 translate to 8.9 million more Americans in corporate-sponsored retirement plans by 1960. Meanwhile, the roughly stable participation rates at about 50 percent from 1996 to the present, during which time private nonfarm employment rose from 100 million to 114 million, reflect the new participation of about 7 million US workers in corporate-sponsored retirement plans.[46] Although less than the rate of participation expansion seen in the 1950s and 1960s, if the goal is expanded participation in corporate pensions, 7 million is hardly a trivial number.

---

41. See the BLS website, www.bls.census.gov, for details of the coverage of the CPS Annual Demographic Survey (March Supplement).

42. This group was chosen as it captures the subset of Americans most likely to be enrolled in a private pension plan; many 16- to 25-year-olds would be in school, and those 65 or older would be retired. However, the choice of survey population matters a lot for the result; as Munnell and Perun (2006, figure 1) illustrate, whether you take full-time workers only or the entire 16+ workforce, may change results for pension plan participation by up to 25 percentage points.

43. The findings of pretty stable coverage rates of approximately 50 percent for US private-sector workers since the early 1980s are validated by several other surveys of different respondent populations. Sanzenbacher (2006) and Purcell (2005) survey establishment data from the Department of Labor Form 5500 filings by all plan sponsors, as well as household data from the Census Bureau's Survey of Income and Program Participation (SIPP), the University of Michigan's Panel Study on Income Dynamics (PSID), and the Federal Reserve Board's triennial Survey of Consumer Finances (SCF). Further analysis of special supplement surveys to the CPS in April 1972, May 1979, 1983, 1988, and April 1993 about the participation of workers in private pension plans yields similar results. See EBRI (1993) and US Department of Labor (1994).

44. See, for instance, Skolnik (1976), Yohalem (1977), and Schultz and Leavitt (1983). See also Gale, Papke, and VanDerhei (2005) for a review of the extensive literature on the shift from defined benefit to defined contribution corporate plans.

45. Data are from the BLS Current Employment Statistics, available at www.bls.gov/ces.

46. McGill et al. (2005, figure 1.6) allude to the same steady rise in the raw number of privately insured Americans.

It is important to note that the participation rate for women has risen substantially from little more than one-third in the late 1970s to close to the male participation rate of 50 percent.[47] And among women working full-time in 2005 (i.e., adjusting for their higher prevalence among part-time workers), their pension plan participation was actually higher (56.4 percent) than that of full-time men (53.7 percent) (Copeland 2006). Thus, with rising female labor force participation, women today are far less dependent on their spouse's retirement income than was true in the 1950s and 1960s in America.[48]

Nonetheless, some of the inequalities of the "good old days" persist, as corporate pension plan participation remains far above average among well-educated, higher-earning, and white workers in America (table 7.1).[49] The notable exceptions to the recent general stability in pension participation rates are the large decline in the participation of unskilled workers (those without a high school diploma) and the continued very low participation of Americans who earn less than the median wage ($25,036 in 2005; US Census Bureau 2006). The decline in participation among Hispanics is largely due to the rise in the non-native-born segment; the participation of native-born Hispanics is comparable to that of other minority groups (Copeland 2006).

In summary, the change in the US employment-based retirement system in recent decades is not one of a decline in participation; ratios are stable and the actual number of Americans with access to a private employer–sponsored plan is higher than ever before. Rather, private corporate pension provision in America is changing because of a qualitative shift from predominantly defined benefit to defined contribution (or hybrid cash-balance[50]) plans.

---

47. See Munnell and Perun (2006) for detailed data on female private pension plan participation in recent decades.

48. For example, recent changes in the Japanese divorce law, which made corporate pension benefits (overwhelmingly allocated to male workers) part of the "family estate," have caused a notable rise in the number of divorces in Japan. This indicates that the dependence power of corporate pensions in some countries remain strong. See Chris Hogg, "Divorce fears for Japan baby boomers," BBC News, Tokyo, March 26, 2007, available at http://news.bbc.co.uk.

49. The data in table 7.1 cover wage and salary workers in both the private and public sectors. Due to the generally higher participation rates among public-sector workers, these data are, therefore, not comparable to the participation rates among private-sector workers presented in figures 7.1, 7.2, and 7.3.

50. Cash-balance plans are a hybrid of both defined benefit and defined contribution plans but combine these such that the employer has a more accurate estimate of potential future obligations. Usually, the employer contributes a preset (defined) amount annually, based on wages, and guarantees a fixed growth rate of these contributions. Upon retirement, the worker can take the accrued amount as either a lump sum or an annuity. In many ways, these plans are similar to the notional defined contribution plans of many governments (see chapters 5 and 6 on private accounts). According to the BLS (2007, table 44), in 2005 23 percent of US private-sector workers covered by a defined benefit pension plan had coverage in the form of a cash-balance plan.

Table 7.1 **Percentage of all wage and salary workers aged 21–64 who participated in an employment-based retirement plan, 1987 and 2005**

Category	1987	2005
By educational attainment		
Graduate/professional degree	65.6	68.3
Bachelor's degree	52.1	58.8
Some college	45.7	46.4
High school diploma	43.9	41.0
No high school diploma	31.5	19.4
By annual income (US dollars)		
50,000 and over	77.6	71.3
40,000–49,999	71.2	65.6
30,000–39,999	60.2	56.2
20,000–29,999	45.7	40.9
15,000–19,999	31.7	27.1
10,000–14,999	20.8	20.1
5,000–9,999	12.4	13.0
Less than 5,000	6.4	8.4
By race		
White	48.0	51.7
Black	43.5	43.1
Other	43.1	43.1
Hispanic	32.2	27.9

Source: Copeland (2006), based on Current Population Survey data.

The PBGC and the Shift from Defined Benefit Corporate Pension Provision in America

The employer-guaranteed defined benefit retirement plan is perhaps intuitively more stable, from the viewpoint of the employee, than the defined contribution plan. However, as pointed out in the 2006 *Economic Report of the President* (Council of Economic Advisers 2006, chapter 3), it is erroneous to assume that participation in a defined benefit plan carries no risk to employees. Defined benefit plans expose participants to:

- *Funding risk:* Employers contribute too little to the plan to cover promised liabilities;

- *Portfolio risk:* Employers invest defined benefit plan assets nonprofitably;

- *Bankruptcy risk:* Employers encounter financial problems and therefore cannot honor their promises;[51]

- *Portability risk:* Employees leave the sponsoring company before acquiring vested pension rights;[52] or

- *Inflation risk (specific to corporate defined benefit plans):* Inflation diminishes the effective value of pension payments. Unlike Social Security, which has automatic annual cost of living allowances (COLAs), or almost all state and local employee pension plans (see appendix table 3B.1[53] in chapter 3), hardly any corporate defined benefit plans include COLAs. Employees with defined benefit coverage, therefore, bear the full inflation risk after retirement. In addition, if a fully funded defined benefit pension plan terminates with no loss of accrued vested pension rights before the age of retirement, employees are subject to additional inflation risk during the intermediate period until retirement.

The switch from defined benefit to defined contribution plans means a shift of the burden of uncertainty about the future from plan sponsors to employees. Yet the termination of a defined benefit plan itself very rarely results in a direct loss of vested benefits, and so any adverse financial effect on plan participants relates almost solely to forgone potential gains during the period after the defined benefit plan termination. Given the lack of COLAs in corporate defined benefit plans, such losses might be considerable when measured in employee purchasing power over the long term. The lack of COLAs in corporate defined benefit plans, however, is a known quantity to both plan sponsors and employees, so the lack of inflation protection for these benefits after a plan termination cannot sensibly be labeled an additional and unforeseen loss of pension benefits, even if the plan termination occurs suddenly before the age of retirement.[54]

---

51. As we pointed out in chapter 3 on public pensions, and contrary to the report of the Council of Economic Advisers (2006, 74), the risk of financial trouble is not restricted to private employers. US public-sector employees will increasingly face the result of this type of risk, too.

52. This risk is particularly pertinent as most private plans rely on "cliff-vesting," in which no vesting of any pension rights occurs until 100 percent of vesting requirements have been fulfilled. BLS (2007, table 57) indicates that in 2005, 84 percent of US defined benefit workers faced cliff-vesting after five years of service.

53. Of the 85 state and local government employee pension plans surveyed in appendix table 3B.1, only one has no COLAs; 19 have only ad hoc COLAs (i.e., similar to Social Security before 1972), and many have CPI-linked COLAs with an annual cap. See also discussion in chapter 5 of the extra cost of indexed annuities.

54. The PBGC does not operate with any benefit payment COLAs for the terminated defined benefit plans that it operates. The maximum defined benefit plan benefit covered by the PBGC does, however, rise with wages (PBGC 2007a).

After the collapse of several private defined benefit pension plans (particularly that of the Studebaker Corporation and its roughly 11,000-member plan in 1963), Congress enacted the Employee Retirement Income Security Act (ERISA) in 1974, in an attempt to mitigate the risks to defined benefit participants listed above (Stewart 2007). ERISA included regulations that defined benefit (and defined contribution) plans had to adhere to in order to qualify for tax-exempt status, but equally important, it established the PBGC. The PBGC is a quasi-governmental body that, through compulsory defined benefit plan sponsor participation, insures the retirement income, within statutory limits, of about 44 million American workers. Its mission is to "[1] encourage the continuation and maintenance of private-sector defined benefit pension plans, [2] provide timely and uninterrupted payment of pension benefits, and [3] keep pension insurance premiums at a minimum."[55] The corporation receives no US government funding but is financed by insurance premiums from legally compelled participating defined benefit plan sponsors, investment returns, the assets of pension plans it takes over, and recoveries from former plan sponsors in bankruptcy.

Under the PBGC statutes, a single-employer plan can terminate in one of two ways: standard or distress/involuntary termination. A standard termination is an option for an employer whose pension plan has sufficient funds to cover its promised defined-benefit benefits; operationally, this means it must be able to either purchase an annuity from a private insurance company covering its vested future benefit payments or (if allowed under plan statutes) issue a single lump-sum payment covering the vested benefit payment.[56] The fact that terminating defined benefit plans must purchase a private insurance annuity covering the entire future benefit stream is important, as private insurance companies, well aware of potential mortality or investment risk in honoring these future commitments, will price their annuities conservatively and hence make plan liabilities on a termination basis higher than on an on-going basis. Liabilities on a termination basis (which, when netted against assets, yield a "buy-out deficit"; see PBGC 2006a, 16ff) are therefore larger than those on an accounting basis, and defined benefit plan sponsors who wish to terminate their plan are thus frequently obliged to put money on the table upfront in order to do so.

---

55. PBGC Mission Statement, available at www.pbgc.gov/about (accessed on September 6, 2008).

56. The idea of workers receiving their vested benefit in a single lump-sum payment upon retirement is similar to the offer in 2006 of up to $140,000 from General Motors to each eligible unionized worker to immediately sever ties with the company. However, a crucial issue for both GM and its workers was the inability to verify whether this upfront lump-sum payment represented the full value (in terms of pension—and especially health care—benefits) of remaining on the company payroll.

Hence it is essential to establish that a standard defined benefit plan termination does not imply a loss of vested pension benefits. Approximately 167,750 defined benefit plans have ceased to exist since 1974 through a standard termination, which represents about 98 percent of all defined benefit plan terminations over this period (Kandarian 2003, PBGC 2007a). Only 3,683 defined benefit plans have terminated in distress (plan sponsor–initiated termination to offload pension liabilities) or involuntarily (PBGC-initiated termination to limit exposure to future losses), affecting 1.1 million active workers and retirees as of 2006.[57] The PBGC as the new plan trustee has ensured that "the vast majority of [these] plan participants . . . receive all the benefits they were promised by their [previous employer-sponsored] plan" (PBGC 2006a, 27). However, in three instances the PBGC will not insure participants' vested benefits:[58]

1. They are a supplemental benefit above the standard life annuity (usually temporary benefits available in case of early retirement until the age of Social Security eligibility; PBGC 2007a, 15); and/or

2. Vested benefits come from increases in benefits during the last five years; and/or

3. They are above the statutory annual limit ($49,500 in 2007) for a single-life annuity starting at age 65 (this limit rises annually with wage growth).

This last exclusion particularly means that some participants in terminating defined benefit plans will immediately lose some of their accrued and vested benefits. Yet, with a $49,500 maximum in 2007—which is almost four times the average annualized March 2007 Social Security benefit of $12,576[59] and more than seven times the annual average PBGC pension payment of approximately $6,400 in 2006 (PBGC 2007a, table S-20)[60]—this loss will affect only the highest-paid employees in the top-

---

57. A further 110,000 workers in PBGC-insured multiemployer plans have been affected through the need for PBGC financial assistance. In 2006 in the single-employer program, actual payments were made to 622,000 recipients, while there were 520,000 with deferred benefits to be paid out at retirement age. About 2 percent (or 13,000 workers) in 2006 opted for a lump-sum payment (PBGC 2007a, table S-20).

58. The statutory maximum benefit is adjusted annually to wage increases and retirement age (i.e., it decreases if the person retires before 65 and is just $39,105 at retirement at age 62 and $22,275 at retirement at age 55), and it is also reduced if paid out instead as a joint and survivor annuity.

59. Available on the SSA website at www.ssa.gov/oact/progdata.

60. Average monthly benefit payment was $531.

income quintile[61] with a very generous defined benefit plan indeed. This is without doubt a small group, likely less than 1 percent of the total number of PBGC payees, according to the latest data.[62]

However, among the few very large pension plan failures (concentrated in the airline and steel industries), which dominate recent PBGC losses, a relatively large share of vested claimants are affected by pension cuts due to the three limitations on PBGC coverage. A survey reported in PBGC (2007a) shows that 8 percent of airline industry workers whose defined benefit pension plans were taken over by the PBGC were affected by the maximum limit of $49,500 and that 14 percent were affected by the five-year benefit increase limitation. The corresponding numbers in the steel industry were 6 and 15 percent.[63] Thus many workers in these two industries have seen their pensions cut due to the annulment of increases in pension benefits during the last five years, when the financial stress of their pension plans ought to have been well-known to interested participants. It is not clear that it is good public policy to insure fully against such losses.

PBGC (2007a) further finds that 60 percent of airline pilots saw their pensions cut because of the $49,500 maximum limit. Yet, again, this threshold is so far in excess of the average pension benefits that it would be unfortunate to believe that the entire group of affected PBGC payees is anything like airline pilots (the "United Airlines fallacy"). It is understandable that the pilots were aggrieved when their pension plan collapsed, but their situation is not at all typical of the average worker participating in a corporate pension program. So although workers eligible for substantial pensions upon retirement should insist on reasonable guarantees for the funding of those pensions—and policy can facilitate that outcome by monitoring corporate pension programs—asking the average taxpayer to subsidize annual pensions of $50,000 or more does not seem appropriate.

Average US Employment-Based Pensions Are Smaller than Many Think

Despite the reported lavishness of some corporate defined benefit pensions, we saw in chapter 3 that only among the highest-income quintile

---

61. The pension and annuity income for the highest-income quintile for the US population at age 65 and above in 2005 was only $15,327. As such, retirees usually risk seeing their benefits cut due to the PBGC maximum benefit guarantee only if they are well into the top income quintile (EBRI databook, chapter 7, available at www.ebri.org).

62. In 2006 the PBGC threshold for coverage was $49,500, indicating a monthly payment of at least $4,125. However, only 1.8 percent, or 11,007 people, of the more than 612,000 retired workers who received their monthly defined benefit pension benefits from the PBGC in 2006 received a monthly benefit above $2,500. What share of the 11,007 were above $4,125 a year cannot be discerned, but the share is almost certainly below 1 percent of the total.

63. Another 7 percent of steel industry workers were also affected by the supplemental benefit restriction.

of Americans did non–Social Security payments make up most retirement income. This finding should serve as a reminder that most US corporate pensions (defined benefit or defined contribution) may not be nearly as generous as some believe. By surveying the distribution of the more than 600,000 PBGC monthly benefit payments in 2006 to retirees in defined benefit pension plans under its administration, it is possible to estimate the average level of private-sector defined benefit pension benefits. However, two things should be noted about this sample. First, it concerns only benefit recipients of defined benefit plans that have terminated. While, as mentioned above, only a fraction of plans have done so under economic stress, several were very big in terms of vested participants.[64] This would indicate a possible upward bias in the size of the individual pension benefits in PBGC-administered plans relative to the national average. Second, these data include benefit payments only to workers who had actually retired by 2006. It is, therefore, possible that the average size of benefit payments will increase once all affected workers start to receive their benefits.

Figure 7.4 presents the latest PBGC data and shows that most US private-sector defined benefit pension plans are quite limited in the extent of their benefits. Indeed, in 2006 only 15 percent of the roughly 612,000 recipients of PBGC benefits received a monthly annuity payment higher than the average monthly Social Security retirement benefit of $1,044. It is not possible from these data to determine the distribution of benefits for all of the more than 30,000 healthy defined benefit plans that cover as many as 44 million Americans, but figure 7.4 does offer at least an indication of the distribution of defined benefit levels. For many recipients, they are far lower than is generally believed. Thus even among American retirees who are eligible for a private defined benefit pension annuity—those usually regarded as among the most privileged of retirees—the median payment in 2006 was only $250 to $300 a month, or $3,000 to $3,600 per year, and for 85 percent of defined benefit–eligible retirees, it is lower than average annual Social Security benefits.[65] Although this benefit level is likely to rise as more fully vested workers in the baby-boomer generation retire, it is nonetheless a decidedly modest defined benefit pension level for most American private-sector recipients, especially as hardly any private-sector defined benefit plans (unlike those in the public sector) include postretirement COLAs.

---

64. PBGC (2007a, table S-5) shows that the 33 plans from the top 10 firms to present claims to the PBGC in 1975–2006 account for over 500,000 of just over 1.7 million vested participants. The eight biggest firms in the top 10 are in the steel and airline industries.

65. Given that workers with vested defined benefit plan benefits seem likely to have had a more stable work life than the average Social Security benefit recipient, they are likely to be eligible for higher-than-average Social Security benefits, indicating than an even higher share than 85 percent will receive more in Social Security benefits than from their defined benefit pension plan.

Figure 7.4   Distribution of PBGC retired workers and beneficiaries from defined benefit plans under administration, by monthly benefit level, 2006

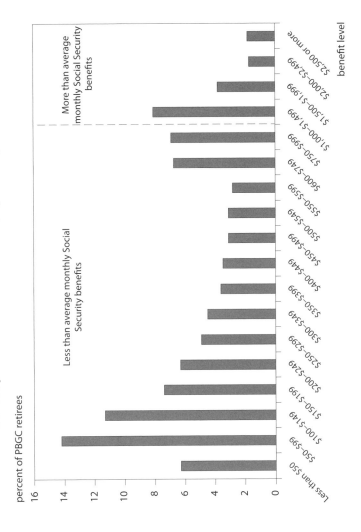

PBGC = Pension Benefit Guaranty Corporation

Note: This figure shows the shares of 611,688 retired payees in the PBGC single-employer program.

Source: PBGC (2007a, tables S-26).

The distribution of defined benefit plan benefits ought to insulate against knee-jerk alarmism when one considers the old age income security impact of the switch from defined benefit to defined contribution corporate pension plans described in this chapter. There simply aren't many "airline pilots" with generous defined benefit pension plans who stand to lose tens of thousands of dollars in annual benefits!

Current PBGC Importance and Financial Situation

It is evident that the number of small defined benefit plans has dramatically declined in recent years, even as the total number of PBGC-insured American defined benefit plan participants has remained relatively stable. So is the glass half full (stable number of defined benefit participants) or half empty (declining number of defined benefit plans)? If one considers the status quo orientation of the PBGC's mission to ensure the continuation and maintenance of defined benefit plans, one might say that the corporation has achieved this goal, as the number of defined benefit participants has risen since 1974. However, the stable number of PBGC-insured US workers masks a steady decline in the share of active (i.e., working under the original defined benefit plan) plan participants. With more defined benefit plan participants in retirement, the share of active workers in defined benefit plans declining, and the overall US workforce expanding, we find the same rapidly declining share of the active US workforce participating in PBGC-insured defined benefit plans, as indicated in figure 7.3. In an expanding economy the PBGC's maintenance and guarantee of existing defined benefit plan benefits for vested members does not prevent the PBGC system as a whole from increasingly failing to provide a guarantee relevant to the broader workforce.

In addition, the PBGC has since 2001 experienced a much publicized deterioration of its financial position as rapidly rising liabilities have been thrust upon it by collapsing private pension plans. This development is shown in figure 7.5. PBGC's net financial position improved somewhat from 2005 to 2007,[66] from −$23.1 billion to −$14.1 billion. But in 2006 the net income of $4.2 billion for both single and multiemployer plans was largely a lobbyist-driven "recovery" of PBGC fortunes. The corresponding improvement in the net financial position comes from a large decline in 2006 PBGC losses from completed and probable termination of single-employer insured plans. In its annual financial report, the PBGC includes its best estimate of its booked losses for the year, net of plan assets and the

---

66. PBGC data are fiscal year data, so the latest data here refer to the situation on September 30, 2007.

Figure 7.5   Combined financial position of PBGC single- and multiemployer programs, 1980–2007 (billions of US dollars)

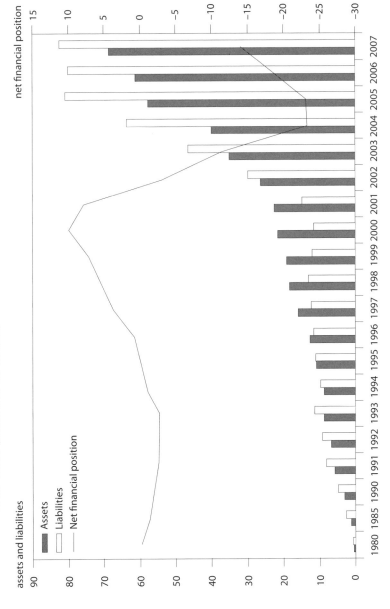

PBGC = Pension Benefit Guaranty Corporation

Source: PBGC (2007a).

present value of expected recoveries from plans likely to terminate within 12 months of the financial statement issuance date.[67] As a direct result of the pension accounting relief options made available to domestic airlines in the 2006 Pension Protection Act (PPA),[68] $8 billion worth of commercial airlines–sponsored pension underfunding was reclassified from "probable" to merely "reasonably possible" terminations in the PBGC's classification, removing them from the booked losses entry in the Corporation's 2006 annual report. In other words, without the accounting rule–based bailout of the US domestic airline industry in the 2006 PPA, there would have been no improvement in the PBGC's net financial position in 2006. The improvement in 2007 was due to strong gains in assets and the absence of additional large plan terminations.

The noteworthy real turnaround in PBGC fortunes is, therefore, not in its net liabilities but rather in the category of "reasonably possible" terminations, which—despite the $8 billion transfer related to commercial airlines—fell by one-third from $108 billion in 2005 to $73 billion in 2006 and $66 billion in 2007 (PBGC 2007b, 48, footnote 7). Thus improving financial conditions of American defined benefit plan sponsors have significantly reduced the PBGC's financial exposure. We shall see below that this improvement is part of a general trend of financial stabilization among US defined benefit plans. The PBGC is not a system facing imminent financial collapse, although it seems clear that the dramatic impact of the financial crisis in late 2008 will put perhaps substantial additional burdens on the PBGC.

Corporate Pension Guarantee Schemes in Other Countries

Other OECD countries have adopted radically different approaches to guaranteeing corporate pension benefits, some of which may be relevant to the US debate.

At one extreme, the Netherlands (where the majority of old age pensions are private defined benefit plans) has shown that through sufficiently stringent regulation, it is possible to do away with the need for a pension benefit guarantor. Dutch authorities, through their new financial

---

67. See PBGC (2005a), note 2 to financial statements, for details about the criteria that the Corporation uses to estimate probable termination in this 12-month period. See detailed note 8, "Contingencies," in PBGC (2004).

68. See PPA Title IV, Section B, "Special Funding Rules for Plans Maintained by Commercial Airlines," which stipulates that commercial airlines may, subject to meeting certain benefit accrual and increase restrictions, adopt a 17- or 10-year amortization schedule to correct pension plan underfunding. This is 3 to 10 years longer than the 7-year amortization schedule and represents a significant reduction in annual required contributions for commercial airlines. See Joint Committee on Taxation (2006, 82ff) for details.

assessment framework in 2007, legislated that "A pension fund must be able at any time and under all circumstances to reinsure its obligations with an insurance company."[69] This means that while minimum funding for Dutch defined benefit plans is always 100 percent of liabilities, a general risk reserve of 5 percent of accrued liabilities must be maintained at all times, and asset-dependent and market price–based solvency tests must show at least a 97.5 percent chance of full funding a year later (i.e., funds have just one year to make up for any underfunding). This regulation stipulates a norm of effective funding levels of 130 to 135 percent of liabilities for defined benefit pension plans in the Netherlands.[70] The unique situation (with such a large share of its total pensions income of this type) in the Netherlands should not be uncritically applied elsewhere, but it nonetheless shows that with sufficient political and regulatory determination, making defined benefit pensions financially secure for participants without a public guarantee is feasible, albeit at high costs to plan sponsors.

At the other extreme, Japan's Pension Guarantee Program (PGP), which provides termination insurance for corporate-sponsored employee pension funds (EPFs), rejects claims from failed plans for intransparent reasons and subjects insured benefits to a reduction formula (based on the funded status of dissolved funds), so that participants of very underfunded plans receive less from the PGP (Stewart 2007). Such provisions undermine the insurance aspect of the program and do not protect participants against the risks of defined benefit plan participation. One may question whether the system warrants the label "guarantee program," as it frequently provides only a small fraction of vested benefits.[71]

Between these two extremes is the German mandatory benefit insurance program, the Pensions-Sicherungs-Verein auf Gegenseitigkeit (PSVaG), which covers vested benefits up to $112,000 (more than twice the PBGC threshold) and is funded by a variable-rate (i.e., fully risk-adjusted) annual insurance premium based on schemes' estimated losses during the previous 12 months. These are then divided by the total insured pension liabilities to provide a contribution rate, which subsequently measured as a share of insured liabilities can vary dramatically from year to year. It

---

69. 2007 Pensions and Savings Act, quoted in Pugh (2006). See Ippolito (2004) for suggestions of a similar compulsory private insurance system in the United States.

70. See Pugh (2006, 44–47) for details. The funding ratio of the two largest Dutch pension funds, the ADP and PGGM, with more than €300 billion in assets, was 134 percent at the end of 2006. In comparison, just 5 percent of US defined benefit pension plans in 2004 had funding levels of 135 percent of liabilities.

71. There are historical reasons for this rather nonchalant view of vested benefits in Japan. Due to reliance on lump-sum payments, retirement benefits have been viewed more as merit-based payments at the discretion of management than a deferred compensation earned by the workers but payable only upon retirement.

averaged about a quarter of a percent since 1975, rose as high as 0.69 percent in 1982, and was close to half a percent in 2005 (PSVaG 2008).

Sweden's Pension Guarantee Mutual Insurance Company (Forsakringsbolaget Pensionsgaranti, or FPG), which covers white-collar employees at Sweden's approximately 1,600 largest companies, operates its own in-house rating agency that determines whether particular types of collateral is required for less credit-worthy companies to (continue to) participate. Otherwise, the insurance premium is uniform for all member companies.[72]

Ontario's Pension Benefit Guarantee Fund,[73] which since 1980 has covered participants in private defined benefit plans, guarantees benefits only up to C$1,000 per month (unadjusted since 1988),[74] a far lower maximum benefit guarantee level than in the United States.

Government guarantee schemes in Germany, Sweden, and Switzerland require that the guarantor purchase private annuities to cover threatened benefits in the event of a bankruptcy (Stewart 2007), and as such, the guarantee entity does not act as an asset manager by taking over the assets of failed pension plans, unlike the PBGC with $68 billion of assets (in 2007; figure 7.5) "under management" from failed plans. The guarantee entities in these countries are thereby shielded from market volatility, but require higher levels of secured funding (in order to be able to purchase annuities) and forfeit opportunities to generate extra investment income.

Finally, the recently established UK Pension Protection Fund (PPF), designed to avoid many of the problems plaguing the PBGC, intends to collect up to 80 percent of its total premium via risk-adjusted component, taking into consideration plan sponsors' financial situation, plan underfunding, and the asset composition of insured plans.[75] Like the PBGC, the PPF is supposed to remain self-financing;[76] unlike the PBGC, the PPF has

---

72. See the FPG/PRI Handbook (available online at www.fpg.se) for details.

73. See Pesando (1996) for discussion of the details and the finding that of Canada's 10 provinces, only the most blue-collar-intensive (Ontario) chose to adopt a model of government-guaranteed defined benefit pension benefits.

74. For details, see Financial Services Commission of Ontario, PBGF Rule P200-001, appendix A (available at www.fsco.gov.on.ca/english/pensions).

75. This is explicitly to reduce the asset-liability mismatch (ALM) inherent in funds with long-term pension liabilities but maintain a high weighting in volatile equity-type assets. See, for instance, Bodie (1996) and PPF (2006) for details concerning ALM. In 2006–07, the PPF estimated that it needed a levy of £675 million to insure probable losses, of which £540 million were to be risk-based.

76. McCarthy and Neuberger (2005), however, raise serious doubts about whether PPF self-financing will be feasible and instead predict that government bailouts will be necessary for large claims.

an independent board of directors[77] with wide discretion in the design of premium structure within the general parameters set in the 2004 Pension Act. It is hoped that this structure, combined with a new independent pension regulator, will insulate the PPF from the political interference that plagues the PBGC.[78]

In summary, this section makes clear that the termination of defined benefit plans in America does not imply a collapse of the US corporate pension system as it does not result in a loss of vested benefits for plan participants. Indeed, 98 percent of terminating defined benefit plans have sufficient funding to pay all vested benefits. Furthermore, transfers of benefit claims from failed defined benefit plans to the PBGC result in losses for only the very highest-paid and most generous defined benefit plan participant. Congressional reforms of funding rules and improvements in financial prospects for US defined benefit plan sponsors have helped PBGC finances.

Why the Switch from Defined Benefit Pension Plans?

Few cost savings are immediately forthcoming to a plan sponsor from terminating a defined benefit plan, and indeed the execution of a standard defined benefit plan termination may, if the plan is underfunded, require substantial upfront sponsor contributions. The principal reason for plan sponsors to terminate their defined benefit plans is longer-term cost saving considerations. There is little evidence that the decline in defined benefit coverage of US workers has been predominantly caused by instances of sudden, acute financial stress on sponsoring companies. Such stress has been behind several large plan terminations with the PBGC, but to assume that it is the main story would be to succumb to the (other) "United Airlines fallacy" of believing that most defined benefit plans have been terminated under circumstances similar to those in United Airlines. We have shown in this chapter that this is not the case.

---

77. The first five nonexecutive directors are two private-sector actuaries, a former CEO, a trade union representative, and a former private corporate lawyer. See UK DWP press release, November 30, 2004, available at www.dwp.gov.uk.

78. We largely agree with the argument in GAO (2007) that congressional interference with the PBGC has had the effect of "filling a vacuum." The GAO (2007, 3) found that "PBGC's Board has limited time and resources to provide policy direction and oversight and has not established comprehensive written procedures and mechanisms to monitor PBGC operations. While the PBGC's board has provided greater attention to the corporation since 2003, the three-member board structure may not be large enough to dedicate the necessary time and attention or provide the skills needed to direct and oversee PBGC. In addition, because the board is composed only of cabinet secretaries, PBGC's board members typically change with each administration, potentially limiting the board's institutional knowledge of the corporation."

Rather than predominantly sudden, acute financial stress, several long-term cost considerations and structural changes are affecting defined benefit plan sponsors:

- financial management costs,
- longevity risk,
- accounting risk,
- asset-liability mismatch risks, and
- defined contribution plan pull factors.

Financial Management Costs for Defined Benefit Plan Sponsors— An Increasingly Uneven Playing Field?

US financial markets have changed considerably since the growth phase of defined benefit plan provision in America in the 1950s, as have the PBGC and preferential tax regulation, the legal environment in which corporate pension plans are organized. Pension plan provision requires record keeping, benefit provision, accounting estimates, and other noncore business activities for plan sponsors. Furthermore, the density and complexity of corporate pension regulation has greatly increased since the 1970s and continues to do so in an unpredictable manner; table 7.2 lists the most important additions and changes to US employee benefits legislation. But to fully grasp the extent of the legal flux in which pension plan sponsors find themselves, one should add innumerable case-law rulings as well as Treasury Department/IRS regulations (both of which are beyond the scope of this book) and the corporate pension accounting changes that we analyze below.

This legislative action has doubtless been well intended and based on desires to improve benefit equity and security, minimize tax evasion, and secure (or even raise) government revenues. But has the cumulative effect led plan sponsors to exit defined benefit plan provision because of spiraling costs (despite the likely administrative cost savings from increased use of information technology)? Or to shift cost advantages of pension plan provision away from defined benefit plans? Analysts' estimates of the average participant cost of sponsors' plan provision suggest that this might indeed have occurred. Such estimates are presented in table 7.3.[79]

Several trends are evident from table 7.3. First, the administrative cost of defined benefit plan provision rose roughly threefold from 1981 to 1996,

---

79. The sources for table 7.2 rely on Form 5500 filed by plan sponsors. Because 1998 is the last year this form routinely asked for the size of the filing plan sponsor, more recent data of this detail are not available. See Popkin and Company (2005, 32) for details.

Table 7.2   Major post-ERISA changes and additions to employee pension benefit legislation

Year	Legislation
1974	Employment Retirement Income Security Act of 1974 (ERISA)
1975	Tax Reduction Act of 1975
1976	Tax Reduction Act of 1976
1977	Social Security Amendments of 1977
1978	Revenue Act of 1978
	Amendments to Age Discrimination in Employment Act
1980	Multi-employer Pension Plans Amendment Act of 1980 (MEPPAA)
	Miscellaneous Revenue Act of 1980
1981	Economic Recovery Tax Act of 1981 (ERTA)
1982	Tax Equity and Fiscal Responsibility Act of 1982 (TEFRA)
1983	Social Security Amendments of 1983
1984	Deficit Reduction Act of 1984 (DEFRA)
	Retirement Equity Act of 1984 (REACT)
1986	Tax Reform Act of 1986
	Single-Employer Pension Plan Amendment Act of 1986 (SEPPAA), including the Consolidated Omnibus Budget Reconciliation Act of 1985 (COBRA 1985)
	Omnibus Budget Reconciliation Act of 1986 (OBRA 1986)
1987	Omnibus Budget Reconciliation Act of 1987 (OBRA 1987)
1988	Technical and Miscellaneous Revenue Act of 1988 (TAMRA)
1989	Omnibus Budget Reconciliation Act of 1989 (OBRA 1989)
1990	Omnibus Budget Reconciliation Act of 1990 (OBRA 1990)
	Older Workers Benefit Protection Act of 1990 (OWBPA)
1992	Unemployment Compensation Amendments of 1992 (UCA)
1993	Omnibus Budget Reconciliation Act of 1993 (OBRA 1993)
	Family and Medical Leave Act of 1993 (FMLA)
1994	Uruguay Round of the GATT
	Uniformed Services Employment and Reemployment Rights Act (USERRA)
1996	Small Business Job Protection Act of 1996 (SBJPA)
1997	Taxpayer Relief Act of 1997
1998	IRS Restructuring and Reform Act of 1998
2000	Community Renewal Tax Relief Act of 2000
2001	Economic Growth and Tax Relief Reconciliation Act (EGTERRA)
2002	Job Creation and Worker Assistance Act of 2002
2003	Jobs and Growth Tax Relief Reconciliation Act of 2003 (JGTRRA)
2004	The Pension Funding and Equity Act of 2004 (PFEA)
2006	The Pension Protection Act of 2006 (PPA)

Source: McGill et al. (2005, table 4.2); authors' calculations.

Table 7.3 Trends in annual plan sponsor administrative cost for US defined benefit and defined contribution plans, 1981–96 and 1998 (current US dollars)

| | Cost per participant of administering pension plan | | | | | | Relative cost trends | | |
| | Participants in defined benefit plan | | | | Participants in defined contribution plan | | Cost ratio of defined benefit/defined contribution provision | | Economies of scale in defined benefit provision: Ratio of 15/10,000 participant plans |
Year	15	75	500	10,000	15	10,000	15-employee plans	10,000-employee plans	
1981	194.67	138.97	67.85	23.32	137.13	25.71	1.42	0.91	8.35
1982	194.80	142.21	69.14	23.37	140.13	26.21	1.39	0.89	8.34
1983	210.67	150.04	72.55	24.12	148.73	27.75	1.42	0.87	8.73
1984	232.40	157.63	76.43	24.96	156.73	29.14	1.48	0.86	9.31
1985	262.47	174.36	85.76	31.57	172.73	33.21	1.52	0.95	8.31
1986	307.60	200.07	102.01	43.35	184.53	35.18	1.67	1.23	7.10
1987	321.80	208.57	117.78	44.73	220.60	37.68	1.46	1.19	7.19
1988	529.47	264.65	139.93	57.88	230.40	38.97	2.30	1.49	9.15
1989	507.80	291.65	151.71	63.72	252.33	44.30	2.01	1.44	7.97
1990	526.60	300.81	155.44	63.85	262.33	45.69	2.01	1.40	8.25
1991	548.93	314.73	163.17	67.87	271.40	46.73	2.02	1.45	8.09
1992	561.47	320.25	165.73	68.39	274.60	47.41	2.04	1.44	8.21
1993	566.13	322.43	166.23	67.82	277.20	47.60	2.04	1.42	8.35
1994	608.53	340.15	171.82	68.82	281.13	48.24	2.16	1.43	8.84
1995	615.07	343.39	172.95	68.66	284.53	48.78	2.16	1.41	8.96
1996	619.93	345.68	173.62	68.33	287.20	49.19	2.16	1.39	9.07
1981–96 change (percent)	218	149	156	193	109	91			

Number of employees at firm, 1998	Defined benefit plan providers	Defined contribution plan providers	Ratio of defined benefit/defined contribution plans
Fewer than 5	959	439	2.18
6–10	541	192	2.82
11–50	405	106	3.82
51–100	217	59	3.68
101–200	232	57	4.07
201–500	218	52	4.19
501–1,000	154	48	3.21
1,001–5,000	147	38	3.87
More than 5,000	159	31	5.13
Cost ratio of 11 to 50/5,000+ plans	2.55	3.42	

Note: Administrative costs include accounting, actuarial, investment advice, and legal fees as well as management fees and trustee expenses.

Sources: Hustead (1998, 166–77), cited in McGill et al. (2005, 90); Popkin and Company (2005).

while roughly doubling for defined contribution plans during the same period. As such, it is clear that the administrative costs of all pension plan provision have risen very rapidly and that defined benefit plan provision has gotten relatively significantly more expensive than defined contribution plans. Second, there are sizable economies of scale in pension plan provision, with large plans five to nine times cheaper to administer per participant, depending on the year and plan characteristics. Third, defined benefit coverage for both small and large plans is significantly more administratively expensive to provide per participant than is defined contribution plan coverage and disproportionally so for small plans. The administrative cost data in table 7.3 suggest that smaller fully funded defined benefit plans would particularly be at risk of termination by cost-conscious plan sponsors, a trend that was also apparent in the analysis of PBGC data above.[80]

It would be erroneous to conclude that rising administrative costs are solely responsible for the shift away from defined benefit plan provision in recent years. However, the changes in pension plan provision after the large legislative reforms enacted through ERISA in 1974 suggest that defined benefit pension plan sponsorship is remarkably sensitive to increases in plan administrative costs. The US Department of Labor (DOL 1977) estimated that ERISA increased the average administrative costs for small plan sponsors by 72 percent—less than may have resulted from subsequent legislation in 1981–96 (table 7.2). This change in plan sponsor administrative costs nonetheless had a dramatic negative impact on the willingness of employers to provide voluntary defined benefit employee retirement benefits (Schieber and George 1981). Figure 7.6 shows that the creation of new defined benefit pension plans peaked in 1974, just before the enactment of ERISA, then declined dramatically before staging a modest (and short-lived) recovery.

These data suggest that US employers are more sensitive to pension plan administrative cost changes than perhaps many believe, something also indicated in GAO surveys of former sponsors of terminated plans about the reasons for terminating their defined benefit plan. GAO's 1977 defined benefit plan termination report shows that more than 85 percent of respondents stated that the enactment of ERISA was partly or fully responsible for their decision to terminate their plan(s), while two-thirds indicated that ERISA's costs were a major consideration.[81] A 1993 American

---

80. A more detailed look at the same PBGC data from 1980 to 2005 reveals the dramatic collapse in the number of small PBGC-insured defined benefit plans, as those with fewer than 100 participants declined by more than three-quarters after the peak in 1985. Declines in mid-size defined benefit plans are smaller—23 percent for plans with 1,000 to 4,999 participants, 52 percent for plans with 250 to 999, and 67 percent for plans with 100 to 250. On the other hand, the number of large defined benefit plans has risen since 1985, with the largest (10,000+) participant plans rising 75 percent, from 354 to 618 (PBGC 2006a).

81. See also Schieber and George (1981, 65ff) for a discussion of this issue.

Figure 7.6 US defined benefit plan creation and termination, 1956–80

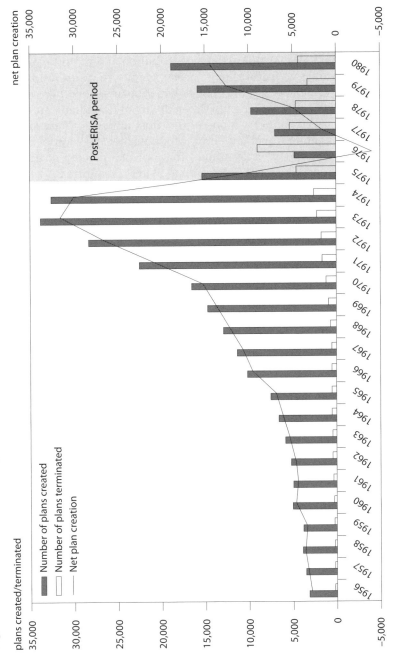

ERISA = Employment Retirement Income Security Act of 1974

Source: Schieber and George (1981, table III-9).

Academy of Actuaries report further found that for 44 percent of defined benefit plan terminations in the late 1980s, "increased government regulation" was the most important factor (AAA 1993).

Moreover, as Ron Gebhardtsbauer (2004) explains, not only have defined benefit plans been saddled since 1974 with increasing regulatory demands (which, in the eyes of plan sponsors, have appeared to favor defined contribution plans), but defined contribution and hybrid plans also offer several attractive features (e.g., pretax employee contributions and matches) not available to private defined benefit plans. Robert Brown and Jianxun Liu (2001) note that the full deductibility of Canadian employees' defined benefit contributions is one of the most important factors in explaining why, among Canadian employer-sponsored pension plans, defined benefit plans in 1998 accounted for about 85 percent of the total against only about 20 percent in the United States (see figure 7.3).

Finally, with the dramatic cuts in recent decades in US capital gains and dividend tax rates, the overall advantage to be derived from tax-benefited status for either defined benefit, defined contribution, or hybrid plans has declined.[82] When effective tax rates are lower, there is less to be gained from tax-benefited status—or more simply put, a smaller bribe is less likely to produce results! While these tax cuts, therefore, may generally have a stimulative and beneficial effect on investment and saving, it is likely they also reduce the incentive for corporate pension plan sponsors to shoulder the burden of administering their plans. Capital gains and dividend tax cuts, therefore, may affect different types of saving in a dissimilar manner.

Given the disproportional rise in administrative costs for defined benefit plans, this decline in tax shelter benefits should have affected defined benefit plan sponsorship most adversely. In short, government regulation of private corporate pensions seems powerfully to have turned against defined benefit plan provision by employers.

Longevity Risk

Companies "want out of it"![83] But how? We define longevity risk here as the risk to the plan sponsor that retirees will live longer and hence be eligible for defined benefit plan benefits for a longer period than expected (in a defined contribution/hybrid plan, the risk is that the retiree will run

---

82. These reductions have lowered the effective total tax rate (corporate and individual tax payments combined) on corporate investments/capital income. See CBO (2005) for details.

83. Quote by UK Pensions Commission Chair Adair Turner, cited in the *Financial Times*, "The Holy Grail of the Asset Classes," November 29, 2006.

out of savings before death). We showed in chapter 2 that average life expectancies in the OECD have risen substantially in recent decades and in chapter 3 the difficulties of predicting future demographic changes. As all private pension funding (unlike PAYGO public systems) occurs ex ante,[84] defined benefit plan sponsors risk exposure to future rises in life expectancies, or longevity risk,[85] and cost-risk-averse companies may seek to offload such risks whenever it is profitable to do so. Regrettably, however, such opportunities have been quite limited. The market for group annuities is very small (Brown, Mitchell, and Poterba 2000),[86] as the purchase of annuities from third-party providers is, as also discussed in chapter 6, typically prohibitively expensive due to the problem of "adverse selection"—annuity providers cannot sort the healthy from the sick among a pool of annuitants and hence cannot predict life expectancies and price the product correctly. But because longevity risk is greater in companies with younger workforces, closing a defined benefit plan to new entrants will improve the options for fair market pricing of a group annuity by limiting this uncertainty and will thus likely stimulate new market entrants.[87] Closing a defined benefit scheme to new entrants is, therefore, likely to be a plan sponsor's first move toward offloading its pension liability with the purchase of a group annuity from a third-party provider.

Some analysts have suggested that integrated pension and life insurance companies offer a natural hedge against longevity.[88] If people live and work longer, they pay into their life insurance policies and do not require a payout, and if they die younger, their pensions (annuities) also do not require a payout. One might hedge longer life spans with assets in companies whose performance is likely to be positively correlated with such eventualities, like elderly care suppliers or some pharmaceutical companies.[89] However, no large-scale market for financial instruments (e.g., mortality bonds, survivor bonds) for hedging longevity risk has

---

84. Ex ante here indicates the time difference between when companies put money into their defined benefit pension plans as employees accrue their pension rights and retirees withdraw them. See also Bodie (1996).

85. This is especially so as many corporate retirement plans, as we saw in chapter 4 is the case in many European countries, have had quite generous access to early retirement.

86. See also Yaari (1965) and Davidoff, Brown, and Diamond (2003). Lane, Clark and Peacock (2008) observe that in the UK annuity market, the most developed in the world, until very recently only two insurance companies were prepared to take over company group annuities, although with the rapid increase in closures of defined benefit plans, the number is rising—in 2007 the company reported 12 transactions in excess of £100 million.

87. This is already happening; see *Financial Times*, "The Holy Grail of the Asset Classes," November 29, 2006.

88. See *Financial Times*, "Death and the Salesmen," February 24–25, 2007, for a recent review.

89. Visco (2005) refers to these types of arrangements as "macro-swaps."

emerged, despite several attempts from private financial companies,[90] because of difficulties in accessing sufficient mortality-related data to enable valid predictions (estimations of life expectancies at age 65 are of relatively recent origin).[91] Moreover, one could easily imagine public relations concerns from participating in a mortality bond market, in which prices would collapse in the fortuitous event of, for instance, the discovery of a cure for cancer. The "merchants of death" label would no longer apply only to arms traders.

The absence of reliable hedging opportunities for longevity risk and of a competitively priced market for group annuities have pushed defined benefit plan sponsors that wish to rid themselves of longevity risk toward defined contribution (or hybrid) plans, in which the retiree bears all or part of the longevity risk. Mervyn King (2004) cited the lack of longevity risk insurance options as a contributory factor to the decline in defined benefit provision among UK plan sponsors in the 1990s, when mortality rates at high ages declined sharply.

Uncertainty about future changes in life expectancies is compounded by uncertainty about the validity of mortality tables used in actuarially estimating existing defined benefit liabilities. There is widespread concern that many defined benefit pension plans have used outdated mortality assumptions and hence may have underestimated their future pension liabilities. The Pension Protection Act of 2006 addressed this issue:

> Under section 430(h)(3)(A), except as provided in section 430(h)(3)(C) or (D), the Secretary is to prescribe by regulation mortality tables to be used in determining any present value or making any computation under section 430. *Those tables are to be based on the actual experience of pension plans and projected trends in such experience* [emphasis added].[92]

The final rules are still to be written by the IRS, but the fact that the Act explicitly requires the future inclusion of projected trends shows an appropriate congressional concern about the effects of the issue on the

---

90. In 2003 BNP Paribas tried to market a bond with payout linked in 25 years to the proportion of UK people aged 65 in 2003. In 2006 AXA issued a bond with a cash flow to bondholders that falls if the mortality rate among AXA policyholders rises. In early 2007 JPMorgan launched its LifeMetrics Index, attempting to benchmark mortality risk (www.jpmorgan .com). See Blake and Burrows (2001), Dowd (2003), and Denuit, Devolder, and Goderniaux (2007) for discussions concerning whether such bonds should be issued by governments. See also *Financial Times*, "Difficulties of Giving Life to Longevity Risk Market," November 26, 2006.

91. The Continuous Mortality Investigation project attempts to systematically collect all new mortality-related data for countries relevant to the financial services sector (www .actuaries.org.uk).

92. *Federal Register* 72, no. 102, May 29, 2007: Proposed Rules. Section 430 specifies the minimum funding requirements that apply to single-employer defined benefit plans.

financial health of US defined benefit plans. According to the Groupe Consultatif Actuariel Européen (2001), only a few countries (including the United Kingdom and France) today require private defined benefit plan sponsors to use forward-looking mortality assumptions. Congress has shown here the legislative foresight it has otherwise frequently lacked on pension accounting issues.

And with good reason, too, as several studies show that different mortality assumptions across countries can have a huge impact on the size of defined benefit liabilities. The Cass Business School (2005) found that, purely due to different mortality assumptions, a £200 million accounting deficit in a typical UK defined benefit pension plan would have been only a £94 million deficit (less than half) in a typical US defined benefit plan but would rise more than 30 percent, to £263 million, in a typical French defined benefit pension plan. Similarly, UBS (2005) estimated that the combined £40 billion defined benefit pension deficit of the companies included in the Financial Times (FT) 100 index would have been a £3 billion surplus with the use of German mortality tables. And if French mortality rates were used, the FT100 deficit would have risen by more than 50 percent, to £63 billion.[93]

The culprit is different assumptions concerning life expectancy at retirement age (proxied by life expectancies at 65) in the typical defined benefit plan. These assumptions all posit continued increases in life expectancy at retirement age, but with quite a bit of variation. One might argue that choosing your mortality assumptions may be more important to defined benefit plan sponsors than Federal Open Market Committee (FOMC) interest rate decisions and even long-term bond market movements. Obviously defined benefit plan sponsors that may have used outdated mortality assumptions face one more reason to switch to a defined contribution or hybrid plan as a way to reduce potential actuarial legacy longevity risk.

Accounting Risk: What Gets Measured, Gets Managed— and May Get Lost!

In recent years, international corporate accounting rules have moved toward more transparency, increased disclosure, and fair value accounting (i.e., the "marking to market" of assets and liabilities, at the expense of accounting assumption–driven estimates). This trend represents an attempt to shift the focus of accounting information from merely a best estimate of the present financial situation/recent performance to a more investor-friendly format that can shed more light on a company's prospects and potential pitfalls. The trend has affected corporate pension accounting

---

93. Antolín (2007) estimates similar magnitudes in differences when using alternative mortality assumptions for a hypothetical defined benefit pension fund.

and, as we saw in chapter 3, has spread to public finances with Government Accounting Standards Board (GASB) Statement 45.

Accounting standards–setting bodies in the United Kingdom, European Union, and elsewhere,[94] in the form of the new Financial Reporting Standard (FRS) 17 (for unlisted companies in Britain) and International Accounting Standard (IAS) 19[95] (for all listed EU companies and elsewhere), have required since 2005 the auditing of all pension schemes according to these principles. However, reflecting the long-standing reluctance in large parts of the US business community and the Congress to introduce additional transparency in US corporate accounting standards, the Financial Accounting Standards Board (FASB) only in September 2006 amended its deeply flawed FAS 87[96] (which had governed US private employers' accounting for pensions since late 1986) by introducing its Statement 158, aimed at enhancing financial disclosure concerning employers' accounting for single-employer pension plans. According to FAS 158, US companies, like their EU and UK counterparts, are now obliged to report defined benefit pension plan assets on a fair value basis[97] and defined benefit plan liabilities on a going-concern projected benefit obligation (PBO) basis,[98] and to recognize the resulting net funded status on their balance sheets. While so far employer pension accounting changes have not affected corporate income statements, this may soon become the case with FASB's pledge to "comprehensively reconsider guidance in FASB Statements No. 87, 88, 106, and 132 in order to improve the reporting of pensions and other postretirement benefit plans in the financial statements by making information more useful and transparent for investors, creditors, employees, retirees, donors, and other users,"[99] while simulta-

---

94. Today more than 100 countries have implemented or begun implementing IFRS rules; and the Securities and Exchange Commission (SEC), on July 25, 2007, published a statement inviting public comments on the possibility of allowing US-listed companies to report their finances using IFRS rules (IAS standards). See "SEC Soliciting Public Comment on Role of IFRS in the U.S.," SEC news release, July 25, 2007, available at www.sec.gov.

95. See IAS-19 (at www.iasb.org) and FRS-17 (at www.frc.org.uk).

96. FAS 87 allowed employers sponsoring defined benefit pension plans numerous "accounting tricks." In particular, it relied on assumed rates of return on pension plan assets, somewhat arbitrary liability discount rates, extensive smoothing (i.e., postponement of the recognition of economically important events) across multiyear periods, and no income statement/balance sheet recognition of changes to plan finances. For an extensive review of the distortive impact of FAS 87 on S&P 500 companies' finances and how to see through it, see Zion and Carcache (2003, 2005).

97. Limited exceptions exist for plan assets used in plan operations and certain insurance contracts. See footnote 2 in FAS 158.

98. Projected benefit obligation (PBO) basis is forward-looking and attempts to capture future wage increases, yet nonvested benefits, actuarial assumptions, and discount rates.

99. See the FASB Project Statement at www.fasb.org/project.

neously pursuing international convergence of accounting standards with the International Accounting Standards Board (IASB).[100]

Combined with Congress's amendment, with the 2006 PPA, of the ERISA minimum funding requirements (it is important to distinguish between legislated ERISA minimum funding requirements and the privately established FASB Generally Accepted Accounting Principles (GAAP), which guide corporate financial reporting generally) for US defined benefit plan sponsors,[101] FAS 158 will introduce additional volatility into US corporate accounting (as we explain below).

It is hardly, however, just a desire to "hide corporate pension accounting skeletons in the closet" that has made business opposition to such changes more entrenched in the United States than in the European Union. There are also fundamental differences in benefit provision between the United States and the rest of the world. As we pointed out in chapter 3, the United States is unique among industrialized countries in its reliance on tax-benefited corporate health care plans rather than a comprehensive government-mandated health care system. The FAS 158 changes to corporate accounting standards and balance sheet recognition concern not only defined benefit pension plans but also other postemployment benefits (OPEBs),[102] which are primarily health care–related expenses.[103] US companies (and state and local governments) have hitherto financed OPEBs out of current cash flow on a PAYGO basis and have rarely prefunded them or even estimated likely future liabilities. Thus only since the adoption of FAS 158 in 2006–07 are US companies recognizing substantial health care–related liabilities on their balance sheets, with resulting large

---

100. IASB and FASB in 2006 signed a memorandum of understanding in which both entities "pledged to use their best efforts (a) to make their existing financial reporting standards fully compatible as soon as is practicable and (b) to co-ordinate their future work programmes to ensure that once achieved, compatibility is maintained" (available at www.iasb.org).

101. In particular, the 2006 PPA's reduction of smoothing periods for assets and interest rates (to two years) and the narrowing of the asset fair value corridor to only 90 to 110 percent of market value will have a volatility-inducing impact on defined benefit plan sponsors' financial statements, similar to that of FAS 158.

102. FASB generally defines OPEBs as "all postretirement benefits expected to be provided by an employer to current and former employees (including retirees, disabled employees, and other former employees who are expected to receive postretirement benefits), their beneficiaries, and covered dependents, pursuant to the terms of an employer's undertaking to provide those benefits. Postretirement benefits include, but are not limited to, postretirement health care; life insurance provided outside a pension plan to retirees; and other welfare benefits such as tuition assistance, day care, legal services, and housing subsidies provided after retirement. Often those benefits are in the form of a reimbursement to plan participants or direct payment to providers for the cost of specified services as the need for those services arises, but they may also include benefits payable as a lump sum, such as death benefits." See FAS 106, paragraph 6.

103. See footnote 5 in FAS 106.

transitional effects to owners' equity[104] (the US experience is unlike that of European companies when they adopted FRS-17 or IAS-19, as EU health care provision is largely a government responsibility).[105]

Compustat data covering the 297 companies in the S&P 500 with either defined benefit plans or OPEB liabilities at the end of 2006 showed a FAS 158–related transitional total accounting loss (i.e., including both pension plans and OPEBs) of $137 billion among 258 companies, while 32 others experienced a total gain of just under $6 billion (seven were unaffected). The top five losers were General Motors ($16.9 billion), IBM ($9.5 billion), Ford ($8.7 billion), Boeing ($8.2 billion), and ExxonMobil ($4.9 billion).[106]

But FAS 158 actually resulted in little additional transparency, as the required information was previously available in footnotes to FASB-compliant financial statements and sophisticated analysts should therefore have incorporated it in company valuations. In other words, the introduction of FAS 158 was an accounting event rather than a market valuation event. However, this will not be the case if FASB's Phase II and international accounting standard convergence compel US employers to recognize pension plan and OPEB servicing expenditures on their income statement. With large unfunded OPEB liabilities and rising health care expenditures in the United States, such a change would introduce both previously unrecognized variable costs and volatility into the earnings statements of US companies, an outcome that they are likely to oppose vehemently.

Looking at accounting standard reforms from the perspective of pension provision, it is tragic that US failure to establish a comprehensive health care system—which, like is currently the case in all other countries, would have removed the vast majority of health care related OPEB liabilities from the list of corporate concerns—may seriously constrain attempts to shore up corporate pension provision and financial reporting.[107] This failure is all the more unfortunate, as US private-sector employers (unlike state and local entities) have recently pretty much eliminated the defined benefit pension plan underfunding that emerged after the collapse of the dot-com bubble in 2001.

---

104. Crucially, FASB allowed OPEBs to be recognized on an accumulated benefit obligation (ABO) basis, which represents accumulated health care expenses but no projected benefits. Given the projected rapid rises in US health care costs, this distinction saved US companies a large amount of owner's equity, as ABO health care liability values would, in general, have been lower than PBO values.

105. Foreign multinational companies with US operations may also be exposed to US OPEB liabilities.

106. All data from Burr (2007).

107. This would be the corporate equivalent of the same phenomenon happening at the US household level already. EBRI (2007) found that 63 percent of Americans had experienced an increase in health care copayments and that a third of this group had reduced retirement savings as a result.

Figure 7.7 illustrates the decline in underfunding of US defined benefit pension plans among S&P 500 participants, from a maximum of $165 billion (16 percent) in 2002 to a combined surplus of $8 billion (1 percent) by the end of 2006.[108] However, volatility in asset markets and interest rates makes year-end snapshots an unreliable gauge for the longer-term health of pension plans. Thus Milliman Consultants and Actuaries (2008) reports that, although in their survey the 100 largest publicly traded companies with a defined benefit plan at the end of 2007 were, on average, overfunded at 106 percent of projected liabilities, by the end of the next quarter funding levels had dropped below 100 percent. It further seems likely that the fall 2008 financial crisis will have seriously affected funding levels, too, through the dramatic decline in global stock markets.[109]

Yet, it is the difference between funding levels of pension liabilities (volatile or not) and health care liabilities that stands out in figure 7.7. The combined net underfunding of health care liabilities was relatively unchanged in 2002–06 at about $300 billion, and had a measly 24 percent funding ratio at the end of 2006. Thus health care liabilities are generally not prefunded and have not benefited from the rise in equity values since 2003 (and in 2006 in discount rates); they, therefore, remain three-quarters unfunded, yielding a potentially much larger impact on annual income statements (after a potential change in US accounting standards) than that of defined benefit pension provisions.[110] This is particularly so as inflation in US health care costs has consistently exceeded that of other sectors of the economy.

Financial markets and US corporate executives generally do not like such volatility in earnings, and so it is not surprising that Jack VanDerhei

---

108. See also Milliman Consultants and Actuaries (2007) for similar results showing that the US corporate defined benefit pension underfunding was eliminated by the end of 2006. Cohen, Moran, and Kim (2007) also show that if one includes non-US defined benefit pension plans sponsored by S&P 500 companies, the funding ratio drops to 97 percent. This occurs as funding levels in non-US S&P 500–sponsored defined benefit plans, due to the lack of pension funding requirements in some countries, were much lower, at 80 percent in 2006, than among US plans.

109. Although, at the same time, it is important to note that another of the principal characteristics of the fall 2008 financial crisis has been the big rise in corporate AA bond yields, used by most pension plans to discount their liabilities. This aspect of the financial crisis, ceteris paribus, improves plan funding levels and works to offset the impact of declines in plan asset values. As such, and not without irony, it is only in the event that corporate AA bond yields decline again (i.e. that financial authorities are successful in their attempts at reintroducing liquidity into the credit markets), but without a corresponding rapid recovery in stock prices, that defined benefit plan sponsors will feel the full adverse effect of the 2008 stock market decline.

110. Kaiser Family Foundation and Hewitt Associates (2006) show that many employers are reducing their retiree health care obligations by increasing retiree premium contributions and cost sharing, drug copayment, out-of-pocket payment limits, or simply terminating subsidized benefits for future retirees.

Figure 7.7   US defined benefit and health care provision net funding levels, S&P 500 companies, 2002–06

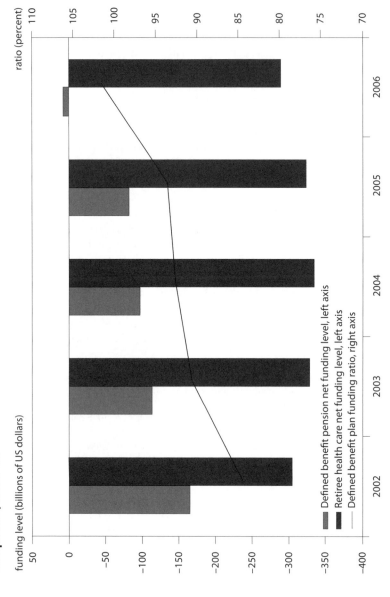

funding level (billions of US dollars)

ratio (percent)

Defined benefit pension net funding level, left axis
Retiree health care net funding level, left axis
Defined benefit plan funding ratio, right axis

Source: Cohen, Moran, and Kim (2007).

(2007) finds that over half of defined benefit pension plan sponsors surveyed in early 2007 either had reduced (in the preceding two years) or were planning to reduce (in the next two years) their level of defined benefit pension provision by (in order of prevalence) closing the defined benefit plan to new hires, freezing their defined benefit plan for all members, reducing the level of defined benefit plan benefits, converting to a hybrid plan, increasing employee contributions, or terminating the defined benefit plan entirely. He also found that defined benefit plan sponsors stated that the two most important drivers for these changes were (1) the desire to restructure the company's benefit strategy and (2) concern over the present and potential future impact of FAS 158 and 2006 PPA on income statements and balance sheet volatility (VanDerhei 2007, figure 5). Thus the accounting risk of additional earnings volatility from new standards provides an important push away from traditional defined benefit pensions.

Asset-Liability Mismatch Risks

Terminating or freezing a defined benefit pension plan is an uncomplicated way for a plan sponsor to either eliminate or significantly reduce exposure to investment risk during the period between contributions to a pension fund and retirees' withdrawal of their benefits (see box 7.2 for details of plan freezing). The risks are passed on to the retiree in the form of defined contribution or hybrid pension plans (or no corporate pension at all), representing a substantial transfer of risk to private households.[111]

Given the convergence of declining equity markets (which reduced asset valuations), declining long-term interest rates (which increased liabilities), and the increasing number of retiring workers that hit corporate pension plans in 2001–02, it may seem rational for plan sponsors to wish to head for the exit. However, as we have indicated, US corporate defined benefit plans actually performed very strongly in 2003–07, thanks to the strong performance of equity markets after 2003, a significant rise in corporate pension contributions,[112] and a rise in discount rates (which are linked to long-term corporate bond rates) in 2006.[113] This strong performance was

---

111. See Visco (2005) for a survey of the literature and in-depth analysis.

112. Zion and Carcache (2005) show that contributions for the S&P 500 were only $10 billion to $15 billion in 1999–2001 before rising to over $40 billion in 2002 and $74 billion in 2003. Cohen, Moran, and Kim (2007) show a decline to $47 billion by 2006. Given that many companies ceased to contribute after the rise in asset values in the late 1990s, this return to pension contributions was belated.

113. The equal-weighted discount rate for the S&P 500 companies fell from 7.2 percent in 2001 to 6.7 percent in 2002, 6.1 percent in 2003, 5.8 percent in 2004, and 5.6 percent in 2005, before rising again to 5.8 percent in 2006 (Cohen, Moran, and Kim 2007).

Box 7.2   The middle ground: Freezing rather than terminating a defined benefit plan

This allows IBM to offer meaningful benefit value for our people at costs we can control over time.

—Randy MacDonald, senior vice president, IBM HR[1]

As an alternative to exiting defined benefit provision entirely by terminating their defined benefit plans and (perhaps) setting up defined contribution or cash-balance plans, sponsors may choose an intermediate option and merely freeze their defined benefit plan partly or completely. They thus continue to support their existing pension benefit commitments but control the costs and uncertainties of these commitments rather than completely removing them from the company's financial statements. Because the standard Pension Benefit Guaranty Corporation (PBGC) termination of a defined benefit pension plan is usually quite expensive (due to the high costs of private group annuity purchases), freezing a pension plan usually carries fewer immediate costs to the plan sponsor.

The PBGC (2005b) distinguishes between several types of defined benefit freeze: a "hard freeze" closes the defined benefit plan to new entrants and prevents existing active participants from accruing any additional benefits. The plan sponsor thus freezes the size of its defined benefit pension liability and achieves complete predictability for it. A "partial freeze" suspends the benefit accrual of some participants but not others, and a "soft freeze" restricts the accrual of pension benefits so that, for example, they no longer rise with seniority, only wages, or vice versa.[2] In both a partial and soft freeze, plan sponsors act to control costs of and uncertainty related to future pension benefit provisions.

Defined benefit plan sponsors may not alter, modify, curtail, or terminate any already accrued benefits,[3] but because defined benefit plan provision is voluntary, sponsors retain the right to at any time alter, modify, or terminate their plan's future benefit provisions. So a decision to freeze a defined benefit plan is probably not a short-term financial fix and cost-cutting measure but rather a long-term strategic attempt by plan sponsors within the legal options available to limit their exposure to the rising costs and uncertainties of defined benefit coverage provision.

Several commentators have noted that healthy US companies have in recent years acted to freeze their defined benefit plans. Munnell and colleagues (2006) list such household corporate names as IBM, Alcoa, Sprint, Verizon, Lockheed Martin, Hewlett-Packard, and Motorola among recent US "defined benefit freezers." Interestingly, Nissan North America, Inc. also did so in 2006 and thus seems to have preemptively moved toward insulating itself from the pension liabilities that have adversely affected its Detroit-based competitors.[4]

The PBGC (2005b) found that 9.4 percent of all insured defined benefit plans were hard frozen in 2003 and were concentrated among smaller plans, affecting 1.8 percent of all active defined benefit plan participants that year. The PBGC study further found that the funding status of frozen plans was, on average, significantly worse than for unfrozen plans. This clearly and unsurprisingly indicates that the cost of defined benefit provision seems to be a major driver of pension freezes. Pension freezes thus provide a cost-control measure for plan sponsors who cannot afford to terminate their underfunded plan in the standard PBGC way, which would require them to fully fund their plan before doing so.

The situation of active participants in a hard-frozen defined benefit pension plan is little different from that of participants in plans that have been terminated in a standard manner under the PBGC. They will get their accrued vested defined-benefit benefits in their entirety but face different pension plan coverage going forward.

1. Comment in relation to IBM's freezing its pension plan in 2005; available online at www.ibmemployee.com.

2. Most defined benefit plans apply a formula linking the number of years of service to the wage level during a particular period, such that benefits, for instance, equal 1.5 percent of the average wage during the last five years of employment times the number of years in employment. See chapter 3 for a detailed discussion of typical defined benefit plan formulas.

3. See McGill et al. (2005, 381ff) for additional standard provisions of defined benefit plan provision.

4. See the Center for Retirement Research website at www.bc.edu for details.

spread across the S&P 500 and especially among larger plans, as illustrated in table 7.4.[114]

Based on the 2006 data, US corporate pension plans seem to be generally well funded and not in any immediate financial distress (that might cause plan sponsors en masse to cease offering defined benefit pensions due to short-term financial concerns). Spectacular United Airlines–style collapses should hence be few and far between. However, it is probably

114. It must again be emphasized that at the time of this writing it seems clear that the effects of the 2008 financial crisis will likely affect pensions plans very negatively if high-grade corporate bond yields decline without a rebound in the stock markets.

Table 7.4 US corporate defined benefit plans, 2003–06

a. S&P 500, funded ratio, by sector (percent)

Sector	Funded ratio			Change, 2003–06
	2003	2005	2006	
Telecommunication services	106	107	118	12
Financials	100	101	108	8
Consumer, discretionary	91	96	104	13
Information technology	91	97	100	9
Industrials	87	92	100	13
Utilities	90	91	97	7
Materials	84	85	94	10
Consumer staples	79	85	91	12
Health care	80	85	90	10
Energy	71	76	87	16
Total S&P 500	90	93	101	11

b. Top 15 plans in the S&P 500, by assets (millions of dollars)

Company	Assets	Obligation	GAAP funded status, end-2006	Funded ratio, end-2006 (percent)
General Motors Corporation	101,392	85,422	15,970	119
AT&T, Inc.	69,284	58,419	10,865	119
General Electric Company	54,758	43,293	11,465	126
IBM Corporation	52,913	46,498	6,415	114
Boeing Company	46,203	45,582	621	101
Ford Motor Company	44,728	45,288	−560	99
Verizon Communications, Inc.	41,509	34,159	7,350	122
Lockheed Martin Corporation	25,735	28,525	−2,790	90
E.I. Du Pont de Nemours & Company	21,909	22,849	−940	96
Northrop Grumman Corporation	21,407	21,484	−77	100
United Technologies Corporation	20,593	21,948	−1,355	94
Bank of America Corporation	16,793	14,025	2,768	120
Honeywell International, Inc.	16,578	17,008	−430	97
United Parcel Service, Inc.	15,374	13,558	1,816	113
Dow Chemical Company	14,958	15,850	−892	94

GAAP = Generally Accepted Accounting Principles

Source: Cohen, Moran, and Kim (2007).

immature to call victory for defined benefit plan sponsorship just yet, as recent developments have not resolved the underlying issues concerning the asset-liability mismatch (ALM) in most defined benefit plans, and 2006's favorable funding levels will not be enough to slow the move away from defined benefit sponsorship.

An inherent ALM emerges as the majority of pension fund assets are invested in equities, while liabilities are discounted using high-grade bond rates and the time for their payout is becoming imminent with an aging workforce. Some commentators worry that this mismatch and the presence of the PBGC introduce moral hazard, as defined benefit plan providers with huge underfunding have an incentive to invest in riskier equities to boost returns. Figure 7.8, which shows the allocation of private US defined benefit plan assets from 1994 to 2007, lends some support to this view. The equity allocation of private defined benefit pension funds rose substantially throughout the bull market of the late 1990s[115] and then continued after the large plan underfunding emerged in 2001–02. The rise is even more pronounced if one includes mutual fund shares in the corporate equity allocation.

However, there are sharply diverging views about the optimal asset allocation for pension funds.[116] Broadly, one school of thought espouses the view that equities are superior because they offer higher returns over the long term and better inflation protection through their valuation, which reflects future profits and wage and price increases. In the other camp are those who opine that a defined benefit pension fund portfolio should be wholly or mostly invested in long-term fixed-income securities, to more closely resemble a fund's long-term fixed-income obligations. This view should gain credibility when, as was the case in 2006 (table 7.4), defined benefit plans are close to full funding levels and hence in a financial position to closely match the full extent of their liabilities.

It is beyond the scope of this book to explore this issue further, except to say that a well-diversified defined benefit portfolio with an equity weight similar to US defined benefit plans in 2006 would not a priori seem excessively risky, even in the longer term, unless the plan sponsor itself experienced significant financial problems in its core operations and would therefore be unable to make required extra pension fund contributions.[117] What is clear, though is that when one compares US defined benefit plan asset allocations with those of other OECD countries, they have the highest of all equity allocations.

Figure 7.9 combines US defined benefit plan data from the Federal Reserve Board with data for corporate pension funds from other OECD countries (as such, they should be viewed with caution, as asset allocations in defined contribution and other plans may differ from those of defined benefit plans).[118] US defined benefit plans have a substantially higher allocation of assets in equities than pension plans elsewhere, although

---

115. These data do not include information about international diversification.

116. See, for instance, Bodie (1995), Siegel (2002), IMF (2004), Feldstein (2005), or Visco (2005).

117. Such high but diversified equity investment ratios would, however, assume that investors in the plan sponsor's stock would be indifferent to additional exposure to unrelated business areas via this pension fund portfolio.

118. There are also substantial differences between countries in the reporting of asset classes. The very high allocation to mutual funds in Australia and Belgium are likely the result of such reporting differences. In US defined contribution plans, the corresponding equity and mutual fund share allocation in 2005 was 76 percent (FRB 2008, table L118C).

Figure 7.8   Asset allocation of US private defined benefit plans, 1994–2007

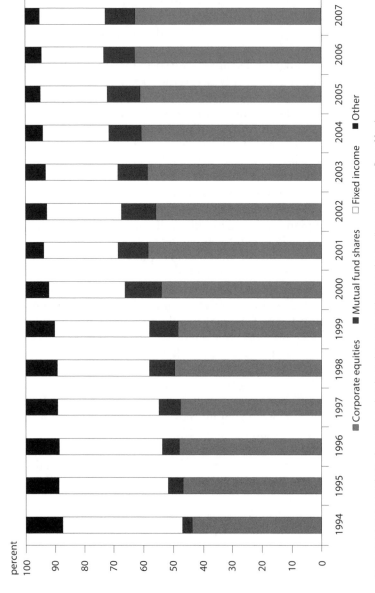

Note: "Fixed income" includes short-term and credit market assets. "Other" equals miscellaneous assets in flow of funds accounts.

Source: Federal Reserve Board (2008).

Figure 7.9 Structure of assets of pension funds in selected OECD countries, 2005

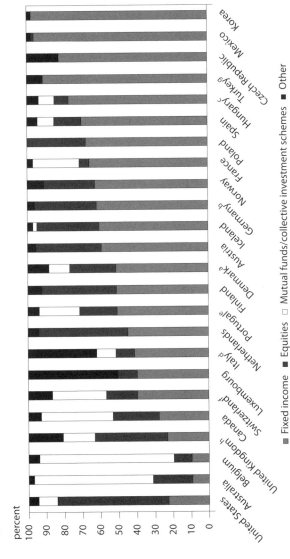

■ Fixed income ■ Equities ☐ Mutual funds/collective investment schemes ■ Other

a. Other investments include value of buildings (not for investment purpose), accounts receivable, provisions for liabilities covered by rein-
surance, as well as accrued income and deferred expenses.
b. Private investment funds, of which 82.3 percent is hedge funds and 17.7 percent is private equity funds.
c. Other investments includes mortgage bonds.
d. Other investments include assets of affiliated companies (with a 100 percent holding) holding land and buildings.
e. Other investments include short-term payable and receivable accounts.
f. Data are estimates; private investment funds, of which 80.3 percent is hedge funds and 19.7 percent is private equity funds.
g. Other investments includes "reverse repo" investments.
h. 2004 data.

Sources: OECD Global Pension Statistics; Federal Reserve Board (2008).

financial markets in the United Kingdom and the Netherlands have relatively high allocations at 40 and 50 percent, respectively.[119] While this difference in allocation may partly result from different regulatory requirements concerning permissible investment assets for pension funds, US defined benefit plans are more exposed to market volatility and ALM than private corporate pension plans elsewhere. Indeed, OECD (2008) estimates that US pension funds lost $2.2 trillion from December 2007 to October 2008, or two-thirds of the total losses among OECD pension funds of $3.3 trillion during this period. Similarly, CBO (2008) estimates that US private-sector defined benefit plans up to 15 percent of the value of their assets in the year to October 2008. Simultaneously, however, the rise in corporate bond yields over the same period (see Kirkegaard 2008 for details on pension liability accounting) cut defined benefit plans' liabilities by 5 to 10 percent. As such, US defined benefit pension plans will likely be significantly more exposed to declines in global equity markets in late 2008 than corporate pension plans elsewhere. Yet US plan sponsors seem unwilling to reduce their ALM by increasing their bond allocation, instead choosing higher risk/returns in their pension funds over reduced volatility in funding ratios, required contributions, and corporate earnings.

Given the increased accounting transparency discussed above and the current full funding ratios, this may yet change, and the age of liability-driven investments by US defined benefit plan sponsors will be upon us soon. However, it seems more likely that US defined benefit plan sponsors want the "upside potential" from a high equity allocation in return. Rather than forgo potential gains from high equities allocations in their defined benefit plans (their autonomous profit center?), they instead reduce volatility in earnings by scaling back or exiting defined benefit plan provision all together.

Defined Contribution Plan Pull Factors

We believe the reasons for a push away from defined benefit plan provision are most important, but there are also "pull" factors toward defined contribution plan provision by private employers. The most important is a desire among many employees for the increased portability and mobility of a defined contribution pension plan: It is easier with a defined contribution plan to leave for a new job without administrative hassles and the risk of financial loss. As we saw in chapter 3, most defined-benefit benefit formulas are designed to encourage long tenures and reduce voluntary job turnover by making it very expensive to quit one's job early in one's career.

---

119. PPF (2006), which breaks out the share of mutual fund investments into other asset classes, suggests that since 2003, UK defined benefit pension plans have had an equity allocation of about 60 percent. Noncomparable data from Watson Wyatt (2007a, figure 5) indicate that the equity allocations of Australia, Canada, and Ireland, in addition to the United States and United Kingdom, are close to 60 percent.

Choice of Corporate Defined Benefit or Defined Contribution/Hybrid Pension Provision in the OECD

When considering the longer-term implications of the US shift away from corporate defined benefit pensions, it makes sense to consider whether there has been a similar trend in corporate pensions in other countries, and if so, what lessons might be learned. However, in order for such international comparisons to be meaningful, it is important to recall just how different countries' pension systems are. The OECD typology (box 2.1 in chapter 2) separated pension provision into three tiers:

1. universal redistributive systems, which are wholly public;

2. mandatory insurance-based systems, which may be either public or privately managed; and

3. voluntary private insurance schemes, which may be occupational (sectorwide) or company-specific, as is the mix of US corporate pensions described in this chapter; or voluntary individual (i.e., purchased by the individual at market prices; excluded from analysis in this book).

Countries whose pension system structures most resemble that of the United States are most relevant to a cross-country comparison of experiences in corporate pension provision, and the statistics in table 7.5 enable us to identify such countries. Because the original OECD sources stress the difficulties of gathering valid and comparable cross-country information, the data presented here are merely the "best available."

Column 2 of table 7.5 shows the ranked coverage (i.e., worker participation) rate of voluntary occupational pension schemes.[120] The US coverage rate of 56 percent[121] is one of the highest in the OECD for purely voluntary corporate pension plans; only Germany and Canada had higher coverage in 2004. Comparable, more detailed cross-country data for the share of workers covered under both defined benefit and defined contribution plans (similar to the US data in figures 7.2 and 7.3) are unfortunately not available. Instead, column 3 provides data for the total size of countries' private corporate pension fund and life insurance assets, to indicate the relative size of this asset class and, by extension, the likely importance of corporate

---

120. Table 7.5 includes Australia and Iceland although they have mandatory systems, which fall outside the tier 3 voluntary pension system. Similarly, the systems in Denmark, the Netherlands, and Sweden are quasi-mandatory. All five countries are nonetheless included in table 7.5 as they have sizable pension assets and hence provide relevant information about the choice between defined benefit and defined contribution plan provision.

121. This OECD cross-country data source has coverage rates slightly higher than the approximately 50 percent from the BLS data in figures 7.2 and 7.3.

Table 7.5   Selected data on voluntary occupational pension plans in the OECD

Country	Coverage of occupational voluntary pensions, 2004 (percent of workforce)	Total private pension fund and life insurance assets, 2006 (percent of GDP)	Share of occupational pension assets, 2006 (percent of assets) In defined contribution plans	Share of occupational pension assets, 2006 (percent of assets) In defined benefit plans
Australia[a]	Mandatory personal	91	83[g]	17
Iceland[a]	Mandatory occupational	138	82	16
Netherlands[b]	90+	136	9[g]	91
Denmark[b]	90+	139	93	7
Sweden[b]	~90	57	5[g]	95
Canada	65	102	9	91
Germany[c]	63	18	0[g]	100
United States	**56**	**120**	**37**	**63**
Ireland	52	50	98[g]	2
Britain[d]	51	88	22[g]	78
Norway	45	7	0	100
Japan[e]	45	23	1[g]	99
Belgium	45	15	25[g]	75
Spain	40	13	97	3
Austria	40	9	75[g]	25
Finland	20	78	0	100
New Zealand	20	13	72	28
France	18	7	0	100
Italy[f]	9	3	85	15
Portugal	5	15	5	95
Greece	n.a.	0.01	50[g]	50
Korea	n.a.	8	0	100

n.a. = not available

a. Schemes in Australia and Iceland are included in this table because, although they are mandatory, they share relevant characteristics of value for this comparison.
b. Coverage is quasi-mandatory via collective bargaining agreements.
c. Includes company book reserves (Direktzusage) for pension provision.
d. Schemes include those contracted out of the state second pension. Thus part of the benefits from these schemes is a component of mandatory retirement-income provision.
e. Includes total covered by tax-qualified pension plans, employees' pension fund, or both.
f. Excludes the severance pay system, Trattamento di Fine Rapporto (TFR), which can be converted into a retirement savings plan. Severance payments are also excluded for Japan and Korea.
g. Data are from 2004.

Note: Countries in italics are those with both coverage ratios and private asset levels above 10 percent.

Sources: OECD Global Pension Statistics; OECD (2007); authors' calculations.

pensions provided from them.[122] Again, the US saving level of 120 percent of GDP for corporate pension provision in 2005 was among the highest in the OECD; only Canada, Denmark, Iceland, and the Netherlands had levels of

122. A note of caution: No cross-country data are available for pension assets for corporate pension plan provision only. The total values for pension plan and life insurance assets presented in table 7.5 thus represent an overstatement of assets available. The extent of this overstatement is unknown and may fluctuate between countries.

more than 100 percent of GDP in 2006. Thus US corporate pension provision, in terms of both coverage and assets accumulated, is of relative prominence within the OECD. In other words, the private leg of the pension stool is quite strong in the United States relative to other OECD countries.

But extensive voluntary corporate pension provision is not a unique US phenomenon, as a number of countries have both extensive coverage ratios and substantial assets. We have illustrated this in table 7.5 by italicizing all countries with a coverage ratio and asset level above approximately 10 percent of workers and GDP, respectively. Fourteen countries meet this admittedly arbitrary threshold, a result that may be useful for comparing developments in the provision of such pensions.

As a reasonable proxy for the missing comparable cross-country data for the breakdown of corporate pension provision in either defined benefit or defined contribution plans, columns 4 and 5 show the breakdown of assets in such plans. We acknowledge, however, that this asset-based indicator is biased in favor of defined benefit plans in countries like the United States, where defined benefit plans are older and thus have accumulated the most assets. Accordingly, this indicator does not illustrate relatively recent shifts from defined benefit to defined contribution plan provision. This bias notwithstanding, what is immediately clear from columns 4 and 5 is the large differences among countries' choices between defined benefit or defined contribution provision, which tend to be polarized as one or the other. Among 15 countries with extensive corporate pension provision, only Belgium, New Zealand, the United Kingdom, and the United States have genuinely mixed defined benefit/defined contribution corporate pension assets and are not relying on either at least 80 percent defined benefit or at least 80 percent defined contribution based systems. This may illustrate that the growth of defined contribution plan provision started earlier in the United States than in many other countries that have relied largely on corporate defined benefit plan provision.[123]

A striking finding in table 7.5 is the fact that five OECD countries with extensive occupational pension plan provisions—Australia, Denmark, Iceland, Ireland, and Spain—relied almost exclusively on defined contribution plans. In other words, it seems entirely feasible to provide extensive occupational/corporate pension primarily, if not exclusively, on a defined contribution basis. Thus it is erroneous to equate occupational/corporate pension provision with defined benefit plan provision only and that the ongoing switch in America to defined contribution/hybrid plans is not to be regarded as the inevitable end of corporate pension but rather merely as the end to corporate pension provision as it has hitherto been known. We shall return below to why it is not clear that such a development towards a "defined contribution world" should be feared in the United States.

---

123. Defined contribution plan provisions grew rapidly in the United States after the creation of 401(k) plans in the 1978 budget bill. See also OECD (2007).

Recent Trends in Corporate Pension Provision in Other OECD Countries

There is some concern that US corporate pension provision and funding requirements place US companies at a competitive disadvantage relative to their global competitors. But table 7.5 shows that companies in several of America's traditional global competitors are involved in extensive pension provision, too. Indeed, the data for Canada, Germany, Japan, and the United Kingdom show that they were at least as or more reliant on defined benefit plan provision than was the case in the United States in 2006. As populations and workforces in these countries are aging even faster than in America (see chapter 2), one should assume that companies here would be exposed to the same corporate pension plan stress experienced in the United States from 2002 until recently. A closer look at all four countries will hence be informative.

Canada

Canada has in recent decades seen a slow decline in the relative membership of employer-sponsored pension plans, known as registered retirement plans (RRPs). While the number of people with RRP coverage has remained steady, it has not kept up with the country's employment growth, and so the coverage rate has declined from 51 percent of the full-time workforce in 1991 to 42 percent in 2006 (figure 7.10).

Figure 7.10 includes memberships of both private- (about 53 percent in 2006) and public-sector plans (47 percent). Among the total public-sector employees, essentially all are covered by a defined benefit plan, and the vast majority of Canadian workers on a defined contribution plan (83 percent) are employed in the private sector.[124] However, despite this, among Canadian private-sector employees covered by an RRP, the share in a defined contribution plan has still increased more slowly than in the United States, and corporate defined benefit plan provision remains the dominant plan type. According to Bob Baldwin (2004), from 1992 to 2002 the share of private-sector Canadian workers in a defined contribution RRP rose from 9 to just 15 percent of the total, implying that the other 85 percent of covered private workforce remains in a defined benefit RRP.[125]

Baldwin (2004) notes further that the decline in Canadian RRP coverage has occurred disproportionally among small defined benefit plans (as in the

---

124. Statistics Canada, daily release, June 21, 2007. See also Department of Finance (2005) and Li (2004).

125. According to Baldwin (2004), it is possible that these data underestimate the corporate shift toward defined contribution plan provision, as some Canadian employers may have shifted toward group-registered retirement savings plans (RRSPs), which are functionally equivalent to a defined contribution plan but as non-RRFs are not captured by these data.

Figure 7.10   Number of members in Canadian employer-sponsored pension plans, by category, 1985–2006

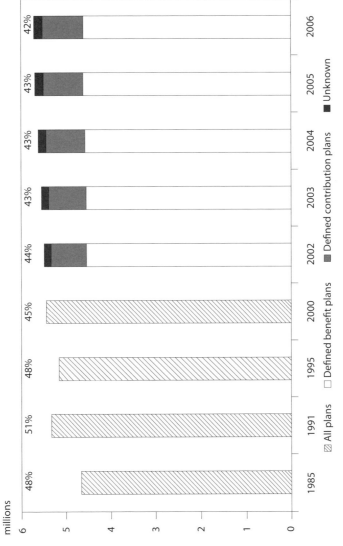

Note: The numbers in percent above the bars is the membership share of full-time employed workforce. While the absolute number of members is stable (the height of the bars), membership share has declined due to Canada's increasing total workforce.

Source: Statistics Canada CANSIM Table 280-0008.

United States). And the country's corporate RRP pension plans have gone through a funding cycle similar to those of the United States and United Kingdom—severe deterioration after 2001, leading to a doubling to C$12 billion of employer contributions from 2000 to 2002, funding rates below 90 percent in subsequent years, and finally an improvement in 2006–07.[126]

In summary, the trend in Canadian corporate defined benefit plans has been toward increased reliance on defined contribution plans, as in the United States, but at a slower rate.

Germany

Germany's 2001 and 2004 pension reforms revolutionized regulation of the country's corporate pension provision to promote the development of supplementary (second-tier) pension schemes. The reform altered regulation of the five defined benefit options for corporate pension provision and funding and for the first time permitted defined contribution plans, although not like those in the United States. Germany's corporate defined contribution plan providers must guarantee the nominal value of all contributions and thus insulate participants against most investment risk so that they risk losing only their investment gains. Zvi Bodie (2007) correctly identifies this as a "consumer protection approach to defined contribution plan provision," a policy approach that the German government adopted as the new supplementary pensions are likely to replace the decreasing government-provided first-pillar benefits.

Two internal options for pension provision—the Direktzusage (plans financed by company book reserves) and Unterstutzungskassen (company-specific benefit funds)—have existed for a long time, are mandatorily insured by the Pensions-Sicherungs-Verein (PSV), and have been the pension vehicles of choice for major German corporations.[127] These options have created substantial balance sheet differences between German and particularly Anglo-Saxon businesses.

There are also three external funding options for German corporations: Direktversicherung (direct insurance contracts[128]), Pensionskassen (staff pension insurance), and Pensionsfonds (pension funds). The first two are subject to the investment regulations (i.e., limitations on permitted

---

126. Watson Wyatt (2007b) estimates that the typical Canadian corporate pension plan was overfunded until early 2002, between 10 and 15 percent underfunded from 2002 to mid-2006, and in the first quarter of 2007 recovered to just below full funding levels.

127. While an internal company benefit fund is a legally separate entity, similar to a book-reserve plan, all retiree benefit claims are directed to the company(ies) sponsoring the benefit fund, or in the case of default, the PSV. See Deutsche Bundesbank (2001) for details.

128. Companies take out an individual or group life insurance policy for their employees, and the insurance company assumes the benefit risk.

asset classes) of the Bundesaufsichtsamt für das Versicherungswesen (the Federal Insurance Supervisory Office) but are not covered by the PSV. Pensionsfonds have no investment restrictions and so can invest heavily in equities, for example, and, since the creation in 2006 of an insurance industry insolvency protection fund, have had the option of such protection.[129]

Figure 7.11 illustrates the recent significant rise in the pension plan coverage of Germany's private workforce, quite unlike the stagnating trend in Canada, the United Kingdom, and the United States. Memberships in Direktzusage, Unterstutzungskassen, and especially in Pensionskassen rose substantially from 2001 to 2006, while Direktversicherung was stable, at just over 4 million members, and Pensionsfonds failed to seriously take off. Overall, coverage of corporate pension plans among the eligible workforce rose by more than 40 percent over this period to a 55 percent coverage ratio. Most German corporate pension plans today are defined benefit plans, while the investment protection requirements for defined contribution plan sponsors make a switch to such plans less financially appealing.[130]

However, several surveys point to the fact that many German companies, like their British or American peers, are nonetheless considering switching fully or partially to defined contribution pension plan coverage.[131] It would thus be erroneous to assume that Germany is unconditionally bucking the trend away from corporate defined benefit plan provision. This conclusion is further buttressed by two important additional factors that set Germany apart from the United Kingdom and United States.

First, it is important to note that the defined benefit pensions provided by German corporations, while highly heterogeneous in structure, are typically less generous than corresponding pensions in, for instance, the US manufacturing industry.[132] German official estimates indicate that workers covered by a corporate defined benefit plan can expect to receive only 6 percent of their retirement income from it, whereas the similar

---

129. The insurance industry insolvency fund is estimated to reach €500 million by 2009 from legally compulsory contributions from German pension funds. Membership, however, is voluntary for individual schemes. See IPE News, "German Pensionskassen Gets Insolvency Protection," May 24, 2006, available at IPE.com.

130. This corresponds to a near 100 percent defined benefit coverage rate for Germany's more than 5 million public-sector employees (TNS Infratest/BMAS 2007, table 6.1).

131. See IPE News, "DC to Take Off in Germany, Watson Wyatt Says," August 24, 2006, and European Pensions and Investment News, "Tempted by the Defined Contribution Carrot," June 18, 2007. Both estimate the share at over 75 percent of surveyed companies. This trend has been spearheaded by several foreign subsidiaries in Germany; for instance, IBM Germany in early 2006 announced that it intended to transfer all its German staff to a new company defined contribution plan (IPE News, "IBM to Transfer German Staff to Defined Contribution Plan," February 1, 2006).

132. This refers to average defined benefit pension plan generosity. Corporate pensions for German executives are likely to be far higher.

Figure 7.11 Membership of corporate pensions in Germany, 2001–06

millions

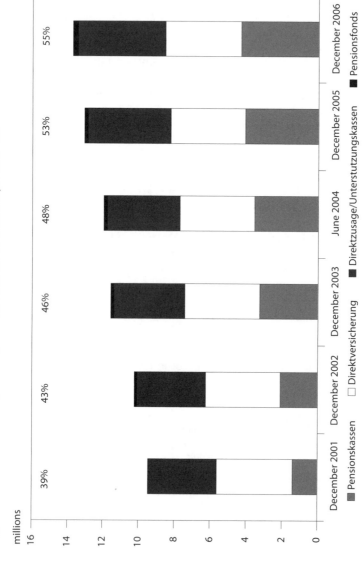

Note: The numbers in percent above the bars are the shares of eligible workforce covered, correcting for some workers having more than one type of coverage.

Source: TNS Infratest/Bundesministerium für Arbeit und Soziales (2007).

number in the United Kingdom is close to 30 percent.[133] Expanding German corporate defined benefit pension provision coverage would therefore not have required these companies to assume new liabilities to the same degree as a corresponding expansion in the United States. It is noteworthy, though, that the expansion of such coverage in Germany has occurred during a period of extensive wage restraint. So a collective bargaining strategy consisting of an exchange of wage restraint in return for improved future (defined benefit) pension guarantees (i.e., postponed expenses) by German employers and unions cannot be ruled out.

Second, another major innovation in German supplemental pension provision, the Riester-Rente, is more like a traditional (IRA-like) defined contribution design than other German pension options and aimed at replacing scheduled cutbacks in the public first-pillar pension.[134] Through a Riester-Rente, German workers can divert up to 4 percent of their wages, on a tax-sheltered basis, into one of the three company-sponsored external pension vehicles mentioned above or create a new individual account. The establishment of the Riester-Rente in 2001 essentially obliged companies that did not have pension plans to provide employees with an opportunity to benefit from the new pension through a corporate pension scheme. Employees may instead set up a personal account and can do so in plans subject to approval by the Federal Financial Markets Authority based on a lengthy list of requirements.[135] The stringent requirements for individual Riester-Renten are a result of their intended replacement function for gradually scaled-back government-guaranteed pensions, and have likely facilitated the rise in corporate pension provision, especially in Pensionskassen, since 2001 (figure 7.11).[136]

Riester-Renten are heavily subsidized, especially for low-wage workers and (unsurprisingly, given Germany's extremely low fertility) families with children. Estimates from Deutsche Bundesbank (2002) show that the savings subsidy can top 90 percent for low-income workers with two children, and is 40 to 50 percent even at much higher income levels. Despite this heavy government backing, the popularity of Riester-Renten was perhaps a little slow to emerge but then rose dramatically, doubling from roughly

---

133. See Social Protection Committee (2005). Old age income is generally higher in Germany than in the United Kingdom, which inflates the UK percentage, and vice versa. As part of the 2001/2004 pension reforms, an increasing role of supplementary pensions is envisioned—and may contribute up to 35 percent of total pension income in Germany by 2050. See Börsch-Supan and Wilke (2004).

134. See Börsch-Supan and Wilke (2004) for details.

135. Börsch-Supan (2004) lists 11 criteria for private individual pension plans to qualify for subsidies/tax relief.

136. Whether a large part of the increase in Pensionskassen is of the newly permitted defined contribution version cannot be discerned from the data available.

5 million in late 2005 to over 10 million in the last quarter of 2007 (figure 7.12). In 2008 the government subsidy for Riester-Renten is scheduled to rise to its final and highest level, with a maximum €2,100 annual tax deduction in addition to several direct subsidies.[137] These subsidies (in effect, a bribe to Germans to kick-start their retirement saving[138]) reflect both the government's determination to promote a supplementary pension system and the difficulties of attempting to "wean" residents off a government-financed pension system. Evidently the German public has belatedly learned to appreciate the lavishly supported switch to private saving for retirement.

Yet figure 7.12 shows that traditional "insurance contract" Riester-Renten, which include corporate pension plans, continue to dominate, indicating the crucial role of corporate pension schemes in supplementary pension provision in Germany. The German experience shows that even a government determined to promote voluntary (as opposed to mandatory) private saving[139] seems unlikely to succeed without extensive use of corporate-sponsored plans, especially if it simultaneously wishes to provide new private savers with a high degree of future income security from their private accounts. Such security seems more likely with Germany's tightly regulated corporate plans than with less restricted individual retirement accounts.

The rising use among many major German corporations of internal "book reserve plans" (Direktzusage) is largely dictated by the tax efficiency of this funding option.[140] However, with the increased focus among investors on companies' pension liabilities in recent years and the implementation of IAS-19, book reserve plans have created some confusion. Non-German investors have wrongly assumed that German companies' defined benefit pension liabilities were unfunded because of the absence of ring-fenced pension fund assets, when, in fact, these liabilities were on the company balance sheet and thus, like any other liability, guaranteed by company business assets (Mercer HR Consulting 2006, 2007).

The problem facing Germany's major corporations has been to combine the tax-optimal status of book reserve plans with a funded status of

---

137. The direct individual subsidy rises from €114 to €154, the child subsidy goes up from €138 to €185 (and an additional €300 for each newborn), and a new special €100 bonus for all under 21 years of age is instituted. See the Bundesministerium für Arbeit und Soziales (BMAS) website at www.bmas.bund.de.

138. The degree to which people simply reshuffle their savings portfolio in order to benefit from these subsidies, rather than contribute additional savings, is a concern. See Börsch-Supan, Ludwig, and Winter (2003) and Börsch-Supan, Heiss, and Winter (2004).

139. Whether such tax concessions for retirement savings are self-financing is highly controversial. See Boskin (2003) and Auerbach, Gale, and Orszag (2004).

140. See Mercer HR Consulting (2007). With a "book reserve plan" and thus no prefunded assets and independent investment income, companies face a rise in their retirement cash expenditures as the number of benefit-receiving retirees increases.

Figure 7.12 Number of Germans with a Riester pension, 2001–07

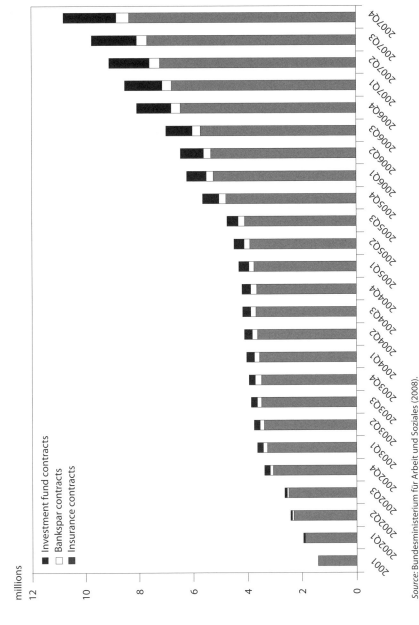

millions

■ Investment fund contracts
□ Bankspar contracts
■ Insurance contracts

2001 2002Q1 2002Q2 2002Q3 2002Q4 2003Q1 2003Q2 2003Q3 2003Q4 2004Q1 2004Q2 2004Q3 2004Q4 2005Q1 2005Q2 2005Q3 2005Q4 2006Q1 2006Q2 2006Q3 2006Q4 2007Q1 2007Q2 2007Q3 2007Q4

Source: Bundesministerium für Arbeit und Soziales (2008).

pension liabilities under IAS-19, which does not recognize internal company (book reserve) assets as eligible for required arm's-length pension funding purposes. The solution has been the contractual trust arrangement (CTA), under which German companies may legally earmark certain of their integrated business assets (i.e., spell out which book reserves they plan to use) for pension provision while retaining their tax-optimal structure. Companies have thus been able to adhere to IAS-19 without any tax implications for themselves or their employees.[141] As a result all companies in the DAX-30 use either a CTA or other external funding options for their pension liabilities (Towers Perrin 2007).

The German tradition of book reserve plans meant that company pension liabilities were frequently internally funded—not necessarily that they were fully funded. German companies have hence not been spared the "adverse impact" of recently increased pension transparency. A watershed event was Standard and Poor's downgrading in February 2003 of German steelmaker ThyssenKrupp to junk status because of its more than €7 billion in pension liabilities.[142] Furthermore, Mercer HR Consulting (2006, 2007) estimates that at the end of 2006 pension liabilities among the 30 German companies in the DAX index may have been as much as 30 to 35 percent underfunded, equal to €80 billion to €85 billion and amounting to a higher percentage of companies' market capitalization than the similar deficit among the FT100 or S&P 500 companies. This despite DAX-30 companies' 2005–06 pension funding contributions of more than €3 for each accrued benefit of €1, more than twice the rate of UK and US firms.

In summary, Germany's move toward an expansion of its supplementary pension system has led to an expansion of corporate pension coverage and defined benefit provision. A move toward increased reliance on corporate defined contribution pension plans seems likely and indeed imminent as businesses move vigorously to improve the funding levels of their pension plans. In this respect, German businesses have shared the pain of their American counterparts in recent years.

Japan

Corporate retirement benefit provision in Japan has traditionally been extensive, with a coverage ratio of close to 90 percent of private-sector workers, although many Japanese companies, in accordance with historical custom, continue to rely on lump-sum payments rather than annuities. According to the Japanese Ministry of Health, Labor, and Welfare (MHLW 2003), 40 percent of Japanese companies in 2003 relied solely on

---

141. This point is crucial, as it allows the corporate implementation of a CTA without having to consult worker representatives on the board and workmen's council.

142. See *Economist*, "Nest Eggs Without the Yolk," May 8, 2003.

lump-sum payments, 17 percent on defined benefit pension plans (annuities), and 30 percent used a combination of the two. The distinction, however, is somewhat blurred as the size of the lump-sum payment is usually estimated in a defined benefit pension-like manner as a function of final salary, years of service, and reason for resignation (Matsubara 2007).[143] Moreover, for funding purposes, this distinction is of less immediate importance, as, both lump-sum payments and defined benefit pension plans are funded through the same vehicles—as in Germany, either company book reserves or separate earmarked assets.

But Japan's reliance on lump-sum payments has fostered the pervasive view of corporate retirement benefits as "merit-based pay" (granted at the discretion of management as a reward for "good service to the company") rather than, as in the United States and elsewhere, as "deferred compensation" earned by the worker and paid upon retirement. As a result, the legal status of Japanese employees' retirement benefits is more uncertain than elsewhere, and the retirement benefit insurance system remains feeble.

Corporate pension plans across the OECD have been adversely affected by both the falls in the world's stock markets after 2001 and the ensuing declines in long-term interest rates. None, however, have been through the financial rollercoaster of Japanese corporate pension plans in the last decade and a half. Japanese plan sponsors have had to contend with both the complete collapse of the country's stock market—the Nikkei Index fell 80 percent, from almost 39,000 at the end of 1989 to below 8,000 in early 2003—and a decline in long-term interest rates to levels unseen elsewhere—the rate on the Japanese 10-year government bond fell from over 8 percent in September of 1990 to below 1 percent in October 1998, a low it reached again in late 2002.[144] Moreover, in this historically hostile investment climate the 5-3-3-2 rule,[145] which severely restrained Japanese pension asset allocation until 1997, further hampered Japanese plan sponsors' efforts to earn the required return on their pension assets.

In addition, in 2000 the Accounting Standards Board of Japan (ASBJ) started to demand increased transparency in corporate pensions. Before then, corporations, regardless of their funding structure and levels, had to merely recognize pension contributions as an expense on the income statement; in contrast, the new standard demands recognition and disclosure

143. Voluntary termination (i.e., employee resignation) usually entails a lower lump-sum payment than does involuntary termination or retirement.

144. The broader Tokyo TOPIX Stock Index fell more than 70 percent from late 1989 to early 2003. The 20-year Japanese government bond fell from 5.7 percent in late 1989 to just above 1 percent in early 2003. All data are from the OECD Main Economic Indicators, available online at www.sourceoecd.org.

145. The 5-3-3-2 rule required at least 50 percent of pension assets to be in fixed income (assets with a guaranteed principal), at most 30 percent in domestic equities, at most 30 percent denominated in foreign currencies, and at most 20 percent in real estate (Nakada 2007).

of the difference between the fair market value of pension assets and pension liabilities (on a PBO basis for both defined benefit annuities and severance payments) as a liability on the balance sheet of pension plan sponsors (see Usuki 2004). This new light on corporate pensions was devastatingly revealing, as the average reported ratio of pension plan assets to liabilities for the fiscal year ending March 2001 was an appalling 54 percent among the more than 1,000 companies on the First Section of the Tokyo Stock Exchange (TSE). And this ratio declined to 46 percent in March 2002 and 42 percent in March 2003, a year in which, according to the Ministry of Health, Labor and Welfare (MHLW 2005a), fully 95 percent of Japanese corporate pension plans were underfunded.[146] In other words, Japanese corporate pensions in 2002 had an average funding ratio of just over half that of the S&P 500 average funding level for pension liabilities, which bottomed out that year at 82 percent (Zion and Carcache 2005). Masaharo Usuki (2003) presents data showing that the total underfunding of 1,024 TSE-listed major Japanese companies in March 2002 was ¥38.9 trillion (almost $300 billion at the prevailing dollar exchange rate of 131), or almost 40 percent more than the estimated $216 billion underfunding in the S&P 500 that year. Of this amount, ¥14.4 trillion (about $110 billion) was still unrecognized on company balance sheets. In light of such catastrophically low average funding levels, and after a decade of abysmal financial returns, the introduction of the new accounting standard in 2000 was a remarkable victory for increased pension transparency—score one for Japanese accountants against Japanese corporate lobbyists! This is all the more impressive when viewed from the United States, where corporate lobbying has prevailed against similar demands for greater pension accounting transparency in the face of much smaller funding deficits.[147]

The funding situation among corporate pension plans in Japan led to two important legislative reforms in 2001–02. The Defined Contribution Pension Law (DCPL) in October 2001 legalized defined contribution pension plans, and the Defined Benefit Corporate Pension Law (DBCPL) in April 2002 significantly shifted the roles of corporate plan sponsors and the government in Japanese defined benefit plans.

Corporate pension provision in Japan traditionally consisted of two types of coverage: tax-qualified pension plans (TQPPs, introduced in 1962) and employee pension funds (EPFs, introduced in 1966[148]). Both emerged because, after the high-growth/high-inflation post–World War II years in Japan (not unlike the situation with nonindexed US Social Security benefits

---

146. The share of underfunded Japanese pension plans rose from 41 percent in 1993 to 91 percent in 2000, 94 percent in 2001, and 95 percent in 2002.

147. Japanese accountants, however, in their interpretations gave other sweeteners to Japanese businesses, as we shall see below.

148. EPFs can be single company funds, allied company (i.e., keiretsu-wide) funds, or multicompany-based funds.

from 1940–50), non-inflation-adjusted benefits from the mandatory second-tier employees' pension insurance (EPI) had declined to near insignificance.[149] Japanese companies, therefore, began to introduce supplementary corporate pensions. With TQPPs and EPFs, company contributions became fully tax-deductible business expenses. Crucially, though, to eliminate a "dual burden" for companies obliged to fund both the mandatory EPI (which saw both benefits and Social Security taxes increase substantially in 1965) and any supplementary pension, companies with an EPF could opt out of the EPI (the "contract-out" option) and manage employees' EPI pensions on a "substitution basis" along with any supplementary pension they wished to institute.[150] This contracting-out would be the (close) equivalent of American companies with a defined benefit pension plan that opted out of Social Security and instead managed corporate and employee contributions to their own pension fund.

This setup essentially allowed EPF plan sponsors to avoid paying Social Security contributions and instead accumulate these and other pension plan contributions on a tax-sheltered basis while servicing benefit payments out of general corporate revenue. Needless to say, this EPF option proved popular, especially among Japan's larger corporations, in times of high economic growth and relatively young workforces, while smaller companies usually relied on purely supplementary TQPPs. Alas, with the financial crisis in 1990 as well as the country's by-then rapidly aging workforce, the contracting-out option turned increasingly against EPF plan sponsors as financial returns collapsed and benefits and liabilities rose rapidly (more on this below).

The DCPL and DBCPL dramatically altered the corporate pension landscape in Japan, as illustrated in figure 7.13. The DCPL paved the way for the introduction of private-sector defined contribution plans in Japan, although differently structured and more limited in scope than US defined contribution plans. Japanese defined contribution plans can be employer or employee sponsored, but not both. In the former plan, the employer may contribute a tax-benefited maximum of ¥46,000 per month (about $420 at the time of introduction in October 2004) if there is no other pension scheme, ¥23,000 per month if the employer simultaneously operates a defined benefit scheme. However, unlike US defined contribution plans, employees are not permitted to make additional contributions to an employer-sponsored defined contribution plan,[151] nor can employers make contributions in excess of the listed amounts (unlike in the United States, where defined contribution plan contributions are, in

---

149. Japan also has had since 1961 a flat rate national basic pension (*kokumin nenkin*), which is a mandatory contributory defined benefit pension system for all residents. The EPI benefits in 1965 were just ¥10,000 per month (Usuki 2003).

150. The government would still pay to the EPF the portion of the EPI covering any subsequent cost of living allowances and costs of wage indexation. See Takayama (2005).

151. This makes the plan similar to a US money purchase plan (Urata 2001).

Figure 7.13 Corporate pension plan options in Japan after passage of the DCPL (October 2001) and DBCPL (April 2002)

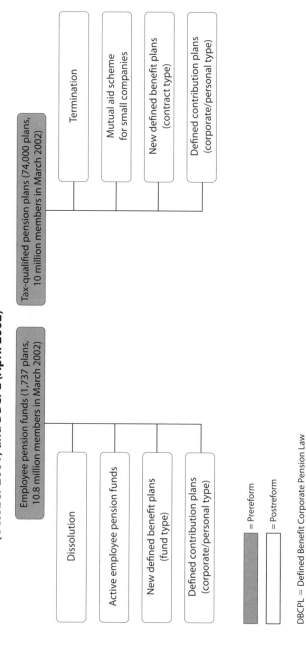

Employee pension funds (1,737 plans, 10.8 million members in March 2002)

- Dissolution
- Active employee pension funds
- New defined benefit plans (fund type)
- Defined contribution plans (corporate/personal type)

Tax-qualified pension plans (74,000 plans, 10 million members in March 2002)

- Termination
- Mutual aid scheme for small companies
- New defined benefit plans (contract type)
- Defined contribution plans (corporate/personal type)

= Prereform

= Postreform

DBCPL = Defined Benefit Corporate Pension Law
DCPL = Defined Contribution Pension Law

Sources: MHLW (2005a); Nakada (2007); authors' calculations.

principle, unlimited, although they lose their tax-benefited status above a certain threshold). And participants in Japan are vested in employer-sponsored defined contribution plans only after three years, not instantly, as in the United States. This delayed vesting for employer-sponsored defined contribution plans is the only reference to legally vested retirement benefits in Japanese law; employers retain the option of retroactively altering all other retirement benefits.

The decision to sponsor a retirement plan is entirely up to the private-sector employer in Japan. If the employer sponsors neither a defined benefit nor a defined contribution plan, employees are eligible for an individual-type defined contribution plan, to which they can contribute up to ¥18,000 per month. Public-sector workers and dependent spouses are not eligible for participation in defined contribution pension plans.[152]

After the termination of a number of underfunded TQPPs in the late 1990s, the DBCPL stipulated the phaseout of these plans by 2012 and provided the legal framework for TQPP sponsors to transfer the plans to defined contribution plans, or to a new contract-type defined benefit plan with more rigorous rules for the protection of plan participant benefits,[153] or, for smaller companies, to mutual aid schemes.[154]

The DBCPL provided EPF sponsors with the option to return the contracted-out substitution part of mandatory employee EPI benefits to the government and instead set up a fund-type defined benefit plan covering only the company's supplemental corporate pension. As shown in table 7.6 there has been a decline of about 25 percent in the defined benefit coverage of private-sector Japanese workers since 2002, when about 20 million enjoyed memberships in either an EPF or a TQPP, to just under 15 million in 2006, split among memberships in a much smaller number of active EPFs and TQPPs as well as new defined benefit plans. At the same time, about 2 million Japanese have gotten access to an employer-sponsored defined contribution pension since 2001, while personal defined contribution plans remain of marginal importance. Thus, as in the United States and elsewhere, Japan's recent experience in corporate provision is one of severe economic strains on plan sponsors and a marked shift from defined benefit to defined contribution plan provision.

However, Japan's regulatory changes to defined contribution plan sponsorship include several oddities. According to Noriyuki Takayama (2005), workers may not receive more than one public pension at a

---

152. Self-employed and dependent spouses may contribute up to ¥68,000 on a tax-benefited basis in a special defined benefit–type pension scheme operated as part of the national pension fund (*kokumin nenkin kikin*).

153. However, actual plan termination insurance for TQPPs or their successors was not initiated.

154. See Takayama (2005) for details.

Table 7.6 Japanese corporate pension provision, 1966–2006

Year	Number of active EPFs	Membership in active EPFs (millions)	Cumulative terminated EPFs	Cumulative EPFs, with "contracted out" EPI pensions handed back to government	Number of active TQPPs	Membership in active TQPPs (millions)	Number of defined benefit plans (contract type)	Number of defined benefit plans (fund type)	Total membership in defined benefit plans (millions)	Number of employer-sponsored defined contribution plans	Membership in employer-sponsored defined contribution plans	Number of individual defined contribution plans
1966	142											
1975	929											
1980	991											
1985	1,091											
1990	1,474											
1991	1,593											
1992	1,735	11.6										
1993	1,804	12.0										
1994	1,842	12.1	18[a]									
1995	1,878	12.1	19									
1996	1,883	12.1	26									
1997	1,874	12.3	40									
1998	1,858	12.0	58									
1999	1,835	11.7	74									
2000	1,801	11.4	103									
2001	1,737	10.9	162							70	88,000	400
2002	1,656	10.4	235		~74,000	~10	15	0	n.a.	361	325,000	14,000
2003	1,357	8.4	327	203	n.a.	n.a.	165	151	n.a.	845	684,000	28,000
2004	838	n.a.	408	641	~59,000	~7.8	479	513	n.a.	1,402	1.3 million	46,000
2005	651	6.3	438	762	n.a.	n.a.	n.a.	n.a.		n.a.	n.a.	n.a.
2006	658	5.3	445	783	45,090	5.7	1,607	603	3.8	1,997	~2 million	69,000

n.a. = not available
EPF = employee pension funds
EPI = employees' pension Insurance
TQPP = tax-qualified pension plans

a. Cumulative terminations from 1966 to 1994.

Sources: MHLW (2005a); Nakada (2007); Yano, Asaoka, and Sakamoto (2007).

time[155] (the inability of employees to contribute to employer-sponsored defined contribution plans and of employers to match contributions to individual defined contribution plans and thereby "participate twice" thus has a legal precedent). Alas, combined with the relatively low contribution thresholds of just ¥43,000/¥23,000/¥18,000 per month (for company-funded plans where no other [defined benefit] corporate plan exists, for company-funded plans where other [defined benefit] corporate plans exist, and individually funded defined contribution plans), this proscription inhibits the ability of defined contribution plans to even approach the replacement value of a reasonably generous defined benefit pension plan. Switches from defined benefit to defined contribution plans in Japan, therefore, seem likely to entail a larger risk of significant benefit reductions for retirees than under a more US-like defined contribution regulatory framework. Moreover, Japanese defined contribution plans have a mandatory rollover in case of job switch, and participants may not access their cash or benefits until age 60.

According to Haruka Urata (2001), the explanation for these apparent attempts to discourage defined contribution plan provision in Japan is partly in atavistic thinking among the Japanese tax authorities and partly in Japan's past as a very high-saving country (the latter is far less true today than in earlier decades, but it does set Japan apart from other countries reforming their pension system[156]). Indeed, to encourage more spending, tax authorities actually attempted to remove incentives to save. Defined contribution plans are viewed as saving and warrant tax-benefited status only when the participant reaches age 60, at which time the savings become old age benefits. In addition, defined contribution plans, like defined benefit plans, are subject to a corporate tax of 1.173 percent of the asset balance. Because this tax discourages both corporations and individuals in times of adverse investment opportunities, it has, however, been suspended since 1999.

In summary, it seems fair to state that the switch from defined benefit to defined contribution plans in Japan has occurred more out of necessity for financially stressed sponsors than as a result of legal or government encouragement, despite a stated desire to increase flexibility in the Japanese labor market through the introduction of corporate defined contribution retirement plans.

However, the DBCPL does include a potentially significant sweetener for Japanese corporate sponsors to alter their old EPFs. As mentioned, this law made it possible for EPF sponsors to hand back to the government the substitution part of the mandatory EPI contracted out in earlier years and, according to Takayama (2005), both financially stressed plan sponsors and labor unions eagerly sought this option. The unions were concerned

---

155. The only exception is people on a disability pension.

156. Japan's household saving rate fell rapidly during the 1980s, to single digits in 2000, and by 2005 to just 3 percent of household disposable income, a level at which it has remained since (OECD *Economic Outlook* 81, available online at www.oecd.org/dataoecd).

about the ability of severely underfunded EPFs to finance contracted-out mandatory EPI pensions, let alone any supplementary corporate pensions and, given the historic lack of real retirement benefit insurance in Japan, this union concern over the fate of otherwise mandatory but "contracted-out" EPI pensions is understandable and resulted in the political demand that the Japanese government ultimately step in and guarantee all parts of the mandatory second-tier pension liabilities.

But at what price did the Japanese government after 2002 agree to take back the EPI pension liabilities it had earlier let EPF sponsors manage? Table 7.6 shows that out of 1,656 active EPFs in 2002 (column 2) 783, or nearly 50 percent, had "handed back" their contracted-out EPI benefits to the government by 2006 (column 5), most of them during the first two years (2003–04). This strong preference for "hand-backs" suggests that the Japanese government offered EPF sponsors beneficial terms for the transaction and, indeed, Usuki (2003) cites several substantial benefits. First, with the extremely low Japanese interest (and hence discount) rates, most EPF sponsors likely welcomed an opportunity to offload long-term pension liability from the corporate balance sheet (recall that as many as 95 percent of pension plans were underfunded in 2002). Second, Usuki (2003) notes that, as in the United States, the semipublic character of contracted-out retirement benefits made regulation both cumbersome and inflexible and resulted in rising administrative and operating costs for EPF sponsors. Third, the rebate premium that EPF sponsors received from the Japanese government to manage the contracted-out benefits were far below market terms, so that EPF sponsors suffered interest rate losses.

The crucial item, though, is the terms of the asset-liability transfer between the underfunded EPFs and the government, in which the government receives the EPF fund assets and in return covers the future benefit liabilities. Usuki (2003, 15) notes that the "hand-back"

> enables a plan sponsor to record one-time profits on the income statement under the new accounting rule, since the amount of the reduced benefit obligation for accounting purposes is larger than the amount of assets a sponsor is required to pay back to the government.

The exact pension accounting details are complex. The ASJB allowed Japanese corporations that handed back the substituted portion of their EPI to the Japanese government to estimate the transferred liabilities on a standard PBO-basis, while estimating the amount of assets (the so-called buy-back reserve) transferred back to the government using a special formula described in the DBCPL.[157] This resulted in potentially large improvements in the consolidated statement of incomes for Japanese

---

157. For the details of this formula, see Sakamoto (2005). We are grateful to Junichi Sakamoto from the Nomura Research Institute for educating us via private correspondence about the effects of the DBCPL.

companies, as the offloaded PBO-basis pension liabilities invariably were much larger than assets transferred to the Japanese government, with the difference bookable as a windfall income gain.

It relevant to consider the general scope of these "hand-back" transactions. To the best of our knowledge, many of the company and government details are not publicly available (or maybe only in Japanese). However, two sources do exist that present a glimpse of the sums involved. The OECD in the online *Sources and Methods for the Economic Outlook* no. 83 lists the value of the capital transfer back to the Japanese government of the handed-back part of their employees' pension scheme as equaling $122.9 billion from 2003 to 2006.[158] Similarly, the annual financial reports of the Japanese Public Pension System to which the contracted-out liabilities were transferred for fiscal years 2003 and 2004 (MHLW 2005b, 2006a, 2006b), when most "hand-backs" occurred, reveal that the book value of the assets amounted to ¥3,496.5 billion ($32.2 billion at FY2003 exchange rates of ¥108.52/dollar) and ¥5,485.4 billion ($52.2 billion at FY2004 exchange rates of ¥105.25/dollar) in 2003 and 2004, respectively—in other words, about $85 billion over these two years alone. No data are available for subsequent years from this source. In total, therefore, a back-of-the-envelope estimate suggests that Japanese corporate EPF plan sponsors handed back to the Japanese government up to $120 billion in book value of pension assets over the four years to 2006 in return for freedom from their contracted-out pension liabilities. It is worth comparing this sum with the approximately $18 billion in net liabilities and $66 billion in reasonably possible exposure of the PBGC as of September 2007 (PBGC 2007b). Hence, the Japanese government from 2003–06 took back pension assets from Japanese corporations worth approximately twice the reasonably possible exposure of the PBGC to all US defined benefit pension plans in 2007!

Two factors remain unknown. First, we do not necessarily know what the market value of that up to $120 billion was at the time of the "handing back." Given the large asset value declines in Japan noted above, the difference might have been very large indeed. Second, and much more important, what was the true size of the other side of the transaction balance sheet—the actual scale of the future pension liabilities assumed by the Japanese government from EPF sponsors in return for the maybe $120 billion in book value assets? The MHLW (2005b, chapter 2, 2) succinctly notes that "It will be important to remind that this [buy-back] money is temporary revenue with future benefit obligations."

Not unlike the situation in France (see appendix 7A), where the government "bought back" all pension liabilities from EDF in 2004, the Japanese

---

158. The OECD describes how the capital transfers reduced the general government financial deficit by 0.1, 1.4, 0.9 and 0.3 percentage points of GDP in 2003, 2004, 2005, and 2006 respectively, equaling a total of $122.9 billion relying on 2003–06 annual dollar-denominated GDP from the IMF *World Economic Outlook* database. See *Sources and Methods for Economic Outlook* no. 83, Annex Database table 26 at www.oecd.org.

with the DBCPL took over parts of the future pension liabilities of a large number of Japanese companies in exchange for an immediate cash-transfer. There seems to be a type of "accounting standards arbitrage" at play here, too, with Japanese corporations taking large (and since 2000, reportable in financial statements) pension liabilities off their books and transferring them to the Japanese government, which does not have to reveal or publish its combined future pension liabilities, according to the System of National Accounts. As all pension liabilities thus "handed back" from Japanese corporations to the government as a result of the DBCPL essentially became a relatively small part of the unpublished total future Japanese government pension liabilities, the true size of this additional future Japanese government fiscal commitment is probably not that important in the short term.

What, on the other hand, mattered a lot almost immediately was the impact on Japanese companies' financial situation. Given the dire financial situation of Japanese EPF plan sponsors in 2002–03, a government bailout seemed not entirely unwarranted and was doubtless good politics at the time. However, the risk of moral hazard in such "across-the-board bailouts" looms large. And certainly many of Japan's largest corporations with large EPFs benefited tremendously from their "hand-back" and the associated PBO-based estimation of eliminated liabilities and special estimation of the transferred "buy-back reserve" assets, even if they were not facing an immediate financial crunch at the time. For example, according to Toyota's 2005 financial reports, in FY2004 and FY2005 the company saw a net positive impact on the consolidated statement of income in its parent company (and certain Japanese subsidiaries) of ¥107 billion and ¥47.2 billion, respectively.[159] At the exchange rates prevailing at the end of the fiscal years, these sums translate to a combined increase of Toyota's reported profits in 2004–05 of about $1.4 billion, solely as a result of the accounting treatment of the "handing back" of some of its pension liabilities to the Japanese government. It seems probable that competing US automakers with large future employee pension liabilities, too, would be interested in offloading these to the public sector under similar terms.

Japan, thus, stands out as the only major defined benefit–intensive country that seems to have instituted a (partial) government bailout of

---

159. These data are from the 2005 Toyota Annual Report, footnote 19 to the consolidated financial statements: Employee Benefit Plans (available at www.toyota.co.jp/en). All of these items are "noncash gains and losses" and accounting for the "hand-back" transaction is complex. Toyota recognized settlement losses to both cost of goods sold (CoGS) and sales, general, and administration (SGA); gains on derecognition of previously accrued salary progression; and gains on differences between the obligation settled (i.e., the scale of the pension underfunding) and the assets transferred back to the Japanese government. As such, the total impact on Toyota's income in 2004 and 2005 is not the same as the "gains from difference between the obligation settled and the assets transferred"; the total for this entry alone was ¥442.4 billion, or $3.85 billion at an exchange rate of ¥115/dollar.

corporate pension plans, as a result of which corporate defined benefit plan provision remains fairly extensive in Japan. Moreover, recent survey data from Greenwich Associates show that 96 percent of Japanese corporate pension funds were fully funded in 2006,[160] thus the voluntary corporate pension system seems to be in more robust financial health compared with earlier years, a trend also found among US defined benefit plans. Yet, other survey data from Greenwich Associates suggest that Japanese pension fund sponsors expect that 50 percent of corporate pensions in Japan will be defined contribution structures by 2015.[161] So although tens of billions of dollars from the Japanese government may well have saved the current defined benefit system from imminent collapse in the early 2000s, they also paved the way for a more orderly longer-term shift toward defined contribution corporate plan provision in Japan.

United Kingdom

The 2004 Pensions Act completely revamped the legal environment for UK defined benefit pension plans, as it introduced a new pension regulation authority as well as the Pension Protection Fund (PPF) to function as a PBGC-like safety net for defined benefit plan participants. These developments have come as a result of a development not dissimilar to what has been experienced in the United States with a long-term decline in the historically dominant corporate defined benefit pension plan provision. This is illustrated in figure 7.14. Generally, the UK defined benefit provision experience mirrors that of the United States: rapid growth in the 1950s and 1960s, followed by a decline in recent decades. A spike in private defined benefit plan provision in the 1980s was related to the privatization of public industries and resulting transfer of public-sector workers on defined benefit plans to the private sector. Nonetheless, defined benefit pension coverage for UK public-sector workers is still 85 to 90 percent,[162] corresponding to private-sector defined benefit coverage in 2005 of just 16 percent, which is even lower than in the United States (figure 7.2). In other words, the shift from defined benefit plan provision among UK companies has been at least as precipitous as among their US brethren.

The first Report of the Pension Commission (Turner 2003) investigated this declining trend in detail and found several key drivers:

- high marginal tax rates for both corporations and individuals initially made pension plans an efficient way to shelter earnings and attract staff;

160. "Japanese Funds in Big Turnaround," *Financial Executive* 23, no. 1, January/February 2007.

161. *BusinessWeek*, "Land of the Dimming Sunset Years," November 7, 2005 (available at www.businessweek.com).

162. Latest data from the UK Office of National Statistics are for 2004.

Figure 7.14 Active membership in UK private occupational schemes, 1953–2005

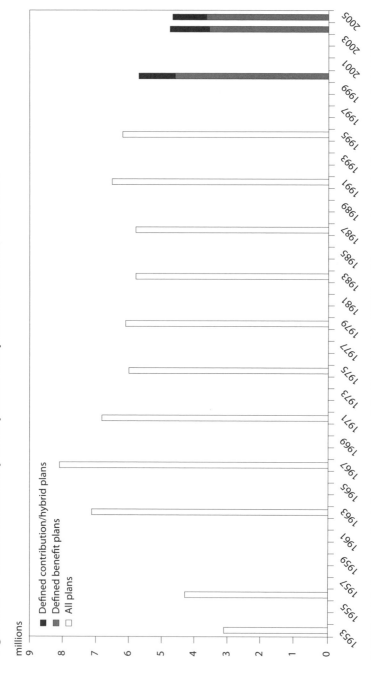

millions

- ■ Defined contribution/hybrid plans
- ■ Defined benefit plans
- □ All plans

Note: Surveys of private occupational schemes have been carried out irregularly since 1953. The split between private and public sectors beginning in 2000 is not perfectly comparable with earlier years, as since 2000 the public-sector figures have included only members of public service schemes. It follows that, from 2000 onwards, figures for the private sector also include members in the wider public sector (such as the Post Office and the BBC) and hence are slightly upwardly biased.

Source: GAD (2003, 2005, 2006).

- enactment in 1975 of the requirement to pay benefits to workers who left a company before retirement raised plan provision costs;[163]
- during the high-inflationary 1970s, benefits were adjusted to prices only at the discretion of plan trustees (compulsory indexation was introduced only in 1987);
- life expectancies have risen;
- regulations have tightened to safeguard equal treatment of workers, early leavers, and survivors; and
- "irrationally exuberant" assumptions of plan asset returns were punctured by the 2001 bear market.

The Turner report concluded that the decline of UK private defined benefit plan provision should be viewed principally as a "postponed result of long-term cost/benefit trends" (Turner 2003, chapter 3 annex).

Also similar to US defined benefit pension plans, the UK plans experienced serious underfunding after 2001, although the same benign financial trends (rising equity markets and rising bond yields after 2006) as in the United States have helped bring the UK plans closer to balance. However, figure 7.15 shows the PPF's Section 179 (S179) monthly balance (essentially equal to liquidation costs for defined benefit pension liabilities with a private-sector third party) for the approximately 7,800 British defined benefit plans from early 2003 to mid-2008, and, as can be seen, that balance fluctuated a lot—approximately £250 billion over this period.

The PPF 7800 index is an estimated value of about 7,800 private-sector defined benefit plans based on changes in market indices for principal asset classes and the fixed interest and index-linked gilt yields.[164] The PPF updates the index estimate monthly, providing a snapshot of the aggregate funding situation of gilt yields of UK defined benefit plans, information frequently missing from the US debate. Its high-frequency data show the volatility of defined benefit pension plans' funding status and the impact of changing prices for financial assets. PPF (2006) estimates that a 100 basis point change in UK government bond rates causes the aggregate PPF 7800 index to change by approximately £13 billion, while a 2.5 percent change in equity prices changes the balance by £11 billion. These estimated pension balance elasticities are cumulative and may thus easily combine for the sizable fluctuations seen in figure 7.15. Such volatility is not likely to be welcomed by UK business executives and, as in the United States, provides a powerful stimulus to exit defined benefit plan provision.

Furthermore, 2006–07 was the first year UK defined benefit plan sponsors had to pay the new mandatory annual PPF levy, estimated at

---

163. The absence of vested pension benefits before 1975 was a blatant transfer from "leavers" to "stayers" in the defined benefit plan.

164. For details, see PPF website at www.pensionprotectionfund.org.uk.

Figure 7.15   Aggregate UK defined benefit plan assets, liabilities, and balance on S179 basis, March 2003–June 2008 (billions of pounds)

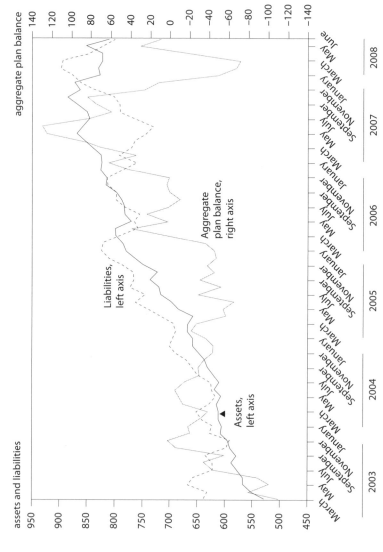

Source: PPF (2008).

£675 million, of which £540 million was to be risk adjusted.[165] PPF (2006) also estimates that UK defined benefit plan sponsors in the first part of 2006 earmarked about £10 billion in "special contributions" aimed at reducing underfunding before the introduction of the levy.

In summary, US and UK corporate defined benefit pension provision broadly share the same long-term concerns: rapidly rising costs, increasing regulation, and increasing volatility.

Conclusions

We draw two clear conclusions from the summaries above of recent trends in corporate pension provision in Canada, Germany, Japan, and the United Kingdom. First, the pension provision problems experienced by some US businesses in recent years are not unique to the United States. Like their US counterparts, corporate defined benefit pension plans in the four Group of Seven (G-7) countries surveyed above have been through the same triple whammy of declining asset prices, declining discount rates, and more transparent accounting standards. It is, therefore, disingenuous to suggest that US corporations are at any discernible pension-related competitive disadvantage in the global market place relative to businesses in other countries. The experience of the four countries surveyed, which are home to the majority of non-US multinational companies, shows otherwise. The one exception is Japan, where the government stepped in to bail out pension plan sponsors; but this followed a far worse domestic recession than experienced in the United States after 2001. Unambiguously, therefore, any global competitive disadvantage to US corporations arising from "social contract commitments" and "corporate welfare" arises not from pension promises but solely from the unfolding cost disaster of US health care provision.

Second, this survey illustrates that the trend away from corporate defined benefit pension provision is not only widespread among the world's major economies but also (in the United Kingdom) as progressed as in the United States. This suggests both that the trend away from defined contribution provision is caused by systemic structural factors (rather than for reasons idiosyncratic to the United States) and that the US trend will continue.

Summary of the Challenges

In this chapter we have described how corporate pensions in America began as a supplement to Social Security, available overwhelmingly to only

---

165. Individual plan risk-based contributions were capped at 0.5 percent of plan liabilities.

higher-income workers or to workers in select industries. The notion that a "golden age" of private employer-based pensions existed perhaps in the 1950s, 1960s, and 1970s is a myth: a lavish (or even comfortable) corporate pension was never a retirement benefit for more than a minority of working Americans. Thus, as is evident in figure 7.16, any change in US corporate pensions will affect only those in the top income quintile, not the vast majority of poor and middle-class Americans in retirement.

Figure 7.16 shows the share of elderly with retirement income from any type of private corporate pension[166] (a more expansive definition than strictly corporate-sponsored retirement plans that will bias these data upward). The two top income quintiles converge at about a 55 to 60 percent coverage rate, the middle quintile is about half that (less than one-third), the second quintile just below 10 percent, and the bottom quintile below 5 percent. At the same time, the share of the US workforce participating in a corporate pension has been relatively stable at just below half since the late 1970s. Access to employer-based pensions of any kind is hence not in precipitous decline. Indeed, combined with the rapidly growing US workforce in the last decade, this stability indicates that perhaps as many as 7 million more American workers have gained access to an employer-based pension since 1996.

Rather than a quantitative decline in access, corporate pensions in America have shifted away from defined benefit plans toward defined contribution, cash balance, and other hybrid-type plans. This transition implies a significant transfer of risk from the employer to the employee. However, in this chapter we have illustrated some mitigating aspects for affected employees and several long-term trends. First, we have laid bare at least two "United Airlines fallacies"—things that were true of that and other high-profile corporate defined benefit plan collapses but that are not representative of the broader picture. Most US corporate defined benefit plans terminated in a standard manner unrelated to any financial difficulties of the plan sponsor and with no loss of accrued vested benefits to the affected workers. Also unlike the experience of United Airlines, most US corporate defined-benefit benefits are relatively modest in size, with a median benefit less than half that of average Social Security benefits. It is, thus, erroneous to assume that the shift from corporate defined benefit pensions must cause economic ruin for affected workers. Thanks to the PBGC, whose financial situation is stabilizing despite the uneven effects of congressional meddling, significant economic losses from this shift will almost exclusively affect Americans well into the top income quintile.

---

166. This includes any non-OASDI employer-based or privately purchased pensions, annuities, or survivors or disability benefits.

Figure 7.16 Share of individuals age 65 or above with income from any private pension, by income quintile, 1975–2006

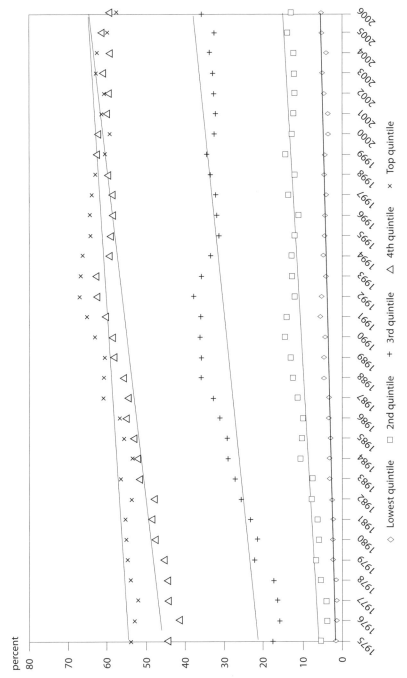

Source: Employee Benefit Research Institute (EBRI) Databook on Employee Benefits, chapter 7.

Second, we have illustrated that the shift away from defined benefit pension sponsorship is not because of short-term financial stress among sponsoring US companies—in fact, surveys of US defined benefit plan providers indicate that as of 2006–07, corporate pension funds were fully funded. Instead, the shift is the result of a combination of five longer-term factors:

- *administrative costs risk* from rapidly rising administrative costs of complying with regulations concerning defined benefit plan provision and related taxation;

- *longevity risk* from both unexpectedly rapid increases in life expectancies and the inclusion of more valid estimations of longevity in plan sponsors' liability calculations;

- *accounting risk* from increased transparency in international accounting standards governing corporate pension provision;

- *market risk* from exposure to volatile asset prices from high equity weights in pension plan portfolios and asset-liability mismatches; and

- advantageous *pull factors* from defined contribution plans, such as increased portability and flexibility.

The switch away from defined benefit plan provision among US corporations is hence a multifaceted development and one that government policy initiatives seem highly unlikely to be able to stop or reverse. On the other hand, the US corporate pension system seems set to continue in its defined contribution/hybrid reincarnation on a much improved financial basis.

However, US corporate pension provision will continue to disproportionally bestow financially more secure benefits on the highest-income Americans, as illustrated in figure 7.17. Those in the highest-income quintile have in the last 30 years seen their private corporate pension income rise in real terms. In 2006 the amount of this income was more than 150 times (!) that of the lowest quintile. The fact that US corporate pensions are regaining their financial footing will therefore benefit the top quintile by securing their future retirement income streams but will be of very limited relevance for lower-income groups. We return to this important finding in chapter 8, when we present our proposal for US pension policy reforms.

Looking beyond US borders, this chapter's brief survey of recent trends in Canada, Germany, Japan, and the United Kingdom revealed that the shift away from employer-based defined benefit pension plans is widespread internationally. In these four G-7 countries, which all have relatively extensive employer-based pension systems, the trend has mirrored that of the United States in recent years: These countries experienced

Figure 7.17   Annual real income of individuals age 65 or above from any private pension, by income quintile, 1975–2006

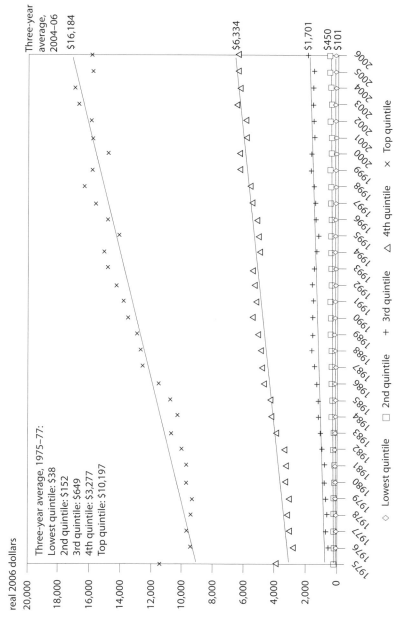

real 2006 dollars

Three-year average, 1975–77:
Lowest quintile: $38
2nd quintile: $152
3rd quintile: $649
4th quintile: $3,277
Top quintile: $10,197

Three-year average, 2004–06
$16,184
$6,334
$1,701
$450
$101

◇ Lowest quintile   □ 2nd quintile   + 3rd quintile   △ 4th quintile   × Top quintile

Source: Employee Benefit Research Institute (EBRI) Databook on Employee Benefits, chapter 7.

substantial underfunding of corporate pension schemes after 2001, accentuated by the same long-term factors at work in the United States. Only in Japan did the longer and more severe economic crisis during the 1990s necessitate a partial government bailout of major employer-based pension plans. These international events underscore the broadness of the shift away from employer-based defined benefit pension provision, and the fact that it is unidirectional despite differing national historical, political, and legal circumstances illustrates the likely limited scope for policy action to stem the tide of this trend.

At the same time, the internationally shared financial problems relating to corporate pension provision show that the playing field in this area is actually quite even and that the pension promises of US businesses do not put them at a competitive disadvantage. Rather, any burdens related to social contract/corporate welfare issues that may affect only US businesses but not those of other major industrial countries are rooted exclusively in the dysfunctional US health care system.

In conclusion, what are the policy implications of this chapter's findings that employer-based pensions will remain disproportionally for the well-to-do and that the shift of such pensions toward defined contribution/hybrid plans seems irreversible? First, it is important to keep this shift in perspective. Employer-based pension provision does not end with defined benefit plans, but it is evident that a system dependent on defined contribution/hybrid plans will require a different type of regulation. The experience of defined benefit plan provision shows an important premium for simplicity in regulation: More complex regulation leads to more employers not bothering to provide coverage for any but their most valued employees.

Second, the seeming inability of the voluntary US employment-based pension system to expand much beyond the top income echelons is a powerful reminder that there are few if any effective voluntary replacements for the Social Security system to provide retirement income to the majority of Americans, a fact that should militate against across-the-board cutbacks in any Social Security reform—indeed, it should argue in favor of a more progressive design for Social Security.

The stability of coverage ratios for all types of corporate pension schemes in the last decades, which has meant that millions of more Americans now have access to it, is largely due to the emergence of defined contribution/hybrid schemes, as the expansion of voluntary corporate defined benefit pension plan provision beyond the highest income groups is simply not realistic. Thus, if, as we believe, the main policy goal is to expand employer-based pension provision to larger groups of workers rather than ensuring the safety of high pension benefits for a small group, the trend toward simpler, cheaper-to-manage defined contribution/hybrid schemes replacing increasingly complex pure defined benefit schemes is in many ways a welcome one.

References

AAA (American Academy of Actuaries). 1993. *The Impact of Government Regulation on Defined Benefit Pension Plan Terminations.* Special Report (March). Washington.

Adema, Willem, and Maxime Ladaique. 2005. *Net Social Expenditure, 2005 Edition: More Comprehensive Measures of Social Support.* OECD Social, Employment and Migration Working Papers no. 29. Paris: Organization for Economic Cooperation and Development.

Antolín, Pablo. 2007. *Longevity Risk and Private Pensions.* OECD Working Paper on Insurance and Private Pensions no. 3. Paris: Organization for Economic Cooperation and Development.

Auerbach Alan J., William G. Gale, and Peter R. Orszag. 2004. *The US Fiscal Gap and Retirement Saving.* OECD Economic Studies no. 39. Paris: Organization for Economic Cooperation and Development.

Baldwin, Bob. 2004. A Shaky Third Pillar: The Vulnerability of Retirement Incomes. In *New Frontier on Research in Retirement*, ed. Leroy O. Stone. Ottawa: Statistics Canada.

Beller, Daniel, J., and Helen H. Lawrence. 1992. Trends in Private Pension Coverage. In *Trends in Pensions 1992*, ed. John A. Turner and Daniel J. Beller. Washington: US Department of Labor, Pension and Welfare Benefits Administration.

Bender, Keith A. 2001. Pension Integration and Retirement Benefits. *Monthly Labor Review* (February): 49–58. Washington: Bureau of Labor Statistics.

Bird, Ronald. 2006. Testimony before the US Senate Committee on the Judiciary, Washington, July 5, 2006.

Blake, D., and W. Burrows. 2001. Survivor Bonds: Helping to Hedge Mortality Risk. *Journal of Risk and Insurance*, no. 68: 339–48.

BLS (Bureau of Labor Statistics). 2007. *Employee Benefits in Private Industry in the United States, 2005.* US Department of Labor Bulletin 2589. Washington.

Bodie, Z. 1995. On the Risks of Stocks in the Long Run. *Financial Analysts Journal* 51, no. 3.

Bodie, Zvi. 1996. What the Pension Benefit Guaranty Corporation Can Learn from the Federal Savings and Loan Insurance Corporation. *Journal of Financial Services Research* 10, no. 1 (March): 83–100.

Bodie, Zvi. 2007. Pension Guarantees, Capital Adequacy, and International Risk-Sharing. Paper presented at conference on Frontiers in Pension Finance and Reform, Amsterdam, Netherlands, March 22–23.

Börsch-Supan, A., A. Ludwig, and J. Winter. 2003. Ageing, the German Rate of Return, and Global Capital Markets. *Demography Special*, no. 273.

Börsch-Supan, Axel H., and Christina B. Wilke. 2004. Reforming the German Public Pension System. Paper prepared for the 2004 General Assembly of the Japan Pension Research Council, Tokyo, Japan, September 9–10.

Börsch-Supan, A., F. Heiss, and J. Winter. 2004. *Akzeptanzprobleme bei Rentenreformen.* Köln: Deutsches Institut für Altervorsorge.

Börsch-Supan, A. 2004. *Mind the Gap: The Effectiveness of Incentives to Boost Retirement Savings in Europe.* OECD Economic Studies, no. 39: 111–44. Paris: Organization for Economic Cooperation and Development.

Boskin, Michael J. 2003. *Deferred Taxes in the Public Finances* (July). Stanford, CA: Hoover Institution.

Brown, Jeffrey R., Olivia S. Mitchell, and James M. Poterba. 2000. *Mortality Risk, Inflation Risk, and Annuity Products.* NBER Working Paper 7812. Cambridge, MA: National Bureau of Economic Research.

Brown, Robert L., and Jianxun Liu. 2001. The Shift to Defined Contribution Pension Plans: Why Did It Not Happen in Canada. *North American Actuarial Journal* 5, no. 3: 65–77.

Bundesministerium for Arbeit und Soziales. 2008. *Entwicklung der privaten Altersvorsorge Stand: 31.12.2007.* Available at www.bmas.de.

Burke, Thomas P., and John D. Morton. 1990. How Firm Size and Industry Affects Employee Benefits. *Monthly Labor Review* (December): 35–43. Washington: Bureau of Labor Statistics.

Burr, Barry. 2007. Winners, Losers in New Accounting Rule. Pensions and Investments (April 30). Available at www.pionline.com.

Cass Business School. 2005. *International Comparative Study of Mortality Tables for Pension Fund Retirees.* Available at www.gcactuaries.org.

CBO (Congressional Budget Office). 2005. *Taxing Capital Income: Effective Rates and Approaches to Reform.* Washington.

CBO (Congressional Budget Office). 2008. The Effects of Recent Turmoil on the Financial Markets on Retirement Security. Statement of Peter R. Orszag before the US House Committee on Education and Labor, Washington, October 7, 2008.

Clark, Robert Louis, Lee Allan Craig, and Jack W. Wilson. 2003. *A History of Public Sector Pensions in the United States.* Philadelphia: University of Pennsylvania Press.

Cohen, A. J., M. A. Moran, and M. A. Kim. 2007. *Pension Review 2007: High-Class Problems.* Goldman Sachs Portfolio Strategy (August 3). New York.

Conyngton, Mary. 1926. Industrial Pensions for Old Age and Disability. *Monthly Labor Review* 22, no. 1: 21–56. Washington: Bureau of Labor Statistics.

Copeland, Craig. 2006. *Employment-Based Retirement Plan Participation: Geographic Differences and Trends 2005.* EBRI Issue Brief 299. Washington: Employee Benefit Research Institute.

Council of Economic Advisers. 2006. *Economic Report of the President.* Washington: Executive Office of the President of the United States.

Davidoff, T., J. R. Brown, and P. Diamond. 2003. *Annuities and Individual Welfare.* Working Paper 2003-11. Boston: Center for Retirement Research, Boston College.

Deloitte. 2006. *Securing Retirement: An Overview of the Pension Protection Act of 2006* (August 3). New York.

Denuit, Michel, Pierre Devolder, and Anne-Cécile Goderniaux. 2007. Securitization of Longevity Risk: Pricing Survivor Bonds with Wang Transform in the Lee-Carter Framework. *Journal of Risk & Insurance* 74, no. 1: 87–113.

Department of Finance (Canada). 2005. *Strengthening the Legislative and Regulatory Framework for Defined Benefit Pension Plans Registered under the Pension Benefits Standards Act, 1985.* Consultation Paper (May). Ottawa.

Deutsche Bundesbank. 2001. *Company Pension Schemes in Germany.* Monthly Report (March): 43–58. Frankfurt am Main.

Deutsche Bundesbank. 2002. *Funded Old-Age Provision and the Financial Markets.* Monthly Report (July): 25–40. Frankfurt am Main.

Dowd, K. 2003. Survivor Bonds: A Comment on Blake and Burrows. *Journal of Risk and Insurance*, no. 70: 339–48.

EBRI (Employee Benefit Research Institute). 1993. *Employment-Based Retirement Income Benefits: Analysis of the April 1993 Current Population Survey.* EBRI Issue Brief 151. Washington.

EBRI (Employee Benefit Research Institute). 2007. *The Future of Employment-Based Health Benefits: Have Employers Reached a Tipping Point?* EBRI Issue Brief 213. Washington.

EDF (Electricité de France). 2004. *Annual Report 2004.* Paris.

EDF (Electricité de France). 2005. *Annual Report 2005.* Paris.

Feldstein, M. 2005. Structural Reform of Social Security. *Journal of Economic Perspectives* 19, no. 2.

FRB (Federal Reserve Board). 2008. *Z-1 Release: Flow of Funds Accounts of the United States* (June 5). Washington.

Frumkin, David, and William J. Wiatrowski. 1982. Bureau of Labor Statistics Takes a New Look at Employee Benefits. *Monthly Labor Review* (August): 41–45. Washington: Bureau of Labor Statistics.

Fullerton, Howard N., Jr. 1999. Labor Force Participation: 75 Years of Change, 1950–98 and 1998–2025. *Monthly Labor Review* (December): 3–12. Washington: Bureau of Labor Statistics.

Gale, William, Leslie Papke, and Jack VanDerhei. 2005. The Shifting Structure of Private Pensions. In *The Evolving Pension System*, ed. W. Gale, J. Shoven, and M. Warshawsky. Washington: Brookings Institution Press.

GAO (General Accounting Office). 1977. *Effects of the Employment Retirement Income Security Act on the Termination of Single Employer Defined Benefit Plans.* Washington.

GAO (Government Accountability Office). 2007. *Pension Benefits Guarantee Corporation: Governance Structure Needs Improvements to Ensure Policy Direction and Oversight.* GAO Report-07-808. Washington.

Gebhardtsbauer, Ron. 2004. What Are the Trade-Offs? Defined Benefit vs. Defined Contribution Systems. Paper presented at AARP/CEPS Forum titled A Balancing Act: Achieving Adequacy and Sustainability in Retirement Income Reform, March 4.

Gordon, Robert S. 1942. Testimony of Robert S. Gordon before the House Ways and Means Committee, Revenue Revision of 1942, 77th Congress, 2nd Session, volume 3, 1942, 2427. Washington.

GAD (Government Actuaries Department). 2003. *Occupational Pension Schemes 2000.* Eleventh Survey by the Government Actuary. London.

GAD (Government Actuaries Department). 2005. *Occupational Pension Schemes 2004.* Twelfth Survey by the Government Actuary. London.

GAD (Government Actuaries Department). 2006. *Occupational Pension Schemes 2005.* Thirteenth Survey by the Government Actuary. London.

Groupe Consultatif Actuariel Européen. 2001. *Actuarial Methods and Assumptions Used in the Valuation of Retirement Benefits in the EU and Other European Countries.* Available at www.gcactuaries.org.

Hacker, Jacob S. 2002. *The Divided Welfare State: The Battle over Public and Private Social Benefits in the United States.* Cambridge, MA: Cambridge University Press.

Hewitt and Associates LLC. 2005. *Micro-History of Employee Benefits and Compensation 1794–2005.* Washington.

Hubbard, Glenn R. 1993. Corporate Tax Integration: A View from the Treasury Department. *Journal of Economic Perspectives* (Winter): 115–32.

IMF (International Monetary Fund). 2004. Risk Management and the Pension Fund Industry. *Global Financial Stability Report* (September). Washington.

Ippolito, R. A. 2004. *How to Reduce the Cost of Federal Pension Insurance?* Policy Analysis no. 253. Washington: Cato Institute.

Joint Committee on Taxation. 2001. *Overview of Present Law and Economic Analysis Relating to Marginal Tax Rates and the President's Individual Income Tax Rate Proposals (JCX-6-01),* March 6. Washington: US Congress.

Joint Committee on Taxation. 2006. *Technical Explanation of H.R.4: The Pension Protection Act of 2006, as Passed by the House and July 28th, 2006 and as Considered by the Senate on August 3rd, 2006.* Washington: US Congress.

Kaiser Family Foundation and Hewitt Associates. 2006. Retiree Health Benefits Examined: Findings of the Kaiser/Hewitt 2006 Survey on Retiree Health Benefits. Washington: Kaiser Family Foundation. Available at www.kff.org.

Kandarian, Steven A. 2003. Testimony of Steven A. Kandarian before the Special Committee on Aging, United States Senate, October 14, 2003, Washington.

King, Mervyn. 2004. What Fates Impose: Facing Up to Uncertainty. 2004 British Academy Lecture, December 1.

Kirkegaard, Jacob Funk. 2008. Will the Financial Bailout Undermine the US Defined Benefit Pension System? Peterson Institute RealTime Economics Issues Watch, November 18. Washington: Peterson Institute for International Economics. Available at www.peterson institute.org.

Lane, Clark and Peacock. 2008. *Pension Buyouts 2008.* Available at www.lcp.uk.com.

Latimer, Murray W. 1933. *Industrial Pension Systems in the United States and Canada.* New York: Industrial Relations Counselors, Inc.

Li, Jinyan. 2004. A Separation, Linkage and Blurring in the Public and Private Pillars of Canada's Retirement Income System. In *New Frontier on Research in Retirement*, ed., Leroy O. Stone. Ottawa: Statistics Canada.

Lindbeck, Assar, and Dennis J. Snower. 1986. Wage Setting, Unemployment, and Insider-Outsider Relations. *American Economic Review* 76, no. 2 (May): 235–39.

Lipset, Seymour Martin, and Gary Wolfe Marks. 2000. *It Didn't Happen Here: Why Socialism Failed in the United States*. New York: W. W. Norton and Company.

Lowenstein, Roger. 2008. *While America Aged: How Pensions Debts Ruined General Motors, Stopped the NYC Subways, Bankrupted San Diego and Loom as the Next Financial Crisis*. New York: Penguin Press.

Maddison, Angus. 2003. *The World Economy: Historical Statistics*. Paris: Organization for Economic Cooperation and Development.

Matsubara, Ryo. 2007. How We Can Keep Employers in the World in Japan. Japanese Society of Certified Pension Actuaries/Hewitt Associates. Photocopy.

McCarthy, David, and Anthony Neuberger. 2005. *The UK Approach to Insuring Defined Benefit Pension Plans*. Pension Research Council Working Paper 2005-8. Philadelphia: Pension Research Council, Wharton School of the University of Pennsylvania.

McGill, Dan M., Kyle N. Brown, John J. Haley, and Sylvester J. Schieber. 2005. *Fundamentals of Private Pensions*, 8th ed. Philadelphia: Pension Research Council, Wharton School of the University of Pennsylvania.

Mercer HR Consulting. 2006. *Pension Liabilities in Tope European Companies—New Research* (August 7). Available at www.mercerhr.com.

Mercer HR Consulting. 2007. *What's New in Germany: Funding Via CTA and Pensionsfonds* (June 22). Available at www.mercerhr.com.

MHLW (Japan Ministry of Health, Labor and Welfare). 2003. *Comprehensive Survey on Working Conditions*. Tokyo.

MHLW (Japan Ministry of Health, Labor and Welfare). 2005a. *Textbook for the Study Programme for the Senior Social Insurance Administrators. Chapter 9: Overview of the Corporate Pension System*. Tokyo.

MHLW (Japan Ministry of Health, Labor and Welfare). 2005b. *Financial Report on The Public Pension System FY 2003 (Actuarial Subcommittee)*. Tokyo.

MHLW (Japan Ministry of Health, Labor and Welfare). 2006a. *Review of the 2004 Actuarial Valuation of the Public Pension Plans*. Tokyo.

MHLW (Japan Ministry of Health, Labor and Welfare). 2006b. *Financial Report on the Public Pension System FY 2004 (Summary)*. Actuarial Subcommittee. Tokyo.

Milliman Consultants and Actuaries. 2007. *2007 Pension Funding Study*. Seattle, WA.

Milliman Consultants and Actuaries. 2008. *2008 Pension Funding Study*. Seattle, WA.

Morris, Charles R. 2006. *Apart at the Seams: The Collapse of Private Pension and Health Care Protections*. Century Foundation Press.

Morton, John D. 1987. BLS Prepares to Broaden Scope of Its White-Collar Pay Survey. *Monthly Labor Review* (March): 3–7. Washington: Bureau of Labor Statistics.

Munnell Alicia H., Francesca Golub-Sass, Mauricio Soto, and Francis Vitagliano. 2006. *Why Are Healthy Employers Freezing Their Pensions?* Issue Brief 44 (March). Boston: Center for Retirement Research, Boston College.

Munnell, Alicia H., and Pamela Perun. 2006. *An Update on Private Pensions*. Issue Brief 50 (August). Boston: Center for Retirement Research, Boston College.

Nakada, Tadashi. 2007. Current Situation of Pension ALMs for Japanese Corporate Pension Plans. Nikko Financial Intelligence, Inc. Photocopy.

OECD (Organization for Economic Cooperation and Development). 2007. *Pensions at a Glance—Public Policies Across OECD Countries 2007*. Paris.

OECD (Organization for Economic Cooperation and Development). 2008. *Pension Markets in Focus* 5 (December). Paris.

PBGC (Pension Benefit Guaranty Corporation). 2004. *Annual Report 2004*. Washington.

PBGC (Pension Benefit Guaranty Corporation). 2005a. *Annual Report 2005*. Washington.

PBGC (Pension Benefit Guaranty Corporation). 2005b. *An Analysis of Frozen Defined Benefit Plans*. Washington.

PBGC (Pension Benefit Guaranty Corporation). 2006a. *Pension Insurance Data Book 2005*. Washington.

PBGC (Pension Benefit Guaranty Corporation. 2006b. *Annual Report 2006*. Washington.

PBGC (Pension Benefit Guaranty Corporation). 2007a. *Pension Insurance Data Book 2006*. Washington.

PBGC (Pension Benefit Guaranty Corporation). 2007b. *Annual Report 2007*. Washington.

PPF (Pension Protection Fund). 2006. *The Purple Book: Pensions Universe Risk Profile*. Croydon, Surrey.

PPF (Pension Protection Fund). 2008. PPF 7800 Data. Available at www.pensionprotection fund.org.uk

Pesando, J. E. 1996. The Government's Role in Insuring Pensions. In *Securing Employer-Based Pensions*, ed. Z. Bodie, O. S. Mitchell, and J. A. Turner. Philadelphia: Pension Research Council, University of Pennsylvania Press.

Popkin, Joel, and Company. 2005. *Cost of Employee Benefits in Small and Large Businesses*. Washington: Small Business Administration. Available at www.sba.gov.

PSVaG (Pensions Sicherungs Verein AG). 2008. *Übersicht über die Entwicklung des Pensions-Sicherungs-Vereins 1 (Januar 1975), Beginn des Geschäftsbetriebs, bis 31. Dezember 2007*. PSV AG. Available at www.psvag.de.

Pugh, Colin. 2006. *Funding Rules and Actuarial Methods*. OECD Working Paper on Insurance and Private Pensions no. 1. Paris: Organization for Economic Cooperation and Development.

Purcell, Patrick, J. 2005. *Retirement Plan Participation and Contributions: Trends from 1998 to 2003*. CRS Report for Congress Order Code RL33116. Washington: Library of Congress, Congressional Research Service.

Root, Lawrence S. 1982. *Fringe Benefits: Social Insurance in the Steel Industry*. Beverly Hills, CA: Sage.

Sakamoto, Junichi. 2005. *Japan's Pension Reform*. Social Protection Working Paper 0541. Washington: World Bank.

Sanzenbacher, Geoffrey. 2006. *An Update on Private Pensions*. Issue Brief 51 (August). Boston: Center for Retirement Research, Boston College.

Sass, Steven A. 1997. *The Compromise of Private Pensions*. Cambridge, MA: Harvard University Press.

Schieber, Sylvester J., and Patricia M. George. 1981. *Retirement Income Opportunities in an Ageing America: Coverage and Benefit Entitlements*. Washington: Employee Benefit Research Institute.

Schultz, James H., and Thomas D. Leavitt. 1983. *Pension Integration: Concepts, Issues and Proposals*. Washington: Employee Benefit Research Institute.

Schreitmueller, Richard G. 1979. History of Pension Plan Integration Rules. Testimony Before the President's Commission on Pension Policy, Washington, October 10.

Siegel, J. 2002. *Stocks for the Long Run*, 3d ed. New York: McGraw-Hill.

Skolnik, Alfred. 1976. Private Pension Plans, 1950-1974. *Social Security Bulletin* 39, no. 6 (June): 3–17. Washington: Social Security Administration.

Social Protection Committee. 2005. *Privately Managed Pension Provision* (February). Brussels.

Steel Industry Board. 1949. *Report to the President of the United States on the Labor Dispute in the Basic Steel Industry* (September 16). Washington.

Stewart, F. 2007. *Benefit Security Pension Fund Guarantee Schemes*. OECD Working Papers on Insurance and Private Pensions no. 5. Paris: Organization for Economic Cooperation and Development.

Takayama, Noriyuki. 2005. *Rise and Fall of the Opting-Out Plan in Japanese Pensions: A Brief Note* (September). Hitotsubashi University.

TNS Infratest/Bundesministerium Für Arbeit Und Sociales. 2007. *Situation und Entwicklung der betrieblichen Altersversorgung in Privatwirtschaft und öffentlichem Dienst 2001–2006*. Berlin. Available at www.bmas.de.

Towers Perrin. 2007. *Germany: Trend to Fund Liabilities Accelerates* (May). Available at www.towersperrin.com.

Turner, Adair. 2003. *Pensions: Challenges and Choices. First Report of the Turner Commission.* London.

UBS. 2005. The Impact of Pension Accounting on Financial Statements and Disclosures. *CFA Institute Conference Proceedings* 2005, no. 3 (April): 19–24.

Urata, Haruka. 2001. New Development in Corporate Pension Schemes in Japan. Paper presented at the Project on Intergenerational Equity (PIE) Conference, Hitotsubashi University, March 17.

US Census Bureau. 2006. *Income, Poverty, and Health Insurance Coverage in the United States: 2005.* Washington: Department of Commerce.

US Department of Labor. 1977. *Final Report Assessment on the Impact of ERISA on the Administrative Costs of Small Retirement Plans.* Prepared by Price Waterhouse and Company, Office of Government Services. Washington.

US Department of Labor. 1994. *Pension and Health Benefits of American Workers: New Findings from the April 1993 Current Population Survey.* Washington.

Usuki, Masaharo. 2003. *Recent Changes to Retirement Benefits in Japan and Relevant Public Policy Issues.* Discussion Paper no. 135. Tokyo: Institute of Economic Research, Hitotsubashi University.

Usuki, Masaharo. 2004. *Risk Management and Pension Plan Choice in Japan.* Pension Research Council Working Paper 2004-17. Philadelphia: Pension Research Council, Wharton School, University of Pennsylvania.

VanDerhhei, Jack. 2007. *Retirement Income Adequacy After PPA and FAS 158: Part One—Plan Sponsors' Reactions.* EBRI Issue Brief 307. Washington: Employee Benefit Research Institute.

Visco, Ignatio. 2005. *Ageing and Pension System Reform: Implications for Financial Markets and Economic Policies.* Report prepared at the request of the Deputies of the Group of Ten, September.

Watson Wyatt. 2007a. *2007 Global Survey of Accounting Assumptions for Defined Benefit Plans.* Available at www.watsonwyatt.com.

Watson Wyatt. 2007b. *Pension Funded Ratios Continue To Improve.* Available at www.watsonwyatt.com.

Wiatrowski, William J. 2004. Medical and Retirement Plan Coverage: Exploring the Decline in Recent Years. *Monthly Labor Review* (August): 29–36. Washington: Bureau of Labor Statistics.

Wyatt, Birchard E., Walter Bjorn, William Rulan Williamson, and Dorrance C. Bronson. 1945. *Employee Retirement Plans.* Washington: B. E. Wyatt Company.

Yaari, M. 1965. Uncertain Lifetime, Life Insurance and the Theory of the Consumer. *Review of Economic Studies*, no. 2: 137–50.

Yano, Tomomi, Yasuchika Asaoka, and Junichi Sakamoto. 2007. Pension Benefit Guarantee Program in Japan. Presentation at OECD Seminar on Reforming Benefit Protection Schemes, Paris, July 2.

Yohalem, Martha Remy. 1977. Employee-Benefit Plans, 1975. *Social Security Bulletin* 40: 19–28. Washington: Social Security Administration.

Yoo, K., and A. de Serres. 2004. *Tax Treatment of Private Pension Savings in OECD Countries and the Net Tax Cost Per Unit of Contribution to Tax-Favoured Schemes.* OECD Economics Department Working Paper no. 406. Paris: Organization for Economic Cooperation and Development.

Zion, David, and Bill Carcache. 2003. *The Magic of Pension Accounting, Part II.* New York: CSFB Equity Research.

Zion, David, and Bill Carcache. 2005. *The Magic of Pension Accounting, Part III.* New York: CSFB Equity Research.

Appendix 7A
An Accounting Standards Arbitrage: How the French Government Took Over the Pension Liabilities of Electricité de France and Made Billions

Above-average pension promises have a direct negative impact on the stock market valuation of a newly privatized company and hence the expected financial proceeds for the selling government. However, by engaging in an "accounting standards arbitrage," the French government turned these large and long-term pension liabilities into an "immediate revenue center" when it partly privatized Electricité de France (EDF) in the early 2000s.

Corporate accounting standards—for instance, the International Accounting Standard 19, which has been in place in Europe since 2005—generally require that publicly listed companies actuarially estimate the size of their implicit liabilities related to defined benefit pension systems and set aside sufficient reserves to meet these obligations. On the other hand, the System of National Accounts (SNA), which regulates how governments account for their revenues, expenditures, assets, and liabilities, demands only that governments recognize the liabilities of fully funded pension schemes (defined contribution or defined benefit plans with reserves close to actuarially estimated liabilities). In addition, the SNA does not require estimation or publication of the liabilities of public pension plans for the general public (i.e., Social Security–like plans).

This transparency differential between corporate and public pension accounting rules allowed the French government to accept a lump-sum payment from newly privatized entities such as EDF in return for transferring their (unreformed formerly public-sector) employee pension liabilities from the company balance sheet, where they would have had to be estimated and reported, to the French government-run National Old Age Insurance Fund (Caisse nationale d'assurance vieillesse, or CNAV), which requires no reporting of these liabilities.

This was a highly lucrative trade for the French government, which in 1997 received $6.6 billion from newly privatized France Telecom in return for taking over its pension liabilities and in 2004 received (on a gross net-present-value basis) €7.7 billion from EDF and Gaz de France for taking over their pension liabilities.[1] In the short term, these proceeds were an

---

1. See *International Herald Tribune*, "Italy's Chances for Euro Improve: Creative Accounting Gets EU's Approval," February 22, 1997. In the financial notes (#2.3.1) to the 2004 EDF annual report (EDF 2004), the pension transfer is described thus: "As of 1 January 2005, the system for benefits relating to pensions, invalidity, death, industrial accidents and work-related illnesses in the electricity and gas sector is managed by the Caisse nationale des industries électriques et gazières (CNIEG). . . . All employees, active or retired, and employees in the French electricity and gas industries are automatically affiliated as of 1 January 2005. The pension liabilities of employees in these industries remain unaffected."

undoubtedly tempting "free lunch" for the French government, such that the EU statistical agency Eurostat in October 2003 approved such lump-sum payments to governments as "capital transfers" to the government and required their inclusion in current revenues, even as incurred liabilities were exempt from reporting.[2]

On the other hand, while France Telecom and EDF had to pay the French Treasury billions of euros upfront, they thus liberated themselves from potentially very large long-term pension liabilities. Much uncertainty typically surrounds long-term pension liability estimates, but considering that the actual immediate financial cost to EDF was just €3.86 billion (€2.4 billion recognized in company equity in 2004, net of taxes) covering pensions for a total workforce of 156,000, with the remainder to be paid over 20 years from 2005,[3] it seems hard to imagine that EDF management did not also leave the negotiating table reasonably satisfied.

This assessment seems particularly clear from the data in table 7A.1 from EDF's 2004 annual report. They show the reconciliation of EDF's balance sheet primo 2004, taking into consideration both the effects of the reform of EDF's pension system and the transition of its corporate accounts from French Generally Accepted Accounting Principles (GAAP) to International Accounting Standards (IAS)/International Financial Reporting Standards (IFRS). Looking at either aggregate assets or equity/liabilities, neither the pension reform nor the transition to IFRS seems to have had much impact—just minor restatements of €56 million and €1.7 billion,

---

2. See "New Decision of Eurostat on Deficit and Debt Payments to Governments by Public Corporations in the Context of the Transfer to Government of their Unfunded Pension Obligations," Eurostat news release STAT/03/120, October 21, 2003. Other European governments have benefited from this type of transaction (e.g., Belgium with Belgacom and Portugal with the postal pension system).

3. The EDF share of the total electricity and gas sector cost of €7.649 billion payable to the CNAV was €6.053 billion. However, €3.329 billion of this cost concerns "regulated activities" related to EDF's status as a fully integrated power company (EDF still owns the French transmission power network). As such, the €3.329 billion will be paid by a special levy (the contribution tarifaire d'acheminement, CTA) on natural gas and electricity transmission and distribution services. The levy will be set in consultation with the French energy sector regulator, the Commission de régulation de l'énergie, CRE), on a price-neutral basis. This means that the levy will be paid not only by EDF but also by possible new entrants on the French power (and gas) market(s) for the next 20 years. In addition to the contributions to CNAV, EDF paid €632 million to the private supplemental pension funds AGIRC and ARRCO in 2005–06. A possible further €327 million contribution "to preserve benefit entitlements" to the latter two is possible, pending negotiations expected in 2010. Only the EDF "exceptional additional pensions," which concern complementary benefits paid annually to retired employees and their dependents, remain directly covered by the company. In 2004 this obligation amounted to €338 million. Hence, under the French GAAP, the company in 2004 presented a pension liability of €13.965 billion (EDF 2004). We note that as EDF in 2005 implemented the new IAS/IFRS standards, several additional changes were made to the accounting for EDF's pension liability under AIS 19.

Table 7A.1 Reconciliation of Electricité de France balance sheet, January 2004 (millions of euros)

Assets and equity/liabilities	French GAAP, January 1, 2004	Restatements to IFRS	Comparative under IFRS, January 1, 2004	Impact of pension reform	Proforma under IFRS, January 1, 2004
Deferred tax assets	216	−58	158	1,677	1,835
Total noncurrent assets	114,883	175	115,058	1,677	116,735
Total assets	146,900	−56	146,844	1,677	148,521
Capital	8,129		8,129		8,129
Consolidated reserves and income	10,796	−58,055	−47,259	46,263	−996
Equity (group share)	18,925	−58,055	−39,130	46,263	7,133
Minority interests	915	−2	913		913
Total equity	19,840	−58,057	−38,217	46,263	8,046
Provisions for employee benefits	2,072	57,949	60,021	−48,093	11,928
Other non current liabilities	92,656	−2524	90,132	151	90,283
Total noncurrent liabilities	94,728	55,425	150,153	−47,942	102,211
Total current liabilities	32,332	2,576	34,908	3,356	38,264
Total liabilities	127,060	58,001	185,061	−44,586	140,475
Total equity and liabilities	146,900	−56	146,844	1,677	148,521

GAAP = Generally Accepted Accounting Principles
IFRS = International Financial Reporting Standards

Source: EDF (2004, 96).

respectively. On the asset side, this remains true even when looking at the individual components. However, on the equity/liability side, the data reveal some significant changes. The transition to IFRS increases the liabilities for employee benefit provision from €2 billion to €60 billion, while the simultaneous effect of the pension reform reduces them by €48 billion, combining for a total increase of roughly €10 billion. A corresponding inverse development is seen in (owner's) equity, which drops dramatically as a result of the switch in accounting standards and increases as a result of the pension reform.

A few basic accounting conventions can help to understand the mechanics of these changes. A company's total assets and total equity/liabilities must always be equal to one another. This balance is calculated by estimating the total assets of the company (i.e., what the company owns) and then subtracting total liabilities (i.e., what the company owes third parties). The difference (the residual plug) equals the (owner's) equity of the company—i.e., what the company is worth to its owners. One could also state that owner's equity represents what the company "owes to its owners."

On January 1, 2004, at the time of the pension reform reconciliation, the sole owner of EDF was still the French government. Table 7A.1 shows that as EDF's owner, the government agreed to let the company reduce its liabilities to a third party—its current and former employees—by more than €48 billion. In return, the government received a massive increase of more than €46 billion from EDF as (owner's) equity.

Of course, in some way this transaction was entirely a "bookkeeping account," in the sense that the liabilities to EDF's current and retired employees were transferred out of EDF but to the French government itself.[4] Yet from the perspective of EDF, the transaction looks quite different. The company was able to transform a nearly €50 billion liability owed to a third party into an IOU to its owners, the French government, and it did so by paying the owner only €2.4 billion after tax.

The reason for this transaction was the government's need to prepare EDF for its initial public offering in October 2005. The French government sold a 10.8 percent share of EDF and raised an additional €6.3 billion of private capital for the French Treasury, while seeing its remaining 87.3 percent share of EDF valued at more than €51 billion.[5] Hence, in the event that the French government would be able to sell its entire stake in EDF to private investors, it would therefore be likely to recover more capital than the estimated €48 billion cost of absorbing EDF's employee pension liabilities (table 7A.1). Such a sale would require a change in French

---

4. This is made explicit in the footnote 2.3.6 to the EDF 2004 Financial Statements, which reads "The State guarantee will be granted in favor of the CNIEG [new pension plan covering old power and gas sector] for all past specific benefits" (EDF 2004).

5. In addition, current and retired employees received 1.9 percent of EDF shares (EDF 2005).

laws. However, with the stock market in mid-2008 valuing the French government's remaining share at more than €125 billion,[6] the financial gains to the government from a well-timed sale could be sizable.

Moreover, the French government is not just any owner, and because of the country's system of mandatory basic and occupational pensions in the private sector, it is better suited than any French private entity to reduce the size of the implicitly estimated €48 billion liability for current or retired EDF workers' pension benefits through reductions in the benefit levels. Indeed, this occurred with the reforms to the "special schemes" in early 2008 implemented by the Nicolas Sarkozy government (see chapter 3). Similarly, future productivity improvements in the French economy as a result of the privatization of the former state power monopoly may justify at least some of the future costs of the assumed liabilities.

Doubtless the French government, under pressure from the European Union to liberalize its power sector and trying to raise money by privatizing its state utilities, had to decide between, on the one hand, privatization and lump-sum pension payment revenue, which would improve government finances by being immediately recognized, and, on the other hand, accepting a substantial long-term pension liability, payable in the future, that would not have to be recognized anywhere in the books. Factoring in the political desire for the French government to avoid social unrest, which was considerable in relation to an earlier possible reduction in EDF pension benefits, it seems understandable that it succumbed to the "moral hazard" of booking the benefits today and pushing the problems into the future.

However, in the longer term, the French government's approach to the EDF pension liabilities may turn out to reap large financial gains, so the case illustrates a starkly different "French way" of dealing with a policy issue that is not that different from the "legacy cost issue" of US smokestack industries in steel, airlines, and autos. Both EDF and these industries were/are laden with long-term employee liabilities that make operating in a competitive business environment[7] increasingly difficult. In a likely attempt to mold a national power champion,[8] the French

---

6. Based on a mid-2008 closing stock price for EDF of €80, a total of 1.8 billion shares, and the government share of 87.3 percent. The EDF stock price has since declined. In addition, the as yet unknown long-term costs of decommissioning EDF's nuclear power plants surround valuation of the company's stock with much uncertainty.

7. EDF in the European Union's newly liberalized power markets, US airlines facing low-cost competition, and "Detroit" and US steel producers in an increasingly competitive global car and steel industry. One crucial difference, though, is that due to the government-provided health care system in France, EDF had no future health care liabilities.

8. EDF has benefited from several additional implicit government regulatory benefits, such as the French government's extreme reluctance to open its domestic power market to foreign entrants and its assumption of the potentially very large long-term liabilities in the decommissioning of French nuclear power plants.

government chose to take over the long-term pension liabilities preemptively and then, with the reforms of the Sarkozy government in 2008, to subsequently reduce them over time, whereas the US government takes over such company pension liabilities in reduced form only after a company bankruptcy, and even so only via the Pension Benefit Guaranty Corporation. In this way, the EDF case illustrates again that pension liabilities are better addressed decisively sooner rather than later.

8

Conclusion

It is essential that we maintain both the forward momentum of economic growth and the strength of the safety net beneath those in society who need help. We also believe it is essential that the integrity of all aspects of Social Security are preserved.

—Ronald Reagan, acceptance speech at the
1980 Republican Convention, July 17, 1980

Based on our analysis of pension reforms in other countries, we conclude that the US Social Security retirement system compares favorably with the systems in other advanced economies and indeed is better than most. Two of its virtues are its modest scale (thus it does not displace a lot of private saving) and its adjustment of benefits based on age of retirement (thus it does not encourage early retirement).

But there are also concerns about the program. First, it is not financially sustainable and is likely to run out of money as the baby-boomer generation retires and lives longer than earlier generations. This is an important problem, although in comparison with many other countries the fiscal challenge for Social Security is not overwhelming; recent estimates released by the Congressional Budget Office (CBO 2008) as this book was being completed in the fall of 2008 suggest that the fiscal shortfall is only about 1 percent of payroll, less than had been thought (the earlier figure was 1.8 percent). In other words, an increase in Federal Insurance Contributions Act (FICA) taxes by 1 percentage point would restore Social Security to a 75-year balance (this is a way of measuring the size of the shortfall and does not necessarily mean that higher payroll taxes are the best solution).

Second, Social Security is not particularly redistributive, in contrast to the retirement programs of other English-speaking countries. This does not mean, however, that there should be an increase in the average size of retirement benefits. Indeed, based on our research and the broad literature on US policy, we conclude that US public support programs are rather more generous to the elderly than they are to younger generations (largely because of Medicare and Medicaid). As many analysts have acknowledged, the distributional issue for Social Security is that upper-income retirees get too much and lower-income retirees too little. The Bush administration proposal for individual accounts recognized the need for additional help for poor elderly Social Security participants; Peter Diamond and Peter Orzsag (2005) have described the poverty risks of elderly widows who rely on Social Security; and Peter G. Peterson (2004) has pointed to the relatively generous benefits for upper-income retirees. In short, there is scope to make the US retirement benefit structure somewhat more progressive.

Third, Social Security does not contribute to national saving—indeed, it may reduce it, to the extent that it discourages private saving. This is an important concern because national saving overall is low in the United States, many American households save little or nothing for retirement and end up dependent on Social Security benefits, and many of the elderly have few financial assets or resources to fall back on when unexpected spending needs arise.

The second and third concerns are relevant to the question of whether there should be a program of individual retirement accounts in the United States. As requested by the Ford Foundation, which funded this research, we examined countries that have adopted such accounts, and we learned much from their experience with these accounts (see chapters 1, 5, and 6). We found that there are two important advantages to such plans. First, as a political tool, they compel people to recognize the link between how much they contribute and how much they draw out. Second, they increase national saving, an advantage in economies that are saving too little, of which the United States is certainly one. The disadvantages of such plans are, first, that they are not at all redistributive but simply translate differences in work-related income into differences in retirement assets. Given the trend in US data showing a substantial widening of the wage and income distribution, we consider this a serious drawback. The second disadvantage concerns transition: Going from a long-established pay-as-you-go plan to a funded individual account plan involves either raising taxes to support the transition (borrowing to do so) or operating a notional plan of the type developed in Sweden. These options are politically easier but reduce or eliminate the advantage of increasing national saving.

Given the disadvantages of replacing the current Social Security program with individual accounts, and given that the current program compares favorably with public pensions in other countries, we conclude that the introduction of an individual account plan to displace the current program is not justified. However, we have been sufficiently impressed by the benefits of individual accounts as they have been used by other countries to suggest that such a program could supplement Social Security, serving mostly low-income savers that do not participate in employer-funded pensions or 401(k) plans. The program would address, in part, the very low national saving rate and the fact that so many households in retirement or approaching retirement have very few financial assets to cover unexpected expenditures.

In this chapter we present our ideas for tackling the key problems facing US Social Security—fiscal imbalance and a lack of adequate household saving. Our ideas are informed and influenced by our research and do not necessarily reflect the views of the Ford Foundation. We believe our reform proposals, if rapidly implemented, would further send a powerful and beneficial signal around the world that America is now determined to address the long-term challenges facing the country.

Based on our assessment of pension reforms in other countries as well as in the United States, we conclude that no single policy tool is sufficient to sustainably "fix" any pension system. The inherent complexity of such systems and the required broad political backing for any reform to work in the long run require the simultaneous use of different policy tools to "distribute the reform pain" across both pension contributors (taxpayers) and beneficiaries (current retirees). The goal is to find a way to put the Social Security retirement program on a sustainable path in a manner acceptable to the broadest possible coalition of constituents.

We, therefore, present four interconnected reform proposals. To deal with the fiscal shortfall, we propose

1. targeted benefit adjustments that better integrate Social Security with private, tax-advantaged pension plans;

2. continued adjustments of the normal retirement age after 2027; and

3. increased Social Security revenues to cover any additional requirements to shore up the program's long-term sustainability.

And to respond to the low saving rate, we propose

4. a system of add-on individual accounts.

Targeted Benefit Adjustments to Deal with the Fiscal Shortfall

Average benefit levels in Social Security are not very high by international comparison, and yet American retirees rely heavily on them for their cash income. Benefit cuts should, therefore, target higher-income rather than lower-income participants. In his book *Running on Empty*, Peter G. Peterson (2004) asks why on earth Social Security is paying benefits to him. Few retirees are as wealthy as Peterson, but many have good incomes and a strong asset base and do not need generous Social Security benefits. In practice, however, these individuals or families do receive pretty generous benefits[1] because they had high income levels for much or all of their lives.

That line of argument suggests that means testing might be appropriate for Social Security benefits, with lower benefits paid to those with higher incomes or higher wealth, a suggestion that takes us back to the discussion of the philosophy behind the program. The Social Security program (as opposed to Supplemental Security Income [SSI]) was introduced by President Franklin D. Roosevelt as a contributory system like the German pension innovation of the late 19th century. The rich get more because they have paid in more.

There are redistributive aspects to the program, so it is not a purely German model, but means testing would represent a major shift that would arouse concern among the program's supporters. One danger of moving to a means-tested program is that over time, it may be perceived as a welfare program and lose its popularity. In our research on other OECD countries we found no evidence of massive public opposition to much more redistributive systems than Social Security, so we are not sure how serious a problem it would be in the United States, but we acknowledge that it would likely motivate opponents of explicit means testing in this country.

There are several ways to make Social Security more progressive without explicit means testing—for example, by taxing 100 percent of benefits (as other OECD countries do; see chapter 2) or increasing the earnings limit on FICA taxes; we do not review them all as our research did not provide additional insight beyond what is already available in the policy literature. Based on what we have learned, however, we do want to make the case that US policymakers should evaluate the large tax breaks for deferred income, including pension contributions. People who have been the beneficiaries of such tax advantages may not need—especially in times of strained government resources—full Social Security benefit levels. Our proposal would function as an implicit cut in the current government subsidies to pension savings through tax provisions.

Integrating Social Security Benefits with Tax-Preferred Private Pension Accumulation

We propose to cut benefits by linking, or integrating, the Social Security benefit that individuals will receive from the public Old-Age, Survivors, and Disability Insurance (OASDI) fund with the funds the same individuals have placed into tax-advantaged private pension savings. The latter include employer pension contributions, which are not counted as part of employees' taxable income, plus individual contributions to 401(k)

---

1. For example, high-income married couples are entitled to monthly benefits of around $3,500 a month, well above the average benefit level.

plans or individual retirement accounts (IRAs), which can be deducted from earnings in computing taxable income. Other forms of deferred compensation, such as awards of restricted stock or stock options, are excluded from income until the stock is converted into marketable securities. The impact of integration for workers who made extensive use of tax breaks for their individual pension savings would be a reduced Social Security pension.

The integration of public and private pensions has a history in the United States. As we noted in chapter 7, private (corporate) pension benefits were often adjusted depending on an individual's level of Social Security benefits—the corporate pension would "top up" the Social Security benefit. We propose something with a similar intent: to make sure people have enough to retire but not provide more than is needed. The big difference is that, historically, the company pension plan benefited from the integration, whereas with our proposal, the Social Security Trust Fund would benefit, an arrangement that would also benefit retirees without significant private pension wealth through the preservation of their Social Security benefit levels.

Specifically, we suggest cutting Social Security benefit levels based on a formula that depends upon the degree to which individuals have already taken advantage of public tax expenditures to augment their private pension saving accounts. We are aware that our proposal runs counter to the US penchant of "conducting social policy via tax breaks," but we believe it is worth it in order to financially safeguard the most important direct public benefit program in America. In essence, we are proposing that well-off individuals—who, partly through the use of government-subsidized tax breaks, have achieved a financially secure retirement—rely less on Social Security.

As we noted in chapter 2, aggregate federal government tax expenditures (i.e., the fiscal cost of granting tax breaks for private pension savings) are substantial, amounting to more than $100 billion a year (and rising), largely for employer-sponsored and 401(k)-type plans (figure 8.1).[2] And the numbers understate the amount because they do not include deferred compensation and stock options. We note as a comparative number that the total federal disbursement in redistributive SSI benefits in 2007 was $39.5 billion (SSA 2008, table IV, C1), significantly less than half of the value of tax breaks that year.

Given the US tax structure, it is not surprising that this country has a larger stock of private pension wealth than almost any other OECD country,

---

2. Some tax breaks granted to corporations may benefit not only individual taxpayers but also shareholders, employees, customers, or other providers of capital, depending on precise economic forces. See OMB (2008, 286). It is important to note that the value (cost to the government) of a tax break rises with the marginal tax rate, hence the decline in federal tax expenditures following the passage of EGTERRA in FY2004, seen in figure 8.1.

Figure 8.1 US federal tax expenditures toward pensions, by category, 1994–2012e

billions of dollars

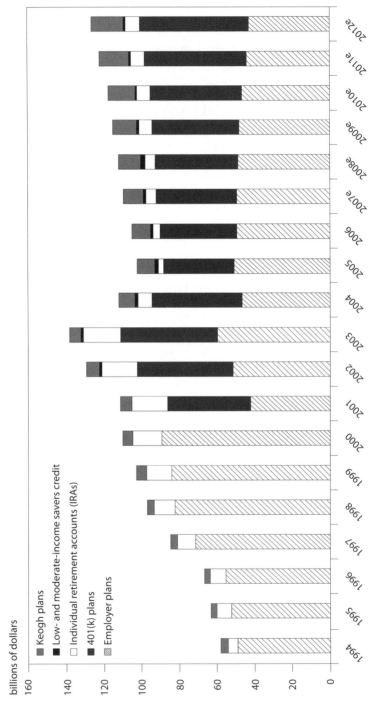

e = estimate

Source: Office of Management and Budget (2008).

at more than 130 percent of GDP. At the same time, we know from chapter 3 that a large group of Americans has no private retirement savings at all, indicating a distributional concern with US retirement savings. A small number of well-to-do Americans will enjoy substantial retirement savings, while a much larger number will have access to only very limited, if any, private savings. Furthermore, as we found in chapter 7, while average US corporate pensions are relatively modest and increasingly in the defined contribution format, they are nonetheless financially reasonably secure and will continue to provide predominantly better-off Americans with additional retirement income.

To a degree, policy is designed to encourage people to do the right thing and set aside enough for their retirement needs. One can argue that those who fail to make such provisions have to expect the consequences of their actions. However, it is a pertinent policy question to ask whether spending $100 billion to $120 billion a year in federal tax expenditures to promote retirement saving is money being allocated correctly, given that it goes overwhelmingly to higher-income groups and that, as we saw in chapter 3, more than a third of Americans have no retirement savings at all and, of those that do, more than a third have less than $10,000.

The results in chapter 3 also showed that only Americans in the top income quintile derive any sizable share of their retirement income from private capital, whereas the overwhelming majority relies almost exclusively on Social Security. Estimating the precise distributional impact of US tax expenditures toward retirement saving is difficult,[3] but updated data from the Congressional Budget Office (CBO 2007) *Utilization of Tax Incentives for Retirement* series provide a glimpse of the situation in 1997–2003.[4]

Table 8.1 shows the rate of participation in tax-favored retirement plans by income group. The share of Americans that save for retirement by participating in tax-favored retirement plans is about 20 percent for those earning less than $20,000 a year, about 50 percent for those earning $20,000 to $40,000, and 70 to 80 percent for income groups over $40,000. As expected, therefore, higher-income groups are overrepresented among participants in tax-favored retirement plans—in progressive tax systems (as in the United States), the benefit of any tax break is greater for higher-income individuals whose tax rate is higher.

---

3. Orszag and Orszag (2000) cite US Treasury data that, as of 2000 (when the maximum IRA contribution was $2,000), nearly two-thirds of tax expenditures toward pension and IRA savings accrue to households in the top fifth of the income scale, while the bottom 60 percent receive only 12 percent of these expenditures. They also note that 70 percent of any new expenditures from a proposed reform to raise the maximum contribution amount to $5,000 would benefit the top fifth of income earners, with only 5.5 percent going to the bottom 60 percent.

4. CBO (2007) presents tabulations of a sample of 1997, 2000, and 2003 individual income tax returns and tax information returns.

Table 8.1 Worker participation in tax-favored retirement plans, by income group, 1997, 2000, and 2003

Annual income (1997 dollars)	Total number of workers	Share of total (percent)	Percent actively participating in any retirement plan	Number of workers contributing	Share of total contributing workers (percent)	Cumulative share of contributing workers (percent)
1997						
Under 20,000	45,686	34	21	9,594	14	14
20,000–40,000	32,066	24	55	17,636	26	40
40,000–80,000	36,720	28	70	25,704	38	78
80,000–120,000	11,474	9	79	9,064	13	91
120,000–160,000	3,491	3	81	2,828	4	95
Over 160,000	3,960	3	77	3,049	4	100
Total	133,397	100	51	68,032	100	
2000						
Under 20,000	44,660	33	20	8,932	13	13
20,000–40,000	31,932	23	51	16,285	24	37
40,000–80,000	37,013	27	67	24,799	36	73
80,000–120,000	13,036	10	79	10,298	15	89
120,000–160,000	4,352	3	83	3,612	5	94
Over 160,000	5,191	4	79	4,101	6	100
Total	136,184	100	50	68,092	100	
2003						
Under 20,000	47,515	34	20	9,503	13	13
20,000–40,000	33,410	24	52	17,373	25	38
40,000–80,000	37,428	27	68	25,451	36	74
80,000–120,000	13,281	9	80	10,625	15	89
120,000–160,000	4,562	3	82	3,741	5	95
Over 160,000	4,612	3	79	3,643	5	100
Total	140,808	100	50	70,404	100	

Note: Participation consists of contributing to an individual retirement account (IRA), self-employed plan, or 401(k)-type plan or being enrolled in a noncontributory plan during the given year. The inclusion of the latter group of noncontributory plan participants is, strictly speaking, irrelevant here and preferably would be avoided. Unfortunately, CBO (2007) does not present data of this kind. It does present data, however, showing that participation in noncontributory plans is relatively stable across income groups, with only a slightly higher participation rate for income categories $20,000–$40,000 and $40,000–$80,000 (CBO 2007, table 2). Hence the inclusion of noncontributory plan participants in these data should not affect the income-based conclusions. The income classifier is adjusted gross income plus excluded contributions to retirement plans less taxable distributions from IRAs.

Source: CBO (2007).

Table 8.1 actually understates the participatory bias in favor of higher-income groups by not considering the magnitude of the participation across income groups. Higher-income groups shelter far larger amounts in tax-favored retirement plans than do lower-income groups, as is evident in the share of each income group that contributes the maximum amount allowed to their tax-favored retirement savings plan.

In 2003, after the passage of the Economic Growth and Tax Relief Reconciliation Act of 2001 (EGTERRA), those with 401(k)-type retirement plans could contribute a total of $12,000 ($14,000 for those over age 50); before passage of the Act, the limit was $11,500 for all participants or a maximum of 25 percent of income (EGTERRA abolished the percentage of income limitation). Also before EGTERRA, participants in IRAs could contribute up to $2,000, an amount that rose to $3,000 with EGTERRA ($3,500 for those over age 50).[5] Table 8.2 shows the share of 401(k)-type and IRA plan participants by income groups that contributed these maximum amounts. Not surprisingly, hardly any low-income participants contributed the maximum, whereas a substantial share of the top income group(s) did. The relatively modest $500 increase (i.e., less than 5 percent) of the maximum contribution level with EGTERRA for 401(k)-type plans significantly lowered the share of maximum contributors.

The data in table 8.2 also indicate that many people do not act entirely rationally when making their retirement saving decisions. Rational decision makers would always attempt to shelter as much of their earnings as affordable in tax-favored retirement plans, and it seems implausible that a significant share of Americans earning over $160,000 (in 1997 dollars) could not afford an extra $500 to reach the new $12,000 contribution ceiling with EGTERRA. Instead, it seems likely that well-off 401(k) investors simply went with the status quo of $11,500.[6] Yet for IRA participants, the increase in maximum contributions from $2,000 to $3,000 meant that only about half as many low-income participants contributed the maximum amount and had very little impact on high-income participants.

Table 8.3 presents data from CBO (2007) for 401(k)-type, IRA, and self-employed retirement plans, and as can be seen, a rising share of total tax-sheltered retirement savings in these three savings vehicles comes from the top income groups. In 1997, 27 percent (about $32.5 billion) of total tax-favored retirement savings came from people with income over

---

5. Data from CBO (2007). These thresholds for maximum savings adjust upwards each year to reflect higher incomes and inflation. In 2007 the maximum contribution in a 401(k)-type plan was $15,500, with an additional $5,000 "catch-up" provision for those over age 50. For IRAs, the 2007 limit is $4,000 ($5,000 for those over age 50).

6. See Kahneman and Tversky (1984) for a description of this "status quo bias."

Table 8.2   Percentage of participants contributing the maximum to tax-favored retirement plans, by plan type and income group, 2003

	401(k)-type plans		Individual retirement accounts	
Annual income in dollars	Pre-EGTERRA	Post-EGTERRA	Pre-EGTERRA	Post-EGTERRA
Under 20,000	1	<1	50	28
20,000–40,000	1	<1	56	33
40,000–80,000	4	1	71	55
80,000–120,000	12	6	81	71
120,000–160,000	26	16	95	87
Over 160,000	52	37	97	87
Total	9	5	71	55

EGTERRA = Economic Growth and Tax Relief Reconciliation Act of 2001

Source: CBO (2007).

$120,000, or essentially the top 5 percent of households that year.[7] This share rose to 31 percent (about $47.6 billion) in 2000 and 32 percent (approximately $60 billion) in 2003. Combining table 8.1 with table 8.3, the top 5 to 6 percent of US workers in 2003 accounted for approximately a third of all tax-favored retirement savings. And this group not only benefits from government-subsidized tax-benefited savings but also receives well-above-average Social Security benefits in retirement. This is, therefore, the group we envision will be most affected by our reform proposal, which calls for reallocating some of the savings subsidies given to this (or a broader definition of) top-income group—say those making over $100,000 a year—of US tax-favored retirement savers and essentially using the savings to shore up the Social Security program.

This group can reasonably be said to be having its cake and eating it too by receiving well-above-average Social Security benefits in retirement as well as benefitting personally from government-subsidized tax-benefited savings. It is important to consider this proposal in the context of the overall tax system. First, the limits on the amount of money that can be set aside in tax-advantaged savings have risen significantly in recent years. Second, tax-advantaged health insurance, tax-advantaged mortgage interest, tax-advantaged retirement saving, and the tax treatment of capital gains all

---

7. In 1997, according to the Census Bureau's income limits, the threshold for inclusion in the top 5 percent of US households by income was $126,500 in current dollars. The CBO (2007) income groups are based on real 1997 income groups (i.e., in 2003, you had to make over $160,000, in 1997 dollars, to be included in the top group), that comparisons of current dollar thresholds across years are difficult.

Table 8.3 Employee contributions to 401(k)-type, IRAs, and self-employed retirement plans, by income group, 1997, 2000, and 2003

Annual income in current dollars	1997			2000			2003		
	Number of participants (thousands)	Average contribution (1997 dollars)	Total contribution (billions of 1997 dollars)	Number of participants (thousands)	Average contribution (2000 dollars)	Total contribution (billions of 2000 dollars)	Number of participants (thousands)	Average contribution (2003 dollars)	Total contribution (billions of 2003 dollars)
401(k)-type plans									
Under 20,000	2,448	546	1.3	2,611	680	1.8	2,976	726	2.2
20,000–40,000	8,331	1,324	11.0	8,248	1,498	12.4	8,806	1,583	13.9
40,000–80,000	14,718	2,482	36.5	15,112	2,822	42.6	15,753	3,162	49.8
80,000–120,000	6,310	4,131	26.1	7,019	4,549	31.9	7,511	5,287	39.7
120,000–160,000	1,958	5,360	10.5	2,561	6,116	15.7	2,741	7,476	20.5
Over 160,000	1,902	7,054	13.4	2,675	7,522	20.1	2,470	9,503	23.5
Total	35,666	2,772	98.9	38,226	3,257	124.5	40,257	3,716	149.6
Individual retirement accounts (IRAs)									
Under 20,000	925	1,428	1.3	1,197	1,352	1.6	1,156	1,689	2.0
20,000–40,000	2,062	1,513	3.1	2,236	1,497	3.3	2,160	1,962	4.2
40,000–80,000	2,631	1,520	4.0	3,736	1,593	6.0	3,688	2,181	8.0
80,000–120,000	1,012	1,741	1.8	2,055	1,744	3.6	1,810	2,444	4.4
120,000–160,000	517	1,863	1.0	911	1,771	1.6	690	2,635	1.8
Over 160,000	670	1,915	1.3	727	1,879	1.4	540	2,941	1.6
Total	7,818	1,593	12.5	10,860	1,620	17.6	10,045	2,197	22.1
Self-employed retirement plans									
Under 20,000	32	2,245	0.1	39	2,057	0.1	35	3,099	0.1
20,000–40,000	93	2,665	0.2	98	2,959	0.3	97	4,021	0.4
40,000–80,000	269	4,098	1.1	319	4,316	1.4	260	6,314	1.6
80,000–120,000	242	6,360	1.5	268	5,821	1.6	268	8,940	2.4
120,000–160,000	145	9,433	1.4	156	9,110	1.4	170	13,315	2.3
Over 160,000	340	14,578	5.0	453	16,058	7.3	443	23,977	10.6
Total	1,159	8,115	9.4	1,332	9,007	12.0	1,274	13,685	17.4

(table continues next page)

Table 8.3 Employee contributions to 401(k)-type, IRAs, and self-employed retirement plans, by income group, 1997, 2000, and 2003 *(continued)*

Annual income in current dollars	Total contributions to 401(k)-type, IRAs, and self-employed retirement plans					
	Percent share of total	Total contribution (billions of 1997 dollars)	Percent share of total	Total contribution (billions of 2000 dollars)	Percent share of total	Total contribution (billions of 2003 dollars)
Under 20,000	2	2.7	2	3.5	2	4.2
20,000–40,000	12	14.4	10	16.0	10	18.6
40,000–80,000	34	41.6	32	50.0	31	59.5
80,000–120,000	24	29.4	24	37.1	25	46.5
120,000–160,000	11	12.8	12	18.7	13	24.6
Over 160,000	16	19.7	19	28.8	19	35.7
Total	100	120.7	100	154.1	100	189.1

Source: CBO (2007).

combine to skew policy such that the largest tax benefits go to the upper-income cohorts, thereby reducing the overall progressivity of the tax system.

Impacts of Pension Integration on Saving Incentives

Integration of the public and private pension benefit systems previously meant the proportional adjustment of private pension benefits to the level of benefits from Social Security. We propose instead an Internal Revenue Service (IRS)/Social Security Administration (SSA) linking mechanism that would reduce the level of Social Security benefits only for those with tax-favored retirement savings (i.e., those who have already benefited from public financial support through their use of federal tax breaks). We believe this selective approach is intuitively fairer (and thus ought to be politically more palatable) than other approaches to targeted Social Security benefit cuts.

One immediate concern with this proposal is that it would reduce the return to private pension saving. Even economists who strongly support the Social Security system have voiced this concern to us, especially given that the United States has such a low saving rate. Do we really want to reduce saving incentives? We offer several observations to allay this concern.

First, we note that we are also supporting the introduction of individual accounts as an add-on to Social Security and that such a program has the potential to increase national saving in a way that benefits lower-income workers. We are aware of the need for a higher saving rate in the United States, but we judge that this should come through a broader-based incentive for saving rather than through a narrow program (together with a plan to balance the federal budget).

Second, the provisions for tax-preferred private saving have become much more generous in recent years. We do not propose eliminating all tax advantages for saving, nor reducing Social Security benefits dollar for dollar based on the extent of the tax preference in any pension saving. Rather, we would scale back the tax advantages, making them comparable to the level of, say, ten years ago (after adjusting for inflation).

Third, the impact of savings tax subsidies on the level of saving is generally small. A tax advantage that increases the rate of return on saving will have offsetting effects on the amount of saving. To illustrate, consider the positive incentive for saving: If I decide to reduce my consumption today and set aside $1,000 for retirement, in 20 years it will yield $1,800 at a 3 percent real rate of return. If, instead, the rate of return is increased to 6 percent because of tax advantages, then the $1,000 will become $3,200 after 20 years, a large difference that will encourage me to save that $1,000 rather than spending it now. With the tax incentive, savers get more for any given dollar level of saving. Thus an increase in the return to saving has a substitution effect that may cause individuals to consume less today and set aside more for tomorrow.

The same tax break, however, creates an incentive for saving less because it makes it easier to reach any given retirement target. For example, if I decide that I need to have $1 million set aside when I retire, a higher rate of return makes it easier for me to reach that goal and I can actually save less. For example, at a 3 percent rate of return, I need to save $3,046 a month for 20 years in order to end up with $1 million, whereas at a 6 percent rate of return I need to save only $2,164 a month. This is the income or wealth effect of a higher rate of return, and it can work to reduce saving.[8]

In practice, the incentives for more and less saving operate at the same time and we would like to know which effect will predominate. That is an empirical question and economists do not agree on what the data show, but generally the answer is that the two effects offset each other, and the net impact of an increase in the rate of return is pretty small either way.

Pension savings tax breaks may have very little positive effect on saving, or even a net negative effect, because for any individual or family that is saving the maximum amount under the tax-advantaged program, there is only the income effect and not the substitution effect. In table 8.2 we saw that a substantial percentage of families with incomes over $160,000 were at the maximum contribution, so we look at an example of this type. Suppose that there are no tax-advantaged saving plans for a very affluent family saving $6,250 a month, or $75,000 a year. They invest at a 3 percent real return and after 20 years with the same annual saving level, they have accumulated a nice retirement nest egg of $2.05 million. Now suppose the government gives them a tax advantage on the first $50,000 a year of their saving ($4,167 a month), so that this level of saving now earns 6 percent a year. This tax-preferred retirement account will accumulate to $1.93 million after 20 years, leaving them nearly as well off as they were before. The first $4,167 per month of their saving ($50,000 a year) will yield a retirement nest egg that is roughly equal to the one they reached by saving $6,250 a month before the tax break. So how much does the family decide to save now that they have the tax break—more or less? If they save more than $50,000 a year, they will earn the lower rate of return on their savings and so the chances are pretty good that they will choose to save less than the $75,000 a year they were setting aside before the tax break.[9] They do not need to save as much (the income effect), and there is no subsidy to their marginal or additional dollars of saving.

---

8. Exactly how rational saving choices change with changes in income depends on the specific attributes of individual preference functions. A general increase in income (a salary increase, for example) is likely to increase both consumption and saving—splitting the extra money. So it is hard to be certain just from theory how people will be affected by policy changes.

9. Rational saving decisions are made on the basis of maximizing welfare over entire lifetimes. When the rate of return rises, people are better off and choose to consume more, including during their retirement years. The saving decisions made over the entire lifespan may be affected either way.

Moreover, because the tax break will also reduce the government's tax revenue, unless there is an increase in other taxes or a decrease in government spending, it is almost certain that it will reduce total national saving.[10]

Is this a realistic example? We have exaggerated the effects a bit to make the case—current tax breaks do not result in a doubling of the rate of return, especially since participants have to pay tax on the withdrawals in retirement[11]; and only a fraction of the population saves the maximum amount allowed to qualify for tax-preferred treatment. But the point is correct and important. When affluent families file their tax returns, their accountants tell them how much they can put into tax-preferred accounts and they move that money from another account in order to reduce their taxes for the year. They do not save an additional amount. The very affluent are a small fraction of the population, but they account for a large fraction of total saving.

Finally, we note again that saving behavior does not always follow the rules of rational economics. Indeed, that is why programs like Social Security require people to contribute to a pension program. An extensive literature of behavioral finance has documented the fact that people are often irrational when making decisions concerning their saving.[12] (These behavioral findings already inform the design of private pension schemes [Benartzi and Thaler 2004]; we attempt to partly introduce them to public pension schemes.) Setting an optimal saving rate is a difficult decision involving an intertemporal choice under a great deal of uncertainty about future income and future rates of return on different assets. As a result, people do not evaluate their future needs but instead make a series of short-term decisions.

Would our proposal to help Social Security cause people to reduce the amount they were setting aside in tax-preferred saving accounts? People would be making a choice between, on the one hand, paying more taxes today and preserving some unknown distant future level of Social Security benefit, and, on the other hand, paying less tax today, knowing that it is still a worthwhile investment overall. This choice is affected by two concepts in behavioral finance, "hyperbolic discounting" and "loss aversion." George Loewenstein and Richard Thaler (1989) describe the notion of hyperbolic discounting, in which people attach too little importance to

---

10. See Engen, Gale, and Scholz (1994) for a more in-depth discussion of the ambivalent effects of savings tax incentives on national savings.

11. Although this is offset with provisions that allow families to pass wealth on to their children and further postpone the taxes.

12. See, for instance, Kahneman and Tversky (1984), Loewenstein and Thaler (1989), Kahneman, Knetsch, and Thaler (1991), Madrian and Shea (2000), Choi et al. (2003, 2005), and Beshears et al. (2006, 2007).

the distant future compared to what would be predicted from a rational evaluation.[13] They give more weight to the immediate benefit of the tax break than to the future loss of benefits, even if the two are equal in present value. They are, therefore, less likely to change their retirement savings in tax-sheltered plans than would be rationally predicted.

Daniel Kahneman, Jack Knetsch, and Richard Thaler (1991) illustrated that people who suffer from "loss aversion" are disproportionally—at a ratio of perhaps 2:1—averse to suffering a loss (relative to their perception of an equal gain). This is important in relation to our proposal, as Daniel Feenberg and Jonathan Skinner (1989) find that one of the most important predictors for whether individuals put money into an IRA is whether they would otherwise have to write a check to the IRS on April 15: Those who owe the IRS money are far more likely to buy an IRA than those getting a refund.[14] Lawrence Summers (1986) further showed that most IRA purchases are made at the last minute, contrary to what a rational person would do, which is to secure tax-sheltered status at the earliest possible date.[15] Thaler (1994) cites this behavior as an example of loss aversion, as would-be savers resist writing a check (i.e., suffering a loss) to the IRS and instead invest the money in an IRA. A similar (lack of) logic will likely cause Americans to take advantage of the tax breaks for retirement saving today despite their awareness of the associated future cuts in their Social Security benefit entitlements. As with hyperbolic discounting, we believe that this will limit any adverse impact of our proposal on the overall level of present savings.

How Much Money Is on the Table?

We saw above that the federal government spends about $120 billion (and rising) annually in tax expenditures for retirement savings, and we have explained why we do not expect our proposal to affect this level of tax expenditure. In other words, this is not the channel through which we intend to cut costs.

We also illustrated that high-income Americans derive most of the economic benefits of tax-benefited retirement plans. We, therefore, propose to cut future Social Security benefits through some proportional formula for Americans earning over $100,000 a year who take advantage of

---

13. Hyperbolic discounting in mathematical terms implies that the discount function is a generalized hyperbola; events τ periods away are discounted with factor $(1 + \alpha\tau)^{-\alpha\delta}$, with α, $\delta > 0$. Such discount functions imply a monotonously falling discount rate. Hereby the near future is discounted too deeply, as too much importance is attached to it.

14. Thaler (1990, 200) describes this as the "I would rather put $2,000 [the 1990 maximum for IRA contributions] in an IRA than pay the government $800" approach to pension saving.

15. See also Akerlof (1991) for a description of self-control and procrastination problems.

tax breaks for their retirement saving. We have chosen the $100,000 threshold because it is a round number, and in 2006 it designated the top income quintile in America.[16] As such, we feel this threshold ensures that we intuitively affect only "high-income Americans" with our proposal. Given that we lack access to linked longitudinal micro-level data for both IRS tax receipts (i.e., data on the degree to which high-income individuals claim tax breaks) and the same individuals' Social Security benefit entitlements later in life, we cannot say with any precision just how much money our reform might save the SSA.

No data are available from the SSA indicating the total dollar figure for benefit payments to Americans who earned more than $100,000 in 2006.[17] However, a look at data for the sources of income for Americans over 65 by income quintile yields some clues. In chapter 3 we saw that only Americans in the top income quintile did *not* derive the majority of their old age income from Social Security benefits. For this top group, Social Security benefits made up only 22 percent of total income. Thus in our proposal we are talking about cutting only a minor source of old age income for high-income Americans.

The Employee Benefit Research Institute (EBRI) publishes an annual dataset for old age income sources by income quintile based on the same Current Population Survey (CPS) data we used in chapter 3.[18] These data allow us to give an approximate dollar figure for the amount of Social Security benefits going to Americans in the top income quintile.[19] However, here we are talking about the top income quintile over age 65, whereas before, when concerned about which Americans took advantage of tax-benefited retirement plans (the $100,000 threshold), we were referring to all ages of the top income quintile. The lack of linked longitudinal micro-level data creates a methodological discrepancy; however, we are fairly certain that the groups will overlap through time, meaning that if you belong to the top income quintile during your working life, you will remain in that group in retirement.

Figure 8.2 shows that the share of Social Security benefit disbursements to the top income quintile has been relatively stable at approximately 25 percent. In 2006 the threshold for inclusion in the top income quintile for those over 65 was $34,570, and this group, on average, had a total income of $70,176.

---

16. The Census Bureau's Income Table H-1 indicates that the lower limit for inclusion in the top income quintile in America in 2006 was $97,033, available at www.census.gov.

17. Data are available for benefit payments only by benefit category, not income group. See the SSA website at www.ssa.gov.

18. See table 7.5 in the EBRI databook, available at www.ebri.org.

19. Some methodological concerns surround the use of CPS income data. See Weinberg (2006) for a detailed discussion of the validity of CPS income data.

Figure 8.2 Share of total Social Security benefit income of individuals age 65 and over, by recipient income quintile, 1975–2006

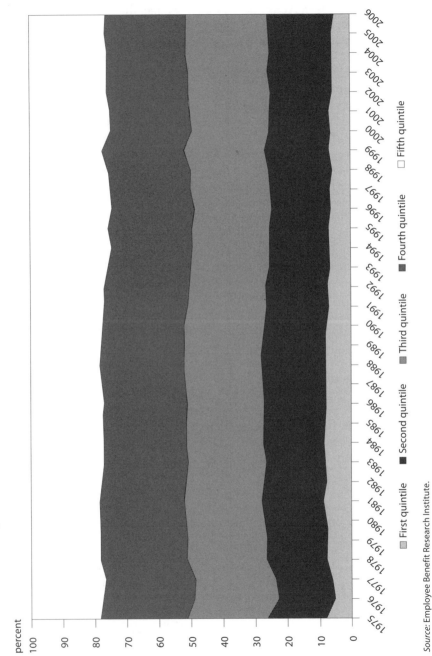

Source: Employee Benefit Research Institute.

The same EBRI data allow us to calculate a rough estimate of the dollar figure for Social Security benefit income for each income quintile. Figure 8.3 illustrates the rising trend in total Social Security benefit payments each year, as more and more Americans retire and begin withdrawing benefits. By 2006 the level of Social Security benefits to the top income quintile had risen to more than $78 billion. These data are derived from CPS income data for Americans age 65 and over, so totals do not necessarily correspond with the data for total SSA disbursements. In 2006, total Old Age and Survivors Insurance (OASI) expenditures were $460 billion, of which $367 billion went to retired workers and dependents, while the remaining almost $100 billion benefited survivors (mostly aged and disabled widowers).[20] This compares with the $320 billion in total recipient income in 2006 indicated in figure 8.3. This difference likely results mostly from OASI expenditures for early retirement benefits for Americans aged 62–65 and benefits to dependents not included in the CPS income data for Americans aged 65 and above. As such, the $78 billion estimate of Social Security benefits to the top income quintile aged 65 years and older is likely biased downward.

How much money would our proposal shift? We do not have the data to spell out the details, so we will only estimate the amount. Given the $120 billion in annual tax expenditures toward retirement saving and at least $80 billion in Social Security benefits to recipients 62 and older in the top income quintile (who benefit the most from tax-favored retirement plans), we believe that a reasonable estimate is that about $30 billion to $40 billion in annual benefit reductions is possible by targeting those who take advantage of tax-preferred pensions. Thus our pension integration proposal would save about 50 percent of the Social Security benefits paid to recipients in the top income quintile.

Through this proposal, we would move the Social Security system away from the German insurance model and toward an income support program. But given the relatively regressive character of the large federal tax expenditures for retirement saving, in our view this is a sound policy. As part of our comprehensive approach to reforming Social Security by looking across a variety of challenges, one might say that we intend to make Social Security itself more progressive, but in reality we believe we would merely be making the entire US old age income security system (i.e. considering the large role of private savings and corporate pensions, too) and the role of the federal government herein less regressive. Moreover, our cross-country evidence concerning the relative progressiveness of OECD public retirement systems (chapter 3) suggests that there is no reason to believe that making US Social Security more progressive will undermine broad political support for the system. There has been no loss

---

20. SSA data, available at www.ssa.gov/oact/stats.

Figure 8.3 Social Security benefit income of individuals age 65 and over, by recipient income quintile, 1975–2006

billions of current US dollars

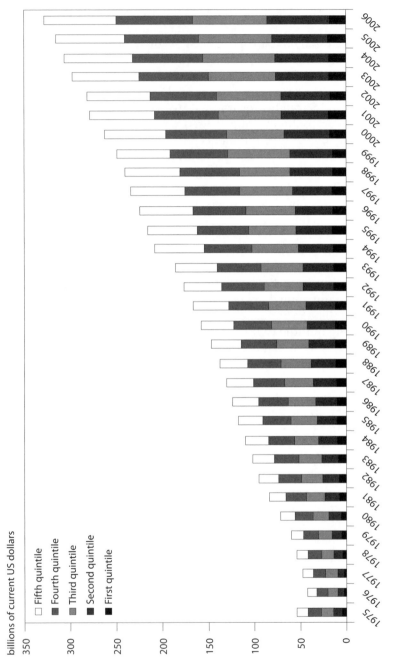

Source: Employee Benefit Research Institute.

of such support in OECD countries with far more progressive public retirement systems, nor was there in the early decades of the US Social Security system, when, as we saw in chapter 3, the system was far more progressive than today.

Our proposal for pension integration addresses only part of the benefit reduction that would be needed, along with some revenue enhancements, to generate fiscal balance for the program into the future. The second part is to adjust the age of retirement.

Adjusting the Retirement Age

There is no economic principle for determining the optimal retirement age or age range for a public retirement program like Social Security. The medical profession tells us that, on average, there is deterioration of physical and mental capacity—vision, hearing, mobility, and memory—with age. But there are tremendous individual variations, with some 80-year-olds able to run marathons that many 30-year-olds cannot. Scientists are said to peak in their 30s, and yet Galileo accomplished some of his finest scientific achievements studying the laws of motion when he was well over 60.[21]

This variation across individuals suggests that differing preferences and circumstances lead to very different choices, and so perhaps the retirement decision should be left to the individual. Social Security does build in some flexibility, allowing people to choose to retire as early as age 62 or to postpone receiving benefits until as late as age 70 in order to receive a higher benefit level. And in recognition that many people remain active and sharp as they age, the United States has abolished most mandatory retirement provisions for companies. Currently, the increases in the "normal" retirement age have not been accompanied by increases in the minimum retirement age to be eligible for Social Security benefits. That creates the danger that some people will retire at 62 without realizing that their monthly benefit level will not suffice to support them as the years pass, especially as their health costs rise. To avoid this problem, it would be better to gradually increase the minimum age for Social Security benefits as well, indeed to let the whole range of retirement ages rise.[22]

We have learned from our cross-country analysis that the age of retirement has a huge impact on the retirement pension budget. While expected lifespan has increased in all OECD countries, the age of retirement

---

21. His book *Dialogues Concerning Two New Sciences* was published in 1638 in Leyden when Galileo was 74. It was "his most rigorous mathematical work, which treated problems on impetus, moments, and centers of gravity," according to a biography by St. Andrews University, available at www-history.mcs.st-andrews.ac.uk.

22. See also Barr (2006) for this issue.

has declined since 1970, and the combination of these two effects has sharply increased the number of years spent in retirement and put tremendous strain on pension budgets. The United States is relatively well off despite these developments because it has not reduced the age at which benefits can be received; indeed it is gradually raising the normal retirement age from 65 to 67 by 2027. But there will be no further increases in retirement age after that unless there is a change in the law.

The SSA has prepared estimates for several types of life expectancy linkages, similar to what we propose, which, as we have found in other OECD countries, illustrate that this is a very powerful policy tool for long-term pension system sustainability. For instance, indexing the Social Security normal retirement age after 2027 to changes in longevity would reduce the long-term actuarial deficit by 0.37 percent of taxable payrolls[23] or, when compared with the new CBO estimates cited at the beginning of this chapter, about one-third of the total necessary adjustment to achieve long-term Social Security sustainability.

We propose to link the range of eligibility ages for Social Security benefits to changes in life expectancies after 2027 in a way that keeps constant the ratio between years spent in retirement and the rest of an individual's lifetime (the "expected time in retirement" to "total life time not in retirement," or ETR-TNR, ratio described in chapter 3). This would mean that the earliest age (now 62) of eligibility would also rise with life expectancy.[24] Such an indexing could occur automatically based on the best available estimates of life expectancy.

However, the Social Security program is based on the idea that people may need guidance in their retirement decisions, so it is important that any public debate on Social Security reform be based on a realistic view of the tradeoffs involved. If participants want to increase the number of years during which they receive benefits, they must expect to contribute more, either by making higher contributions or by working for more years. While economic theory does not provide a definitive answer to which of these choices people would make if they acted rationally, it does suggest pretty strongly that increases in expected lifespan should

---

23. See SSA Long-term Solvency Provision, C-7, available at www.ssa.gov. This scenario increases the normal retirement age by one month every other year. Another SSA scenario (C-6) suggests that a constant ratio of expected retirement years to potential work years would yield savings of similar magnitude.

24. It is important to note, however, that we do not foresee many future savings to the OASDI Trust Fund from linking the earliest age of eligibility (62) to life expectancy. This is due to the fact, discussed in chapter 3, that many people in the age group of 62 and up who retire early would likely instead seek and receive disability benefits. The SSA thus estimates that the total savings to the OASDI Trust Fund from raising the earliest age of eligibility from 62 to 65 would lead to an improvement in the Trust Fund's long-term balance of only 0.01 percent of payrolls. See SSA Long-term Solvency Provision, C-8, available at www.ssa.gov.

be met in part by increases in the number of years at work. We, therefore, believe that the rule of thumb should say that the retirement age should be increased in response to expected lifespan increases in such a way that the proportion of life spent in retirement remains constant. If Social Security participants, through their representatives, decided that the expectation of extended working years imposed too great a burden on the elderly, then the rule could be changed, provided tax contributions were adjusted to sustain solvency. Individuals would retain the right to choose their retirement age from within a range, as in the current system.

Increasing Revenues for the Social Security System

As discussed in chapter 1, we do not believe that an internationally comparative methodology, such as the one used in this book, can provide us with the insights into how to potentially raise additional revenues in the future for the Social Security system. The differences between individual countries' revenue-raising laws and traditions are simply too great. As such, we do not feel we are in a position as part of this project to provide any guidance as to the specifics of the design of any new revenue-raising measures for Social Security. However, we do believe that any additional revenue needed to "fix Social Security for the long term" should be raised as a "plug" to fill any additional long-term financial shortfall left over from the implementation of our first two proposals to remedy the current Social Security financial imbalance.

Our proposals will appropriately distribute the "reform pain" over as broad a range of groups as we deem possible. We are confident that the need for additional revenues for Social Security would be relatively modest after the implementation of our reform proposals concerning tax breaks and retirement ages, especially in comparison to the need for increased revenues to finance projected levels of accelerating Medicare and Medicaid costs as well as continuously rising levels of discretionary spending. In this context, any additional revenue-raising measures needed to balance Social Security's finances in perpetuity are undoubtedly among the lesser of the fiscal challenges facing the United States today.

Add-On Program of Individual Accounts

The United States has a market economy and generally allows individuals to make their own spending decisions. On that basis, perhaps people should decide for themselves if they want to set aside part of their disposable income to save for their retirement years. We disagree, however, and build the case for a government-sponsored program of individual accounts based on three elements.

First, most low- and middle-income households lack the information and training necessary to make good investment decisions. Many people do not know the difference between stocks and bonds, do not know how to pick a mutual fund suitable for retirement, and can, therefore, benefit from guidance on retirement saving. Although employers with sponsored retirement plans frequently provide such guidance, many workers and the self-employed do not have this advantage. Second, low- and middle-income households that start small retirement accounts face management or transaction fees that are large relative to their contributions. This is one of the lessons learned from the experience of other countries. Small savers would benefit if the government pooled funds and covered administrative costs, thereby enhancing the returns earned by small accounts. Third, many households are not able to project their future and decide rationally how much they will need. Even sophisticated and educated individuals have trouble doing this and make rule-of-thumb decisions instead. As explained above, one of the ways people fail to make rational long-term decisions is that they favor current consumption over the future.

Do these points make an economic case for a compulsory saving system for those who do not save enough voluntarily? There is a case for compulsory auto insurance because otherwise, uninsured drivers involved in accidents lack the resources to reimburse the parties they have damaged. Their lack of insurance makes them a burden on others. Similarly, there is a case for compulsory health insurance because otherwise, those who have coverage pay for those who receive treatment without it. Those who lack health insurance are a financial burden on others. Similarly, there is a case for compulsory retirement saving because people who reach old age without having saved enough to support themselves have to be supported by the rest of society. The alternative of allowing the elderly poor to starve or become homeless is a socially unacceptable outcome.

The latter argument was part of the reasoning behind the creation of Social Security and the SSI program in the first place: Americans were unwilling to see the elderly become destitute. So the case for a compulsory add-on individual account system has to be made on the grounds that the programs introduced in the 1930s and expanded since then do not provide adequate incomes to the elderly going forward, especially considering future health care cost increases and likely restrictions on Medicare and Medicaid spending. An alternative approach would be to expand Social Security or the SSI program to provide more support to the elderly. However, a compulsory saving plan would provide distinct advantages in the form of increased national saving and greater transparency—workers would see where their money was going and would be less likely to consider the contributions as taxes.

How would an add-on saving program work? Employers and employees would be required to contribute a percentage of Social Security payroll to the plan with the funds collected by the IRS and turned over to the SSA, just as FICA taxes are collected today (2.5 percent of taxable payroll from employees and employers, for example). Instead of being put in the current trust fund, however, the money would be passed to private fund managers for investment in an age-adjusted standard portfolio, the default choice for all participants. The standard portfolio would consist of US and international stocks and bonds, with the selection made by the investment managers. Those who wanted a different portfolio choice could request it, subject to limits; if participants wanted to choose green funds, for example, they could do so provided there are fund managers willing to create such funds. An independent board of trustees, charged with maximizing returns without regard to other goals, would select and supervise the managers. The government would be prohibited from voting any equities or of influencing the choices of the investment fund managers.

We believe that compulsory add-on savings accounts are justifiable but that, given the popular aversion to taxes and the need for fiscal adjustment, it would not be politically feasible to introduce a compulsory program now. Instead, we propose a voluntary program in which workers are automatically enrolled unless they opt out. Such an approach can encourage enrollment, as evident in recent pension reforms in the United Kingdom and New Zealand, which implemented auto-enrollment features in their national pension schemes.[25] Workers should also receive information about the advantages of the IRS and SSA coverage of the program's administrative costs, enabling market returns with smaller fees than would be available for small individual accounts in the marketplace. Higher-income workers enrolled in employer-sponsored plans would probably choose to opt out. Employers that provided matching funds in a preexisting retirement program would not be required to contribute to a government plan on behalf of their employees.

It may also be possible to create an additional incentive for participation. Although we have argued that there should be increases in the normal retirement age, they would create "leakage" between pension systems: If the age of earliest retirement is also increased (from 62, where it is today), then some workers needing to retire early will retire on disability instead, thus eliminating any revenue savings from the later retirement age. If the age of earliest retirement is not increased but the benefits are actuarially reduced, then some workers will retire early, and then either they or their spouses will be in poverty when they become very old. To address these problems, the rules for early retirement could be adjusted depending

---

25. See chapters 5 and 6 for discussion of the New Zealand KiwiSaver program and recent UK pension reforms.

on whether or not the worker had participated in the add-on savings plan. Workers who had participated would automatically be eligible to receive benefits at age 62; those who had not would have to demonstrate that they had adequate funds to avoid poverty in retirement, and if not, they would have to start receiving benefits at a later age. This provision would encourage the development of the add-on individual accounts.

Timing the Reform of Social Security and Automatic Balancing Mechanisms

> *Without corrective legislation in the very near future, the Old Age and Survivors Insurance Trust Fund will be unable to make benefit payments on time beginning no later than July 1983.*
>
> —OASDI Trustees (1982, 2)

Based on our cross-country research, we are fairly optimistic about the potential for reforms of the Social Security system, as we believe that solutions are feasible with only a modest amount of pain for both current and future US taxpayers and retirees. Yet the simple stubborn fact is that the problems with Social Security are of a magnitude that require cautious, workable, and farsighted reform, and the feasibility and timeliness of such reform are hindered by political factors. The quotation above indicates that the last reform of Social Security came about only in the nick of time before the exhaustion of the OASI Trust Fund,[26] suggesting that a "crisis" was necessary for reform to be politically possible.[27] Similarly, we have seen that in other OECD countries (and the United States in 1983) there is a tendency to implement pension reforms with a substantial time lag so that any potentially painful alterations affect voters long after the reformers have left office.

Although such delays reflect the political necessity of getting any pension reform passed by the legislature, they also pose potentially significant intergenerational fairness issues. Therefore, we make the case for a prompt reform of Social Security by briefly touching on the timing of pension reforms and reviewing the use of automatic balancing mechanisms (ABMs), a policy tool to eliminate pension reform procrastination among policymakers. Because future policymakers may opt to suspend or

---

26. Romig (2006) describes how, as part of the 1983 reform, the OASI Trust Fund in November and December 1982 to avoid cash-flow problems had to borrow $17.5 billion from the Disability Insurance and Hospital Insurance (Medicare) Trust Funds. The money was repaid by 1986, after the 1983 reform had restored the solvency of the OASI Trust Fund.

27. There is a large political economy literature exploring the impact of economic crises on the prospects of structural reforms. See Williamson (1994) for an overview.

annul an ABM when the going gets tough, these mechanisms require the approval of a large majority in national parliaments or, in the United States, broad bipartisan support in Congress.

ABMs, an innovative recent development in other OECD countries, ensure that national pension systems entering a fiscal imbalance are brought back to long-term financial stability in an expeditious manner. They work in much the same way that the automatic cost of living allowances (COLAs) adapt Social Security benefit levels annually for inflation.[28] But whereas COLAs automatically protect the benefit adequacy and thus living standards of retirees, ABMs automatically secure the long-term financial sustainability of the pension system and thus also safeguard the intergenerational fairness of the pension system.

Well-designed ABMs have the political advantage of being automatic (as their name indicates) and transparent, and they go into effect long before a crisis point. They also specify how any future financial shortfall in a pension system will be made up and thus efficiently allocate any "pain" among workers and retirees.

Sweden has introduced an ABM for its new notional defined contribution (NDC) pension system (see chapter 6),[29] but of more direct interest to US policymakers are the ABM reforms introduced in Germany and Japan (the employees' pension insurance [EPI] system) in 2004. These countries' pension systems share the basic defined benefit design of Social Security and, as we saw in chapter 3, have mandatory pension systems that aim to provide average mandatory pension replacement levels roughly similar to Social Security.[30]

All mandatory OECD defined benefit pension systems that want to remain solvent at a fixed tax/contribution rate face at least three similar long-term challenges: rising life expectancies, leading to beneficiaries receiving benefits for longer periods; declining support ratios, as the number of workers per retiree drops with the retirement of the baby-boomers and long-term declines in fertility levels; and the financing of the inevitable

---

28. We saw in chapter 3 that the "automaticity" of Social Security's COLAs was introduced only in the 1970s and that prior to that, Congress had to legislate separately for each inflation adjustment.

29. Given that Sweden' introduced an NDC pension system, the country was able to base its ABM on the concept of "turn-over duration," the difference between the earnings-weighted average age of contributing workers and the benefit-weighted average age of pension recipients. If the turnover duration is, say, 33 years, then the pension system is, based on annual contributions, able to finance 33 years of pension liabilities. However, turnover duration as defined here is a meaningful concept only in an NDC system and not applicable to a standard defined benefit pension system. See Settergren (2001) for the technical details of the Swedish ABM.

30. See figure 3.1. All three countries target average mandatory pension replacement rate levels of 33 to 40 percent of average economywide earnings.

"legacy debt" carried forward to future generation from the inception of any defined benefit pension system, where the "first-generation" recipients receive more benefits than they contributed to the system.[31]

However, two major factors differentiate the situation that faced the German and Japanese defined benefit pension systems in 2004 from that of Social Security today. First, both Germany and Japan, as we saw in chapters 2 and 3, face a future of populations ageing much faster than in the United States and are likely to see large absolute declines in their workforces. Second, neither country had an earmarked "OASDI-type" public pension trust fund. For these reasons the outlook for their mandatory public defined benefit pension systems in 2004 was more serious than that facing Social Security today, and the scope of their ABMs correspondingly far-reaching. The latter matters, as ABMs are potentially very potent policy instruments with direct implications on the daily lives of millions of people.

The ABMs introduced in Germany (called the sustainability factor[32]) and Japan (termed macroeconomy indexation[33]) in 2004 were similar in design. Both aimed to guarantee that the future tax/contribution level required to maintain the pension system's fiscal solvency did not rise above a certain percentage of wages. In Germany, these maximum limits (split equally between employers and employees) were set at 20 percent in 2020 and 22 percent by 2030, up from 19.5 percent in 2005. In Japan, the ABM will prevent the tax/contribution rate (also split evenly between employers and employees) from rising above 18.3 percent of wages by 2017, up from 14.64 percent in 2006. In other words, the introduction of ABMs in Germany and Japan also possessed some of the traditional "delayed introduction of pension reforms" characteristic described in chapter 4. In both countries an additional purpose of the mechanisms is to moderate scheduled future increases in tax/contribution levels (already at levels significantly above US payroll taxes) to the mandatory public defined benefit pension system and thus ease future burdens on workers.[34]

---

31. Note that, as discussed in chapter 3, it is improper to directly equate the narrow accounting-like concept of "legacy debt" carried forward in a country's defined benefit pension scheme with the much broader notion of "intergenerational fairness." Certainly, a defined benefit pension system that causes a premature collapse of government finances or requires a rapid rise in future contribution levels due to excessively generous benefit levels for initial generations of retirees is intergenerationally unfair. However, a defined benefit pension system is only one (admittedly large) public institution with the longevity to transfer wealth between generations. School systems, health care, and physical infrastructure are other examples, as are earlier public norms of elderly being cared for within the family.

32. See Börsch-Supan, Reil-Held, and Wilke (2003) and European Commission (2005).

33. See Sakamoto (2005) and Fukawa (2006).

34. Estimates for Germany indicate that without the ABM, the required tax/contribution rate would rise to 28 percent of wages by 2040, while for Japan the tax/contribution rate required without the ABM would be 23 percent of wages by 2025. See Sakamoto (2005).

Germany and Japan also chose measures that adjust the annual COLA benefit increase for any future change (i.e., decline) in the pension system contributor/beneficiary ratio.[35] They will thus cut pension benefits in proportion to the projected decline in the ratio of workers contributing to the pension system and the number of pensioners drawing benefits from it. But, as we saw in chapter 2, if Germany and Japan increase their current low labor force participation by tapping unused labor reservoirs and, in particular, raising the level of participation among women, the two countries will be able to blunt the effects of their projected decline in working age population and of the ABM. Nonetheless, the effects of ABMs in both countries are potentially very large. In Japan, for instance, the Ministry of Health, Labor, and Welfare estimates that the ABM would cause average replacement rates for the EPI pension to decline 2 to 14 percentage points by the 2040s, depending on the economic scenario (Sakamoto 2005). Axel Börsch-Supan, Anette Reil-Held, and Christina Wilke (2003, figure 4.3) similarly estimate potential gross benefit cuts in Germany of up to 15 percentage points by 2040.

The ABM design chosen by Germany and Japan works in a way that reduces pension benefits for both current and future retirees and thus secures the long-term financial sustainability of the German and Japanese mandatory defined benefit pension systems exclusively via benefit cuts. However, as noted above, this seemingly one-sided ABM fiscal remedy was only one part of broader reforms in the two countries and, in fact, will work only to reduce the effects of already decided future tax/contribution increases. As such, the German and Japanese ABMs, in truth, are not one-sided measures aimed solely at retirees but rather can be said to be a balancing factor that ensures that long-term pension system sustainability is not achieved solely through continuously and already legislated rises in tax/contribution levels. They are subsequently a tool to help to begin distributing "the pain" of long-term pension system sustainability over as many generations as possible.

This distinction is crucial to US policymakers because current US law also has a de facto ABM in place to guarantee the long-term sustainability of Social Security. Figure 8.4 shows the most important financial indicators for Social Security from 1970 to the end of current projections in 2085 (intermediate scenario). We include disability pensions and show the relevant numbers for the entire OASDI program(s). As can be seen, the income rate[36] (thick grey line) rose rapidly from 1970 to 1990 and has surpassed

---

35. See Sakamoto (2005) and European Commission (2005) for detailed descriptions of how ABMs will adjust annual benefit indexation in Germany and Japan.

36. Equals the ratio of income from tax revenues on a liability basis (payroll tax contributions and income from the taxation of scheduled benefits) to the OASDI taxable payroll for the year. OASDI interest income is not included.

Figure 8.4   OASDI income and cost rates and Trust Fund size, projected to 2085

income rate, cost rate (percent of taxable payroll)

Trust Fund (trillions of US dollars)

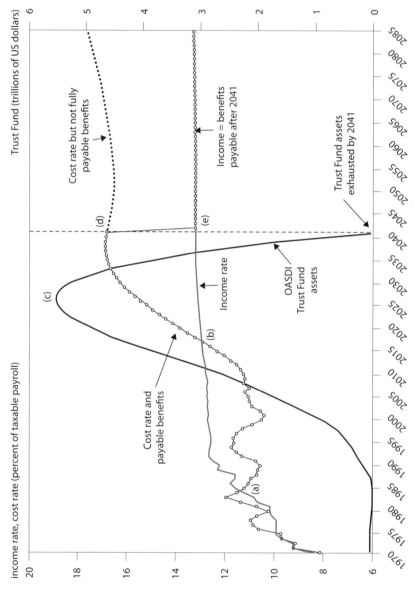

OASDI = Old Age, Survivors, and Disability Insurance

Source: OASDI Trustees (2008).

the cost rate[37] since the early 1980s, when the last major reform of Social Security brought forward scheduled increases in payroll taxes[38] (point a) and will continue to so until 2017 (point b). These higher levels of income led to the intended buildup of the OASDI Trust Fund, which rose (thick black line, right axis) from essentially nothing in the mid-1980s to a projected peak of over $5.5 trillion in 2026 (point c).[39] However, after 2026, with the larger numbers of Americans retiring and resulting increases in the OASDI cost rates to levels significantly above the income rates, the Trust Fund declines rapidly and will be exhausted in the year 2041. The retirement of the baby-boomer generation will lower the Social Security contributor/beneficiary ratio from its historical level (since 1974) of 3.2–3.4 to just 2.2 from 2030 on (OASDI Trustees 2008, figure II.D.3). Thus, although Social Security in 2017–41 goes through the same transition period that in Germany and Japan would lead to automatic adjustments in annual pension indexation, no automatic changes occur *during* the transition process (as in Germany and Japan); instead, in part because of the existence of the OASDI Trust Fund, they are postponed until the process is essentially finished by 2041.

At the point of OASDI Trust Fund exhaustion in 2041 (point d), Social Security can no longer continue to pay out benefits according to the original schedule,[40] and payments are automatically reduced to match only the continuous level of payroll tax income (point e). As a result, the Social Security Trustees in the 2008 report project the ability to pay only about 78 percent of scheduled Social Security benefits after 2041, dropping to 75 percent by 2082. This means that US Social Security has a built-in ABM that "guarantees" its long-term sustainability and function by imposing a universal benefit cut of 25+ percent beginning in 2041. Thus the entire "pain" of balancing Social Security's books will be borne by retirees after 2041.

But contrary to the ABMs in Germany and Japan, the US ABM is not part of a broader pension reform, such as increases in retirement ages and tax/contribution levels, which might distribute "the pain" among workers and current retirees. The US approach is thus extremely one-sided in

---

37. Defined as the ratio of the cost of the program(s) to the taxable payroll for the given year.

38. See overview of the 1983 amendments to Social Security legislation, available at www.ssa.gov/history.

39. The reason the Trust Fund continues to increase between 2017 and 2026 is that interest income from Treasury Securities held by the OASDI Trust Fund is included in the Fund's assets but excluded from the calculation of the OASDI income rate as it does not relate to payroll taxation.

40. See box 6.2 for the legal details of what happens, according to current US law, when the OASDI Trust Fund is exhausted. See also Romig (2006).

its use of automaticity to fix the Social Security solvency problem by simply cutting benefits for future retirees after 2041.

The crucial question is, who benefits from the current pension system design, implemented with the last big reform in 1983, which restored Social Security to long-term solvency solely by cutting benefits for retirees after 2041? Who benefits from the lack of either increases in contributions for present-day workers or cuts in benefits for today's retirees? The answer is that those (relatively old) current participants in Social Security, who will be dead—and thus have ended both contributions to and benefits from Social Security—before 2041 are the winners here. They will have contributed to Social Security at today's unsustainable rate of payroll taxation (given today's benefit levels) and will have received their unsustainable Social Security benefits (given today's payroll tax levels) and will thus be completely unaffected by the 2041 ABM. It is, perhaps, not a coincidence that these rules were written this way in 1983, as the principal beneficiaries will be the large and politically decisive American generations born after 1946.

Many argue that "Congress will never allow this to happen," that it is inconceivable that Social Security benefits would simply be cut by a quarter come 2041. Indeed, as we have shown in this book, such an across-the-board cut would certainly lead to wholly unacceptable increases in old age poverty. Yet for each year that Social Security reform is postponed, an ever greater number of Americans will avoid sharing any of the "pain" from putting Social Security back into long-term balance. If, for instance, the last minute reform scenario of 1983 were to repeat itself by the late 2030s in order to avoid unacceptable imminent benefit cuts in Social Security, the baby-boomer generation would have already largely passed from the scene and thus have avoided sharing any of the reform pain of making Social Security sustainable for the longer term. Therefore, while we have found that Social Security is not facing imminent financial collapse or "bankruptcy," this is not an argument in favor of not doing anything to reform it as soon as possible. The reason is one of simple intergenerational fairness—the longer any reform is postponed, the larger the share of the ABM effect borne by future generations. The fact that the current Social Security system will continue to function for several more decades must, therefore, never be a politically expedient excuse for failure to reform the system now.

Furthermore, while there are limitations to comparing reforms for very different pension systems, it is nonetheless illustrative to see that the ABMs in Germany and Japan, which operate much sooner than in the United States, may lead to a decline of approximately 15 percent in benefit levels by the 2040s, as compared to the roughly 25 percent benefit cut projected for US retirees in one fell swoop by 2041. In other words, postponement of the Social Security ABM so that it affects retirees only after 2041 will impose a significantly larger benefit cut on this group than is the case for retirees in Germany and Japan, where the "pain" is distributed already today and across many more retirees.

Given the feasible reform options available today, US policymakers who push Social Security reform into the future impose an unnecessarily large and intergenerationally unfair burden on future generations. We acknowledge that Social Security reform is a political challenge, but, in the words of Abraham Lincoln, "You cannot escape the responsibility of tomorrow by evading it today."

References

Akerlof, George A. 1991. Procrastination and Obedience. *American Economic Review* 81, no. 2 (May): 1–19.

Barr, Nicholas. 2006. Non-Financial Defined Contribution Pensions: Mapping the Terrain. In *Pension Reform: Issues and Prospects for Non-Financial Defined Contribution Schemes*, ed. Robet Holtzmann and Edward Palmer. Washington: World Bank Publications.

Benartzi, Schlomo, and Richard H. Thaler. 2004. Save More Tomorrow™: Using Behavioral Economics to Increase Employee Saving. *Journal of Political Economy* 112, no. 1: 164–86.

Beshears, John, James J. Choi, David Laibson, and Brigitte C. Madrian. 2006. *The Importance of Default Options for Retirement Savings Outcomes: Evidence from the United States.* NBER Working Paper 12009. Cambridge, MA: National Bureau of Economic Research.

Beshears, John, James J. Choi, David Laibson, and Brigitte C. Madrian. 2007. *The Impact of Employer Matching on Savings Plan Participation Under Automatic Enrollment.* NBER Working Paper 13352. Cambridge, MA: National Bureau of Economic Research.

Börsch-Supan, A., A. Reil-Held, and C. B. Wilke. 2003. *How to Make a Defined Benefit System Sustainable: The "Sustainability Factor" in the German Benefit Indexation Formula.* Mannheim, Germany: University of Mannheim Institute for the Economics of Aging.

Choi, James J, David Laibson, Brigitte C. Madrian, and Andrew Metrick. 2003. *Passive Decisions and Potent Defaults.* NBER Working Paper 9917. Cambridge, MA: National Bureau of Economic Research.

Choi, James J, David Laibson, Brigitte C. Madrian, and Andrew Metrick. 2005. *Optimal Defaults and Active Decisions.* NBER Working Paper 11074. Cambridge, MA: National Bureau of Economic Research.

CBO (Congressional Budget Office). 2007. *Utilization of Tax Incentives for Retirement Saving: Update to 2003.* Washington.

CBO (Congressional Budget Office). 2008. *Updated Long-Term Projections for Social Security, August 2008.* Washington.

Diamond, Peter A., and Peter R. Orszag. 2005. Saving Social Security. *Journal of Economic Perspectives* 19, no. 2 (Spring): 11–32.

Engen, Eric M., William G. Gale, and John Karl Scholz. 1994. *Do Saving Incentives Work?* Brookings Papers on Economic Activity 25, no. 1994-1: 85–180. Washington: Economic Studies Program, Brookings Institution.

European Commission. 2005. *Modeling the Impact of Ageing Populations on Public Spending: Country Fiche on the German Pension System* (November). Brussels.

Feenberg, Daniel, and Jonathan Skinner. 1989. *Sources of IRA Saving.* NBER Working Paper 2845. Cambridge, MA: National Bureau of Economic Research.

Fukawa, Tetsuo. 2006. Sustainable Structure of the Japanese Public Pension System Viewed from a Germany-Japan Comparison. *Japanese Journal of Social Security Policy* 6, no. 1: 131–43.

Kahneman, Daniel, and Amos Tversky. 1984. Choices, Values and Frames. *American Psychologist*, no. 39: 341–50.

Kahneman, Daniel, Jack L. Knetsch, and Richard H. Thaler. 1991. Anomalies—The Endowment Effect, Loss Aversion and Status Quo Bias. *Journal of Economic Perspectives* 5, no. 1 (Winter): 193–206.

Loewenstein, George, and Richard H. Thaler (1989). Anomalies—Intertemporal Choice. *Journal of Economic Perspectives* 3, no. 4 (Autumn): 181–93.

Madrian, Brigitte C., and Dennis F. Shea. 2000. *The Power of Suggestion: Inertia in 401(K) Participation and Savings Behavior*. NBER Working Paper 7682. Cambridge, MA: National Bureau of Economic Research.

OASDI Trustees. 1982. *The 1982 Annual Report of the Board of Trustees of the Federal Old-Age and Survivors Insurance and Federal Disability Insurance Trust Funds*. Washington: Social Security Administration.

OASDI Trustees. 2008. *The 2008 Annual Report of the Board of Trustees of the Federal Old-Age and Survivors Insurance and Federal Disability Insurance Trust Funds*. Washington: Social Security Administration.

OMB (Office of Management and Budget). 2008. *Annual Budgets of the US Government, Analytical Perspectives FY2008*. Washington: White House.

Orszag, Peter, J., and Jonathan M. Orszag. 2000. *Would Raising IRA Contribution Limits Bolster Retirement Security for Lower- and Middle-Income Families or Is There a Better Way?* Washington: Center on Budget and Policy Priorities.

Peterson, Peter G. 2004. *Running on Empty: How the Democratic and Republican Parties Are Bankrupting Our Future and What Americans Can Do About It*. New York: Farrar, Straus and Giroux.

Romig, Kathleen. 2006. *What Would Happen If the Trust Funds Ran Out?* CRS Report for Congress. Washington: Congressional Research Service.

Sakamoto, Junichi. 2005. *Japan's Pension Reform*. Social Protection Discussion Paper 0541. Washington: World Bank.

Settergren, O. 2001. *The Automatic Balance Mechanism of the Swedish Pension System*. Stockholm: National Social Insurance Board.

SSA (Social Security Administration). 2008. *2008 Annual Report of the SSI Program*. Washington.

Summers, Lawrence H. 1986. Summers Replies to Galper and Byce on IRAs. *Tax Notes* 31, no. 10 (June 9): 1014–16.

Thaler, Richard H. 1990. Saving, Fungibility, and Mental Accounts. *Journal of Economic Perspectives* 4, no. 1: 193–205.

Thaler, Richard H. 1994. Psychology and Savings Policies. *American Economic Review* 84, no. 2: 186–92.

Weinberg, Daniel H. 2006. Income Data Quality Issues in the CPS. *Monthly Labor Review* (June): 38–45. Washington: Bureau of Labor Statistics.

Williamson, John, ed. 1994. *The Political Economy of Policy Reform*. Washington: Institute for International Economics.

Abbreviations

AARP	American Association of Retired People
ABM	automatic balancing mechanisms
ABO	accumulated benefit obligation
ASBJ	Accounting Standards Board of Japan
AFOREs	*administradoras de fondos para el retiro* (private financial institutions in charge of the administration and investment of retirement savings in Mexico)
AFPs	*administradores de fondos de pensiones* (private pension fund managers in Chile)
AIME	average indexed monthly earnings
AITR	average itemized tax rates
ALM	asset-liability mismatch
APW	average production worker
ARC	annual required contribution
AW	average worker
BLS	US Bureau of Labor Statistics
BMAS	Bundesministerium für Arbeit und Soziales (Germany's Ministry for Labor and Social Affairs)
BSP	basic state pension (UK)
CBO	Congressional Budget Office
CES	BLS Current Employment Survey
CNAV	Caisse nationale d'assurance vieillesse (French government–run National Old Age Insurance Fund)
COLA	cost of living allowance
CONSAR	Comisión Nacional del Sistema de Ahorro para el Retiro (Mexico's National Commission for the Pension System)

CPI	consumer price index
CPI-U	consumer price index for urban consumers
CPS	BLS Current Population Survey
CTA	contractual trust arrangement
DB	defined benefit
DC	defined contribution
DBCPL	Defined Benefit Corporate Pension Law (Japan)
DCPL	Defined Contribution Pension Law (Japan)
DWP	UK Department for Work and Pensions
EBRI	Employee Benefit Research Institute
EBS	BLS Employee Benefits Survey
ECB	earnings continuation benefit (Japan)
EDF	Electricité de France
EET	exempt-exempt-taxed
EGTERRA	Economic Growth and Tax Relief Reconciliation Act of 2001
EIRO	European Industrial Relations Observatory
EPFs	employee pension funds
EPI	employees' pension insurance
EPL	employment protection legislation
ERISA	Employee Retirement Income Security Act of 1974
ETR	expected time in retirement
FASAB	US Federal Accounting Standards Advisory Board
FASB	Financial Accounting Standards Board
FICA	Federal Insurance Contributions Act
FMLA	Family and Medical Leave Act of 1993
FOMC	Federal Open Market Committee
FPG	Forsakringsbolaget Pensionsgaranti (Sweden's Pension Guarantee Mutual Insurance Company)
FRS	Financial Reporting Standard
FRTIB	Federal Retirement Thrift Investment Board
GAAP	Generally Accepted Accounting Principles
GAO	Government Accountability Office (formerly General Accounting Office)
GASB	Government Accounting Standards Board
HI	Hospital Insurance
HRS	University of Michigan Health and Retirement Study
IAS	International Accounting Standards
IASB	International Accounting Standards Board
IFRS	International Financial Reporting Standards
IMSS	Instituto Mexicano del Seguro Social (Mexico's Institute of Social Security)
INFONAVIT	Instituto del Fondo Nacional de la Vivienda de los Trabajadores (Mexico's National Workers' Housing Fund Institute)

IRAs	individual retirement accounts
IRS	Internal Revenue Service
IVCM	Seguro de Invalidez, Vejez, Cesantía en edad avanzada y Muerte (Disability, Old Age, and Survivors)
JGTRRA	Jobs and Growth Tax Relief Reconciliation Act of 2003
LABREF	European Commission's Labor Market Reforms database
MHLW	Japanese Ministry of Health, Labor, and Welfare
MPG	minimum pension guarantee (Chile)
NCS	BLS National Compensation Survey
NDC	notional defined contribution
NIPA	US national income and product accounts
NMR	net migration rate
NMS	new member states (of the European Union)
NPS	Korean National Pension Scheme
NPSS	National Pension Savings Scheme (UK)
OASDI	Old-Age, Survivors, and Disability Insurance
OASI	Old-Age and Survivors Insurance
OECD	Organization for Economic Cooperation and Development
OMB	Office of Management and Budget
OPEBs	other postemployment benefits
PASIS	Pensión Asistencial (Chile's program of welfare pensions)
PATC	BLS Survey of Professional, Administrative, Technical, and Clerical Pay
PAYGO	pay as you go
PBGC	Pension Benefit Guaranty Corporation
PBO	projected benefit obligation
PBS	Basic Solidarity Pension (Chile)
PGP	Japan's Pension Guarantee Program
PIA	primary insurance amount
POBs	pension obligation bonds
PPA	2006 Pension Protection Act
PPF	UK Pension Protection Fund
PSID	University of Michigan's Panel Study on Income Dynamics
PSVaG	Pensions-Sicherungs-Verein auf Gegenseitigkeit (Germany)
RCS	EBRI Retirement Confidence Survey
RGAVTS	Régime général d'assurance vieillesse des travailleurs salaries (France's universal pension scheme)
RRP	registered retirement plans (Canada)
SAFP	Superintendencia de Administradores de Fondos de Pensiones (Mexico's Superintendency of Pension Fund Managing Companies)

SCF	Federal Reserve Board's triennial Survey of Consumer Finances
SEC	Securities and Exchange Commission
SERPS	State Earnings-Related Pension Scheme (UK); since 2002 called the State Second Pension, or S2P
SIEFORE	Sociedad de Inversión Especializada en Fondos para el Retiro (specialized mutual funds for pensions)
SIPP	US Census Bureau's Survey of Income and Program Participation
SNA	System of National Accounts
SOCX	OECD Social Expenditure database
SPPRFs	sovereign and public pension reserve funds
SPS	New Solidarity Pension System (Chile)
SSA	Social Security Administration
SSI	Supplemental Security Income
SSW	Social Security wealth
TEE	taxed-exempt-exempt
TNR	time not in retirement
TPAM	Technical Panel on Assumptions and Methods to the Social Security Advisory Board
TPATPP	total prefunded assets toward pension provision
TQPP	tax-qualified pension plans
TTE	taxed-taxed-exempt
UF	*unidades de fomento* (unit of account used in Chile)
UI	unemployment insurance
UAW	United Auto Workers
UMW	United Mine Workers
USW	United Steel Workers

Index

avoiding low-wage workers, 299
collecting clients' contributions directly, 300
noncompliance among, 293
products offered by, 299
African-American mortality rates. *See* blacks
after-housing poverty rates, 122*n*
age discrimination
by employers, 221
practices, 349, 351
age distribution, of total social spending, 138*b*, 140*f*–42*f*
age of retirement. *See* retirement age(s)
age thresholds, for initial pension benefit eligibility, 258
age-specific rates
assumptions about the future, 169
for a given population, 168
aging. *See* population aging
Aging and Employment Policies Project, 221–22
aging populations
effects of by 2030, 225
of Europe, 226*b*
rapidly growing size of, 64
agricultural workers, in Japan, 245
AIME estimation, 118*b*, 119*b*
AITR (average itemized tax rates), 47*n*
Alfred Dodge Company, 349, 349*n*
ALM (asset-liability mismatch), 380*n*, 400–401
American welfare capitalists, 349
annual hours worked, freezing, 224–25
annual required contribution (ARC), 192
annuities
Americans not covered by, 211
as a bad deal for many people, 342
in Chile, 284
compared with lump-sum payouts, 315
vs. lump-sum payments in Japan, 416–17
market for group, 389
Vanguard-AIG inflation-indexed, 281
annuity market, 342
Antideficiency Act, 328*b*
antipoverty program, Social Security as, 3
antipoverty provisions, of Bush proposals, 340
APS (Solidarity Pension Contribution), 305
ARC (annual required contribution), 192
arduous work, offering retirement for, 173

ASBJ (Accounting Standards Board of Japan), 417–18, 424
ASBL (self-administered pension funds), in Belgium, 355*b*
asset(s), of pension funds, 403*f*
asset allocation
for pension funds, 401
of US private defined benefit plans (1994–2007), 402*f*
asset classes, reporting of, 401*n*
asset liability mismatch risks, 397–404
asset ownership, underreporting of, 211
asset value tax, in Belgium, 354*b*
asset-liability mismatch. *See* ALM
asset-liability transfer, 424
at-risk plans, returning to full funding, 352*b*
Australia
allowing lump-sum withdrawals, 18
child bonus payment, 70*b*
goal of increasing national saving not realized, 316
individual accounts, effect on national saving, 310
individual accounts in, 282–84
lump sum withdrawal problem, 341–42
lump-sum payments, 315
participation rates in individual accounts, 291–92
Austria, 267
automatic balancing mechanisms. *See* ABMs
automatic stabilizers, 241, 327, 328*b*
autonomous funded pension plans, 36
average indexed monthly earnings (AIME) estimation, 118*b*, 119*b*
average itemized tax rates (AITR), 47*n*
average pension benefit level, 115
average production worker (APW), 56*n*
average worker (AW), 56*n*
averaging period, for pensions, 267

baby-boomers, as a voting group, 329*b*
back doors, to early retirement, 254, 255*f*
balance sheet, of EDF, 445*t*
Balladur reform, 161*b*, 162*b*
bankruptcy risk, of defined benefit plans, 370
Basic Solidarity Pension (PBS), in Chile, 305
basic state pension (BSP), in the United Kingdom, 290
behavioral finance, literature of, 463
Belgium, 255*f*, 354*b*, 355*b*

COLA (cost-of-living allowance)
  abandoned in Germany, 328*b*
  compared with ABMs, 475
  in Germany and Japan, 477
  not part of corporate defined benefit
    plans, 370
  to Social Security benefits, 117*b*, 119*b*
College Board, costs of college, 106*n*
Comisión Nacional del Sistema de
    Ahorro para el Retiro (CONSAR),
    287
commercial airlines–sponsored pension
    underfunding, reclassified, 378
commission rate, AFPs charging the
    same, 299
Commission to Strengthen Social
    Security, report of, 4*n*
company pension plans, US workforce
    covered by, 19–20
company-specific private insurance
    schemes, 405
compliance, enforcing in Chile, 294–95
compulsory contribution, to retirement
    accounts, 28
compulsory retirement saving, case for,
    472
compulsory superannuation system, in
    Australia, 283
CONSAR (Comisión Nacional del
    Sistema de Ahorro para el Retiro),
    287
constant decliners, in fertility rate, 67
constitutional provisions, about state
    indebtedness, 194*n*
consumer price index (CPI)
  changes in, 119*b*
  indexing initial benefit levels to, 339
  monthly benefits indexed to, 339
consumer protection approach, 410
consumption
  direct and indirect taxation of, 47–48
  measuring individual comfort and
    welfare, 121
consumption smoothing, 166
continued work, increasing benefit levels,
    243
continuing employment, income derived
    from, 134
Continuous Mortality Investigation
    project, 390
contractual trust arrangement (CTA), 416
contributions
  density of in Mexico, 295
  ensuring no future increases in rates, 241

making up for mixed, 332
  pooling before passing on to private
    investment managers, 17
  by state and local governments to
    pension funds, 189, 190*f*
  structure in Mexico, 287
contributory insurance, 114
corporate AA bonds, yields of, 395*n*
corporate accounting rules, changing
    toward transparency, 391
corporate benevolence, 349
corporate defined benefit pension plans
  global shift from, 21
  performing strongly in 2003-07, 397,
    399, 400*t*
corporate health care provision, 351
corporate pension(s)
  assumption of a single-earner nuclear
    family, 362
  challenges to the provision of, 347–436
  coverage of US, 349, 350*f*
  coverage to blue-collar workers, 361–62
  creation of voluntary supplementary,
    357
  decline in the provision of, 348
  exclusions from, 362–63
  findings on, 19–22
  funds, assets of, 401, 403*f*, 404
  guarantee schemes, 378–81
  introduced as supplements to Social
    Security, 20
  liabilities, financing, 38
  rapid growth years (1940-70), 351
  regulation, 382
  shifting away from defined benefit
    plans, 432
  unions role in expanding, 360–63
  in the US, 7
corporate pension plans
  coverage rate for, 405
  finances and funding of, 29
  financial rollercoaster of Japanese,
    417
  as generally well funded, 399
  integration with Social Security, 358
  introduction in the US, 348–49
  options in Japan, 420*f*
  participation in, 365, 366*f*, 368, 369*t*
  volatility of funding levels, 20
corporate pension provision
  benefits on the highest-income
    Americans, 434, 435*f*
  challenges facing, 431–36
  historical chronology of, 351

defined contribution plans, 21, 158, 418, 421
administrative cost for, 382, 384t–85t
compulsory in Australia, 283
countries relying almost entirely on, 407
easier to leave for a new job, 404
features not available to private defined
benefit plans, 388
integrating using excess and step-wise
excess integration plans, 359n
introduction in Japan, 419
oddities in Japan's regulatory changes
to, 421, 423
protected, 97
provision, 423
pull factors, 404
retirees bearing all or part of the
longevity risk, 390
switching from defined benefit to, 370
unprotected, 97
defined-contribution pensions, real rate of
return on, 102
demographic challenge
synthesizing with fiscal, 85–91
as unevenly distributed, 66
demographic outlook, 64–78
adverse for government sector in
general, 189
adverse in Eastern and Southern
Europe and Northeast Asia, 10–11
by OECD country, 86t–89t
Denmark, 47, 158, 159b–60b
dependency ratio approach, in Germany
and Japan, 328b
dependent benefits, 116b
differential indexing proposal, 6n
direct age link, implementing, 164
direct eligibility age qualifications, 158,
159b–63b
direct tax benefits, to older population, 45
direct taxation data, 47n
Direktvericherung (direct insurance
contracts), 410, 411
Direktzusage (plans financed by
company book reserves), 410, 411,
414
disability benefits
incentives for workers to seek, 253n
Mexican workers retiring under, 286,
287t
disability pension beneficiaries, in US, 253n
disability pensions
availability of, 230n
excluded in tracking pension spending,
43n

medical access criteria to, 253
progressivity of, 113
disability program, benefits of, 25
discount rates, rise in, 397
dissaving, 310, 322
distributional challenges, 108
distributional issue
of individual accounts, 16
of US Social Security, 23
distributional problem, in individual
account plans, 18–19, 280
distributive challenge, 11–14
diversified equity investment ratios,
401n
dual public pension system, in Denmark,
159b
dualism, of public pension systems, 176
DWP (UK Department of Work and
Pensions), 308

early retirement
adjusting rules for, 473–74
in Australia's retirement system, 291
back doors to, 254, 255f
benefit reductions for, 81n
costs to treasuries of, 43
effects of eliminating, 227b–28b
examples of country reforms of,
261t–63t
impact on the fiscal challenge, 81
incentivizing, 114
in Japan, 242
linking to life expectancies in Denmark,
159b
not subsidized by Social Security, 23
phasing out for older workers,
226b–27b
plans, 25
policy implications of, 24–25
scaling back options for, 269
schemes, 258–60, 261t–63t
subsidies for, 269
earnings continuation benefit (ECB), in
Japan, 244
EBRI data. See Employee Benefit Research
Institute (EBRI)
EBS. See BLS Employment Benefits
Survey
economic assumptions, for OECD
pension modeling, 102
economic dependency ratios, 222
in the EU population, 225
for OECD countries, 222–25, 223f
OECD in 2030, 229f

5-3-3-2 rule, in Japan, 417, 417*n*
fixed contribution rate, 241
fixed costs, of continuing to live, 130*b*
flat rate mandatory systems, 56
flat rate means-tested pension plan, 282
flat rate national basic pension (*kokumin
    nenkin*), in Japan, 419*n*
flat rate national pension benefit, to
    agricultural workers in Japan, 245
follow-the-money principle, 183
Förster and Mira d'Ercole, old age income
    data from, 205–207
401(k)-type plans, 457–58, 459*t*–60*t*
France
    buying back pension liabilities from
        EDF, 426
    compared with US in terms of pension
        sustainability, 41
    effective retirement age compared with
        Japan, 82
    elimination of progressive early
        retirement, 262*t*
    extending average estimation period,
        267
    linking quarters of contributions to life
        expectancies, 158
    persons in early retirement schemes
        or on unemployment benefits
        without work search
        requirements, 255*f*
    phasing out end of career leave, 262*t*
    public and private pension in, 161*b*–63*b*
    social spending on the highest-earning
        elderly, 138*b*, 142*f*
    threats from aging populations, 42
    turning pension liabilities into an
        immediate revenue center, 443–48
France Telecom, 444
freeze concept, of gender- and age
    category-specific employment
    rates, 226*b*
French *functionnaires*, compared with US
    state and local employees, 189
French government, agreeing to let
    companies reduce liabilities, 446
frictional departures, 228*b*
FRS (Financial Reporting Standard) 17,
    392
full pension, age of initial eligibility,
    257–58
Fuller, Ida May, 144
fund accounting, 194*n*
fund hopping, in Mexico compared with
    Chile, 287, 289

fund managers. *See also* investment
    managers
    in Chile, 299
    competition among, 18
    investing in an age-adjusted standard
        portfolio, 473
funded defined contribution plans.
    See defined contribution plans
funded ratio, 400*t*
funding risk, of defined benefit plans, 369
funding shortfall, of Social Security, 5

G-7 countries
    immigrants needed to stabilize old age
        support ratio, 74*f*
    stopping the aging process via
        immigration, 75
GASB (Government Accounting
    Standards Board)
    organization of, 191*n*
    requiring pension plan sponsors
        account for OPEB expense, 192
    requiring state and local governments
        to use accrual basis for pension
        costs, 191–93
    Rule No. 45, 14
GDP
    New Zealand growth and employment
        rates by gender and age group,
        236*f*
    percent of Finland's in TPATPP, 97, 100
    percentage going to gross public
        pensions in 2005 and 2050, 9
    TPATPP as percent of, 41
general government fiscal positions
    (2006), 33*f*
Generally Accepted Accounting
    Principles (GAAP), 183*n*, 393
generational accounting, 137, 139, 143–44
generosity
    cross-country differences in, 56
    of mandatory pension levels, 111
    of the mandatory pension promise,
        62–63
Germany
    ABM reforms in, 475
    ABMs introduced in, 476
    contributory insurance model, 110
    corporate pension provision trends in,
        410–16
    corporations, external funding options,
        410
    educational improvement among older
        male workers, 248, 251

initial age of pension eligibility, 257–58
in-kind benefits, 43*n*
Instituto del Fondo Nacional de la
    Vivienda de los Trabajadores.
    See INFONAVIT
Instituto Mexicano del Seguro Social
    (IMSS), 285
insurance-based mandatory systems, 56
insurance-based Social Security, 117*b*
integration, of public and private
    pensions, 453
integration percentage, 359*n*
interest rates, Japanese decline in, 417
intergenerational distributional effects,
    155
intergenerational fairness
    compared with legacy debt, 476*n*
    of delays in reform, 474
    not evident in the US political system,
        329*b*
    requiring reform of Social Security, 480
intergenerational transfers, 108
    comprehensive measure of, 145–66
    related distributional issues and,
        137–66
Internal Revenue Service (IRS)/Social
    Security Administration (SSA)
    linking mechanism, 461
International Accounting Standard (IAS),
    392, 414, 416, 443
International Labor Office, pension
    system typology, 60*b*
intertemporal budget constraint, 143
intrinsic rate of return, in Poland
    compared with Sweden, 334
investment advice, colored by self-
    interest, 315
investment management companies
    (*administradores de fondos de ahorro*).
    See AFOREs
investment managers. *See also* fund
    managers
    selection of, 27
investment risk, transferring, 365
investments, no evidence of excessively
    risky, 18
investors, workers not informed or
    skilled, 281
involuntary termination, of defined
    benefit plans, 372
IRAs
    employee contributions to, 457–58,
        459*t*–60*t*
    last minute purchases of, 464

Ireland, 43, 66*n*, 126
Italy, 17, 42, 325*b*–26*b*

Japan
    ABM reforms in, 475
    corporate pension provision, 416–27,
        422*t*
    divorce law, 368*n*
    early retirement, 242
    effective retirement age, 82, 238, 239*f*
    employment rates, 15, 15*n*
    financial situation for prefectures and
        municipalities, 185*n*
    government bailout of pension plan
        sponsors, 431
    government rescue of corporate
        defined benefit plans, 21
    increase in residents 65 or older, 77
    karoshi risk, 256
    mandatory government pension
        benefits, 8
    older workers remaining employed,
        238–46
    pension distribution among men, 243*f*
    Pension Guarantee Program (PGP),
        379
    positive developments and future
        concern, 244–46
    public pension system, 240–44
    retirement incentives critical to, 246
    retiring later, 81
    sustainability of, 41
    taking back pension assets, 425
    view of vested benefits, 379*n*
    workforce declines, 66
Japanese Labor Force Survey, 244
job search assistance, 221
jobs, pensions by type of, 173–74

karoshi
    risk of in Japan, 256
    translated, 256*n*
KiwiSaver program, 238
Korea
    decline in total fertility, 67, 72–73, 72*f*
    increase in the effective retirement age,
        151
    low public expenditure on pension
        provision, 43*n*
    workforce declines, 66
    workforce under different fertility
        scenarios, 72–73, 72*f*
Korean National Pension Scheme (NPS),
        43*n*

race, impact on mortality rates, 172
rates of return
  on individual accounts in Chile, 302
  for nonfinancial accounts
    in Latvia, 336
    in Poland, 334
rational long-term decisions, 472
rational saving choices, 462n
RCS (Retirement Confidence Survey), 129b, 131f, 131t
real estate, role in total wealth, 37n
real income, from private pensions, 435f
real poverty rates, in Chilean households, 303, 304t
recognition bonds, 310–11, 310n, 312
recoverers, in regard to fertility rate, 67
redistribution
  built into a pension system, 110
  facilitating cross-country comparison of, 111
  in insurance-based pension systems, 115
  lack of with retirement payments, 5
  principle of, 12
  relation with generosity, 111
redistributive aspects
  of early Social Security, 116b
  to Social Security, 452
reference age, changes in life expectancies as, 163–64
reform pain, distributing, 471
registered retirement plans (RRPs), 408
Renault, 25n
replacement birth rate, 67
replacement fertility rate, 72
replacement rates
  in Chile, 302
  under current Social Security, 339
  for full-career civil servants, 177, 178t
  incentive effects of, 264
  of the Japanese pension, 240
  in the mandatory UK public system, 307
  in Mexico, 306
  under Mexico's social security system, 286t
  in pension schemes, 264, 266
retiree health care net funding level, 396f
retirees
  continuing to work after retirement, 52b–53b
  number increasing rapidly in most countries, 2
  ratio of workers to, 64
  redistributing in favor of lower-income, 119b

social spending bias in favor of, 138b
supported by few hours of work, 9
retirement
  amount of lifetime, 165
  circumstances of, 129b
  composition of years spent in, 151, 152f
  decision about, 256–68
  estimated years spent in, 147, 148f
  incentives for, in Japan, 246
  income during, 6, 42
  increase in expected years in (1970–2004), 147, 150f, 151
  linking to life expectancies, 196
  percent of expected lifetime in, 165
  rates of, 257–58
  reform of, underlying economics of, 326
  savings for in the US, 129b–30b
  time spent in, 13, 145–66
retirement age(s)
  adjusting, 469–71
  adjustment of benefits based on, 449
  comparing, 79
  different for men and women, 166–67
  erasing distributional differences in, 167
  increasing, 26, 29
    from 60 to 65 in New Zealand, 235
    as life expectancy increases, 5
    normal, 166
    as a powerful tool, 28
  life expectancies linked to, 13, 108, 155, 156f–57f
  mattering more than demographics for labor supply, 11
  PIA as adjustment formula for, 120b
  possible stratifications of, 171–74
  raising, 151, 153
  in the US compared with European countries, 15
retirement benefits
  levels of, impact of pension integration on, 358–59
  sought by unions, 361
retirement funds, in Australia, 283
retirement plans
  decisions to sponsor in Japan, 421
  US worker participation in, 364f
  workers' participation by income group, 456t
retirement policies, employment rate and, 14–15
retirement promises, to state and local workers, 192

retirement saving
with after-tax dollars, 5
distributional concern with, 455
promoting, 455
US encouraging tax-advantaged
private, 20
revenue forgone method, 49
reverse compounding, practice of, 194*n*
Riester pension, number of Germans
with, 413–14, 415*f*
RRPs (registered retirement plans), in
Canada, 408

S&P 500 companies, benefits and health care
provision net funding levels, 396*f*
S179 basis, 430*f*
S2P (State Second Pension), 290
replacing SERPS in the UK, 307
SAFP (Superintendencia de
Administradores de Fondos de
Pensiones), 294, 300
SAR (Retirement Savings System), in
Mexico, 285
savings
generated by an individual account
system, 315
incentives for, impacts of pension
integration on, 461–64
increase in Chile, 311
individual accounts addressing, 277
irrational decisions regarding, 463
positive incentive for, 461
tax subsidies for, 461
saving rate
higher, need for, 461
in Japan, 423, 423*n*
in US, 23
Scandinavian countries, public
expenditures on pension
provision, 48
SEC (Securities and Exchange
Commission), allowing IFRS
rules, 392*n*
self-employed retirement plans, 457–58,
459*t*–60*t*
self-employed workers, in Chile, 295
SERPS (State Earnings-Related Pension
Scheme), 290, 297
75+ age cohort, negative savings rate
among, 122
76 and older cohort, poverty rates for,
126
shadow economy. *See also* informal
economy; nonobserved economy

in Chile, 303
effects of a large, 314
sickness and disability benefits, serving
as early retirement programs, 25
SIEFOREs, rates of return on Mexican, 306*t*
silo'ing, avoiding, 7
65+ age cohort, heterogeneity of, 126
65+ income distribution, by source and
income group, 208*t*–10*t*
65+ population
sources of income by income group, 133*f*
sources of income for, 132*f*
smoke and mirrors solution, Swedish
reform plan as, 333
SNA. *See* System of National Accounts
social benefits
alternate sources of, 259
expenditures remaining very low until
retirement, 138*b*
tax treatment of across OECD
countries, 45–48
social capital thesis, 172*n*
social insurance, tax preferences
supporting, 5
social protection, meaning old age
protection, 138*b*
social quota, in Mexico, 287, 312
Social Security
benefit income, by recipient income
quintile, 466*f*, 468*f*
benefits indexed to wages and
inflation, 280
compared with other advanced
countries, 10
comparing favorably with systems in
other advanced economies, 449
computing benefits, 118*b*
concerns about, 449
contributions, avoiding payment of, 52*b*
current legal environment of, 328*b*
difficulty in reforming, 329*b*
distributional issue for, 450
financial situation of, 184
historical overview of, 116*b*–17*b*
as a hybrid pension program, 115
increasing revenues for, 471
inflation adjustment of benefits, 361
insurance-based, 117*b*
linking to life expectancies, 164
making more progressive, 452
moving away from the German
insurance model toward an income
support program, 467
not adding to national saving, 23

as not particularly generous, 63
penalizing beneficiaries receiving labor
    income, 268
people relying overwhelmingly on, 211
phase-in of retirement ages, 153n
redistribution, room for additional, 111
redistributive
    as less, 12
    as not particularly, 449
reform of, as third rail of American
    politics, 137, 138b–39b, 451
restoring solvency to, 29
state and local government workers not
    participating in, 188
targeting benefit cuts, 196
unfunded liabilities, 321
virtues of, 3
Social Security Act, implemented as an
    insurance-based system, 114
Social Security Act of 1935, 11–12
Social Security Administration (SSA)
    efficiency of, 27
    Long-term Solvency Provision, C-7, 470
    old age income data from, 205, 207, 210
    sources of income data, 177, 179f
Social Security benefits
    automatic markdown on, 29
    cutting for Americans earning over
        $100,000 a year, 464–65
    increasing the minimum age for, 469
    integrating with tax-preferred private
        pension accumulation, 452–61
    levels of, 453
Social Security Reform (1983), 153
Social Security Trust Funds
    assets of, 194n
    current surpluses of, 35–36
Social Security Trustees, immigration
    level assumptions, 76
Social Security wealth (SSW), 256
Social Security-based accrual accounting,
    long-term cost estimates for, 184
social spending
    classification, from Adema and
        Ladaique, 347n
    individual benefits accruing from,
        138b–39b
socioeconomic status, positive impact on
    mortality risk, 171–72
socioeconomic stratification, of mortality
    rates, 173
socioeconomic variables
    correlated with differentials in life
        expectancies, 171

intertwined with race on mortality
    rates, 172–73
soft freeze, 398b
Solidarity Pension Contribution (APS),
    305
solvency
    lessons for dealing with, 28–29
    restoring to Social Security, 22
SOSI (Statement of Social Insurance), 183n
South Korea. See Korea
Soviet bloc, pension reform in, 334–38
Spain, 267–68
special schemes, in France, 161b, 162b
SPPRFs, OECD countries with, 37
SPS (New Solidarity Pension System), 305
SSA. See Social Security Administration
SSI (Supplementary Security Income)
    program, 12, 117b
SSW (Social Security wealth), 256
standard termination, 371
starting points. See fiscal starting points
state and local employees
    defined benefit component alone, 188
    generous pension coverage, 188
    retirement plans, 188
state and local governments
    accounting rules changes, 191–93
    choosing to renege on pension
        promises, 195
    cost of benefits per hour worked, 187f
    effects of accounting transparency,
        185–95
    pension coverage compared with
        private industry, 186f
    spending on defined benefit
        compensation, 185
    underfunding
        of pension funds, 189, 189n
        of pension promises, 14
state debt, low level of US, 191
State Earnings-Related Pension Scheme.
    See SERPS
State Second Pension. See S2P
Statement 158, introduced by the FASB,
    392
Statement 45, of the GASB, 192
Statement of Social Insurance (SOSI), 183n
state-owned enterprises (SOEs), 182
states, with financially healthy pension
    systems, 191
statutory retirement ages
    compared with effective age of
        retirement, 79
    lower for public pensions, 176–77

wage contribution threshold, 355
wealth effect, in the United Kingdom, 313
welfare, maximizing over entire lifetimes, 462*n*
welfare program, perceiving a means-tested program as, 452
welfare state, US corporate-sponsored as myth, 363
well-off individuals. *See also* higher-earning groups
   relying less on Social Security, 453
West Virginia Teachers Retirement System, 191
widow problem, 124*n*
women
   addressing inequality for, 314
   allowing to retire earlier than men, 108
   educational attainment, fertility levels and, 69*b*, 71*f*
   effective old age support ratio, 84*f*
   effective retirement ages, 157*f*
   excluded from corporate pensions, 362
   increasing pension system participation in Chile, 295
   living significantly longer, 166
   lower retirement incomes in Chile, 302
   MPG discriminating against in Chile, 304
   old age support ratio, 82*n*
   participation rate in corporate pensions, 368
   pension promise made to, 63
   retiring early, 79, 81, 253
   working outside the home and fertility, 69*b*, 71*f*
work disincentive, reducing, 277
work ethic, in Japanese culture, 238*n*
work history, linking to pension receipts, 342

work incentive provisions, 332
work performed, decline in, 151*n*
work search requirements, 254, 255*f*
workforce
   amount of work done by in Europe, 9
   contributors to the diversity of projections, 66
   defining potential, 79
   employing aging, 221
   issues affecting the quantity of a country's, 64
   most exempt from Italian pension reform, 325*b*
   outlook for the size of, 64–76
   participation
     in US corporate pension plans, 367
     in US retirement plans, 364*f*
     in selected OECD countries, 65*f*
     withdrawing early from, 251–56
     women's prolonged periods of absence from, 63
workforce size
   fertility and, 67–73
   immigration and, 73–76
working age population. *See* workforce
working pensioner, in Japan, 242, 244
working population, support burdens for, 227*b*
World Bank, typology of pension plans, 60*b*
World Health Report, life expectancies in, 167

years of life, allocating the benefits of additional, 155

zaishoku earnings test, 241, 244
zaishoku penalty, 242

Other Publications from the Peterson Institute

66 Managed Floating Plus   Morris Goldstein
    March 2002   ISBN 0-88132-336-5
67 Argentina and the Fund: From Triumph to
    Tragedy   Michael Mussa
    July 2002   ISBN 0-88132-339-X
68 East Asian Financial Cooperation
    C. Randall Henning
    September 2002   ISBN 0-88132-338-1
69 Reforming OPIC for the 21st Century
    Theodore H. Moran
    May 2003   ISBN 0-88132-342-X
70 Awakening Monster: The Alien Tort
    Statute of 1789   Gary C. Hufbauer/
    Nicholas Mitrokostas
    July 2003   ISBN 0-88132-366-7
71 Korea after Kim Jong-il
    Marcus Noland
    January 2004   ISBN 0-88132-373-X
72 Roots of Competitiveness: China's Evolving
    Agriculture Interests
    Daniel H. Rosen, Scott Rozelle, and Jikun
    Huang
    July 2004   ISBN 0-88132-376-4
73 Prospects for a US-Taiwan FTA
    Nicholas R. Lardy and Daniel H. Rosen
    December 2004   ISBN 0-88132-367-5
74 Anchoring Reform with a US-Egypt Free
    Trade Agreement   Ahmed Galal
    and Robert Z. Lawrence
    April 2005   ISBN 0-88132-368-3
75 Curbing the Boom-Bust Cycle: Stabilizing
    Capital Flows to Emerging Markets
    John Williamson
    July 2005   ISBN 0-88132-330-6
76 The Shape of a Swiss-US Free Trade
    Agreement   Gary Clyde Hufbauer/
    Richard E. Baldwin
    February 2006   ISBN 978-0-88132-385-6
77 A Strategy for IMF Reform
    Edwin M. Truman
    February 2006   ISBN 978-0-88132-398-6
78 US-China Trade Disputes: Rising Tide,
    Rising Stakes   Gary Clyde Hufbauer,
    Yee Wong, and Ketki Sheth
    August 2006   ISBN 978-0-88132-394-8
79 Trade Relations Between Colombia and the
    United States   Jeffrey J. Schott, ed.
    August 2006   ISBN 978-0-88132-389-4
80 Sustaining Reform with a US-Pakistan Free
    Trade Agreement   Gary C. Hufbauer
    and Shahid Javed Burki
    November 2006   ISBN 978-0-88132-395-5
81 A US–Middle East Trade Agreement: A
    Circle of Opportunity?   Robert Z. Lawrence
    November 2006   ISBN 978-0-88132-396-2
82 Reference Rates and the International
    Monetary System   John Williamson
    January 2007   ISBN 978-0-88132-401-3
83 Toward a US-Indonesia Free Trade
    Agreement   Gary Clyde Hufbauer
    and Sjamsu Rahardja
    June 2007   ISBN 978-0-88132-402-0
84 The Accelerating Decline in America's
    High-Skilled Workforce
    Jacob Funk Kirkegaard
    December 2007   ISBN 978-0-88132-413-6
85 Blue-Collar Blues: Is Trade to Blame for
    Rising US Income Inequality?
    Robert Z. Lawrence
    January 2008   ISBN 978-0-88132-414-3
86 Maghreb Regional and Global Integration:
    A Dream to Be Fulfilled
    Gary Clyde Hufbauer and Claire Brunel, eds.
    October 2008   ISBN 978-0-88132-426-6

BOOKS

IMF Conditionality*   John Williamson, editor
1983   ISBN 0-88132-006-4
Trade Policy in the 1980s* William R. Cline, ed.
1983   ISBN 0-88132-031-5
Subsidies in International Trade*
Gary Clyde Hufbauer and Joanna Shelton Erb
1984   ISBN 0-88132-004-8
International Debt: Systemic Risk and Policy
Response*   William R. Cline
1984   ISBN 0-88132-015-3
Trade Protection in the United States: 31 Case
Studies*   Gary Clyde Hufbauer, Diane E.
Berliner, and Kimberly Ann Elliott
1986   ISBN 0-88132-040-4
Toward Renewed Economic Growth in Latin
America*   Bela Balassa, Gerardo M. Bueno,
Pedro Pablo Kuczynski, and Mario Henrique
Simonsen
1986   ISBN 0-88132-045-5
Capital Flight and Third World Debt*
Donald R. Lessard and John Williamson, editors
1987   ISBN 0-88132-053-6
The Canada-United States Free Trade
Agreement: The Global Impact*
Jeffrey J. Schott and Murray G. Smith, editors
1988   ISBN 0-88132-073-0
World Agricultural Trade: Building a
Consensus*
William M. Miner and Dale E. Hathaway, editors
1988   ISBN 0-88132-071-3
Japan in the World Economy*
Bela Balassa and Marcus Noland
1988   ISBN 0-88132-041-2
America in the World Economy: A Strategy
for the 1990s*   C. Fred Bergsten
1988   ISBN 0-88132-089-7
Managing the Dollar: From the Plaza to the
Louvre*   Yoichi Funabashi
1988, 2d. ed. 1989   ISBN 0-88132-097-8
United States External Adjustment
and the World Economy*   William R. Cline
May 1989   ISBN 0-88132-048-X
Free Trade Areas and U.S. Trade Policy*
Jeffrey J. Schott, editor
May 1989   ISBN 0-88132-094-3

Dollar Politics: Exchange Rate Policymaking
in the United States*
I. M. Destler and C. Randall Henning
September 1989   ISBN 0-88132-079-X

Latin American Adjustment: How Much Has
Happened?*   John Williamson, editor
April 1990   ISBN 0-88132-125-7

The Future of World Trade in Textiles and
Apparel*   William R. Cline
1987, 2d ed. June 1999   ISBN 0-88132-110-9

Completing the Uruguay Round: A Results-
Oriented Approach to the GATT Trade
Negotiations*   Jeffrey J. Schott, editor
September 1990   ISBN 0-88132-130-3

Economic Sanctions Reconsidered (2 volumes)
Economic Sanctions Reconsidered:
Supplemental Case Histories
Gary Clyde Hufbauer, Jeffrey J. Schott, and
Kimberly Ann Elliott
1985, 2d ed. Dec. 1990   ISBN cloth 0-88132-115-X
          ISBN paper 0-88132-105-2

Economic Sanctions Reconsidered: History
and Current Policy   Gary Clyde Hufbauer,
Jeffrey J. Schott, and Kimberly Ann Elliott
December 1990   ISBN cloth 0-88132-140-0
          ISBN paper 0-88132-136-2

Pacific Basin Developing Countries: Prospects
for Economic Sanctions Reconsidered: History
and Current Policy   Gary Clyde Hufbauer,
Jeffrey J. Schott, and Kimberly Ann Elliott
December 1990   ISBN cloth 0-88132-140-0
          ISBN paper 0-88132-136-2

Pacific Basin Developing Countries: Prospects
for the Future*   Marcus Noland
January 1991   ISBN cloth 0-88132-141-9
          ISBN paper 0-88132-081-1

Currency Convertibility in Eastern Europe*
John Williamson, editor
October 1991   ISBN 0-88132-128-1

International Adjustment and Financing: The
Lessons of 1985-1991*   C. Fred Bergsten, editor
January 1992   ISBN 0-88132-112-5

North American Free Trade: Issues and
Recommendations*
Gary Clyde Hufbauer and Jeffrey J. Schott
April 1992   ISBN 0-88132-120-6

Narrowing the U.S. Current Account Deficit*
Alan J. Lenz/June 1992   ISBN 0-88132-103-6

The Economics of Global Warming
William R. Cline/June 1992   ISBN 0-88132-132-X

US Taxation of International Income:
Blueprint for Reform   Gary Clyde Hufbauer,
assisted by Joanna M. van Rooij
October 1992   ISBN 0-88132-134-6

Who's Bashing Whom? Trade Conflict
in High-Technology Industries
Laura D'Andrea Tyson
November 1992   ISBN 0-88132-106-0

Korea in the World Economy*   Il SaKong
January 1993   ISBN 0-88132-183-4

Pacific Dynamism and the International
Economic System*
C. Fred Bergsten and Marcus Noland, editors
May 1993   ISBN 0-88132-196-6

Economic Consequences of Soviet
Disintegration*   John Williamson, editor
May 1993   ISBN 0-88132-190-7

Reconcilable Differences? United States-Japan
Economic Conflict*
C. Fred Bergsten and Marcus Noland
June 1993   ISBN 0-88132-129-X

Does Foreign Exchange Intervention Work?
Kathryn M. Dominguez and Jeffrey A. Frankel
September 1993   ISBN 0-88132-104-4

Sizing Up U.S. Export Disincentives*
J. David Richardson
September 1993   ISBN 0-88132-107-9

NAFTA: An Assessment   Gary Clyde
Hufbauer and Jeffrey J. Schott/rev. ed.
October 1993   ISBN 0-88132-199-0

Adjusting to Volatile Energy Prices
Philip K. Verleger, Jr.
November 1993   ISBN 0-88132-069-2

The Political Economy of Policy Reform
John Williamson, editor
January 1994   ISBN 0-88132-195-8

Measuring the Costs of Protection
in the United States   Gary Clyde Hufbauer
and Kimberly Ann Elliott
January 1994   ISBN 0-88132-108-7

The Dynamics of Korean Economic
Development*   Cho Soon
March 1994   ISBN 0-88132-162-1

Reviving the European Union*
C. Randall Henning, Eduard Hochreiter, and
Gary Clyde Hufbauer, editors
April 1994   ISBN 0-88132-208-3

China in the World Economy
Nicholas R. Lardy
April 1994   ISBN 0-88132-200-8

Greening the GATT: Trade, Environment,
and the Future   Daniel C. Esty
July 1994   ISBN 0-88132-205-9

Western Hemisphere Economic Integration*
Gary Clyde Hufbauer and Jeffrey J. Schott
July 1994   ISBN 0-88132-159-1

Currencies and Politics in the United States,
Germany, and Japan   C. Randall Henning
September 1994   ISBN 0-88132-127-3

Estimating Equilibrium Exchange Rates
John Williamson, editor
September 1994   ISBN 0-88132-076-5

Managing the World Economy: Fifty Years
after Bretton Woods   Peter B. Kenen, editor
September 1994   ISBN 0-88132-212-1

Reciprocity and Retaliation in U.S. Trade
Policy   Thomas O. Bayard
and Kimberly Ann Elliott
September 1994   ISBN 0-88132-084-6

The Uruguay Round: An Assessment*
Jeffrey J. Schott, assisted by Johanna Buurman
November 1994   ISBN 0-88132-206-7

Global Electronic Commerce: A Policy Primer
Catherine L. Mann, Sue E. Eckert, and Sarah
Cleeland Knight
July 2000   ISBN 0-88132-274-1
The WTO after Seattle   Jeffrey J. Schott, ed.
July 2000   ISBN 0-88132-290-3
**Intellectual Property Rights in the Global
Economy**   Keith E. Maskus
August 2000   ISBN 0-88132-282-2
**The Political Economy of the Asian Financial
Crisis**   Stephan Haggard
August 2000   ISBN 0-88132-283-0
**Transforming Foreign Aid: United States
Assistance in the 21st Century** Carol Lancaster
August 2000   ISBN 0-88132-291-1
**Fighting the Wrong Enemy: Antiglobal
Activists and Multinational Enterprises**
Edward M. Graham
September 2000   ISBN 0-88132-272-5
**Globalization and the Perceptions of American
Workers**   Kenneth Scheve/Matthew J. Slaughter
March 2001   ISBN 0-88132-295-4
World Capital Markets: Challenge to the G-10
Wendy Dobson and Gary Clyde Hufbauer,
assisted by Hyun Koo Cho
May 2001   ISBN 0-88132-301-2
Prospects for Free Trade in the Americas
Jeffrey J. Schott
August 2001   ISBN 0-88132-275-X
**Toward a North American Community:
Lessons from the Old World for the New**
Robert A. Pastor
August 2001   ISBN 0-88132-328-4
**Measuring the Costs of Protection in Europe:
European Commercial Policy in the 2000s**
Patrick A. Messerlin
September 2001   ISBN 0-88132-273-3
Job Loss from Imports: Measuring the Costs
Lori G. Kletzer
September 2001   ISBN 0-88132-296-2
**No More Bashing: Building a New
Japan–United States Economic Relationship**
C. Fred Bergsten, Takatoshi Ito, and
Marcus Noland
October 2001   ISBN 0-88132-286-5
Why Global Commitment Really Matters!
Howard Lewis III and J. David Richardson
October 2001   ISBN 0-88132-298-9
**Leadership Selection in the Major
Multilaterals**   Miles Kahler
November 2001   ISBN 0-88132-335-7
**The International Financial Architecture:
What's New? What's Missing?**   Peter Kenen
November 2001   ISBN 0-88132-297-0
**Delivering on Debt Relief: From IMF Gold
to a New Aid Architecture**
John Williamson and Nancy Birdsall,
with Brian Deese
April 2002   ISBN 0-88132-331-4
**Imagine There's No Country: Poverty,
Inequality, and Growth in the Era
of Globalization**   Surjit S. Bhalla
September 2002   ISBN 0-88132-348-9

Reforming Korea's Industrial Conglomerates
Edward M. Graham
January 2003   ISBN 0-88132-337-3
**Industrial Policy in an Era of Globalization:
Lessons from Asia**   Marcus Noland
and Howard Pack
March 2003   ISBN 0-88132-350-0
Reintegrating India with the World Economy
T. N. Srinivasan and Suresh D. Tendulkar
March 2003   ISBN 0-88132-280-6
**After the Washington Consensus:
Restarting Growth and Reform
in Latin America**   Pedro-Pablo Kuczynski
and John Williamson, editors
March 2003   ISBN 0-88132-347-0
**The Decline of US Labor Unions and the Role
of Trade**   Robert E. Baldwin
June 2003   ISBN 0-88132-341-1
**Can Labor Standards Improve under
Globalization?**   Kimberly A. Elliott
and Richard B. Freeman
June 2003   ISBN 0-88132-332-2
**Crimes and Punishments? Retaliation
under the WTO**   Robert Z. Lawrence
October 2003   ISBN 0-88132-359-4
Inflation Targeting in the World Economy
Edwin M. Truman
October 2003   ISBN 0-88132-345-4
**Foreign Direct Investment and Tax
Competition**   John H. Mutti
November 2003   ISBN 0-88132-352-7
**Has Globalization Gone Far Enough?
The Costs of Fragmented Markets**
Scott Bradford and Robert Z. Lawrence
February 2004   ISBN 0-88132-349-7
**Food Regulation and Trade:
Toward a Safe and Open Global System**
Tim Josling, Donna Roberts, and David Orden
March 2004   ISBN 0-88132-346-2
**Controlling Currency Mismatches
in Emerging Markets**
Morris Goldstein and Philip Turner
April 2004   ISBN 0-88132-360-8
**Free Trade Agreements: US Strategies
and Priorities**   Jeffrey J. Schott, editor
April 2004   ISBN 0-88132-361-6
Trade Policy and Global Poverty
William R. Cline
June 2004   ISBN 0-88132-365-9
**Bailouts or Bail-ins? Responding to Financial
Crises in Emerging Economies**
Nouriel Roubini and Brad Setser
August 2004   ISBN 0-88132-371-3
Transforming the European Economy
Martin Neil Baily and Jacob Kirkegaard
September 2004   ISBN 0-88132-343-8
**Chasing Dirty Money: The Fight Against
Money Laundering**
Peter Reuter and Edwin M. Truman
November 2004   ISBN 0-88132-370-5

WORKS IN PROGRESS

DISTRIBUTORS OUTSIDE THE UNITED STATES

**Australia, New Zealand,
and Papua New Guinea**
D. A. Information Services
648 Whitehorse Road
Mitcham, Victoria 3132, Australia
Tel: 61-3-9210-7777
Fax: 61-3-9210-7788
Email: service@dadirect.com.au
www.dadirect.com.au

India, Bangladesh, Nepal, and Sri Lanka
Viva Books Private Limited
Mr. Vinod Vasishtha
4737/23 Ansari Road
Daryaganj, New Delhi 110002
India
Tel: 91-11-4224-2200
Fax: 91-11-4224-2240
Email: viva@vivagroupindia.net
www.vivagroupindia.com

**Mexico, Central America, South America,
and Puerto Rico**
US PubRep, Inc.
311 Dean Drive
Rockville, MD 20851
Tel: 301-838-9276
Fax: 301-838-9278
Email: c.falk@ieee.org

Asia *(Brunei, Burma, Cambodia, China,
Hong Kong, Indonesia, Korea, Laos, Malaysia,
Philippines, Singapore, Taiwan, Thailand,
and Vietnam)*
East-West Export Books (EWEB)
University of Hawaii Press
2840 Kolowalu Street
Honolulu, Hawaii 96822-1888
Tel: 808-956-8830
Fax: 808-988-6052
Email: eweb@hawaii.edu

Canada
Renouf Bookstore
5369 Canotek Road, Unit 1
Ottawa, Ontario KlJ 9J3, Canada
Tel: 613-745-2665
Fax: 613-745-7660
www.renoufbooks.com

Japan
United Publishers Services Ltd.
1-32-5, Higashi-shinagawa
Shinagawa-ku, Tokyo 140-0002
Japan
Tel: 81-3-5479-7251
Fax: 81-3-5479-7307
Email: purchasing@ups.co.jp
*For trade accounts only. Individuals will find
Institute books in leading Tokyo bookstores.*

Middle East
MERIC
2 Bahgat Ali Street, El Masry Towers
Tower D, Apt. 24
Zamalek, Cairo
Egypt
Tel. 20-2-7633824
Fax: 20-2-7369355
Email: mahmoud_fouda@mericonline.com
www.mericonline.com

United Kingdom, Europe
(including Russia and Turkey), **Africa,
and Israel**
The Eurospan Group
c/o Turpin Distribution
Pegasus Drive
Stratton Business Park
Biggleswade, Bedfordshire
SG18 8TQ
United Kingdom
Tel: 44 (0) 1767-604972
Fax: 44 (0) 1767-601640
Email: eurospan@turpin-distribution.com
www.eurospangroup.com/bookstore

Visit our website at:
www.petersoninstitute.org
E-mail orders to:
petersonmail@presswarehouse.com